LABOR
RELATIONS

LABOR RELATIONS

Fifth Edition

Arthur A. Sloane

Professor of Industrial Relations
University of Delaware

Fred Witney

Professor of Economics
Indiana University

Prentice-Hall, Inc., Englewood Cliffs, N.J. 07632

Library of Congress Cataloging in Publication Data

SLOANE, ARTHUR A.
    Labor relations.

    Bibliography: p.
    Includes index.
    1. Industrial relations—United States.
2. Collective bargaining—United States.
I. Witney, Fred.   II. Title.
HD8072.S6185 1985   331.89′0973   84–11734
ISBN   0-13-519562-4

Editorial/production supervision and text design: Pamela Wilder
Cover and chapter opening design: Judith A. Matz-Coniglio
Manufacturing buyer: Ed O'Dougherty

Printed in the United States of America

10   9   8   7   6   5   4   3   2

ISBN 0-13-519562-4   01

Prentice-Hall International, Inc., *London*
Prentice-Hall of Australia Pty. Limited, *Sydney*
Editora Prentice-Hall do Brasil, Ltda., *Rio de Janeiro*
Prentice-Hall Canada Inc., *Toronto*
Prentice-Hall of India Private Limited, *New Delhi*
Prentice-Hall of Japan, Inc., *Tokyo*
Prentice-Hall of Southeast Asia Pte. Ltd., *Singapore*
Whitehall Books Limited, *Wellington, New Zealand*

To Louise, Amy, and Laura
and Judy, Eileen, and Frank

Contents

PART TWO *The Environmental Framework*

2 The Historical Framework 55

3 The Legal Framework 98

4 Union Behavior: Structure, Government, and Operation 139

PART THREE *Collective Bargaining*

PART FOUR *Some Final Thoughts*

APPENDIX

Preface

There are no prerequisites to this book beyond an interest in labor–management relations. We have designed it to serve as an aid to all readers who desire a basic understanding of unionism in its natural habitat. With such a thrust, however, the volume focuses on certain areas, which necessarily minimizes the treatment of others.

Labor Relations brings in, for example, sufficient economic material to allow a fundamental appreciation of the union–management process and stops at that point. We have, throughout, tried to implement our belief that all the various topic treatments should be short enough to be interesting while at the same time long enough to cover the subject.

On the other hand, our offering in no way *restricts* itself to what is commonly described as "collective bargaining." Its focus is on the negotiation and administration of labor agreements, with emphasis on the development and application of the more significant bargaining issues as they now appear between the covers of the contracts. Further, our own teaching experiences have shown us that these topics cannot profitably be studied in isolation. Labor relations, in the sense in which we use the term, can best be viewed as an interaction between two organizations—management and the labor union—and the parties to this interaction are always subject to various, often complex, environmental influences. Only after the reader gains an understanding of the evolving management and labor institutions, and only after the environment surrounding their interactional process has been appreciated, can he or she attempt to understand bargaining itself in any satisfactory way.

The book consequently begins with a broad overview of the general nature of the labor–management relationship as it currently exists in the United States (Part I). It then moves to a survey of the historical, legal, and structural environments that so greatly influence contractual contents and labor relations behavior (Part II). Finally, it presents a close examination of the negotiation, administration, and major contents of the labor agreement itself (Part III). Through description, analysis, discussion questions, and, in the later stages of this volume, selected arbitration cases drawn from our own experiences, we hope to impart understanding of all these aspects of labor relations.

Numerous changes, primarily additions, mark this fifth edition. Even in the few years since the 1981 publication of our fourth edition, developments in the field have dictated the inclusion of new material relating to technological change and robotics, plant closings, the quality of work life, concessionary bargaining, unions on corporate boards, public employees and harder times, and unions in the world of sports (among other new subjects). We have also, with the benefit of some hindsight, substantially enlarged upon our prior treatment of such topics as seniority versus affirmative action, women and minorities in unions, right-to-work laws, OSHA, antilabor consultants, and union leadership, and we have considerably updated the discussion of a host of other issues ranging from decertification elections to pensions. Twelve new and recent arbitration cases are presented (in addition to two cases retained from the fourth edition), along with a significantly revised bibliography, an amended mock negotiation problem, and many new discussion questions. Nonetheless, we have exercised self-restraint in the rewriting: only changes that can be defended on grounds of general improvement of *Labor Relations* have been incorporated. We are strong believers in the old Puritan dictum that "nothing should ever be said that doesn't improve upon silence" while also sharing with the late Calvin Coolidge the conviction that "if you don't say anything, no one will ever call upon you to repeat it."

When a book has reached the stage of a fifth edition, it stands indebted to so many people that individual acknowledgment is futile. As in the prior editions, students, friends from the ranks of both management and labor, and colleagues at other educational institutions have all offered suggestions, many of them highly constructive and consequently implemented by us. Rita Beasley, who cheerfully and competently provided secretarial services on behalf of the volume, does deserve a special citation, however, and so too, for her probing research regarding Samuel Gompers, does Amy J. Sloane.

ARTHUR A. SLOANE
FRED WITNEY

LABOR
RELATIONS

chapter 1

Organized Labor and the Management Community: An Overview

Our society has historically placed a high premium on property rights. Because of this, and perhaps also because the American soil has nurtured a breed of highly individualistic and aggressive businesspeople, employers in this country have accepted unionism through the years approximately as well as nature tolerates a vacuum.

The evidence for this phenomenon is not in short supply. Symbolic of management sentiments in the mid-nineteenth century were, for example, the comments of the editors of the *New York Journal of Commerce* relating to current demands of the printers in that locality:

> Who but a miserable craven-hearted man, would permit himself to be subjected to such rules, extending even to the number of apprentices he may employ, and the manner in which they shall be bound to him, to the kind of work which shall be performed in his own office at particular hours of the day, and to the sex of the persons employed, however separated into different apartments or buildings? For ourselves, we never employed a female as a compositor and have no great opinion of apprentices, but sooner than be restricted on these points, or any other, by a self-constituted tribunal outside of the office, we would go back to the employment of our boyhood, and dig potatoes, pull flax, and do everything else that a plain, honest farmer may properly do on his own territory. It is marvelous to us how any employer, having the soul of a man within him, can submit to such degradation.[1]

[1] *New York Journal of Commerce,* February 7, 1851, as quoted in Neil W. Chamberlain, *The Labor Sector* (New York: McGraw-Hill, 1965), p. 341.

Five decades later, George F. Baer, president of the Philadelphia and Reading Railroad, relied on God rather than ridicule in setting forth views that were no less representative of many employers of *his* time. In a 1903 letter, Baer replied to a citizen who had requested him "as a Christian gentlemen" to make concessions to the striking workers on his railroad, as follows:

> I see you are evidently biased in your religious views in favor of the right of the working man to control a business in which he has no other interest than to secure fair wages for the work he does. I beg of you not to be discouraged. The rights and interests of the laboring man will be protected and cared for, not by the labor agitators, but by the Christian men to whom God in His infinite wisdom has given control of the property interests of the country. Pray earnestly that the right may triumph, always remembering that the Lord God Omnipotent still reigns and that His reign is one of law and order, and not of violence and crime.[2]

Sinclair Lewis used the medium of fictional satire to make his points, but real-life counterparts of his small-town businessman George F. Babbitt were sufficiently in supply to make *Babbitt* an instant success when it was published in 1922. Babbitt's opinions on the subject of organized labor were quite forthright, if not entirely consistent:

> A good labor union is of value because it keeps out radical unions, which would destroy property. No one ought to be forced to belong to a union, however. All labor agitators who try to force men to join a union should be hanged. In fact, just between ourselves, there oughtn't to be any unions allowed at all; and as it's the best way of fighting the unions, every businessman ought to belong to an employer's association and to the Chamber of Commerce. In union there is strength. So any selfish hog who doesn't join the Chamber of Commerce ought to be forced to.[3]

In our own day, management views on the subject are considerably more sophisticated and far less emotion-laden. Over the past few decades, major changes have affected the employment relationship and contributed to the lessening of overt antiunionism. The findings of the behavioral sciences, particularly industrial sociology and applied psychology, have led to an employee-centered management approach that was unknown to an earlier era. Far greater worker expectations have been fostered by a new social climate derived from the ending of mass immigration, growing levels of education, and the spread of the world's most ambitious communications network. Moreover, the old-time owner–manager, holding a major or exclusive proprietary interest in his business, has now been substantially displaced. He has been succeeded by the hired administrator, oriented toward management as a profession, as much an employee as the people far below him in the

---

[2] Herbert Harris, *American Labor* (New Haven, Conn.: Yale University Press, 1939), pp. 126–27.
[3] Sinclair Lewis, *Babbitt* (New York: Harcourt Brace Jovanovich, 1922), p. 44. (Rights for the British Commonwealth excluding Canada have been granted by Jonathan Cape Limited, Publishers, London, England, on behalf of the Estate of Sinclair Lewis.)

company hierarchy, and increasingly aware that profitability is not the only test of company performance today (and that community responsibilities are also prime considerations). Finally, the right of workers to organize and bargain collectively, free of employer restraint or coercion, has been protected by statute since the mid-1930s.

In this new setting, progress in union–management relations has undeniably been made. Considerably more enlightened management policies toward organized labor are in effect today than was the case even thirty years ago. A large measure of contractual stability has been achieved in many situations. Violence in labor disputes has all but disappeared. The incidence of strikes has been almost steadily decreasing, and strikes now consume a minuscule portion of total working time— less than 0.15 percent in most recent years. A greater willingness by both parties to resort to facts rather than to power or emotion as a basis for bargaining is in evidence. And, indeed, unions have now been completely accepted by some managers, with outspoken attacks on organized labor in general being relatively rare from *any* employer quarter.

For all these sanguine developments, however, the fact remains that unions are still far from welcome in the eyes of the employer community. If the attacks on unionism are more muted and less belligerent than they were in the past, they nonetheless exist on a wide scale. Over two decades ago, one observer of the labor scene summed up what he saw as the modal situation at that time in words that are wholly appropriate even now:

> Even if the manager does not view the union as a gang, he often still feels that they strike a discordant note in the happy home. Once there, unrest develops. A peer group outside the home becomes more important to the children than the parents; the father's powers are challenged; the child begins to think his goals are not synonymous with those of the parents (he may even want his allowance raised); and, perhaps worst of all, he wants to have his voice heard in how the home should be run.[4]

In the face of this management enmity, on the other hand, unionism has shown absolutely no tendency to retreat. Owing primarily to the inroads of changing technology and the resulting employment decline, as well as to changing market demands affecting the manufacturing sector, organized labor has, it is true, expanded its membership barely at all in the past few years. And despite some claims by labor relations analysts that the fast-growing white collar sector will soon become more hospitable to collective bargaining, it is equally true that union penetration in this area thus far has fallen considerably short of its potential. But it is no less a matter of record that more than seven times as many workers are union members today as was the case in 1932, and it is quite apparent that the 22 million employees who currently constitute the labor movement in this country exhibit no notable signs of disenchantment with it. Whatever one's speculation about the problems

[4] Albert A. Blum, "Management Paternalism and Collective Bargaining," *Personal Administration*, XXVI (January–February 1963), p. 38.

awaiting unionism as the nature of our labor force changes (and, as will be shown, the speculation is both optimistic and pessimistic from the union viewpoint), the labor union seems to be very much here to stay.

In this introductory chapter, then, we shall want to examine several questions. Why do workers, apparently in complete disregard of their employers' wishes, join and remain in unions? Why, for that matter (beyond the extremely general reasons suggested by the preceding paragraphs), do employers so steadfastly continue to oppose the concept of unionism? Assuming that managers have no choice other than to deal with a labor organization, what alternative methods for this collective bargaining are open to them? And what, if any, trends in their concrete dealings with unions have managements exhibited in recent years? Before we discuss these questions, however, we must assess the current status and strategic power of the American labor movement itself.

THE STATE OF THE UNIONS TODAY

Completely reliable statistics relating to union membership in this country have never been available. Some unions in reporting their figures have traditionally exaggerated, to gain respect and influence for the union itself within the total labor movement, to make the union officers look better by showing a rise in enrollments during their term of office, or merely to hide a loss of membership. Other unions have been known to report fewer members than they actually have, for financial reasons (for example, to avoid paying per capita taxes to labor federations to which they may belong, particularly the AFL–CIO), or because of bookkeeping practices that exclude workers currently on strike (or those on layoff from work) from the list of present members.

The figure of 22 million workers, offered above as constituting the present extent of union organization, is commonly accepted as an appropriate one, however. This total includes some 20.5 million U.S. members of national and international unions[5] and roughly 1.5 million American members of independent local unions (those not affiliated with any national or international union). It excludes the approximately 1.2 million Canadians who belong to internationals with headquarters in the United States.[6]

In 1984, in terms of relative labor force penetration, the 22 million in the unionized work force represented about 20.9 percent of all U.S. workers, a statistic that was down somewhat from the 24.7 percent of the nation's labor force that unions had represented only fourteen years earlier. In speaking for the 22 million, unions accounted for over one-quarter of the employers in nonagricultural establishments (where union organizing has historically been concentrated). They also

---

[5] The terms *national* and *international* will be used interchangeably in this volume as, indeed, they are used in practice.

[6] Unofficial data furnished by U.S. Department of Labor, Bureau of Labor Statistics.

represented somewhat less than one-third of "organizable" American industrial employees (our nonprofessional and nonsupervisory employees, although some union representation from both the professional and supervisory sectors does exist).[7]

More specifically, about 40 percent of the nation's blue collar workers, those whose job duties are primarily manual in nature, are now represented by unions, and in some blue collar sectors—notably transportation, municipal utilities, and manufacturing—the nonunionist is definitely a rarity. Almost all manual workers in such "smokestack" industries as automobiles and steel, for example, carry union cards. And the same can be said for their counterparts in rubber, aerospace, agricultural implements, the needle trades, paper, and brewing. Organization also covers a substantial, if somewhat lesser, percentage of the blue collar employees in the printing, oil, chemical, electrical, electronic, pharmaceutical, and shoe industries, and significant numbers of workers in construction, mining, and communications.

States and cities with a high percentage of their workers in these industries show, not surprisingly, a high proportion of unionized employees. Indeed, five states alone—New York, California, Pennsylvania, Illinois, and Ohio—account for almost half of all union members in this country (while employing just over one-third of the U.S. nonagricultural work force). There are, in fact, more union members in New York alone than there are in eleven southern states, including Texas, combined. And Washington, Michigan, and Massachusetts also have ratios of union membership to nonagricultural employment that place them well above the national average of just under 30 percent. Several major cities, too, that are heavily dependent on the industries cited—Pittsburgh, Detroit, and Seattle, among others—currently have at least 90 percent of their manufacturing-plant workers covered by union contract. States and cities without large representation from these industries tend to show considerably lower figures: In both North Carolina and South Carolina, less than 7 percent of the nonagricultural labor force belongs to a union, for example, and anyone who wagers that a random work group in Charlotte or Charleston (or Jacksonville or New Orleans, for that matter) is a nonunion one is very likely going to win.

Union strength, then, is highly concentrated in areas that are strategic to our economy. If organized labor has thus far been notably unsuccessful in its attempt to organize such white collar (and fast-growing) sectors as trade, services, and finance, and such remaining great pockets of nonunionism in manufacturing as the textile industry, unions *have* been cordially greeted by the workers in much of large-scale industry. Indeed, the labor movement today bargains with many of the most influential managements in the country, those that regularly take the lead in price and wage movements. From trucking, whose importance to the nation is such that the American Trucking Associations can boast in its motto "If you got it, a

---

[7] *Ibid.*

truck brought it," to the focal points of any advanced industrialized nation in durable goods production, unions are dominant. They have power, accordingly, where the possession of power is particularly important.

Union membership related directly to industrial category also illustrates the high percentage of labor organization accounted for by the groups cited above, and the relatively small successes enjoyed by labor organizers in white collar industries. The figures in the following partial industrial listing relate to the *total* work forces in each industry. In fairness to unions, it should be recognized that each industry includes a varying but never inconsequential number of employees who would consider joining the ranks of organized labor, if at all, only in their wildest dreams (managers and other administrators, higher-echelon specialists, and in some cases political officeholders). But the discrepancy between the blue and white collar sectors is vivid nonetheless.[8]

Industry	Percentage Unionized
Railroads	78.6%
Automobiles	66.2
Primary metals	59.8
Postal	52.2
Paper	48.7
Other transportation	42.9
Telephone communication	40.1
Stone, clay, and glass	39.6
Construction	39.2
Fabricated metals	38.2
Local government	19.6
State government	13.3
Wholesale, retail trade	10.2
Hospitals	8.4
Services, finance	7.8

Titles do not always accurately portray the kind of worker represented by a union (teachers in Oklahoma City belong to the Laborers Union, for example, and taxicab drivers in Chicago are members of the Seafarers' International Union). But they generally do so, and a reading of the names of the eight largest 1984 internationals offers further evidence of the importance of blue collarites to the labor movement. Of these eight largest (which collectively today account for over 40 percent of all union members), only two even appear from their names to be outside of labor's main blue collar mold, and in both cases this is somewhat misleading: The United Food and Commercial Workers, formed by a 1979 merger of the Retail Clerks and Meat Cutters, represents mainly manual workers; and substantial numbers of State, County and Municipal Employees perform such definitely blue collar assignments as stock-handling and pothole patching.

---

[8] Figures furnished by the U.S. Department of Labor.

Union	Members
Teamsters (Independent)	1,800,000
Automobile Workers (AFL–CIO)	1,300,000
Steelworkers (AFL–CIO)	1,300,000
Food and Commercial Workers (AFL–CIO)	1,200,000
State, County and Municipal Employees (AFL–CIO)	950,000
Electrical Workers (AFL–CIO)*	900,000
Machinists (AFL–CIO)	820,000
Carpenters (AFL–CIO)	800,000

* International Brotherhood of Electrical Workers.
Source: Authors' estimates based on data published by the U.S. Department of Labor.

WHITE COLLAR EMPLOYEES

If the labor movement is predominantly a blue collar one, however, this is no longer true of the U.S. labor force itself. In 1956, the number of white collar workers exceeded that of blue collar workers in this country for the first time in our nation's history. And the gap has been steadily widening ever since. Such sectors as trade, services, finance, and government have continued to expand, while the blue collar sectors—particularly manufacturing, mining, and transportation, but with the construction sector as a conspicuous exception—have actually, in the face of improved technologies and changing consumer demands, shown employment declines.

Fewer than 16 percent of workers in U.S. industry are now employed in manufacturing, as compared with some 23 percent two decades ago, while that graphic symbol of the nation's service sector, the McDonald's hamburger empire, has now expanded to the point where it employs more than three times as many workers as does United States Steel. In fact, employment in the iron and steel industry, which peaked at 952,000 in 1957, had fallen to 653,000 twenty-five years later,[9] whereas jobs in automobiles, chemicals, apparel, and many other older industries, while often taking longer to peak (and in many cases not actually doing so until the late 1970s) had demonstrated similar decline by the mid-1980s. Whether or not smokestack America was actually in its sunset years at the time of this writing, most experts *believed* that it was and that all the grim employment trends would only continue.

More than any other factor, this changing complexion of the labor force has given organized labor cause for concern. Its inability to recruit white collar workers on any significant scale has been primarily responsible for its slippage from representing just under 25 percent of the labor force to its above-noted position of representing closer to 20 percent. Unless it can do far better than it has to date in organizing the nation's millions of clerical, sales, professional-technical, and other employees, it will by simple mathematical logic see the percentage drop even more, perhaps to the 15 percent level.

[9] *New York Times,* May 8, 1983, Sec. 3, p. 1.

This is not to say, of course, that unions do not exert a major collective bargaining influence on behalf of some groups of white collar workers. Such white collar types as musicians and actors have for years been willing joiners of labor organizations. In recent years, two unions in particular have shown significant gains in this quarter: the State, County and Municipal Employees, whose estimated 950,000 members (as noted) now place it just below the very largest labor organizations in the country; and the American Federation of Teachers, which grew from 60,000 members in 1960 to over a half million members a quarter-century later. Also exhibiting no small amount of organizational success have been the Postal Workers and the Letter Carriers (each with current memberships in the vicinity of 250,000). Some 125,000 college faculty members and 16,000 physicians, too, are in the ranks of unions at the present time, as are almost 50,000 engineers and several thousand lawyers. Nurses on the East and West Coasts are far more often bargained for collectively than they are not. Moreover, many of labor's largest internationals—most notably the Teamsters and the Steelworkers—do represent large numbers of white collar employees in addition to their traditional types of constituents.

In addition, as even the most casual reader of the sports pages must be fully aware, professional athletes in all major league sports are not only nowadays collectively bargained for, as essentially none of them were a relatively few years ago, but they have in the case of both baseball and football engaged in notable and long-lasting work stoppages in the 1980s. The 650 members of the Major League Baseball Players Association struck their 26 owners for fifty days in 1981, wiping out a third of that year's schedule. And the next year, not to be outdone, the National Football League's Players Association, with some 1,500 members, went head to head with the owners in its sport in an eight-week suspension of play. In a third round of bargaining, so to speak, the National Basketball Players Association in 1983 won a promise from the basketball team owners to guarantee 53 percent of their gross to pay players' salaries in the future, without a strike, and since these salaries in 1983 averaged some $246,000 (roughly $50,000 more than the baseball average and about two and one-half times the football one), this promised only to make a good thing better for them.

Nonetheless, there has been no particularly impressive change in total union penetration of the white collar field in recent years. In 1956, some 2.42 million white collar workers were in unions; a decade later, the figure had risen only to approximately 2.7 million, despite the growth of this sector by several million more jobs, to over 26 million by the late 1960s. And by 1984, with an even more rapid growth in total white collar employment in the intervening years, the union rolls had advanced only to about the 5 million mark, a point clearly far short of the saturation level. Nor had even these modest gains of organized labor been evenly spread throughout the white collar world. Most of them had been gained strictly from the public-service sector, where, as we shall see, in many cases favorable legislation had made the enrollment of new members both comparatively easy and comparatively meaningless: In Texas, for example, public-sector unions can neither bargain collectively for wages nor—even in the case of teachers' unions—strike, and any resemblance between these labor organizations and, say, the Teamsters in Michigan is strictly coincidental.

SOME PROBABLE EXPLANATIONS

Why has the white collar world been so relatively unreceptive to the union organizer when its blue collar counterpart has been so hospitable? Many theories have been advanced, by almost as many theorists. All bear some risk of oversimplification, given both the variety of ever-changing needs and wants that play on human behavior and the heterogeneity of the white collar population itself (including as it does such dissimilar occupational categories as engineers, professional salespeople, medical and other health workers, clerical and office employees, members of the teaching profession, and government workers). But among the many explanations for labor's general failure to date in penetrating the White Collar Frontier, the following may well be the most accurate. Taken collectively, they also constitute some rather formidable grounds for union pessimism in the years ahead.

1   The public has in recent years been inundated with news of seemingly irresponsible union strikes and commensurately unstatesmanlike settlements, union leaders' criminality, and featherbedding situations. The resulting poor image of the labor movement, as conveyed by the mass media, may well have alienated hundreds of thousands—and, conceivably, even millions—of potential white collar union joiners. In an age when even the occupant of the White House can be determined by public image, this factor—although it is not only unquantifiable but even basically unprovable—cannot be overlooked.

This topic should in any event receive far more attention than it has heretofore been given. Certainly, as has long been observed by thoughtful students of labor relations, unions most often get into the headlines for activities that cover them with discredit. A union leader's criminality will invariably do the trick. And so, too, will news of any seemingly irresponsible union strike, or almost any charge, if made with sufficient vigor, that unionized employees are receiving pay for work that is not performed (or "featherbedding").

Thus, there may well be significant numbers in the general population who believe that "Construction Strike Threat Looms" is a regular, if somewhat repetitious, column appearing in their local newspaper. (*Looms,* from all available evidence, is the only verb utilized in such situations, a phenomenon similar to that pertaining to "Prison Riots," which can only be "Quelled"—or for that matter "Last Minute Settlements," which can do only one thing to strikes, namely, "Avert" them.) And one can only guess at how many Americans think that "Featherbedding" is part of the official job designation of the "Railroad Firemen." It is also true, as the late A. J. Liebling once commented, that the public is regularly informed that "Labor *Demands*" but that "Management *Offers*"; and few can argue with a further observation of this famous journalist that when General Motors workers go out on strike for more wages, this is major news throughout the nation (if not the world), whereas the president of General Motors takes his considerably larger income home quietly.

From the labor point of view there is, of course, an intrinsic unfairness in such a factor. It is conflict, as more than one media member has observed, that makes the headlines. The large majority of union agreements that are peacefully renegotiated year after year go virtually unnoticed by the reporters of the news, but the few strikes of any dimensions are treated with the journalistic zeal of a Tolstoy. The overwhelming proportion of union officials continue to lead their lives in full compliance with the laws of the land, but this seems insignificant to the news compilers in the face of the conviction of a single Jimmy Hoffa or Tony Boyle, with whose blemished records all informed citizens have become amply familiar. And charges that unions demand pay for work that is not performed totally dwarf the large body of evidence that featherbedding is engaged in by only a small segment of unionized employees.

Yet what editor can justify headlines proclaiming that "Local 109 of the Rubber Workers Is a Very Statesmanlike Local," that "Business Agent Duffy Gabrilowitz of the Plumbers Union Is One Hundred Percent Honest," or that "Management Says That Pulp, Sulphite, and Paper Mill Workers Are Giving a Fair Day's Work for a Fair Day's Pay"? Only, we suspect, a journalist with a strongly developed suicidal urge. Accordingly, the large segment of the population that allows its opinions of unionism to be molded only by those labor activities receiving wide publicity is undestandably—if, for organized labor, unfortunately—less than enthusiastic about the institution. An incalculable but undoubtedly formidable number of white collar workers—unlike their blue collar counterparts, who are generally in a better position by virtue of proximity to perceive strengths as well as weaknesses in unionism—fall into this population category.

2   The labor movement has in recent years been distinguished in the main by uninspiring, rather bureaucratic leadership that seems only dimly aware of the white collar problem and totally unimaginative about discovering any solutions. The complaint of labor scholar J.B.S. Hardman that "superannuated leaders, who have outlived their usefulness, are probably met more frequently in the labor movement than in any other militant social movement,"[10] although it was made almost sixty years ago and intended to apply exclusively to the late 1920s, could fit into any typical outsider's critique of labor's current performance without doing violence to the basic theme. Hardman's words constitute, as Jack T. Conway could say much more recently, "the lingering lament of an aging officialdom, which too frequently symbolizes—to the public and to its membership—dried-up idealism and a stalled drive for reform."[11]

[10] J.B.S. Hardman, *American Labor Dynamics* (New York: Harcourt, Brace & Co., 1928), p. 95.
[11] Jack T. Conway, "Challenges to Union Leadership in an Era of Change," in *Proceedings of the Twenty-first Annual Winter Meeting, Industrial Relations Research Association,* December 29–30, 1968, p. 183.

And, with considerable accuracy, the journalist A. H. Raskin could write not long ago that

> . . . few among the field marshals of labor have much appetite for . . . battle [with management]. Like Willie Loman in "Death of a Salesman," they like to be liked . . .
>
> Thus, [former AFL–CIO President George] Meany plaintively asks the captains of industry why they are "seeking to destroy a labor movement that has always supported and promoted free enterprise . . ."
>
> Calls for reviving the old Franklin D. Roosevelt coalition of labor, liberals, blacks, religious groups, youth, women and the like will lack meaning unless unions start by redefining their own goals along lines that will convince space-age workers that labor has dug itself out of the 19th century. Then labor leaders will have to get off their duffs and do some systematic organizing instead of feeling aggrieved . . .[12]

Nor has this condition entirely escaped the attention of labor leaders themselves. There are many more top leaders in their sixties now than there are septuagenarians and octogenarians, and the observation once made by a United Automobile Worker secretary–treasurer that "some of the board members of some of the unions, when they have a board meeting, they look like a collection of a wax museum" no longer basically applies. But there is still much validity to the charge made by the UAW when it withdrew from the AFL–CIO some years ago in a now-concluded dispute with its leadership, that the federation "has become isolated from the mainstream and too often acts like a comfortable, complacent custodian of the status quo."[13]

For those who continue to believe strongly in the potential of the labor movement as a force for accomplishment in our society, there is something quite sad about the current state of union leadership. All the trappings of success surround it—as Raskin could accurately point out, "The hair shirt has given way to white-on-white broadcloth, imported fabrics, and custom tailoring"[14]—and the expense-account perquisites of labor's major officials are totally indistinguishable in their lavishness from those of the leaders of the business community. But somewhere in the transformation from crusader for the underdog to accepted member of the Establishment, both the sense of mission and the creative spark to implement it seem to have been severely dampened by affluence. The senior citizens who constitute the bulk of current labor leadership appear, in short, to be resting quite comfortably on their hard-earned laurels, lacking motivation to reenter the organizational arena and expend the energy, money, and, perhaps above all, imagination that are required by such an elusive potential constituency as the white collar sector. Wilfrid Sheed's thoughts are relevant: "The widespread impression

---

[12] A. H. Raskin, "Management Comes Out Swinging," in *Proceedings of the Thirty-first Annual Meeting, Industrial Relations Research Association*, August 29–31, 1978, pp. 230–31. Meany resigned his presidency in November 1979 and died in early 1980.

[13] *Business Week*, May 31, 1969, p. 77.

[14] A. H. Raskin, "The Unions and Their Wealth," *Atlantic Monthly*, April 1962, p. 89.

that Labor consists of aging white men guarding their gains may be an exaggeration verging on libel; but it *is* widespread."[15] And so, too, are those of a union staff aide: "[Union leaders are] too worried about appearances, about losing battles instead of trying new things, and they spend too much time talking to each other at . . . receptions."[16]

Sheed's "widespread impression" may not be so close to libel, either, at least as far as labor's attitude toward the declining percentage of union members is concerned. On this topic, George Meany could observe in the 1970s that

> to me, it doesn't mean a thing. I have no concern about it, because the history of the trade union movement has shown that when organized workers were a very, very tiny percentage of the work force, they still accomplished and did things that were important for the entire work force. The unorganized portions of the work forces has no power for the simple reason that they're not organized.[17]

And Meany's successor as AFL–CIO president Lane Kirkland could elaborate as follows:

> Frankly, I don't care whether the salesmen are organized. If they want to be organized, fine. If they don't I don't feel any ideological compulsion to organize them. I don't feel any compulsion to organize foremen, plant managers, advertising men, hustlers, what have you.[18]

3   White collar workers possess certain unique general properties that may tend to work against unionization in any event. Any citation of these ingredients automatically incurs all the risks of generalization alluded to earlier, but there is agreement among scholars of the white collar population that they definitely exist.

a   White collar employees have long felt superior to their blue collar counterparts and have tended to believe that joining a union (an institution traditionally associated with manual workers) would decrease their occupational prestige. This goes well beyond the issue of labor's currently poor image cited above. A certain autonomy at work, however little it may be in many cases, is imparted to the holder of the white collar job as it is not to the factory or even construction worker. Prior educational achievements, modes of dress and language, relative cleanliness of the work situations, and even job locations within the enterprise also typically give the white collar jobholder much more in common with management than with the blue collar employee. Income based on salary rather than wages further weakens the potential bonds between the two submanagerial classes. Nor, clearly, can the sheer fact that society generally looks down upon manual work and places its premium upon mentally challenging employment be disregarded in explaining the superiority complex of the white collarite.

In an economy such as ours—where for most people the more basic needs have now been relatively well satisfied—the role of such status considerations can

[15] Wilfrid Sheed, "What Ever Happened to the Labor Movement?" *Atlantic,* July 1973, p. 69.
[16] *Business Week,* August 17, 1981, p. 28.
[17] Haynes Johnson and Nick Kotz, *The Unions* (Washington, D.C.: Washington Post Company, 1972), p. 175.
[18] *Ibid.,* p. 176.

be considerable. To ask the white collar worker to identify by unionization with the steel worker, truck driver, and hod carrier—and to follow in the traditions of Samuel Gompers or John L. Lewis (to say nothing of the leadership of the Teamsters, three of whose last four national presidents have been convicted of crimes, or of former Mine Worker president Tony Boyle, of whom it was once said that he could immeasurably increase the moral level in a room simply by leaving it) is consequently, by its very nature, no small undertaking.

b However tenuous it may be, white collar workers can at least perceive some opportunity to advance into managerial ranks, whereas blue collar employees are typically limited in their most optimistic advancement goal to the "gray area" of the foremanship. Unlike the wearers of the white collar, the blue collar workers sense (usually quite accurately) that educational and social deficiencies have combined to limit their promotional avenues within the industrial world, and they can adjust to the fact that they are permanently destined to be apart from and directed by the managerial class. Since such a fate is often not nearly as clear to the white collar workers (partially for the reasons cited in the previous paragraphs), they are understandably more reluctant to join the ranks of unionism and thus support what is potentially a major constraint on employer freedom of action.

c The considerably higher proportion of women in white collar work than in blue collar work has served as a dampening force for organization. By and large, women have always been notoriously poor candidates for unionism. In many cases until now (although the situation is changing), the job has been thought of as temporary—either premarital or to supplement the family breadwinner's paycheck (often on a sporadic basis)—and, consequently, the union's argument of long-run job security has had little appeal. In other cases—perhaps as high as 25 percent at the time of this writing—the job is a part-time one, also to the detriment of the union organizer. Nor can the labor movement's traditional aura of militant masculinity be eliminated as a possible causal factor in explaining the female response to organizational attempts. ("We have," one concerned union president has said, "to get rid of the old baseball bat, T shirt, tattooed image.")[19] Here, however, one moves wholly into the realm of speculation.

d Finally, many white collar workers with professional identifications—engineers, college professors, and institutionally employed doctors, for example—continue to believe that for them there is still much more to be gained from individual bargaining with their employer than from any form of collective bargaining. Viewing the latter as an automatic opponent of individual merit rewards, they tend to perceive the relatively few unionists within their professions as either mediocrities in need of such group support, or masochists.

SOME GROUNDS FOR UNION OPTIMISM

If it is thus tempting to begin sounding the death knell for the labor movement on the grounds that its failure to penetrate the critical Collar Frontier can be explained by a combination of factors that seem to be at least collectively insurmountable, realism dictates that several other factors also be pondered. And these additional

[19] *Time,* September 4, 1978, p. 39.

considerations can lead one to an entirely different conclusion regarding the future
of organized labor in the white collar area.

1 The same newsprint, television, and radio announcements that have brought
news of union misdoings to the white collar population have also informed this
primarily nonunion audience of highly impressive income improvements in the
unionized sector. For example, few nonunionists are entirely unaware of the gains
in the heavily organized construction sector that by the 1980s were adding $4.50
per hour and more to the wages of skilled craft workers over the next three years,
or in many cases as much as the monies received as *total* hourly wages by workers
in wholesale and retail trade, finance, insurance, real estate, and many other parts
of the white collar world. The imminence of a situation where the lowest wage for
even a common laborer in the construction industry would soon be $20,000 or
more could only have been received with considerable envy by the unrepresented
insurance-company debit agent whose current earnings, despite his college degree,
placed him at not much more than two-thirds of this figure. And knowledge of the
fact that substantial overtime opportunities at hefty premiums were also available
to such unionists—as they were most frequently not to white collar workers—
could only increase the latter's flow of adrenalin.

In fairness, it must be recognized that the historically overtight labor markets
and fractionalized bargaining structure of construction have made it a labor union
extreme from the viewpoint of wage aggrandizement. It is also true that workers
in this sector were sometimes paying a significant penalty in recent years for the
munificence of their earlier settlements: They were not always employed, their
labor costs having made their employers noncompetitive with nonunion contractors.
But the kind of invidious comparisons engendered by the construction totals clearly
extends to other situations. By the 1980s, for example, the U.S. Bureau of Labor
Statistics could show gross average weekly earnings for nonsupervisory production
workers in petroleum and coal products, mining, primary metal industries, transportation equipment, transportation and public utilities, machinery (except electrical), chemical, and allied products and ordinance and accessories all exceeding
$300 per week, in some cases by very large margins. In contrast to the situations
in these heavily unionized areas, the comparable statistics for wholesale and retail
trade, services, the predominantly nonunionized "textile mill products" and "apparel and other textile products" sectors, and finance, insurance, and real estate
(lumped together by the Bureau of Labor Statistics in its reporting) remained below
$200, frequently well below.

Nor can the white collar population indefinitely be expected to be indifferent
to truck-driver incomes (symbolically, the *International Teamster* magazine could
report some years ago that "recently a professor at ivy-covered Williams College
in New England returned to the Teamsters as an over-the-road driver because he
could double his salary at Williams")[20] and to various other highly remunerated

---

[20] *International Teamster,* September 1960, p. 16.

(and overwhelmingly unionized) workers such as longshoremen, tool and die makers, and airline mechanics. For that matter, San Francisco sanitation workers were receiving $21,000 in annual base wages alone by the early 1980s, and this figure, even though far from the poverty level, paled by comparison with the $29,120 contractually guaranteed to Port of New York Authority longshoremen, whether or not there was any work for them.[21] And not one of the 85,000 United Parcel Service drivers—unionists all—was making less than $25,000 as this section was being written, with many of these employees earning considerably above that figure.

The responsibility for the relatively high standards of living involved here does not rest completely with unionism. Clearly, one must also examine such a variety of other factors as skill levels, industrial ability to pay, community wage structures, imperfections in the product market, and industrial productivity (among others) in explaining these wage levels. And one can readily cite such unionized areas as the New England boot and shoe industry and the meatpacking industry, where the overall situation often allows no real wage improvement at all and, consequently, none is received by organized labor.

But the hazards of accepting the more impressive union bargaining totals at their face value are not particularly relevant in this context. Misleadingly or not, such dollar amounts often symbolize in a highly visible fashion the ability of unionism to effect dramatic wage gains. And, as the gap between the incomes of the blue collar and white collar worlds continues to widen, a greater willingness to consider union membership may conceivably be the result. Indeed, appreciation of the fact that snobbishness neither purchases groceries nor pays the rent seems already to have accounted for some of the increased willingness of at least teachers and lower echelons of hospital work forces to undertake such a consideration.

2 The definite upsurge in unionism among government employees—although probably attributable far more to enabling legislation not only at the federal but at many state and local levels than to any pronounced rank-and-file militancy—is combing with the (lesser) emergence of collective bargaining in other white collar areas to gradually weaken the nonmember's traditional association of organized labor with manual work. As previously implied, the process is still an excruciatingly slow one from labor's viewpoint. But the growing presence of these higher-status, better-educated federal civil servants and state employees (to say nothing of those paragons of brainwork, the local schoolteacher and the previously mentioned college faculty members, physicians, engineers, lawyers, and nurses) in union ranks can only be expected to erode the older images in time. Whether this psychological change will be sufficient in itself to win over more than a fraction of the untapped white collar market for the labor movement is another question. But, certainly, one of the grounds for labor's failure until now will have been dissipated.

3 It is probably also only a question of time before considerably more aggressive, imaginative, and empathetic leadership than organized labor now pos-

---

[21] Thus, many longshoremen might well go without work during slack periods for weeks or even months at a time and in some cases—if protected by enough security—more or less permanently while still drawing the pay.

sesses comes to the fore, which would also make widespread white collar unionization far more likely.

For all the apparent apathy and conservatism at the highest levels of labor in the 1980s, there was no dearth of people in the second and third tiers of union leadership who exhibited these more positive characteristics. Far more attuned to the aspirations and values of our increasingly sophisticated labor force than were their currently more influential colleagues, they had become more and more frustrated by labor's lack of progress in recent years (as well as, often, by the tepid responses of their own memberships to the official goals of their particular unions). They fully appreciated the necessity for an immense outpouring of financial, institutional, and personal effort in the quest for the white collarite. And, in the best traditions of Samuel Gompers and John L. Lewis, they exhibited no lack of ideas as to how such unionization could be effected, even advocating wholly different organizational structures to attain this goal, should these become necessary. The vicissitudes of union politics clearly ensured that not all, or even many, of these leaders would ever actually achieve ascendancy in the labor movement. Those who would, however, would undoubtedly abet the chances of white collar unionism.

4 Finally, the working conditions of white collar employment are themselves now changing in a direction that may weaken both the superiority complex and promanagement proclivity of the white collar wearer.

The very individuality of white collar work is itself now disappearing from much of the industrial scene. An accelerating trend toward organizational bigness has already combined with the demands of technological efficiency to make cogs in vast interdependent machines of many clerks, comptometer operators, technicians, and even engineers, rather than allowing them to remain as individuals working alone or in comfortably small groups in these categories. White collar workers, no less than blue collar ones, are increasingly becoming bureaucratized. More and more, as a general statement, they are the victims of routine. Ever larger numbers of their jobs have become less desirable. Blue collar workers by no means covet the white collar positions as they once did.

In the years ahead, all of this should only accelerate. The advance of technology, in various forms from word-processing equipment to elaborate computerized design systems, is now proceeding at a faster rate in offices than in factory atmospheres, and many of the analytical and decision-making challenges once allowed the white collarite are slowly disappearing as it does so. The enormous productivity gains that such new developments have brought about have also caused, quite justifiably, considerable job uncertainty and can of course also generate a definite decrease in the economic value of job skills. Awareness that remote computer terminals can remove the work from the office altogether and assign it to such homebound subcontractors as mothers of small children and the physically handicapped is hardly cause for celebration among currently employed white collar workers. Nor is a common prediction that the computer (since it constitutes an indefensible luxury if allowed to be idle) may even force many white collar employees into one of the thus far most distinguishing features of factory work, shift work. It does not seem overly rash to assume that these changes could radically alter the complacent self-image of the white collar wearers by blurring the traditional perceived differences between the nature of their work and that of their blue collar counterparts.

And, in such an atmosphere, it may well be that the white collar workers' longstanding feeling of affinity with management as well as their sense of self-actualization on the job will also evaporate, to the point of rendering the white collarites far more susceptible than they have been in the past to the overtures of the union organizer.

Thus a case can be made for either position. It is difficult to deny that future white collar unionization does face great obstacles. But it is probably no less advisable to hedge one's bets before writing off organized labor as an institution doomed to an ultimate slow death because, having long ago captured the now-shrinking blue collar market, it has realized its only natural potential. If the grounds for union optimism as expressed above must necessarily remain speculative, nonetheless there are enough of them and there is sufficient logic to each of them to justify at least some amount of hopefulness on the part of the labor movement.

LABOR'S PRESENT STRATEGIC POWER

Other formidable obstacles also confront organized labor today. It is undeniable that unions have in recent years fallen from public favor, owing perhaps above all to various public exposures of corruption at the top levels of a few but nonetheless highly visible unions, and also to their own bargaining excesses. These latter topics will be discussed on subsequent pages. Here, it is relevant to note that the publicity involved, temporary or not, has cost the labor movement thousands of friends among the general public (and, presumably, in the ranks of potential union members): In one major recent study,[22] only 55 percent of the American people showed themselves as being favorable to unions, a figure that represented a significant decrease from 1967 (when the comparable statistic was 66 percent) and 1959 (when it was 76 percent). And, as one observer could point out with considerable accuracy in the 1980s, "Perhaps the last major . . . employee strike that enjoyed any measure of public sympathy was the walkout by postal workers in 1970.")[23]

Labor's fall from popular grace has also led to restrictive federal and state legislation that can in some ways be construed as "antilabor" (see Chapter 3).

Finally, labor has been handicapped to some extent by such current factors as the national trend to smaller, decentralized plants, resulting in more-personalized worker treatment; industry's present tendency to locate new plants in smaller, semirural, and often southern communities, climates not conducive to a hearty reception for the union; and the growing levels of income across the nation, strip-

[22] *Time,* November 16, 1981, p. 124.
[23] *Ibid.*

ping union promises of a "living wage" of some of their effect.

Yet, for all these adverse factors, it is still of some relevance for anyone who attempts to predict the labor movement's future that in their century and three-quarters on the American scene, unions have faced even greater obstacles than these and have ultimately surmounted them. As Chapter 2 relates, the history of U.S. labor is in many ways a study of triumph over economic, social, and political adversity.

However one views organized labor's future, its present strategic power cannot be denied. The labor movement's concentration of membership in the economy's most vital sectors has meant that the 20.9 percent of the labor force that bargains collectively has been an extremely influential minority. One may not agree with the newspaper headlines that a particular strike has "paralyzed the economy," but it appears to be an acceptable generalization that the wages or salaries and other conditions of employment for much of the remaining 79.1 percent of the labor force are regularly affected to some degree by the unionized segment.

Thus, if the exact future dimensions and membership totals of organized labor are today in some doubt, the importance of collective bargaining is not. Nor can one dispute labor's staying power, given the labor movement's deep penetration into virtually all the traditional parts of our economy and its continuing hold upon these areas. The reports of collective bargaining's death are, as Mark Twain cabled from Europe following reports of his own demise, "greatly exaggerated." And if modern managers are unhappy with unionism, realism dictates not that they wait for it to vanish from the scene, but that they apply their efforts toward improving the collective bargaining process by which they are so likely to be directly affected.

WHY WORKERS JOIN UNIONS

Questions concerning human behavior do not lend themselves to simple answers, for the subject itself is a highly complex one. "Why do workers join unions?" clearly falls within this category.

In his widely accepted theory of motivation, however, the late psychologist A. H. Maslow has provided us with helpful hints, although the theory itself relates to the whole population of human beings rather than merely to those who have seen fit to take out union membership.[24]

Maslow portrays man (a category that presumably also encompasses "woman") as a "perpetually wanting animal," driven to put forth effort (in other words, to work) by his desire to satisfy certain of his needs. To Maslow, these needs or wants can logically be thought of in terms of a hierarchy, for only one type of need is active at any given time. Only when the lowest and most basic of the needs in this hierarchy has been relatively well satisfied will each higher need become, in turn,

---

[24] A. H. Maslow, *Motivation and Personality* (New York: Harper & Row, 1954). Much of Maslow's concept was originally presented in his article "A Theory of Human Motivation," *Psychological Review*, L (1943), 370–96. See also Douglas McGregor, *The Human Side of Enterprise* (New York: McGraw-Hill, 1960), pp. 36–39, for an excellent restatement of Maslow's theory.

operative. Thus, it is the *unsatisfied* need that actively motivates man's behavior. Once a need is more or less gratified, man's conduct is determined by new, higher needs, which up until then have failed to motivate simply because man's attention has been devoted to satisfying his more pressing, lower needs. And the process is for most mortals unending, since few people can ever expect to satisfy, even minimally, all their needs.

At the lowest level in this Need Hierarchy, but paramount in importance until they are satisfied, are the *physiological* needs, particularly those for food, water, clothing, and shelter. "Man lives by bread alone, when there is no bread"; in other words, any higher needs he may have are inoperative when he is suffering from extreme hunger, for man's full attention must then necessarily be focused on this single need. But when the need for food and the other physiological essentials is fairly well satisfied, less basic or higher needs in the hierarchy start to dominate man's behavior, or to motivate him.

Thus, needs for *safety*—for protection against arbitrary deprivation, danger, and threat—take over as prime human motivators once man is eating regularly and sufficiently and is adequately clothed and sheltered. This is true because (1) a satisfied need is no longer a motivator of behavior, yet (2) man continues to be driven by needs, and (3) the safety needs are the next most logical candidates, beyond the physiological ones, to do this driving.

What happens when the safety needs have also been relatively satisfied, so that both the lowest need levels no longer require man's attention? In Maslow's scheme of things, the *social* needs—for belonging, association, and acceptance by one's fellows—now are dominant, and man puts forth effort to satisfy *this* newly activated type of want.

Still higher needs that ultimately emerge to dominate man's consciousness, always assuming that the needs below them have been gratified, are in turn *self-esteem* needs, especially for self-respect and self-confidence; *status* needs, for recognition, approval, and prestige; and finally, *self-fulfillment* needs, for realization of one's own potential and for being as creative as possible.

All this constitutes an oversimplification of Maslow's Need Hierarchy. Maslow himself qualified his concept in several ways, although only one of his reservations is important enough for our purposes to warrant inclusion here: He recognized that not all people follow the pattern depicted and that both desires and satisfactions vary with the individual.

Even in the capsule form presented above, however, Maslow's contribution is of aid in explaining why workers join unions. The many research findings that now exist on this latter topic[25] basically agree that all employees endeavor to

---

[25] The most timeless of these studies are E. Wight Bakke, "To Join or Not to Join," in E. Wight Bakke, Clark Kerr, and Charles W. Anrod, eds., *Unions, Management and the Public* (New York: Harcourt Brace Jovanovich, 1960), pp. 79–85; Joel Seidman, Jack London, and Bernard Karsh, "Why Workers Join Unions," in *The Annals of the American Academy of Political and Social Science*, 274, No. 84 (March 1951); and Ross Stagner, ed., *Psychology of Industrial Conflict* (New York: John Wiley, 1956). See also Henry S. Farber and Daniel H. Saks, "Why Workers Want Unions: The Role of Relative Wages and Job Characteristics," in *Journal of Political Economy*, 88, No. 21 (1980), 349–69. Jeanne M. Brett's "Why Employees Want Unions," in Kendrith M. Rowland, Gerald R. Ferris and Jay L. Sherman, *Current Issues in Personnel Management*, 2nd ed. (Boston: Allyn and Bacon, 1983) is also instructive on the subject.

gratify needs and wants that are important to them, because of dissatisfaction with the extent to which these needs and desires have been met. They also agree that, while what is "important" among these needs and wants varies with the individual employee, much of the answer depends upon what has already been satisfied either within the working environment or outside it. Many of these studies also support Maslow's hierarchy for the majority of workers in approximately the order of needs indicated by Maslow.

It should not be surprising that dissatisfaction with the extent of physiological need gratification is no longer a dominant reason for joining unions in this country. In our relatively affluent economy, few people who are working have any great difficulty in satisfying at least the most basic of these needs. In an earlier day, before the advent of minimum wage laws and other forms of legal protection, this was not as true, and, as has already been suggested, union promises of a "living wage" were of great appeal to many workers. However, those members of the labor force who today are frustrated in trying to satisfy their minimal needs for food, clothing, and shelter are those who are *unemployed,* not the most logical candidates for union membership. The research substantiates the downplaying of the role of physiological needs rather conclusively. Significantly, one of the most thorough of the studies found that not one employee out of 114 workers in a large industrial local union became a union member primarily for this purpose.[26] (This is hardly to say that union members have lost interest in higher wages and other economic improvements. As will be shown later, the desire for these benefits persists as strongly as ever. The point is, however, that this desire now stems from higher need activation. Money can satisfy more than just the physiological needs.)

On the other hand, research suggests that dissatisfaction with the extent of gratification of (1) safety, (2) social, and (3) self-esteem needs—in approximately that order—has motivated many workers to join unions. To a lesser extent, status and self-fulfillment needs have also led to union membership.

Unions are uniquely equipped, in the eyes of thousands of workers, to gratify safety needs. If very few of the 200,000 labor–management contracts currently in force in the United States are identical, at least this much can be said for virtually all of them: They are generally arrived at through *compromise,* and they define in writing the "rules of the game" that have been *mutually agreed upon* to cover the terms and conditions of employment of *all* represented workers for a specific future period of time. The union thus acts as an equal partner in the bilateral establishment of what the late Sumner H. Slichter called the "system of industrial jurisprudence." And in the interests of minimizing conflict among the workers it represents, it strives to inject uniformity of treatment—particularly in the area of job protec-tion—into the contract.

Union membership can consequently provide workers with some assurance against arbitrary management actions. The union can be expected to push for curbs against what it calls "management discrimination and favoritism" in, for example,

---

[26] Seidman, London, and Karsh, "Why Workers Join Unions."

job assignment, promotional opportunity, and even continued employment with the company. However well-meaning are a management's intentions, the company cannot guarantee that it will not at times act arbitrarily, for in the absence of such checks as the union places on its actions, it is always acting unilaterally. Satisfaction of the safety needs—in the form of considerable protection against arbitrary deprivation, danger, and threat—is thus offered by the union in its stress on uniformity of treatment for all workers. Many employees, particularly after they have perceived "arbitrary" action by management representatives, have found the appeal irresistible.

The social needs are also known to be important, if secondary, motivators of union membership. Especially where the work itself must be performed in geographically scattered locations (as in many forms of railroad employment, truck driving, or letter-carrying) or where the technology of the work minimizes on-the-job social interaction (as on the automobile assembly line), the local union can serve the function of a club, allowing the formation of close friendships built around a common purpose. But even when the work is not so structured, local unions foster a feeling of identification with those of like interests, often in pronounced contrast to the impersonality of the large organization in which the worker may be employed. Increasingly, unions have capitalized upon their ability to help satisfy social needs. As the latter have become more important to members of the labor force (not only because of the declining frustration of the lower needs but also because general leisure time has increased), unions have become increasingly ambitious in sponsoring such activities as vacation retreats, athletic facilities, and adult education programs "for members only." But unions have never been reluctant to publicize the social bonds they allow: It is not by accident that internal union correspondence has traditionally been closed by the greeting "Fraternally yours," that the official titles of many unions have always included the word "Brotherhood," and that several labor organizations continue to refer to their local unions as "lodges."

Social *pressure* has also been instrumental in causing workers to join unions. Employees often admit that the disapproval of their colleagues would result from their not signing union application cards. Normally, the disapproval is only implied. One study, for example, unearthed such explanations from workers who had joined unions as "I can't think of a good reason, except everybody else was in it," and "I suppose I joined in order to jump in line with the majority." On occasion, however, the pressure has been considerably more visible, as witness this quotation from the same study: "They approached you, kept after you, hounded you. To get them off my neck, I joined."[27]

Other workers, at higher levels, have explained their union membership as being attributable mainly to their desire to ensure that they will have a direct voice, through union election procedures, in decisions that affect them in their working environment. Such employees tend to participate actively in union affairs and to

[27] *Ibid.*

use rather freely such phrases as "I wanted to have a voice in the system." The underlying rationale of this behavior is a clear one: Managements do not normally put questions relating to employment conditions to worker vote; unions, however imperfectly, purport to be democratic institutions. To these workers, representation by a labor organization has appeared to offer the best hope in our complex, interdependent, and ever-larger-unit industrial society that their human dignity will not be completely crushed. On this basis, self-esteem needs can, at least to some extent, be appeased.

Finally, a relatively few other employees have found in the union an opportunity for realization of their highest needs—for status and self-fulfillment. They have joined with the hope of gaining and retaining positions of authority within the union officer hierarchy. For the employee with leadership ambitions, but with educational or other deficiencies that would otherwise condemn that employee to a life of prestige-lacking and unchallenging work, opportunities for further need satisfaction are thus provided.

Unionization, then, results from a broad network of worker needs. The needs for safety, social affiliation, and, to a lesser extent, self-esteem appear to be of primary importance to employees in contemporary America. And it would appear that these needs are being relatively well met by unions, or workers would have exercised their legally granted option of voting out unions in far greater measure than they have done.

This in no way minimizes the role of money and other economic benefits, for these emoluments—which unions have not been reluctant to seek, even with their members' incomes at today's high levels—are clearly related to needs beyond the physiological. Health insurance and pensions lend protection against deprivation, for example, and wages themselves can increase not only safety but status. But it does emphasize the role of protection against arbitrary treatment, formal group affiliation beyond the framework of the company, and—for some workers—an opportunity for participation in "the system." By definition, management can never itself satisfy either of the first two worker needs. Thus far, in unionized establishments, it has failed to satisfy employees on the last ground.

Two final remarks are in order. First, it has often been hypothesized that many workers join unions for *none* of the reasons cited above, but simply because they work where union membership is required for continued employment after their probationary period (the so-called "union shop" arrangement). Although it is undeniable that some workers do join for this reason, the facts do not support the belief that they are numerous. Beginning in 1947, the American labor laws provided that only if a majority of workers in the bargaining unit voted for the union shop in a secret-ballot election supervised by the government would such a shop be permitted in a labor contract. In the next four years, 46,000 elections were held: 97 percent of them favored the union shop and 91 percent of the workers eligible to vote voted in favor of the arrangement. In 1951, the election provision was repealed as a waste of the taxpayer's money.

Second, although an explanation of why workers join unions can be reduced (as was done here) to relatively uncomplicated statements, for a specific worker the motivations may be considerably more involved, even encompassing several levels of need satisfaction at once. The summary offered, if the research on which it is based is valid, is sufficiently accurate to meet our own needs. By the same token, however, unionization is at times derived from a variety of complex variables, and complete understanding of it must therefore necessarily rest on a situational foundation.

WHY MANAGERS RESIST UNIONS

Some time ago, after years of successfully withstanding union organization attempts, a small-scale New York City dress manufacturer discovered that a majority of his workers had finally become union members. Immediately thereafter, these employees struck for increased job security and improved pension benefits. On the very first morning of the strike, the manufacturer's wife—who was also the firm's bookkeeper—reported to work at her customary hour of 8 A.M. She was amazed to see her husband out on the picket line, addressing the strikers as follows: "Sam, you stand over there; Harry, you stand eight yards in back of Sam; and Leo, you come over here, eight yards behind Harry." The puzzled woman posed the natural question, "Jack, what on earth are you doing?" And the manufacturer replied, "I want they should right away know who's boss!"

The outcome of this particular labor–management struggle is unknown. But the episode nonetheless furnishes a clue as to one reason why managers are considerably less than enthusiastic about unions. As we have already seen, collective bargaining necessarily decreases the area of management discretion. Every contractual concession to the union subtracts from the scope that the management has for taking action on its own. As Bakke observed many years ago, "A union is an employer-regulating device. It seeks to regulate the discretion of employers . . . at every point where their action affects the welfare of the men."[28] Yet it is the manager who tends ultimately to be held responsible for the success or failure of the business, and not the union. Hence, employers feel it essential that they reserve for themselves the authority to make all major decisions, including those the union might construe to be affecting "the welfare of the men." In short, they feel that they must still be allowed to remain, on all counts, "the boss."

Behind such a sentiment is a managerial awareness, continuously reinforced for all administrators of profit-making institutions by day-to-day realities, that management hardly owes its exclusive allegiance to its employees. Clearly, employee needs are important and, for that matter, can be ignored for any length of time only with complete disregard for the continued solvency of the enterprise. But exactly the same can be said of the pressures exerted on management by the firm's customers, stockholders, competitors, and suppliers. Were those pressures

---

[28] E. Wight Bakke, *Mutual Survival: The Goal of Unions and Management* (New York: Harper & Row, 1946), p. 7.

not opposing ones, management's job would be far easier than it is. But because there are so many points of conflict, an aggressive union can make the managerial role a highly difficult one.

The desire to retain decision-making authority is by no means, however, strictly attributable to a managerial desire for peace of mind. Unions undoubtedly do add to the personal unhappiness and consequent morale problems of managers, but the resistance to unionism is often based also on a genuine and deep concern for the welfare of society. Countless managers believe that only if management remains free to operate without union-imposed restrictions can American business continue to advance. And only through such progress, they believe, can it provide employment for our rapidly growing labor force, let this nation compete successfully in world markets, and increase general living standards. By decreasing company flexibility (in the form of work-method controls, decreased workloads, increased stress on the seniority criterion in the allocation of manpower, and various other ways), it is argued, unions endanger the efficiency upon which continued industrial progress depends. And this is no less true, managers contend, just because these union demands are made in the name of such euphemistic goals as "job security," "equitability," and "democracy in the workplace."

A related employer fear is also held by many managers, although it is understandably given somewhat less publicity by them than is the previous argument. Such executives feel that in the absence of management's unhampered freedom to manage, the optimum utilization of manpower will be lost to society. This argument assumes that there are strong elements of a process of natural selection at work in the industrial world and that, admittedly with some exceptions, those who rise to levels of great authority within it are those who have proved that they are best equipped to hold such places. Any attempt to undercut this authority—on the part of, for example, labor unions—consequently makes society the poorer.

On four different grounds, then—(1) that managers must be allowed authority commensurate with their responsibility, (2) that unchecked union pressures may totally frustrate managers in their role as the recipients of cross-pressures from many other institutional and market forces, (3) that unions limit company flexibility and thus endanger economic progress, and (4) that only by allowing managers maximum opportunity to manage is society furnished with an optimum allocation of manpower—union inroads are typically resisted by management. There is, however, a common denominator to all four: Each argument seeks to ward off encroachments on management's *decision-making* powers.

Admittedly, even in the absence of unionism, management's ability to make decisions in the employee-relations area is not an unlimited one. A widespread network of federal, state, and community legislation now governs minimum wages, hours of work, discrimination, safety and health, and a host of other aspects of employee life with complete impartiality as to whether or not the regulated firms are organized or nonunion. Moreover, where employers encounter tight labor markets (those in which new employees are difficult to recruit), they tend to accommodate at least their more visible personnel practices—wages and other economic benefits, in particular—to what the market demands. Finally, the prevalent values of our times must always be considered. The mores of society have an important influence on employers. And it is a hallmark of our ever more sophisticated society that workers expect to be governed by progressive personnel policies that are based on objective standards whenever possible. Most nonunion firms have attempted to conform to these values no less actively than have most unionized enterprises.

The fact remains, however, that managers who are not bound by the restrictions of labor agreements, and who do not have to anticipate the possibility of their every action in the employee relations sphere being challenged by worker representatives through the grievance procedure, have considerably more latitude for decision making than do their counterparts at unionized companies. One need not in any way sympathize with the management fear of unionism to understand this fear. Given the importance of the decision-making prerogative to managements, the managerial resistance to labor organizations—whether it stems directly from management self-interest or from a concern for the welfare of society—can at least be appreciated.

If the previous paragraphs help to explain the major reasons for management's jaundiced view of the labor union, they do not acknowledge other reasons that frequently bolster this view. There are, undoubtedly, several such reasons.

In the first place, many employers tend to look upon the union as an *outsider,* with no justifiable basis for interfering in the relationship between the company and its employees. The local union, with which the firm is most apt to engage in direct dealings, typically represents workers of many competitive companies, and hence by definition it cannot have the best interests of any particular firm at heart. Worse yet, runs this charge, the local is often part of a large, geographically distant international union, by which it is closely controlled, and thus is not allowed to give adequate consideration to unique problems within its locality.[29] Beyond this, the union (whether local, international, or some intermediate body) has objectives and aspirations that are very different from those of the particular company: Where the company seeks to maximize profits within certain limits, the union seeks such goals as the maximization of its own membership and of its general bargaining power. These are objectives that the company can at best greet with apathy and at worst (when the pursuit of such goals is "subsidized" by the company in the form of its own concessions to the union) can view only with unhappiness.

Second, the manager may look upon the union as a *troublemaker,* bent upon building cleavages between management and workers where none would otherwise exist. Even aside from the previously noted fact that the union grievance procedure allows all management actions affecting areas delineated in the labor contract to be challenged, and therefore regularly provides an opportunity for controversy that

[29] Not all employers lament the "outside" aspects of unionization. Many prefer the more detached viewpoints of international union representatives who *are* removed from the tensions and political considerations involved in day-by-day local labor relations. Some managers welcome, in addition, the stabilization of labor terms among otherwise competitive employers that frequently accompanies wider-scale bargaining.

is normally absent in nonunion situations, there is some truth in this charge. Particularly where the union occupies an insecure status in the plant (possibly in the absence, for example, of the union shop), its leaders may find it essential to solicit grievances in order to keep the employees willing to pay union dues. But even where the labor organization does have such security, grievances may still be encouraged by union officials and for several logical reasons: Ongoing grievances can later be dropped in return for management concessions; individual union leaders can point to a record of effective grievance handling as they seek to rise within the union hierarchy; and unpopular managers can be displaced if *their* superiors are sufficiently uneasy about high grievance rates within their units. And, of course, union representatives may simply prefer to have management—or, if need be, an arbitrator—deny the grievance rather than do it themselves: Managers and arbitrators do not have to stand for reelection and can more easily afford to incur worker wrath.

Third, many managers view unions as *underminers of employee loyalty* to the company. In order to understand this point of view, one does not have to fully embrace the philosophy that high worker motivation levels depend upon appreciative employees who view the employer as a benefactor and work for him to a great extent out of gratitude. It is sufficient for the reader to imagine the reactions of any employer who has prided himself on providing good wages and working conditions and showing a personal concern for the individual problems of his employees (perhaps tangibly evidenced by the voluntary payment of medical expenses to meet health emergencies and unsolicited loans to meet other financial crises) upon learning that a majority of his work force has suddenly decided to "go union." This employer may use such epithets as "ingrates" in speaking of his own employees, but it is more likely that the union itself will bear the brunt of his censure. It is human nature to attribute one's defeats to forces beyond one's own control ("an irresponsible union misleading our employees and turning them against the company") rather than to factors looked upon as controllable ("employee attitudes"). The previously cited fact that management can *never* itself provide either full protection against arbitrary treatment or formal group affiliation independent of the company is overlooked by managers at such moments. So, too, is a silver lining in the situation—namely, that it is entirely possible for workers to have dual loyalties, to the union *and* to the employer.[30] In at least the early stages of the union–management relationship, unions may be resisted for having subverted employee allegiance fully as much as they are opposed on the other grounds that have been noted.

A fourth root of tension, although it is applicable to only a minority of

---

[30] The most exhaustive study on the subject of "dual loyalties" is that of Father Theodore Purcell, conducted in the mid-1950s. Interviewing 202 workers in various departments at Swift and Company, he discovered that whereas at least 79 percent felt a definite allegiance to the union as an institution, 92 percent felt allegiance to the company. "Allegiance" was construed as an attitude of approval of the overall objectives of each institution, rather than strict loyalty. See Theodore V. Purcell, *Blue Collar Man* (Cambridge, Mass.: Harvard University Press, 1960); and also *The Worker Speaks His Mind on Company and Union* (Cambridge, Mass.: Harvard University Press, 1953), by the same author. More recently, a 1975 poll of several thousand Burlington Northern Railroad employees (made in this case by the management itself) showed that workers with a "favorable attitude" toward their union also had a favorable attitude toward their boss, to a very large extent.

company executives, may arise simply because the previously discussed *reputation* of the labor movement has preceded the arrival of unionism in the plant. This has been a particularly influential factor in the resistance of some managers to collective bargaining in the recent past. Not being forced to deal with a union until now and, primarily because of this freedom, knowing little more about labor unions than they have been told by the mass media, such relatively unsophisticated employers have been alarmed by the widely publicized reports of irresponsible union strikes, union-leader criminality, and featherbedding charges that have found their way onto newspaper front pages and television screens over the past decade. These managers have asked, in effect, "How can you expect us to welcome an institution whose representatives engage in such activities?"

Fifth, and rounding out the list of major causes of the corporate executive's opposition to organized labor, are the *major values of the labor movement* as these are perceived by management. Some of these values—a stress on seniority, work-method controls, and decreased workloads—have already been mentioned in the context of "threats to decision making." There are, however, many other such shared union values that rankle management at least as much.

"Security," for example, has far more favorable connotations to unionists than it does to employer representatives. Higher managers by definition have a history of successful achievement behind them and hence are willing to take chances because they are relatively optimistic as to the outcome. The average union member, feeling that the probabilities of his success in risk taking are low, and, indeed, often believing that he is running in a race that is fixed, presses the union leadership to obtain even greater protection for him in his *current* job.

"Democracy" is a hallmark of the union value structure, and union representatives who bargain with managements are usually elected, as indicated, through a process that at least claims to be democratic. Managers, whose hierarchy is based on merit and experience, are thus forced to bargain, often on issues with major ramifications for the organization, with unionists who may have no better credentials for their role than the possession of a plurality of votes in a popularity poll.

And where the management representative speaks glowingly of "individualism" and declares that America's economic triumphs have been based on it, the union sees itself as part of a social movement and places a premium on "group consciousness."

As for "efficiency," which scores high on the management scale of values, to the union it smacks of a callous disregard for worker dignity and even worker health. Accordingly, it is something to be regarded with deep suspicion by employee representatives and to be resisted whenever resistance is practicable.

(To this list of reasons why employers resist unionism, a desire for *status* in the managerial community could probably be added. It is, in certain management circles, quite a mark of distinction to be able to stay what is typically nowadays called "union-free." And while such a reason is somewhat less visible and thus less demonstrable than are the reasons outlined in the body of this section, such nonunion employers as IBM, Texas Instruments, Eastman Kodak, Delta Airlines, and DuPont regularly support its existence by proudly citing the fact that they have not as yet been vulnerable to any appreciable unionization. DuPont has been nothing if not enthusiastic in pointing out that national unions have succeeded in only 13 out of 235 representation elections there since 1940, for example, and Delta's chairman is given to the use of such declarations as "If we ever become unionized, this will be because we've made mistakes.")

Such comments as those above, as with our treatment of "Why Workers Join Unions," can be offered only as generalizations. For a specific union–management relationship, the value differences may hardly be as pronounced; the writers are personally familiar, for that matter, with several relationships in which the unions seem to place far higher values on ability and efficiency than do the managements. Such value conflicts as the ones enumerated are, however, quite genuine in many union–management situations and thus represent the realities of labor relations rather than its stereotypes. As such, they serve to reinforce management's opposition to unionism, however much this opposition may be anchored to such other reasons as the decision-making issue.

LABOR RELATIONS CONSULTANTS

When an employer's opposition to unionization is implacable, it may succumb to an urge to use "labor relations consultants," retaining their services either to prevent a union from gaining bargaining rights or to get rid of an established union through a decertification election (about which more will be said in Chapter 3). And in fact the number of such specialists (who are usually either lawyers or psychologists) has risen appreciably in recent years. By some estimates, there are currently over 1,500 of them and they collectively receive many millions of dollars annually for their services from employers who engage them.

At times consultants advise their clients to engage in activities that are quite illegal under national labor policy, such as placing agents in the workplace to spy on employees; harassing and discharging union members; avoiding the hiring of black people (who are—in the opinion of at least one practitioner in this line of work—"more prone to unionization than whites"); and initiating decertification elections. Given the state of labor relations law, however, consultants have a wide area of lawful tactics and strategies to place at their clients' disposal.

Consultants, some of whom earn as much as $250,000 annually, often hold seminars stressing such topics as "Making Unions Unnecessary," "Avoiding Unions," and "Putting the Union Organizer on the Defensive." They also produce a wide variety of articles and books that find a lucrative market among antiunion managements.

MANAGEMENT PHILOSOPHIES TOWARD UNIONS

Given the many different roots of management opposition and the pervasiveness of so many of these, it is tempting to speculate that, deep in their corporate hearts, the basic attitude of *most* business enterprises must be one of intransigent hostility. Were this presumed attitude, in other words, to be stated as an official policy, it would read approximately, "We seek to weaken organized labor by any and all means at our command, to frustrate it in its demands, to grant it nothing that is not absolutely necessary, and under no circumstances to make any attempt at accepting the union as a permanent part of our employee relations. If we adhere to this approach consistently and with sufficient patience, our workers will see that the union offers them nothing. And they will ultimately arise and vote the union out at least as enthusiastically as they have voted it in."

There can be no denying that some executives do espouse this policy, as above, and that at an earlier time in American labor history, many managers did so. The irony of contemporary labor relations, however, is that despite management's continuing opposition to unionism and its constant resistance to new labor inroads, much of the employer community has substantially departed from such a provocative stance. It has moved instead to what Professor Lloyd Reynolds of Yale has called a "defensive endurance" philosophy: "If this is what our workers want, I guess we'll have to go along with it." In a word, the union is *accommodated,* however unwelcome and even unpalatable its presence may be. Management remains ever on guard as to "matters of principle," seeks to prevent the union from "intruding" in areas that are "the proper function of management," and frequently is highly critical of certain union actions. *But* the labor organization is taken for granted, harmony with it is sought wherever possible, and the employer can deal with the union on a day-to-day basis without feeling that conciliation has made him a traitor to his class. When people speak of "maturity" in labor relations, they are frequently thinking of this rapidly growing managerial posture—and organized labor's reciprocation of it.

A specific union–management relationship even today, however, need not necessarily be marked by *either* employer attitude depicted above. Variety is still the essence of our labor relations system, and so many variables can influence management policies that it is unrealistic to assume that the only possibilities are (1) intransigence and (2) accommodation. Variations in the abilities of managers to accurately understand the membership goals and leadership desires of the unions with which they are dealing, and in the skill with which companies have met these union aspirations—to say nothing of the nature of these goals and desires themselves—have led to a wide diversity of management positions. So, too, have variations in the managers' own relative degrees of security within the corporate framework, and the economic health of the companies involved. Obviously, variations in union attitudes may be highly relevant. And the same can be said of such other variables as the past labor relationships between the parties, the technological environments of both the industry and the employer, and even the role of the government, where this is a factor. Most of these topics will receive fuller treatment in later chapters of this book. Here it is pertinent to note the many grounds for differing attitudes toward unions among managerial groups.

Thus, although accommodation today is the dominant attitude in many relationships, having followed an era of intransigence, there are many variations on the theme of "management labor relations philosophies." And even among the more general of these different philosophies, at least six separate types (including the two above) can be distinguished.[31]

In reviewing these different possibilities for management policy, let it be clearly understood that in each case the employer's ability to adopt the avenue under description depends upon a factor that is beyond its direct control: the union's own basic policy for its dealings with management. The labor organization, obviously, must reciprocate in kind, and in the absence of such reciprocation, at least in the long run, management's chosen approach becomes a completely fruitless one. In short, the employer can *work toward* each of the following approaches, but this managerial project will always be subject to some modification, depending upon the union's response.

1 *Conflict,* or the intransigent, uncompromising attitude depicted previously, is now fast fading from the labor relations scene. Nonetheless, this attitude existed on a wide scale prior to World War II. Such a managerial stance arose to a great extent because many companies had been newly organized before that time, and because union organizational campaigns have never been notable for their sensitivity to personal feelings. Unions rarely resist the temptation in these circumstances to engage in negative stereotyping of those who run the organization. The top managers are painted as ruthless, greedy profiteers, ready to do almost anything to increase return on investment and wholly insensitive to the most obvious of human problems. Any actual incidents that might support such charges are, of course, produced as accompaniments to such charges, but lack of available evidence is not necessarily any kind of obstacle at all.

The union, consequently, does more than "undermine employee loyalty to the company" at such a time; it frequently goes well beyond the borders of the factual and bruises management egos in the process. Add managerial fears of decision-making encroachments and of union values that are antithetical to those of management, as well as the other grounds for management's opposition to unionism on top of such an emotion-charged atmosphere, and it should not be surprising that many companies in the period immediately following their unionization embraced a philosophy of "no acceptance" of the union. Only in the face of the law and union power could unions extract concessions from such managements, and then only quite begrudgingly and on as temporary a basis as possible.

Some companies and an ever-growing number of public servants are, of course, even today among the newly organized, since new union conquests hardly ended with the unionization of the major mass-production industries in the 1933–1941 period. And it is in the labor relations of these, indeed, that one is most apt today

---

[31] The late Benjamin M. Selekman was justifiably considered one of the foremost theoreticians in this field, although he generally portrayed "bargaining relationships" and not merely the management portion of these relationships. The exposition that follows bears a strong indebtedness to his work (although it departs from it on several major points), and particularly to his *Labor Relations and Human Relations* (New York: McGraw-Hill, 1947) and his "Framework for Study of Cases in Labor Relations," in *Problems in Labor Relations*, 3rd ed., coauthored with S. H. Fuller, T. Kennedy, and J. M. Baitsell (New York: McGraw-Hill, 1964), pp. 1–11.

to encounter the Conflict philosophy. But this managerial attitude is not confined to new bargaining relationships: A minority of long-organized companies also currently adheres to it, owing to changes in management personnel, changes in union personnel, or various other factors—including the particular management's sheer refusal to abandon the hope that if unions are never really accepted by their companies, they will eventually also lose acceptance from their worker–members. In recent years, various newspaper publishers throughout the country have seemed, to many observers, to epitomize this latter situation. So, too, have the owners and operators in the world of organized professional sports, most particularly baseball.

The mammoth Litton Industries, at least if allegations from the several unions that deal with it are to be believed, by repeatedly closing plants before unions can get in, and refusing to negotiate contracts even after unions have been successful in organizing Litton locations, has also represented the intransigent approach masterfully. Other deserving current nominees for the "Best Representative of a Conflict Philosophy Award" are Caterpillar Tractor, the world's largest construction equipment maker, and Allis-Chalmers, whose recent battles with the United Automobile Workers have been nothing if not nasty ones.

Such an attitude not only does not lead to amicable labor relations but can also be expected to foster union militancy, as the union reacts by engaging in various pressure tactics (often including slowdowns of production and sudden "wildcat" strikes) to gain through these means what it cannot hope to procure at the bargaining table. Finally, managements embracing a Conflict philosophy run a decided risk of being found in violation of the labor laws, particularly those involving "refusal to bargain" and discrimination against employees for the purpose of discouraging membership in a union.

It is primarily for these reasons that many Conflict philosophies have either been dismissed as realistic management alternatives in the first place or given way to:

2 An *Armed Truce* attitude. Here, employer representatives are motivated by approximately the following logic: "We are well aware that the vital interests of the employer and the union are poles apart, and that they always will be. But this doesn't mean that every action we take in our labor relations should be geared to weakening the union and thus forcing head-on conflict with it. Instead, since we can expect the union to firmly press to extend its fields of interest, our basic mission is to press, just as ambitiously, toward containing it within limits. We will honor the law immaculately, and therefore deal with the union without any subterfuges on the subject of wages, hours, and conditions of employment; but we will hold our bargaining practice strictly within the boundaries of these legal obligations and thus define our negotiation scope as rigidly as possible. Moreover, we will interpret any agreements emerging from these negotiations strictly and insist upon the union's observing, in its day-to-day conduct, its contractual obligations 100 percent."

What the management members (and those on the union side, too) really want here is, as Barbash has aptly pointed out, a "workable adversary relationship," and because they do seek such a situation, they have "*normalized*" it.[32] Indeed, Barbash is hardly alone in believing that this adversary principle endures "because it reflects the objective reality of modern industrial organization—its competitiveness, its pervasive command-and-obey organization, and its zero-sum efficiency ethic, all of which by their nature pit participants against one another. We must not exclude the final possibility that there is something in the human psyche that infuses every human situation with latent aggressiveness."[33]

Even today, many union–management relationships have made no more progress than this. The union representatives return the feelings of their management counterparts, and the struggle for power goes on indefinitely. Wages, hours, and other rigidly construed employee-relations areas are dealt with as their issues arise, but the more crucial question of union security versus management rights, being insoluble in such an atmosphere, continually blocks more constructive dealings. With some justification, the General Electric Company has frequently been regarded as an excellent example of a company that has espoused this Armed Truce philosophy, at least until recently. The Timken Company, too, might be said to meet the criteria. ("If you need mercy, forget about it," a steelworker leader asserted with some bitterness not long ago. "You're not going to get it from Timken.")[34]

3 *Power Bargaining,* as an alternative, is more conducive to solving labor relations problems than is the Armed Truce approach. As is *not* the case under either Conflict or Armed Truce, managers in Power Bargaining can "accept" the union and, in fact, tend to pride themselves on their sense of "realism," which leaves them no choice but to acknowledge the union's power. (A prerequisite for this philosophy, obviously, is that the union *have* significant power.) By the same token, such executives press their own company's bargaining power to the maximum that economic and other conditions at any one time allow. The managerial rationale is, more or less: "We face strong and deeply entrenched unions squarely and with an accurate perception of their power—and we accept them as sovereign spokespersons for their side. We are practical people and economic realists, not crusaders with naïve faith in idealistic trimmings. Our task is not to pursue the fruitless approach of directly opposing and limiting the union, but to increase and then use our own power to offset that of the other side where we can."

Might does not necessarily make right, but it can lead to agreement at the bargaining table. And on this basis it can be argued that continued controversy is minimized in Power Bargaining. However unenthusiastically, managements in such a relationship can live with their unions, for at least the short run, in most areas affecting employee relations.

[32] Jack Barbash, "Values in Industrial Relations: The Case of the Adversary Principle," in *Proceedings of the Thirty-third Annual Meeting, Industrial Relations Research Association,* September 5–7, 1980, p. 1.
[33] *Ibid.,* pp. 2–3.
[34] *Business Week,* November 9, 1981, p. 44.

On the other hand, any relationship focused upon a balance of power is a highly tenuous one. It always contains the danger of regression to one of the earlier approaches when the power ratios change. As such, Power Bargaining has not been widespread at any one time in American labor relations, although many industries marked by small employers and highly centralized unions have at one time or another seen it. In such cases, the employers have typically associated in an attempt at a united front to counter the union's strength.

In short, for the reasons indicated, most managements in the current economy view all three previous alternatives as unsatisfactory. Since, needless to say, their unions wholeheartedly agree with them on this point, the climate for a more harmonious relationship—in the form of Accommodation—exists.

4 *Accommodation*, however, is hardly the same as cooperation. As pointed out earlier, management remains constantly vigilant as to "principle" and, as does the union, clings to such values as "orbits of respective equities and privileges." In this regard, Accommodation differs little from Armed Truce. Moreover, the management gaze is still riveted upon the traditional agenda of collective bargaining—wages, hours, and conditions of employment—and there is a self-conscious employer unwillingness to *officially* discuss anything that cannot rather rigidly be construed as falling within these topics.

The property of Accommodation that makes it unique lies in the area of everyday practice rather than in formal declarations. The late Benjamin M. Selekman provided a definitive description of what results in daily affairs when a management philosophy of "meeting the union halfway" is reciprocated by the labor organization:

> . . . Within these bounds [of "principles," "equities," and "privileges"] the leaders, the ranks, and the organizations . . . interact with comfortable, "customary," familiar patterns of behavior. They have evolved their routines of recognizing functions and settling differences. They have learned how to adjust one to another . . . , to accept the reduction of conflict as an accomplishment without demanding its total elimination. They have proved themselves willing to . . . conciliate whenever necessary, and to tolerate at all times.[35]

Such a definition in no way implies that the employer need go out of its way to *help* organized labor. For that matter, opposition to the concept of unionism in general may still remain the hallmark of management's philosophy, as it frequently does. In an atmosphere of Accommodation, however, the roles of both emotion and raw power are minimized, in favor of the management's *adjusting* to the union *as it is*. Extreme legalism in at least the basic areas of wages, hours, and conditions is supplanted by compromise, flexibility, and "toleration." As such, Accommodation constitutes a considerably more positive approach to labor relations than do any of the previous alternatives.

There is ample evidence that the mainstream of American management has

[35] Selekman, Fuller, Kennedy, and Baitsell, *Problems in Labor Relations*, p. 7.

today entered the Accommodation stage in its dealings with unions. All the major automobile and steel employers now exhibit Accommodation characteristics—if not in every labor relations matter (subcontracting, production standards, and the possibility of plant shutdowns remain definite sticking-points, as we shall see), at least in the great bulk of them. And so, too, do most managements nowadays in such long-unionized industries as petroleum, construction, railroading, the airlines, trucking, rubber, and textiles. Not surprisingly, there is still wide variation in the nature and quality of contract administration among companies, and even among locations within the same company. But the growth of Accommodation has quite visibly resulted in the significant development of mutually acceptable policy and in more orderly day-to-day union–management relations, results that even the great diversity of labor relations cannot obscure.

5 *Cooperation,* involving full acceptance of the union as an active partner in a formal plan, is for exactly that reason decidedly rare. It necessitates a management (as well as a union) that is willing to extend matters of everyday union–management relations beyond the traditional areas to such broader fields as technological change, waste, and business solvency. And this, in turn, calls for corporate executives who genuinely believe that unions can make definite and positive contributions to the success of the firm, through furnishing management with information it would not otherwise have, through winning over worker support for management goals, and in various other ways.

In a formal plan for Cooperation, the management supports not only the right but the *desirability* of union participation, and the union reciprocates by actively endorsing the employer's right and need for an adequate return on its investment. The two labor relations parties *jointly* deal with both personnel and production problems as they occur. Suggestions pertaining to cost reduction and productivity improvement are typically solicited from all worker levels. And whatever economic gains in increased efficiency may be realized from such cooperation projects are normally shared by the employer with the work force.

Most managements that have adopted this approach to labor relations have, by and large, been well publicized, either as participants in rather formalized "Scanlon Plans" or, as in the case of the Tennessee Valley Authority and the city of Jamestown, New York, independently. But the very fact that so much publicity has been given to thse plans based on the cooperative approach graphically symbolizes how few in number they have been thus far. Moreover, the approach is still so incompatible with present-day management (and, often, union) value systems that, to date, most such plans have been implemented only as a last resort when the management was faced with a severe financial crisis. The word "cooperation" is frequently used in management addresses to worker groups, but in the manager's lexicon of today, it obviously has a meaning that is considerably more restricted than the one depicted here.[36]

---

[36] Chapter 9 will inspect another form of "cooperation": Quality of Work Life programs, whose ultimate acceptability to labor–management relations in general has yet to be determined.

As different as each of the previous five approaches to labor relations is from the four others, there is a common denominator: Whichever one is selected is, subject to its ability to meet management goals, at the outset strictly the company's business. Ultimately, a Conflict approach may lead to a strike involving government intervention, or an amassing of strength in a Power Bargaining situation may have other legal ramifications, and in any of the five cases, the union may, of course, react in such a way to make the approach unsuitable. The company can hardly do much with Accommodation if the union is Conflict oriented. But at least at the outset, the employer is perfectly free to experiment with any of the various approaches.

6 The same cannot be said of one other approach, *Collusion.* If, up until now, the enumerated management alternatives can be viewed as leading to successively more union–management harmony (from Conflict on the one hand to Cooperation on the other), this one can be looked upon as generating "too much harmony."

Under Collusion, employers have been known to bribe union officials to agree to bargaining table concessions and substandard (or "sweetheart") contracts, and sometimes to waive the formality of actually having a contract altogether. And these bribes have on occasion taken imaginative forms: interest-free loans, ownership interests (invariably disguised) in the company, and the placement of company insurance contracts with insurance agencies owned by the union officials.

But such activity has almost exclusively been confined to narrow sectors of local-market industries, with marginal and intensely competitive employers for whom a small difference in labor cost can mean the difference between solvency and insolvency, and where visibility to the public law-enforcement agencies is relatively slight. Having named the least ethical sectors of the garment trades, building trades, trucking, waterfront, and entertainment industries, one has almost exhausted the list.

LABOR RELATIONS IN THE PUBLIC SECTOR

If the unionized percentage of the total civilian labor force has registered some slippage in recent years, and if the figures from the overall white collar frontier in the recent past can be described as essentially unchanged, organized labor can point with satisfaction to its organizational successes in the fastest-growing employment sector of all, that of the public employee.

In 1940, according to the official figures of the U.S. Department of Labor, the nation's governmental work force at all levels (federal, state, and local) numbered 4.2 million, or 9.6 percent of total payroll employment. By 1960, the figure had exactly doubled, to 8.4 million. And, rising even more dramatically when compared with overall labor force figures, it reached the 12.5-million mark by the end of the 1960s. By 1976 it had climbed to almost 15 million (and over 18 percent of total payroll employment in the country), although this was to be its high-water mark for at least a few years. After the late 1970s, negative reaction from the taxpayers to the rapid growth caused the figures to hit a plateau, albeit in no way to decrease.

Undoubtedly, many factors explain the strong upward curve. But Loewenberg and Moskow seem to have their fingers on the foremost three of them in pointing out that (1) all else being equal, a growing population (the U.S. figures grew by 55 percent between 1940 and 1970, for example) requires an even larger growth in public services; (2) technological progress and relative affluence have produced a whole new gamut of challenges (for instance, air-lane regulations, water pollution, mass urban transport); and (3) changes in concepts of what government can do or should do vary over time, but generally in a more ambitious direction.[37]

No reliable figures for union membership among government employees are available for the period before 1956, when civil servants in the Bureau of Labor Statistics began collecting this kind of data. But where the BLS's information reveals 915,000 governmental unionists in 1956 (heavily concentrated in the federal service, and particularly among its postal, shipyard, and arsenal employees), the same agency reported almost 1.5 million organized workers only eight years later, and by 1983 was estimating that somewhat over 3.0 million public employees—widely distributed throughout all levels of government and embracing a spectrum that included such disparate types as engineers, zoo keepers, firefighters, jail guards, teachers, sewage workers, and common laborers—were in union ranks.

It should thus come as no surprise to the reader that the greatest rate of growth in the entire labor movement has occurred among unions that represent, either exclusively or primarily, public employees. The American Federation of State, County and Municipal Employees (AFSCME), gaining 1,000 new members a week through most of the 1970s and up to a total membership of some 950,000 by the mid-1980s, as noted earlier (from only 210,000 in 1961), has until quite recently been the fastest-growing union in the nation. An almost comparable success story has been registered by the American Federation of Teachers, which increased (as also noted earlier) from 60,000 members in 1960 to over a half-million some twenty-five years later. And the labor movement can also take considerable encouragement from the quadrupling of members recorded by the American Federation of Government Employees during the 1960s (to 280,000 ten years later), although the size of this organization—with little growth in its primary potential membership market of defense and Pentagon installations—has essentially been unchanged from its 1970 figure in more recent years.

Even the foregoing statistics understate the degree of recent union penetration of the public sector, however. It was generally estimated at the time of this writing that at least another 3 million employees belonged to professional and civil service associations that were outside the official ranks of organized labor but in many cases distinguishable from bona fide unions only by their titles. Into this latter

[37] J. Joseph Loewenberg and Michael H. Moskow, *Collective Bargaining in Government* (Englewood Cliffs, N.J.: Prentice-Hall, 1972), p. 3.

category would certainly fall the fast-growing and increasingly militant 1.8-million-member National Education Association, the heavy majority of whose members are now covered by collective bargaining agreements. So, too, would the Assembly of Government Employees (estimated strength of over 600,000 members in various state employee subunits), the American Nurses Association (representing the interests of almost 250,000 employees), and the Fraternal Order of Police (with over 125,000 members), all of these also having shown rapid rises in organizational size over the past few years.

One must freely acknowledge that organized labor still has a long way to go before its penetration of the public sector can be deemed to be anywhere near complete. Based only on official union-membership figures, the 3 million unionized public employees probably constitute no more than 20 percent of the total membership potential. And even if all 3 million association members are included (and, as indicated above, not all of them should be, since an indeterminate although doubtless minority percentage of them are not bargained for collectively), the figure still comes to not much more than about 40 percent of the total public-sector employee population. But the gains of the recent past are nonetheless highly impressive and deserve exploration.

The Growth of Public-Sector Unionism: Some Explanations

In all likelihood, three factors have been particularly responsible for this new union thrust.

First and probably foremost, *legal developments* since 1960 have given organized labor both a protection and an encouragement that were previously conspicuous by their absence. At the federal level, a highly influential event was President John F. Kennedy's 1962 issuance of Executive Order 10988, constituting the first recognition ever on the part of the federal government that its employees were entitled to join unions and bargain collectively with the executive agencies for which they worked. Three types of union recognition were provided—informal, formal, and exclusive—depending upon the percentage of employees in the bargaining unit represented by the union. And, if the latter could gain exclusive recognition (by showing that it represented at least 10 percent of the employees involved and then being selected or designated by a majority of employees within the bargaining unit), the employing agency was compelled to meet and confer regularly with such a union on matters affecting personnel policy and practices and working conditions.

The order did remove many key topics from the scope of this collective bargaining—among them, mandatory union membership, agency budgetary negotiations, and new technology—and it had certain deficiencies in the dispute-settlement area (in case of a bargaining impasse, should mediation efforts fail, the only available procedure was an appeal to a higher level of the agency's own management). But E.O. 10988, nonetheless, by attempting to provide organizational and bargaining rights for employees of the federal government in essentially the same way as these rights had been established for employees in the private sector almost three decades earlier by the Wagner Act, provided a significant stimulus to union growth not just in the federal employee province but, in short order, also at the state and local government levels. As former President John F. Griner of the American Federation of Government Employees could succinctly observe, "No matter that the collective bargaining rights [under E.O. 10988] were modified, truncated, almost emasculated, E.O. 10988 was the . . . Magna Charta. The workers saw their opportunity. They grasped it. They joined the union in droves."[38]

The White House, moreover, liberalized its "Magna Charta" a very few years later. Richard M. Nixon's Executive Order 11491, effective as of January 1, 1970, abolished both informal and formal union recognition on the grounds that these two types had proved to have had little meaning. It provided, instead, that any union could gain exclusive recognition if selected by a majority of the bargaining-unit employees in a secret-ballot election. It also created a three-member Federal Labor Relations Council to decide major policy matters and to administer and interpret the order itself, substituting these officials for the large potpourri of department heads who had handled—often quite inconsistently—these activities under E.O. 10988. And it gave the assistant secretary of labor for labor–management relations authority to settle disputes over the makeup of bargaining units and representation rights, to order and supervise elections, and to disqualify unions from recognition because of corrupt or undemocratic influences; formerly, these matters had been handled by the particular federal agency involved, and its ultimate judgment on them was not subject to appeal.

E.O. 11491 also established an impartial Federal Services Impasses Panel to settle disputes arising during contract negotiations, by final and binding arbitration if necessary. As stated above, the old order had provided for no such impartial procedure in the case of bargaining deadlocks (except for mediation), effectively placing unions at the ultimate mercy of the federal agency with which they were negotiating (and thus allowing one labor leader to compare the whole process to "a football game in which one side brings along the referee"). Since federal employees lack the right to strike, the new system for arbitration by neutrals seemed both equitable and realistic.

For all this liberalization contained in E.O. 11491, Congress in 1979 enacted a law that supplanted it. For many years, indeed since President Kennedy's original executive order, the government unions had pressured Congress to provide a *statutory* basis for the federal labor relations program, and their persistence paid off when Congress enacted the Civil Service Reform Act of 1978, Title VII of which superseded E.O. 11491 in January of the following year. Though it carried forward the basic rights and duties of federal employees and agencies as contained in the executive order, it made a number of important changes in the federal labor relations program. Functions formerly performed by the Federal Labor Relations

[38] *Ibid.*, p. 57.

Council and the assistant secretary of labor were lodged in an independent Federal Labor Relations Authority (FLRA). In large measure, the FLRA duplicates the functions of the National Labor Relations Board, which has jurisdiction in the private sector. By protecting the tenure of the members of the FLRA, and by making it independent from any existing federal agency, the law placed the new agency in a better position to administer objectively and effectively.

The new law also made a number of substantive changes. In the "management rights" area, federal agencies are now expressly prohibited from bargaining on mission, budget, organization, number of employees, and matters of internal security. Permitted but not required are negotiations concerning the methods, means, and technology of conducting agency operations. The law also expands the scope of matters subject to negotiated grievance and arbitration procedures including, for the first time, employee discharge, demotion, and long-term suspensions. When an employee alleges discrimination in violation of the Civil Rights Act, the employee may elect either to use the negotiated procedure or file charges with the Equal Employment Opportunity Commission, but not both. Upon a union's request, the federal agency involved is required to deduct dues of its members provided the employees sign the necessary dues checkoff authorization cards. To balance the scales, official time (work time) may be used by employees representing the union in negotiations (including attendance at impasse settlement proceedings) to the extent that management officials are on paid time.

These changes, significant improvements over the predecessor executive orders, have generally been welcomed by both federal employee labor unions and agency management.

At the state level, although the influence of the developments in Washington can be clearly detected, the trend toward giving legal protection to civil servants in their efforts to organize and bargain collectively has been even more pronounced. Prior to the enactment of the Kennedy order, only one state, Wisconsin in 1959, had extended such a right to public employees. By the time of this writing, virtually all other states had sanctioned collective bargaining for at least some types of public workers. Indeed, some forty of them had enacted legislation conferring such protection upon all (or almost all) state and local employees, and laws in eight states (Alaska, Hawaii, Minnesota, Montana, Oregon, Pennsylvania, Vermont, and Wisconsin) even allowed—in different degrees—some strikes. Court decisions in three other states (Michigan, New Hampshire, and Rhode Island) had effectively also made the strike weapon a viable tool for some public workers in those jurisdictions.

And no signs of a reversal are on the horizon of either this trend or the significant increase in state and local employer union membership that it has generated.

A *second* factor behind the explosion in public-sector unionism has been the public servant's increasing unhappiness as the *remuneration package has fallen* farther and farther *behind* that of private employment.

Wages in the two sectors had historically been quite comparable, but by the mid-1960s the gap, even going beyond that of the general union–nonunion discrepancy already touched on in this chapter, was fully in evidence. In San Francisco, for example, journeymen electricians earned on the average $12,979 in 1966, whereas city librarians with M.A. degrees there could expect a top salary of $12,150. In the same year, city laborers in Boston averaged a significant $737 less than manufacturing laborers. And in Detroit in 1967, city stock clerks received for their annual average incomes a full $1,085 less than did stock clerks in the automobile industry.[39] As a general statement, public employees in these years earned from 10 to 30 percent less than their exact counterparts, who perhaps worked down the street from them, in private industry.[40]

Even more jarring to the civil servants, however, was the lag in working conditions underpinning this wage package, since these conditions had for years been far *superior* in the public sector. For their traditionally comparable pay, the public servants had been asked to work shorter hours (with appreciably more liberal holiday and vacation entitlements than their private counterparts), had been given a degree of job security that almost no other workers possessed, and could look forward to a pension entitlement that in most instances would dwarf that of private-industry employees—if, in fact, the latter even had a pension expectation. By the 1960s, all these relative advantages had eroded, as public-sector fringe benefits and working conditions saw little further liberalization, while these areas in private industry first caught up with and then slowly eclipsed the public emoluments. If the public employees were not completely disgruntled in the face of this development, they were certainly—to paraphrase the late P. G. Wodehouse—a long distance from being gruntled. Increasingly, they turned to their newly legalized avenue of collective bargaining to redress what was viewed as a clear injustice.

Third, and finally, one cannot disregard the *general spirit of the times* in explaining the rise of public unionism. These same growth years were marked throughout American society by a degree of social upheaval rare in the nation's history. No part of the established order was seemingly immune from attack, as blacks, Hispanics, women, homosexuals, student activists, an increasingly broad spectrum of citizens opposed to the Vietnam War, and even older people organized—often, militantly—to exert in support of their respective causes a collective pressure that could hardly be overlooked. The results were, as in the case of the black demands upon organized labor that will be dealt with in Chapter 2, generally mixed. But sufficient progress was certainly made to bring home to many public employees who had eschewed organization until that point the advantages to be gained by collective action.

To this trio of key explanations, readers might care to add others of their choosing: The increasing vulnerability to unionization of many public-sector managers because of archaic personnel policies; a fear on the part of government workers in the latter, inflation-dominated years of this period that their jobs would be the first to be eliminated in the face of growing taxpayer resistance to the higher

---

[39] Thomas R. Brooks, *Toil and Trouble*, 2nd rev. ed. (New York: Dell Publishing, 1971), p. 306.
[40] *Ibid.*

costs of public administration (an issue that will be touched upon shortly); the changing complexion of the government work force itself, with an ever-higher percentage of younger and often more aggressive jobholders; and perhaps the sheer numerical growth in public employees, making them a more tempting target for the union organizer. In any case, however, the reasons for the demonstrable, if to date incomplete, successes of labor in the public-employee arena appear at the very least to have been understandable. As such, they seem destined to continue, certainly for a while.

The Public-Employee Unionist: The Strike Issue

"If you treat public employees bad enough," said George Meany in late 1974, on the occasion of the founding convention of the AFL–CIO's new Public Employee Department, "they'll go on strike and they'll get the support of the union movement." Meany, a man rarely accused of mincing words, also told the same audience that public workers involved in labor disputes should feel free to strike "any damn time you feel like going on strike."[41] This was not the first time that year that the (then) AFL–CIO chief executive had registered these sentiments. Nor did he depart from the views expressed by many other, if less influential, labor chieftains in advancing them. But the setting this time—the new department symbolized the conquests of the recent past by uniting under its aegis 24 AFL–CIO-affiliated unions representing more than 2 million workers—gave a special impact to his words.

Ironically, had Meany said exactly the same thing only a few years earlier, he would very likely have been either publicly vilified as a nihilistic demagogue or dismissed as a droll master of hyperbole (this being the same Meany who on an earlier occasion had offered his observation that "most college professors, when given a choice of publish or perish, tend to make the wrong decision"). For, throughout labor's long history in this country, public policy toward the public-sector strike had been clear, unequivocal, and resoundingly negative. Calvin Coolidge had deemed such work stoppages "anarchy": In a famous statement referring to the 1919 Boston police strike, he had also declared, "There is no right to strike against the public safety by anybody, anywhere, at any time"; Franklin D. Roosevelt had called them "unthinkable"[42]; all relevant government regulations (including E.O. 11491) for federal employees had historically banned the public-worker strike; and as Barrett and Lobel have asserted, "In the mid-1960s, it would be accurate to say that public policy in all states clearly prohibited work stoppages of public employees by statute, court decision, or attorneys' general opinion."[43] Indeed, public-employee organizations themselves showed their general agreement with this constraint by including, in almost all cases, total bans on work stoppages in their own constitutions.

---

[41] *Wall Street Journal,* November 7, 1974, p. 29.
[42] Jerome T. Barrett and Ira B. Lobel, "Public Sector Strikes—Legislative and Court Treatment," *Monthly Labor Review,* 97, No. 9 (September 1974), 19.
[43] *Ibid.*

What was past was definitely not prologue in this case, however. If, prior to 1960, public-sector strikes were all but unknown, and if, even as late as 1960, only 36 such strikes were recorded, the 1970 totals showed 412 of them,[44] including an unprecedented eight-day strike by the nation's postal employees and another nationwide one by airport flight controllers. The trend was accelerating when Meany advanced his views on the subject, and it would not visibly diminish in the later years of the decade. An all-time record of 593 public-employee strikes actually took place in 1979, and as a publication of that year could assert, fairly enough in view of the "reality so vividly communicated by the media":

> We may see firemen watching homes burn down as they pursue their labor relations goals, or nurses walking a picket line to achieve proper union recognition. Your local police may suddenly begin giving out traffic tickets for everything as they carry out a planned slowdown. . . . Sanitation workers might leave your garbage to pile up in your driveway, or the guards at the correctional facility might decide to withhold their services. It may be the postal employees who become reluctant to handle your mail unless collective bargaining works for them, or the teachers who carry out a strike action to effect an increase. There are a dozen other examples of the criticality of labor relations in the public sector . . .[45]

Yet the harsh punishments all but universally called for by the various laws were essentially being ignored by civic authorities. (For example, in the federal government, any striker is subject to up to five years in jail plus a fine and dismissal, but as A. H. Raskin has pointed out in speaking of the aforementioned postal and flight controllers' stoppages, "No striker ever got close to Leavenworth or Lewisburg,"[46] and no striker has since.) It was, indeed, in recognition of this fact—that except in the rarest of instances, the antistrike laws could be violated with impunity given the political realities—that the several states mentioned earlier had legalized the public strike for at least some workers. And, of potentially great significance, it was because of this awareness also that an increasing number of U.S. congressmen appeared to be in basic agreement with the view of the new AFL–CIO department that *all* public-sector strikes except for those creating a demonstrable peril to the public health should be legalized.

On the other hand, not quite *every* public-sector strike has violated the laws with impunity. When the nation's 11,500 flight controllers waged a second strike eleven years later—in August 1981—President Ronald Reagan aggressively reacted by firing them and also by setting the wheels in motion for their union (the Professional Air Traffic Controllers Organization, or PATCO) to be removed as the controllers' legally recognized bargaining representative (as it ultimately was). PATCO, which displayed surprising ineptness in not trying to win support from other unions in advance of its stoppage and whose major demand (for higher wages

[44] U.S. Department of Labor, Bureau of Labor Statistics, *Report 1727*, 1972.
[45] Marvin J. Levine and Eugene C. Hagburg, *Labor Relations in the Public Sector* (Salt Lake City: Brighton Publishing Company, 1979), p. xv.
[46] *New York Times*, September 22, 1974, p. E-2.

than the controllers' current $35,000–$40,000 annually and shorter hours) was not one calculated to win much support from outsiders anyhow, was hardly typical in any of its actions. But Reagan's actions were well received by a heavy majority of all Americans, and some experts thought that future political figures might heed a lesson here and act similarly in the years ahead.

Whatever happens, the next decade will presumably see a resolution of the inevitably emotion-laden issue of public-sector strikes. And, given the general ineffectuality of the present strike bans (PATCO notwithstanding), this resolution will quite probably be on the side of the right to strike except for (1) such clearly indispensable civil servants as policemen and firefighters and (2) cases in which the peril to health and safety is otherwise shown to exist; in these cases, most likely, binding arbitration by third parties will be utilized to resolve bargaining impasses.

Supporters of such a development—and in their ranks are many neutrals—contend that this right to strike would only recognize reality. They argue also that only the strike threat can guarantee that public officials will bargain in good faith. And they point out that the many private-sector unionists who perform jobs identical to those in the public arena (for example, transit employees, teachers, and maintenance workers), since they do have the right to strike, possess an inequitable bargaining advantage over their government counterparts.

Arguments on the negative (or antistrike) side focus on these factors: (1) In the private sector, the employer can counter the strike weapon with a lockout of his own, but he can hardly do this as a government official, and hence the legalized public strike would create a large labor relations imbalance; (2) public pressures on the public official to end a strike are infinitely greater than those on the private administrator, and thus the former is forced to capitulate more quickly, to the ultimate detriment of the community; and (3) the monopolistic nature of virtually all public-sector employment makes almost all of it "essential," and thus the public should be guaranteed against its legalized interruption.

Whatever the merits of these latter contentions and supplementary antistrike ones,[47] the momentum definitely belonged to those taking the other side of the argument as this was being written.

Public Employees and Harder Times

Something that was far *less* to labor's liking was also happening in the public sector at the time of this writing, however. A combination of a widespread taxpayers' revolt, severe decreases in federal payments to state and local governments, and a definite animus on the part of citizens to perceived public employee excesses (symbolized, indeed, by the popularity of Reagan's PATCO actions) was taking a good deal of clout away from public-sector unions—ironically, even amid the improved prospects for their right to strike.

In mid-1978, embittered taxpayers in California—increasingly upset by ever-

---

[47] See John F. Burton, Jr., and Charles Krider, "The Role and Consequences of Strikes by Public Employees," in Loewenberg and Moskow, *Collective Bargaining,* pp. 274–88, for a lucid treatment of many of these considerations.

higher tax burdens and also mindful of the ravages of inflation on their own budgets—approved a severe limitation on the swollen property taxes in their state by voting by a landslide margin for a so-called Proposition 13. And the consequences of this popular referendum verdict—which was remarkable as much for its one-sidedness as for its direction—were rapidly assimilated across the nation as voters all over the country registered similar sentiments and politicians from Massachusetts to Montana found themselves with far fewer resources than they had previously been allocated to administer governmental services. Labor costs—typically accounting for 65 to 85 percent of governmental budgets—were obviously prime targets for diminution as it became painfully obvious to all public figures that standing up to union demands (even when these were perhaps warranted) would be a much more profitable course of action for them than would accommodating such demands.

When it took office in 1981, the Reagan administration compounded labor's woes by rapidly cutting almost $20 billion in federal payments to state and local governments for programs running the gamut from education to public employment. Coming on top of the Proposition 13 occurrences, the cuts were likened by one union leader to "the San Francisco fire on top of the earthquake."[48] While in theory there was nothing to stop the state and local governments from making up for this federal niggardliness by raising revenue in other ways, in fact the latter course of action was rarely followed. Consequently, employment in government—until then, as mentioned above, one of the nation's great growth industries—no longer increased at all and even decreased in some places (if not on a national aggregate basis).

Amid all of this taxpayer unwillingness to part with money and White House-engineered austerity, some amount of spine-stiffening by politicians in their dealings with public-sector unions was inevitable. And the generous settlements of earlier years were now replaced in short order by hard-nosed bargaining by governmental officials—something that may well have led the unions themselves to agree with Oscar Levant's dictum that "a politician is a person who will double-cross a bridge when he comes to it," but that was clearly what the public in the 1980s wanted. As one seasoned labor lawyer could comment regarding the Reagan administration's highly publicized firing of the PATCO strikers, it "just put the frosting on the cake. It was all public employers needed to hear because they were beginning to feel more confident anyway about their ability to deal with unions."[49]

The trend was an ominous one for labor—which initially chose to react by actively engaging in more strikes than ever, although by the mid-1980s public resentment had caused some decrease in this activity in favor of union lobbying for new taxes around the country. But, given the basic union successes in public-sector bargaining in the pre-Proposition 13 years, there were grounds for union optimism, too. Under any conditions, it did not seem to be too much to hope that the current, newer, and not especially appealing situation would itself be replaced

[48] *Business Week*, November 23, 1981, p. 49.
[49] *Wall Street Journal*, November 30, 1981, p. 34.

by a more responsible bargaining system, administered by parties whose maturity had been hastened by adversity, and fairer to all concerned. (Exhibit 1-1 indicates one union's feelings about all this.)

Military Unionism: An Exception to the Public-Sector Explosion,
Being an Idea Whose Time Has Not Come

"If we want to hire mercenaries and have a [servicemen's] union," said the U.S. congressman from the large naval community of San Diego in 1976, "then the whole idea of service to one's country is out the window. I oppose it very strongly."[50] "If the time came when a military commander's decision was subject to a union vote," asserted one of his colleagues later that year, "you might as well not even have an armed forces."[51] At about the same time, Senator Strom Thurmond stated that "if military unions have proved irresponsible in other countries, we can hardly permit them to be organized in the United States on the flimsy hypothesis that they may possibly be more responsible here."[52] And the Veterans of Foreign Wars said in an official statement that "unions would interfere with the chain of command, would impair discipline and response to orders,"[53] while the Chief of Naval Operations proclaimed that "unionism in the sense that there would be collective bargaining to determine whether or not certain operations would be undertaken is unthinkable in the military sense."[54]

These remarks were all inspired by the general direction of labor relations in the public sector, to be sure, but there were also some unique circumstances. Dependent fully on volunteers in these peacetime years, armed forces recruiters could hardly count on patriotism to fill their openings and instead had understandably emphasized the material benefits of military service. They had thereby created on the part of service people a strong interest in gaining and increasing such benefits (an interest that was further expanded by the dearth of taxpayer enthusiasm in all areas, of course). Moreover, six countries (the Netherlands, Belgium, West Germany, Norway, Sweden, and Denmark) had in the relatively recent past seen the formation of soldier unions, and there had been considerable successes by most of these in extracting both economic and job condition improvements from their respective governments. Finally, directly influenced in turn by *these* developments, the American Federation of Government Employees (AFGE) had decided to poll its 280,000 members as to whether or not it should establish military locals.

But military unionism was, in stark contrast to so much other public-sector unionism, simply not to be (at least for a while). It was overwhelmingly opposed by all senior armed force officials and by most congressmen as well, essentially for the reasons advanced in the statements quoted above. Almost three-quarters of the general public informed the Gallup Opinion Index pollsters that they were

[50] *San Diego Union,* January 24, 1976, p. A-1.
[51] *Navy Times,* December 27, 1976, p. 3.
[52] *New York Times,* March 4, 1977, p. D-13.
[53] *Ibid.*
[54] *Ibid.*

EXHIBIT 1-1

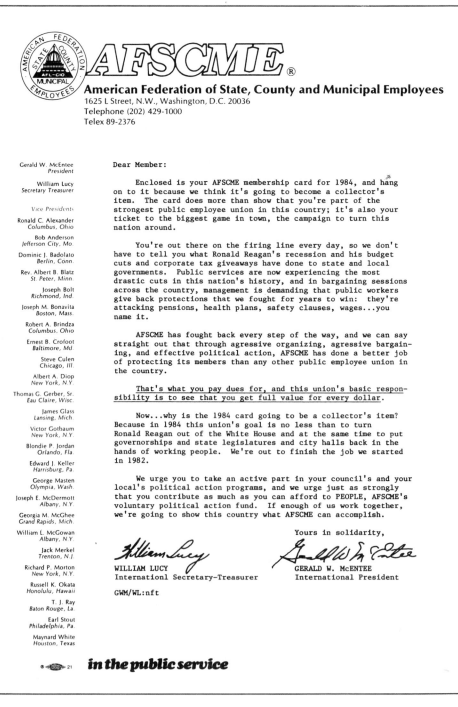

AFSCME ®

American Federation of State, County and Municipal Employees
1625 L Street, N.W., Washington, D.C. 20036
Telephone (202) 429-1000
Telex 89-2376

Gerald W. McEntee
President

William Lucy
Secretary Treasurer

Vice Presidents

Ronald C. Alexander
Columbus, Ohio

Bob Anderson
Jefferson City, Mo.

Dominic J. Badolato
Berlin, Conn.

Rev. Albert B. Blatz
St. Peter, Minn.

Joseph Bolt
Richmond, Ind.

Joseph M. Bonavita
Boston, Mass.

Robert A. Brindza
Columbus, Ohio

Ernest B. Crofoot
Baltimore, Md.

Steve Culen
Chicago, Ill.

Albert A. Diop
New York, N.Y.

Thomas G. Gerber, Sr.
Eau Claire, Wisc.

James Glass
Lansing, Mich.

Victor Gotbaum
New York, N.Y.

Blondie P. Jordan
Orlando, Fla.

Edward J. Keller
Harrisburg, Pa.

George Masten
Olympia, Wash.

Joseph E. McDermott
Albany, N.Y.

Georgia M. McGhee
Grand Rapids, Mich.

William L. McGowan
Albany, N.Y.

Jack Merkel
Trenton, N.J.

Richard P. Morton
New York, N.Y.

Russell K. Okata
Honolulu, Hawaii

T. J. Ray
Baton Rouge, La.

Earl Stout
Philadelphia, Pa.

Maynard White
Houston, Texas

Dear Member:

Enclosed is your AFSCME membership card for 1984, and hang on to it because we think it's going to become a collector's item. The card does more than show that you're part of the strongest public employee union in this country; it's also your ticket to the biggest game in town, the campaign to turn this nation around.

You're out there on the firing line every day, so we don't have to tell you what Ronald Reagan's recession and his budget cuts and corporate tax giveaways have done to state and local governments. Public services are now experiencing the most drastic cuts in this nation's history, and in bargaining sessions across the country, management is demanding that public workers give back protections that we fought for years to win: they're attacking pensions, health plans, safety clauses, wages...you name it.

AFSCME has fought back every step of the way, and we can say straight out that through agressive organizing, agressive bargaining, and effective political action, AFSCME has done a better job of protecting its members than any other public employee union in the country.

That's what you pay dues for, and this union's basic responsibility is to see that you get full value for every dollar.

Now...why is the 1984 card going to be a collector's item? Because in 1984 this union's goal is no less than to turn Ronald Reagan out of the White House and at the same time to put governorships and state legislatures and city halls back in the hands of working people. We're out to finish the job we started in 1982.

We urge you to take an active part in your council's and your local's political action programs, and we urge just as strongly that you contribute as much as you can afford to PEOPLE, AFSCME's voluntary political action fund. If enough of us work together, we're going to show this country what AFSCME can accomplish.

Yours in solidarity,

WILLIAM LUCY
Internationl Secretary-Treasurer

GWM/WL:nft

GERALD W. McENTEE
International President

in the public service

against the idea.[55] Interestingly enough, military unionism was also attacked by the top officers of the AFL–CIO, chronically fervent believers in the values of a strong military, as not being conducive to national defense. And it was even opposed by some of the AFGE leadership itself, the union's ranking national vice president, for example, arguing that the AFGE not only did not have the resources to organize servicemen but trying to do so would net the union too many enemies in Congress.

In late 1977, the AFGE announced that its members had voted by the significant margin of 4 to 1 to reject the idea of organizing the armed forces. The U.S. Senate shortly thereafter passed a bill (with only four senators dissenting) prohibiting union organizing and collective bargaining in the military, presumably to guarantee that no such projects as the AFGE one would recur. The far-reaching categories of public-sector unionists would thus not in this country, surely not soon and possibly never, include the armed forces. And whether or not the dire consequences predicted by many would actually have resulted from such unionism would as a result not be known.

Yet is is still possible that armed forces unionism will some day become a reality after all. As William Gomberg has argued in a thoughtful essay on the subject, "no bureaucracy—not even the military dedicated to country and honor—can be trusted to monitor itself and . . . a system of checks and balances is required for this purpose." Perhaps, he hypothesizes, the public will some day understand this—as its elected officials did in the case of so much other public-sector bargaining after being unalterably opposed to it in earlier years—and "what is forbidden at the present time may well emerge as conventional behavior in the future."[56]

But such a change in attitudes is, as Gomberg fully recognizes, quite conjectural. For now, both those who shudder at the thought of military unionism and those who supported it when the AFGE looked into the matter must deal in "what might have beens" and "ifs," not the most useful of commodities. If bullfrogs had wings . . . If "ands" and "buts" were candied nuts . . .

Labor Relations in the Public Sector: An Assessment

To experienced neutral Sam Zagoria, the overall boom in public-sector unionism (the military failure and the recent hard times befalling public unions notwithstanding) has constituted "a quiet revolution of government . . . [with] workers . . . effectively building some new passageways into the executive and council chambers where public policy is determined."[57] To former government manager Frederick O. R. Hayes, it "is only one manifestation of the powerful social forces that have swept the nation. . . . Community participation and militant unionism in the public sector are clearly bedfellows."[58] The late president of AFSCME, Jerry Wurf, viewed

[55] Report No. 146 (Princeton, N.J.: American Institute of Public Opinion, September 1977), pp. 1–4.

[56] William Gomberg, "Unionization of the U.S. Armed Military Forces—Its Development, Status, and Future," in *Proceedings of the Thirteenth Annual Winter Meeting, Industrial Relations Research Association,* December 28–30, 1977, p. 55.

[57] Sam Zagoria, *Public Workers and Public Unions* (Englewood Cliffs, N.J.: Prentice-Hall, 1972), pp. 1–2.

[58] *Ibid.,* p. 99.

the dramatic unionization story as proof that "the day when the service worker was destined to be a grub is gone forever,"[59] and former secretary of labor Peter Brennan observed that it "may be the single most important development in labor–management relations in the past generation."[60]

Probably all these comments are valid, and our society is not necessarily the loser for their being so. Public employers, long the wielders of unquestioned authority and unilateral decision-making powers, are now being forced by unions and quasi unions to share these perquisites much as private employers were in the turbulent decades of the 1880s and 1930s. However one feels about unionism, it is undeniable that in the private sector labor has encouraged not only more enlightened and responsible management but also a satisfactory sense of worker participation while generally producing conditions of employment that both parties can comfortably live with. There is no reason to believe that these consequences—for all the obvious (if lessening) differences between public and private employment and for all the major problem areas in the public arena at the moment (most conspicuously, of course, those involving the strike and the budget)—will not, for government work, ultimately be the same.[61]

SOME CONCLUDING REMARKS ON THE CURRENT QUALITIES OF LABOR–MANAGEMENT RELATIONS

"Anyone," the arbitrator Theodore W. Kheel once remarked, "who starts a sentence by saying that 'the trouble with labor or management is' is bound to be partially right but mostly wrong." Such sweeping generalizations as the one cited are highly hazardous in most areas of life, but in a field as varied as labor relations, they are wholly unwarranted.

It is hoped that in pointing up the various "multiplicities"—of causes for workers joining unions, of reasons why managers resist unions, and of employer philosophies themselves—the dangers of being too cavalier in *interpretation* have also been implied. Maslow's Need Hierarchy does not always fall neatly into place in linking Specific Employee X to a labor organization. And when analyzing the motivations of "workers" as a general grouping, a person may be equally far off base unless he or she recognizes that a variety of different need-motivated reasons may be simultaneously at play. The management resistance to union inroads is, in turn, also derived from a wide array of specific causes, even though the desire to retain decision-making authority in managerial hands lies at the heart of most of

---

[59] *Business Week,* July 27, 1974, p. 54.

[60] *U.S. News & World Report,* October 14, 1974, p. 66.

[61] One measure of the vitality of public-employee organization and collective bargaining is the ever-growing number of cases that are arbitrated by public-sector unions. As in the private sector, the cases cover the gamut of day-to-day labor relations problems. Later two public-sector cases will be presented. The first, placed at the end of Chapter 8, Case 6, is called "Teacher Contracts: The Case of the Girls' Gymnastics Coach." The second, placed at the end of Chapter 10, Case 11, is called "Relatively Equal Ability: The Case of the Illinois Prison." Depending upon the judgment of the instructor, these cases might be handled at this point, even before the labor relations matters involved in them are explored, or they might await fuller treatment of the underlying technical issues.

them. And employer philosophies concerning unionism can run the gamut from intransigent hostility on the one hand to complete "togetherness" in the form of collusion on the other, although neither of these extremes is common. The various frameworks presented in this chapter can serve as useful guides for specific analyses, but a little knowledge has at times been known to be a dangerous thing. Let the student beware!

Moreover, if variations in (1) workers' expectations from their unions, (2) employer grounds for resisting unionism, and (3) management attitudes in implementing this resistance account *by themselves* for much present-day diversity in labor relationships, other factors augment this diversity. To recall only a few that were cited in this chapter, the current financial states of the individual companies (and industries and, increasingly, public employers) may serve as an influential variable. So, too, may technological change confronting both the industry and the employer, past relationships between the parties, the goals of the leaders themselves on both sides of the bargaining table, management's degree of perception regarding labor situations, and, of relevance for some relationships, the prospects for government intervention, including an assessment of the form this is likely to take.

And this is to say nothing of the differences between one union *as an institution* and another, a topic that has been intentionally deferred for extensive treatment in Chapter 4. Let it suffice to state here that unions exhibit a heterogeneity all their own. In a very important sense, indeed, there has never been a literal "labor movement" in this country. The AFL–CIO is a loose federation with very limited power. Bargaining is carried out by the highly diverse international unions, each with its particular traditions, structure, and government, and by the constituent locals and other subgroups of the internationals. Even today, despite a strong trend toward international union control over local union activities, a few international unions perform little more than bookkeeping functions, with the locals exercising almost complete autonomy. Other internationals are highly centralized, and local independence in any sphere is virtually nonexistent. Organized labor is broad enough, too, to contain both (1) the Teamsters Union, which has long represented to many people a prime form of "business unionism," with its leaders utilizing the union as "a marketing cooperative to sell so many head of labor to employers at the highest market price"[62] and in no way being concerned with general social reform (of running the union, former Teamster president Hoffa once said, "Everyone who writes about me seems amazed that I call it a business instead of a crusade or something. Well it is a business. We are not labor statesmen. We are not humanitarians or longhairs";[63] and (2) the United Automobile Workers, whose leadership for many years has stressed "social unionism," or the achievement of gains benefiting all of society, not just its own membership. It also includes not only the garment unions, which have—through ambitious union-financed projects ranging from cooperative housing to adult education programs—made unionism

[62] Lester Velie, *Labor U.S.A.* (New York: Harper & Row, 1959), p. 14.
[63] Steven Brill, *The Teamsters* (New York: Simon & Schuster, 1978), p. 96.

for their constituents a "way of life" but also the United Electrical Workers, whose members still lock arms to sing such old labor songs as "Solidarity Forever" and "Which Side Are You On?" and some of whose leaders are believed to have ties with the Communist party (although the leaders themselves adamantly deny this). In short, there are unions and there are unions.

Any of the variables enumerated above can be crucial to the molding of a specific labor–management relationship. At any one time, several of them are apt to be at work in influencing the nature of this relationship. And, given this situation, the great variety in the subject areas, wordings, and lengths of the nation's 200,000 labor–management contracts, which serve as tangible (if, as will be seen, not always completely accurate) symbols of labor relationships, is understandable.

Certainly, there is no reason to expect a contract for the five waitresses in a New Hampshire restaurant to bear any resemblance to the International Brotherhood of Teamsters' nationwide trucking agreement. Any great similarity between the General Electric Company–International Union of Electrical Workers document and that negotiated by the Lace Workers and their marginal employer in Honeysuckle, Mississippi, would likewise constitute a striking coincidence.

Can *any* remarks, then, in the face of all of these variables, be applied to the majority of the contracts in this country? Some statements *can* still be made, and even as ambitious a phrase as "the *vast* majority of all agreements" will support them.

For all their variations, almost all labor contracts today validate a particular institutional status for the union, and well over two-thirds of them incorporate the union-shop arrangement, requiring union membership for continued employment. The vast majority of the agreements reveal what the parties have agreed to as being "vested exclusively in the company," either explicitly (in a so-called "management rights" article) or implicitly (in indirect language scattered throughout the contract). They announce, in more or less detail, the increasingly broad range of wage, hour, and other economic-related employment conditions under which the employees have agreed to be governed. They incorporate a variety of administrative clauses dealing with work rules and job tenure. And they outline the procedures for settling the disputes that will inevitably arise during the life of the agreement, as well as providing for a renegotiation of the contract when its duration has been exhausted.

These are no small accomplishments. Real or imaginary threats to job security, to the union's existence, to what managers deem their freedom to run their own businesses, and to what employees refer to as fair conditions are regularly involved. Yet the signing of any contract requires some form of mutual agreement and, most often, some major concessions by both the management and the union. It is a tribute to the increasing maturity of both parties that so much progress has been made in this direction over the past few decades. This is particularly true when one considers not only the drastic technological and economic changes that have taken place in our society since the Great Depression but also the many direct grounds for open conflict between labor and management that have existed ever since.

A host of other accomplishments, which will be given liberal treatment in the pages that follow, also bear testimony to the ability of the labor relations system to adjust itself to accommodate new needs and desires. The spread of the seniority principle, under which the employee with the longest service receives preference in various employment matters, has minimized employee demands for both "justice" and "objective personnel management." On these morale-building grounds, it has also had considerable appeal—when used in moderation—to many managements. Moreover, the almost complete acceptance by the parties of binding arbitration by a neutral as the final step in the grievance procedure, thus normally ruling out work stoppages during the term of the agreement, has also injected much stability into labor relations. And the same can be said of the growth of long-term contracts—now commonly three years in duration instead of the traditional one-year basis. Nor can one overlook the contractual adjustments to the spread of the many new employee fringe benefits that have arisen in this period. Bilateral statesmanship must receive some credit, too, for the satisfactory contractual resolution, at least over time, of many knotty problems involving technological change and unionized workers.

The labor contract, admittedly, forms only the bare skeleton of the total relationship between a union and a management. As is also true of both the marriage contract and the citizen's income tax report, it is little more than a legal prerequisite to harmony; by itself, it does not produce rapport. To evaluate any labor relationship accurately, one must know the degree of mutual trust and good will that lies behind the written agreement, to say nothing of the extent to which supplementary documents and verbal understandings may affect the wording printed on the contract pages. Finally, no contract is any better than its *administration:* The contract incorporates a body of rules, but this does not guarantee that both parties will always interpret these rules in the same way. Moreover, the fact that agreements can never hope to explicitly cover all contingencies means that there will always be at least the chance for future disagreement. In short, a variety of problems affecting the relationship can surround even the most harmonious-appearing labor contract.

Judged by any available standard, however, the considerable progress and increasing maturity that is at least *symbolized* by the contractual contents has marked *all* portions of union–management relations over the past very few decades. One can accept the Slichter, Healy, and Livernash verdict that the process of accommodation is "neither complete nor uniform" and recognize that judgment involving the public sector must as yet remain suspended, without in any way negating the more basic conclusions of these three scholars that

> . . . the American collective bargaining system must be regarded as one of the most successful economic institutions in the country. In the great majority of

plants it has produced rules and policies that are fair to both sides and that permit managements to conduct operations efficiently. Although there is wide variation in the results of bargaining, the concentration of settlements that are good compromises is large . . . [and] experience to date evidences a degree of social progress that few would have predicted [at the end of the 1930s].[64]

The reader is invited to postpone any agreement (or disagreement) with these opinions until the contents of the various areas cited in the preceding paragraphs are treated more fully. Part III's six chapters are totally reserved for this latter purpose: Chapter 5, for an examination of management and union behavior at the bargaining table; Chapter 6, for the treatment of contract administration; Chapters 7 and 8, for description and analysis of the major economic issues with which collective bargaining is now involved; and Chapters 9 and 10, for relatively detailed inspection of the basic institutional and administrative issues in the current labor–management sphere.

If one does acquiesce at this early point, however, is there also justification for assuming that the mainstream of our labor relations system today stands on the threshold of a great new era to which strikes will be entirely foreign and where harmony will be the universal guiding rule?

Despite all the progress to date, such a prophecy would, we think, be extremely naïve. It can be expected that managements will continue to oppose the concept of unionism and to resist new union inroads as energetically as ever, for the roots of this opposition are essentially rational ones *as judged by management values.* By the same token, there is little reason to believe that unions will not continue to press for an ever-greater narrowing of the scope of management discretion, in the interests of obliging worker wants and needs as *they* view them. Indeed, in the years immediately ahead, the stresses between the parties seem destined to grow: The recent intensification of industrial price and technological competition (and, in the public sector, of severe budgetary pressures) has already pitted an accelerated employer search for greater efficiency against an equally determined union campaign for increased job security.

Since a labor relations millennium is far distant, it seems a safe prediction that occasional impasses will continue to be reached by labor and management, and that these will result in strike actions, as they have in the past.

There is both an irony and a serious threat for our system of free collective bargaining in the inevitability of future strikes. If labor relations progress has clearly been evident, the community has also increased its expectations from union–management relations. It has become increasingly less tolerant of work stoppages, and it regularly shows itself as favoring greater governmental control over union activities.

Despite an ever-deeper penetration of governmental regulations (described in Chapter 3 and elsewhere), our labor relations system—the public sector obviously excepted—has nonetheless thus far essentially remained in private hands.

[64] Sumner H. Slichter, James J. Healy, and E. Robert Livernash, *The Impact of Collective Bargaining on Management* (Washington, D.C.: Brookings Institution, 1960), pp. 960–61.

This toleration for private decision making is consistent with the dominant values of our society, particularly with its premium on maximum freedom of action for both individuals and organizations. But the possibility that a tripartite labor relations system, with the government as a full-fledged participant, will ultimately supplant the present bipartite system can never be overlooked. Whether or not what is still "free collective bargaining" will be allowed to continue will depend to no small degree on the current system's ability to continue its progress sufficiently and in time to satisfy the increasingly high level of public expectation. The fact that there is still much room for improvement in labor–management relations makes the entire system as it currently exists a vulnerable one.

Discussion Questions

1 "No one except union officers and union staff members would suffer one iota if unions were to be outlawed in the United States, and enormous numbers of people would gain immeasurably if this should happen." Discuss.

2 "There is no reason on earth why lower and even middle managers should not consider joining a labor union, and it is really just a fluke that they, at least to date, have not." Comment fully.

3 "From the labor point of view, there is an intrinsic unfairness in the fact that it is essentially only conflict that attracts attention from the mass media." How valid, in your opinion, is this statement?

4 "The blue collar worker is the only natural habitat of unionism in the United States, and union failures to date outside of this sector prove this statement conclusively." Do you agree? Why or why not?

5 "Managers resist unions for a variety of entirely logical and rational reasons, and thus they can be expected to continue this opposition indefinitely, since the reasons will presumably continue to be logical and rational." Comment, with specifics.

6 More than a few public officials in recent years have argued that any police officer, firefighter, or sanitation worker who goes out on strike in defiance of the law should be fired on the spot. How does such a viewpoint accord with yours?

7 Under what, if any, circumstances, would you personally consider joining a union?

8 It has occasionally been argued that the United States is, in the words of a major rubber industry executive, "experiencing the cult of the individual." Do you accept this position and, if so, do you think that its continuation would significantly hurt labor's efforts in the years immediately ahead?

9 "The great variety in the subject matter, language, and length of the nation's 200,000 labor–management contracts is entirely understandable." Discuss the validity of this quotation.

Selected References

AARON, BENJAMIN, et al., eds., *Public Sector Collective Bargaining*. Madison, Wis.: Industrial Relations Research Association, 1979.

BLUM, ALBERT A., ed., *White Collar Workers*. New York: Random House, 1971.

BOK, DEREK C., and JOHN T. DUNLOP, *Labor and the American Community*. New York: Simon & Schuster, 1970.

FREEMAN, RICHARD B., and JAMES L. MEDHOFF, *What Do Unions Do?* New York: Basic Books, Inc., 1984

HORTON, RAYMOND D., *Municipal Labor Relations in New York City: Lessons of the Lindsay-Wagner Years*. New York: Praeger, 1973.

LOEWENBERG, J. JOSEPH, and MICHAEL H. MOSKOW, *Collective Bargaining in Government*. Englewood Cliffs, N.J.: Prentice-Hall, 1972.

LUBERMAN, MYRON, *Public Sector Bargaining: A Policy Reappraisal*. Lexington, Mass.: Lexington Books, 1980.

NESBITT, MURRAY B., *Labor Relations in the Federal Government Service*. Washington, D.C.: Bureau of National Affairs, 1976.

PURCELL, THEODORE V., *Blue Collar Man*. Cambridge, Mass.: Harvard University Press, 1960.

SERRIN, WILLIAM, *The Company and the Union*. New York: Knopf, 1973.

SLICHTER, SUMNER H., JAMES J. HEALY, and E. ROBERT LIVERNASH, *The Impact of Collective Bargaining on Management*. Washington, D.C.: Brookings Institution, 1960.

SOMERS, GERALD G., ed., *Collective Bargaining: Contemporary American Experience*. Madison, Wis.: Industrial Relations Research Association, 1980.

STEIBER, JACK, *Public Sector Unionism: Structure, Growth, Policy*. Washington, D.C.: Brookings Institution, 1973.

STERRETT, GRACE, and ANTONE ABOUD, *The Right to Strike in Public Employment* (2nd ed., rev.). Ithaca, N.Y.: ILR Press, Cornell University, 1982.

WOLFBEIN, SEYMOUR L., ed., *Emerging Sectors of Collective Bargaining*. Braintree, Mass.: D. H. Mark, 1970.

ZAGORIA, SAM, *Public Workers and Public Unions*. Englewood Cliffs, N.J.: Prentice-Hall, 1972.

chapter 2

The Historical Framework

As is true of other established disciplines, there is still some controversy as to the returns inherent in the study of history. For every Shakespeare asserting that "what is past is prologue," or a Santayana who proclaims that "those who do not understand history are condemned to repeat its mistakes," there is a Henry Ford declaring that "history is a pack of tricks that we play on the dead" and that the field is, in fact, "bunk."

No one can claim to understand present-day institutions, however, without having at least some basic knowledge of their roots. It would make a considerable difference to those who are either hopeful or fearful that labor unions will ultimately fade from the industrial scene, for example, if unions were purely a phenomenon of the last few years (and thus potentially destined for extinction when environmental conditions change), rather than being—as they are—organizations of relatively long standing in the economy. Similarly, only by recognizing what workers have expected of their unions in the past is one entitled even to begin to pass judgment on the present performance of organized labor. This chapter thus attempts to provide the reader with a necessary working knowledge of American labor history.

THE EIGHTEENTH CENTURY: GENESIS OF THE AMERICAN LABOR MOVEMENT

If labor unions connote *permanent* employee associations that have as their primary goal the preservation or improvement of employment conditions, there were no such institutions in America until the closing years of the eighteenth century. Concerted actions of workingmen in the form of strikes and slowdowns were not unknown to the colonial period, but these disturbances were, without exception, spontaneous efforts. They were conducted on the spur of the moment over temporary grievances, such as withholding of wages. Generally unsuccessful, they were never undertaken by anything resembling permanent organizations.

Given the dimensions of the labor movement today and the variety of seemingly compelling reasons why workers have attached themselves to it, this total absence of labor unions for well over a century calls for an immediate explanation.

In those years of simple handicraft organization, there were, in fact, at least four forces at work that served to weaken any motivation that workers might otherwise have had for joining together on a long-term basis.

In the first place, the market for the employer's product was both local and essentially noncompetitive. Workingmen were thus allowed close social ties with the owner, often performing their work in the owner's home. In addition, they could maintain a comparatively relaxed pace of production in such an atmosphere.

Second, both the laws of supply and demand and government regulations allowed employees a large measure of job security at this time. Labor of all kinds, and particularly skilled craft labor, was in short supply in the colonies. A series of colonial labor laws calling for apprenticeship service prior to many kinds of employment and carefully circumscribing the conditions under which employees could be discharged offered further protection to jobholders.

Third, the existence of ample cheap land in the West meant that the dissatisfied artisan or mechanic could always move on should either local adversity or the spirit of adventure strike him. Many workers did migrate to the ever-expanding frontier, allowing even more advantageous employment conditions for those who remained: Incomes increased all the more in the East, to the point where, by some estimates, wages were twice those paid to workers in Britain.

Finally, the low ratio of labor to natural resources in the frontier nation helped ensure that price rises would lag behind the wage increases. Assistant Secretary of the Treasury Coxe, sounding very much like a twentieth-century Chamber of Commerce manager, could—even at late as 1790—assert with considerable justification that "though the wages of the industrious poor are very good, yet the necessaries of life are cheaper than in Europe, and the articles used are more comfortable and pleasing."[1]

Ironically, however, the development of the frontier laid the groundwork for the birth of bona fide labor organizations. An expanded system of transportation built around canals and turnpikes was simultaneously linking the new nation's communities and allowing the capitalists of the late eighteenth century to enlarge their product markets into the beginnings of nationwide ones. The merchant who was unwilling or unable to respond to the challenge was left by the wayside as competitive pressures forced each businessman to find cost-cutting devices in the newly unsheltered atmosphere. The more imaginative employers located such de-

---

[1] Lloyd Ulman, *American Trade Unionism—Past and Present* (Berkeley, Calif.: Institute of Industrial Relations, 1961), p. 367.

vices: To decrease labor costs, they introduced women and children to their work-places, farmed out work to prison inmates, and generally cut the wages of males who remained in their employ. For good measure, they frequently increased the hours in the workday (at no increase in pay), minutely subdivided the work into more easily assimilated (but commensurately more repetitive and monotonous) operations, and hired aggressive overseers to enforce newly tightened work stand-ards.

The less-skilled workingman could react to these unwelcome changes by mov-ing to the frontier. Not having invested much in the way of time or education in learning his current job, he might also attempt to move occupationally to more desirable kinds of work. The skilled worker, on the other hand, had mastered his craft through years of apprenticeship and was no longer occupationally mobile.

Some skilled craftsmen did move to the frontier. But the extension of the product market meant that their new masters were still not free to ignore labor cost-cutting methods; suits tailored in Ohio competed now with those made in Boston. Nor could the craftsmen count any longer on advancing into the class of masters themselves; the scope of manufacturing was necessarily greater, and to enter the employer ranks it now took capital on a scale not ordinarily available to most wage earners. Basically, the skilled workers' alternatives were to passively accept the wage cuts, the competition of nonapprenticed labor, and the harsh working conditions or to join in collective action against such employer innovations. Increasingly, by the end of the eighteenth century, they chose the latter course of action.

THE FIRST UNIONS AND THEIR LIMITED SUCCESSES

These early trade unions—individually encompassing shoemakers, printers, car-penters, tailors, and artisans of similar skill levels—waged blunt attacks on the changes brought about by the extension of markets. Their members agreed upon a wage level and pledged not to work for any employer who refused to pay this amount. They also bound themselves not to work alongside any employee who did not receive the basic minimum or who had not served the customary period of apprenticeship for the trade. In addition, most of these craft unions attempted to negotiate closed-shop agreements, whereby only those who were union members in the first place would be employed at all.

Generally proving themselves willing to strike, if need be, in support of their demands, the early unions were at times surprisingly successful in achieving them. And although work stoppages of the day were typically both peaceful and short in duration, the new worker aggressiveness they symbolized was sufficient to bring on considerable countervailing action from the employers.

The masters turned to two sources: organization in employers' associations and aid from the courts. Societies of otherwise competitive master masons, car-penters, shoemakers, printers, and other employers of skilled labor were quickly established in most urban areas where union activity was pronounced, for the purposes of holding down wages and destroying labor combinations wherever these existed. Attacking on a second front, the masters also turned to the judges and urged prosecution of their workers' organizations as illegal conspiracies in restraint of trade. The jurists were quickly convinced: The Journeyman Cordwainers (shoe-makers) of Philadelphia were found guilty of joining in such a conspiracy by striking in 1806, and within the next decade a variety of similar court cases had also resulted in shattering defeats for the worker organizations. Not until 1842, indeed, with the famous *Commonwealth* v. *Hunt* decision in Massachusetts that strikes could be legal if they were undertaken for legal purposes, did the judges even begin to modify the harsh tenets of the "Cordwainer doctrine" when requested to rule on union affairs by employers.

If the criminal conspiracy doctrine and the varying successes of the employer associations crimped the growth of the incipient labor movement, moreover, an economic event temporarily sent unionism into almost total collapse. In 1819, a major nationwide depression occurred and, as was to be no less the case in later nineteenth-century periods of ecomomic reversal, labor organizations could not withstand its effects. Union demands that might be translated into employer conces-sions when the demand for labor was high could be safely dismissed by the masters with jobs now at a premium. Employers once again cut rates with impunity and showed little hesitation in dismissing workers who had joined unions in earlier years. Under the circumstances, the worker cry was "Every man for himself," rather than "In union there is strength," and virtually no union could, or did, survive mass desertion.

REVIVAL, INNOVATION, AND DISILLUSIONMENT

The return of economic health to the country by late 1822 was paralleled by a revival of unionism. Their bargaining power restored, skilled employees in the trades that had previously been organized once again turned to union activity.

More significantly, the process of unionization now spread to new frontiers, both geographic and occupational. Aroused by the same merchant-capitalist threats to living standards and status that had previously given incentive for collective bargaining to their East Coast counterparts, craftsmen in such newly developed cities as Buffalo, Pittsburgh, Cincinnati, and Louisville established trade union locals at this time. And new (and widely publicized) victories of the skilled worker unions in both the older and newer cities had by the mid-1830s generated the formation of unions among such previously nonunion groups as stonecutters, hat-ters, and painters.

These years also saw other innovations made by organized labor. Prior to 1827, each local craft union had operated on its own as a totally separate organi-zation. In that year, however, representatives of fifteen different trades in the city of Philadelphia formed the country's first central labor union, for joint action on a citywide basis. The original goal of the Philadelphia group was a ten-hour day for its trade union members, but this was soon displaced as a major demand: In 1828, the organization converted itself into a political party, endorsing "workingmen's candidates"—with only limited success—for public office.

Workingmen's parties were also organized in other eastern states in this period of Jacksonian democracy. Political associations of workers seeking such goals as universal free education and the abolition of imprisonment for debt arose in New York, Massachusetts, and Delaware. Most of their objectives were soon realized, but the workingmen's parties themselves—often torn by internal dissension and always confronted by competition from the two major national parties—were generally short-lived.

The original form that the Philadelphia "city central" had taken—as a purely economic joint undertaking of several trade unions in a single city—had a more lasting influence on workers in other locations. Similar bodies were quickly set up throughout the East and, despite the frequent divergence of opinion among the various trades represented, showed remarkable staying power. By the mid-1830s, at least twelve cities had such "city centrals," most of which provided their affiliated local unions with financial and moral encouragement in times of strikes and co-ordinated such ancillary activities as the promotion of union-made goods.

Even the beginnings of national worker organization were attempted at this time. In 1834, delegates from the city centrals of several eastern cities met in New York to form the National Trades' Union. This pioneering workers' project quickly proved fruitless—industry had not yet itself significantly organized on a national basis and would not for three more decades—but the scope of the NTU's activities nonetheless symbolizes the ambitiousness of the worker representatives involved.

Indeed, the initiative displayed by leaders of both the city centrals and the local unions had led to impressive union membership totals by 1836. It has been estimated that there were in the country as a whole in that year 300,000 unionized workers, constituting 6.5 percent of the labor force.[2] One can only guess to what heights the total figures would have risen had not the following year brought a national economic depression that was even more severe than the business slump of 1819.

The hard times that began in 1837 were to last for almost thirteen years. In the face of them, trade union activity vanished almost as completely as it had two decades earlier. Moreover, a new factor now arose to compound union ills: The 1840s saw waves of immigrants—themselves often the victims of economic diversity in such countries as Ireland, Germany, and England—enter the United States. American business conditions by themselves had been sufficient to wipe out most unions of the day, but this new source of job competition and low wages ensured that not even the strongest of unions could endure.

Now so severely frustrated in their economic actions and distrustful of the free-enterprise system for having failed to safeguard their interests, some workers

---

[2] Foster Rhea Dulles, *Labor in America,* 2nd rev. ed. (New York: Thomas Y. Crowell, 1960), p. 59.

transferred their energies to a series of ambitious political schemes for redesigning the economy. "Associationists" set up socialistic agricultural communities; George Henry Evans preached the virtues of "land reform" through direct political action by workingmen ("Vote Yourself a Farm"); and still other advocates of a new social order promulgated producers' cooperatives—employee-owned industrial institutions—as the workingman's salvation.

None of these programs succeeded, however. As Dulles has astutely observed, they did not "in any way meet the needs of labor. In spite of the enthusiastic propaganda, the answer to industrialization did not lie in an attempt to escape from it."[3]

THE LAYING OF THE FOUNDATION FOR MODERN UNIONISM AND SOME MIXED PERFORMANCES WITH IT

With the return of prosperity in 1850, unions once again became a factor to be reckoned with. Profiting from the past, they eschewed political diversions, concentrated on such now traditional goals as higher wages, shorter workdays, and increased job security and regained much of their former membership.

The first major national unions, often superseding the economic functions of the city centrals, were also established at this time. Although the "Golden Age" of American railroading still lay ahead, the construction of the first complex rail systems was now accelerating. As a result, not only were product markets once more widening but so too were labor markets, bringing workers within the same crafts and industries into direct economic competition with each other. National coordination to standardize wages, working conditions, membership rules, and bargaining demands was deemed necessary by labor leaders; the alternative was cutthroat competition among individual local unions, eager for new members and expanded work opportunities and therefore willing to undercut the terms of other locals (to the employer's distinct advantage). The International Typographical Union, the country's oldest permanent national, dates from 1850. By 1860, at least fifteen other crafts had organized on a national basis. In addition to the Typographers, the Machinists and the Iron Molders have continued as labor organizations to this day, although the last-named is currently anything but a giant in labor circles.

The 1861 advent of the Civil War brought a new spurt in union membership growth, to a post-1836 high of over 200,000 unionists by the end of hostilities in 1865. Some of this organizational success was due to the labor shortages brought on by military mobilization: The economy's demand for labor commensurately increased, thus enlarging labor's bargaining power and union economic gains. There were undoubtedly at least two other reasons, however: (1) wartime inflation always threatened to counteract the wage increases achieved by unions, and many workers (somewhat unsuccessfully) looked to collective bargaining as a force for staving off

---

[3] *Ibid.*, p.81

this menace; and (2) organized labor was further helped by the prolabor sentiments of President Lincoln, who firmly resisted employer and public pressure to intervene in the occasional wartime strikes and instead offered as his opinion that "labor is the superior of capital and deserves much the higher consideration."

At war's end, however, the labor movement still comprised less than 2 percent of the country's labor force (as against 6.5 percent in 1836) and had yet to make any real penetration into the factories of the land and their huge organizing potential. But the foundation for the unionism of the next seventy years had now been laid. Few skilled-worker types were totally unrepresented by unions in 1865: More than 200 local unions, individually encompassing such widely divergent craftsmen as cigar makers, plumbers, and barrel makers, were founded in the war years alone. In addition, the logical necessity of forming *national* unions had now been almost universally recognized by labor leaders, and some thirty new ones had been added to the several that had preceded the war. And labor had achieved, through Lincoln, at least a measure of government support for its right to strike.

Labor's momentum, moreover, was sustained in immediate postwar years. The war-generated nationwide prosperity continued virtually unabated until 1873 and, aided by its favorable economic conditions (as in earlier business booms), labor's bargaining strength again increased. New members were attracted by announcements of new union gains, but there were now also other reasons for the increased membership totals. The broader organizational foundations that had been laid prior to 1865, particularly in the multiplication of national unions, allowed both more efficient and more varied organizing campaigns. Moreover, the post–Civil War period unleashed formidable threats to the workingman in the form of (1) accelerated waves of immigrants (increasingly, now, from southern and eastern Europe) who were willing to work for low wages; (2) changing technology, with the machine downgrading many skill requirements and allowing the employer to substitute unskilled labor for craftsmen and women for men; and (3) the continued widening of the gap between wages and prices that had begun in the wartime years. Workers thus had more incentive to join in collective bargaining, and acted upon it.

On the other hand, not every union shared in these gains. Particularly unsuccessful, in fact, was the new Molders national union, whose embittered president, William Sylvis, now turned away from "pure and simple" collective bargaining to espouse cooperative foundries. He was totally convinced that workers "must adopt a system which will divide the *profits* of labor among those who produce them," and was soon instrumental in the establishment of a number of producers' cooperatives.

These undertakings proved no more successful than they had in the 1840s, however. By 1870, most of the worker-owned associations had been forced by competitive pressures to cut wages, hire lower-cost labor, and—in general—act very much like the management-run business that Sylvis had so lamented.

Sylvis then transferred his energies to a new organization, which had been founded in 1866. The National Labor Union, riding the crest of union optimism at the close of the war, constituted the first major attempt at uniting all national unions, city centrals, and locals into a single central federation of American labor since the ill-fated National Trades' Union of 1834. Its first leaders, drawn mainly from the building and printing trades, had unsuccessfully urged legislative enactment of the eight-hour working day. They had also sought, again without tangible success, such further political goals as currency reform and women's suffrage.

Sylvis drew the organization even further from economic action to such new political objectives as the reservation of public lands for actual settlers only and abolition of the convict labor system. But the National Labor Union could not sustain membership enthusiasm with a credo that was so far removed from worker pocketbooks; one by one, its constituent labor organizations deserted it, and by 1872 the NLU had passed from the scene.

The failures of the cooperative and political movements were harbingers of more wide-sweeping labor disasters. Business collapsed in 1873, beginning a new period of deep depression that lasted for more than five years. In its wake, most of the local unions (as well as the city centrals) once more disappeared. Many of the nationals fared no better, but the greater financial resources and more diversified memberships of these broader organizations did allow them to offer greater resistance to the slump; not only did eleven of the nationals, in fact, weather these years but eight new nationals were established during this time. Consequently, for the first time, a depression did not completely stop unionization. Nonetheless, five-sixths of total union membership did erode in the 1873–1878 period; only 50,000 unionists remained in 1878.

Encouraged by the depression-caused weakening of union bargaining power, employers also turned—in the 1870s—to weapons of their own, in an all-out frontal attack on what was left of organized labor. Acting both singly and through employer associations, they engaged in frequent lockouts, hired spies to ferret out union sympathizers, circulated the names of such sympathizers to fellow employers thorugh so-called black lists, summarily discharged labor "agitators," and engaged the services of strikebearers on a widespread scale.

The results of these efforts varied. Most of the labor organizations that were strong enough to withstand the depression could also frustrate the employer onslaughts. But there was at least one notable effect of the management campaign. Retaliating in kind to the quality of employer opposition (as well as to the widespread unemployment of the times), both unionists and nonunionized workers engaged in actions that for bitterness and violence were unequaled in American history. A secret society of anthracite miners, the Molly Maguires, terrorized the coal fields of Pennsyvlania in a series of widely publicized murders and acts of arson. Railroad strikes paralyzed transportation in such major cities as Baltimore, Pittsburgh, and Chicago and, with mob rule typically replacing organized leadership as these ran their course, were most often ended only with federal troops being called out to terminate mass pilaging and bloodshed. Public opinion was almost always hostile to such activities, and lacking this support the demonstrations could not succeed. It is probably also true that employers were more easily enabled, by the general resentment directed toward worker groups for these actions, to gain still another weapon in their battle against unions: The labor injunction, first applied by the courts during a railway strike at this time, was to be quite freely granted— as Chapter 3 will bring out—by the judges for more than five decades thereafter.

THE RISE AND FALL OF THE KNIGHTS OF LABOR

Prosperity finally returned to the country in 1878, and with it union growth once again resumed. Over the next ten years, sixty-two new national unions (or "international" unions, as many of these were now calling themselves, in recognition of their first penetration of the Canadian labor market) were established. Locals and city centrals also resumed their proliferation. Even more significantly, the early 1880s marked American labor's most notable attempt to form a single, huge "general" union, the Noble and Holy Order of the Knights of Labor.

The Knights had actually been established before the depression. In 1869, a group of tailors had founded the organization's first local in Philadelphia. Its avowed goal was "to initiate good men of all callings"—unionists as well as those not already in unions, craftsmen, and (unlike virtually all other labor organizations of the day) totally unskilled workers. It particularly desired such a broad base of membership to "eliminate the weakness and evils of isolated effort or association, and useless and crushing competition resulting therefrom." But the Knights' definition of "good men of all callings" was not all-inclusive; the founders specifically wanted "no drones, no lawyers, no bankers, no doctors, no professional politicians."

Surviving the depression as a secret society, the Knights abolished their assortment of rituals and passwords in the late 1870s and thenceforth openly recruited in all directions.

Such aggressiveness, combined with what now was the normal increase in union bargaining strength amid general economic prosperity, allowed a slow but steady growth of the order's membership. There were roughly 9,000 Knights in 1878 and over 70,000 by 1884. Then, following a major 1885 strike victory against the Wabash Railroad, the growth became spectacular. Workers of all conceivable types clamored for membership, and by mid-1886 there were 700,000 people in the wide-sweeping organization.

The aftermath of the Wabash strike was to be the high-water mark for the Knights, however. The leaders of the order proved wholly unable to cope with the gigantic membership increase, and as the new Knights sought to duplicate the Wabash triumph with one ill-timed and undisciplined strike after another, a steady stream of union defeats ensued. The very diversity of backgrounds among the members also drained the effectiveness of the organization: The old skilled trade unionists found little in common with the shopkeepers, farmers, and self-employed mechanics who shared membership with them, and they rapidly deserted the order. Nor did the presence of thousands of unskilled and semiskilled industrial workers, often of widely varying first-generation American backgrounds, add anything to group solidarity.

Greatly discouraged by the schisms within their organization, many such workers soon followed the path set by the skilled tradesmen and left it.

Although each of the factors above was undoubtedly influential in the Knights' rapid decline after 1886—to 100,000 members by 1890 and to virtual extinction by 1900—still another factor was probably even more responsible for the fall of the order. The system of values held by the Knights' leadership was considerably at variance with the values of rank-and-file Knights. For all their diversity and essential lack of discipline, the latter could (employers and the self-employed always excepted) at least unite on the desirability of higher wages, shorter hours, and improved working conditions. Under Knights President Terrence V. Powderly, however, these goals were significantly minimized in favor of such "social" goals as the establishment of consumer and producer cooperatives, temperance, and land reform. Even the strike weapon, despite its great success against the Wabash management and its popular appeal to Knights' members, was viewed with disdain by Powderly to the end; he considered it both expensive and overly militant. Why was this Knight different from all other Knights? The historical records lack a definitive explanation. But whatever the reason the philosophical gap between leadership and followers was thus a wide one, and Powderly was forced to pay the supreme penalty for perpetuating it. Ultimately, he was left with no one to lead.

By the late 1880s, a wholly new organization—the American Federation of Labor—had won over the mainstream of the Knights' skilled-trade unionists, and the once vast array of other membership types, disillusioned, was again outside the ranks of organized labor. Taft has written an appropriate epitaph:

> The Knights of Labor can best be regarded as a producers', and not specifically as a wage earner's, organization. It had no program around which workers in industry could rally for a long campaign. . . . The Knights of Labor expired because it could not fulfill any function.[4]

THE FORMATION OF THE AFL AND ITS PRAGMATIC MASTER PLAN

Almost from its inception in 1881, the American Federation of Labor was a highly realistic, no-nonsense organization.

Even in that year, the more than 100 representatives of skilled-worker unions who gathered at Pittsburgh to form what was originally entitled the Federation of Organized Trades and Labor Unions included many dissident Knights, disenchanted with Powderly's "one big union" concept and political-action emphasis. The rebels were already convinced that the future of their highly skilled constituents lay completely outside the catchall Knights. They recognized that such craftsmen possessed considerably greater bargaining power than other, less-skilled types of Knights members because of their relative indispensability to employers. Consequently, they were anxious to exercise this power *directly* in union-management

[4] Philip Taft, *Organized Labor in American History* (New York: Harper & Row, 1964), p. 120.

negotiations. Powderly's idealistic and somewhat hazy legislative goals might be appropriate for workers who could not better their lot in any other way, but they seemed to many FOTLU founders to be a poor substitute for strike threats and other forms of economic action when undertaken by unionists who were not so easily replaceable. Well versed in American labor history, these early advocates of an exclusive federation of craft unions were also well aware of the fates of earlier organizations that had subordinated economic goals to political ones.

However logical these arguments for a more homogeneous and "pure collective bargaining" federation of skilled craft unions may seem to present-day readers, the FOTLU was not immediately a smashing success. It was initially torn by both personality and philosophical schisms. More important, the built-in weaknesses of the Knights had not yet become widely apparent to the large body of American craftsmen; paradoxically, the craft confederation's ultimate triumph had to await the first real victories—and then the rapid downfall—of the Powderly organization.

Indeed, the basic issue that was to split irrevocably the craft unions from the Knights involved the jurisdiction of the national unions themselves. The dramatic spurt in Knights membership following the 1885 Wabash victory threatened to entirely submerge the craft "trade assemblies" and the parent national craft unions, which had thus far retained their separate identities within the order, in a throng of numerically superior semiskilled and unskilled workers. Nor would Powderly, never the compromiser and now at the pinnacle of his short-lived success, grant any assurances that the Knights would not violate the jurisdictions of the existing national unions. Rubbing salt into the nationals' wounds, the Knights' leadership even went so far now as to organize rival national unions and to try to absorb both these and the established nationals into the "mixed" assembly and the district structures of the order.

The rupture was soon complete. In late 1886, representatives of twenty-five of the strongest national unions met at Columbus, Ohio, transformed the somewhat moribund FOTLU into the American Federation of Labor, unanimously elected Samuel Gompers of the Cigar Makers as the AFL's first president, and thereby ushered in a new era for the American labor movement. Despite their moment of glory, the Knights were soon to begin their rapid decline—with some of the impetus toward their dissolution, to be sure, being directly lent by the secession of the skilled-worker nationals. For the next fifty years, the basic tenets of the AFL were to remain unchallenged by the mainstream of labor in this country.

Samuel Gompers, the Dutch–Jewish immigrant who was to continue as president of the federation for all except one of the next thirty-eight years,[5] has frequently been referred to as a supreme pragmatist, a leader convinced that any supposed "truth" was above all to be tested by its practical consequences. Careful consideration of the basic principles upon which he and his lieutenants launched

---

[5] In 1894, he lost his try for reelection by a narrow margin and had to wait a year before he could return to office.

the AFL does nothing to weaken the validity of this description. Essentially, Gompers had five such principles.

In the first place, the national unions were to be autonomous within the new federation: "The American Federation of Labor," Gompers proudly announced, "avoids the fatal rock upon which all previous attempts to effect the unity of the working class have split, by leaving to each body or affiliated organization the complete management of its own affairs, especially in its own particular trade affairs."[6] The leader of a highly successful national himself, Gompers felt particularly strongly that questions of admission, apprenticeship, bargaining policy, and the like should be left strictly to those directly involved with them.

Second, the AFL would charter only one national union in each trade jurisdiction. This concept of "exclusive jurisdiction" stemmed mainly from the unpleasant experiences of the nationals with rival unions chartered by the Knights. It was also, however, due to Gompers's deep concern that such competitive union situations would give the employer undue bargaining advantages by allowing him to pit one warring union against another.

Third, the AFL would at all costs avoid long-run reformist goals and concentrate instead only upon immediate wage-centered gains. As noted above, its founders were determined not to suffer the fates of earlier, reform-centered organizations: "We have no ultimate ends," asserted Gompers's colleague Adolph Strasser on the occasion of his testimony before a congressional committee at this time. "We are going on from day to day. We are fighting only for immediate objects—objects that can be realized in a few years."

Fourth, the federation would avoid any permanent alliances with the existing political parties and, instead, "reward labor's friends and defeat labor's enemies." Gompers was willing, however, to accept help for the AFL from any quarter, with only one major exception: He had at one time been a Marxian Socialist, but familiarity had bred contempt and, long before 1886, he had permanently broken with his old colleagues. At the 1903 AFL convention, he was to announce to the relative handful of Socialists present: "Economically, you are unsound; socially, you are wrong; and industrially, you are an impossibility."[7] To the end, Gompers's philosophy was firmly embedded in the capitalistic system.

Finally, Gompers placed considerable reliance on the strike weapon as a legitimate and effective means of achieving the wages, hours, and conditions sought by his unionists. Shortly before his election to the AFL presidency in May 1886, he had been one of the leaders of a general strike designed to obtain the eight-hour day. More than 300,000 workers had participated in this action, and almost two-thirds of them had achieved their objective through it. Gompers's own Cigar Makers, too, had rarely hesitated to resort to strikes when bargaining impasses had been reached. And, generally speaking, these demonstrations of economic strength had also been successful.

[6] Taft, *Organized Labor*, p. 117. Quoted from a speech by Gompers to the Web Weavers Amalgamated Association, March 5, 1888.
[7] *AFL Convention Proceedings*, 1903, p. 198.

Profiting from the lessons of history, Gompers's federation thus represented a realistic attempt to adjust to an economic system that had become deeply embedded in the United States. National union autonomy, exclusive jurisdiction, "pure and simple" collective bargaining, the avoidance of political entanglements, and the use of strikes where feasible—these proven sources of union strength were to be the hallmarks of the new unionism. The federation would provide the definition of jurisdictional boundaries for each national and give help to all such constituent unions in their organizing, bargaining, lobbying, and public relations endeavors. But it would otherwise allow a free hand to its national union members as they pursued their individual goals. And the stress was to be on the needs of skilled workers, not those of "good men of all callings," as the Knights had placed it: Some semiskilled and unskilled workers within a relatively few industries (such as mine workers and electricians, because of the strategic power of their national unions) were encouraged to join, but basically the AFL made no great efforts to organize workers with less than "skilled" callings and was to admit them only if they organized themselves and had no jurisdictional disputes with craft unions.

So successful did this master plan prove to be that, except for slight modifications that will be described later, it was not until the mid-1930s that its logic was in any way seriously questioned.

THE EARLY YEARS OF THE AFL AND SOME MIXED RESULTS

Even in the short run, the policies of the AFL were so attractive to the nationals that within a few years virtually all of them had become members of the new organization. Given this reception, the Gompers federation grew steadily, if not spectacularly: It had counted 140,000 members in 1886; by 1889, the figure had risen to 278,000.

It is also noteworthy that the economic depression that swept the country between 1893 and 1896 did not drastically deplete union membership totals, as had been the case in earlier hard times. The new principles of Gompers, reflected at both the federation and national levels, gave labor significant staying power. Moreover, the now centralized control held by the nationals over their locals both lessened the danger that local monies would be dissipated in ill-advised strikes and provided the locals with what were normally sufficient funds for officially authorized strikes.

On the other hand, organized labor still had a severe problem to contend with in the 1890s: the deep desire of the nation's industrialists, now themselves strongly centralized in this era of trusts and other forms of consolidation, to regain unilateral control of employee affairs. Not since the 1870s had the forces of management been as determined, as formidable, or, particularly in the case of two widely heralded strikes of the time, as successful in opposing unionism.

The first of these two union disasters involved the long-established Amalgamated Association of Iron and Steel Workers and the Homestead, Pennsylvania, plant of the Carnegie Steel Company (predecessor of the United States Steel Corporation). Here, in 1892, the company attempted to reduce wages as part of its renegotiation of an expiring agreement with the union. When the workers refused to agree to the pay cut, the Carnegie management locked them out and imported some 200 Pinkerton detectives to safeguard 2,000 strikebreakers who had been hired to replace the Amalgamated members. In a subsequent pitched battle between detectives and unionists, ten men were killed, several on each side. But the company successfully resumed operations with the strikebreakers, aided by the presence of the state militia, and thus dealt a crushing blow to the once powerful Amalgamated: The union's morale was badly broken, and not for forty-five more years would Carnegie, or most of the other fast-growing mills in the Pittsburgh area, again operate under a union contract. Adding insult to injury, the Carnegie management also permanently blacklisted many of the defeated strikers and thereby denied them reemployment throughout the industry.

The Pullman, Illinois, strike of 1894 was unlike Homestead in that it involved the fast-growing American Railway Union, not an AFL affiliate. Otherwise, however, it differed essentially only in degree of violence and exact method of company victory. As in 1892, it was precipitated when the company (here, the Pullman Palace Car Company) attempted unilaterally to cut wages. The workers, not originally ARU members, then walked off their jobs and requested the railway union to intervene in their behalf. The union, welcoming the opportunity for new members, promptly instituted a boycott against all Pullman cars throughout the country. In Chicago, violence ensued when the railroad executives there imported Canadian strikebreakers. Considerable railroad property was destroyed and most train operations were completely halted. When total mob rule then threatened, the U.S. Department of Justice intervened and obtained a federal court injunction outlawing further union activities. President Grover Cleveland also dispatched federal troops to the scene, despite the objections of the governor of Illinois. Only after a month of further violence, plant destruction, and the killing and wounding of several soldiers and rioters was the boycott finally ended. But, as at Homestead, the defeat was a crushing one for the union. The railroads refused to reinstate the strikers, and within a few years the union had permanently vanished from the scene.

Other managers, impressed by the triumphs of the Carnegie and railroad managements, and at times alarmed by what they felt was the overly belligerent stance of the AFL unions, also became more aggressive in their battles with labor. Employers in the metal trades formed a Metal Trades Association to defeat the Machinists in their quest for a nine-hour day and then adopted a policy of "no outside interference" with their company operations. Builders in Chicago, no less strongly united, completely ousted their workers' union representatives and regained full control of construction activities following a one-year 1899 strike. And the employers in the job foundry industry banded together in the National Founders' Association, which successfully terminated not only longstanding Molders Union work rules but, for all practical purposes, the existence of the union itself. In addition, the general public tended to be no more sympathetic, normally, to the aims of the labor movement; symbolically, the eminent president of Harvard University, Charles W. Eliot, reportedly "went so far as to glorify the strikebreaker as an example of the finest type of American citizen whose liberty had to be protected at all costs."[8]

Despite all these adverse factors, union membership growth in this period was unparalleled. From 447,000 unionists in 1897, the figure increased almost fivefold to 2,073,000 in 1904—a rate of expansion that has never been equaled since. The figures reflect the national prosperity of the day and the success of many of the national unions (their problems notwithstanding) in organizing their official jurisdictions along the lines of the AFL principles.

But the labor movement could not indefinitely withstand the continuing employer opposition, now augmented by a series of devastating court injunctions on the one hand and rival union challenges from leftist workingmen's groups on the other. Total union membership dropped to 1,959,000 in 1906, and even its ultimate growth to 3,014,000 by 1917 was quite uneven and—considering the fact that 90 percent of the country's labor force still remained unorganized—unspectacular.

Intensified employer campaigns for the open (nonunion) shop, led by the National Association of Manufacturers, resulted in a number of notable union strike losses after 1904 in the meatpacking and shipping industries, among others. Violence often occurred—most drastically at the Colorado Fuel and Iron Company's Ludlow location, when in 1913 eleven children and two women were found burned to death in strikers' tents that the state militia, summoned by the company, had set afire. These were also the peak years of yellow-dog contracts (under which employees promised in writing never to engage in union activities); labor spies; immediate discharge of workers at the slightest evidence of union sympathies; and the use of federal, state, and local troops on a wholesale scale to safeguard company interests in the face of strike actions.

The courts, too, were not particularly restrained in their conduct toward unions. Injunctions banning specific union activities often appeared to unionists to be issued quite indiscriminately.

Still another threat to the established unions, in the years between 1904 and 1917, came from workers themselves. Sometimes impatient with what they considered to be the slow pace of AFL union gains, and sometimes wholly antagonistic toward the very system of capitalism, radical labor groups arose to challenge the Gompers unions for membership and influence. This was the heyday of immigration into the United States—some 14 million newcomers, mainly from Europe, arrived in the first two decades of the twentieth century—and the European political socialism that many of the radical groups espoused found some recruits in this quarter. But the most significant of these radical organizations was essentially a native American one, the colorful Industrial Workers of the World.

The IWW was founded in 1905 by a wide array of dissidents: western metal miners, loggers, and out-and-out drifters; Socialist Labor party members; and a

---

[8] Joseph G. Rayback, *A History of American Labor* (New York: Free Press, 1966), p. 215.

few disenchanted AFL union leaders from locals of longshoremen and barbers, among others. Its militant organizers placed no faith in the free-enterprise system and asserted in the very first line of the IWW preamble that "the working class and the employing class have nothing in common." They also put a premium on inviting all types of workers to join (including, with a hospitality reminiscent of the Knights of Labor, farmers, industrial workers, and intellectuals); were willing to support what they called a "genuine labor party"; and strongly advocated militant direct economic action.

The "Wobblies," as IWW members were termed, achieved several tangible victories. They made major inroads among the miners and lumber workers of the West. Most notably, they assumed leadership of a spontaneous 1912 walkout of Lawrence, Massachusetts, textile workers and led them to victory in the form of wage-cut restorations, despite considerable management opposition and police intervention. But an equally bitter fight, marked by much violence, was lost the following year by the IWW-sponsored silk mill workers in Paterson, New Jersey, and from then on Wobblie membership—never more than perhaps 70,000—rapidly declined. By 1917, strongly opposing U.S. entry into World War I, the IWW had lost virtually all public support, and the federal government was in the process of obtaining convictions against its leaders for sedition. Yet, despite its ultimate failure and comparatively small membership, the IWW did demonstrate in its few years of gains that many unskilled and even migratory workers were now beginning to look to collective bargaining to safeguard their interests—indeed, given no alternative by the AFL, that they would support a bargaining agency as removed from their other values as the revolutionary IWW. Gompers's original principles were still quite adequate to meet the needs of the basic labor movement, but the day would come when the concept of skilled-worker paramountcy would be more seriously challenged.

For the time being, however, Gompers and the AFL could point with satisfaction to some signal gains. As previously noted, these did not lie primarily in the area of overall organizational growth: In the face of the onslaughts from the employers and the courts, as well as the abortive threats of radical dual unionism, AFL union membership rose only slowly in the pre–World War I years. Rather, the gains rested to a great extent on the outstanding organizing and bargaining successes of a few specific AFL member nationals, particularly in the building trades, the ladies' garment industry, and coal mining. Ironically, two of these unions (the International Ladies' Garment Workers and the United Mine Workers) owed much of their new strength to membership policies that took in many semiskilled and even unskilled workers, although skilled-worker needs were still emphasized (and although both these unions were definite exceptions to AFL union practice in their actions).

The AFL's further grounds for satisfaction rested on another irony: Despite the continuation of the policy against active involvement in politics, AFL lobbying activities at both the federal and state levels had been instrumental in the enactment of significant progressive labor legislation. Among other such achievements, by

1917 some thirty states had introduced workmen's compensation systems covering industrial accidents, and almost as many had provided for maximum hours of work for women. On the federal level, the 1915 LaFollette Seamen's Act had greatly ameliorated conditions on both American vessels and foreign vessels in American ports, and the 1916 Owen–Keating Act had dealt a severe blow to child-labor abusers. But Gompers was destined not to be successful in what had appeared at first to be an even greater triumph: Although the Clayton Act of 1914 had seemed to exempt labor from antitrust laws and the penalties of the injunction, in 1921 the Supreme Court was to interpret the Clayton Act in such a way as to render it toothless in labor disputes.

WARTIME GAINS AND PEACETIME LOSSES

From 1917 to 1920, the time of World War I and the months of prosperity following it, the AFL grew rapidly. The 3 million workers in the AFL unions on the eve of the hostilities increased to 4.2 million by 1919 and 5.1 million only one year later.

During the war, military production, the curtailment of immigration, and the draft combined to create tight labor markets and thus gave unions considerable bargaining power and commensurate gains. Real wages for employees in manufacturing and transportation increased by more than 25 percent during the war.

Even more significantly, labor received for the first time official government support for its collective bargaining activities. The rights to organize and bargain collectively, free of employer discrimination for union activities, were granted AFL leaders by the Wilson administration for the length of the war.

But the immediate postwar months were even more conducive to union growth than the war years. The economy's production needs remained high, now to satisfy pent-up consumer demands, and the cost of living hit an all-time high. Company profits also burgeoned, freed of artificial wartime restraints. No longer obliged to honor the no-strike pledges, unions aggressively struck in pursuit of worker wages attuned to both profits and cost of living, and, with their bargaining power now so high, they generally succeeded. As in earlier times of demonstrated labor triumphs, victory brought further conquest: New recruits flocked into the labor movement to gain their share in prosperity through collective bargaining.

Despite this auspicious entrance into the 1920s, however, the decade was to be one of great failure for unionism. Total union membership rapidly dwindled from the 1920 peak of 5.1 million to 3.8 million three years later and, steadily if less dramatically declining even after this, hit a twelve-year low of 3.4 million at the close of the decade. The drop is even more remarkable given the fact that the economy generally continued to flourish during this period; in every prior era of national prosperity, unions had gained considerable ground.

Nonetheless, there were understandable reasons for the poor performance of unionism in the 1920s. A combination of five powerful factors, most of them as unprecedented as organized labor's boom-period decline, was now at work.

First, after the beginning of the decade, prices remained stable, and, with workers generally retaining their relatively high wage gains of the 1917–1920 period, the cries of labor organizers that only union membership could stave off real wage losses fell on deaf ears.

Second, employers throughout the nation not only returned to such measures for thwarting unionization as the yellow-dog contract and the immediate discharge of union "agitators" but now embarked on an antiunion, open-shop propaganda campaign so extensive that one contemporary observer was moved to remark that never before in its history had

> . . . America seen an open shop drive on a scale so vast as that which characterizes the drive now sweeping the country. Never before has an open shop drive been so heavily financed, so effectively organized, so skillfully generated. The present drive flies all of the flags of patriotic wartime propaganda. It advances in the name of democracy, freedom, human rights, Americanism.[9]

The campaign, typically conducted under the slogan of the "American Plan," portrayed unions as alien to the nation's individualistic spirit, restrictive of industrial efficiency, and frequently dominated by radical elements who did not have the best interests of America at heart. Particularly in regard to the last of these charges, the public appeared to be impressed: It was still mindful of the IWW, and now its attention was also called, freely by the newspapers, to the relatively few other significant leftist inroads into labor circles. To many citizens, too, organizations that could even remotely be construed as going against individualism and the free-enterprise system in this day of laissez-faire Republicanism were also highly un-American.

Third, but often tied into their "American Plan" participation, many companies introduced what became known as "welfare capitalism." Intending to demonstrate to their employees that unions were unnecessary (as well as dangerous), they established a wide variety of employee-benefit programs: elaborate profit-sharing plans, recreational facilities, dispensaries, cafeterias, and health and welfare systems of all kinds. Employee representation plans were also instituted, with workers thus being offered a voice on wages, hours, and conditions—the companies being thereby enabled to satisfy many grievances before they became major morale problems. Although the managements could withdraw the benefits at any time, and although the employee representatives normally had only "advisory" voices, union ills were undeniably compounded by these company moves.

In the fourth place, the courts proved themselves even less hospitable to labor unions than they had been in labor's dark days preceding World War I. Having denied in 1921 that the Clayton Act exempted unions from the antitrust laws and the injunction, the Supreme Court proceeded to invalidate an Arizona anti-injunction law the same year and then struck down state minimum-wage laws as violations of liberty of contract in 1923. Encouraged by the implied mandate from

---

[9] Savel Zimand, *The Open Shop Drive* (New York: Bureau of Industrial Research, 1921), p. 5.

Washington, lower-court judges now issued injunctions more freely than ever.

Fifth, and finally, some of the union losses were due to unimaginative leadership in the labor movement itself. Gompers died in 1924, and his successor, William Green, lacked the aggressiveness and the imagination of the AFL's first president. Labor's troubles were clearly not to be viewed with equanimity, but Green and most of his AFL union leaders were, as Rayback has tersely commented, "content to rest upon past performances, to confine membership to the elite among workingmen, and to remain the junior partner of management in the nation's economic system."[10]

On the eve of the Great Depression in late 1929, then, organized labor remained almost exclusively the province of the highly-skilled-worker minority, apathetic in the face of the loss of one-third of its members in a single decade, militantly opposed by much of the employer community, severely crimped by judicial actions, and often suspected by the general public of possessing traits counter to the spirit of America. It appeared to have a superb future behind it.

THE GREAT DEPRESSION AND THE AFL'S RESURGENCE IN SPITE OF ITSELF

The stock-market collapse of October 1929 ushered in the most severe business downturn in the nation's history. Between 1929 and the Depression's lowest point in 1933, the gross national product dropped from over $104 billion to around $56 billion, and a staggering 24.9 percent of the country's civilian labor force was out of work by 1933, compared with an unemployment rate of only 3.2 percent in 1929.[11]

Figures specifically relating to organized labor were equally gloomy. Between 1929 and 1933, the average twelve-month membership loss rate for organized labor accelerated to 117,000, and by 1933 union membership stood at 2,973,000—only 200,000 above the 1916 level.[12]

Given this severe loss of dues-payers, plus the necessity of sustaining strikes against the inevitable wage cuts of workers still employed, it is not surprising that many unions soon became as impoverished as their constituents. Symbolically, Ulman reports that "one forlorn strike against a small steel mill had to be called off after the contents of the strikers' soup kitchen had been depleted by a group of hungry children."[13]

It is surprising, however, that the mood of the workers themselves seemed to be one of bewildered apathy. The atmosphere was now marked by constant mortgage foreclosures (resulting in thousands moving into shanty towns on city dumps, which were bitterly called "Hoovervilles" after the incumbent president).

[10] Rayback, *History of American Labor,* p. 303.
[11] Stanley Lebergott, *The Measurement and Behavior of Unemployment* (Princeton, N.J.: National Bureau of Economic Research, 1957), p. 215.
[12] Ulman, *American Trade Unionism,* p. 397.
[13] *Ibid.,* pp. 397–98.

It was characterized by the constant fear of starvation on the part of many of those not working and the fear of sudden unemployment on the part of many of those still employed. Virtually all remnants of welfare capitalism were being abruptly terminated. Under these conditions, one might have expected a reincarnation of such militant organizations as the IWW, seeking to overthrow the capitalistic system that was now performing so poorly. Some workers did indeed turn to such radical movements as Communism, but, in general, the nation seemed to have been shocked into inaction.

It is still more surprising, even considering its uninspiring performance in meeting the challenge of the 1920s, that the leadership of the AFL did not noticeably change its policies in these dark days. Through 1932, Green and the AFL executive council remained opposed to unemployment compensation, old-age pensions, and minimum-wage legislation as constituing unwarranted state intervention. They asked only for increased public-works spending from the government. So far was the AFL from the pulse of the general community at this time that, although the great bulk of union officials were and had long been Democratic party supporters, it refused, with scrupulous official neutrality, to endorse either candidate in the 1932 presidential election that swept Democrat Franklin D. Roosevelt into office with what was then the largest margin in American history.

Roosevelt's one-sided victory symbolized the country's (if not the AFL's) willingness to grant the federal government more scope for participation in domestic affairs than it had ever been given before. The business community, upon which the nation had put such a premium during the prosperous years of the 1920s, was now both discredited and demoralized. It had become painfully apparent, too, to the millions who had been steeped in the values of American individualism, that the individual worker was comparatively helpless to influence the conditions of his employment environment. In short, the Depression allowed labor unions—which had been so greatly out of favor with their countrymen only a few years earlier— a golden opportunity for revival and growth, now with government encouragement.

Even before the election, such a climate had resulted in one notable gain for unions. The Norris–La Guardia Act of 1932 satisfied a demand Gompers had originally made in a petition to the president and Congress some twenty-six years earlier: The power of judges to issue injunctions in labor disputes on an almost unlimited basis was now revoked. Severe restrictions were placed on the conditions under which the courts could grant injunctions, and such orders could in no case be issued against certain otherwise legal union activities. In addition, the yellow-dog contract was declared unenforceable in federal courts.

The 1932 act marked a drastic change in public policy. Previously, except for the temporary support that unions received during World War I, collective bargaining had been severely hampered through judicial control. Now it was to be strongly encouraged, by legislative fiat and—after Roosevelt took office in early 1933—by executive support.

Roosevelt and the first "New Deal" Congress wasted little time in making known their sentiments. The National Industrial Recovery Act of mid-1933, in similar but stronger language than that already existing in the Norris–La Guardia Act, specifically guaranteed employees "the right to organize and bargain collectively through representatives of their own choosing . . . free from the interference, restraint or coercion of employers." Green, in what for him was unusual enthusiasm, immediately praised the act as giving "millions of workers throughout the nation . . . their charter of industrial freedom" and launched a moderate drive to expand AFL membership among craft workers. More remarkable, however, was the response to the NIRA by rank-and-file workers themselves: Almost overnight, thousands of laborers in such mass-production industries as steel, automobiles, rubber, and electrical manufacturing spontaneously formed their own locals and applied to the AFL for charters. By the end of 1933, the federation had gained more than a million new members.

The largest single gains at this time were registered by those established AFL internationals that had lost the most members during the 1920s and could capitalize upon the new climate in public policy to win back and expand their old clientele. Both the men's and women's clothing unions fell into this category. Most impressive of all, however, was the performance of the United Mine Workers under their aggressive president, John L. Lewis. Lewis dispatched dozens of capable organizers throughout the coal fields, had signs proclaiming that "President Roosevelt wants you to join the union" placed at the mine pits, and not only regained virtually all his former membership but organized many traditionally nonunion fields in the Southeast. There were 60,000 Mine Workers at the time of the NIRA's passage; six months later, the figure had grown to over 350,000.

The employers, however, did not remain docile in the face of this new union resurgence. Terming collective bargaining "collective bludgeoning," many of them responded to the NIRA by restoring or instituting the employee representation plans of the previous decade. Such "company unions," although bitterly assailed by bona fide unionists as circumventing the law's requirements concerning "employer interference," spread rapidly. By the spring of 1934, probably one-quarter of all industrial workers were employed in plants that had them. Many other managements simply refused, the law notwithstanding, to recognize any labor organizations. On many occasions, this attitude led to outbreaks of violence, ultimately terminated by the police or National Guard units.

The National Industrial Recovery Act was itself declared unconstitutional by the Supreme Court early in 1935, but Congress quickly replaced it with a law that was even more to labor's liking. The National Labor Relations Act, better known (after its principal draftsman in the Senate) as the Wagner Act, was far more explicit in what it expected of collective bargaining than was the NIRA, in two basic ways. First, it placed specific restrictions on what management could do (or could not do), including an absolute ban on company-dominated unions. Second, it established the wishes of the employee majority as the basis for selection of a bargaining representative and provided that in cases of doubt as to a union's majority status, a secret-ballot election of the employees would determine whether or not the majority existed. To implement both provisions, it established a National

Labor Relations Board, empowered not only to issue cease-and-desist orders against employers who violated the restrictions but also to determine appropriate bargaining units and conduct representation elections.

Considerably less than enthusiastic about the Wagner Act, many employers chose to ignore its provisions and hoped that it would suffer the same fate as the NIRA. They were to be disappointed: In 1937, the Supreme Court held that the 1935 act and its congressional regulation of labor relations in interstate commerce were fully constitutional.

THE CIO'S CHALLENGE TO THE AFL

Meanwhile, however, the AFL itself almost snatched defeat from the jaws of victory. The leaders of the federation clashed sharply as to the kind of reception that should be accorded the workers in steel, rubber, automobiles, and similar mass-production industries who had spontaneously organized in the wave of enthusiasm following the NIRA's passage. The federation had given these new locals the temporary status of "federal locals," which meant that they were directly affiliated with the AFL rather than with one of the established national unions. The workers involved, however, wanted to form their own national industrial unions covering all types of workers within their industries, regardless of occupation or skill level. And this, obviously, meant a radical departure from the fifty-year AFL tradition of discouraging nonskilled workers and essentially excluding noncraft unions (the mining and clothing industries, as noted earlier, always excepted because of their particular situations).

John L. Lewis, who had shown such initiative in expanding the ranks of his Mine Workers in the preceding months, led the fight for industrial unionism within the federation. Allied with Sidney Hillman of the Clothing Workers and David Dubinsky of the Ladies' Garment Workers, he argued that changing times had now made skilled-craft unionism obsolete, that the AFL could no longer speak with any political power as long as it confined itself to what was (with the acceleration of mechanization and the replacement of craftsmen by semiskilled machine operators) a steadily dwindling minority of the labor force, and that, should the federation fail to assert its leadership over the new unionists, rival federations would arise to fill the vacuum. Holding perhaps the greatest oratorical powers ever possessed by an American labor leader (and very possibly the only one to begin sentences with "Methinks"), Lewis ridiculed the AFL president for not being able to decide the issue: "Alas, poor Green. I knew him well. He wishes me to join him in fluttering procrastination, the while intoning *O tempora, O mores!*" Moreover, in a dramatic speech at the 1935 AFL Atlantic City convention, he warned that should the federation fail to "heed this cry from Macedonia that comes from the hearts of men" and refuse to allow industrial unionism or to organize the millions still unorganized, "the enemies of labor will be encouraged and high wassail will prevail at the banquet tables of the mighty."

Lewis spoke to no avail. The convention was dominated by inveterate craft-unionists, many of whom possibly believed that Macedonia was somewhere east of Akron and who at any rate were opposed to admitting what Teamster president Daniel Tobin described as "rubbish" mass-production laborers. The demands of industrial unionism were defeated by a convention vote of 18,024 to 10,933. And Lewis, never one to camouflage his emotions for the sake of good fellowship with his AFL colleagues, left Atlantic City only after landing a severe uppercut to the jaw of Carpenter Union president William L. Hutcheson in a fit of pique.

Within a month, Lewis had formed his own organization of industrial unionists. The Committee for Industrial Organization (known after 1938 as the Congress of Industrial Organizations) originally wanted only to "counsel and advise unorganized and newly organized groups of workers; to bring them under the banner and in affiliation with the American Federation of Labor."[14] But the AFL, having already made its sentiments so clear, was to deny the new organization the latter opportunity; almost immediately, Green's executive council suspended the CIO leaders for practicing "dual unionism" and ordered them to dissolve their group. When these actions failed to dissuade the CIO, the AFL took its strongest possible action and expelled all thirty-two national member unions.

Lewis and his fellow founders—themselves heads of such nationals, in addition to those in the garment industries, as the Textile Workers, the Hatters, and the Oil Field Workers—were spectacularly successful in realizing their objectives. Armed with ample loans from the rebel nationals, aggressive leadership, experienced organizers, and, above all, confidence that mass-production workers enthusiastically *wanted* unionism, the AFL offshoot was able to claim almost 4 million recruits as early as 1937.

By 1941, even more remarkable conquests had been registered. One by one, virtually all the giant corporations had recognized CIO-affiliated unions as bargaining agents for their employees: all the major automobile manufacturers, almost all companies of any size in the steel industry, the principal rubber producers, the larger oil companies, the major radio and electrical equipment makers, the important meatpackers of the country, the larger glassmakers, and many others. Smaller companies that had also been unionized in this period could at least take comfort in the fact that they were in good company.

Still, the CIO's organizing campaigns were not welcomed by many of these companies with open arms. United States Steel recognized the CIO's Steel Workers Organizing Committee without a contest in 1937 (ostensibly because it feared labor unrest at a time when business conditions were finally improving). But the other major steel producers unconditionally refused to deal with unionism, the law notwithstanding. In 1941, the National Labor Relations Board ordered these companies to recognize what had by then become the United Steelworkers of America, but four years of company intimidation, espionage, and militia-protected strike-breaking—highlighted by a Memorial Day 1937 clash between pickets and police

---

[14] *Minutes of Committee for Industrial Organization,* Washington, D.C., November 9, 1935.

that resulted in the deaths of ten workers, injuries to many more, and substantial damage to property—had then elapsed.

The use of professional strikebreakers often served as a particularly potent employer weapon in these years. Such temporary payroll members were entrusted with such missions as the conveying of the impression that the struck organization was actually operating (to demoralize those out on strike) and the inciting of violence (to encourage the public authorities to take action against the unionists). In pursuit of the first goal the strikebreaker might, for example, burn paper in a plant furnace so that the smoke of the chimney would give the appearance of plant production. The driving of empty trucks to and from the plant was another frequently used ploy. Actually, the professional strikebreaker was often incapable of performing the struck worker's regular job and generally merely amused himself in the plant to while away the time.

And these strikebreakers frequently adopted such tactics as the hurling of stones into picket lines and the spitting at strikers to provoke violence, facts that explain why such individuals were at times termed "agents provocateurs." If the strikers were goaded into counterviolence, as they often were, the state militia or National Guard—rarely friendly to labor organizations—could then be summoned to the scene.

It was not the most honorable kind of occupation, and many of its practitioners in fact possessed prior criminal records. As one of them—the well-known professional strikebreaker Sam "Chowderhead" Cohen—once commented about his own lengthy record of imprisonment, "You see, in this line of work they never asked for no references."[15]

But where there was a will on the part of unionists there was generally a way. In some industries, workers turned to "sit-down" strikes—protest stoppages in which the strikers remained at their places of work and were furnished with food by allies outside the plant. Such stoppages, now illegal as trespasses upon private property, were of considerable influence in gaining representation rights for the unions in the historically nonunion automobile, rubber, and glass industries.

Nor, more significantly, was the AFL itself placid in the face of its new competition. Abandoning its traditional lethargy, it now terminated its "craftsmen only" policy and chartered industrial unions of its own in every direction. AFL meatcutters emerged to challenge CIO packinghouse workers for members of all skill levels within the meatpacking industry. AFL papermill employees competed against CIO paper workers. AFL electricians tried to recruit the same workers, from all quarters of the electrical industry, as did the CIO electrical-union organizers. And the story was much the same in textiles and automobiles. Moreover, many of the long-established AFL unions now broadened their jurisdictions; most notable were the Teamsters, whose president had apparently become oblivious to his former charge that mass-production workers were "rubbish," and who now waged aggressive organizational campaigns among workers in the food and agri-

[15] R.R.R. Brooks, *When Labor Organizes* (New Haven: Yale University Press, 1937), p. 146.

cultural processing industries. Aided by the same favorable climates of worker opinion and public policy that had originally inspired Lewis, and now also helped by improving economic conditions, the AFL actually surpassed the CIO in membership by 1941. By that time, however, the CIO had paid its parent the supreme compliment: It had modified its framework to include craft unionism as well as industrial unionism, and the lines separating the two rival federations had become permanently clouded.

At the time of Pearl Harbor, in December 1941, total union membership stood at 10.2 million, compared with the less than 3 million members of only nine years earlier. The CIO itself—representing some 4.8 million workers at this time—was destined to achieve little further success, as measured by sheer membership statistics; it would enroll only 6 million employees at its zenith in 1947 and then gradually retreat before the onslaught of a further AFL counterattack. But if Lewis's organization failed to live up to its founder's expectations as the sole repository of future union leadership, neither could it in any satisfactory way be described as a failure. When America entered World War II in late 1941, the labor movement not only was a major force to be reckoned with but, for the first time, was to a great extent representative of the full spectrum of American workers. And for this situation, the CIO's challenge to the AFL's fifty years of dominance deserves no small amount of credit.

WORLD WAR II

As in the case of World War I, the years after Pearl Harbor saw a further increase in union strength. Although the country's economic conditions had improved considerably in the late 1930s, only after the start of hostilities and the acceleration of the draft did a tight labor market arise to weaken employer resistance to union demands.

Other factors favorable to organized labor were also present. The federal government, sympathetic enough with the goals of unionism for almost a decade, now went even further in its tangible suport: In return for a no-strike pledge from both AFL and CIO leaders, labor was granted equal representation with management on the tripartite War Labor Board, the all-powerful institution that adjusted collective bargaining disputes during this period. It was also given an unprecedented form of union security—the still-utilized "maintenance of membership" arrangement, requiring all employees who are either union members when the labor contract is signed or who voluntarily join the union after this date to continue their membership for the length of the contract (subject to a short "escape" period). Finally, unions further profited in the membership area from the fast growth of such wartime industries as aircraft and shipbuilding and the reinvigoration of such now crucial sectors as steel, rubber, the electrical industry, and trucking. By the end of the war in 1945, union ranks had been increased by more than 4 million new workers, or by almost 40 percent.

By and large, labor honored its no-strike pledge during hostilities. Somewhat less than one-tenth of 1 percent of total available industrial working time was lost to the war effort through union economic action. However, with the cost of living continually rising, and with the War Labor Board nonetheless attempting to hold direct wages in check (not always successfully, and frequently at the cost of allowing such "nonwage" supplements as vacation, holiday, and lunch-period pay), the incidence of strikes did increase steadily after 1942. Particularly galling to the general public were several strikes by Lewis's own Mine Workers, all in direct defiance of President Roosevelt's orders and all given substantial publicity by the mass media.

Managers themselves, regaining much of their lost stature with the stress on war production at this time, could also point to other evidence that labor had become "too powerful." The competition between the AFL and CIO, officially postponed for the duration of the war, in practice continued almost unabated. Such rivalry on occasion temporarily curtailed plant output, as unions within the two federations resorted to "slowdowns" and "quickie strikes" to convince employers of their respective jurisdictional claims. Instances of worker "featherbedding"—the receipt of payment for unperformed work—marked several industries, notably construction. And members of the Communist party, originally welcomed by some CIO unions because of their demonstrated organizational ability, had now gained substantial influence if not effective control within several of these unions, including both the United Automobile Workers and the Electrical, Radio, and Machine Workers.

The public's attention was also called, by forces unhappy with the labor movement's rapid growth, to union political strength. The AFL had not yet abandoned its traditional policy of bipartisanship, but Lewis had led the CIO actively into political campaigning and had, in fact, resigned his federation presidency (while retaining his Mine Workers leadership) when the CIO rank and file had refused to bow to his wishes and vote for Republican Wendell Willkie in 1940. Under Lewis's successor, Philip Murray, and particularly through the direct efforts of Clothing Worker president Sidney Hillman, the CIO had become even more aggressive and influential—within the Democratic party. It now held considerable power within most northern Democratic state organizations, and such was its influence at the national Democratic level that when a fabricated story swept the country to the effect that Roosevelt had ordered his 1944 party convention to "clear everything with Sidney," it was widely believed. So effective had Hillman's CIO Political Action Committee become by this time that attacks upon it emanated from the highest of places: The Republican governor of Ohio claimed that the PAC was "trying to dominate our government with radical and communistic schemes," and the House Un-American Activities Committee (with a membership unfriendly to Roosevelt) called it "a subversive . . . organization."[16]

The American man and woman in the street seemed to be impressed. By the

[16] Rayback, *History of American Labor*, p. 386.

end of the war in 1945, public opinion polls showed more than 67 percent of the respondents in favor of legislative curbs on union power.

PUBLIC REACTION AND PRIVATE MERGER

Organized labor fell even further from public favor in the immediate postwar period. Faced with income declines as overtime and other wartime pay supplements disappeared, with real wage decreases as prices rose in response to the huge pent-up consumer demand, and with layoffs as factories converted to peacetime production, workers struck as they had never done before. Although the violence of earlier-day labor unrest did not recur often, the year 1946 saw new highs established in terms of number of stoppages (4,985), number of employees involved (4.6 million), and person-days idle as a percentage of available working time (1.43). The month of January 1946 alone was marked by almost 2 million workers on strike. And by the end of the year, noteworthy stoppages (many of them simultaneously) had occurred in virtually every sector of the economy, including the railroads, autos, steel, public utilities, and even public education.

Such strikes were not well received by a frequently inconvenienced public that had already voiced reservations about union strength. The sentiments that the Wagner Act and other public policies of the 1930s had been too "one-sided" in favor of labor grew rapidly and soon became compelling. In 1947, a newly elected Republican Congress passed, over President Truman's veto, the Taft–Hartley Act.

Taft–Hartley drastically amended the Wagner Act to give greater protection to both employers and individual employees. To the list of "unfair" labor practices already denied employers were added six "unfair" *union* practices, ranging from restraint or coercion of employees to featherbedding. Employees could now hold elections to decertify unions as well as to certify them. Provisions regulating certain internal affairs of unions, explicitly giving employers certain collective bargaining rights (particularly regarding "freedom of expression" concerning union organization), and sanctioning government intervention in the case of "national emergency strikes" were also enacted.

A fuller discussion of Taft–Hartley is reserved for later pages; however, it might be added here that the 1947 act was at least as controversial as the Wagner Act had been. Its proponents, consistent with the views of Senator Taft, asserted that it "reinjected an essential measure of justice into collective bargaining." Less friendly observers of Taft–Hartley, including the spokespeople of organized labor, were less happy and hurled such epithets as "slave labor act" at it. That the act has proved generally satisfactory to the majority of Americans, however, may be inferred from the fact that in the 1980s, Taft–Hartley, essentially unchanged from its original edition, remained the basic labor law of the land.

Speaking with the self-assurance always allowed one who can draw on hindsight, it is tempting to argue that the AFL–CIO merger of 1955 was inevitable. The issue that had led to the birth of the CIO was, as noted, blunted even by the late 1930s when the AFL rapidly chartered its own industrial unions and the CIO began to recognize craft unions as part of its structure. By 1939, indeed, ten of the twenty-nine existing CIO unions were craft organizations, and the AFL encompassed possibly as many noncraft workers as it did craftsmen. But sixteen more years were to elapse before merger became a reality, and significant differences of values, political opinions, and personalities still had to be bridged in this period.

In the first place, the new unions that had been formed, first by the CIO and later by the AFL, were often meeting head-on in their quests for new members and enlarged jurisdiction. Any merged federation would have to resolve not only this kind of overlap but also the membership raiding that was frequently carried on by such rival unions. For a long while, compromise seemed impossible: The AFL tended to regard all jurisdictions as exclusively its own and to insist that the CIO unions be fully absorbed within its framework; on its part, the CIO strongly suggested that its affiliates would participate in a merger only if their existing jurisdictions were given official protection.

Second, the conservative AFL leaders displayed deep hostility toward the Communist-dominated unions within the CIO. Such unions reached a peak in the immediate postwar months, when a special report of the Research Institute of America listed eighteen of them in this category. And Taft has gone so far as to assert that for a short while in that period, "it was a question whether the anti-Communists in the CIO could muster a majority."[17]

Finally, personalities played a role. Murray (still influenced by his predecessor as CIO president, Lewis) and Green were mutually suspicious leaders. Each was quite unwilling to take the initiative in any merger move that would involve subordination of infuence to the other.

By 1955, however, most of these cleavages had been resolved. Murray, his patience with the Communist unions exhausted as they became more aggressive and (in particular) strongly opposed the government's Marshall Plan, had taken the lead in expelling most such unions from the CIO in 1949 and 1950. Virtually all other Communist-influenced unions, presumably taking the hint, had voluntarily left the federation shortly thereafter. Murray's move cost the CIO an estimated 1 million members, but new unions were quickly established to assume the old jurisdictions, and Murray claimed to have regained most of the lost membership within the next two years.

Further preparing the way for ultimate merger were the 1952 deaths of Murray and Green, both suddenly and only eleven days apart. The two successors—Walter Reuther of the United Auto Workers, for Murray, and AFL secretary-treasurer George Meany, for Green—were relatively divorced from the personal bitterness of the earlier presidents.

And beyond these factors were growing sentiments on the part of both AFL and CIO leaders that only a united labor movement could (1) stave off future laws of the Taft–Hartley variety, (2) avoid the jurisdictional squabbles that were in-

---

[17] Taft, *Organized Labor*, pp. 623–24.

creasingly sapping the treasuries of both federations, and (3) allow organized labor to reach significant new membership totals for the first time since 1947.

In December 1955, culminating two years of intensive negotiations between representatives of the two organizations, the AFL–CIO became a reality. The new constitution respected the "integrity of each affiliate," including both its "organizing jurisdiction" and its "established collective bargaining relationships." Consolidation of the rival unions was to be encouraged but was to be on a voluntary basis. And it was agreed that the new giant federation would issue charters "based upon a strict recognition that both craft and industrial unions are equal and necessary as methods of trade union organization." Three decades later, as will be seen, complete harmony between the AFL and CIO wings had yet to be achieved. But with the act of merger, the open warfare that had first revitalized and then damaged the labor movement passed from the scene.

ORGANIZED LABOR SINCE THE MERGER

Although some observers predicted that the original 15-million membership total (two-thirds of it provided by the AFL) of the AFL–CIO would rapidly double, the figure was actually no different in 1984, still 15 million.

It is true that the united federation had expelled the International Brotherhood of Teamsters in 1957 for alleged domination by "corrupt influences," thereby depriving itself of 1.8 million members in terms of 1984 statistics. But the fact remains that organized labor *overall* has been anything but impressive in terms of membership growth since the merger. The current 22-million figure for all union members (counting those in unions currently outside the ranks of the AFL–CIO— Teamsters, Mine Workers, railroad operating employees, and others) is, in fact, less than 3 million higher than it was in the mid-1950s. And since the nation's total labor force has been growing at a much faster clip than organized labor's membership since the merger, labor has clearly been losing ground on a relative basis. At the time of this writing, as mentioned earlier in this book, unionists made up under 30 percent of America's total nonagricultural employment, the lowest percentage since 1942.

Several formidable obstacles undoubtedly serve to explain this situation. Paramount among them is, of course, the fact that blue collar workers, traditionally constituting that sector of the labor force most susceptible to the overtures of the union organizer, have now been substantially organized. And this sector has, it will be recalled, been declining as a source of jobs in recent years, due mainly to the onslaughts of automation and to changes in demand. It remains to be seen whether new approaches, fresh leadership, and environmental changes adversely affecting worker morale can gain for organized labor the allegiance of the growing white collar sector. As the statistics in the preceding chapter indicated, however, unions to date have not been spectacularly successful in recruiting this wave of the future (their performance in the public sector excepted).

Beyond this, labor's fall from public favor, which began in the 1940s and led initially to the enactment of Taft–Hartley, had yet to be arrested four decades later. Congressional disclosures of corruption in the Teamsters and several smaller unions (among them, the Laundry and Bakery Workers) in the late 1950s hardly improved labor's image. The AFL–CIO quickly expelled not just the Teamsters but all the offending unions. But the public seemd to be far more impressed by the disclosures than by the federation's reaction to them, as indeed had been the case following the CIO's expulsion of its Communist-dominated affiliates.

Union resistance to technological change, sometimes taking the form of featherbedding and insistence on the protection of jobs that seemed no longer to be needed (those of diesel firemen and certain airline and maritime employees, for example), also was anything but calculated to regain widespread public support. Nor was it easy to generate sympathy outside the labor movement on behalf of plumbers who threatened to strike for wage rates in excess of $20 per hour, electricians demanding a twenty-hour workweek, and New York City transit workers seeking a 50 percent wage increase, a thirty-two-hour workweek, and some seventy-five other demands. These few examples were among the extremes; most unionists showed considerably more concern for the welfare of their industries in the post-merger years. But such actions as the ones illustrated, being more newsworthy, attracted more attention. It is conceivable that, through this combination of factors ranging from corruption to excessive demands, countless potential union members had been alienated.

The continuing lack of public confidence in unionism had also led, in the relatively recent past, to new legislation restricting labor's freedom of action. In particular, the Landrum–Griffin Act of 1959 stemmed from this climate and, directly, from the union-corruption revelations of Congress that were cited above. Among its other provisions, Landrum–Griffin guarantees union members a "Bill of Rights" that their unions cannot violate and requires officers of labor organizations to meet a wide and somewhat cumbersome variety of reporting and disclosure obligations. It also lays out specific ground rules for union elections, rules that have been deemed too inhibiting (as have most other parts of the act) by many labor leaders.

It is perhaps also true that labor's conspicuous recent lack of success has stemmed from the fact that the new breed of manager has acted a great deal more responsibly in employee relations, thereby making the organization considerably less vulnerable to unionization. Objective and essentially uniform standards for discipline, promotion, layoffs, recalls, and a host of other personnel areas have now all but totally replaced even the palest efforts at tyranny, and in the face of the change relatively few workers seem to feel the need for a collective bargaining agency as a curb on supervisory ruthlessness.

Whatever the reasons, it was obvious that organized labor could not count the three decades after the merger among its golden years and that many of the conditions that could explain unionism's lack of success in these years persisted at the end of this period.

UNIONISM AND THE BLACK WORKER

Inevitably, in the late twentieth century, organized labor was also forced to devote considerable attention to an issue that was far less parochial in its thrust: the increasingly intense quest of the black community for genuine equality of opportunity. Employment expectations that were initially (if indirectly) raised by the landmark Supreme Court school-desegregation decision of 1954 had been considerably heightened by the broad equal-employment-opportunities legislation of the Civil Rights Act of 1964. And since in subsequent years the gap between expectation and reality remained significant, the labor movement found itself under growing attack as frustrated blacks charged it with bigotry and racism, collusion with an equally insensitive managerial community to exploit the black worker, and total inadequacy in the field of integrative social action.

Not all blacks, of course, shared this dim opinion. The Urban League's late, highly respected Whitney Young undoubtedly echoed the sentiments of a significant sector of the black world in stating that "when we look at the whole picture, labor is strongly on the side of social justice and equal rights. . . . All unions ought to be educating their members to the dangers of bigotry, and to the fact that racism damages white workers as well as blacks. But on the whole, organized labor is as good a friend of black efforts for equality as exists in our imperfect society."[18] Nor would objective blacks deny not only that AFL–CIO leadership, and particularly Meany and Reuther, had been in the forefront of efforts to enact the equal-employment-opportunities provisions into the Civil Rights Act of 1964 itself but that for a time these federation chieftains had waged this campaign almost entirely alone. As the head of the NAACP's Washington Bureau, Clarence Mitchell, could later testify in this regard, "Organized labor gave unfailing, consistent and massive support where it counted most. . . . The members of organized labor were always present at the right time and in the right places."[19] And most blacks would presumably acknowledge that the approximately 2.5-million-member black contingent within the ranks of unionism by the early 1980s constituted—in aggregate figures—not only roughly the same proportion as that for blacks in the total U.S. population but substantial progress from 1928, when black membership was 2.1 percent, and even from 1956, when the figure had climbed to 8.6 percent.[20]

To the growing body of black militants, however, the Youngs and Mitchells could quickly be dismissed as Uncle Toms, whose laudatory statements only proved that they had been captured by the Labor Establishment. And the significant numerical growth in black unionists in no way touched the heart of the problem—that even where the admissions bars were down, a highly disproportionate number of blacks' jobs were at the bottom of the skills ladder, situations shunned by whites and entirely lacking in career progression opportunities. Above all, they could

---

[18] "John Herling's Labor Letter," *Washington Daily News,* November 30, 1968, p. 4.
[19] Ray Marshall, *The Negro Worker* (New York: Random House, 1967), pp. 40–41.
[20] Derek C. Bok and John T. Dunlop, *Labor and the American Community* (New York: Simon & Schuster, 1970), p. 120.

point with considerable bitterness to the building trades, where many years after the passage of the Civil Rights Act, little more than 5 percent of all black apprentices were enrolled in skilled-craft training programs (the remainder being in the so-called "trowel trades"—general laborers, cement masons, and kindred occupations, whose pay scales averaged much less and whose status was lowest). This was an especially jarring situation to blacks, given the large number of projects financed with public money.

Thus, while black militants had espoused picketing and (on occasion) disrupted production as a protest against alleged discrimination in the automobile, steel, and appliance sectors, it was in the nation's huge construction industry that the most potentially explosive confrontations had occurred.

In the tension-packed year of 1969, especially notable and highly publicized black coalition protests had closed major construction projects in Chicago and Pittsburgh. Accompanied by some violence, these had generated union (and employer) pledges to hire and train black journeymen not only immediately but in considerably greater numbers than ever before. Other cities also witnessed such direct action and a similar resolution of the action.

But the unlikely prospects for an amicable or imminent solving of the national construction employment issue had been accurately indicated by the enthusiastic reception accorded the president of the AFL–CIO Building and Construction Trades Department immediately after the Chicago and Pittsburgh confrontations. On this occasion, he defiantly declared to 300 cheering delegates at the department's convention, "We wish to make it clear that we do not favor acceptance of unreasonable demands. . . . We should make it clear again that the conduct, curriculum, and control of our training programs are going to remain in the hands of our crafts and our contractors. They are not going to be turned over to any coalition."[21]

And vastly compounding the construction industry problem was the deeply embedded building trades tradition of restrictive membership, designed not only to limit competition for jobs and to increase the asking price for the existing members' performances of services but in part also to nurture a certain amount of father–son employment situations. In support of such goals, and also because much employment in the industry had been intermittent and seasonal, hiring had historically been done through the union hiring hall. Racial intolerance itself had, indeed, not often been easily provable in the face of these other exclusionary considerations—as, presumably, in the case of the Philadelphia building trades local whose leader some years ago countered black charges of discrimination with the outraged declaration that "we don't take in *any* new members, regardless of color."[22]

Adding a final complexity to the building trades issue, moreover, was the fact that, by craft union definition, journeymen cannot be created instantaneously. Skilled ironworkers, plumbers, electricians, steamfitters, and similarly highly renumerated

[21] *Business Week,* September 27, 1969, p. 31.
[22] Marten Estey, *The Unions* (New York: Harcourt Brace Jovanovich, 1967), p. 68.

workers by and large have emerged only after rigorous apprenticeship programs, often lasting five or more years (and paying relatively low trainee wages during the period). Only through this process, the unions had argued, could the high standards of the craft be upheld. To many blacks, who had long viewed much of the apprenticeship philosophy as primarily a restrictive device (racial or otherwise) anyhow, the unions owed the black community considerable accelerated upgrading to journeymen status as compensation for years of total exclusion. To many whites already in unions, such a concession would greatly dilute the quality of craftmanship and thus devastate morale among the present skilled-trades workers.

The gap separating the two positions was, consequently, a very large one. And given its dimensions, few observers predicted much success even from the federal government's much-heralded Philadelphia Plan, which was also implemented in 1969. This innovative concept established minority-group quotas for six building trades unions working on federal construction jobs in the Philadelphia area, beginning with a 4 percent quota in 1969 and scheduled to rise to a 19 percent average by 1973. It was, however, immediately assailed by unions and some contractors as an illegal system denying to other prospective employees equal protection of the Constitution, as a mechanism that would undermine the crafts and decrease the efficiency of building-trades work, and as an impractical device requiring the hiring of blacks either not available at all or unacceptable as employees if available. Ironically, civil rights groups also quickly attacked the plan as insufficient in ensuring jobs, and also as making no provisions for training or upgrading to journeyman status within the unions. They also viewed it negatively as being geared only to temporary employment. And the influential black spokesman Bayard Rustin, in fact, went so far as to describe the plan as one that "actually does nothing for integration. . . . It is designed primarily to embarrass the unions and to organize public pressure against them."[23]

Although plans similar to Philadelphia's had by the 1980s been implemented in Atlanta, San Francisco, St. Louis, Camden, N.J., and Washington, D.C., as well as Chicago (although not Pittsburgh), support for the basic concept involved had long before steadily eroded. It had become a victim not only of the sharp attacks upon it from both sides but of a national white backlash in general. It had also been substantially weakened by the Nixon administration's preference in the 1970–1974 period for a voluntary approach to construction industry hiring. "It's best," said Secretary of Labor Peter J. Brennan in 1973, "when labor and management honestly agree on a plan and work together to make it succeed,"[24] and under the Nixon "hometown plan" approach to minority hiring, some seventy such plans—based on having labor, management, and minority leaders work out their own "goals and timetables" for integration—were implemented with mixed but generally very unimpressive results.

The deep national recessions culminating in 1975 and 1983, particularly severe

[23] Bayard Rustin, "The Blacks and the Unions," *Harper's*, May 1971, p. 79.
[24] *Business Week*, December 1, 1973, p. 86.

ones for construction and ones whose further employment ramifications for minority-group members will be explored in the last chapter of this book, further dampened whatever optimism remained for significant building-trades job improvement on the part of blacks. And by the mid-1980s, while some progress had obviously come about—overall, about 15 percent of all jobs in construction were then held by black workers—blacks had not significantly increased their proportion of jobs in the *skilled* trades. Indeed, the national labor director of the NAACP could say in the late 1970s, in comparing this latter area with its situation regarding blacks several years earlier, "If it was bad then, it's worse now."[25] From all available evidence, there was nothing to give blacks any additional encouragement at the time of this writing.

Nor were the building trades unique in having aroused the ire of blacks. Several of the railway brotherhoods continued even in the 1980s to show an almost total absence of blacks on their membership rosters (a situation that could primarily be explained by the strong southern historical ties of these unions), as did some printing and entertainment industry crafts and the Air Line Pilots Association. And black holders of major union-leadership posts, even in unions with substantial black memberships, remained conspicuous by their absence. The Teamsters and the Steelworkers, for example, had no blacks at all on their executive boards until the last years of the 1970s (when each union installed one) despite the large percentages of blacks in both of these large internationals; the Automobile Workers, over one-third black, could point to not much more progress, with only two blacks on their twenty-six-member board until recently (although one of these, Vice President Marc Stepp, was in charge of relations with the Chrysler Corporation and thus bargained for 90,000 UAW members); and the powerful, policy-making AFL–CIO Executive Council, with just two of its thirty-five members black, also remained a sea of white faces.

In fact, there is currently only one black president of an international union—Frederick O'Neal, head of the 78,000-member Actors and Artistes of America—and his union is obviously not one of the nation's more important ones.

As the editors of a major Industrial Relations Research Association project could say—in speaking of the total discrimination picture—"the problem simply will not recede very quickly."[26] The choice of words seemed quite apt, given the fact that they were written almost one-quarter of a century after the Supreme Court's school decision, and thirteen years after passage of the Civil Rights Act.

Yet the "problem," at least as it involved the labor movement, should also be viewed in perspective. Generally speaking, industrial unions had rarely practiced membership discrimination in either admission or job assignment. They had recognized that in most industries (as opposed to crafts), large numbers of blacks already existed and that the price of discrimination in such a situation would be the sacrifice of organizing potential. Thus, even prior to the rise of the CIO, the needle trades unions and coal miners aggressively fought off efforts on the part of

---

[25] *Washington Post,* February 20, 1977, p. F-9.
[26] Leonard J. Hausman et al., eds., *Equal Rights and Industrial Relations* (Madison, Wis.: Industrial Relations Research Association, 1977), p. vi.

their more biased rank and file to restrict membership to whites, and essentially all industrial unions, following the great waves of organization in the 1930s, had espoused a policy of full equality regarding both admission and occupational level for blacks. The attitude of the AFL–CIO has already been cited, in reference to the 1964 Civil Rights Act, and it is no less a matter of record that the federation had consistently upheld as a cardinal principle ever since the 1955 merger, "to encourage all workers without regard to race, creed, color, national origin or ancestry to share equally in the full benefits of union organization."[27] Finally, the effective alliances forged between labor and civil rights groups—which resulted most notably in improved conditions for black Memphis, Tennessee, sanitation workers in 1968, and one year later (under the banner of "Union Power Plus Soul Power Equals Victory") union recognition and considerable economic betterment for black hospital employees in Charleston, South Carolina—cannot be overlooked in any summary of this more positive side of labor's efforts.

Even the federation and industrial unions, however, had been unable to uproot occasional discriminatory practices (as opposed to policies) within the lower levels of their hierarchies. The federation, as Chapter 4 will attempt to show, has limited powers over its affiliates and has stopped short of using its ultimate penalty of expulsion both out of consideration of "overkill" and because of a realistic fear that many craft unions might voluntarily leave the federation fold in sympathy with the disciplined organizations. And the elected leaders of local industrial unions have had, as Bok and Dunlop have accurately pointed out, "much to lose and little to gain by fighting against racial prejudice" where it does exist among their members at the lower levels, particularly "given the high rate of turnover in local union office, and the natural inclination to remain in power."[28] Again, however, the problem was nowhere near as blatant as in the case of the craft unions.

Perhaps it was asking too much of organized labor to exhibit a record that was above reproach in regard to its treatment of black employees, considering that no other sector of our society had performed any better—or possibly, indeed, as well. But in view of the understandable unhappiness of the black community with labor's performance to date, it was nonetheless obvious that this issue remained in the 1980s, for unionism, a great one.

WOMEN IN LABOR UNIONS

Women make up some 25 percent of union membership in the United States but hold only 12 percent of the leadership positions in their organizations,[29] and even these statistics overstate how well they have done. Most of the positions are at the local as opposed to the national level, and even in locals the jobs are most often at the very bottom of the hierarchy, shop stewardships.[30]

[27] *AFL–CIO Constitution*, Article II, Sec. 4.
[28] Bok and Dunlop, *Labor and the American Community*, p. 135.
[29] *AFL–CIO News*, May 1, 1982, p. 7.
[30] Karen S. Koziara and David A. Pierson, "The Lack of Female Union Leaders: A Look at Some Reasons," *Monthly Labor Review*, 104, No. 5 (May 1981), 30.

Until 1980, indeed, the thirty-five-member AFL–CIO Executive Council, made up basically of the presidents of the major national unions affiliated with the federation, had remained an all-male province (and, as we know, almost an all-white one as well). And while two women now belong to this key governing body, both inevitably held secondary union positions at the time of their appointments, as they still do, since no woman can even now be said to hold anything but such a slot. Joyce D. Miller is one of several vice presidents of the Amalgamated Clothing and Textile Workers, and Barbara B. Hutchinson—who by being a black as well as a woman gives the federation double mileage in a single person—holds a comparable position within the American Federation of Government Employees.

One hundred years after the formation of the American Federation of Labor, moreover, only four national unions (all of them small ones) had female presidents, and offsetting even this modest performance was the fact that the number of women national union secretary–treasurers, never large, had actually fallen over the previous three decades. The latter had been nine in 1952; at the start of the 1980s it had dwindled to seven.

Had women not become significantly more numerous both in the civilian labor force and within union ranks in the years since the merger, such statistics could well have been received with aplomb by all but perhaps the most militant of women. As it was, however, female unionists according to Bureau of Labor Statistics figures numbered just under 5.2 million by 1983, up from a meager 1.1 million in 1956. And in these same years, the female percentage of the total civilian labor force had risen from just over 30 percent to almost 45 percent. Justice had accordingly, in the eyes of many women, not been remotely rendered.

It had been in recognition of this lack of progress, and a deeply harbored belief that the masculine leaders of labor had not fought aggressively enough for higher wages and improved working conditions for their female constituents, that more than 3,000 women members from fifty-eight international unions had met at Chicago in 1974. In general agreement with the sentiments of one speaker (Linda Tarr-Whelan, deputy director for program development for the American Federation of State, County, and Municipal Employees, and as such, symbolically, one of the more prominent female unionists) that "the union presidents understand power,"[31] they had formed the Coalition of Labor Union Women (CLUW) to work within the union movement for change.

In particular, they had pledged that the new organization's objectives would focus upon increased union efforts to organize women workers; greater participation of women in union affairs, particularly in policy-making positions; positive action by unions against sex discrimination in pay, hiring, job classification, and promotion; and adequate child-care facilities. Not one union initially had specifically endorsed the new women's group. But the founders of CLUW had made it very clear that they harbored no thoughts of engaging in a direct confrontation with organized labor. "Working through the union" was the dominant theme of

[31] *Business Week*, March 30, 1974, p. 102.

this convention, and no one questioned the declaration of the CLUW's new vice-president, Addie Wyatt, that "our unions are not really our enemies, since we are the unions. Our real job is to see to it that our bosses respond in a more meaningful way to our needs." Nor was any challenge lodged to the assertion of another CLUW leader that "men aren't going to resign their posts. They're just going to have to make room for more people on the boards."[32]

Talk, as has been observed by many evaluators of it, is cheap. And almost a decade later it still remained to be seen if all of this original oratory would lead to concrete results. CLUW itself was still very much in business in the mid-1980s: Indeed, it had grown to sixty-five chapters, more than half of which had been formed since 1979 alone, and its most recent biennial convention had drawn delegates, alternates, observers, and visitors from twenty countries. But there was little to show that, for many unions, much had really changed at all in these years. For every union that was clearly devoting more concern to women than it had in the past (for example, the United Automobile Workers with its increasingly active women's department, and the Communications Workers), there might well have been another (such as the Ladies' Garment Workers or Joyce Miller's own Amalgamated Clothing and Textile Workers, despite both unions' overwhelmingly female memberships) that appeared to be far less aggressive in pursuing the interests of women than it once was.

Some overall progress had certainly been made, however. By all accounts CLUW was instrumental in converting the AFL–CIO from a stance of opposition to the Equal Rights Amendment to one of aggressive support. It had also helped effect 1978 legislation forbidding employers to discriminate against pregnant employees and—although to date without success—had proven an energetic lobbyist (usually in tandem with other unionists) for federal actions effecting equal pay for "comparable" (as opposed to "identical") work. Even George Meany had been sufficiently impressed to announce at the 1977 CLUW convention that he had become "a closet feminist" and to tell his audience there that "if supporting a living wage for all workers makes a feminist, move over, sisters, I've been called a lot worse."[33]

On the other hand, tales of sexism among male union power-holders still abounded. ("When we went shopping around for a union," one leader of a national organization devoted to organizing female office workers could report, "one [union] official said to us: 'If I had a girl here to do the typing, I'd have more time to organize women.' ")[34] And, as indicated, the men had by no means actually made "room for more people on the boards."

Yet the women's increasing interest in their own jobs—not just through CLUW but through such other new organizations as the ambitious National Association of Working Women, whose 10,000 members had recently joined forces with the 650,000 Service Employees International Union in an attempt to organize

[32] Ibid.
[33] New York Times, October 19, 1977, p. 55.
[34] New York Times, March 29, 1981, p. 8-F.

the nearly 20 million female clerical workers in the United States—was nonetheless highly significant. Women had now shown themselves, really for the first time in a sustained way, as being willing to engage in employment-improvement action on many fronts. As in the case of minorities' demands for more attention, it was clear in the 1980s that organized labor could now afford to ignore their increasing self-awareness only to its definite detriment.

AN ANALYSIS OF UNION HISTORY

It is impossible to explain the history of unionism in this country with a single or all-encompassing theory. Economic, structural, and philosophical factors have all been at work, in varying degrees at various times—as has, occasionally, the sheer force of circumstances.

In earlier years, the highly sporadic growth of the American labor movement depended to a great extent on the basic *health of the economy,* and one can rather closely correlate the years of union success and failure with the periods of good and bad times for general business conditions. Union bargaining power, and thus the basic attractiveness of union membership, was high in the essentially prosperous periods of the years immediately prior to 1819, the 1822–1837 era, and in 1850–1873 (with the exception of brief recessions in the late 1850s); in each of these intervals, union membership lists significantly rose. By the same token, it was not until the depression of 1873–1878 that the labor movement could even moderately withstand the slumping demand for labor services engendered by periods of economic reversal; the depressions of 1819–1822 and 1837–1850 all but eradicated collective bargaining for their durations.

Nor does such a correlation end with 1878. The record fivefold expansion in union ranks between 1897 and 1904 occurred simultaneously with another economic boom period, and the tight labor markets of the two world wars clearly fostered union growth and labor organization effectiveness. After the late 1870s, however, there are as many exceptions to this rule of "as the economy goes, so goes unionism" as there are illustrations of its accuracy. Organized labor rode out the drastic 1893–1896 depression without major depletions of either its ranks or its previously acquired bargaining strength; it was forced into an ignominious retreat in the highly prosperous 1920s; and it enjoyed its greatest successes during the most formidable of all American depressions, in the 1930s. It is clear that the analyst of labor history can take the economic conditions factor only so far.

Room must also be reserved for recognition of the pronounced *structural changes* that unionism has been willing to make throughout its existence to accommodate the changing nature of industry. Some of these attempts were premature and consequently abortive—notably the National Trades' Union in 1834, whose ambitious concept had to await the nationalizing of industry in the 1860s. But just as the widening of product markets had given impetus to the growth of local unions at the turn of the nineteenth century, the extension of labor markets following the construction of comprehensive railroad networks ultimately made the coordination of local unionism through the national union structure no less mandatory. Had labor been either unwilling or unable to establish its countervailing power in this fashion, the existence of the movement on any significant scale might have ended with the rise of the large national corporation in the closing decades of the century. It is equally tempting to speculate as to the sanguine effects for labor of the establishment of the AFL's "exclusive jurisdiction" concept; it is a matter of record, however, that the rival unionism of the pre-1886 period had proven highly detrimental to many national unions.

Above all, it is undeniable that labor faced a critical juncture in the midst of the Great Depression, when the continuing wisdom of its craft unionism structure was severely questioned—and that, however begrudgingly the peak federation moved to accommodate the millions of industrial-unionist constituents who desired acceptance, an ultimate willingness to adapt to a changing situation was for labor the only logical decision. High wassail did not prevail at the banquet tables of the mighty.

Major *philosophical decisions*, too, have exerted a strong influence on the state and shape of American unionism as it appears nowadays. In many ways, Samuel Gompers was not only the father of the modern labor movement but its supreme spiritual symbol. A pronounced strain of pragmatism runs, in fact, through all of labor's history, just as it motivated so many of Gompers's actions. The mainstream of labor, with or without Gompers, has always stressed the practical at the expense of the ideal, shunning, as he and his fellow AFL founders did, "objects that cannot be realized in a few years." To George Meany, ideology was "baloney."

Thus, such presumed social panaceas as the socialistic agricultural communities, land reform, and producers' cooperatives that were proposed by the zealous reformers of the 1840s had no great appeal to the typical workingman; their connection with his on-the-job happiness and their relevance to solving the pressing problems of industrialization were too remote to be appreciated. The same can be said of the National Labor Union's advocacy of the termination of the convict-labor system, currency reform, and women's suffrage three decades later, and of Terrence V. Powderly's campaign for cooperatives and temperance. Nor does the notable failure of the IWW and its revolutionary credo that "the working class and the employing class have nothing in common" detract from this common denominator. Such lofty goals as these and their latter-day reincarnations in the various radical groups that have on many occasions dotted the periphery of the labor movement have been received with total apathy by the average rank-and-file unionist.

What *has* historically concerned the union member has been more in the here and now: more economic benefits, improved working conditions, and, above all else, a maximum of job security. These great motivators of support for organized labor accounted directly, it will be remembered, for the rise of the first American unions, and no labor organization of any lasting influence since 1800 has ever lost sight of such mundane "bread-and-butter" but also (to the union constituent) vitally important goals.

So greatly does this stamp of "pure and simple," "more and more" unionism permeate labor history that whole schools of academic thought in the labor area have been built around it. Most notable of them is the John R. Commons–Selig Perlman, or "Wisconsin School," theory, which holds that the key to understanding union growth and survival rests primarily on undertanding the American worker's "consciousness of scarcity" and of limited opportunity, which in turn fostered a deep desire for improved "property rights" on the job itself. To protect the dignity and security of the individual jobholder, collective bargaining appears to this school to have been accepted by employees as a vital first step.

History seems to support this basic Commons–Perlman thesis as at least a major further explanation of American labor history. It has not been by sheer coincidence that all major periods of union growth, excepting only wartime ones, have been marked by widespread job insecurity; this situation was as true of both 1800–1819 and 1822–1837, when the worker fears stemmed primarily from employer cost-cutting devices necessitated by the new scope of product markets, as it was two decades later, when the menace of interworker competition on a geographic basis due to widened labor markets was the major cause of alarm. It was as much in evidence when the immigrant waves from Europe accelerated in the late 1860s as in the 1897–1904 period, marked by its myriad of "scientific management" innovations. And the booming union totals of the 1930s coincided, of course, with the Great Depression. The fact that equally great "consciousness of scarcity" characterized other, *less* successful periods for labor (for example, the 1904–1916 period, when European immigration hit its peak) in no way negates the "Wisconsin School" thesis.

But just as some attention must be paid to the economic and structural factors in addition to these philosophical ones in understanding the growth of unionism, and just as Maslow's Need Hierarchy can hardly be ignored in dealing at least with contemporary unionism, so too must one recognize that some key aspects of labor history defy any theoretical generalizations at all. One can attempt to account for the huge success of AFL and CIO organizational drives in the 1930s, for example, in terms of "willingness to adjust to organizational forms" (structural) or "job consciousness" (philosophical)—if not in terms of the "economic conditions" framework—but in doing so one has only a partial explanation. In retrospect, the evidence is clear that *both* of the factors above combined with a variety of special economic, public-policy, and labor-leadership circumstances to foster this great period of union growth, and that in many ways each further factor was unprecedented in its order of magnitude. Similarly, the adverse technological, public relations, and legal obstacles with which labor has been confronted over the past few decades also hinge on unparalleled conditions.

Thus what is past may not necessarily, the declaration of Shakespeare notwithstanding, be prologue. And hopes for a resurgence of union growth that are anchored only to the propositions that labor's growth has "always" been sporadic, that unionism has "always" been able to adapt itself structurally to changing needs, and that worker job consciousness has "always" guaranteed collective bargaining a firm place in our society are not necessarily justified.

What, then, can one say about labor's future in terms of its past? Even with the high degree of uncertainty that such predictions inevitably involve, and despite all the unprecedented circumstances since the 1930s, at least one factor emerges clearly from a reading of labor history in this country. And it suggests that the current reports of unionism's impending doom may indeed be grossly exaggerated. Organized labor has been surrounded by conditions at least as bleak as those confronting it today many times in its 185-year history, and on each occasion it has proved equal to the challenge. It has fully recovered not only from the disastrous economic depressions that at various times have wiped out most of its membership but from the inroads of reformers who temporarily succeeded in divorcing it almost entirely from its collective bargaining functions. It has overcome devastating victories won by employers, and formidable weapons in the hands of the courts. It has incurred deep-rooted public disfavor before, particularly in the 1870s and 1920s, and ultimately surmounted it. And at perhaps the two most critical junctures of all in its still-short history—(1) in the 1880s, with the rapid disintegration of the Knights and their "one big union" concept, and (2) on the eve of the Great Depression, when an apathetic AFL remained almost exclusively the province of the highly skilled amid severe membership losses and concerted attacks from without—a Gompers and a Lewis could emerge to lead unionism to heights previously thought unreachable.

It is entirely possible that labor's remarkable staying power has been due to the single fact that to many workers, from the early nineteenth century to the present, there has really been no acceptable substitute for collective bargaining as a means of maintaining and improving employment conditions. Whatever its deficiencies, the labor union has offered millions of employees in our profit-minded industrial society sufficient hope that their needs, not only as employees but as individuals, would be considered to warrant their taking out union membership. At the very least, these employees have been satisfied that the only theoretical alternative to collective bargaining—individual bargaining—has for them been no alternative at all from a practical viewpoint.

Thus, the strongest of cases can be built, as the earliest pages of this book have indicated, that collective bargaining is here to stay—most probably in the highly pragmatic "bread-and-butter" form from which its successes have always emanated, and quite probably also with future structural modifications (however belated at times these may be in coming) to accommodate future institutional needs—but at least here in some form that is not dramatically different from its present character for the foreseeable future.

From this it necessarily follows that, as Kheel has pointed out, "Our objective must be not to find a substitute for bargaining but to discover ways of making it work better."[35] And the latter can be located only after one fully understands not only the labor relations process but the framework in which it operates. Toward this understanding such a book as this is, of course, directed.

Discussion Questions

1 "Without the rise of the merchant–capitalist in this country, there could have been no genuine labor movement." Comment.

2 It has been said that "unions are for capitalism for the same reason that fish are for water." Elaborate upon this statement, drawing from the historical record.

3 Explain the following paradox: Until relatively recent years, skilled workers who enjoyed comparatively high levels of income and status constituted the main source of union membership.

4 "If the Knights of Labor expired because it could not fulfill any function, the American Federation of Labor succeeded because it could admirably fulfill many functions." Elaborate, qualifying this statement if you believe that qualifications are needed.

5 One scholar of labor history has offered as his opinion that "even with the New Deal . . . union development experienced, not a marked mutation, but a partial alteration and expansion in leadership, tactics, and jurisdiction. The adjustment in basic union philosophy was neither profound nor completely permanent." Do you agree?

6 If a Gompers and a Lewis could emerge to rescue unionism at critical times in the past, cannot a case be made that there is nothing basically wrong with organized labor today that imaginative leadership could not cure? Discuss fully.

7 "American unionism has very definitely been a war profiteer." Do you agree or disagree?

8 How valid, in your opinion, is the basic Commons–Perlman thesis regarding union growth and survival?

Selected References

ARONOWITZ, STANLEY, *False Promises: The Shaping of American Working-Class Consciousness.* New York: McGraw-Hill, 1973.
BERNSTEIN, IRVING, *The Turbulent Years: A History of the American Worker, 1933–1941.* Boston: Houghton Mifflin, 1970.

[35] Theodore W. Kheel, "A Labor Relations Policy for 1964," *Personnel Journal,* April 1964, p. 181.

BIMBA, ANTHONY, *The Molly Maguires*. New York: International Publishers, 1970.

BROOKS, THOMAS R., *Toil and Trouble: A History of American Labor* (2nd ed., rev.). New York: Delacorte Press, 1971.

DUBINSKY, DAVID, and A. H. RASKIN, *David Dubinsky: A Life with Labor*. New York: Simon & Schuster, 1977.

DULLES, FOSTER RHEA, *Labor in America* (3rd rev. ed.). New York: Thomas Y. Crowell, 1966.

FINLEY, JOSEPH E., *The Corrupt Kingdom: The Rise and Fall of the United Mine Workers*. New York: Simon & Schuster, 1972.

GALENSON, WALTER, *The CIO Challenge to the AFL: A History of the American Labor Movement, 1935–1941*. Cambridge, Mass.: Harvard University Press, 1960.

GARNEL, DONALD, *The Rise of Teamster Power in the West*. Berkeley: University of California Press, 1972.

GOULD, WILLIAM B., *Black Workers in White Unions*. Ithaca, N.Y.: Cornell University Press, 1977.

GOULDEN, JOSEPH C., *Meany*. New York: Atheneum, 1972.

HENRY, ALICE, *Women and the Labor Movement*. New York: Arno, 1971.

HILL, HERBERT, *Black Labor and the American Legal System*, Volume I: *Race, Work, and the Law*. Washington, D.C.: Bureau of National Affairs, 1977.

LENS, SIDNEY, *The Labor Wars: From the Molly Maguires to the Sitdowns*. Garden City, N.Y.: Doubleday, 1974.

LYND, ALICE, and STAUGHTON LYND, *Rank and File*. Boston: Beacon Press, 1974.

NIELSEN, GEORGIA PANTER, *From Sky Girl to Flight Attendant*. Ithaca, N.Y.: ILR Press, Cornell University, 1982.

RAYBACK, JOSEPH G., *A History of American Labor*. New York: Free Press, 1966.

REUTHER, VICTOR G., *The Brothers Reuther and the Story of the UAW*. Boston: Houghton Mifflin, 1976.

TAFT, PHILIP, *Organized Labor in American History*. New York: Harper & Row, 1964.

ULMAN, LLOYD, *American Trade Unionism—Past and Present*. Berkeley: Institute of Industrial Relations, University of California, 1961.

———, *The Rise of the National Trade Union*. Cambridge, Mass.: Harvard University Press, 1955.

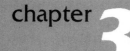

chapter *3*

The Legal Framework

As previous pages have suggested, today's manager is hardly free to deal with the union as he or she wishes. A growing body of federal and state laws and the judicial and administrative interpretations of these laws now govern the employer at virtually all points at which the manager comes into contact with organized labor. Legislation today has much to say about management's role in union organizational campaigns and its bargaining procedures in negotiating contracts once a union has gained recognition. It is also outspoken about the acceptable contents of the company's labor agreements, and even its actions in administering these agreements. As is also true of the union, whose conduct is at least equally regulated by public policy, the employer can scarcely afford to be poorly informed in the area of labor law.

If the laws have become extensive, however, they have also become complex and often nebulous. Labor lawyers have been forced to undertake herculean tasks, not always successfully, in attempting to assess what is legal and what is not in the sphere of collective bargaining. And inconsistent interpretations of the labor statutes—stemming from the National Labor Relations Board, the various state and lower federal judiciaries, and the Supreme Court itself—continue to mark the field. There is, in fact, some justification for those who have termed the last major piece of federal labor legislation, the Landrum–Griffin Act of 1959, the "Lawyers' Full Employment Act."

But if it is impossible to state definitively the exact constraints on union–management relations that the law now imposes, at least what might appropriately be described as "currently useful generalizations" can be offered. Moreover, not only such basic principles but also their paths of development must be dealt with if the environment in which labor relations now operate is to be fully appreciated. If the lessons of general labor history have greatly influenced the nature of the bargaining process as it exists today, the ever-greater thrust of the laws has had an equally pervasive effect.

THE ERA OF JUDICIAL CONTROL

In view of the present scope of labor legislation, it is somewhat ironic that little more than five decades ago, employers were virtually unrestrained by law from dealing with unions as they saw fit. There was, as we have seen, almost no statutory treatment of labor–management relations from the days of the American Revolution until the Great Depression of the 1930s. Instead, individual judges exercised public control over these relations. And the courts' view of union activities was, for the most part, as unsympathetic as was that of most businessmen of the times.

The employers' traditional weapons for fighting labor organizations—such as formal and informal espionage, blacklists, and the very potent practice of discharging "agitators"—were normally left undisturbed by the judges. However, if the members of the judiciary believed that union activities were being conducted either for "illegal purposes" or by "illegal means," they were generous in extracting money damages from the unions and in ordering criminal prosecution of labor leaders.

The qualifications for "illegality" varied to some extent from court to court. In general, however, most aggressive union activities of the day—strikes to obtain agreements whereby the employer would employ only union members (the closed shop), picketing by "strangers" (those not in a direct superior–subordinate relationship with the employer), and the secondary boycott (the exercise of economic pressure against one company to force it to exert pressure on another company that is actually the subject of the union's concern)—were held to be illegal. Many courts went even further. Through the 1920s, such remarks as "Judicial actions against even peaceful picketing are merely declaratory of what has always been the law and the best practice in equity" flowed freely from the judges. And although it was President Calvin Coolidge who asserted that "the business of the United States is business," the remark could readily have emanated from most members of the judiciary well into the third decade of this century. The courts, viewing their primary role as that of protecting property rights, allied themselves with few exceptions squarely with the employer community to neutralize the economic power of organized labor.

Fully as welcome to employers, too, was the extensive court use of the injunction. This device, a judicial order calling for the cessation of certain actions deemed injurious and for which the other forms of court-provided relief appeared to be unsuitable remedies, was often invoked by the judges following employer requests for such intervention. To unionists, such restraining orders seemed to be issued quite indiscriminately. Even the relatively detached observer of legal history, however, would very likely conclude that it did not seem to take much to convince the judges that union activities should be curbed: The jurists issued their restraining decrees almost as reflex actions; and strikes, boycotts, picketing—virtually any form of union "self-help" activity—thus ran the risk of being abruptly ended if in any way present or imminent damage to the employer's property could be shown as being threatened.

THE NORRIS–LA GUARDIA ACT OF 1932

Despite its 1932 date, the Norris–La Guardia Act is of considerably more than historical interest. As is true of the later labor laws that will be discussed in this chapter, most of its provisions are still valid and continue today to govern labor relations in interstate commerce.

At the time of its passage, however, the act was particularly noteworthy. Not only did it constitute the first major interindustry federal legislation to be applied to collective bargaining, but—as stated earlier—it marked a significant change in public policy *from repression to strong encouragement of union activity*. Implemented in the final days of the Hoover administration, it owed its birth mainly to the widespread unemployment of the times and to a general recognition that only through bargaining collectively could many employees exercise any satisfactory influence on their working environments. It also stemmed, however, from popular sentiment that justice had not been served by allowing the courts their virtually unlimited authority to issue injunctions in labor disputes.

Accordingly, the act greatly narrowed the scope of the courts for issuing such injunctions. Peaceful picketing, peaceable assembly, organizational picketing, payment of strike benefits, and a host of other union economic weapons were now made nonenjoinable. Also enacted within the new law were procedural requirements for injunctions issued on other grounds.

Even more symbolic of the major shift in public policy was the act's assertion that it was now necessary for Congress to guarantee to the individual employee "full freedom of association, self-organization, and designation of representatives of his own choosing, to negotiate the terms and conditions of his employment . . . free from interference, restraint, or coercion of employers." All the federal labor laws passed since 1932 have embodied this same principle.

Nor was the new treatment of unionism destined to be confined only to the federal arena. Within a short period of time, twenty states (including almost all the major industrial ones) had independently created their own "little Norris–La Guardia Acts" to govern labor relations in intrastate commerce.

Norris–La Guardia and its state counterparts did not by themselves, however, greatly stimulate union growth. They clearly expanded union freedoms and placed legal limits on judicial capriciousness, but they did little to restrain employers directly in their conduct toward collective bargaining. Only the previously cited

"yellow-dog" contract arrangement, whereby managements had been able to require nonunion membership or activity as a condition of employment, was declared
unenforceable by the 1932 act. Otherwise, employers remained at liberty to fight
labor organizations by whatever means they could implement, despite the ambitious
language of Norris–La Guardia.

THE WAGNER ACT OF 1935

It remained for the National Labor Relations Act of 1935, more commonly known
as the Wagner Act, to alter this situation by putting teeth in the government's
pledge to protect employee collective bargaining rights. The Wagner Act, it will
be recalled, accomplished this through two basic methods: (1) It specifically banned
five types of management action as constituting "unfair labor practices"; and (2)
it set forth the principle of majority rule for the selection of employee bargaining
representatives and provided that, should the employer express doubt as to the
union's majority status, a secret-ballot election of the employees would determine
if the majority existed. It also created an independent, quasi-judicial agency—the
National Labor Relations Board (NLRB)—to provide the machinery for enforcing
both these provisions.

Employer Unfair Labor Practices

The five employer unfair labor practices, deemed "statutory wrongs" (although
not crimes) by Congress, have been modified to some small extent since 1935, as
noted below. They remain, however, a significant part of the law of collective
bargaining to this day, and they constitute an impressive quintet of "thou shalt
nots" for employers who might otherwise be tempted to resort to the blunt tactics
of prior eras in an effort to undermine unionism. The Wagner Act (1) deemed it
"unfair" for managements to "interfere with, restrain, or coerce employees" in
exercising their now legally sanctioned right of self-organization; (2) restrained
company representatives from dominating or interfering with either the formation
or the administration of labor unions; (3) prohibited companies from discriminating
"in regard to hire or tenure of employment or any term or condition of employment
to encourage or discourage membership in any labor organization"; (4) forbade
employers to discharge or otherwise discriminate against employees simply because
the latter had filed "unfair labor practice" charges or otherwise offered testimony
against company actions under the act; and (5) made it an unfair labor practice
for employers to refuse to bargain collectively with the duly chosen representatives
of their employees.

In the years since 1935, the NLRB and the courts (to which board decisions
can be appealed by either labor relations party) have had ample opportunity to
make known their interpretations of all five of these provisions. In dealing with
some of them, both public bodies have been quite consistent in their decisions,
and what the framers of the Wagner Act had in mind is no longer seriously ques-

tioned by either management or union representatives. In other cases, however, the board members and judges have had some difficulty in issuing rulings that have been perceived by the labor relations parties as being compatible with prior rulings on the same subject. But the judges have at least generally proved themselves to be reluctant to reverse the original NLRB decisions when these have been appealed to the courts, and the inconsistencies would in most cases appear to stem more from the changing membership of the five-member board through the years and from inherent difficulties in the words of the laws themselves than from this "opportunity for appeal" factor.

Relatively clear-cut decisions have been rendered by the NLRB and courts in two of the five areas:

1 The interpreters of the Wagner Act have consistently held a wide variety of employer practices to be in violation of the "interfere with, restrain or coerce employees" section. Among other management actions, bribery of employees, company spy systems, blacklisting of union sympathizers, removal of an existing business to another location for the sole purpose of frustrating union activity, and promises by employers of wage increases or other special concessions to employees should the latter refrain from joining a union have all historically constituted "interference" contrary to the act. The same can be said of board and court treatment of employers who have threatened to isolate ("like a rotten apple," in one case) prounion workers, engaged in individual bargaining with employees represented by a union, or questioned employees concerning their union activities in such a way as to tend to restrain or coerce such employees. When satisfied that any such violations have occurred, the board has issued cease-and-desist orders against the guilty employer with no hesitation. And when it has found that employees have been discharged unlawfully in the process, the NLRB has most frequently required their reinstatement with full back pay.

Particularly in this area, the courts have proved unwilling, by and large, to reverse board decisions upon appeal, moreover, and the fact that failure to "cease and desist" after the courts have called for this action constitutes contempt of court has at times dissuaded employers from carrying an appeal to the courts in the first place. However, under normal circumstances, the employer who both refuses to comply with an adverse board order and decides not to appeal it (so as not to bring the matter to the court's attention) stands to gain little; the NLRB itself can be counted upon to take the initiative and ask the judges for an order calling for employer compliance with the original board decision.

2 The board and courts have also had no apparent difficulty in deciding what constitutes evidence of employer discrimination related to the fourth unfair labor practice. They long ago concluded that such management actions as the layoff of an employee shortly after his testimony before the board and the discharge of a woman worker immediately after her husband had filed unfair labor practice charges (on other grounds) against the company could be taken as discriminatory, and they have consistently ruled in this direction ever since. The board has further concluded, apparently also without much hesitation, that a company's belief that charges filed by an employee are false in no way justifies its taking punitive action against the employee. On the other hand, considerably fewer cases have had to be decided concerning this fourth unfair practice than any of the others, presumably because employers have themselves recognized that violations here are normally quite obvious to all concerned and have therefore refrained from taking such action in the first place.

Interpretation seems to have been somewhat more difficult when the issues have involved the three other portions of the employer unfair labor practice section.

1 The restriction on employer discrimination "in regard to hire or tenure of employment or any term or condition of employment to encourage or discourage membership in any labor organization" has clearly made it unlawful for employers to force employees who are union members to accept less desirable job assignments than nonunionists, or to reduce the former type of employee's pay because of the union affiliation. Similarly, it is obvious that companies that demand renunciation of union membership as a condition of continued employment, or in order to be promoted within the nonsupervisory ranks, do so only at their peril. But the legality of other types of employer conduct has proved to be anything but as clear-cut.

Where, for example, there is conclusive evidence that an employee has falsified an employment application and thus failed to reveal a previous criminal record, can the person be properly discharged for this offense? Not always, according to at least one NLRB decision covering exactly this situation. Here, the board cited the company's "antiunion bias," its knowledge of the employee's union activities, and its treatment of nonunion employees who had committed comparable offenses, in deciding that the company's official reason for the discharge was only a pretext for discrimination against union members.[1] Case of this kind have proved to be thorny ones for the board and the courts and have often caused considerable flows of adrenalin on the part of employers.

2 The proviso restraining company representatives from dominating or interfering with both the formation and the administration of labor unions—included because of Congress's unhappiness with the widespread creation of employer-influenced company unions in the years preceding 1935—has been the basis of much complex litigation since that date. Obviously, when an employer has control over the union sitting on the other side of the bargaining table, genuine collective bargaining cannot take place. But determining just when an employer has such control has proven to be no easy matter. Among specific management actions that the board and courts have looked unfavorably upon as evidence of employer control have been the following: the solicitation of company–union membership by supervisory employees, the company's payment of membership dues for all employees joining the union, and an employer gift to a union of $400 and the right to operate a canteen that made a monthly profit—none of these company moves being es-

---

[1] *Photoswitch*, 99 NLRB 1366 (1962).

pecially notable for their subtlety. On the other hand, interpretations have found nothing unlawful in the mere fact that, for example, a labor organization limits its membership to employees of a single employer; the test for unfair practice pivots exclusively upon the question of which party *controls* the organization, and in a case such as this only much closer inspection (and the standards for "control" established by the interpreters) can reveal whether or not the employer is in violation of the law.

3 The fact that the 1935 legislation said little more on the subject of an employer's "refusal to bargain collectively with the representatives of his employees" than can be gleaned from these words perhaps guaranteed that controversies would result from this last section of the Wagner Act's "Rights of Employees" section, and this has indeed been the case. As such new topics for potential bargaining as pensions, health insurance, seniority, and subcontracting have arisen in the years since 1935, the NLRB and courts have been freely called upon to make known their opinions as to what must be bargained by employers, and what need not be. The courts have also been asked for a more precise definition of "bargaining" itself than the act provided. The issue is still far from resolved, and with new possibilities for bargaining constantly emerging, perhaps it never fully will be. But the board and judicial decisions of the past half-century have at least ambitiously attempted to shed light on the scope for employer action in this area, and certain statements can now be made with some authority.

In brief, there are today many "mandatory" subjects of bargaining with which the employer must deal in good faith. Such subjects include wages, hours of employment, health insurance, pensions, safety practices, the grievance procedure, procedures for discharge, layoff, recall and discipline, seniority, and subcontracting. Managers are not required to make concessions or agree to union proposals on any of these (or various other) subjects. They *are* obligated, however, to meet with the union at reasonable times and with the good-faith intention of reaching an agreement. On "nonmandatory" or "voluntary" subjects—those that are lawful but not easily related to "wages, hours and other conditions of employment"— employers are not so obligated and are free to refuse to bargain about them.

Where there is a duty to bargain, the employer must supply—upon union request—information that is "relevant and necessary" to allow the labor representatives to bargain "intelligently and effectively." The NLRB and courts have ruled, for example, that a union is entitled to information in the employer's possession concerning wage rates and increases, on the grounds that it cannot deal intelligently with the subject without such information. Similarly, if a company claims financial inability to honor the union's demands, it must stand ready to supply the union with authoritative proof of this inability.

The employer's duty to bargain also entails the duty to refrain from taking unilateral action on the "mandatory" subjects. Companies that have announced a wage increase without consulting the employees' designated representatives, or have subcontracted work to another employer without allowing their own union a chance to bargain the matter, violate this portion of the law.

Yet the apparent finality of such remarks as these is highly deceptive. Not only is considerable uncertainty left as to what else is a "mandatory" subject for bargaining (beyond the specific topics cited and the few others that the NLRB and judges have thus far dealt with affirmatively) and what is "nonmandatory," but the question of what constitutes "the good-faith intention of reaching an agreement" on the employer's part is left an open one.

It remains to be seen what further subjects the board and courts will ultimately assign to the "mandatory" category. A union demand for moving allowances for workers transferred by the company? A proposal that all production workers be placed on a salaried basis, rather than being paid by the hour? A request by the labor organization that all foreign production of the company's product be terminated? Guarantees by the company that pension funds will be invested in low-cost housing for union employees? Each of these demands has been raised on several occasions in actual bargaining situations in recent years. Except for the first, company negotiators have been notably reluctant to accommodate any of them, or numerous similarly ambitious union proposals. Yet as Fleming, who raises the possibility of all of them ultimately going before the interpreters of public policy, has pointed out, "In the changing and very real world of bargaining, all [of these and similar demands] may be close to the felt needs of the parties . . . [and] deciding which of [them] falls into the mandatory category will not be an easy task. Job security and internal union affairs pose extremely delicate issues."[2]

If disposition of such issues as these must thus await future board and court treatment, it at least appears safe to predict that the books have not yet closed on the list of "mandatory" topics; most of the subjects with which employers are now required to deal in good faith are themselves relative newcomers to such status, and the NLRB and jurists today appear to be more activistic in this regard than ever.

Indeed, a previous edition of this book declared with absolute confidence that (among other situations forbidden them) unions could not make the prices charged by employers for food in plant cafeterias and vending machines subject to the bargaining process. A mere four years from the time that those words were written, the U.S. Supreme Court made them obsolete by ruling, in a mid-1979 case involving the Ford Motor Company, that employers could in fact be required to bargain over such prices (and related services, too). Speaking for the Court, Justice Byron White said that "the availability of food during working hours and the conditions under which it is to be consumed are matters of deep concern to workers, and one needn't strain to consider them to be among those 'conditions' of employment that should be subject to the mutual duty to bargain."[3] Nothing is guaranteed except change.

---

[2] Robben W. Fleming, "The Obligation to Bargain in Good Faith," in Joseph Shister et al., *Public Policy and Collective Bargaining* (New York: Harper & Row, 1962), p. 83; see also Guy Farmer, *Management Rights and Union Bargaining Power* (New York: Industrial Relations Counselors, 1965).
[3] *Ford Motor Company* v. *NLRB*, 441 U.S. 488 (1979).

Another fact is of significance. When the NLRB or a court determines that an issue does *not* fall within the mandatory category, it means that such an issue will probably not be included in a collective bargaining contract. With respect to these subjects, the parties may agree *voluntarily* to include them, but neither side may force such an issue to an impasse. For example, a union may not strike on an issue that is held to fall within the nonmandatory category. Thus, if such a proposal is not to the liking of one party, it may simply refuse to bargain over the issue, and the other side may not use economic power (such as a strike, lockout, or picketing) to force the issue. Over the years, the NLRB and the courts have found that many issues fall within the nonmandatory category. Employers may not insist that a union withdraw fines previously imposed upon union members who have crossed picket lines during a strike; demand that a national union be a party to the contract where a local union affiliated with the national union is the lawful and certified bargaining representative; require a union to post a performance bond; require that nonunion employees shall have the right to vote on the provisions of the contract negotiated by the union; or demand a strike-vote election among employees before a strike occurs.

Unions may not insist that the employer increase pensions and other benefits of those employees already retired; require a company to contribute to an industrywide promotion fund; or require a bank to continue a free investment counseling service for employees whom the bank terminated. At least, not yet.

The steadily increasing types of tests adopted by the board and courts for "good faith"—for example, whether or not employer delaying tactics were used in the bargaining, some evidence of management initiative in making counterproposals, and employer willingness to accommodate completely routine demands (such as the continued availability of plant parking spaces)—have often been attacked for their naïveté, if not for the spirit behind them. Anyone who thinks that such tests by themselves can definitively reveal whether or not "good faith" has actually occurred at the bargaining table would probably believe almost anything.

At the very least, however, it is obvious that in being forced to plug the existing gaps in the Wagner Act's "refusal to bargain" interpretations, representatives of public policy have projected themselves more and more into the labor–management arena in the years since 1935, perhaps to an extent that was never contemplated when the Wagner Act was passed.

Employee Representation Elections

Despite all the interpretative difficulties that have been involved in the employer unfair labor practice provisions, the latter clearly were—and are—wide-sweeping in their implications for collective bargaining. However, they still represent an *indirect* approach to the protection of employee bargaining rights: By themselves, they clearly restrict employer action in the labor relations area, but they say nothing explicit about the key question of initial union recognition.

The authors of the Wagner Act were well aware of this gap and proceeded to deal directly with the issue in another section of the act, that pertaining to the secret-ballot election. As noted previously, the NLRB was authorized to conduct such an election should the employer express doubt that a majority of its employees had chosen to be represented by any union at all. Prior to this time, a union could gain recognition from an unreceptive employer only through the successful use of such economic weapons as the strike and boycott.

As this part of the act now stands, the board can conduct a representation election if requested to do so by a single employee, by a group of employees, or by a labor organization acting for employees. In any of these three cases, the petition must be supported by "a substantial number of employees" who desire collective bargaining representation, and it must allege that the employer refuses to recognize such representation. Employers may also petition for such an election, presumably with the objective of proving that the employees do *not* desire union representation or for various reasons of scheduling strategy (such as trying to get the board to hold the election at the time least favorable to the union).

It it also possible for an election to involve two or more unions, each claiming "substantial" employee support. The employees then have the choice of voting for any of the unions on the ballot or for "no union." If none of these choices (including "no union") wins a majority of the votes cast, a runoff election is then conducted between the two choices that have received the highest number of votes.

In administering this portion of the law, the NLRB itself ultimately framed a few further rules designed to foster labor relations stability. Should any union win an NLRB-conducted election and then execute a valid contract with the employer, rival unions may now not seek bargaining rights (through a subsequent election) for a period of three years following the effective date of the contract or for the length of the contract—whichever is the shorter. However, the victorious union is still not guaranteed its bargaining rights for this period of time: If the employees themselves have second thoughts about the desirability of retaining the union's services, they can—after one year—petition the NLRB for a decertification election. A majority vote in this election rescinds the union's bargaining agency.

Unions lose a majority of decertification elections, and the trend here is very much against them. In the first two years of Taft–Hartley's operation, they lost bargaining rights in 144 out of 229 such elections, thereby "winning" (in the sense of staving off defeat) some 37 percent of them. In 1970, according to the National Labor Relations Board's annual report for that year, they won only 30.2 percent of some 301 decertification elections. In 1980, an unprecedented total of 902 such contests took place, and workers voted for retention of the union in a mere 25 percent of them. And since in the 1980s organized labor was annually winning only about 45 percent of all *new* certification elections, or significantly fewer than the 55 percent certification victory record commonly registered until the 1970s, there was double cause for concern in the labor movement.

Employers cannot legally start the decertification process, but antiunion consultants are amply available—in fact, as noted earlier, they constitute a new growth industry by themselves in the 1980s—to help management make the environment "right" for decertification. Forcing the union to go out on a costly strike is only a single example. And something of a process of contagion may also abet the chances of a given union being thrown out as this trend continues: As one AFL–CIO official has commented, "Employers realize the company down the street has decertified the union and they're encouraged to do the same."[4]

Although winning an election is by far the most common way for a union to secure bargaining rights, there are circumstances under which the NLRB now orders an employer to bargain collectively even though it does not conduct an election. These occur when a union is successful in getting a majority of employees in a bargaining unit to sign union-membership authorization cards, and the employer engages in serious unfair labor practices the effect of which destroys the union's majority. For example, the employer may discharge employees who are union sympathizers. In such situations, the NLRB theory is that a union would win the election were it not for the unfair labor practice, and the holding of the election would not reflect the actual sentiment of the employees. In 1969, the Supreme Court sustained this doctrine in *NLRB* v. *Gissel Packing Company*.[5] In 1982, the NLRB pushed the *Gissel* doctrine a step further. When an employer commits "outrageous and pervasive" unfair labor practices, the board will grant bargaining rights to the union *even though the union did not persuade a majority of the employees to sign authorization cards during the organizational campaign.*[6] In such a hostile environment, the board believes that the employees would be fearful of signing the cards.

Employers and management groups have bitterly criticized this NLRB policy. They contend that the NLRB should not order collective bargaining on the basis of authorization cards; the test of the union's majority should be determined only through an election. Employers contend that employees may sign cards because of social pressure or could be misled by a union organizer as to the purpose of the authorization card. Of course, employers can avoid the effect of the policy by not engaging in serious unfair labor practices during the time a union conducts its organizing campaign. In the last analysis, therefore, it depends upon employer conduct as to whether the NLRB will order collective bargaining based on authorization cards. Also, if frequency is used as a standard, the issue of bargaining orders based on authorization cards has been exaggerated. In the typical year, the NLRB orders collective bargaining on this basis in only about 1 percent of the cases. In all other cases, the board determines the majority status of unions through the election process.

FROM THE WAGNER ACT TO TAFT–HARTLEY

As established by the Wagner Act, then, the scope of National Labor Relations Board activities was to be twofold. The board was charged with investigating employer unfair labor practices, and it was given the authority to conduct employee representation elections.

The NLRB's members (appointed by the president, subject to confirmation

---

[4] Anne Field, "Seceding from the Unions," *Forbes,* October 26, 1981, p. 40.
[5] 395 U.S. 575 (1969).
[6] Conair Corp., 261 NLRB No. 178 (1982).

by the Senate) and its various regional officials outside Washington, even in their earliest years of existence, undertook both these assignments zealously. By 1947, they had processed almost 44,000 unfair labor practice cases, running the gamut in their decisions from dismissing complaints as having no merit to issuing cease-and-desist orders against guilty employers. In the area of representation cases, the board was even more active. Almost 60,000 such cases were dealt with between 1935 and 1947. In addition to determining whether or not elections should be held and conducting such elections if the answer was in the affirmative, the NLRB often had the further duty of deciding the type of unit appropriate for the particular labor relationship (such as employer, craft, or plant).

Although its activities were necessarily controversial, as was the act sanctioning them, there is general agreement today that in this twelve-year period the board performed its basic mission of protecting the right of employees to organize and bargain collectively quite creditably. Even at the time, many contemporaries had been impressed; as in the case of Norris–La Guardia, "little Wagner Acts" were soon enacted in many states to govern labor relations in intrastate commerce.

The modern labor movement in this country can, in fact, justifiably be said to have begun in 1935. Union membership totals boomed after that year, due in no small measure to the Wagner Act and its state counterparts. Other factors were, of course, also responsible: the improving economic climate, the generally liberal sentiments of the times, the keen competition between the American Federation of Labor and the newly born Committee for Industrial Organization, and dynamic union leadership. And it is equally true that prior legislation—not only Norris–La Guardia but also the ill-fated national Industrial Recovery Act of 1933—had paved the way for the new era and had independently led to much spontaneous union organization before 1935. But it is no less a fact that employers could still legally try to counteract unionism by almost any means except the yellow-dog contract and the arbitrary injunction process—up to and including sheer refusal to grant the union recognition under any circumstances—before the passage of the Wagner Act. It is extremely doubtful that organized labor could have grown as it did—from 3.6 million unionized workers in 1935 to more than 14 million by 1947—without the Wagner Act's protection.

Certainly public opinion as registered in Congress did not debate this last point. As the average citizen gradually turned against unionism in the mid-1940s, he blamed existing public policy for the union excesses of the times, most notably for the postwar strike waves. As the last chapter has described, his voice ultimately became a compelling one: Congress overrode President Truman's veto and passed the Taft–Hartley Act of 1947, thereby stilling the cries that the Wagner Act had become too "one-sided" in favor of labor.

THE TAFT–HARTLEY ACT OF 1947

With the advent of Taft–Hartley, officially known as the Labor–Management Relations Act, a new period in public policy toward labor unions began: that of *modified encouragement coupled with regulation.*

Much as the Wagner Act was to a great extent designed to correct weaknesses in Norris–La Guardia, which nonetheless was not repealed and remains a part of the legal environment of collective bargaining to this day, Taft–Hartley amended but did not displace the Wagner Act. The Wagner Act, essentially as adjusted by the 1947 legislation, governs labor relations today.

Indeed, the old unfair employer practices were continued virtually word for word by the new legislation. The only significant changes were that the closed shop (and its requirements that all workers be union members at the time of their hiring) was no longer allowed and that the freedom of the parties to authorize the *union shop* (which, as noted earlier, allows the employer to hire anyone but provides that all new employees must join the union after a stipulated period of time) was somewhat narrowed. The intention of this amendment related to the third employer unfair labor practice: In its ban on employer hiring and job condition discrimination in order to encourage or discourage union membership, the Wagner Act *had* authorized employers to enter into union and closed-shop agreements. The changes clearly symbolized public policy's new attitude toward unions.

Far more indicative of the public's less enthusiastic sentiments toward unions, however, were those portions of Taft–Hartley that dealt with (1) *union unfair labor practices,* which were now enumerated and prohibited in the same way that the employer practices had been; (2) *the rights of employees as individuals,* as contrasted with those rights that employees now legally enjoyed as union members; (3) *the rights of employers,* a subject the Wagner Act had glossed over in its concentration on employer duties; and (4) *national emergency strikes.* To some extent, other major parts of the new law—those relating to internal union affairs, the termination or modification of existing labor contracts, and suits involving unions—also demonstrated a hardening of congressional attitudes toward labor organizations. We shall consider these various provisions separately.

Union Unfair Labor Practices

Going the framers of the Wagner Act one better, Taft–Hartley enumerated six labor practices that the unions were prohibited from engaging in. Labor organizations operating in interstate commerce were now officially obliged to refrain from (1) restraining or coercing employees in the exercise of their guaranteed collective bargaining rights; (2) causing an employer to discriminate in any way against an employee in order to encourage or discourage union membership; (3) refusing to bargain in good faith with their employer about wages, hours, and other employment conditions; (4) certain types of strikes and boycotts; (5) charging employees covered by union-shop agreements initiation fees or dues "in an amount which the board finds excessive or discriminatory under all the circumstances"; and (6) engaging in "featherbedding," the requirement of payment by the employer for services not performed.

As in the case of the unfair employer labor practices, interpretative difficulties have marked the subsequent treatment of some of those provisions. In addition, the six unfair labor practices directed against unions appear to have varied considerably more widely than in the case of the Wagner Act employer provisions in their effects on labor relations practice.

Two of the six provisions have perhaps had the greatest influence on collective bargaining, and, undoubtedly a salutary one, in the years since the enactment of Taft–Hartley:

1 The ban on union restraint or coercion of employees in the exercise of their guaranteed bargaining rights, which also entails a union obligation to avoid coercion of employees who choose to refrain from collective bargaining altogether. What constitutes such restraint or coercion? The myriad of rulings rendered by the NLRB and courts since 1947 has at least indicated that such union actions as the following will always run the risk of being found "unfair": the stating to an antiunion employee that the employee will lose his job should the union gain recognition; the signing with an employer of an agreement that recognizes the union as exclusive bargaining representative when in fact it lacks majority employee support; and the issuing of patently false statements during a representation election campaign. Union picket-line violence, threats of reprisal against employees subpoenaed to testify against the union at NLRB hearings, and activities of a similar vein are also unlawful.

Despite this ban against union coercion of employees who do not desire to engage in union activities, the Supreme Court in 1967 did hold that a union may assess and collect fines from union members who work during a strike.[7] However, whatever tangible benefit unions received from the ruling proved short-lived, because the same court in 1972 held that strikebreaking union members may not be fined when they resign from the union before crossing the picket line.[8] To get around the latter decision, unions amended their constitutions and bylaws forbidding members to resign just before and during a strike. So far, though the U.S. Supreme Court has not yet ruled, such limitations on the right of employees to withdraw from unions are illegal.[9]

This first unfair union practice also extends to the coercion of the employer in the latter's selection of his own bargaining representative. Post-1947 rulings have stated, for example, that unions cannot refuse to deal with former union officers who represent employers or insist on meeting only with the owners of a company rather than with the company's attorney. On the other hand, unions have every right to demand that the employer representative with whom they deal have sufficient authority to make final decisions on behalf of the company; the interpreters of public policy have clearly understood that to have this any other way would be to frustrate the whole process of bargaining.

2 The Taft–Hartley provision that makes it unfair for a union to cause an employer to discriminate against an employee in order to influence union membership. There is a single exception to this prohibition: Under a valid union-shop

[7] *NLRB* v. *Allis-Chalmers*, 388 U.S. 1975 (1967).
[8] *NLRB* v. *Granite State Joint Board*, 409 U.S. 213 (1972).
[9] *Pattern Makers' League*, 265 NLRB No. 170 (1982).

agreement, the union may lawfully demand the discharge of an employee who fails to pay his or her initiation fee and periodic dues. Otherwise, however, unions must exercise complete self-control in this area. They cannot try to force employers to fire or otherwise penalize workers for any other reason, whether these reasons involve worker opposition to union policies, failure to attend union meetings, or refusal to join the union at all. Nor can a union lawfully seek to persuade an employer to grant hiring preference to employees who are satisfactory to the union. Subject only to the union-shop proviso, Taft–Hartley sought to place nonunion workers on a footing equal to that of union employees.

Occupying more or less middle ground in its degree of influence upon the labor relations process stands the third restriction on union practices, pertaining to union refusal to bargain. Here, clearly, Taft–Hartley extended to labor organizations the same obligation that the Wagner Act had already imposed on employers.

To many observers, the law's inclusion of this union bargaining provision has meant very little; unions can normally be expected to pursue bargaining rather than attempt to avoid it. Nevertheless, the NLRB has used it to some extent in the years since Taft–Hartley to narrow the scope of permissible union action. The board has, for example, found it unlawful under this section for a union to strike against an employer who has negotiated, and continues to negotiate, on a multi-employer basis, with the goal of forcing that employer to bargain independently. It has also found a union's refusal to bargain on an employer proposal for a written contract to violate this part of the law. To the employer community, in short, at least some inequities seem to have been corrected by this good-faith bargaining provision.

The fourth unfair union practice has given rise to considerable litigation. Indeed, of all six Taft–Hartley union prohibitions, the ban on certain types of strikes and boycotts has proven the most difficult to interpret. Even as "clarifed" by Congress in 1959, this area remains a particularly murky one for labor lawyers.

Briefly, Section 8(b)(4) of the 1947 act prohibits unions from striking or boycotting if such actions have any of the following three objectives: (1) forcing an employer or self-employed person to join any labor or employer organization or to cease dealing with another employer (secondary boycott); (2) compelling recognition as employee bargaining agent for another employer without NLRB certification; (3) forcing an employer to assign particular work to a particular craft.

Particularly in regard to the secondary boycott provision, it does not take much imagination to predict where heated controversy could arise. To constitute a secondary boycott, the union's action must be waged against "another" employer, one who is entirely a neutral in the battle and is merely caught as a pawn in the union's battle with the real object of its concern. But when is the secondary employer really neutral and when is he an "ally" of the primary employer? The board has sometimes ruled against employers alleging themselves to be "secondary" ones on the grounds of common ownership with that of the "primary" employer and, again, when "struck work" has been turned over by primary employers to secondary ones. But board and court rulings here have not been entirely consonant.

In its other clauses, too, the Taft–Hartley strike and boycott provision has led to intense legal battles. When is a union, for example, unlawfully seeking recognition without NLRB certification and when is it merely picketing to protest undesirable working conditions (a normally legal action)? Is a union ever entitled to try to keep within its bargaining unit work that has traditionally been performed by the unit employees? On some occasions, but not all, the board has ruled that there is nothing wrong with this. The histories of post-1947 cases on these issues constitute a fascinating study in the making of fine distinctions. At least, however, the large incidence of litigation might indicate that the parties have not been able to totally overlook the new rights and responsibilities bestowed upon them by Taft–Hartley (whatever these might exactly be).

Last, and least in the magnitude of their effect, stand the relatively unenforceable provisions relating to union fees and dues, and to featherbedding.

The proscription against unions charging workers covered by union-shop agreements excessive or discriminatory dues or initiation fees included, it will be recalled, a stipulation that the NLRB could consider "all the circumstances" in determining discrimination or excess. Such circumstances, the wording of the Taft–Hartley Act continues, include "the practices and customs of labor organizations in the particular industry and the wages currently paid to the employees affected." Without further yardsticks and depending almost exclusively on the sentiments of individual employees rather than irate employers for enforcement, this part of the act has had little practical value. In one of the relatively few such cases to come before it thus far, the board ruled that increasing the initiation fee from $75 to $250 when other unions in the area charged only about one-eighth of this amount was unlawful. In another case, it was held that the union's uniform requirement of a reinstatement fee for ex-members that was higher than the initiation fee for new members was *not* discriminatory under the act.

The sixth unfair labor practice for unions has proved even less influential in governing collective bargaining: Taft–Hartley's prohibition of unions from engaging in "featherbedding." The board has ruled that this provision does not prevent labor organizations from seeking *actual* employment for their members, "even in situations where the employer does not want, does not need, and is not willing to accept such services." Mainly because of this interpretation, the antifeatherbedding provision has had few teeth; the union would be quite happy to have the work performed, and the question of need is irrelevant. Employer spokespersons for some industries, entertainment and the railroads in particular, have succeeded in convincing the public that their unwanted—but performing—workers are "featherbedding," but under the interpretation of the law as this now exists they are engaging in inaccuracies.

Even these least influential of the six union prohibitions, however, clearly indicate the philosophy in back of Taft–Hartley—in the words of the late Senator Robert A. Taft, "simply to reduce special privileges granted to labor leaders."

The Rights of Employees as Individuals

In other areas, too, the act attempted to even the scales of collective bargaining and the alleged injustices of the 1935–1947 period.

Taft–Hartley, unlike the Wagner Act, recognized a need to protect the rights of individual employees against labor organizations. It explicitly amended the 1935 legislation to give a majority of the employees the right to refrain from, as well as engage in, collective bargaining activities. It also dealt more directly with the question of individual freedoms—even beyond its previously mentioned outlawing of the closed shop, union coercion, union-caused employer discrimination against employees, and excessive union fees.

RIGHT-TO-WORK LEGISLATION Perhaps most symbolically, Taft–Hartley provided that should any state wish to pass legislation more restrictive of union security than the union shop (or in other words, to outlaw labor contracts that make union membership a condition of retaining employment), the state was free to do so. Many states have proved themselves as so willing: Twenty states, mainly in the South and Southwest, now have so-called "right-to-work" legislation. Advocates of such laws, which will be discussed at greater length in Chapter 9, have claimed that compulsory unionism violates the basic American right of freedom of association; opponents of "right-to-work" laws have pointed out, among other arguments, that majority rule is inherent in our democratic procedure. There has thus far, however, been an impressive correlation between stands on this particular question and attitudes toward the values of unionism in general. People opposed to collective bargaining have favored "right-to-work" laws with amazing regularity. Prounionists seem to have been equally consistent in their attacks on such legislation. It is still unproven, at any rate, that "right-to-work" laws have had much effect on labor relations in the states where they exist.

DIRECT PRESENTATION OF GRIEVANCES Also designed to strengthen the rights of workers as individuals was a Taft–Hartley provision allowing any *employee* the *right to present grievances directly* to the employer without intervention of the union. The union's representative was to be given a chance to be present at such employer/ employee meetings, but the normal grievance procedure (with the union actively participating) would thus be suspended. Few employees have thus far availed themselves of this opportunity: The action can clearly antagonize the union, and since the employer's action is normally being challenged by the grievance itself, the employee may have a formidable task ahead.

RESTRICTED DUES CHECKOFF Finally, the act placed a major restriction on the fast-growing dues-checkoff arrangement. Through this device (which will also be discussed in more detail later), many employers had been deducting union dues from their employee's paychecks and remitting them to the union. Companies were thus spared the constant visits of dues-collecting union representatives at the workplace, and unions had found the checkoff to be an efficient means of collection. Under Taft–Hartley, the checkoff was to remain legal, but now only if the individual employee had given his or her own authorization in writing. Moreover, such an authorization could not be irrevocable for a period of more than one year. This restriction has hardly hampered the growth of the checkoff; it is today provided for in over 80 percent of all labor contracts, compared with an estimated 40 percent at the time of Taft–Hartley's passage. The new legal provision had undoubtedly minimized abuse of the checkoff mechanism, however.

Other Employee Rights

Employees have gained other rights based on the language of Taft–Hartley or by NLRB and court construction. *When a labor agreement requires membership in a union as a condition of employment,* and should a member protest the stance of the union in political elections or lobbying activities, the U.S. Supreme Court has held that the union must rebate to the member that proportion of his or her dues allocated for political purposes. Though the dues rebate policy for political dissenters arose originally under the Railway Labor Act, it is fully applicable to unions covered by Taft–Hartley.[10] For example, the union member who supports the Republican candidate for political office has the right to have rebated the proper proportion of dues expended for political purposes when the organization supports the Democratic candidate. One union, despairing of the complicated problem of calculating the proper proportion of rebated dues, a few years ago established a flat 5 percent rebate plan which it said covered the amount of dues it spends for political campaigns and lobbying.

Taft–Hartley confers a special benefit on professional employees, who under its terms are defined in part as those whose work is primarily intellectual in character and who utilize considerable judgment and discretion in the performance of their jobs.[11] When employees meet requirements of the definition, the NLRB must poll them in a special election to determine whether they desire to be represented by a rank-and-file union, an organization composed exclusively of professionals, or by no union. Whatever their verdict, the board must comply with their wishes. Thus, the agency may not place professional employees in a bargaining unit composed of production and maintenance employees unless a majority of the professionals polled vote for that kind of representation. Over the years the NLRB has struggled with the definition of professional employees. It has held that a college

---

[10] *Machinists* v. *Street,* 367 U.S. 740 (1961); *Brotherhood of Railway and Steamship Clerks* v. *Allen,* 373 U.S. 113 (1963). See also Benjamin J. Taylor and Fred Witney, *Labor Relations Law,* 4th ed. (Englewood Cliffs, N.J.: Prentice-Hall, 1983), pp. 396–98.

[11] Here is the complete definition of a professional employee: "any employee engaged in work (i) predominantly intellectual and varied in character as opposed to routine mental, manual, mechanical, or physical work; (ii) involving the consistent exercise of discretion and judgment in its performance; (iii) of such a character that the output produced or the result accomplished cannot be standardized in relation to a given period of time; (iv) requiring knowledge of an advanced type in a field of science or learning customarily acquired by a prolonged course of specialized intellectual instruction and study in an institution of higher learning or a hospital, as distinguished from a general academic education or from an apprenticeship or from training in the performance of routine mental, manual, or physical processes; or any employee, who (i) has completed the courses of specialized intellectual instruction and study described in clause (iv) or paragraph (a), and (ii) is performing related work under the supervision of a professional person to qualify himself to become a professional employee as defined in paragraph (a)."

degree does not necessarily place the person in the professional category, and by the same token the lack of a college degree does not automatically exclude the employee from the professional category. Rather than formal educational achievement, what counts is the kind of work the employee actually performs on the job.[12] In the professional category, for example, the board has included non-college-trained plant engineers, time study men, and employees who estimate the needs and cost of material used by their employers. In the nonprofessional category, the NLRB has—not without some controversy—placed general accountants, newspaper journalists, radio announcers, singers, and continuity writers.

Finally, pursuant to a mandate incorporated in Taft–Hartley, the NLRB under certain circumstances permits craft employees (electricians, machinists, carpenters, plumbers) to break away from an industrial bargaining unit and establish their own unions. In each case, the NLRB will consider the specific situation involved before ruling on separate craft union representation.[13] In one case the agency denied separation of a group of craft employees from the production workers unit on the grounds that their work was closely integrated in the employees' operation.[14] That is, the work of the skilled employees was so highly integrated into the productive process that a strike of the skilled group would cause a shutdown of the entire plant. In another case the NLRB permitted a group of craft employees to break out of the industrial unit because the evidence demonstrated that their work was not closely integrated. Equally important was the fact that the industrial union did not represent the craft employees fairly in collective bargaining.[15] As expected, industrial unions because of loss of membership and employers because of the problems involved in dealing with many unions in the same plant normally argue that craft employees should not be separated. Despite these claims, however, under the proper set of circumstances the NLRB permits craft employees to select their own bargaining agent.

The Rights of Employers

In still a third area, Taft–Hartley circumscribed the union's freedom of action in its quest for industrial relations equity. In this case, it explicitly gave employers certain collective bargaining rights.

For example, although employers are still required to recognize and bargain with properly certified unions, they could now give full freedom of expression to their views concerning union organization, as long as there was "no threat of reprisal or force or promise of benefit." Thus an employer may now, when faced with a representation election, tell employees that in his opinion unions are worthless, dangerous to the economy, and immoral. An employer may even, generally speaking, hint that the permanent closing of the plant would be the possible aftermath

---

[12] *Ryan Aeronautical Company,* 132 NLRB 1160 (1962).
[13] *Malinckrodt Chemical Works,* 162 NLRB 48 (1966).
[14] *Firestone Tire & Rubber Company,* 222 NLRB 1254 (1976).
[15] *Buddy L. Corporation,* 167 NLRB 808 (1967).

of a union election victory and subsequent high union wage demands. Nor will an election be set aside, for that matter, if the employer plays upon the racial prejudices of the workers (should these exist) by describing the union's philosophy toward integration, or if the employer sets forth the union's record in regard to violence and corruption (should this record be vulnerable) and suggests that these characteristics would be logical consequences of the union's victory in that plant—although in recent years the board has attempted to draw the line here between dispassionate statements on the employer's part and inflammatory or emotional appeals.[16] An imaginative employer can, in fact, now engage in almost any amount of creative speaking (or writing) for employees' consumption. The only major restraint on the employer's conduct is that he must avoid threats, promises, coercion, and direct interference with the worker-voters in the reaching of their decision. Two lesser restrictions also govern, however: The employer may not hold a meeting with employees on company time within twenty-four hours of an election; and the employer may never urge employees individually at their homes or in the office to vote against the union (the board has held that the employer can lawfully do this only "at the employees' work area or in places where employees normally gather").

An employer may avoid these two minor restrictions by holding a "captive audience" meeting before the twenty-four-hour limit on company property and during working time. And the employer need not give equal time to the union to reply to the employer's statements.[17] At such meetings, with all the employees assembled, the employer by the use of representatives has an excellent opportunity to influence the vote in the impending election. In a case involving the J. P. Stevens Company, the NLRB moved further to protect the right of employers to hold effective captive audience meetings. At a Stevens meeting a number of employees sympathetic to the union got up and asked questions. When they refused to sit down and stop asking questions, the company discharged them and the NLRB subsequently sustained the discharges.[18]

In an effort to balance the opportunity of unions to reach the employee, the NLRB has ruled that within seven days after an election is scheduled the employer must make available to a regional director of the agency the names and addresses of the employees eligible to vote in the election. Then the list is furnished to the union.[19] In other words, instead of granting unions equal time at captive audience meetings, the agency has provided unions with an alternative method of contacting employees—home visitation and letter writing. However, unions claim that these techniques do not measure up to the effectiveness of the captive audience meeting. Undoubtedly the captive audience doctrine is one factor explaining why unions currently lose a majority of NLRB elections.

[16] For a fuller discussion of these and various related organizational matters, see Taylor and Witney, *Labor Relations Law*, Chap. 12.

[17] *Livingston Shirt*, 107 NLRB 400 (1953).

[18] *J. P. Stevens*, 219 NLRB 850 (1975).

[19] *Excelsior Underwear, Inc.*, 156 NLRB 1236 (1966). Sustained by U.S. Supreme Court in *NLRB* v. *Wyman Company*, 394 U.S. 759 (1969).

Taft–Hartley afforded employers additional benefits. Under the Wagner Act, foremen had the right to organize and bargain collectively under the protection of the statute. As rank-and-file employees they had the opportunity to utilize the facilities of the NLRB when employers discharged them for union activities or refused to recognize and bargain with their unions. When the U.S. Supreme Court affirmed their protection under the law, it said that the fact that foremen are "employees" for purposes of the Wagner Act "is too obvious to be labored."[20] Protected by the NLRB, the foremen union movement grew to 32,000 members during World War II. Responding to employer pressure, however, Congress excluded foremen from the scope of the Taft–Hartley Act. Under the 1947 law the NLRB no longer has the authority to provide foremen with protection in their union activities. Employers may discharge foremen if they show an interest in union organization, and the employer is no longer legally required to recognize or bargain with foremen unions. Stripped of legal protection, the foremen union movement has virtually disappeared.

Subsequently, the U.S. Supreme Court held that all managerial employees are excluded from the scope of Taft–Hartley.[21] Previously, the NLRB held that managerial employees who were not foremen were covered by the statute. The agency ruled that way because whereas Congress expressly removed foremen from the scope of the law, defining foremen as those who handle labor relations problems, it did not expressly remove managerial employees who have nothing to do with labor relations matters. In any event, by a 5–4 vote, the high court held that the protection of Taft–Hartley is not to be extended to any management employees. Though it is not likely that many managerial employees desire collective bargaining, those who do may lawfully be discharged by their employers should they engage in union activities. Nor is a private-university employer required to recognize or bargain with a union composed of its faculty. In a decision that must have surprised and shocked college teachers, the U.S. Supreme Court held 5–4 that such employers are "managers" and, therefore, deprived of legal protection in *their* union activities.[22]

In addition, under Taft–Hartley employers may lock out their employees when an impasse occurs in collective bargaining.[23] At times, employees are willing to work on a day-to-day basis after the labor agreement expires. This procedure offers the parties additional time to reach an agreement without a work stoppage. Under the law, however, the employer may use the lockout to shock employees into accepting management's last offer. Even if employees are willing to work after the contract expires, the employer may deny them this opportunity and lock them out of the plant. The only qualification on this right is that the employer must have

[20] *Packard Motor Car Company* v. *NLRB*, 67 S. Ct. 789 (1947).
[21] *NLRB* v. *Bell Aerospace Company*, 416 U.S. 267 (1974).
[22] *NLRB* v. *Yeshiva University*, 444 U.S. 672 (1980). This decision generated sharp criticism among faculty groups. See, for example, John William Gercacz and Charles E. Krider, "NLRB v. Yeshiva University: The End of Faculty Unions?" *Wake Forest Law Review*, 16, No. 6 (December 1980), 891–914; and American Association of University Professors, "The Yeshiva Decision," *Academe*, Bulletin of the AAUP, 66 (May 1980), 188–97.
[23] *American Ship Building Company* v. *NLRB*, 380 U.S. 300 (1965).

engaged in good-faith collective bargaining prior to the lockout. What makes the employer's lockout right even more effective is that it is all right to continue to operate the plant with temporary replacements.[24] Under these circumstances, the locked-out employees are under pressure to capitulate to the employer's final contract offer. Such changes understandably were favorably received by the employer community.

National Emergency Strikes: An Overview

Of most direct interest to the general public, but of practical meaning only to those employers whose labor relations can be interpreted as affecting the national health and safety, are the national-emergency strike provisions that were enacted in 1947. As in the case of most Taft–Hartley provisions, these remain unchanged to this day.

Sections 206 through 210 of the act provide for government intervention in the case of such emergencies. If the president of the United States believes that a threatened or actual strike affects "an entire industry or a substantial part thereof" in such a way as to "imperil the national health and safety," he is empowered to take certain carefully delineated action. He may appoint a board of inquiry, to find out and report the facts regarding the dispute. The board is allowed subpoena authority and can thus compel the appearance of witnesses. It cannot, however, make recommendations for a settlement. On receiving the board's preliminary report, the president may apply, through the attorney general, for a court injunction restraining the strike for sixty days. If no settlement is reached during this time, the injunction can be extended for another twenty days, during which period the employees are to be polled in a secret-ballot election as to their willingness to accept the employer's last offer. The board is then to submit its final report to the president. Should the strike threat still exist after all these procedures, the president is authorized to submit a full report to Congress, "with such recommendations as he may see fit to make for consideration and appropriate action."

By 1984, the national emergency provisions of the law had been invoked thirty-five times (only twice, however, since 1972), and thirty injunctions had been issued. On four occasions, the president did not elect to seek injunctions after receiving board of inquiry reports, and on one occasion a court refused to grant the president an injunction. In 1971, a Federal district judge turned down President Nixon's request for an order sending 200 Chicago grain elevator operators back to work on the grounds that the strike posed no threat to the national health or safety. Injunctions, however, have not always been effective in bringing about settlements; six strikes started or were resumed after the injunction expired.

People with professional expertise in the field of labor relations have not been enthusiastic about this portion of the law through the years. For example, W. Willard Wirtz, secretary of labor during most of the 1960s, believed that "what

---

[24] *Ottawa Silica,* 197 NLRB 53 (1972).

Taft–Hartley comes down to is simply a polished-up, embroidered form of relief by court injunction . . . the real question is to get a settlement of the strike issue, and on this the injunction procedure seems to me to hurt, rather than to help."[25] The late George W. Taylor, a highly respected academician–arbitrator, was adamant in his longstanding position, based to a great extent on firsthand observation, that "devices such as the injunction, designed to get production resumed prior to the settlement of a dispute, add additional complexities to the negotiating process which has already bogged down."[26] And virtually every session of Congress over the past thirty-five years has been asked to consider "national-emergency disputes" revision bills from those of its members with special interests and/or proficiency in the area. The procedures themselves, however, continue on the books, in their unadulterated 1947 form.[27]

It would be naïve to predict that this gap between complaint and remedial action will continue in its present dimensions for many decades more. Certainly a public that has greatly increased its level of aspiration as to union behavior, and shouts that "there ought to be a (new) law" almost as a reflex action in the face of public inconvenience, cannot be held at bay indefinitely.

This consideration, however, cannot erase the record. In a period of unparalleled government inroads into a host of other fields of once-private endeavor (clearly including many other areas of union–management relations), our national emergency strike provisions have—with few supporters and no shortage of both influential and active antagonists—at least until now been left entirely alone.

Several reasons have been widely advanced to explain this paradox. A necessary prerequisite for altering existing legislation is the reopening of Taft–Hartley to congressional debate; a cogent case can be made that organized labor, despite its attacks upon the existing legislation, now views such action as a potential Pandora's box that might bring into the spotlight such issues as labor's present exemption from antitrust laws, a nationwide right-to-work law, and even new congressional treatment of industrywide bargaining. Nor has industry, by and large, welcomed congressional exploration of the industrial relations scene in the years since 1947. Management spokespersons have frequently voiced fears of compulsory arbitration, price control, and generally increased government intervention in the sphere of private enterprise. And although conjectures must remain unproven that this combined labor–management trepidation has significantly influenced the federal gov-

---

[25] *U.S. News & World Report,* 47 (October 19, 1959), 74.

[26] George W. Taylor, "The Adequacy of Taft–Hartley in Public Emergency Disputes," *Annals of the American Academy of Political and Social Science,* 333 (January 1961), 78.

[27] Nor has much applause been heard for the emergency strike machinery of the Railway Labor Act of 1926, which governs the airlines as well as the railroads. General agreement exists that at least since World War II, the mediation, voluntary arbitration, ad hoc emergency board appointments, and sixty-day "cooling-off" periods provided by this legislation have settled few of the major disputes in these two transportation sectors. Even worse, the parties can get the emergency boards established with relative ease—more than 200 such boards have been appointed in railroad disputes alone since 1947—and this fact has been widely blamed for depriving managements and unions involved of incentive to live up to their own collective bargaining responsibilities. Why bargain in good faith when the whole dispute can be dumped handily into the lap of the government boards, whose recommendations, although they may be of great help to one or the other of the parties, are not binding? As in the case of the Taft–Hartley provisions, however, the criticism continues unabated, and the emergency procedures remain wholly intact.

ernment in its preservation of the status quo, the joint opposition to changes in laws has undoubtedly had some restraining effect.

It is also a matter of record that agreement has been lacking as to the right solution, even though many have been proposed, primarily by representatives of the academic community. This, too, has presumably acted as a major deterrent to remedial action by our public officials.

And the all-but-patent futility of the task, if balancing the objectives of public policy is considered, must surely be thought of as a further explanation for the continuing gap between words and action in Washington. As Lloyd G. Reynolds, who has suggested that "anyone who could devise an equitable and enforceable method of handling these disputes would deserve a Nobel prize for industrial peace," has forcefully argued:

> The policy objective is not just to prevent stoppages of production, which can always be done by use of force. The objective is rather to prevent strikes by methods that are orderly and uniform in their application, that involve a minimum of direct compulsion, that do not impose greater pressure on one party than on the other, and that leave maximum scope for settlements to be reached through direct negotiation between the parties.[28]

Any solution falling short of satisfying all these requirements would, to most thoughtful American citizens, be deficient. Recognition that such an ideal may be impossible to achieve, however, has undoubtedly acted as an additional restraining force for public officials.

But to the explanations for the laissez-faire stance adopted, however reluctantly, by both Democratic and Republican administrations, must be added one that has been advanced with considerably less frequency; the extralegal weaponry in the hands of our presidents. It is a major irony that White House improvisation, having realized a significant amount of success in the past, may also have decreased the incentive in Washington to locate something better.

National Emergency Strikes: The Weapons of Extralegality

It is not generally appreciated, particularly amid the abundance of current pleas to give the president an "arsenal of weapons" for handling national emergencies, that our chief executives do not now lack for alternative courses of action, even if these are not framed explicitly by the laws. Nor have presidents, in general, hesitated to use these weapons when political pressures to "do something" have loomed large enough and prospects of warding off or ending a strike through the machinery of Taft–Hartley (or the Railway Labor Act) have appeared sufficiently dim.

A few examples illustrate these workings of extralegality. The 116-day 1959 basic steel strike was settled above all by high-level mediation efforts and ultimate settlement-term recommendations by Vice President Nixon with the aid of Sec-

---

[28] Lloyd G. Reynolds, *Labor Economics and Labor Relations,* 7th ed. (Englewood Cliffs, N.J.: Prentice-Hall, 1978), p. 600.

retary of Labor Mitchell. It has been generally agreed that both Nixon's prestige and his pressure ended this dispute after the Taft–Harley procedures had failed. Nixon's pressure was felt through such actions as those later depicted by Mitchell in his comments upon these sessions:

> Reviewing the Waldorf [Astoria Hotel] conference, Mitchell said that Nixon did not threaten the [steel company] executives but that he did paint "a very realistic picture of what might happen" if they failed to avail themselves of a chance to settle—conjuring up many possibilities of the kind of legislation that might result." . . . He left "many things" to their imagination, Mitchell said.[29]

In the Lockheed Aircraft–Machinist dispute three years later, President Kennedy not only personally requested a sixty-day truce and appointed a three-man extralegal board of public citizens to assist federal mediators in negotiations but— according to one authoritative source—when Lockhead "declined to accept . . . [this] board's recommendation for an election to determine the union shop issue, the Defense Department announced, in effect, that its defense contracts were being especially reviewed and placed on an *ad hoc* basis."[30]

President Johnson virtually locked up the 1965 steel industry and United Steelworkers' negotiators for five days in quarters near his White House office. He constantly requested the parties during personal visits (at times with the secretaries of labor and commerce) to come to terms in the process and ultimately provided his own "statistical referee" in the person of the chairman of the Council of Economic Advisers to institute suggestions, which led to White House recommendations accepted by both sides.

In 1977, fearful that the apparent paranoia of Mine Workers president Arnold Miller by itself would bring about a strike in Miller's critical coal mining sector, the Carter administration—in an unprecedented move—itself quietly recruited staff members and consultants for the union after Miller had fired much of his corps of assistants. To Carter and his labor advisers a union in chaos (as the Mine Workers threatened to be) simply could not bring negotiations to a successful conclusion.[31]

Such a list could be extended considerably. Special mediation efforts on the part of highly respected private citizens were utilized with beneficial results in the maritime disputes of 1961 and 1962. Prior to invocation of Taft–Hartley in the 1962–1963 Boeing Company–Machinist impasse, an extralegal board made recommendations, a privilege denied official Taft–Hartley boards. In 1978, following more than a bit of governmental prodding, the Postal Service and its three negotiating unions agreed to let Harvard professor James J. Healy mediate that dispute for fifteen days and impose an arbitrated settlement should agreement not be

---

[29] *Business Week,* January 9, 1960, p. 28.
[30] Herbert R. Northrup and Gordon F. Bloom, *Government and Labor* (Homewood, Ill.: Richard D. Irwin, 1963), p. 369.
[31] The strike, an 111-day one indeed, ensued anyhow. Without the governmental moves, on the other hand, it might well have lasted longer.

forthcoming within the fifteen-day period (as it was not). And the record hardly lacks for instances of presidential exhortations, made both publicly and privately, for self-restraint in the face of national defense (cold war, Korean, Vietnamese, or oil crisis) exigencies; of executive suggestions that an unhappy Congress could be forced into drastic ad hoc remedial action (most notably carried out in the case of 1963, 1967, 1970, and 1982 railroad strike prevention orders); or of White House expressions of dissatisfaction with existing strike legislation and broad hints of less palatable laws to come should labor statesmanship not prevail on a bipartite basis.

If these extralegal weapons have not been universally successful in achieving their immediate goal of strike settlement or strike avoidance, they have at least combined with the existing labor statutes—and on many occasions with the entirely independent actions of the two contractual parties—to realize this objective. Although some of the settlements may have added to unwanted inflationary movements or may otherwise have had publicly undesirable consequences, the basic missions of dissipating a national emergency dispute has always been accomplished. Extralegal avenues now open to our chief executives have invariably produced labor peace when all else has failed.

National Emergency Strikes: The Risk of Relative Success

Obviously, however, the problem can hardly be dismissed in as cavalier a fashion as the preceding paragraph might suggest. At least three additional factors must be considered.

First, successful executive improvisation has often been implemented only after the "emergency" has existed for some time. The extralegal avenues performed effectively, for example, only after 116 days of strike activity (plus passage of almost the full Taft–Hartley injunction period) in the case of steel in 1959, and after a one-month strike following the injunction period in the case of the 1962–1963 Atlantic and Gulf Coast longshoring impasse. Improvisation was tried earlier in these and many other national disputes with a notable lack of success, and the fact that such "emergencies" have not been terminated as rapidly as chief executives would have liked—with attendant adverse consequences for the economy—should not go unnoticed.

Second, although the efficacy of each of the successful extralegal weapons can hardly be debated, the question can be raised whether or not all have been consistent with the dominant values of our private enterprise society: How appropriate, for example, is a threat to deprive an aircraft manufacturer of defense contracts essentially because of its presumably sincere aversion to the principle of the union shop? How advisable is the imposition of ad hoc compulsory arbitration in peacetime, as in the case of the railroads? And would threatened new and essentially punitive legislation, directed primarily against the party deemed by government representatives as the recalcitrant in the bargaining, in any way be guaranteed an objective—or equitable—basis?

Third, the fact that the extralegal actions have until now produced labor peace when all else has failed obviously provides no assurance that the nation will not be confronted ultimately with an "emergency" strike that no existing presidential weapon—legal or extralegal—will be able to terminate easily. It is entirely conceivable that at some future time, a major labor relations impasse will combine with the imperviousness of one or both parties to existing executive weapons and the unwillingness of Congress to supply tailor-made back-to-work legislation, forcing the nation to wait until the strike burdens become completely intolerable. This unhappy state of affairs was almost reached in the case of the 1974 coal strike (as opposed to the one in 1977–1978), which fortunately terminated after a short period of time. A long coal strike then, taking into consideration soaring prices and a high unemployment rate, could have had serious consequences for the nation.

In short, the existing weapons of extralegality do not constitute a panacea for the problem of "national emergency" disputes. And if their successful exercise in the past as a frequently used supplement to our official legislation helps explain the remarkable staying power of these all but friendless laws, the existence of the defects in the improvised weapons would still seem to make some overhaul in our present machinery highly desirable. The danger may lie in the strong possibility that the relative efficiency of these weapons in achieving their immediate purpose of ending an "emergency" is depriving us of sufficient incentive to search seriously for a better way to serve the national interest.

Other Taft–Hartley Provisions

Taft–Hartley also devoted attention to *internal union affairs,* the first such regulation in American history. Its impetus came not only from the previously cited Communistic taints attached to several unions but also from the fact that, in the case of a few other labor organizations, lack of democratic procedures and financial irregularities (often involving employer wrongdoing as well) had become glaringly evident. Accordingly, the act set new conditions for unions thenceforth seeking to use the NLRB's services: (1) All union officers were obligated to file annual affidavits with the board, stating that they were not members of the Communist party; (2) certain financial and constitutional information had to be annually filed by unions with the secretary of labor; and (3) unions (as well as corporations) could no longer contribute funds for political purposes in connection with any federal election. The affidavit requirement, judged to be ineffective, was repealed in 1959. The other stipulations were allowed to remain in force until that date, when they were only slightly amended and then substantially enlarged upon (as further discussion will indicate). Essentially, aside from what unionists vocally termed a nuisance value, the provisions are notable for the first recognition of public policy that some internal regulation of the union as an institution was in the public interest— and as a harbinger of more such regulation to come.

Another Taft–Hartley provision that has upset some union leaders involves the *termination or modification of existing labor contracts.* Applicable to both labor organizations and employers, it requires the party seeking to end or change the agreement to give a sixty-day notice to the other party. The law further provides that, during this time period, the existing contract must be maintained without strikes or lockouts. In addition, the Federal Mediation and Conciliation Service and state mediation services are to be notified of the impending dispute thirty days after the serving of the notice. Workers striking in violation of this requirement lose all legal protection as "employees" in collective bargaining, although the law also asserts that "such loss of status for such employee shall terminate if and when he is reemployed" by the employer.

In some instances, leaders of labor organizations have found it both difficult and politically unpopular to restrain their constituents from violating this provision. Unionists have also, on occasion, frankly pointed out that the scheduling prerequisites for striking have deprived their organizations of some economic power, at least insofar as the element of surprise is concerned. Yet many representatives of both parties would undoubtedly agree that these provisions have let mediators intervene before it is too late to help and have generally aided in the resolution of disputes by allowing more time for thoughtful consideration of what is involved. From the point of view of the public interest, it is clearly on this basis that the effectiveness of the notice provisions should be judged.

Section 301 of Taft–Hartley decreed that "*suits for violations of contracts* between an employer and a labor organization representing employees in an industry affecting commerce" could be brought directly by either party in any U.S. district court. Labor agreements, in short, were to be construed as being legally enforceable for the first time in American history. Damage suits are not calculated to increase mutual trust or offset misunderstandings between the parties in labor relations, however, and unions and managements have generally recognized this. Consequently, relatively few such suits have come to the courts in the years since this provision was enacted. Many contracts today, in fact, contain agreements *not* to sue, a perfectly legal dodge of Section 301. More will be said about this issue in Chapter 9.

Though employer suits against unions under Section 301 for violation of no-strike provisions have been comparatively infrequent, the U.S. Supreme Court has established some applicable policies. Only the union, and not individual members or officers, is liable for any damages assessed in court proceedings.[32] Also, a national union is not responsible for damages when its local unions engage in wildcat strikes.[33] Since local unions normally do not have huge treasuries, employers understandably seek damages from the national union. However, the high court has held that national unions are not liable when they do not provoke or encourage wildcat strikes. To get around this policy, employers would have to negotiate specific contractual language placing an affirmative obligation on national unions to end

[32] *Complete Auto Transit, Inc.* v. *Reis*, 451 U.S. 401 (1981).
[33] *Carbon Fuel* v. *United Mine Workers of America*, 444 U.S. 212 (1979).

wildcat strikes, and making them liable even when they do not provoke or encourage such work stoppages. Of course, not many national unions would agree to such a provision.

Coverage of Private Hospitals

In 1974 Congress extended the coverage of Taft–Hartley to private nonprofit hospitals and nursing homes. This was no small matter. About 2 million employees work in about 3,300 nonprofit hospitals. Before that time the NLRB assumed jurisdiction over proprietary (profit-making) health-care institutions. However, until Congress amended Taft–Hartley, the agency was not authorized to handle cases in the nonprofit sector because the original law expressly excluded it from the coverage of the statute.

Recognizing that hospitals supply a critical public service, the new legislation (which now covers profit and nonprofit hospitals) established a special set of dispute-settling procedures. Unions representing hospital employees must give ninety days' notice before terminating a labor agreement, thirty days more than Taft–Hartley requires in other industries. In addition, a hospital union may not strike or picket unless it gives ten days' notice. This notice requirement, not found in other industries, provides hospital management with the opportunity to make arrangements for the continuity of patient care. Furthermore, a labor dispute in a health-care facility is automatically subject to mediation efforts of the Federal Mediation and Conciliation Service. Finally, unlike its authority in other industries, the FMCS is empowered to appoint a fact-finding board to make recommendations to settle hospital labor disputes.

As a result of the unique character of health-care institutions, the NLRB was required to establish special policies in the application of the 1974 amendment. These involved the establishment of the bargaining unit, union solicitation of members on hospital property, enforcement of the ten-day notice requirement, and the application of its protection to interns and resident physicians. In the matter of the bargaining unit, the agency struck a balance between a "wall-to-wall" unit and a multitude of units that would make collective bargaining and the operation of a hospital very difficult. In general, for collective bargaining purposes, the agency establishes six types of bargaining units: physicians employed by a hospital (other than residents and interns), registered nurses, professional employees, technical employees, business office personnel, and general service and maintenance employees. Each group of employees, classified in separate units, may select its own union for collective bargaining purposes.

To avoid disturbing patients, hospital management can forbid the solicitation of union members and the distribution of union literature in patient rooms and other patient-care areas such as X-ray, operating, and therapy rooms even if the activity occurs during nonworking time. In contrast, within industry in general, employers may not forbid such union activities during nonworking time. The more difficult problem involves patient-access areas, such as hallways, gift shops, cafeterias, and visitors' lounges. So perplexing and controversial is this problem that the matter has been before the NLRB and the courts many times. Using two U.S. Supreme Court decisions as the authority, it would appear that unions may not solicit members in hospital corridors and in lounges on floors occupied by patients. However, unions may solicit in cafeterias, gift shops, and the main lobby even though patients may have access to them.[34]

With regard to the ten-day notice rule, the NLRB has applied the provision literally. Hospital employees who strike or picket without filing the notice may be discharged by the hospital. It does not matter whether or not the employees are represented by a union or whether or not the union had knowledge of their illegal conduct.[35]

In a highly controversial decision, the NLRB has held that hospital interns and resident physicians are excluded from the protection of Taft–Hartley.[36] It said that such persons are not "employees" within the meaning of the law but are students pursuing a graduate medical education. Though the nation's 12,000 interns and 48,000 residents receive salaries for their work, pay federal income taxes on their earnings, and devote a great deal of their time to patient care, the agency held that they have no rights under Taft–Hartley. Should they strike for union recognition, being denied access to the NLRB election procedures, this NLRB policy may well prove not to be in the public interest.

Administrative Changes in the Law

Taft–Hartley also enlarged the NLRB from three to five members and, in the interests of a faster disposition of cases, authorized the board to delegate "any or all" of its powers to any group of three or more members. In addition, the office of independent General Counsel was created within the NLRB, to administer the prosecution of all unfair labor practices. This last change was made to satisfy the increasingly bitter charges (particularly from employers) that the same individuals had exercised both prosecution and judicial roles.

As the NLRB machinery now operates, the board members and General Counsel delegate most of their work in processing unfair labor practice charges (which have tripled in number in the last fifteen years, up from 17,000 in the late 1960s) and conducting representation elections to thirty-one regional and two subregional offices scattered throughout the country. Each office deals with these two problems as they arise in its particular geographic area. The General Counsel supervises the work of the offices, and the board members' efforts are thus saved for those issues appealed to it from the regional level. As will be recalled, board decisions can themselves be appealed to the courts (and ultimately to the Supreme Court).

From what has been said, it is obvious that the NLRB has considerable

[34] *Beth Israel Hospital* v. *NLRB,* 434 U.S. 1033 (1978). *NLRB* v. *Baptist Hospital,* 440 U.S. 943 (1979).
[35] Office of the General Counsel (NLRB), Release No. 1385, March 27, 1975, p. 2.
[36] *Cedars-Sinai Medical Center,* 223 NLRB 251 (1976).

authority to apply the provisions of the law. What the legislation does is to establish broad guidelines, but it is up to the agency to apply the law to particular situations. In the vast majority of the cases, the courts have sustained the decisions of the board on the grounds that the agency possesses expertise that should be given full faith and credit by the judiciary. It follows, therefore, that how the law will be applied depends to a great extent on who sits on the board. It is a matter of common sense that presidents will choose members who generally represent the socioeconomic philosophy of the nation's chief executive office, and thus, over the years, employers and unions alternatively have been bitterly critical of board policies. In general, unions have criticized the policies of Republican-appointed NLRB members, and employers have displayed the same attitude toward the board when directed by appointees of Democratic chief executives.

THE LANDRUM–GRIFFIN ACT OF 1959

As might have been expected, the Taft–Hartley Act generated considerable controversy. In the years immediately after its passage, labor leaders bitterly assailed the new law as being—in addition to a "slave labor act"—a punitive one, and invoked such statements in regard to its authors as "the forces of reaction in this country want a showdown with free American labor." Taft–Hartley supporters, on the other hand, frequently referred to the act as a "Magna Charta" for both employers and employees and widely praised its efforts to "equalize bargaining power." Unable to see any appropriateness in these latter remarks, spokespersons for organized labor, until roughly a decade ago, in turn responded by pressing for the repeal of the act—or occasionally, for its drastic amendment—in every session of Congress. Their complete failure to realize this goal and their recent unwillingness even to pursue it attests to the basic acceptance of Taft–Hartley's provisions in the recent past by the American public, as well as to labor's concern that an even less desirable law might be the outcome.

The framers of public policy themselves, however, did not long remain satisfied that existing labor legislation was fully adequate to uphold the public interest. In 1959, the national legislature passed another significant law, the Landrum–Griffin Act (officially, the Labor–Management Reporting and Disclosure Act). This act was the direct outgrowth of the unsatisfactory internal practices of a small but strategically located minority of unions, as revealed by Senate investigations, and it can be said to have marked the beginning of quite *detailed regulation* of internal union affairs, going far beyond the Taft–Hartley treatment of this subject.

Under Landrum–Griffin provisions, as noted earlier, union members are guaranteed a "Bill of Rights" that their unions cannot violate, officers of labor organizations must meet a variety of reporting and disclosure obligations, and the secretary of labor is charged with the investigation of relevant union misconduct.

The "Bill of Rights" for union members is an ambitious and wide-sweeping one. It provides for equality of rights concerning the nomination of candidates for union office, voting in elections, attendance at membership meetings, and participation in business transactions—all, however, "subject to to reasonable" union rules. It lays down strict standards to ensure that increases in dues and fees are responsive to the desires of the union membership majority. It affirms the right of any member to sue the organization once "reasonable" hearing procedures within the union have been exhausted. It provides that no member may be fined, suspended, or otherwise disciplined by the union except for nonpayment of dues, unless the member has been granted such procedural safeguards as being served with written specific charges, given time to prepare a defense, and afforded a fair hearing. And it obligates union officers to furnish each of their members with a copy of the collective bargaining agreement, as well as full information concerning the Landrum–Griffin Act itself.

Not content to stop here in prescribing internal union conduct, the 1959 legislation laid out specific ground rules for *union elections*. National and international unions must now elect officers at least once every five years, either by secret ballot or at a convention of delegates chosen by secret ballot. Local unions are obligated to elect officers at least once every three years, exclusively by secret ballot. As for the conduct of these elections, they must be administered in full accordance with the union's constitution and bylaws, with all ballots and other relevant records being preserved for a period of one year. Every member in good standing is to be entitled to one vote, and all candidates are guaranteed the right to have an observer at the polls and at the ballot counting.

Landrum–Griffin also made it more difficult for national and international unions to place their subordinate bodies under *trusteeships* for purely political reasons. The trusteeship, or the termination of the member group's autonomy, has traditionally allowed labor organizations to correct constitutional violations or other clearly wrongful acts on the part of their locals. The Senate investigations preceding Landrum–Griffin had found, however, that this device was also being used by some unions as a weapon of the national or international officers to eliminate grassroots opposition per se. Accordingly, the act provided that trusteeships could be imposed only for one of four purposes: (1) to correct corruption or "financial malpractice"; (2) to assure the performance of collective bargaining duties; (3) to restore democratic procedures; and (4) to otherwise carry out "the legitimate objects" of the subordinate body. Moreover, the imposition of a trusteeship, together with the reasons for it, was now to be reported to the secretary of labor within thirty days, and every six months thereafter until the trusteeship was terminated.

The extent of Landrum–Griffin control of the internal affairs of unions is perhaps best illustrated by the act's policing of the kind of person who can serve as a union officer. Persons convicted of serious crimes (robbery, bribery, extortion, embezzlement, murder, rape, grand larceny, violation of narcotics laws, aggravated assault) are barred for a period of five years after conviction from holding any union position other than a clerical or custodial job. The period of exclusion may be shortened if the person's citizenship rights are fully restored before five years or if the U.S. Department of Justice decides that an exception should be made.

A fair question to ask is whether or not this policy should be applied to officers of other kinds of institutions, such as business, government, universities, and churches. On the surface, at least, it would appear that if government controls the moral character of union officers, it should apply the same policy across the board. To do otherwise makes it appear that union officers are being held to a higher standard of personal conduct than is required of, say, corporation officials. Should a corporation official who has been convicted of a serious crime, including violations of the nation's antitrust and pure food and drug laws, be treated in the same way as a union officer? This could be the subject for a lively debate in any student group.

To curb financial corruption, the law requires that union officers must each year file reports with the secretary of labor containing the purpose for which union funds are spent. The objective is to discourage union officers from using the organization's treasury for items of a personal nature. Since financial reports are made available to union members, they can learn whether or not their dues are being used in the interest of the membership. Should it be determined that a union officer has used union funds for personal items, the law authorizes court suits to recover the money from the officer. If a report is not filed, or if the information contained is not true, the responsible union officer is subject to criminal penalties. Outright embezzlement of union funds may also result in imprisonment and/or fines. In addition, all union officers must be bonded by a private bonding company in which the union has no interest.

Although most of Landrum–Griffin was aimed at union behavior, the act does include provisions that cover employer activities. Landrum–Griffin made employers responsible for reporting annually to the secretary of labor all company expenditures directed at influencing employee collective bargaining behavior. Employer bribery of union officers and other such blunt tactics had actually constituted federal crimes since the passage of Taft–Hartley, but the new act expanded the list of unlawful employer actions. Bribes by companies to their own employees so that they do not exercise their rights to organize and bargain collectively were added to the list of crimes. So, too, were many forms of employer payment aimed at procuring information on employee activities related to labor disputes. Violations by employers of their reporting obligations invite the same criminal penalties as are provided for union representatives.

In a way, the law attempted to fill the gap created by union-membership apathy. It can be argued that a more effective way to promote union democracy and financial responsibility is by active participation of members in union affairs. The members of any union, local or international, have it in their power to require that their organizations adhere to democratic procedures and financial responsibility through the existing internal machinery of their unions. It is debatable that the federal government should protect union members against abuse by the organization when these members are not particularly concerned as to how their unions in fact operate.

In any event, few would now argue for repeal of the legislation. Even union opposition against Landrum–Griffin has subsided. Control of the internal affairs of unions by government is now an established feature. Possibly, no law will convert unions into models of democracy; still, the effect of the law has eliminated some of the more flagrant abuses of undemocratic practices and financial irresponsibility. For example, in 1969, the United Mine Workers held an election to choose their international officers. This was the first such national election ever conducted in this union in over forty years, and it is not likely that it would have been held in the absence of the law's requirements.[37] And, undoubtedly, the act has curtailed the activities of the comparatively small number of union officers who would regard the union's treasury as something to be used for their personal aggrandizement. Although there still exist some undemocratic practices and some corruption in the house of labor, there have been fewer flagrant instances of such conduct since the passage of the legislation. If nothing else, the law has educated union officers as to their responsibilities to their members. To this extent, the law has apparently accomplished its major objectives, and does for union members what they have failed through apathy to do for themselves.

Landrum–Griffin—Title VII

Quite apart from regulating internal union affairs and imposing obligations on employers, the Landrum–Griffin law in Title VII made some important changes in the Taft–Hartley Act. It authorized the NLRB to decline cases involving small employers engaged in interstate commerce, and permitted the states to take jurisdiction of such cases. The theory here was that the NLRB should conserve its funds and manpower for those cases that have a substantial impact on interstate commerce.

It also closed the so-called loopholes that developed under Taft–Hartley's secondary boycott provisions. As we have seen, one purpose of the Taft–Hartley law was to outlaw secondary boycotts. However, the NLRB and the courts permitted unions to engage in certain types of secondary boycott activity. The reason for this was the character of the language of the 1947 law that regulated these activities. Under the 1959 law, Congress adopted new language that generally closed these loopholes, and under the present state of affairs, a union's opportunity to engage in secondary boycott activities has virtually been eliminated.

Landrum–Griffin also outlawed the "hot-cargo" arrangement. Under a hot-cargo clause, an employer agrees with a union not to handle products of or otherwise deal with another employer involved in a labor dispute. Accordingly, the hot-cargo arrangement is a form of secondary boycott. The difference is that an employer agrees by contractual provision to engage in secondary boycotts upon receiving a signal from its union that another employer should be boycotted. Such arrange-

---

[37] However, the election had tragic consequences. On New Year's Eve 1970, Joseph Yablonski (who opposed Tony Boyle, the incumbent president), his wife, and his daughter were murdered. Subsequently, Boyle and other officers of the union were convicted of the crime.

ments are now illegal, and unions that force an employer to negotiate hot-cargo clauses engage in an unfair labor practice. For reasons peculiar to the nature of the construction and garment industries, however, Congress excepted these two industries from the hot-cargo proscription.

Title VII imposed another important restriction upon unions. It pinned down and controlled recognition and organizational picketing. At times, unions have found this kind of picketing effective to force employers to recognize unions and to persuade employees to join unions. Such picketing is particularly effective in a consumer business, such as a department store or a restaurant. A picket line thrown around a department store could persuade customers not to buy at the store, and this kind of union pressure could force the employer to recognize the union. Under Taft–Hartley, there was no restriction on this kind of picketing, and unions could picket for recognition and organizational purposes for an indefinite length of time.

Under the 1959 law, the opportunity for unions to picket for such purposes was sharply reduced. Such picketing activities now constitute an unfair labor practice if (1) the employer is lawfully recognizing another union; (2) a valid election has been conducted by the NLRB in the previous twelve months; or (3) no election petition has been filed with the NLRB within thirty days after the picketing began.

This provision is of particular importance to employers who want to be freed from the pressure of picketing. Thus, within thirty days after the start of the picketing, the union must file a petition for an election. If it loses the election, recognition and organizational picketing may not be engaged in for one year. Consequently, the opportunity of a union to picket for an indefinite period of time is eliminated.

However, there is one major qualification to this proscription. A union may picket for informational purposes after thirty days without filing an election petition. Informational picketing is defined by the law as the kind that advises the public that the employer involved does not employ members of the union or have a contract with it. Of course, the picket-sign legends must be truthful. For example, they may not state that the employer does not employ members of the union if in truth he does. Also, informational picketing, as distinct from recognition and organizational picketing, may not interfere with pickup and delivery of products at the site of the company being picketed.

The Title VII amendments to Taft–Hartley caused unions unhappiness in yet another way: in their letting the NLRB decline cases of small employers engaged in interstate commerce, thereby eliminating the opportunity for the employees of such employers to exercise their organizational and collective bargaining rights under the federal law. If a state does not have a law similar to Taft–Hartley (and many states do not), these employees now have no legal forum to protect them in their efforts to organize and bargain collectively.

In only one major way did unions, indeed, *benefit* from the enactment of Title VII. The Title did redress a promanagement inequity that was created by Taft–Hartley. Under the earlier law, workers out on an economic strike (wages, pensions, seniority, and the like) were not permitted to vote in NLRB elections held during the course of a strike if the employer replaced them with other employees. What was inequitable about this provision is that the replaced economic strikers could not vote, *but the replacements were entitled to vote*. The replacements would, of course, vote to decertify the union, since, if the union maintained bargaining rights, it would insist as a condition of settling the strike that the regular employees be reinstated in their jobs and the replacements ("strikebreakers," "scabs," "finks" in union talk) be fired. Thus, the only way the replacements could be assured of holding their jobs would be to vote the union out. This would not be hard to do, provided that the employer hired a sufficient number of replacements during the strike.

Assume that the bargaining unit is composed of 500 employees, all union members. A strike takes place, and the 500 employees go out on strike. The employer then hires 400 replacements, and an election is held by the NLRB to determine whether the union still represents a majority of the bargaining unit. Under this illustration, the 400 replacements vote in the election, but, of the regular employees, only the 100 who have not been replaced can vote. When the votes are counted, it should occasion little surprise that the 400 replacements vote to destroy the union. And, with this result, the employer will no longer need to recognize the union.

Indeed, under the original Taft–Hartley law, some employers provoked economic strikes, hired replacements, and then petitioned the NLRB for an election. It is easy to see why organized labor looked upon this provision as a real threat to its existence.

Unions received some relief from this state of affairs in the 1959 law. Under its terms, replaced economic strikers may vote in NLRB elections, provided the election is held within one year from the start of a strike. If the strike lasts longer than one year, the replaced strikers are not eligible to vote. Under the assumption that most strikes would terminate before one year, it is understandable that the AFL–CIO stated in 1960 that "although most of the Taft–Hartley amendments were severely damaging to labor unions, [this one] was favorable."

LABOR LAW REFORM AND THE FILIBUSTER

With the 1976 election of President Carter and a Congress dominated by the Democratic party, organized labor believed that the time was ripe to enact amendments to Taft–Hartley that would correct what it called major deficiencies in the operation of the law. For many years, the labor movement had complained about unreasonable delays in the processing of election petitions and unfair labor practice cases. It had also deemed inadequate the remedies that the National Labor Relations Board could impose on employers who violate the law.

In the summer of 1977, President Carter announced his support of the Labor Law Reform Act and pledged to fight particularly for its portions that would make organizing easier. He also said that the proposed legislation would make the laws that govern labor–management relations work more efficiently, quickly, and equitably.[38]

In the view of the president of the U.S. Chamber of Commerce, by contrast, the act constituted

an ill-advised attempt to further the interests of organized labor at the expense of individual worker rights.[39]

As originally introduced in the House of Representatives, the proposed legislation would have expedited the election process and imposed stiffer penalties against employers who violate national labor policy. To speed up representation elections, the measure placed strict deadlines on the NLRB. Were a union to provide authorization cards from more than half the employees in the bargaining unit, the election had to be held within fifteen days after the election petition was filed. In cases where the union had authorization cards from more than 30 percent but less than 50 percent of the employees, the NLRB would be required to hold the election within forty-five days after the petition was filed. Should the NLRB determine that the issues involved in a representation case were of exceptional novelty or complexity, the election might be delayed as long as seventy-five days. These deadlines satisfied the union complaint regarding alleged employer stalling tactics in the matter of elections.

Under the terms of the House measure, the NLRB would have been required to seek an injunction from a federal court reinstating promptly employees discharged for union activities during an organizational campaign or in the period after an election and before the signing of the first collective bargaining agreement. Also, such employees would have been entitled to double back pay with no deduction for outside earnings gained during the period of discharge. Under normal NLRB procedures, an unlawfully discharged employee must wait about one year before the agency directs reinstatement, and should the employer appeal the NLRB decision to the courts (an employer right frequently used), the delay can consume several years. By being required to effect prompt reinstatement of unlawfully discharged employees, employers would have lost a commonly used antiunion weapon.

Another unfair labor practice of employers would have been subject to a more effective remedy. This involves employers who do not bargain in good faith and unlawfully delay the negotiation of a labor agreement. To deal with this problem, under the terms of the legislation, the NLRB would be authorized to require an employer who refused to bargain in good faith for the first labor agreement to pay damages to the employees by this formula: an amount equal to the average wage negotiated at similar plants where collective bargaining proceeded lawfully.

[38] *Congressional Record,* July 18, 1977, pp. H7257–58.
[39] "Proposed Amendments to the National Labor Relations Act," American Enterprise Institution, Washington, D.C., February 1978, p. 2.

Data needed to determine the amount would be supplied by the U.S. Bureau of Labor Statistics. Faced with such a remedy, employers would lose whatever profit could be gained by deliberately stalling in collective bargaining.

Even a more serious penalty would have been assessed against employers who willfully violated a final order of the NLRB or the federal courts. These employers would face a loss of federal contracts for up to three years. An exception could be made by the secretary of labor only for national defense reasons.

The House passed the bill by a vote of 257 to 163. However, much to the disappointment of organized labor, a filibuster in the summer of 1978 blocked passage in the Senate. Supporters of the legislation lacked only two votes to stop the filibuster. What must have been frustrating for them was that the Senate bill had been watered down and took into consideration some of the employers' objections to the House version. At this writing it does not appear that another attempt will be made in the near future. Despite the support of the president of the United States and a Democratic Congress, the effort failed, and given failure under these circumstances the chance of future enactment of any such change in labor law is dim indeed.

SOME CONCLUSIONS

What are some reasonably safe conclusions based on the long experience of public policy recited on these pages? Can we make some predictions about future developments in the area of labor law? The first and perhaps the most accurate conclusion that can be made is that public policy toward organized labor and collective bargaining has changed significantly over the years. It has moved from legal repression to strong encouragement, then to modified encouragement coupled with regulation, and, finally, with Landrum–Griffin, to detailed regulation of internal union affairs. It seems a safe prediction not only that further shifts in this public policy can be expected but that these changes, as was not always the case in earlier times, will depend for this direction strictly on the acceptability of current union behavior to the American public.

This point is particularly important to the unionists of today. Especially since 1937, when it held the Wagner Act wholly constitutional, the Supreme Court has permitted the legislative branch of government the widest latitude to shape public policy. Congress and the state legislatures are judicially free to determine the elements of the framework of labor law. To most citizens, such a situation is only as it should be; our judiciary is expected to interpret law but not to make it, and we generally expect actions of the legislative branch to be voided only when the particular statute clearly and unmistakably violates the terms of the Constitution. But since today the polls, and not the courts, do constitute the forum in which our policies toward labor are determined, and since the public has in the recent past apparently increased its level of aspiration as to union behavior, labor organizations have been forced to become increasingly conscious of the images they project.

Such a situation accounts to a great extent for the growing union stress on such nontraditional labor concerns as charity work, college scholarships, Boy Scout troops, and Little League teams, which will be discussed in the next chapter. It also accounts for the entire labor movement's uneasiness whenever strikes arousing the public ire, or such notable black marks as James R. Hoffa's jury-tampering and pension-fund defrauding convictions, occur. And it undoubtedly has been one major factor in leading to more maturity and self-restraint on the part of some labor leaders at the bargaining table. As Chapter 1 noted, however, whether this progress will continue sufficiently and in time to satisfy the increasingly high level of public expectation and thereby ward off further laws of the Taft–Hartley and Landrum–Griffin variety remains an unanswred question.

Second, every law since Norris–La Guardia has expanded the scope of government regulation of the labor–management arena. To the curbs on judicial capriciousness enacted in 1932 have been added, in turn, restrictions on employer conduct, limitations on union conduct, and governmental fiats closely regulating internal union affairs. Most of the other parts of the later laws—to cite but two examples, Taft–Hartley's modification of the Wagner Act's closed- and union-shop provisions and Landrum–Griffin's new conditions regarding the "hot-cargo" clauses—represent ever-finer qualifications of the freedom of action of both parties. Given both the electorate's impatience with the progress of collective bargaining and Congress's apparently deep-seated reluctance to decrease the scope covered by its laws, future legislation can be expected to move *further* in the direction of government intervention. This should hold true whether the future laws are enacted with the implicit goal of "helping" or of "hurting" unions.

Individual value judgments clearly determine the advisability of such a trend. But if one believes that stable and sound industrial relations can be achieved only in an environment of free collective bargaining, wherein labor and management—the parties that must live with each other on a day-to-day basis—are allowed to find mutually satisfactory answers to their industrial relations problems, there is cause for concern. Government policy that limits this freedom strikes at the very heart of the process.

This is not to say that the more recent labor statutes are entirely barren of provisions that are valuable additions to the law of labor relations. The union unfair labor practices relating to restraint and coercion of employees and to union-caused employer discrimination are clearly a move in the right direction. So, too, are Taft–Hartley's curbs on strikes and boycott activity engaged in at times by some unions for the objective of increasing the power of one union at the expense of other labor organizations, despite all the litigation that has surrounded these curbs since 1947. Nor does the requirement that unions bargain collectively embarrass anyone except the union leader who is uncooperative and recalcitrant.

At the same time, however, the government intervention in regard to such issues as union security, the checkoff, and the enforcement of the collective bargaining agreement (to cite but three), and the decreasing scope for union and management bargaining-table latitude in general, do raise the question of ultimate government control over *all* major industrial relations activities. For one who believes in "free collective bargaining," the increasing reach of the statutes may be steering labor policy in a very dangerous direction.

Third, even if one does conclude that the gains of our present dosage of government regulation outweigh its losses and inherent risks, this hardly proves that the current statutes and their interpretations constitute the most *appropriate* ones to meet each specific labor relations topic now being dealt with.

Finally, and probably also as an inevitable consequence of the increased coverage of public policy, labor laws have become anything but easy to comprehend. The inconsistent NLRB and judicial rulings that have plagued them in recent years may be based to some extent on philosophical and political differences, but they undeniably also stem from the built-in interpretative difficulties in the laws themselves.

What consitutes "refusal to bargain"? When are companies discriminating in regard to "hire or tenure of employment or any term or condition of employment" to influence union membership? What constitutes unlawful union recognition picketing? It is hard to disagree with the commonly heard lament of unionists and labor relations managers that it has become ever more risky to state definitively what is legal in bargaining relationships and what is not; and the most valuable information available to the management or labor union representative who is concerned with labor law may very possibly be the telephone number of an able labor attorney. But, given the dimensions of this law today, however unpalatable many of its tenets may be to one or the other party, and whatever dangers may be inherent in present trends, the managers and unionists who are *not* concerned with public policy remain so only at their peril.

Discussion Questions

1 Why, do you think, did the courts so squarely ally themselves with the employer community and against organized labor from the days of the American Revolution until the Great Depression of the 1930s?

2 "The Norris–La Guardia Act conferred no new rights on workers. It merely adjusted an inherently inequitable situation." Comment.

3 How much truth do you feel lies in the statement that "there was great need for the Wagner Act . . . its sole defect lay in the fact that it was not slightly broadened from time to time to regulate a few union practices of dubious social value"?

4 It has been argued that whatever deficiencies may have accompanied the Taft–Hartley Act, it did "free workers from the tyrannical hold of union bosses." Do you agree?

5 Do you feel that the Wagner Act or the Taft–Hartley Act has been more influential in leading to the current status of organized labor in this country?

6 "In the last analysis, the public must judge the relative merits of the collective bargaining process." Discuss.

7 If all existing national labor legislation could instantly be erased and our statutory regulation could then be completely rewritten, what would you advocate as public policy governing labor relations—and why?

8 Whether or not you agree with the exact scope and specific wording of the present laws, do you consider these laws to be essentially equitable to both management and labor?

9 "If union members were to attend union meetings regularly and take an active role in the operation of the union, there would be no need for Landrum–Griffin." Defend your position whatever it may be.

10 What do you believe to be the most important right that the Taft–Hartley Act offers (a) the employee (b) the employer? In each case, defend your selection.

Selected References

AARON, BENJAMIN, and K. W. WEDDERBURN, eds., *Industrial Conflict: A Comparative Legal Survey*. New York: Crane, Russak, 1973.

BELLACE, JANICE R., ALLAN BERKOWITZ, and BRUCE D. VAN DUSEN, *The Landrum–Griffin Act*. Philadelphia: University of Pennsylvania, 1979.

CULLEN, DONALD E., *National Emergency Strikes*. Ithaca, N.Y.: New York State School of Industrial and Labor Relations, 1968.

FELDACKER, BRUCE S., *Labor Guide to Labor Law*. Reston, Va.: Reston Publishing Co., 1980.

GETMAN, JULIUS, STEVEN GOLDBERG, and JEANNE B. HERMAN, *Union Representation Elections: Law and Reality*. New York: Russell Sage Foundation, 1976.

GOULD, WILLIAM B., *A Primer on American Labor Law*. Cambridge, Mass.: MIT Press, 1982.

MCCULLOCH, FRANK W., and TIM BORNSTEIN, *The National Labor Relations Board*. New York: Praeger, 1974.

MCLAUGHLIN, DORIS B., and ANITA W. SCHOOMAKER, *The Landrum–Griffin Act and Union Democracy*. Ann Arbor: University of Michigan Press, 1979.

MILLER, EDWARD B., *An Administrative Appraisal of the NLRB* (3rd ed.). Philadelphia: University of Pennsylvania, 1981.

SCHLOSSBERG, STEPHEN I., and FREDERICK E. SHERMAN, *Organizing and the Law* (rev. ed.). Washington, D.C.: Bureau of National Affairs, 1971.

SWANN, JAMES P., JR., *NLRB Elections: A Guidebook for Employers*. Washington, D.C.: Bureau of National Affairs, 1980.

TAYLOR, BENJAMIN J., and FRED WITNEY, *Labor Relations Law* (4th ed.). Englewood Cliffs, N.J.: Prentice-Hall, 1983.

WELLINGTON, HARRY H., *Labor and the Legal Process*. New Haven, Conn.: Yale University Press, 1968.

4

Union Behavior: Structure, Government, and Operation

Simplicity does not mark the structure of organized labor in this country. The movement is a complex one, with layers upon layers (some of them important and others inconsequential) of governmental instruments. But this complexity does have a basis that is historically rational. Labor's internal system has emerged only through the years. And it is in fact still undergoing what is at times significant face-lifting as the movement continuously exercises what it has believed to be the winning approach ever since Samuel Gompers pointed the way: doing whatever is felt to be necessary to improve the lot of the American worker, and by whatever means seems to offer the greatest chances of success at the time. The system is, in short, based on pragmatism, and it has consistently attempted to adapt itself to changing conditions as these conditions have arisen.

Given this paramount fact, the reader should hardly be surprised to learn that unionism in this country includes a variety of different functions, levels of authority, and governing practices.

For example, the AFL–CIO is a federation that contains many different sectors exercising different duties and authority. Most of the 160 national or international unions in existence in the United States belong to the federation, although 65 of them, including such mighty ones as the International Brotherhood of Teamsters and the United Mine Workers, do not.[1] National unions, in turn, are themselves subdivided into regions or districts for more efficient management and administration. And although the vast majority of the country's more than 70,000 local unions belong to national unions, the several hundred of them that do not

---

[1] From figures furnished by the Bureau of Labor Statistics, U.S. Department of Labor.

are commonly described as "independent" unions.[2] Finally, some unions are craft in character, others industrial, and some are both craft and industrial.

Because unions are not similar in terms of heritage, size, geographic location, the personalities of their officers, and the kinds of workers who are members, it should be expected that they will differ widely in terms not only of their governments but of their day-to-day operations. Some (perhaps most notably the International Typographical Union, which is unique among unions in having an organized two-party system, and the Newspaper Guild) both before and after Landrum–Griffin have operated very democratically, whereas a few (including most but not all segments of the International Brotherhood of Teamsters) have always maintained a highly autocratic system of internal government. Unions are different in terms of the intensity of their political activities, although events of the past three decades have made virtually all labor organizations conscious of a need to become relatively active in political campaigns and thus in influencing the selection of lawmakers. Some unions have engaged in considerably more "social" activities of the type alluded to in the preceding chapter than have others. Above all, unions vary in terms of their internal rules, dues and initiation fees, and qualifications for membership. Thus, although in the following pages an effort will be made to present a systematic analysis of union behavior, structure, and government, one should recognize that diversity rather than uniformity characterizes the American labor movement. We must be concerned with common principles and trends, but there are many exceptions to them.

THE AFL–CIO

Relationship to National Unions

The decision of the former AFL and CIO to unite forces into a consolidated AFL–CIO in 1955 was made by the affiliated national unions of the two federations; the officers of the AFL and the CIO did not themselves have the power to bring about such a consolidation. This observation demonstrates a very important principle of the structure of the American labor movement—the autonomy of the national unions. The federation can exist only as long as the national unions that belong to it agree to stay in this labor body.

In a sense, the relationship of the national unions to the federation compares closely with the relationship of member nations to the United Nations. No nation *must* belong to the United Nations; any nation *may* withdraw from the international organization at any time and for any reason whatsoever. Nor does the UN have the power to determine the internal government of any of its affiliates, its tax laws, its foreign policy, the size of its military establishment, and similar national specifications. Nations affiliate and remain members of the world body for the advantages that the organization allows in the pursuit of world peace, and for other

---

[2] A number of such "independents" nonetheless belong to the AFL–CIO as federal locals.

purposes, but they continue to exercise absolute sovereignty in the conduct of their own affairs.

The same is true of the relationship of the AFL–CIO to its affiliated national unions. A union belongs to the federation because of the various advantages of affiliation, but the national union is autonomous in the conduct of its own affairs. Each union determines its own collective bargaining program, negotiates its contracts without the aid or intervention of the federation, sets its own level of dues and initiation fees, and may call strikes without any approval from the AFL–CIO; nor, conversely, can the federation prohibit a strike that an affiliated member desires to undertake.

Moreover, the federation cannot force a merger of two of its affiliates that have essentially the same jurisdiction. For example, the International Brotherhood of Electrical Workers of the old AFL and the International Union of Electrical Workers of the old CIO have what strikes the disinterested observer as virtually identical jurisdictions in manufacturing. It may seem logical that these two national unions should merge their forces, and in the process further consolidate with the smaller, independent United Electrical Workers; in fact, all three of these unions have in recent years discussed such a consolidation. To date, however, the conversations have produced no action, and perhaps they never will. As Jerry Wurf, late president of the American Federation of State, County, and Municipal Employees, once observed:

> Mergers and consolidations are, of course, easier to talk about than to bring about. At stake are the bread-and-butter questions that always impede institutional change: What will happen to the elected officers, the paid staff, the local and regional structures, and the assets and traditions to which all unions, meek or mighty, cling? There still would be jobs and titles. But even the most selfless politician (and we labor leaders are, after all, political creatures) often sees himself as peerless when it comes to occupying a union presidency. The power, the payroll, the trappings—these are the real obstacles. . . .[3]

On the other hand, two or even more unions within the AFL–CIO may merge voluntarily if they do desire to do so, and, since 1955, some sixty of them have. Most notable in recent years were the 1969 joining together of four of the five railroad operating brotherhoods into the 220,000-member United Transportation Union, now the largest AFL–CIO affiliate concerned solely with transportation, and the 1979 amalgamation of the Retail Clerks International Union and the Amalgamated Meat Cutters and Butcher Workmen into the 1.2 million-member United Food and Commercial Workers. Consolidations of some importance have also taken place in the past few years in printing, the postal service, chemicals, steel, and textiles.

Steadily rising administrative costs have motivated many of these merger actions; almost half of the federation's ninety-five national unions have fewer than

---

[3] *Washington Post*, October 14, 1973, p. C-1.

50,000 members and thus fall below what AFL–CIO officials have estimated to be the minimum dues-paying base necessary to support effective action. In other cases, technological change or the changing desires of the marketplace have simply made a union obsolete, and the merger becomes a device to provide what Weber has accurately deemed "a decent burial."[4] Examples in this latter category would surely be the Cigar Makers, whose remaining 2,500 members merged with the Retail, Wholesale, and Department Store Workers in 1974, and the Sleeping Car Porters, who disappeared by merger into the Brotherhood of Railway and Airline Clerks four years later.

In still other situations, the growth of the managerial conglomerate—with ownership spanning several different product markets—has been the spur. The Tobacco Workers and Bakery and Confectionery Workers merger and the absorption by the Steelworkers of not only the Mine, Mill, and Smelter Workers but also the Aluminum Workers and District 50 of the Mine Workers can all be explained on this latter basis. The mergers were triggered by a desire to match the bargaining strength of employers whose own boundaries had themselves been significantly expanding. Obviously, such a multifaceted conglomerate as the LTV Corporation (to use only one example), which today controls—among other operations—Jones & Laughlin Steel, Youngstown Sheet and Tube, Kentron International, Lykes Bros. Steamship, Continental–Emsco, and Vought Corporation could not be met on equal terms by narrowly jurisdictioned unionism.

Lately, mergers for all of these reasons have been increasing a bit. Between 1956 and 1982, there were sixty-two mergers involving separate national unions (or, on occasion, independent employee associations); of these sixty-two, ten occurred after 1979. Not all of them involved the AFL–CIO, but the heavy majority did, and some observers of the trend now predict that within another decade the federation will comprise only fifteen to twenty large unions—perhaps one for the communications field, one for retailing, another single union for the metalworker trades, and so on.

It must be stressed again, however, that all mergers under the decentralized AFL–CIO system have been voluntary. The affiliated unions are masters of their own fates, and each of them can pursue its own objectives, conduct its own affairs, and devise what policies and programs it desires to follow without intervention by either the federation or any other national union. Least of all can any outsider compel them to merge.

Enforcement of Federation Rules

The AFL–CIO constitution does, however, contain certain rules of conduct that a national union must respect if it desires to remain a member of the federation. Each affiliate must pay to the federation a per capita tax of 27 cents per member per month. No union may "raid" the membership of any other affiliate, nor may

---

[4] Arnold R. Weber, "Mergers: Union Style," *Wall Street Journal*, May 14, 1979, p. 20.

it be officered by Communists, Fascists, or members of any other totalitarian group. Among other rules, an affiliate is obligated to conduct its affairs without regard to "race, creed, color, national origin, or ancestry." Each affiliate is further expected "to protect the labor movement from any and all corrupt influences."

The practical question immediately arises as to what powers the AFL–CIO may exercise when an affiliated national union does not comply with these and various other rules of the federation. If the AFL–CIO had wide-sweeping powers over the national unions, the federation officers could swiftly compel the errant union to correct its improper conduct. It could still belong to the federation, but its violation of the federation's constitution would be abruptly terminated.

The realities of the situation, however, are such that the federation is not empowered to correct violations by exercise of such power. It can do no more than to suspend or expel a national union that persists in the violation of the federation's constitution.

The expulsion weapon has been used in several instances, but never rashly. Before the AFL–CIO expelled the Teamsters Union, for example, that union was put on notice that it stood in flagrant violation of the anticorruption provision of the federation's constitution. AFL–CIO officials instructed the Teamsters that they would face expulsion unless certain of their national officers were removed and the corrupt practices eliminated. Only when the Teamsters adamantly refused to comply did the AFL–CIO convert the threat into actuality and take the ultimate step of expelling the union from its ranks. And even though the UAW actually withdrew from the AFL–CIO in 1968 (and would not return until 1981) because of its claim that the AFL–CIO was not doing enough in organizational work and had not been militant enough in areas of social affairs, the federation technically expelled the UAW only on the entirely understandable ground that it had refused to pay its per capita dues.

Moreover, as a practical matter, the federation is compelled to use even this amount of authority sparingly and with discretion. The expulsion of the Teamsters was prompted by the corrupt practices of union officers who were highly visible to the public. The AFL–CIO could not tolerate such a situation in the light of the existing public clamor against dishonest union leadership and practices; it was fully aware that the retention of the Teamsters would reflect adversely on *every* affiliated union. One would be naïve, however, to believe that all unions scrupulously adhere to the letter and spirit of each rule incorporated in the federation's constitution. It is, for example, common knowledge that many affiliated unions still discriminate against blacks, although—as has been noted earlier—in recent years progress has been made in eliminating such practices and although certain provisions of the Civil Rights Act of 1964 (which make it unlawful for unions to discriminate because of race, color, or creed) have further helped in this regard. Despite all this improvement, however, some unions still prohibit blacks from joining, fail to represent them fairly and equally in collective bargaining, and otherwise discriminate against them. Such practices, of course, conflict not only with legality but with the AFL–CIO constitutional proscription against racial discrimination. But the federation is faced with a major dilemma under such circumstances: If it were to expel each union found to be in any way discriminating against blacks, the size of the federation would be drastically reduced and its influence as a labor body would be seriously impaired. Indeed, to date no union has been expelled from the federation for racial discrimination; about all the federation officers have done has been to use moral suasion to deal with the problem. Such an approach has not yet been particularly effective in many cases, but to do more than this would jeopardize the entire federation.

Member-union autonomy is also evident from the ease with which national unions have left the federation voluntarily. The peripatetic United Mine Workers well illustrate this situation. After they were expelled from the AFL for spearheading the formation of the CIO through the efforts of their president, John L. Lewis, the Mine Workers became a CIO affiliate when Lewis was elected the latter federation's first president. As part of Lewis's resignation as CIO president following the defeat of Wendell Willkie in 1940, however, the Mine Workers disaffiliated from the CIO and shortly thereafter rejoined the AFL. Yet Lewis *once again* pulled his union out of the AFL, in 1947, after he had attempted to persuade the AFL to pass a resolution to the effect that no union leader should sign the non-Communist affidavit that was then required of union officers by the Taft–Hartley law, and the Mine Workers have continued to be independent to this day.

Nor have the Mine Workers been unique in their actions. Even since 1955, several other affiliates have withdrawn from the AFL–CIO (and, in some cases, returned to it), each time pointing up the fact that the federation has no power whatsoever to force any of its affiliates to remain in its ranks.

Why, then *do* most national unions seek to belong to the federation? What do they get for their per capita tax money?

Advantages of Affiliation

By far the chief benefit associated with membership is protection against "raiding." One provision of the AFL–CIO constitution states that "each such affiliate shall respect the established collective bargaining relationship of every other affiliate and no affiliate shall raid the established collective bargaining relationship of any other affiliate." This means that once an affiliated union gains bargaining rights in a company, no other union affiliated with the federation may attempt to dislodge the established union and place itself in the plant. Such a stricture frees unions from the task of fighting off raids from sister unions of the federation. Time and money conserved in this way can be used to organize the unorganized or devoted to other union programs. Unions that violate the no-raiding provision of the constitution may realistically expect to be expelled from the AFL–CIO; and because mutual self-interest of all members is involved, the amount of raiding has in fact decreased sharply since the formation of the federation.

Thus, before a union withdraws voluntarily from the AFL–CIO or engages in conduct that could result in expulsion, the officers of the union must weigh the consequences of operating outside the federation as these consequences concern proneness to raiding. Such considerations have been particularly influential in maintaining AFL–CIO membership for most smaller and weaker nationals, whom protection against raids benefits to a greater degree than it does larger national unions. But considerations of the money, time, and energy involved in counter-attacking raiding attempts have also convinced most larger nationals of the wisdom of continued federation membership.

Federation membership involves still other advantages. With the federation as the spearhead, the union movement has comparatively more power in the po-litical and legislative affairs of the nation—a particularly influential consideration, given the thrust of the laws today—and labor's impact upon elections and congres-sional voting is correspondingly greater than if each national union went its own way. In addition, by coordinating political efforts, the federation can use union funds, and such other sources of political persuasion as letter-writing campaigns, more effectively. Moreover, the AFL–CIO helps national unions in organizing campaigns, although the nationals are expected to bear the chief responsibility for new organization. And affiliated national unions also receive some help from the federation in the areas of legal services, educational programs, research, and social activities.

On the other hand, in the best tradition of Gompers, the federation does not negotiate labor agreements for the affiliated national unions. It is not equipped to render such services; nor do the autonomous national unions desire such inter-vention. In only one way does a national union directly benefit on the collective bargaining front from its membership in the federation: A framework is provided whereby unions that bargain in the same industry or with the same company can consolidate their efforts. A large company such as General Electric, for example, bargains with many different unions, and affiliated unions that deal with General Electric can thus more easily adopt common collective bargaining goals (such as uniform expiration dates of labor agreements and the attainment of similar eco-nomic benefits) than would be the case without the availability of federation co-ordination; the joint 1966, 1969, 1973, 1976, 1979, and 1982 bargaining endeavors of (in most of these years) eleven major unions with General Electric (and sub-sequently with Westinghouse) were in fact conducted under AFL–CIO auspices, through the coordinating efforts of the federation's increasingly active Industrial Union Department, and this has been true of several other joint union efforts, which are summarized in the next chapter under "Coordinated Bargaining."

Structure and Government of the AFL–CIO

As the chart on page 146 indicates, the supreme governing body of the federation is its *convention*, held once every two years. Each national union, regardless of size, may send one delegate to the convention, and unions with more than 4,000 members may send additional delegates in proportion to their size. Each national

STRUCTURAL ORGANIZATION OF THE AFL–CIO

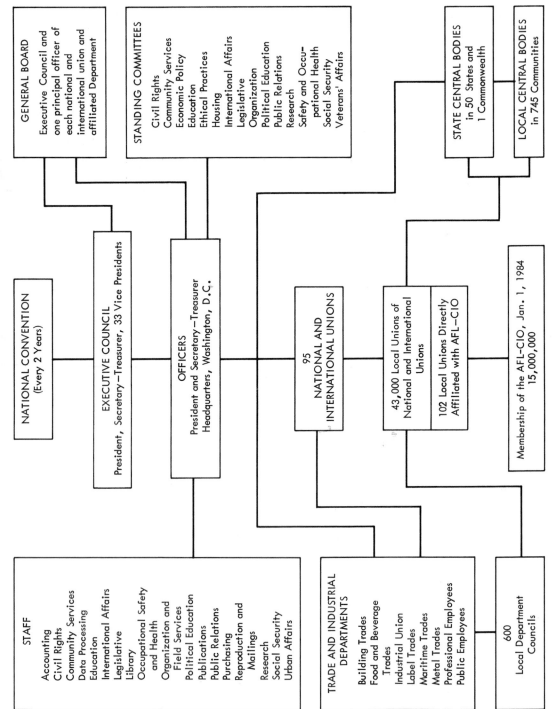

GENERAL BOARD

Executive Council and one principal officer of each national and international union and affiliated Department

STANDING COMMITTEES

Civil Rights
Community Services
Economic Policy
Education
Ethical Practices
Housing
International Affairs
Legislative
Organization
Political Education
Public Relations
Research
Safety and Occu-
pational Health
Social Security
Veterans' Affairs

STATE CENTRAL BODIES
in 50 States and
1 Commonwealth

LOCAL CENTRAL BODIES
in 745 Communities

NATIONAL CONVENTION
(Every 2 Years)

EXECUTIVE COUNCIL
President, Secretary–Treasurer, 33 Vice Presidents

OFFICERS
President and Secretary–Treasurer
Headquarters, Washington, D.C.

95
**NATIONAL AND
INTERNATIONAL UNIONS**

43,000 Local Unions of
National and International
Unions

102 Local Unions Directly
Affiliated with AFL–CIO

Membership of the AFL–CIO, Jan. 1, 1984
15,000,000

STAFF

Accounting
Civil Rights
Community Services
Data Processing
Education
International Affairs
Legislative
Library
Occupational Safety
and Health
Organization and
Field Services
Political Education
Publications
Public Relations
Purchasing
Reproduction and
Mailings
Research
Social Security
Urban Affairs

**TRADE AND INDUSTRIAL
DEPARTMENTS**

Building Trades
Food and Beverage
Trades
Industrial Union
Label Trades
Maritime Trades
Metal Trades
Professional Employees
Public Employees

600
Local Department
Councils

union delegate casts one vote for every member represented, an arrangement that allows larger unions, such as the Steelworkers and Automobile Workers, more influence in the affairs of the convention.

Financial expenses of the delegates are defrayed by their individual national unions and not by the federation. Such expenses can at times be quite high and may even dissuade nationals from sending their full quotas of delegates; the convention lasts two weeks, is held in first-rate hotels in a major city, and often involves considerable travel.

The convention reflects any convention of any large group. Federation officers are elected; amendments to the AFL–CIO constitution are proposed and at times adopted; committee reports are rendered; internal policies of the federation are deliberated and at times changed; and countless resolutions, ranging from purely trade-union affairs to such weighty topics as U.S. foreign policy, are voted upon. There are speakers and more speakers. Delegates must be able to sit for long periods and be capable of absorbing rhetoric that is, while occasionally inspirational, far more often soporific.

The decisions and policies adopted by the convention are implemented by the AFL–CIO *executive council,* composed of the president, secretary–treasurer, and thirty-three vice presidents of the federation. The vice presidents are elected at the convention and are usually selected from the presidents of the major affiliated national unions, although the 5,000-member Sleeping Car Porters (until its afore-mentioned 1978 disappearance by merger into the Brotherhood of Railway and Airline Clerks) constituted a notable exception in this regard—primarily because of the personal respect in which its black president, A. Philip Randolph, was held. Only the president of the federation and its secretary–treasurer devote full time to the affairs of the organization, however; the vice presidents meet with the executive council at least three times a year but remain as presidents of their own national unions.

Among its chief duties, the executive council interprets and applies the federation constitution; plays a "watchdog" role in legislative matters that affect the interests of workers and unions; assembles, through a full-time staff of legal and economic experts, the data needed for testimony before congressional committees; keeps in contact with the many federal agencies that have authority in the labor field; and ensures that the federation is kept free from corrupt or Communistic influences. If it suspects that a union or its officers are in violation of the federation's constitution, it may investigate the matter, and if it finds that the charges are valid, it may, by a two-thirds majority, vote to suspend the guilty union. It may also recommend the ultimate penalty of expulsion of the union, but only the full convention may actually expel the union from the federation.

The executive council also selects six of its membership who, along with the AFL–CIO president and secretary–treasurer, constitute the federation's *executive committee.* This smaller group meets every two months and has the major function of advising and counseling the president and secretary–treasurer on issues involving the federation and its policies. Only the president and the secretary–treasurer receive a salary for their duties—$110,000 and $90,000 per year, respectively. All other federation officers serve without salary, although they are compensated for their expenses when attending to federation business.

A fourth decision-making body within the federation is the AFL–CIO *general board,* which consists of all members of the executive council and one principal officer of each of the national unions and the affiliated departments (to be described below). Usually, the affiliated national union designates its chief officer as its representative to serve on the general board, which must meet at least once a year and may meet more often at the discretion of the federation's president. Its chief duty is to rule on all questions and issues referred to it by the executive council.

The federation constitution also requires that the president appoint a number of *standing committees,* and AFL–CIO custom dictates that each committee chairman be president of a national union and that all members be active trade unionists. At present, such committees (which are in all cases supplied with full-time professional staffs) deal with such issues as civil rights, community services, economic policy, education, ethical practices, housing, international affairs, legislation, organization, political education, public relations, research, safety and occupational health, Social Security, and veterans' affairs. The federation's growing scope of interests is illustrated by the character of these committees, some of which are relatively new and virtually all of which clearly extend well beyond strictly trade union affairs.

Eight constitutional departments, trade and industrial groupings for unions with strong common interests, are currently in existence: Building Trades, Industrial Union, Maritime Trades, Metal Trades, Union Label and Service Trades, and—most recently—Professional Employees, Public Employees, and Food and Beverage Trades. National unions may belong to more than one of these departments, and many of them with memberships in two or more areas of interest do exactly that (for example, the International Brotherhood of Electrical Workers, with some members who work in the building trades and others who work in factories), but in each case the national is required to pay to the respective department a per capita tax based on the number of its members whose occupations or jobs fall under the department's jurisdiction. These dues are in addition to those the national union pays as a condition of belonging to the AFL–CIO.

Each department is concerned with problems of its particular industry. Such problems can involve collective bargaining issues, new organizational drives, legislative matters, or more specialized areas with which the unions of a particular branch of industry are uniquely confronted. The Union Label and Service Trades Department, for example, has as its primary objective the education of the consuming public with regard to the desirability of purchasing union-made goods. It is composed of all AFL–CIO affiliates that stress use of a union label to show that union members produced the product; to many union members, and to many suporters of unionism also, such a label is particularly persuasive before a purchase is made. (Exhibit 4-1 shows one effort of this AFL–CIO unit.)

EXHIBIT 4-1

Courtesy of Union, Label and Service Trades Department, AFL–CIO

State and City Bodies

Even though most of the activities of the AFL–CIO are centered in Washington, the federation has also established state and city bodies to deal with problems at the state and municipal levels. There are now state bodies in each of the fifty states and one in Puerto Rico; and, on the city level, the federation has created city centrals in some 745 communities.

Note that these state and city central bodies are established *directly* by the AFL–CIO; they are not created by the national unions affiliated with the federation or by local unions that belong to these national unions. Local unions that belong to national unions affiliated with the AFL–CIO may join a state or a city central body, but the national union must be affiliated with the AFL–CIO; and should a national union be expelled from or withdraw voluntarily from the federation, its local unions lose membership in the state and city central bodies. Thus, when the Teamsters Union was expelled from the AFL–CIO, the locals of this union were likewise expelled from the state and city bodies.

Similar to the AFL–CIO, also, the state and city bodies have no executive power over their affiliated unions. They do not engage in collective bargaining, call or forbid strikes, or regulate the internal affairs of their affiliated local unions. Instead, the chief concern of the state and city bodies is political and educational activities. They lobby for or against legislation, offer testimony before state legislative committees, and promote political candidates favored by organized labor. Almost all state organizations now hold schools for representatives of their affiliated unions—the classes being taught by union officials, university instructors, government officials, and, on some occasions, representatives of the business community. The city bodies, in addition to participating in similar legislative and educational activities, engage in a wide variety of community service work—promoting the United Way, Red Cross, and similar community projects, among other endeavors. In many cities and towns, such bodies have sponsored Boy Scout troops and Little League baseball teams, as well as art institutes, musical events, day-care centers for children of working mothers, and even the purchase of Seeing-Eye dogs for blind people. Although genuine altruism doubtless motivates many of these good deeds, so, too, does the need for an improved public image which is today so keenly felt by many unionists.

Functions and Problems of the Federation

For all that the AFL–CIO voluntarily abstains from doing so or is restricted by its constitution from attempting, there can be no denying the aggressiveness with which the federation pursues the activities it does undertake. In the political arena, this is particularly true. As do most other major interest groups in the United States, the federation now employs a large corps of full-time lobbyists whose mission is to exert pressure upon members of Congress to support legislation favored by the AFL–CIO and to oppose those bills the federation regards as undesirable. Its principal officers themselves frequently testify before congressional committees and make public declarations of federation political policies. And, by its very dimensions, the federation provides a powerful sounding board for all of organized labor. Ostensibly, when the president of the AFL–CIO speaks, he represents some 15 million union members and their families, 95 national unions, 43,000 local unions, 51 state federations, and over 700 citywide labor bodies. No other labor leader can claim as much attention and exert as much influence. He and other important federation officials are from time to time invited to the White House and are regularly invited by U.S. senators, congressmen, and heads of major federal agencies dealing with labor matters to specify labor's position on vital issues of the day. It is doubtful that representatives of any other interest group make as many appearances at the nation's presidential residence as do members of the AFL–CIO high command.

At times of federal and state elections, the federation's role is equally important. The federation has created a Committee on Political Education (COPE) that coordinates the political action of organized labor during such periods. This political arm of the federation operates at the national, state, and local levels, where (since the Taft–Hartley law, as we know, forbids unions to contribute union dues to political candidates) it raises money on a voluntary basis from union members through so-called "political action committees." Some of this money is given directly to political candidates who are regarded as friends of organized labor; the rest is expended for radio and TV programs of a political nature, the publication of voting records of candidates who have previously served in elective offices, the distribution of campaign literature, and kindred activities.

It is difficult to assess exactly how effective the federation has been in the political arena, since both successes and failures are amply in evidence. In 1980, for example, an estimated 44 percent of all union members voted for Ronald Reagan, whose candidacy was about as welcome to the bulk of the AFL–CIO leaders as Martin Luther King's would have been to the Ku Klux Klan.[5] On the other hand, between 60 and 70 percent of all COPE-endorsed congressional candidates (approximately 400 of them in most recent election years) have been victorious in each biennial election over the past decade, and for many of these candidates labor's support was a critical factor. Certainly, the federation has been sufficiently encouraged by the results to continue to play an active political role.

COPE, under any conditions, has never thought small. It was responsible for most of the $20 million that labor as a whole pumped into the 1982 campaign, through some 350 political action committees, for example, and in election years it can regularly be counted on in the 1980s to recruit as many as 125,000 volunteers to work in community political activities. The federation estimates that such volunteers in each of these elections have placed over 10 million telephone calls from their more than 20,000 telephones (operating at COPE offices, local union and council offices, and the private homes of union members) during registration and get-out-the-vote campaigns, and have distributed hundreds of COPE films. COPE activity nowadays is, in short, something that neither its friends nor its foes can ignore. (Exhibit 4-2 shows one of COPE's many efforts.)

The political objectives of organized labor and the federation are varied in character. The AFL–CIO supports legislation that strengthens the role of organized labor in collective bargaining, organizational drives, the strike, picketing, and boycotting. To these ends, the federation has, for example, consistently advocated such measures as the repeal of state "right-to-work" legislation and has lobbied for other changes in the federal and state laws that would strengthen the use of such union self-help methods as boycotts and picketing in labor's direct relationship

---

[5] A slight irony to this is the fact that Reagan was the first U.S. chief executive who was at one time a union president. He was head of the Screen Actors Guild from 1947 to 1952 and again in 1959.

EXHIBIT 4-2

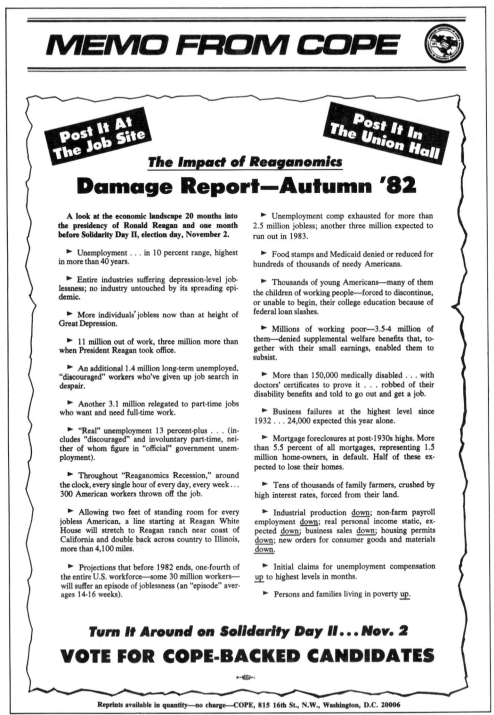

MEMO FROM COPE

Post It At The Job Site

Post It In The Union Hall

The Impact of Reaganomics
Damage Report—Autumn '82

A look at the economic landscape 20 months into the presidency of Ronald Reagan and one month before Solidarity Day II, election day, November 2.

► Unemployment . . . in 10 percent range, highest in more than 40 years.

► Entire industries suffering depression-level joblessness; no industry untouched by its spreading epidemic.

► More individuals' jobless now than at height of Great Depression.

► 11 million out of work, three million more than when President Reagan took office.

► An additional 1.4 million long-term unemployed, "discouraged" workers who've given up job search in despair.

► Another 3.1 million relegated to part-time jobs who want and need full-time work.

► "Real" unemployment 13 percent-plus . . . (includes "discouraged" and involuntary part-time, neither of whom figure in "official" government unemployment).

► Throughout "Reaganomics Recession," around the clock, every single hour of every day, every week . . . 300 American workers thrown off the job.

► Allowing two feet of standing room for every jobless American, a line starting at Reagan White House will stretch to Reagan ranch near coast of California and double back across country to Illinois, more than 4,100 miles.

► Projections that before 1982 ends, one-fourth of the entire U.S. workforce—some 30 million workers—will suffer an episode of joblessness (an "episode" averages 14-16 weeks).

► Unemployment comp exhausted for more than 2.5 million jobless; another three million expected to run out in 1983.

► Food stamps and Medicaid denied or reduced for hundreds of thousands of needy Americans.

► Thousands of young Americans—many of them the children of working people—forced to discontinue, or unable to begin, their college education because of federal loan slashes.

► Millions of working poor—3.5-4 million of them—denied supplemental welfare benefits that, together with their small earnings, enabled them to subsist.

► More than 150,000 medically disabled . . . with doctors' certificates to prove it . . . robbed of their disability benefits and told to go out and get a job.

► Business failures at the highest level since 1932 . . . 24,000 expected this year alone.

► Mortgage foreclosures at post-1930s highs. More than 5.5 percent of all mortgages, representing 1.5 million home-owners, in default. Half of these expected to lose their homes.

► Tens of thousands of family farmers, crushed by high interest rates, forced from their land.

► Industrial production <u>down</u>; non-farm payroll employment <u>down</u>; real personal income static, expected <u>down</u>; business sales <u>down</u>; housing permits <u>down</u>; new orders for consumer goods and materials <u>down</u>.

► Initial claims for unemployment compensation <u>up</u> to highest levels in months.

► Persons and families living in poverty <u>up</u>.

Turn It Around on Solidarity Day II . . . Nov. 2
VOTE FOR COPE-BACKED CANDIDATES

Reprints available in quantity—no charge—COPE, 815 16th St., N.W., Washington, D.C. 20006

AFL–CIO News, Oct. 2, 1982, pp. 11–12.

with business. It has also, however, regularly supported such bills as those favoring national health insurance, low-cost public housing, liberalized minimum-wage laws, more comprehensive unemployment-compensation statutes, and more effective public education—all of which measures are intended to benefit all the workers of the nation and their families, rather than strictly those within the ranks of unionism. The AFL–CIO today fully recognizes that many of these less parochial objectives cannot be achieved through face-to-face union–management collective bargaining and has consequently supported such measures as the ones cited to gain additional leverage in its efforts to improve the status of the American wage earner.

Beyond the legislative and political function, the federation carries out a massive research program—the results of which are embodied in its regular publications, above all the weekly *AFL–CIO News,* as well as in special bulletins, briefs for the courts of the nation, and a series of pamphlets, monographs, and books. Through these varied publications, the federation tries to keep union members and others abreast of labor developments from the union point of view.

Another important function is that of promoting new organizations. Although the basic responsibility for such new organizations falls upon national unions, the federation also organizes on its own and helps affiliated unions in their organizational drives. When the AFL–CIO organizes a union by itself, it charters such a local union directly with the federation in much the same fashion that the old AFL did in the 1930s. There are 102 such directly affiliated labor unions now in existence, and through its field officers the AFL–CIO bargains contracts for these local unions and aids them in time of strikes and other difficulties with management. In return, members of such locals pay dues directly to the AFL–CIO. This collective bargaining function for directly affiliated local unions should not, however, be confused with the principle already established: The AFL–CIO does not bargain collectively for affiliated national unions or for locals that belong to such affiliated national unions. Moreover, most of these directly affiliated local unions are themselves ultimately assigned by the federation to a national union that has appropriate jurisdiction over the jobs and occupations of its members.

In recent years, the American labor movement has also demonstrated increasing concern with the labor movement in foreign nations. Two major factors lie behind this development. In the first place, the increasing tempo of international trade, now increasingly also tied into the rise of the "multinational," has threatened the job security and welfare of American workers. The impact in the United States of products produced by foreign labor under conditions of comparatively lower wages and poorer working conditions makes it more difficult for American unions to retain benefits already secured and to obtain improvements in them. American unions understand full well that benefits secured in their contracts are placed in jeopardy because of such competition from low-wage foreign nations. Hence, by strengthening the foreign labor movement, American unions not only improve the status of workers within foreign nations but at the same time protect the advances that have been gained through collective bargaining in this country.

The second reason concerns the threat of Communist domination of foreign labor movements and, through this tactic, the possible seizure of the governments of foreign nations by Communists. Even in the United States, as Chapter 2 has demonstrated, organized labor has been faced with such a threat, although in this country it has been successfully surmounted. The 1949–1950 expulsion from the CIO of the several Communist-controlled unions, and the establishment of new unions to take over the membership of such unions, dealt a telling blow to Communism's influence on the American labor movement. The AFL, too, when it was the only federation in the nation, waged a continuous and bitter battle against the left and managed to maintain its basically conservative philosophy and objectives. There are today only a handful of American labor unions, all of them relatively minor in strategic power (for example, the Furriers Union and, as noted earlier, the United Electrical Workers), that are even remotely believed to be dominated by Communists. But the problem is much more severe in foreign lands: In such nations as Italy and France, Communistic elements do have considerable influence on the affairs of the labor movements. And the important officers of America's labor movement, well schooled in the potential consequences of Communism, believe with considerable justification that should such totalitarianism spread to the governments of these countries, the first casualties would be the free labor movement, collective bargaining, and the right to strike. For such reasons, the AFL–CIO works hard to help foreign trade unions remain free from Communist domination.

Critics currently charge the AFL–CIO with being "isolationistic"—because it was highly instrumental in persuading the United States to withdraw from the International Labor Organization in 1977 (although it was also instrumental in the U.S. decision to rejoin the ILO three years later) and because it also pulled out of the International Confederation of Free Trade Unions in 1969 (although it rejoined the latter in 1982), in both cases primarily because of a belief that Soviet-dominated worker organizations were unduly influencing these bodies. But the charge thus has little validity.

The federation and its affiliates contribute considerable monies to aid in the organization of foreign workers, the training of foreign labor leaders, the education of foreign union members, and the promotion of a variety of similar activities. In addition, the AFL–CIO has representation on various committees of the United Nations, hosts many visiting labor delegates from foreign nations who are sent by their governments or by higher trade-union bodies in their respective nations, and even on frequent occasions itself finances the trips of these foreign labor leaders. The AFL–CIO and many of its affiliated national unions have also financed trips of their own representatives to foreign lands to see at first hand the problems of other labor movements.

Conflict Between Craft and Industrial Unions

If the main benefit associated with federation membership is protection against raiding, one of the major problems of the AFL–CIO has been that of maintaining peace between affiliated unions in their jurisdictional disputes over jobs. Frequently, craft unions (formerly, for the most part, AFL affiliates) and industrial unions (CIO members when the two groups were separate ones) have battled each other avidly over such jurisdiction, particularly in establishments where an industrial union holds bargaining rights but where some jobs could be carried out more efficiently by members of a craft union. Such jobs as those involving the routine maintenance of machinery or other equipment, the major overhaul or installation of equipment, and the construction of new facilities often fall into this category.

What could spark a conflict is the desire of members of craft unions whose members are not employees of the industrial company to do the work that is being performed by the skilled tradesmen on the payroll of the factory. At times, employers find it cheaper to hire these outside craftsmen to perform the work and therefore seek out contractor–employers who control such skilled employees. On other occasions, a skilled-trade union, through a contractor–employer, makes overtures to the industrial employer. However, the problem could also arise from the other direction. That is, the industrial employer may have customarily subcontracted certain maintenance work to outside skilled tradesmen. To secure this work for its own membership, the industrial union that holds bargaining rights in the factory puts pressure upon the employer to cease this practice and to award the work to the employer's own employees who are, of course, members of the industrial union. It is not difficult to understand that when jobs are scarce, the conflict between craft and industrial unions can achieve major dimensions.

Indeed, the problem became so serious in the recession-marked first months of the 1960s that many observers predicted the imminent collapse of the entire federation through craft–industrial warfare. Remarkably, however, the important leaders of the craft and industrial unions were able to arrive at a workable solution to the problem at the 1961 AFL–CIO convention and thereby rescue the federation from such a collapse. They adopted an "Internal Disputes Plan," often also referred to as the "Live and Let Live" plan, and incorporated it into the constitution of the AFL–CIO. More technically, the constitutional amendment officially preserved the integrity of past practices in work assignments. Henceforth a union's right to jobs would depend on what relevant customs or practices had been in force where it sought such jobs. If the members of an industrial union had held jurisdiction over new construction in the past, this customary work assignment would be respected by craft unions. If an employer had customarily subcontracted out maintenance work, this practice was to be respected by industrial unions, who were not to put pressure upon employers to change it.

An elaborate procedure has been adopted to implement this new constitutional provision. In the event that a union charges that another union is violating the terms of the new policy, the AFL–CIO assigns a federation official to mediate the dispute. If this effort fails, an impartial umpire is appointed to make an award. Once the umpire hands down the decision, the rival union is expected to abide by the award. However, the losing union has the right to appeal to a three-person subcommittee of the AFL–CIO executive council. This subcommittee may disallow the appeal, in which event the umpire's decision is final and there is no other appeal procedure. But if the subcommittee is not fully satisfied with the umpire's award, it may refer the case to the entire executive council, which will decide the issue by majority vote. The council may uphold the award, reverse it, or modify it. In any event, however, the executive council's decision is final and binding on the unions involved in the dispute.

If a union fails to comply with the decision rendered through this procedure, the amendment to the constitution provides that the federation may impose sanctions on the noncomplying union, and if the violation persists, the union can be expelled from the federation.

In the many years since the Internal Disputes Plan was implemented, noncompliance has been all but nonexistent. Of the first 2,200 complaints filed with the AFL–CIO president's office, in only 26 cases (involving fifteen unions) did affiliates even initially fail to heed the decisions of the umpire or directions of the subcommittee, and even in most of these instances compliance was later achieved. The threat of sanctions (preventing the penalized union from using all AFL–CIO services and facilities including the filing of charges to protest that *its* customary job jurisdiction is being violated by another union) appears to have been a potent weapon. No union has ever been expelled for a continuing violation.

And it is safe to say, accordingly, that the craft–industrial conflict, once one that threatened disaster for the labor movement, has now been satisfactorily resolved. The AFL–CIO, with this conflict basically behind it, will undoubtedly continue to exist as a permanent federation in the United States, and this can only be advantageous, since—from the viewpoint of stability in industrial relations—the preservation of the federation is a public necessity.

THE NATIONAL UNION

Relationship to Locals

If the national union is quite autonomous in the conduct of its affairs, the story is quite different when one examines the relationship between the national union and its local unions. Although there are many exceptions, most national unions exercise considerable power over their locals. Before a local union may strike, it must normally obtain the permission of the national union. And, should the local union strike in defiance of national union instructions, the national union can withhold strike benefits, refuse to give the local union any other form of aid during the strike, and in extreme cases even taken over the local on a trusteeship basis. In addition, consistent with the regulations of many national unions, all local collective bargaining contracts must be reviewed by the national officers before they may be put into force. All national union constitutions today contain provisions that establish standards of conduct and procedures for the internal operation of their constituent locals—usually, the dues that the locals may charge, the method by which their officers may be elected and their tenures of office, the procedures for the discipline of local union members, the conduct of union meetings, and other rules of this kind.

Violation of these national union standards can result in sanctions placed upon the local union officers and on the local union itself. Recently, for example, many national unions have been at least as conscious of the problem of racial discrimination within the union movement as has the AFL–CIO, and almost all national constitutions now contain a nondiscriminatory clause, designed to guarantee blacks equal and fair treatment from the local unions. Several local unions have been seized by their nationals when they have discriminated against blacks through such mechanisms as providing segregated local union facilities or when they have failed to afford blacks equal protection in the negotiation of labor agreements or in the grievance procedure.

In addition, within the collective bargaining process, the national union is currently exercising considerably greater control and influence over the contracts that locals negotiate. This is particularly true when the members of the locals work for companies that sell their products in national product markets—an ever-increasing number. Nationals desire that companies over whose employees they have jurisdiction and that compete in national product markets operate under common labor-cost standards. They are less likely to exercise control over the unions whose members produce for local markets—for example, in the construction industry, because the labor costs involved in the construction of a building in one city do not directly compete with those affecting the construction of a building in another.

Service in Collective Bargaining

The national exercises much of its influence over the local in the direct collective bargaining process through the service that the national union provides its locals in the negotiation of labor agreements. To understand this national–local relationship, however, one should not regard the negotiation service of the national union as a function that is performed against the will of the local union. On the contrary, local unions not only generally desire and expect the help of the national union when they negotiate labor agreements with the employer, but should the national union either refuse to provide these services or perform them in an ineffective way, the local union members and their officers can be counted upon to be sharply critical of the national union. The officers of the national could safely assume, in fact, that such a disgruntled local union would attempt to take political reprisal against the officers of the national in the next election of national officers.

The chief reason for the local union's desire for help from the national union in collective bargaining involves the complexities of the contemporary collective bargaining process. As will be made more evident in future chapters, many of the issues of collective bargaining have become increasingly intricate. Most contracts focus upon such involved items as adjustment to technological change, pension plans, insurance programs, supplementary unemployment benefit plans, job evaluation, production standards, subcontracting, and complicated wage incentive programs. Beyond the complex character of the issues, moreover, the modern process is obviously made more difficult because of the character of the laws of labor relations. In short, it takes an expert to negotiate under current circumstances.

For effective representation, it is necessary to find people who are knowledgeable and experienced and have a professional understanding of the collective bargaining process; few local unions are fortunate enough to include such people in their membership. Each local union elects a negotiating committee, but the members of such committees are typically employed in the plant and work full time on their jobs. They simply do not have the opportunity to keep abreast of current developments in collective bargaining and to make a searching study of the problems involved in the negotiation of the difficult issues. On the company side, moreover, there are normally management representatives who are well trained and equipped to handle the contemporary collective bargaining negotiation. Many of them have received special training in labor relations (although most avoid living up to Ambrose Bierce's definition of *specialist,* "one who knows everything about something and nothing about anything else"), and some devote full time to the problems of negotiation and administration of collective bargaining contracts.

Indeed, without the services of the national union, there would be a sharp disparity of negotiating talent at the bargaining table. In this light, it is easy to understand why the local union does not regard the intervention of the national union at the bargaining table as an invasion of the rights of the local, but rather views this service as indispensable to the effective negotiation of the labor agreement.

Most national unions have well-qualified people to render this service: the so-called staff representatives, who devote full time to union affairs. They are hired by the national union, paid salaries and expenses for their work, and expected to provide services to the local unions of the national. All of them are union members, and they normally reach their position of staff representative by having demonstrated their ability as union members and local union officers. They are not, however, elected to their jobs but are hired because of their special talents.

Although the staff representatives perform a variety of duties, such as organizing new plants, engaging in political-action work at times of federal and state elections, directing strikes, and representing the union and its members before the federal and state labor agencies, helping the local unions to negotiate labor agreements constitutes one of their primary functions.[6] Staff representatives gain much bargaining experience because they normally service several local unions, and in the course of one year they may be called upon to negotiate many different labor agreements, thus gaining on-the-job training that serves as an invaluable asset to them when they confront a specific management at the bargaining table. Many national unions also send their staff representatives to special schools, some of which are held on university campuses and are taught by specialists in the labor education field, for additional training. Moreover, the staff representative is invariably backed up by experts within the national union. Almost every national union has several departments that concentrate on the major issues involved in collective bargaining. For example, the United Automobile Workers has depart-

[6] A major exception to all these remarks involves craft unions in local product market industries; here, local business agents are normally elected to perform such duties.

ments that deal with pensions, wage systems, insurance, and other critical areas. The specialists assigned to these national departments may be freely called upon by the staff representatives, should their services be needed.

The Regional or District Office

Staff representatives may work out of the headquarters of the national union, but more frequently they are assigned to a regional or district office. Almost every national union divides the nation into regions or districts, and locals of the national union that are located in the geographical area or the district obtain services from their respective district offices. For example, District 30 of the United Steelworkers of America, headquartered in Indianapolis, covers most of Indiana and Kentucky and is administered by a district director elected by the local unions of the district. About twenty staff representatives are assigned by the national union to District 30 and work under the immediate supervision of the district director.

Each staff representative services about seven local unions. The representative attends the local union meetings, works closely with the negotiating committees, hears the problems of the workers in the plant in which the local holds control, and attempts to understand the values and objectives of the members. The representative is the liaison between the national and the local union, and in this capacity can do much to influence the local in the acceptance of national union collective bargaining policies. In such a capacity, moreover, the staff representative can serve as a mediator between local unions and the national when differences arise between them.

A good staff representative wins the confidence of local officers and members, and the local union will thus rely heavily upon this individual's counsel in collective bargaining matters. The representative can exert great influence upon the local to reject or accept the last offer of an employer. Indeed, frequently this person can provoke a strike or prevent one by the way in which he or she reports to the local union and makes recommendations to the members. The representative is, in short, often in an excellent position to influence the decision-making process in collective bargaining.

Multiemployer Bargaining

Although most multiemployer bargaining is in relatively small bargaining units in local-product markets, at times national unions bargain with employers on a multiemployer basis. That is, a group of managements band together as a unit to negotiate with the national union. Employers find this structure of collective bargaining valuable because it prevents a given union from "whipsawing" each employer: Usually, under a multiemployer bargaining structure, each employer is comparatively small in size and unimpressive in financial resources, and the companies compete fiercely in the product market; in the absence of multiemployer collective bargaining, the union could pick off one employer at a time. Such employer-association–national-union collective bargaining is found in industries such as clothing, coal, and shipping—all of which contain large measures of the unstabilizing factors noted.

When multiemployer collective bargaining exists and where the product market is not a local one, the national officers themselves typically bargain for the contract, and the local unions play a comparatively passive role—a situation that also holds at the other extreme, when unions bargain with industrial giants of the nation (such as General Motors and United States Steel). The national unions negotiate the agreement in the latter instance, since no one local union could possibly measure up to the strength of these companies. Bargaining logic dictates that in both cases, the national union rather than the local union play the paramount labor relations role.

Additional National Union Services

Beyond providing considerable help in the negotiating of labor agreements, the national union renders other valuable services to its local unions. The national usually awards benefits to employees on strike, although the actual amount of money paid in strike benefits is invariably modest: Approximately $75 weekly (usually awarded to strikers with a minimum number of dependents, with other strikers getting less) constitutes the ultimate in union largesse and even it, of course, is dispatched only until the strike fund is exhausted. More important, the national union intervenes with the strikers' creditors so that the automobiles, furniture, and other holdings of the union members will not be repossessed. And it ensures that no striking employee or his or her family goes hungry, even if this guarantee involves the actual distribution of food to the strikers. Management should be aware that unions in these days do not lose strikes because of hunger or unpaid bills. If there are insurance premiums to be paid, doctors to see, rent to be paid, or school tuition to be met, the national unions will see to it that the worker does not suffer. This is true despite the obvious fact that the national unions themselves have financial limitations, for virtually all nationals do under normal circumstances have the resources to assure that the minimum physiological needs of their member–workers are met, and many larger unions are quite amply financed. The Automobile Workers, for example, paid out over $160 million in strike benefits during a sixty-seven-day 1970 General Motors strike.[7] In addition, if a national union does run out of money, labor custom dictates that other national unions will lend it money to finance the strike.[8]

---

[7] Some of this money went to liquor stores. In Michigan, where 170,000 strikers lived, liquor sales increased 4 percent in the first week of the strike. And as the manager of the state Liquor Control Commission told the *Detroit Free Press* (according to William Serrin, in *The Company and the Union*, New York: Vintage, 1974, pp. 187–88), "the history of major strikes seems to be that right at the start the men get paint and materials to fix their houses and buy a few extra jugs . . . it's probably just an expression of relief from the daily grind."

[8] In this regard, it should also be appreciated that striking workers usually have income sources beyond the aid that they might receive from their own union. Some get welfare payments. Some have working spouses and/or they themselves can rather easily find full-time or part-time jobs. In two states—New York and Rhode Island—strikers are eligible for unemployment compensation. And while it can hardly be called an income source, the fact that this is, in addition, the age of widespread charge accounts must also be placed into the equation.

The national union also aids the locals in the grievance procedure and in arbitration, both of which subjects will be discussed in detail in Chapter 6. Normally, the staff representative represents the local in the last step of the grievance procedure. Along with the local union grievance committee, the staff representative attempts to settle the grievance to the satisfaction of the complaining worker, and if the case does ultimately go to arbitration, he or she usually directly represents the grievant. In general, whether they win or lose their arbitration cases, staff representatives present the union's case very effectively. This fact is often offered by labor leaders as one reason why unions employ lawyers less frequently than do employers when cases go to arbitration. There is no need to incur the expense if the staff representative can do the job as competently as an attorney.

Of course, at times local unions *are* in need of an attorney, as when the local union has a case that requires testimony in the courts. For example, employers may sue a union for breach of contract, or workers may be indicted because of violence in picketing. When attorneys are needed, the local union can normally obtain the services of the national union's legal staff, whose members, although invariably paid less than comparable lawyers who work for corporations, are frequently highly competent and usually quite dedicated to the union movement. Several prominent attorneys, Clarence Darrow most notably, made their mark by representing labor organizations.

The fact that the local does so readily receive such services from its national constitutes the reason why the vast majority of local unions belong to a national union. Indeed, less than 2 percent of all locals are not affiliated with a national, and all these "independents" (except for the relative handful of them belonging directly to the AFL–CIO and thus enabled to make use of the federation's services) must rely upon their own resources, whereas the many local unions that do belong to nationals can use the considerable resources of the latter.

Other Functions of the National Union

Although national union officers and staff representatives devote the major share of their time to providing services to the local unions, the range of the national union's activities includes many other important functions. Today, the major concern of all unions is that of increasing membership, in the face of the relative plateau of the past few years. Responsible labor union officials understand that the unorganized must be organized, and the chief burden for this also falls to the national union staff representatives. Although the AFL–CIO does do some organizational work, it does not have the staff to perform this function effectively; nor can the responsibility for the organization of new plants be undertaken by local officers or members. At times, local union people help in organizational drives, but because they are full-time employees, they do not have much opportunity to carry out this function.

Accordingly, the catalyst for new organization falls to the staff representatives of the national unions, upon whom constant pressure is exerted to organize nonunion plants. Indeed, in some national unions, not only the advancement but even the continued job tenure of the staff representative is determined by his or her success in organizing such plants.

The task is hardly an easy one. Most nonunion employers can be counted upon to wage a fierce fight against organization. Many employees who are not members of unions do not want a labor union, because management provides them with many of the benefits they would receive if organized. And the staff representative's organizing mission becomes even more difficult if attempts are made to organize in the South or in small communities regardless of sectional location. In any event, the representative must make contacts among the workers, convince them of the value of unions, and dispel notions that unions are corrupt, Communistic, or otherwise undesirable institutions. Many workers are ready to believe the worst about organized labor, and staff representatives often admit that these conceptions are difficult to erase. "Today," says one veteran, "the workers insult you, they spit at you, they throw [union membership] cards in your face."[9] And as a union leader could recently point out from his own unhappy experiences, even such institutions as church-administered hospitals can become formidable foes when faced with union organizers: "The Little Sisters of the Poor," as Leon Davis of the Hospital and Health Care Employees has observed, "can be hard as nails."[10]

Moreover, the potential union member "doesn't have the background in unionism his or her parents had; he doesn't view himself as a 'worker,' he probably doesn't even use the word 'worker,'" as the organizing director of the Teamsters has said. "We have to do more to show him the relevance of the union situation."[11] Even otherwise friendly employees often equate unions, as was pointed out earlier in this volume, with manual workers, and while this is by definition no obstacle if the target work force is made up of steelworkers or truck drivers, it can clearly handicap organizers who go after the growing body of office, professional and other non-blue-collar types.

Staff representatives are thus forced to use their powers of imagination, and any understanding of law and psychology that they might have, to the fullest. The representative may initially attempt to organize "from inside," through the informal leaders in the plant. The next step may be to visit workers in their homes, distribute leaflets, and arrange organizational meetings (which frequently are poorly attended). Subsequently the representative must counteract whatever management does to block the organizational attempt; even in today's more enlightened atmosphere, some employers warn employees of dire consequences if they organize, tell their employees that unions exist only to collect dues for the personal benefit of the union "bosses," and—the organizing tactic laws cited in Chapter 3 notwithstanding—on occasion even threaten workers with loss of their jobs if a union is established, as well as promise them benefits if they reject the union. In 1974,

[9] New York Times, July 19, 1977, p. 22.
[10] New York Times, January 7, 1982, p. A-18.
[11] Wall Street Journal, July 28, 1980, p. 13.

the Farah Manufacturing Company was organized by the Amalgamated Clothing Workers (not yet merged with the Textile Workers) following a two-and-one-half-year struggle that included a boycott of Farah products. The victory, however, came only after a National Labor Relations Board administrative law judge had criticized Farah for carrying on "a broad-gauged antiunion campaign consisting of glaring and repeated violations" of the National Labor Relations Act and acting as if "there were no act, no board and no Ten Commandments."[12]

There are other formidable obstacles for the organizer. If the plant is located in a comparatively small community, there may be a concerted attempt among the leaders of the community to keep the union out. The target employer may have good friends who run the newspaper, the radio and TV stations, the Chamber of Commerce, and the local stores, and these power centers may join forces to do what they can to keep the union from gaining a foothold. Indeed, it is not uncommon for the clergy in a town to be enlisted in the fight against the union.

The organizational mission of the staff representative is thus a highly challenging one and, in recent years, this person has probably experienced more failures than successful ventures. Often, in pondering the results of emotion-draining efforts, the staff representative doubtless feels like Marius contemplating the ruins of Carthage. But he or she is typically persistent, and this tenaciousness occasionally reaps its reward: Illustratively, although clearly also an extreme, in late 1980, J. P. Stevens and Co. (the second largest textile manufacturer in the nation) signed an agreement with the Amalgamated Clothing and Textile Workers in the culmination of a seventeen-year concerted organizational campaign by the union. The company, the real-life backdrop for the 1979 film *Norma Rae,* had fought the union so aggressively that a New York court had branded it "the most notorious recidivist in the field of labor law" and the NLRB had cited it twenty-two times for violating the federal labor statutes.

Another major function of the national union concerns political action, although the nationals vary widely in the vigor that they display in this regard. At one extreme, the Machinists and Automobile Workers (which between them contributed over $3 million to favored congressional candidates in 1982) are constantly engaged in politics—not only in helping to elect endorsees but through such projects as the UAW's recent, not yet successful, one of getting Congress to approve a "domestic content" bill requiring foreign firms to use a high percentage of American parts and labor in automobiles sold in the United States. The Steelworkers, too, impelled by recent hard times, have also made intense political action a way of life. At the other end of the spectrum, many of the building trades unions have rarely shown much interest in this area.

The trend, however, is definitely in the direction of more rather than less activity. As has already been noted, national leaders understand that the success of the union depends in large measure upon the fashioning of a favorable legal

---

[12] *Wall Street Journal,* April 8, 1974, p. 25.

climate for new organization and for the implementation of traditional trade union weapons when conflicts arise with employers. Moreover, a growing number of national unions share the belief of AFL–CIO leaders that the political programs of organized labor in the areas of Social Security, medicine, low-cost public housing, full employment, and the like are in the best interests of the nation as a whole. (The Teamsters, not in the AFL–CIO, must rely on their own efforts to advance particular union interests, and they do so by an ambitious counterpart to the AFL–CIO's COPE. It is known by the appropriate acronym of DRIVE, and Exhibit 4-3 shows how it is financed.)

When the national union officers are politically motivated, they are normally aggressive in exerting pressure upon the local unions and their members to take an active role in political affairs. Their union newspapers are filled with political news, voting records of the candidates, and the union point of view when elections are impending. National unions also arrange political rallies, purchase radio and television time to get the national's story across to the members and the public, and issue a barrage of political leaflets and pamphlets. In some national unions, during the weeks before important elections, the staff representatives are ordered to suspend collective bargaining negotiations, grievance meetings, and arbitrations and devote their full time to political work. The fact that each national union employs many staff representatives—in such large unions as the Automobile Workers and Steelworkers, the numbers run into the hundreds—serves as an important advantage; and if the staff representatives are adroit and hard-working, the favored political candidate can benefit greatly from such support.

Depending upon their size and leadership policies, national unions perform other functions. Some arrange educational programs for their staff representatives and local union officers. Most of the courses in these programs deal exclusively with the practical aspects of labor relations—how to bargain labor agreements, the best way to handle grievances, and the like. At times, however, the courses deal with foreign affairs, taxation, economics, government, and other subjects not directly related to the bread-and-butter issues of trade unionism. In addition, some national unions administer vacation resorts for their members, award university scholarships to children of members, organize tours to foreign nations, and sponsor a variety of social functions that are similar to those maintained by the state and city labor bodies but more tailored to the specific interests and aptitudes of the particular national union's members.

In recent years, there has also been a trend on the part of some nationals to engage in media campaigns to build a more favorable institutional image and often to attract members directly as well. Television, radio, billboard, and newspaper projects of some magnitude have been conducted by such unions as the Carpenters (whose ads here have concluded with the message "We're building the 20th Century"), Teamsters, Garment Workers, Communications Workers, Teachers, and an increasing number of others. Not alone among organizations in our society, they have learned the value of communications.

EXHIBIT 4-3

SILENCE ISN'T GOLDEN
WHEN YOUR RIGHTS ARE AT STAKE!

The right of free speech is one granted Teamsters and other American citizens by the U.S. Constitution. But if we don't use that right, we silence our own voices and lose our chance to be involved in the decision-making process on critical issues.

DRIVE, the Teamsters Political Action Committee, is dedicated to making Congress aware of members' positions on issues that vitally affect them, and on giving support to candidates for federal, state and local offices who do listen to and support labor's positions on key issues.

With recession, high unemployment, deregulation and other problems threatening Teamster jobs, and a whole range of legislative issues such as Hobbs Act amendments threatening our rights, we can't allow ourselves to be silenced this year!

**NATIONAL MASTER FREIGHT
UNITED PARCEL SERVICE
CAR HAUL
TANK HAUL
KROGER
MONTGOMERY WARD**

Teamsters covered by these national contracts have the perfect vehicle already for making their voices heard. Their contracts contain a DRIVE checkoff clause that allows them to donate dollars to DRIVE simply by signing the attached card and mailing it to Teamsters headquarters (c/o DRIVE, 25 Louisiana Ave., N.W., Washington, D.C., 20001). It's that easy. Decide what you want to give and your union and employer will do the rest.

The rest of us can get involved, too, first by checking our own contracts to see whether we have a voluntary DRIVE checkoff clause we can utilize, and if we don't, by sending a voluntary donation of our own to the national DRIVE program. Finally, it's important, too, to remember to register, so you can vote in the important races upcoming this election year.

If you're tired of bad government, joining DRIVE can help make your voice heard amid the crowd. By staying silent, you may lose your rights!

- -

DRIVE—Democrat Republican Independent Voter Education

Classification _____   Local Union # _____   Date _____

I subscribe, freely and voluntarily and not out of fear of reprisal, the sum, indicated below, each year to DRIVE with the understanding that this voluntary contribution may be used for political purposes in accordance with the constitution and rules of DRIVE.

I further hereby authorize and request my employer to deduct from my earnings the sum indicated below each year during any payroll period to be remitted to my local DRIVE Chapter.

I reserve the right in accordance with the applicable State or Federal laws to revoke this voluntary authorization at any time by giving written notice of such revocation to my DRIVE Chapter in accordance with such laws or otherwise.

Suggested voluntary contribution.

____ $5   ____ $10   ____ $15   ____ $20   ____ $25

A copy of our report is filed with the Federal Election Commission and is available for purchase from the Federal Election Commission, Washington, D.C. 20463.

Name of Company—Please Print _____   Name—Please Print _____   Social Security Number _____

Address _____   City _____   State ____   Zip ____   Signature _____

The International Teamster, Feb. 1982 issue.

Government of the National Union

When a national union is formed, a constitution is adopted that spells out the internal government and procedures of the union. Virtually every constitution provides that a convention should be held, and it designates this convention as the supreme authority of the union. Under the rules of most national unions, each local union sends delegates to the convention, with the number of delegates permitted to each local being dependent upon the local's paid-up membership totals. Hence, as in the AFL–CIO, the larger locals are more influential than the smaller units. Within most unions the locals range in size from several thousand to a literal handful of members in some locals that have contracts with small employers.

Ordinarily, the chief officers of the local unions are elected as delegates, although in the very large locals, which have the opportunity to send many delegates, rank-and-file members are chosen because the quota cannot be filled by the officers alone.

Many rank-and-filers consider being sent to a convention a definite plum, and not simply for the honor involved. Few national conventions rival for high living those of the Teamsters, about whose last convention—held in Las Vegas— a *New York Times* reporter wrote:

> Like others who come to this desert city, the teamsters went to lavish parties, ate lobsters and platters of spareribs, meatballs and finger sandwiches, and consumed immense quantities of beer and mixed drinks. They listened to the country songs of Tammy Wynette and the jokes of Joan Rivers, the comedienne. They received a filmed greeting from President Reagan and warm salutes from two White House emissaries.[13]

But almost all national conventions, which are usually held in resort locations, contain most of these elements if in lesser degree. When the delegates lose time from work the local union normally pays their lost wages, and the convention often lasts a week or so, allowing a welcome change of pace from what is often a humdrum employment life. Many delegates, even at their own expense, take their families along and look on the entire experience as money well spent.

Although under the terms of the Landrum–Griffin Act the delegates must be chosen by secret ballot, the officers of the nationals themselves may be selected in either of two ways: In about three-fourths of the national unions, the constitution requires that the principal officers (president, vice president, and secretary–treasurer) be elected by the convention. In the others, the officers are elected by a direct referendum wherein each member of the union may cast a ballot. Some of the largest unions in the national follow the latter procedure, including the United Steelworkers of America, the Amalgamated Clothing and Textile Workers, and the International Association of Machinists, but, even among the larger unions, most utilize the convention election system.

[13] *New York Times,* June 7, 1981, p. 4-E.

Union business dealt with at national conventions, in addition to the election of chief officers, runs a wide gamut. At the 1983 convention of the UAW, for example, the 2,500 delegates were asked to consider avenues for improving job security of their members in upcoming negotiations with the Big Three automobile makers and ways of making the diminished UAW budget (diminished because the union had lost some 400,000 members in the previous five years) go further in the field of organizing. They also pondered the authorization of a major new lobbying effort designed to rebuild America's basic industries (including, needless to say, the automotive sector). Cutting membership contributions to the union's hefty $500 million strike fund, from 30 percent of each member's monthly dues to 15 percent, was another item on the agenda.

Special problems of the various locals are also aired, and this provides an excellent opportunity for an exchange of ideas and experiences and for otherwise breaking down the provincialism of the local unions; delegates from a large local union in, say, Chicago can learn of the problems of a small local in a small southern community, for example. The convention also permits local union officers to display themselves to their best advantage. Most of them would like to rise in the union hierarchy, and the convention offers a testing ground for their talents. A rousing speech by a local union president may attract the attention of the delegates, and this favorable showing may stand the local person in good stead later when an attempt at higher office is made.

The actual business of the convention may be initiated either by the national officers or by the delegates. Decision making takes the form of resolutions, proposals, and reports on which the delegates vote. As in any large convention, the officers have a distinct advantage in this respect, since the president appoints the committees that bring important issues before the delegates and is in a position to select members for these committees who the leadership knows are favorable to the national officers' point of view. On the other hand, a determined local union, or even individual delegates who feel strongly about their cause, can bring to the attention of the convention a resolution, a recommendation, or even an amendment to the constitution. There is a limit, in fact, to how far any national president can go in bottling up the resentment of determined delegates. And, particularly if a delegation from a local can enlist the support of delegates from other locals, there is an excellent chance that the entire convention will hear its point of view. For all the authority and control the nationals exert over the locals, if national officers gain the enmity of a sufficient number of local unions, the delegates of these locals can band together and cause an upheaval at the convention; and, if the issues are of extreme importance, the resentment of these locals could result in a change in national union leadership. Thus, the local unions do have a political check against their national officers. There is a line the latter can cross only at the risk of losing their jobs.

In short, as long as the national union holds regularly scheduled conventions, the democratic process has an opportunity of working. The convention provides the forum wherein the policies, behavior, and competency of the national union officers can be evaluated, and the key to the democratic operation of a national union therefore lies in the regularity with which conventions are held. More than half the national unions hold conventions either annually or biennially, and most of the rest hold them every three or four years. A small number of national unions, however, simply do not hold conventions at all, and this clearly eliminates almost entirely any practical opportunity for the local unions to participate in the government of their unions. Nothing in the Landrum–Griffin law, indeed, requires unions to hold regular and reasonably frequent conventions. The law does require that the union membership be afforded the opportunity to elect its national officers at least every five years, but a union managed by autocrats can legally avoid the holding of conventions indefinitely.

National Union Officers

The chief of the national union is, of course, its president, who administers the organization with the assistance of such other major officers as the vice president (or vice presidents), secretary–treasurer, and members of the executive board. The latter group is ordinarily composed of the district or regional directors (who, in some national unions, are also called vice presidents), and its members have a variety of official tasks: enforcing the constitution of the national, implementing its policies, filling a national officer's position when vacant, voting on important matters referred to it by the president, placing items on the agenda for deliberation and voting, and a host of related duties. Normally, the executive board of a national union meets regularly and frequently, according to the provisions of a constitution, and on occasion also meets at the call of the president to deal with some pressing problem. Since the members of the executive board are from all over the nation and have direct supervision of the locals in their particular districts, the board mechanism provides an excellent way for the national union officers to learn of the problems of all locals throughout the country. Likewise, it provides a channel for communicating policies of the national union to its locals and membership.

In some unions, however, executive boards merely rubber-stamp decisions of the national officers. This is true most often when a president, either by union custom or because of the person's particular personality, is allowed to exercise autocratic leadership. It is safe to say, however, that in most unions the executive board directs the affairs of the union and establishes the union's basic policies, which the president is then obliged to carry out. The exceptions in recent years— James R. Hoffa of the Teamsters and W. A. "Tony" Boyle of the Mine Workers, in particular—have in fact generally been succeeded in office by leaders who appear to have taken extra efforts to alter the old images of power imbalance and to encourage the executive boards to participate more fully in policy-making decisions.

A responsible, devoted, and active national union president has a difficult job. One day the executive may be negotiating a contract with a major corporation, and the next day speaking at an important meeting of the union, or to the members of some other labor organization. The union president is also, typically, obligated to testify before congressional committees, preside over the union's executive board meetings, and travel to foreign nations as a participant in international labor organization bodies. He is expected to take an active role in important national political elections, constantly put pressure upon the staff representatives to organize nonunion plants, mollify companies that are disgruntled because of wildcat strikes or other forms of unauthorized union behavior, and perform a variety of other duties that may either be of major importance or strictly routine in character, but that also take up a great deal of time. Indeed, the management of even a small or medium-sized national union is a difficult one; the job becomes immensely more complicated and difficult in a large union.

The union president, moreover, is constantly torn between duties of a pressing character. In many cases, the leader must make the hard decision alone and hope it is the right one. As any chief executive, the president bears the ultimate responsibility for the organization's efficient, honest, and prudent management. Above all, the president must satisfy the membership, and at times this is a much more difficult job than dealing with management.

For all of this, union presidents hardly grow rich on the salaries of their offices. Their average annual pay at the time of this writing was in the neighborhood of $76,000—only 77 percent higher than the average a decade earlier, compared with a 100 percent increase for rank-and-file workers.[14] The lastest figures did show figures that were anything but modest for a few top officials: the Teamster president, Jackie Presser, was at the apex, with a $225,000 salary, and a dozen officers of other national unions (plus the Teamsters' own secretary–treasurer) also topped $100,000 (although in no case but that of the Teamsters by very much). But even in the mid-1980s only thirty officials at the national level made $80,000 or more, and these amounts were easily balanced by the salaries of the presidents of such major unions as the Automobile Workers, Communications Workers, Clothing and Textile Workers, Machinists, Mine Workers and Rubber Workers: In these unions the range was between $50,000 and $72,000. It is clear that money was not the motivator, either, for the president of the United Electrical Workers: Limited in what he could get by the union's constitution to no more than the highest weekly wage in the industry, he earned a far from staggering $22,032 plus an equally unimpressive expense allowance.

It is certainly true that a few national leaders have taken things too far, financially speaking, while in office. Before the passage of the Landrum–Griffin Act, for example, President David Beck of the Teamsters succumbed to an urge to buy items of a personal nature in copious amounts and charge them to his union. In more recent years, the authoritarian Mine Workers president Boyle also flagrantly misused union money for his personal benefit. And although receiving pay from the holding of several union jobs simultaneously is not in itself illegal—in the Teamsters, it is almost a way of life for the top officials, at least ten of whom in 1983 got paychecks from four or more positions—some element of good judg-

[14] *Business Week,* May 10, 1982, p. 118.

ment might be brought into question when the total derived incomes go well into the six-figure area. The same can be said of the practice in some unions (the Laborers, most conspicuously) of placing relatives in high-paying jobs with no seeming correlation of such placements with any merit on the part of the relatives.

Yet these are definitely the exceptions. No union leader remotely approximates the more than one hundred chief executive officers of American businesses who currently make more than $1 million per year, to say nothing of the more than twenty who now top $2 million on an annual basis.[15] And even the highest-paid union leader in the country—in a recent year, Harold Friedman of the ever-generous Teamsters, who was paid $195,000 as a Teamsters official and another $233,803 from an affiliated Bakery Workers Union local that he headed—was several light-years away from the ranking management recipients: Federal Express Chairman Frederick W. Smith, who got a handsome $51.5 million (almost all of it from exercising options) and the four top officials of Toys 'R' Us, all of whom got at least $7.5 million (with the chairman here landing a hefty $43.7 million).[16]

Workers pay the salaries of their union officers, however. And the employee who earns $16,000 in a good year may still assess a $60,000 salary as being exorbitant. But an objective assessment must turn more toward a conclusion that the typical national union leader is, if anything, underpaid given his responsibilities. When measured by the number of members, number of locals, and his own very formidable list of duties, even the Teamsters president does not seem to be getting an unreasonable salary (whatever might be said of the lower-echelon Mr. Friedman's).

Although modestly paid, the national president wants to keep that job. Union leaders have power and prestige and play an important role in our society. Many presidents do indeed remain in office for considerable lengths of time, and some of them stay in the chief executive chair for so long that memory does not recall another president. Daniel J. Tobin was president of the Teamsters for forty-five years; William Hutcheson, of the Carpenters for forty-two years; John L. Lewis, of the Mine Workers for forty years. James C. Petrillo, president of the Musicians, gave up his job, involuntarily at that, only when he grew so old and feeble that it is doubtful that he had the strength to play his instrument. Only a relative handful of unions—including the Automobile Workers, Steelworkers, and Machinists—have any provision for compulsory retirement of their national officers even now, and if national union board meetings can no longer be confused with "a collection of a wax museum," youth does not exactly hold sway in them, either. Richard L. Trumka, a lawyer and third-generation miner who was elected in 1982 at age 33 to head the 220,000-member United Mine Workers, is the youngest leader of a major union in the United States, by some distance: Only a handful of other national presidents are even below the half-century mark and most are in their sixties or beyond. (Exhibit 4-4 illustrates the hard-fought election that took place for the

---

[15] *Compensation Review*, 15, No. 1 (First Quarter, 1983), 75.
[16] *Business Week*, May 9, 1983, p. 84.

presidency of the once fully autocratic Mine Workers. Neither candidate could find much good to say about the other, and after the incumbent, Church, was ultimately defeated he was conspicuously absent from the Trumka inauguration ceremonies.)

Most national union officers stay in power for years, in fact, and it is not difficult to explain why they do so. Once in office, they possess sufficient power to minimize centralized opposition and to make it extremely difficult for new candidates to present themselves to the membership in an effective manner. The point has been made that when conventions are not held regularly and frequently, it is difficult for a new face to get much backing. In addition, staff representatives are hired by the national union and can usually be removed at the pleasure of the national officers. It would take rare courage for a paid representative to oppose the incumbent president, and the tendency is, in fact, understandably in the other direction. In addition, most incumbent presidents get personal mileage out of their union newspapers. The editor of the national union newspaper is also a hired person, and subject to control of the national officers. Any upstart candidate could not expect much favorable publicity, if indeed the candidate received any publicity at all, in the union press. As Wilfrid Sheed once commented, "The [president] controls the newspaper and assorted promo material, which is likely to feature pictures of himself peering knowingly into a mine face or welding machine, like a bishop at a confirmation. (In the Steelworkers, I'm told, a man could go mad staring at I. W. Abel. It's worse than *Muhammed Speaks.*)"[17]

In short, the incumbent national officers have a political machine that tends to perpetuate them in office. However, it would be incorrect to believe that this is the only reason for long tenure of office. Sophisticated union members understand that frequent changes of national union officers and open displays of factionalism weaken the position of the union against management in collective bargaining. Beyond this, a national union officer may have genuinely earned reelection to office over the years because the officer has been doing a good job for the membership. A national union president who is devoted, honest, courageous, and competent does not need a political machine to be reelected. Many national union officers fall within this category, and representatives of management should not regard national union officers as incompetent people who hold office only because of political machination.

THE LOCAL UNION

Where the People Are

Although we leave for the last an analysis of the character and functions of the local union, it does not follow that the local union is the least important of the labor bodies in the union movement. On the contrary, it could be argued successfully that for the individual union member, the local union is the most important

---

[17] Wilfrid Sheed, "What Ever Happened to the Labor Movement?" *Atlantic*, July 1973, p. 62. Abel was president of the union until June 1977, when he retired.

EXHIBIT 4-4

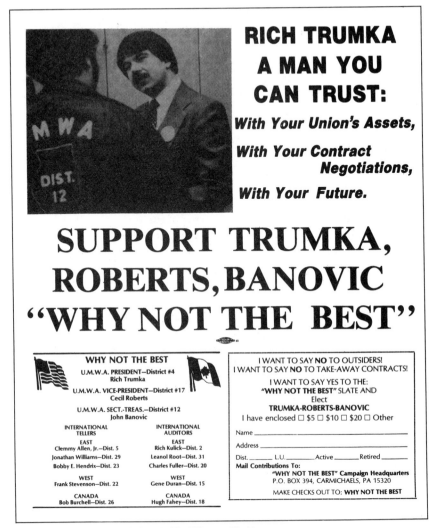

unit of all. In a sense, the federation, the national union and its district organizations, and the other labor bodies discussed previously are administrative and service organizations. Although they are vitally important and carry out a variety of significant activities, as we have seen, no union member really "belongs" to such larger bodies. Unionists are members of these organizations only by reason of their membership in a local union, are geographically close only to the local, and largely condition their loyalty toward an image of the total labor movement by what they perceive to transpire within the confines of the local union. Many

EXHIBIT 4-4 (continued)

A Message From Sam

Dear Brothers and Sisters,

I trust the men and women of the United Mine Workers. I trust you to make intelligent and aware decisions based on facts. I trust you to be able to find the truth.

I believe you trust me, even those who disagree with me on some issues. One thing I have always done since I became president has been to be truthful, to be honest with you. You are the people who are the heart and soul of this Union. You deserve honest leadership.

A campaign should be based on ideas, achievements, records and plans. You know my record and achievements. You have seen my plans for the future (in the last UMWA Journal). You may not agree with all of them, b u t those things are out front for you to judge.

My opponent has suddenly found himself slipping from the solid ground of truth into quicksand of deception. Much of this you have probably already read about in your newspapers or have seen or heard on television and radio.

These stories have concerned his qualifications to be president of the UMWA. They are not what he has said they were.

The individual issues are not the main point.

The main point is the pattern of deliberate deception of every coal miner in the United Mine Workers of America.

I feel sorry for a young man who wants something so badly that he would go these lengths to get it. Ambition is a terrible master.

But you cannot lead a union by deception. When the membership begins to doubt your word, your honesty and your truthfulness, then there is no leadership, there is no progress, there is no future.

Let us continue to build our future together.

Fraternally,

Sam Church J

Sam Church Jr.

union members do not, indeed, even know the names of their national and federation officers, but they do know their local union president, business agent, and stewards. They know them because they see them where they work and because these are the people who handle the union member's day-to-day problems.

Local Union Officers

Although some locals are formed before the employer is organized, a local union typically comes into existence when there is organization of an employer. After it has organized and secured bargaining rights, a local typically applies for and receives a national union charter. This document establishes the local's affiliation with the national union and entitles the local to its services, and by the same token it subjects the local to the rules and discipline of the national union. Depending upon the unit of organization, a local union may be confined to a single plant or several plants of a single company or may include workers of a single craft, such as electricians who perform their duties in a given geographic area.

There is absolutely no correlation between the size of a national union and its number of locals. The Teamsters, with 1.8 million members, have 745 locals, but the Steelworkers, considerably smaller with a membership of 1.3 million, have almost 5,000 of them. And while the Food and Commercial Workers have chartered 790 locals to support their 1.2 million constituents, the Barbers and Beauticians have almost as many locals (702) for their 41,000 members, allowing those who belong to the latter union the unusually small member-to-local ratio of about 59 to 1.

Once the local is established, the members, in accordance with their bylaws (which are usually specified in the national union constitution), elect their officers— typically a president, vice president, secretary–treasurer, and several lesser officials. Since such election procedures almost invariably allow direct participation by all union members, the local union officers are elected on a much more democratic basis than are those chosen to lead the national union. Moreover, the union member knows much more from firsthand experience about the local union candidates for office than he or she does about the national union officers. The vast majority of local union officers, in fact, work in the plant along with the other union members and are under constant and often highly critical observation by them. Both democracy and a far higher turnover rate for local officers than for the union's national officials also stem from the fact that the local union officer, unlike the national union president, has little if any patronage to dispense. Local leaders do not have a paid staff as does the national counterpart; nor, generally speaking, can the local officer make use of any other powers of patronage or the purse, since neither exist in any measure.

In general, the local union officers work without pay. In only the large local unions are such officers reimbursed for their work, and, even then, their salaries tend to approximate the wages they would have earned from their employers. And in the relatively infrequent instances when the local union president and secretary– treasurer do receive some small compensation for their duties even when they are full-time employees in the plant, the amount of money is comparatively small when measured against the duties they perform. For example, in Bloomington, Indiana, one local's secretary–treasurer receives the far from awesome salary of $2,000 per year for taking care of the books, making financial reports, answering all correspondence, and assuming a volume of other miscellaneous duties. The size of his job is measured by the fact that the local has over 3,000 members and by the union's requirement that all his duties must be conducted on his own time.

A fair question, then, is why union members desire to acquire and retain local union officer jobs. Despite their nominal or totally nonexistent financial rewards, they must perform a variety of duties and assume considerable responsibility, and they are constantly being pressured by the membership under whose direct surveillance they labor. The question is not an easy one to answer, since the motivations are obviously different with different people. A leading reason, however, is that the local union officers acquire prestige and status in the company and in the community. Virtually all people desire recognition once lower needs have been relatively well satisfied, and the attainment of a local officer's job accomplishes this objective for some workers.

Another reason may involve the local union officer's devotion and dedication to the union movement. "In general," Koziara, Bradley, and Pierson have concluded from their study of this topic, those who become union officers "are people who believe unions have a meaningful function to perform in our society."[18] If the local officer really believes in unions, he or she has the opportunity of making the movement work by carrying out the position's duties in an honest and effective manner.

Still other union members may genuinely court the competitive character associated with the office: The local union officers deal with the employer on a day-to-day basis, and many of the dealings regularly involve what some workers view as "the struggle" with management.

Finally, the reason may be a political one, involving the future of the local union officer in the national union. As stated, national union officers are elected officials, and staff representatives are union members who are hired by the national union. Thus, to go up the ladder, the union member must normally start at the local union level; a local union officer's job is commonly the first step in the long and hard pull toward the top. The large majority of all current national union officers and staff representatives have held a local union officer's job at some earlier period of their careers.

Functions of the Local Union: Relations with Management

The duties of local union officers are dependent, of course, upon the functions of the particular local union, but unless contracts are negotiated on a multiemployer basis or with a very large corporation, local union officers directly negotiate the labor agreement with the employer. If the national union staff representative often aids the local in carrying out this function and usually plays a highly visible role in the process, the fact remains that the local union officers who are also involved in negotiations are directly responsible to the members of the local union. The staff representative, a hired hand, does not face political defeat if he or she exercises poor judgment or fails to negotiate a contract that the membership feels is suitable. Should a contract, however, hurt the local union members, it is very likely that in the next election the local union officers will be changed. Because of its local character, factionalism in the local is, in fact, a constant problem. It is comparatively

[18] Karen S. Koziara, Mary I. Bradley, and David A. Pierson, "Becoming a Union Leader: The Path to Local Office," *Monthly Labor Review*, February 1982, p. 46.

easy for a dynamic, aggressive, and ambitious newcomer to use a poor contract as a weapon to dislodge an incumbent officer.

Another important function of the local is that of negotiating grievances. Indeed, most of the union's time is devoted to this task; the labor agreement is negotiated only periodically, but, through the grievance procedure, it must be administered every day. To this end, each local union has a number of stewards— usually one steward to a department of the company, elected by the union members of that department—who serve as administrative personnel.

In most plants, the members also elect a chief steward to be chairman of the grievance committee. At the lower steps of the grievance procedure, the worker's complaint is handled by the department steward, and, normally, the local union president or chief steward does not enter the picture until the grievance has reached the higher levels. But at the last step of the grievance procedure, the local union president and the union grievance committee (composed of the chief steward and several other stewards) will negotiate the grievance, typically with the staff representative of the national union also being present. Moreover, if a grievance goes to arbitration, the local union president and the union committee will attend the hearing, and although at this forum the national staff representative usually presents the union's case, the representative depends heavily upon the local union officers and the committee for the data that will be presented to the arbitrator.

It is difficult to overestimate the vital importance of the effective use of the grievance procedure as a function of the local union. Indeed, to the union member who has a grievance, the handling of that grievance means more to the individual than what the union secured in the collective bargaining agreement. This is particularly true when the grievant complains agianst a discharge or against an alleged company violation of an important working condition.

In this capacity, however, the local union officers are also vulnerable. Take, for example, a grievance that, though important to the employee, does not have merit. If the local union president tells this to the union member, the president risks offending a constituent. And if this happens frequently and with many different workers, the union members can demonstrate their resentment in the next election. This appears completely unfair and senseless, but it is what the local union officers have to contend with, and explains why local union officers frequently take up grievances that do not have merit.

At times, too, the local officers are forced to deal with "borderline" grievances—complaints that may or may not have merit but that, for a variety of reasons, the local union officers cannot persuade the employer to grant. Often, the local does not want to risk losing the grievance in arbitration. It therefore refuses to handle the grievance, and the job now is to pacify the employee, who may have some justification for being resentful—not an easy mission when the grievance deals with an important issue and has some basis under the labor agreement. Consequently, the local officials may change their minds and take such grievances into arbitration, hoping for the best; if the arbitrator denies the grievance, the local union officers can always use the arbitrator as the scapegoat. However, in spite of an effective presentation at the arbitration hearing, the disgruntled union member may still blame union officers. It is said that victory has many fathers, but defeat is an orphan. Fortunately, unions win their share of grievances in the grievance procedure and in arbitration, and in the campaign before the next election, the local union officer can point with pride to successes and minimize or explain away defeats.

Judicial Procedures

Another function of the local union is that of disciplining union members who are alleged to have violated union rules. As does every organization, unions have standards with which members must comply. These standards are incorporated by the national union's constitution and are duplicated in the local union's bylaws. If a union member violates any of these rules, he or she may be disciplined by the local union membership in the form of a reprimand, a fine, suspension, or, in extreme cases, expulsion from the union.

Commonly proscribed standards of conduct that frequently merit expulsion include the promotion of dual unionism (when a union member seeks to take the local out of one national union and place it in another—true treason in unionism!); participating in an unauthorized or "wildcat" strike; misappropriating union funds; strikebreaking; refusing to picket; sending the union membership list to unauthorized persons; circulating false and malicious reports about union officers; and providing secret and confidential information to the employer. Under the official rules of some unions, a member may also be expelled because of membership in a Communistic, Fascistic, or other totalitarian group. We may quarrel with the justice or fairness of one or more of these rules, but the fact remains that they must be obeyed, since they have been adopted by the union at large. From the union point of view, each of them pertains to an important area of conduct.

The procedures used at the local level to enforce the rules of the union differ widely, but the following would probably reflect most local union procedures: Any union member may file charges against any other member, including the local union officers. When this occurs, the president has the authority to appoint a so-called "trial committee," composed of union members belonging to the local in question and normally including officers, stewards, and rank-and-file members who take an active role in the affairs of the union. The trial committee has the job of investigating the complaint, holding a hearing if it believes that the charge has substance, and reaching a decision that it will ultimately present to the entire local union body for final determination. To protect against a political situation within the local wherein favorites of the local union officers, or the officers themselves, may not be brought to account for a violation, the union members initiating the charge may appeal to the national union. Thus, a "not guilty" verdict, the dismissal of charges by the local union officers, or the pigeonholing of complaints does not necessarily end the disciplinary process.

After its investigation of the charges, the local union's trial committee holds a hearing at which the accused member is present. The accused may select another union member to act as his or her spokesperson. As in most other private or semiprivate organizations, the union member may not hire a defense lawyer while the case is being processed within the union, but witnesses are called, and cross-examination is permitted. And, although no oath is administered for the same reason (since the hearing is not in a court of law), union members who deliberately lie or who grossly misrepresent the facts may themselves be charged with a violation. After the hearing, the trial committee reports its decision and the reasons for the verdict to the local union membership. At this point, the membership may adopt, reject, or modify the committee's decision. At times, the trial is in effect reheld before the local membership, since some members might desire to review the evidence that the trial committee used to arrive at its decision.

If the decision is "not guilty," the member or members who filed the charge may appeal to the executive board of the national union. By the same token, when the decision of the local goes against the charged union member, that member may appeal to the national union and, under the provisions of virtually every constitution, the member can also ultimately appeal the decision of the national union officers to the national convention.

On the surface, this judicial procedure appears fair and calculated to protect the accused union member. It would seem that the accused receives a full and fair hearing and gains further protection through provisions for the right of appeal. In practice, however, there have been several instances of serious abuses of the local union judicial procedure, although, with more than 70,000 locals to consider, it is absolutely impossible to make any kind of accurate judgment of the relative extent to which the abuse has existed, and any opinion is sheer speculation.

It was because of such union actions, however, that the Landrum–Griffin Act specified that no member could be disciplined, fined, or expelled without having first received a written list of charges, a reasonable time to prepare the defense, and a full and fair hearing. Today, if these legal standards are violated, a union member may bring suit in the federal courts for relief. Under the law, the union member may not go to court before he or she attempts to settle the case through union procedures, although to check dilatory union tactics, the law also specifies that if the internal procedure consumes longer than four months, the union member need not exhaust the internal remedies of the union before going to court.

In 1957, the United Automobile Workers dealt with the problem of abuse in the disciplinary procedure in a different manner. It established a "Public Review Board," composed of seven citizens of respected reputation and impeccable integrity and having no other relationship with the union. Usually, such citizens have been nationally known members of the clergy, the judiciary, or university faculties. Under the amendment to the UAW constitution that established the plan, the president of the national union selects the board members, subject to the approval of the national union's executive board and ratification by the national convention. Among other duties, this watchdog committee may reverse the decision of the executive board of the national union that has upheld the discipline of a union member, and experience has shown that the board has been quite willing to reverse the national union's executive board when it has believed that such a reversal was justified. To date, however, only the Upholsterers International Union has followed the pattern of the UAW. If each national union were to establish such an agency, and if each agency were allowed the same freedom to act that has been granted the UAW Public Review Board, there would clearly be less need for legislation to protect the status of union members.

Political Activities

Although the AFL–CIO and national union officers and staff representatives play an effective role in lobbying and in supporting candidates in their campaigns for political office, it can be argued with much justification that the political efficiency of the union movement depends above all upon the vigor of the local. After all, the number of the federation and national officers and staff representatives is very small in comparison with the number of local union members. And much of the legwork during the national and state elections must necessarily be performed by local union members if it is to be performed at all on any large scale. Indeed, the success of the union movement in "rewarding its friends and punishing its enemies" depends in large measure on the willingness of local union officers and members to engage in politics.

Nonetheless, the degree to which local unions participate in politics is often determined by the basic philosophy of the national union. If the national union officers do not want their union to engage in politics, or if they merely go through the motions of indicating such a preference, the local unions of the nationals will reflect this kind of leadership. On the other hand, when the national union officers do take an active role in the political affairs of the nation, the local unions typically respond by placing a major emphasis on such political action of their own. However, even when the national unions do cajole their locals into taking this active role in politics, the members themselves may or may not follow the instructions of the national union officers, and the national's efforts must consequently be geared in two directions: toward the local leadership and toward the local membership.

If a constant problem of the national union that is politically inclined is thus to motivate the locals to follow its example, even within the ranks of such active unions as the UAW and Machinists, there are many dozens of local unions that either refuse to participate or participate in a lackadaisical way. Locals of less politically conscious nationals often show even greater reluctance. Moreover, just because the AFL–CIO leadership or a national union president supports a candidate for elective office, this does not mean that every union member will vote that way. Some may not vote at all, of course, and postelection analyses of union member districts show that many others vote for the opposite candidate, as the millions of unionist votes for Ronald Reagan in 1980, noted earlier, vividly illustrate. There is no permanent "labor vote," as is sometimes claimed by people who view the political participation of the union movement as an evil.

Indeed, as long as we maintain secret elections, even the most homogeneous groups in the nation can never rest assured that their members or followers will vote as the organization urges them to. And if members of the most closely knit of unions do not lockstep to the polls and vote in accordance with the recommendations of their leadership, members of less cohesive labor groups are often significantly divided in their election choices.

Our society is, moreover, pluralistic in character, and its countless pressure groups have their own favored candidates. Each group has the right and, indeed, the obligation to participate in the election process. These are the hallmarks and the dynamics of a democratic society wherein each group seeks the votes of its members and those of the public. Under such a system of checks and balances, any one group or organization is prevented from dominating the political life of the nation, moreover, and this is clearly to the good.

A union member may be a good trade unionist and support with vigor the union's collective bargaining policies and its strikes. He or she may enthusiastically take a place on the picket line. However, when that member casts a ballot for the president of the United States, a senator, congressman, governor, and other political candidates, the vote cast will reflect the individual's political heritage and interpretation of the political situation at the time. Union members share in common with their counterparts in a myriad of other groups the fact that they are not isolated from the multitude of pleas for votes that arise from countless organizations and sources of political information. The daily press, radio and television, the political candidate, the worker's traditional political affiliation, and many more factors will influence each person's vote, and the individual's labor organization is only one of many factors that are involved in political determination at election time.

Nonetheless, a local union that takes an active role in politics can be of great help to a favored candidate, and, in a close election, the support can tip the scales in the candidate's favor. The local union will encourage each member to register and to cast a ballot at election time. Prior to the election, it will do all in its power to "educate" the union member as to how to vote, through publications, meetings, house-to-house visits, and other forms of active political activity. In addition, the local union may legally make expenditures from union dues for such purposes as the holding of meetings of a political character and the publication and distribution of politically inspired newspapers and leaflets, although (as stated earlier) only money that is raised on a voluntary basis from the membership can be contributed directly to the people running for political office.

Other Functions and Problems

Beyond the major functions discussed above, local unions at times engage in a variety of social, educational, and community activities. Of late, as in the case of higher labor bodies, the last area has become increasingly important. Union leaders realize that the welfare of their members depends in part on a progressive and well-run community. How the schools are run, for example, is of vital interest to the local unionist who must pay taxes to operate the schools and who may have children attending the schools. As in the case of city labor bodies, representation of local union officials on United Way committees, Red Cross drives, and similar endeavors is also increasing in frequency. Moreover, unions recognize that the public image of organized labor, which has been tarnished in recent years, tends to improve to the extent that unions engage in such community services. Labor's various forms of participation in community service programs demonstrate that union members are not only collectively a socially oriented group but also individually responsible and interested citizens of the community. Likewise, the integration of unions in community work tends to lessen the tensions between management and organized labor. If a union leader can work effectively with the management representatives on the school board or in the United Way drive, there is a better chance for harmonious labor relations at the workplace.

Many local unions also conduct regularly sponsored and generally effective educational programs for the benefit of their officers and stewards. As noted previously, the need for these programs arises primarily from the complexity of the contemporary labor–management relationship, but it also stems to a great extent from the brisk turnover of the local union officers and stewards. Some of the programs are sponsored by the national unions, although in many cases the local itself arranges the educational program. Indeed, no union is considered modern today unless it has devised a well-planned educational program for its leadership. Such educational programs frequently bring to the surface workers of talent and high native intelligence. Through education, not only are they capable of doing a better job for their membership and acting more responsibly and rationally at the bargaining table, but education tends to make them more useful citizens. Of at least as much practical interest to many workers, union members who acquire such measures of education tend to rise more rapidly to important jobs at both the local and national levels.

One of the most important problems of the local is that of interesting the membership in attending regular monthly meltings of the union. Attendance at these meetings is frequently very poor, and the problem is not easy to solve. The vast majority of union leaders sincerely want their members to turn out at the meeting. They believe that the union has nothing to hide and that, by regular attendance and discussion at meetings, the members become more active, tend to be more devoted, and in general allow the local to deal with both employers and representatives of the public from a considerably stronger position than would otherwise be the case. The fact remains, however, that union members normally stay away from their meetings in droves; for the regular monthly meetings, only about 5 to 10 percent of the membership turns out (even a smaller percentage is common enough, especially in large locals); and one wonders why there has been so much said about union democracy when the union member does not seem sufficiently interested to participate in the affairs of his or her own union. When unions are poorly managed, when corruption exists, when leadership is second-rate, the fault is essentially that of the union member who does not care enough to attend the regular union meeting.

Thus, although from the days of the earliest unions labor organizations have undertaken a variety of measures (ranging from more convenient hours to the incorporation of social activities into the meeting schedule) to encourage attendance, in all these years unions have not found the solution to the problem of worker apathy toward attendance at meetings, and there is every likelihood that it will persist in the future. The only notable exception involves meetings at which a strike vote is scheduled to be taken. In general, the union members will turn out at this time because this issue of striking or working is, of course, of crucial importance.

On the other hand, management should not interpret poor attendance at the regular monthly meetings to mean that in crisis situations the members will not support their union. In a showdown, the typical union member will actively support the union; a management that makes a decision to chance a strike solely on the grounds of poor attendance at union meetings makes a very unwise choice. The members will invariably rally to the union's cause when there are issues involved that vitally affect their welfare, no matter how little interest they have demonstrated in the day-to-day operation of their local at more peaceful times.

UNION FINANCES

As do all other organizations, the union makes many expenditures and must meet its financial obligations. Chief expenditures of unions include the payment of salaries for their full-time officers and staff representatives, travel expenses, clerical expenses, office equipment and supplies, telephones, telegrams, postage, arbitration fees, and rent or mortgage payments for office space and the union hall. Beyond this, the strike fund must be built up to pay strike benefits when needed.

At the international level, where the lion's share of the dollars is spent, most of the money paid out goes to staff members who provide direct and indirect services. It has been estimated that in the case of the United Automobile Workers, for example, about 85 percent of the spending is for this purpose. In a recent year, the UAW's research budget was approximately $500,000; its sixteen-member Washington staff spent about the same amount; the union's public relations expenditures were running at an annual rate of just under $1 million; and this second largest union in the country was even financing a six-man staff of safety experts who were flying around the country upon request from local unions to check for hazards.

The Teamsters, who have never been pressed for cash, spend it even more lavishly on services. Some 550 staff persons employed in fifteen different departments at the block-long union headquarters in Washington work in such fields of endeavor as lobbying, education (including the administration of a 20,000-volume library), communications (including the issuance of an impressively packaged quarterly publication, the *International Teamster*), and a large legal department (itself supervising the activities of some 400 Teamster lawyers scattered throughout the country). They also staff a research wing (to compile information, above all, to back up contract bargaining demands), a steadily growing health and safety unit, an organizing department, and even an electronic data-processing department (supplying computer support nationwide to the several hundred Teamster locals).

At times, people are impressed by the relatively large amounts that unions collect in dues and initiation fees, foregetting that the union dispenses formidable amounts of money to meet its bills. By some estimates, the annual income of American unions from all sources—special assessments and earnings from investments, as well as the regular monthly dues paid by constituents, and initiation fees—amounts to about $3 billion. And there is little question but that $3 billion looks like a lot of money, particularly when you don't have it. But when one considers the net worth of unions, a more accurate picture is gained. Such worth, for all unions in the United States, still remains under the $1 billion mark and in no way comes close to paralleling the wealth of corporations, at least a dozen of which have net assets that *individually* exceed this billion-dollar figure. Of the General Motors Corporation, it has been written, "In the 1960s, when it had some 1.6 billion dollars in cash and bonds and, embarrassingly, seemed unable to find ventures in which to invest these funds, a General Motors executive, asked by a *Wall Street Journal* correspondent what the corporation planned to do with that vast sum of money, laughed and said General Motors was 'saving up to buy the federal government.'"[19] GM, one of the world's largest private industrial corporations (in the first quarter of 1983 alone, it earned the better part of a billion dollars in profits), is admittedly an extreme, but it is impossible to imagine any labor organization's being placed in the same anecdotal situation.

In general, the dues paid by union members holding semiskilled and unskilled jobs in manufacturing are less than those paid by members who work in the skilled trades. The obvious reason for this is that electricians, plumbers, carpenters, and kindred skilled employees earn higher wages than do employees whose jobs require lesser skill levels. A substantial majority of union members now pay dues that come out to roughly two hours' wages per month, and two major unions—the Steelworkers and Automobile Workers—have in fact officially set their monthly dues figures at exactly this two-hour level, thereby building automatic increases into the dues structure. Initiation fees—by definition, a one-shot affair—tend to be in the $50–$100 range, with only a small handful of unionists (primarily in the building trades, airline pilot profession, and similarly highly remunerated groupings) being charged more than $200 in such fees by their labor organizations.

In the light of all that has been said about the functions of unions, the amount of money the typical member pays is thus comparatively small. Nonetheless, like everyone else, the union member desires maximum and ever-improving services for the least cost possible. Indeed, union leadership must be very careful when it

---

[19] William Serrin, *The Company and the Union* (New York: Vintage, 1974), p. 72.

seeks to raise the monthly dues. Even a modest increase of 50 cents per month could cause an upheaval among the membership. With increasing expenses and sometimes declining memberships, unions *must* at times raise dues if they desire to maintain the same level of services for their membership, but this is a step normally taken only as an extreme last resort. Illustratively, during one recent period of declining union membership, the UAW laid off many staff representatives and otherwise tried to curb expenses drastically before requesting a modest dues increase. (Exhibit 4-5 illustrates one of many union efforts that failed. In 1983, the Newspaper Guild tried to raise its minimum dues schedule to 5.5 percent and ultimately to 6.0 percent of each member's regular weekly compensation, a rate that most of its members already paid. As mandated by its constitution, it sent an official referendum ballot to all of its members. The exhibit comes from the union's newspaper, the *Guild Reporter,* which officially reported the final tally in its February 11, 1983, issue.)

A CONCLUDING WORD

The American labor movement *is* vast and complicated, but its elements fit together in a systematic fashion and provide the framework for the carrying out of the basic functions and objectives.

In a day of increasing union dependence upon the sentiments of the general public, particularly as these sentiments are translated into legislative actions, these objectives have increasingly encompassed social and community activities that clearly extend well beyond labor's traditional campaigns for improved "property rights" on the job itself. These more broadly based endeavors can in no way be expected to diminish in the years ahead, for the advantages for the labor movement that can potentially be derived from them are certain to continue.

Yet this newer emphasis should not obscure either the pronounced strain of "bread-and-butter" unionism that has marked organized labor throughout its history or the internal union political considerations that continue to generate this more basic behavior. If unions are, by and large, not fully democratic, they are nonetheless highly political in nature. The union leader must above all be conscious of the general wishes of his or her constituents. And these wishes, particularly at the lower levels of the union structure where the collective bargaining process itself takes place, continue to be closely related to wages, hours, and conditions.

Just as internal political considerations have dictated national union autonomy within the AFL–CIO, so too have such considerations led to the complete responsibility of virtually all national union executives to at least the most pressing desires of local unionists, and to such commonly observed phenomena as the high turnover rates of local officers themselves.

It has often been said that a union "is a political animal operating in an economic framework." The story of a union that a while ago sent its hospitalized

EXHIBIT 4-5
Official Dues-Referendum Returns

Following are the official results in the Jan. 20-25 Guild-wide referendum on increasing the Minimum Dues Schedule mandated for Guild locals by TNG's Constitution.	*The local by local and overall vote totals listed are those certified by the International Election & Referendum Committee, which met Feb. 7 and 8 at TNG headquarters in Washington.*	*Votes in the "For" column were in favor of the increase in the Minimum Dues Schedule.* *Votes in the "Against" column were opposed to the increase.*

LOCAL[1]	ELIGIBLE VOTERS	FOR	AGAINST	LOCAL[1]	ELIGIBLE VOTERS	FOR	AGAINST
Akron	133	5	101	Memphis	402	204	66
Albany	273	133	53	Montreal	283	73	45
Bakersfield	96	21	26	New York	4,941	438	1,487
Battle Creek[2]	1	—	—	Northern Ontario			
Boston	289	109	81	(Sudbury)[2]	28	—	—
Brockton	127	65	34	Ottawa	319	44	24
Buffalo	706	120	135	Pacific Northwest			
Canadian Wire Service	774	340	68	(Seattle, Tacoma)	1,112	200	276
Central California	756	182	19	Pawtucket	32	8	4
Chattanooga	42	3	34	Peoria	89	7	13
Chicago	521	42	107	Philadelphia[5]	1,280	191	212
Cincinnati	111	25	39	Pittsburgh	138	20	25
Cleveland	450	173	51	Portland	292	154	51
Columbus	147	45	81	Providence	414	91	133
Denver	600	27	72	Pueblo	117	4	42
Detroit	978	93	233	Puerto Rico[2]	1,063	—	—
Erie	164	41	75	Rochester[2]	2	—	—
Eugene	72	5	47	Rockford	46	10	32
Gary	64	5	42	St. Louis	920	315	278
Great Falls	21	12	4	Salem	66	56	0
Harrisburg	67	8	53	San Antonio	91	3	13
Hawaii	457	160	35	San Diego	842	109	234
Hazleton	24	0	21	San-Francisco-Oakland	1,359	339	146
Hudson County				San Jose	781	171	51
(Jersey City)[3]	52	—	—	Scranton	90	45	9
Indianapolis[2]	1	—	—	Sheboygan	64	24	24
Kenosha	48	14	19	Sioux City[2]	6	—	—
Kingston[4]	31	—	—	Southern Ontario			
Knoxville	51	0	16	(Toronto)	1,804	143	263
Lake Superior (Duluth)	30	11	11	Terre Haute	90	25	1
Lansing	36	5	11	Toledo	352	39	107
Lexington	44	20	7	Twin Cities	822	267	168
Los Angeles	353	47	43	Utica	21	4	6
Lynn	31	14	11	Vancouver-			
Manchester	110	67	3	New Westminster	1,116	164	264
				Victoria	178	89	5
				Washington-Baltimore	1,796	253	110
				Wilkes-Barre	103	84	15
				Wire Service (U.S.)	1,196	82	250
				Woonsocket	45	0	37
				Yakima	23	4	3
				York	75	10	36
				Youngstown	155	26	70
				At-Large	3	2	0
				TOTALS	**30,216**	**5,490**	**6,032**

[1] Locals not listed had no members eligible to vote.

[2] No official return received by close of International Election & Referendum Committee meeting Feb. 7-8.

[3] Official return postmarked two days after deadline; ballots not received by close of IERC meeting.

[4] No postmark on official return; ballots not received by close of IERC meeting.

[5] Ballots from Wilmington and Pottstown units not counted due to discrepancy between number cast and number of signatures on voter eligibility lists. Ballots would not be determinative in outcome of referendum.

Source: The Guild Reporter, Feb. 11, 1983.

management adversary a basket of fruit with a card stating that the "members of Local 25 wish you a speedy recovery by a vote of 917 to 648" may or may not be fictitious: corroboration is now impossible. But unions are by any standard highly "political." And no one who loses sight of this most fundamental labor relations factor can truly appreciate union behavior. Union members do have the ultimate control of their labor organizations—however much in-practice union *leadership* has been the catalyst of the policies, programs, and operation of the union—and the leadership can never ignore this fact of life.

Discussion Questions

1 J.B.S. Hardman once described labor organizations as being "part army and part debating society." What considerations on his part might have led to this description?

2 It has been argued in many nonlabor quarters that it is socially undesirable for unions to take the initiative in organizational campaigns and that the public interest is served only when unorganized workers initially seek out the union. Is there anything to be said for this point of view? Against it?

3 "There are both advantages and disadvantages to AFL–CIO affiliation for national unions." Comment.

4 "The increasing sophistication and enlightenment of modern top business executives in dealing with their subordinates has led to a state of affairs wherein managements today are more democratic than unions." Do you agree? Why or why not?

5 "Unions are no less private institutions than country clubs or Masonic lodges, and as such should be no more subject to government regulation of their internal affairs than these other organizations." The present thrust of the laws notwithstanding, is there any validity to this argument?

6 Albert Rees has pointed out that it is "paradoxically true that the presence of strong unions may improve the operation of democratic processes in the general national or state government even if the internal political processes of the union are undemocratic." Explain this paradox.

7 Daniel Bell, the former labor editor of *Fortune* magazine, once commented that in taking over certain power from management, "the union also takes over the difficult function of specifying the priorities of demands—and in so doing, it not only relieves management of many political headaches but becomes a buffer between management and rank-and-file resentments." Is there any justification for such a comment?

Selected References

BARBASH, JACK, *American Unions*. New York: Random House, 1967.

BRILL, STEVEN, *The Teamsters*. New York: Simon & Schuster, 1978.

ESTEY, MARTEN, *The Unions: Structure, Development, and Management* (3rd ed.). New York: Harcourt Brace Jovanovich, 1981.

GOULDEN, JOSEPH E., *Meany; The Unchallenged Strong Man of American Labor*. New York: Atheneum, 1972.

GREENSTONE, J. DAVID, *Labor in American Politics*. Chicago: University of Chicago Press, 1977.

HALL, BURTON H., ed., *Autocracy and Insurgency in Organized Labor*. New Brunswick, N.J.: Transaction Books, 1972.

HERLING, JOHN, *The Right to Challenge: People and Power in the Steelworkers Union*. New York: Harper & Row, 1972.

HUTCHINSON, JOHN, *The Imperfect Union: A History of Corruption in American Trade Unions*. New York: Dutton, 1972.

NASH, ALLAN, *The Union Steward: Duties, Rights and Status*. Ithaca, N.Y.: New York State School of Industrial and Labor Relations, 1977.

ROTH, HERRICK, *Labor: American's Two-Faced Movement*. New York: Petrocelli/Charter, 1975.

SAYLES, LEONARD R., and GEORGE STRAUSS, *The Local Union* (rev. ed.). New York: Harcourt Brace Jovanovich, 1967.

SEIDMAN, JOEL, ed., *Trade Union Government and Collective Bargaining*. New York: Praeger, 1970.

TAFT, PHILIP, *The Structure and Government of Labor Unions*. Cambridge, Mass.: Harvard University Press, 1954.

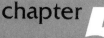

chapter 5

At the Bargaining Table

However much specific unions may differ in their exact structures, governments, and general operations, virtually all labor organizations share at least the same primary objective. Whatever in the way of concrete demands may be sought from the employer, the union's major goal is to negotiate with the latter a written agreement covering both employment conditions and the union–management relationship itself on terms that are acceptable to the union. But the employer, too, must be able to live with these terms, and it is because of this second requirement that bargaining sessions almost unavoidably contain stresses and strains; more for one party—not only in the economic areas of the contract but, as will be seen, in many of the so-called "institutional" and "administrative" areas—all but invariably means less for the other. Moreover, the labor–management tensions are *recurrent* in their nature, since contracts are regularly renegotiated—most commonly, today, every two or three years. No contractual issue can thus ever be said to have been permanently resolved.

There is always a certain glamour to any interorganizational bargaining situation, particularly when such conflicts as those above can be anticipated. Labor–management negotiations constitute no exception to this rule, and, indeed, the process of arriving at a labor relations agreement has been viewed in a number of rather colorful ways.

Dunlop and Healy, for example, have pointed out that the labor contract negotiation process has been depicted as (1) a poker game, with the largest pots going to those who combine deception, bluff, and luck, or the ability to come up with a strong hand on the occasions on which they are challenged or "seen" by the other side; (2) an exercise in power politics, with the relative strengths of the parties being decisive; and (3) a debating society, marked by both rhetoric and name calling. They have also noted that what is done at the union–management bargaining table has, at other times, been caricatured in a somewhat less dramatic way—as (4) a "rational process," with both sides remaining completely flexible and willing to be persuaded only when all the facts have been dispassionately presented.[1]

In practice, it is likely that *all* these characteristics have marked most negotiations over a period of time. Occasionally, indeed, one such description seems to be extremely apt. Some bargaining sessions within the automobile industry have had all the attributes of the poker game except that the "losers" and "winners" have not been quite as easily identifiable. No one present at negotiations between the Teamsters and representatives of the over-the-road trucking companies can fail to be impressed by the influence of the relatively far greater economic strength of the union. There are those who see a parallel between bargaining in the men's clothing industry and debating society activities. And the General Electric Company for years prided itself on its firm resolution to "let the facts govern," although its unions strongly disagreed that GE in fact adhered to this policy.[2]

Nor, since bargaining will always by its very nature pit the conflicting interests of the two parties against each other, is there any reason to expect any of these factors to die out. The increasing "maturity" of collective bargaining implies enlargement of the rational process, but it is doubtful that there can ever be such a thing as complete escape from the other elements.

Moreover, a number of additional factors will also, almost inevitably, have a bearing upon the conduct of the negotiations. Items such as the objectives of the parties, the personalities and training of the negotiators, the history of labor relations between the union and management, the size of the bargaining unit, and the economic environment operate to influence the character of collective bargaining negotiations.

Some negotiators try to bluff or outsmart the other side; others would never even think of employing such tactics. Some employer or union representatives try to dictate a labor contract on a unilateral basis—"take it or else"—but most bargainers recognize that such an approach is ultimately self-defeating. In most instances, unions presenting their original proposals will demand much more than they actually intend to get, and managements' first counterproposals are usually much lower than the employers are actually prepared to offer. In other situations, however, managements and unions do not engage in these practices to any appreciable extent, and original proposals and counterproposals are relatively realistic.

[1] John T. Dunlop and James J. Healy, *Collective Bargaining,* rev. ed. (Homewood, Ill.: Richard D. Irwin, 1955), p. 53.
[2] General Electric's unique and controversial bargaining approach, known as "Boulwarism," will be discussed later in this chapter.

Representatives of employers and labor organizations differ in training, preparation, education, experience, personality, concept and standard of equity, and labor relations philosophy.

There are still other sources of variation. In some negotiations, the predominant feature might be union factionalism; in others, disagreement between management officials concerning objectives and policies. The history of labor relations in one situation might reveal that each side has had implicit faith in the other. In other negotiations, because of past experience, the bargaining might be conducted in a climate of mutual distrust, suspicion, and even hatred. Certainly, if the objective of the parties is to find a solution to their mutual problems on the basis of rationality and fairness, the negotiations will be conducted in an atmosphere quite different from one in which the fundamental objective of the union is to "put management in its place" or in which the chief objective of the company is to weaken or even destroy the union. All these factors, as well as others, will have a profound influence upon the conduct of collective bargaining negotiations.

Two other preliminary remarks are in order. First, because so many variables do have a bearing upon the negotiations, a portion of the following discussion highlights some procedural practices that might help to reduce friction between employers and unions, to minimize the possibility of strikes, and to promote better labor relations. Nonetheless, if labor relations in a company have been harmonious in the past, and if collective bargaining negotiations have been conducted with a minimum of discord, there is little reason to change procedures. "Let sleeping dogs lie" is a sound principle of collective bargaining negotiations. These observations should be kept in mind throughout the following discussion.

Second, there has been a marked change in the general atmosphere of negotiations in relatively recent years. Perhaps thirty-five years ago, the typical collective bargaining session involved a tussle between table-pounding, uninformed, and generally ill-equipped people. Possibly the side that came out better was the one whose representatives shouted louder or could use overt power threats more effectively. And conceivably the typical negotiation was a matter of each side's taking the adamant position of "take it or else."

At present, however, collective bargaining is most commonly an orderly process in which employee, employer, and union problems are discussed relatively rationally and settled more or less on the basis of facts. There is less and less place in modern collective bargaining sessions for emotionalism, name calling, table pounding, and the like. Not many negotiators use trickery; distortion, misrepresentation, and deceit are not dominant characteristics of the modern bargaining session. Advantages gained through such devices are temporary, and the side that sinks to such low levels of behavior can expect the same from the other party. Such tactics will merely serve to produce bad labor relations and to encourage the possiblity of industrial strife. Certainly, one objective of collective bargaining sessions should be the promotion of rational and harmonious relations between employers and unions. To achieve this state of affairs, those to whom negotiations are entrusted should have the traits of patience, trustworthiness, friendliness, integrity, and fairness. If each party recognizes the possibility that it may be mistaken and the other side right, a long stride will be taken in the achievement of successful collective bargaining relations.

PREPARATION FOR NEGOTIATIONS

By far the major prerequisite for modern collective bargaining sessions is preparation for the negotiations. Both sides normally start to prepare for the bargaining table long before the current contract is scheduled to expire, and in recent years the time allotted for such planning has steadily lengthened. Six months or even a year for this purpose has become increasingly observable in both union and management quarters.

The now general recognition of the need for greater preparation time rests on the previously cited fact that contents of the "typical" labor agreement have undergone a major transformation in the comparatively recent past. In recognizing and attempting to accommodate new goals of the parties, contracts have steadily become more complex in the issues they treat. (Exhibit 5-1, the Table of Contents for the current bargaining agreement between United Food and Commercial Workers Local 56 and the Packaged Convenience Foods Division of the General Foods Corporation, indicates the wide range of topics now dealt with by the typical contract.)

Take, for example, wage clauses—which have appeared in almost all contracts since the days of the earliest unions. Today, they make anything but easy reading. Where once such clauses noted the schedule of wages (generally the same for all workers within extremely broad occupational categories) and the hours to be worked for these wages, and usually little more than this, over the past few years they have become both far lengthier and considerably more complicated. Today, subsections relating to labor-grade job clasifications, rate ranges, pay steps within labor grades, differentials for undesirable types of work, pay guarantees for employees who are asked to report to work when no work is available for them, and a host of other subjects are commonplace in contracts. Moreover, most of these subsections spell out their methods of operation in detail.

Nor can the question of hours any longer be cavalierly disposed of. The extension of premium pay for work on undesirable shifts, holidays, Saturdays, and Sundays has increased the room for further bargaining. In addition, the contract must resolve the question of remuneration for hours worked in excess of a "standard" day or week: All nonexempt workers in interstate commerce today receive, by law, time-and-one-half pay after forty hours in a single week, but an increasing number of contracts have more liberal arrangements from the worker's viewpoint. And having opened these issues to the bargaining process, the parties must now anticipate a whole Pandora's box of further but related issues. Do workers qualify for the Sunday premium when they have not previously worked the full weekly schedule? Where employees are normally required for continuous operations or

EXHIBIT 5-1
Table of Contents from Current Bargaining Agreement Between the United Food and Commercial Workers Local 56 and the Packaged Convenience Food Division of the General Foods Corp.

TABLE OF CONTENTS

TABLE OF CONTENTS

are otherwise regularly needed for weekend work (firefighters, maintenance men, and watchmen in certain operations, for example), can they collect overtime for work beyond the standard week? The bargainers on both the labor and the management side must prepare their answers, and their defenses of these answers, to such questions and many similar ones; all may reasonably be expected to arise during the actual bargaining. And this necessity for anticipation is no less true merely because a previous contract has dealt with these matters, for each party can count on the other's lodging requests for modifications of the old terms in the negotiations.

The same can be said concerning the wide range of employee benefits, from paid vacations to pension plans, which have increased dramatically over the past two decades. This benefit list promises to become even lengthier. Job insecurity in an age of automation should lead to increased income-security devices. Collectively bargained profit-sharing plans have received some recent impetus as either partial or total substitutes for wage increases at such companies as General Motors, Ford, Uniroyal, and International Harvester and may now— after years of achieving only a foothold in industry—realistically be expected to spread. But it is even more likely that the continuous liberalization in the existing benefits, and the attendant costs and administrative complexities involved in all of them that have marked the history of each since its original negotiation, will continue. No one is more aware of this fact than the experienced labor relations negotiator.

Finally, increasingly thorny problems have arisen at the bargaining table regarding the so-called "administrative clauses" of the contract. These provisions deal with such issues as seniority rights, discipline, rest periods, work-crew and workload sizes, and a host of similar subjects that vary in importance with the specific industry. All these topics involve, directly or indirectly, employment opportunities; and, therefore, treatment of them has become ever more complicated in a competitive industrial world that pits a management drive for greater efficiency and flexibility against a commensurately accelerated union search for increased job security.

Fuller discussion of all these areas is reserved for Chapters 7 through 10. Even the cursory treatment offered here, however, offers ample evidence that bargaining the "typical" contract necessitates far more sophistication than in an earlier, less technical age. Labor agreements can no longer be reduced to the backs of envelopes, and ever-more-specialized subjects confront labor negotiators. Accordingly, the need for thorough and professional preparation well in advance of the bargaining is no longer seriously questioned by any alert union or management.

In today's increasingly data-conscious society, much general information can aid the parties in their advance planning. The U.S. Department of Labor's Bureau of Labor Statistics is a prolific issuer of information relating to wage, employee benefit, and administrative clause practices—and not only on a national basis but for many specific regions, industries, and cities. (Two examples of the BLS's handiwork are shown as Exhibit 5-2, which presents a national picture, and Exhibit 5-3, which deals with the building trades in each of many different cities.) Many employer groups stand ready to furnish managers with current and past labor contracts involving the same union with which they will be bargaining, as well as other relevant knowledge. International unions perform the same kind of function for their local unions and other subsidiary units where the bargaining will be on a subinternational basis. And for both parties there is also no shortage of facts emanating from such other sources as the Federal Reserve Board, the U.S. Department of Commerce, private research groups, and various state and local public agencies.

Each bargaining party may also find it advisable to procure and analyze information that is more specifically tailored to its needs in the forthcoming negotiations. Most larger unions and almost all major corporations today enlist their own research departments in the cause of such special data gathering as the making

EXHIBIT 5–2
Distribution of 1983 Deferred Wage Increases by Industry[1]

	Total Contracts[2]	0 Cents	1–10 Cents	11–20 Cents	21–30 Cents	31–40 Cents	41–50 Cents
MANUFACTURING							
Apparel & other finished textiles	14	—	—	1	2	5	3
Chemicals & allied products	46	—	—	—	3	2	4
Electrical machinery & equipment	18	—	—	1	2	3	1
Fabricated metals	22	—	—	5	5	1	2
Foods & beverages	27	—	1	3	2	2	1
Furniture	6	—	—	—	—	—	2
Leather & leather products	1	—	—	—	—	—	—
Lumber & wood products	12	—	—	—	—	1	—
Machinery (except electrical)	31	—	2	2	8	2	—
Miscellaneous manufacturing	2	—	—	—	—	—	—
Ordnance	1	—	—	—	—	1	—
Paper & allied products	43	—	—	—	3	—	3
Petroleum & allied products	1	—	—	—	—	—	—
Primary metals	19	—	6	3	4	1	—
Printing & publishing	36	—	1	2	1	3	1
Professional, scientific & controlling instruments	5	—	1	—	—	—	—
Rubber products	3	—	—	—	2	—	1
Stone, clay & glass	29	—	—	1	2	—	15
Textile mill products	10	—	—	—	—	2	6
Tobacco	—	—	—	—	—	—	—
Transportation equipment	37	—	2	3	14	7	—
Total manufacturing	363	—	13	21	48	30	39
NONMANUFACTURING (Excluding Construction)							
Agriculture	2	—	—	—	1	—	—
Communications	9	—	—	2	1	—	—
Insurance	7	—	1	—	—	—	2
Mining	12	—	—	3	1	1	—
Services							
Except health care	40	—	—	5	4	6	3
Health care	19	—	—	1	2	2	3
Transportation services	—	—	—	—	—	—	—
Transportation (combined)	25	—	—	2	1	—	—
Airline	7	—	—	1	—	—	—
Railroad	—	—	—	—	—	—	—
Street car, bus & taxi	3	—	—	1	—	—	—
Water & other	15	—	—	—	1	—	—
Trucking & warehousing	4	—	—	—	—	—	—
Utilities (light, power, gas & water)	9	—	—	—	1	—	2
Wholesale & retail trade	85	—	2	4	8	8	15
Total nonmanufacturing excluding construction	212	—	3	17	19	17	25
Total all industries excluding construction	575	—	16	38	67	47	64
CONSTRUCTION	112	—	—	—	—	3	1
Total all industries	687	—	16	38	67	50	65

[1] Figures pertain to new or revised fringe provisions.
[2] Includes some contracts carrying wage increases of unspecified amounts; not included in tabulations of medians.
—Sufficient data to compute median increase unavailable.
Source: Bureau of Labor Statistics.

EXHIBIT 5–2 (continued)
Distribution of 1983 Deferred Wage Increases by Industry[1]

51–60 Cents	61–70 Cents	71–80 Cents	81–90 Cents	91 Cents–$1.00	$1.01–1.10	$1.11–1.20	$1.21–1.30	Over $1.30	Median Adjustment (Cents per Hour)	Median Adjustment (Percentage)	Cost-of-Living Clauses
1	1	—	1	—	—	—	—	—	37.6	8.0	1
2	10	6	8	3	1	—	—	—	67.6	7.5	5
2	5	1	1	—	—	—	—	—	56.5	6.4	8
7	1	1	—	—	—	—	—	—	37.6	4.7	7
3	4	3	2	—	1	3	—	—	62.2	8.0	4
1	—	—	1	—	—	—	—	1	—	—	—
1	—	—	—	—	—	—	—	—	—	—	—
2	3	1	1	1	—	—	—	1	70.0	8.0	2
5	5	2	—	2	—	1	—	—	51.5	5.0	14
1	—	1	—	—	—	—	—	—	—	—	—
—	—	—	—	—	—	—	—	—	—	—	1
6	7	8	11	1	—	1	—	1	72.0	8.0	2
—	—	1	—	—	—	—	—	—	—	—	—
2	2	—	—	—	—	—	—	—	22.0	2.2	14
8	2	2	4	2	—	1	1	2	60.1	7.2	11
1	—	—	3	—	—	—	—	—	—	—	1
—	—	—	—	—	—	—	—	—	—	—	1
4	3	1	3	—	—	—	—	—	50.0	5.6	19
—	1	1	—	—	—	—	—	—	48.0	8.0	—
—	—	—	—	—	—	—	—	—	—	—	—
1	4	2	2	—	2	—	—	—	30.3	3.0	18
47	48	30	37	9	4	6	1	5	55.7	6.9	108
—	—	—	—	—	—	—	—	—	—	—	1
—	1	—	—	1	1	2	—	1	—	—	1
1	—	1	—	1	—	—	—	—	—	—	1
2	3	—	1	—	—	—	—	—	40.0	3.4	7
4	2	—	5	—	1	—	1	1	43.2	8.0	7
4	1	1	1	2	—	—	—	—	53.1	8.0	—
—	—	—	—	—	—	—	—	—	—	—	—
7	2	—	—	1	—	1	3	2	56.0	7.5	12
—	—	—	—	—	—	—	1	2	—	—	—
—	—	—	—	—	—	—	—	—	—	—	—
—	1	—	—	1	—	—	—	—	—	—	1
7	1	—	—	—	—	1	2	—	56.0	7.5	11
1	—	1	—	—	—	—	—	2	—	—	—
1	—	—	1	1	3	—	—	—	—	—	4
23	10	4	2	3	—	3	—	—	55.0	6.0	25
43	19	7	10	9	5	6	4	6	56.0	7.2	58
90	67	37	47	18	9	12	5	11	56.0	7.0	166
1	3	1	—	5	—	3	12	80	150.0	9.1	8
91	70	38	47	23	9	15	17	91	60.0	7.4	174

EXHIBIT 5–3
Union Wage Scales in the Building Trades: July 1, 1981[1]

City	Bricklayers	Building Laborers	Carpenters	Electricians	Painters	Plasterers	Plumbers
Akron, Ohio	*$14.500	*$13.670	*$15.350	*$14.697	*$14.250	*$12.960	*$15.240
Albany, N.Y.	*13.000	*11.200	*12.180	*14.850	*12.070	*13.000	*13.289
Albuquerque, N.M.	12.310	8.480	11.400	12.509	10.300	10.610ʳ	13.250
Anchorage, Alaska	18.930[2]	15.870[2]	*19.930	22.150	19.950[2]	18.250[2]	*22.000
Atlanta, Ga.	*11.370	*8.560	*12.500	12.950	*12.100	*11.900	12.450
Baltimore, Md.	12.580	*8.800	*12.050	*13.800	*10.700	*12.000	12.120
Birmingham, Ala.	11.830	7.570	10.930	12.778	11.550	10.530	12.450
Boise, Idaho	12.690	*10.160	*12.100	*14.550	10.870[2]	*11.640	*12.720
Boston, Mass.	11.400	*10.800	12.250	13.680	*13.710	*11.870	15.350
Buffalo, N.Y.	*14.930	*11.795	*14.030	*14.452	*13.000	*16.060	*14.760
Burlington, Vt.	*9.450	*7.850	*11.360	*11.450	*10.730	*9.450	*12.200
Butte, Mont.	15.940	*10.160	*12.230	*15.278	*11.560	*12.750	13.750[2]
Charleston, S.C.	9.400	(3)	*9.750	10.450	*8.500	9.100	10.800
Charleston, W.V.	*14.100	*10.530	*13.100	*16.860	*11.400	13.600	*13.210
Charlotte, N.C.	*9.500	*6.300	*10.800	*10.400	*8.500	*8.300	*11.400
Chattanooga, Tenn.	13.720	*8.100	*11.780	*12.873	*10.100	*12.250	*13.350
Cheyenne, Wyo.	12.280[2]	*8.780	11.520[2]	*14.250	*14.010	11.280[2]	11.970[2]
Chicago, Ill.	*15.200	*12.250	*15.400	*17.050	*13.200	*13.845	*15.800
Cincinnati, Ohio	*15.195	*13.700	*15.800	*15.364	*14.650	*14.645	*14.970
Cleveland, Ohio	*14.440	*13.490	*14.670	*15.840	*15.060	13.250	*14.480
Columbia, S.C.	(3)	(3)	9.600	*10.200	*8.500	(3)	*12.020
Columbus, Ohio	*15.090	*11.240	*13.920	*15.550	*13.290	*14.340	*15.840
Corpus Christi, Tex.	10.700	*6.960	*10.440[4]	12.730	*9.600	12.100	12.250
Dallas, Tex.	*13.670	*8.300	*13.140	*13.632	*12.490	*11.950	*13.230
Dayton, Ohio	*12.980	*11.140	*13.400	*15.630	13.210	*14.700	*15.860
Denver, Colo.	*13.150	*9.400	*13.115	15.069	*14.010	12.340[2]	*14.470
Des Moines, Iowa	*13.400	*11.645	*12.500	*13.850	*13.320	*13.355	*14.900
Detroit, Mich.	*15.570	*11.840	*15.500	*16.198	*14.300	*14.740	*14.150
Duluth, Minn.	12.410[2]	9.850[2]	11.350[2]	*14.590	12.060[2]	12.400[2]	12.360[2]
El Paso, Tex.	8.650	6.210	9.310	11.900	7.900	8.980	10.780
Erie, Pa.	13.050	*11.550	*12.800	14.550	*11.500	12.960	*15.970
Evansville, Ind.	14.280	10.750	13.500	*14.800	*12.032	13.880	*16.398
Fargo, N.D.	*13.200	*8.600	*11.490	11.550[2]	*10.950	*13.500	12.860[2]
Flint, Mich.	*14.520	*10.460	12.530	*15.082	*12.100	*12.520	*14.540
Fort Worth, Tex.	*13.860	*8.300	*13.140	*13.800	*13.440	*13.930	*13.530
Fremont, Calif.	*18.050	*12.940	15.350[2]	17.135[2]	*17.620	*15.080	*20.850
Fresno, Calif.	*16.350	*12.940	*16.050	*15.224	*12.970	12.400	16.500[2]
Grand Rapids, Mich.	*13.400	*9.460	*13.040	12.208	*11.150	*12.540	*13.890
Hammond, Ind.	*15.050	11.500	*15.000	*16.128	*13.700	13.310	*14.820
Hartford, Conn.	*12.800	10.000	12.750	*13.870	*12.150	*12.800	12.710
Honolulu, Hawaii	12.380	*10.160	12.750	*12.860	*13.050	12.340	13.000
Houston, Tex.	*14.600	*10.850	*14.450	12.825	*14.130	12.975[2]	*13.490
Huntsville, Ala.	*12.750	7.440	9.850	*13.100	9.350	*12.250	12.900
Indianapolis, Ind.	*13.750	10.350	*14.580	*15.010	*12.700	14.180[2]	*15.350
Jackson, Miss.	11.150	6.650	*10.550	*12.750	8.500	*9.750	12.500
Jacksonville, Fla.	*11.650	*7.220	*11.320	12.150	*10.950	*10.310	12.000
Kansas City, Mo.	13.390	11.200	14.050	14.680	*13.590	*16.050	*14.544
Knoxville, Tenn.	*12.710	*7.420	*10.690	*12.260	*10.400	*11.830	*12.550
Lansing, Mich.	*14.350	*10.600	*13.970	*13.968	12.700	*12.320	*14.430
Las Vegas, Nev.	15.570[2]	11.750[2]	*15.310	*18.360	*17.340	*13.420	*17.350
Little Rock, Ark.	*11.800	7.650	10.850	12.397	9.850	10.900	*13.300

(See footnotes at end of table)

EXHIBIT 5–3 (continued)
Union Wage Scales in the Building Trades: July 1, 1981[1]

City	Bricklayers	Building Laborers	Carpenters	Electricians	Painters	Plasterers	Plumbers
Long Beach, Calif.	*17.050	*11.880	*14.940	14.420[2]	*15.290	*16.345	*16.850
Los Angeles, Calif.	*17.050	*11.880	*14.940	14.420[2]	*15.290	*16.345	*16.850
Louisville, Ky.	*12.840	*10.150	*13.350	*15.333	*11.070	10.850	14.220
Lubbock, Tex.	10.850	6.960	*11.900	12.455	*10.150	10.000	*12.700
Madison, Wis.	10.940[2]	*11.270	*13.120	*14.140	*13.610	*11.100	*13.710
Manchester, N.H.	*11.410	*9.070	*11.360	*13.850	*10.000	*11.410	*14.000
Memphis, Tenn.	13.250[r]	*8.915	*11.830	*15.480	*12.375	11.300[5]	*15.670
Miami, Fla.	12.550	8.470	11.350	13.350	11.050	12.550	*13.460
Milwaukee, Wis.	*14.470	*12.170	*14.120	*15.490	*12.850	*13.220	*15.190
Minneapolis, Minn.	*13.310	*11.250	11.660[2]	*15.170	*13.010	*13.400	*13.540
Mobile, Ala.	11.980	7.480	11.570	13.570	*11.090	12.140	12.650
Montgomery, Ala.	9.250	*6.600	10.550	*10.783	9.250	10.530	9.250
Nashville, Tenn.	*12.400	*8.100	*12.300	*13.300	*10.350	*10.400	*12.700
New Bedford, Mass.	11.400	*10.800	*12.820	*12.400	*11.630	11.400	*12.890
New Haven, Conn.	*13.050	10.000	12.950	*14.500	*11.450	*13.050	11.470
New Orleans, La.	*13.250	*10.200	*12.350	*13.253	9.845	*11.030	12.950
New York, N.Y.	*14.170	10.650[2]	*14.590	*15.750	*12.000	*13.300	*14.060
Newark, N.J.	*13.210	*9.500	*14.100	14.570	*12.400	*13.210	*15.425
Norfolk, Va.	*11.680	*7.000	*10.850	*11.700	*10.250	*11.960	11.050
Oakland, Calif.	*18.050	*12.940	15.350[2]	17.135[2]	*17.620	*15.080	*20.850
Oklahoma City, Okla.	*12.800	*9.750	*12.550	12.282	*11.650	*14.200	*14.240
Omaha, Neb.	*12.990	*9.760	*13.820	*13.929	*12.420	*12.720	*13.690
Peoria, Ill.	*14.240	*13.640	*14.560	*16.000	*14.370	*14.460	*14.830
Philadelphia, Pa.	*13.280	9.800	*12.520	*15.160	*12.400	*13.960	*14.230
Phoenix, Ariz.	12.520[2]	*10.150	*12.685	*17.150	12.380	*14.620	15.490[2]
Pittsburgh, Pa.	*14.850	*12.040	*13.750	13.350	*14.580	*12.840	*15.050
Portland, Maine	9.300	*7.920	*10.890	*13.000	9.250	9.000	11.700
Portland, Ore.	*16.060	*11.970	*15.200	17.990	*13.730	*14.420	*18.330
Providence, R.I.	12.300	*10.550	*12.750	*13.850	11.150	*12.350	*13.300
Raleigh, N.C.	*9.500	*6.250	*10.800	*10.750	*8.500	*8.400	*11.400
Reading, Pa.	*12.150	*9.550	*11.980	13.390	*11.050	*12.410	*14.230
Richmond, Va.	*12.500	*7.000	*10.850	*13.650	*10.000	*11.650	12.400
Riverside, Calif.	*16.500	*11.880	*14.940	*17.540	*16.740	*18.445	*16.850
Rochester, N.Y.	*14.820	*10.000	*13.360	*15.200	*13.090	*14.820	*14.410
Rock Island, Ill.	*14.060	*12.530	*14.910	·15.686	*13.770	15.400	14.867
Rockford, Ill.	*13.930	*12.450	*13.650	*14.611	*13.950	*14.310	*15.660
Sacramento, Calif.	14.860[2]	*12.940	15.350	18.600[2]	*17.620	*15.660	*16.820
Salt Lake City, Utah	12.900[2]	9.070[2]	*12.650	*13.865	11.100	*13.340	14.310
San Antonio, Tex.	*12.780	7.870	11.740	*12.778	*10.450	13.100	13.900
San Diego, Calif.	*17.590	*12.600	*16.310	*16.590	*16.740	16.160	*16.850
San Francisco, Calif.	*15.620	*12.940	15.350[2]	*20.180	*17.510	*15.840	*22.340
Santa Ana, Calif.	*17.050	*11.880	*14.940	*17.370	*16.740	*17.245	*16.850
Santa Fe, N.M.	12.310	8.480	11.400	12.509	10.300	10.610	13.250
Savannah, Ga.	10.450	*7.470	*11.500	11.300	9.850	9.000	12.200
Schenectady, N.Y.	*13.020	*11.390	*13.180	*14.200	*13.070	*13.020	*14.500
Scranton, Pa.	*12.000	*10.800	*12.990	*11.950	*11.350	*14.030	12.190
Seattle, Wash.	*16.870	*14.300	*15.470	*18.443	*15.060	*14.480	*18.010
Shreveport, La.	*11.800	*7.930	*11.500	*13.160	10.750[2]	9.750	12.690
Sioux Falls, S.D.	*13.100	9.690	11.360[2]	*12.450	9.750[2]	12.340	*12.450
South Bend, Ind.	*13.410	10.550	*13.850	*14.400	*11.690	*12.990	*14.280
Spokane, Wash.	15.180	*11.500	*15.160	*16.510	*14.980	*14.930	18.810

(See footnotes at end of table)

EXHIBIT 5–3 (continued)

City	Bricklayers	Building Laborers	Carpenters	Electricians	Painters	Plasterers	Plumbers
Springfield, Mass.	*12.400	*10.550	12.150	12.430	*10.821	*12.400	12.250
St. Louis, Mo.	12.350²	*11.975	*14.460	*14.790	12.990ʳ	*12.995	*14.005
St. Paul, Minn.	*13.310	*11.250	11.660²	*14.630	*12.520	11.600²	*14.670
St. Petersburg, Fla.	*12.250	*8.330	*11.550	10.300	*9.250	*9.400	*14.030
Stamford, Conn.	11.470	10.000	*11.900	*15.790	*12.100	11.470	*14.750
Syracuse, N.Y.	11.940²	*10.630	*12.990	*14.700	*11.770	*12.450	*13.930
Tampa, Fla.	*12.250	*8.330	*11.550	12.750	*9.250	*9.400	*12.460
Toledo, Ohio	*16.015	*13.780	*15.810	*16.800	*13.450	*16.520	*16.900
Topeka, Kans.	*13.140	8.450	*11.300	13.630	*12.590	*13.100	*13.530
Trenton, N.J.	14.050	10.150	*13.200	15.270	*12.400	14.050	14.310
Tulsa, Okla.	12.440	8.850	11.480	13.250	12.250	13.050	12.770
Washington, D.C.	*14.750	*10.420	*13.420	*14.700	*13.520	13.400	12.850
Wichita, Kans.	12.400	8.050	*11.250	*13.680	*12.140	11.400	13.480
Wilmington, Del.	*12.900	*10.500	*14.550	14.030	*11.620	12.870	*15.890
Worcester, Mass.	11.500	*10.800	12.500	*14.280	13.430	11.500	*13.330
York, Pa.	*11.050	*8.100	*11.490	*12.940	*9.750	11.080	*12.200
Youngstown, Ohio	*14.195	*11.880	*13.270	*14.600	*13.450	13.610	*13.590

¹ These rates represent the minimum wage rates (excluding holiday and vacation payments regularly made or credited to the worker each pay period) agreed upon through collective bargaining between employers and trade unions.

² New rate in negotiation on survey reference date.

³ No union wage rate in effect on survey reference date.

⁴ Part of basic rate transferred to insurance, pension, and/or vacation plans.

⁵ Includes contributions to annuity. Supplemental Unemployment Benefits, training, and industry advancement funds; separate data not available.

* Represents either a newly negotiated or deferred increase.

ʳ Revision of data previously reported.

Source: Bureau of Labor Statistics.

of community wage surveys. On occasion, outside experts may also be recruited to make special studies for one of the parties; much of the bargaining stance taken by the Maintenance of Way Employees a few years ago, for example, rested on a painstaking analysis of employment trends in that sector of railroading, conducted at union expense by a highly respected University of Michigan professor. Many managements have also made major use of the research services of academicians and other outsiders on an ad hoc basis. In multiemployer bargaining situations, whether or not an official employers' association actually handles the negotiations, the same premium on authoritative investigation has become increasingly visible.

The computer has now become an invaluable assistant to both parties in these preparations. As one management organization recently informed its clients in this regard:

> With programmed information on wages, workers, and various economic sce-
> narios, the computer has raised the calculation of contract costs to a fine art.
> Negotiators can approach the bargaining table with accurate knowledge of the
> cost of each of their proposals. Perhaps even more important . . . costs can be
> calculated in minutes instead of hours or even days. As a result, negotiators
> can consider many options in a short period of time, can work with reasonable

assurance that hidden costs will not show up at a later date, and can avoid many of the delays which painstaking cost calculations created in the past.[3]

The list of uses to which such research can be put is literally endless. Depending upon its accuracy and stamp of authority, it can be used to support any stand, from a company's avowal that certain pension concessions would make it "noncompetitive" to a union's demand for increased cost-of-living adjustments. The management may find support for a desired subcontracting clause in the revelation that the union has been willing to grant the same clause to other employers. The union may gain points in its argument for a larger wage increase by mustering the bright outlook for the industry that has been forecast by the Commerce Department. On the other hand, where poker, power, or debating traits mark the bargaining, and the "rational process" of appeal to facts counts for little, the whole effort may seem a fruitless one. Most frequently, however, negotiators who approach the bargaining table without sufficient factual ammunition to handle the growing complexities of labor relations operate at a distinct disadvantage: The burden of proof invariably lies with the party seeking contractual changes, and in the absence of facts, "proof" is hard to come by.

As painstaking a task as the fact-accumulation process may seem to be, farsighted managements and labor leaders recognize that considerably more must be done to adequately prepare for bargaining.

Increasingly, the top echelons within both union and company circles have come to appreciate the necessity of carefully consulting with lower-level members of their respective operating organizations before framing specific bargaining table approaches. Superintendents, foremen, industrial engineers, union business agents, union stewards, and various other people may never become directly involved in the official negotiation sessions,[4] and the distance separating them from the top of the management or union hierarchy is usually a great one. But the growing maturity of labor relations has brought with it a stronger recognition by the higher levels of both organizations that the success or failure of whatever agreement is finally bargained will always rest considerably upon the acceptance of the contract by such people. In addition, unless the official negotiators are well informed on actual operating conditions in advance of the bargaining, there is every chance that highly desirable modifications in the expiring agreement will be completely overlooked.

On the management side, since the daily routines of the operating subordinates require their close contact with the union, such people are in a position to provide the bargainers with several kinds of valuable information. They can be expected to have knowledgeable opinions as to what areas of the expiring contract have been most troublesome; they can, for example, provide an analysis not only of grievance statistics within their departments but of employee morale problems

---

[3] Drawn from "The Impact of the Computer on Employee Relations," a paper issued by Organization Resources Counselors, Inc., in 1983.

[4] This depends on the scope of the negotiations, however. Where the bargaining is on the local level (as opposed to areawide, industrywide, or nationwide bargaining), the business agent (for example) will very likely be an active union participant in the formal sessions. The same can be said for many management superintendents.

that may lie behind the official grievances that have been lodged. They presumably have some awareness as to the existing pressures on the union leadership, and their knowledge of these political problems can help management to anticipate some of the forthcoming union demands. They may be able to assess how the union membership would react to various portions of the contemplated management demands.

Not to be dismissed lightly, either, is the fact that this process of consultation allows lower managers genuine grounds for feeling some sense of participation in at least establishing the framework for bargaining. The employer thus stands to gain in terms of morale, as well as in information.

For the union, the need for thorough internal communication may be even more vital. The trend to centralization of bargaining in the hands of international unions has in no way lessened the need of the union officialdom to be responsive to rank-and-file sentiments. It has, however, made the job of *discovering* these sentiments, and incorporating them into a cohesive bargaining strategy, considerably harder; and "middlemen" within the union hierarchy must be relied upon to perform this assignment. Thus, business agents, grievance committee members, and other lower union officials can play a key role even where the negotiations themselves have passed upward to a higher union body, for only they are in a position to take the pulse of the rank and file.

The long list of widely varying and frequently inconsistent rank-and-file demands cannot, however, be passed upward to the international level without some adjustment. Most internationals screen these workers' proposals—inevitably giving more weight to those of important political leaders at the lower levels than to those stemming from totally uninfluential constituents—through committees composed of the subordinate officials at successively higher levels within the union hierarchy. Ultimately, a "final" union contract proposal may be placed before the membership of each local, or at least before representatives of these locals, for their official stamps of approval. And here again, the support of lower union officialdom is vitally needed by the union negotiators—to rally rank-and-file support behind the finalized union demands and to gain membership willingness to strike, if need be, in support of these demands. Aside from the fact that the local unionists may be as well equipped to help the negotiators plan their strategy as are their management counterparts, local leaders who have been bypassed in the consultation process do not typically make loyal supporters of the union's membership-rallying effort.

Finally, both legal and (on many occasions) public relations considerations now clearly demand a major place in preparation for bargaining. Specialists in both these areas must be engaged and utilized by both sides to ensure that bargaining demands will be compatible with the labor statutes, and that public support (or, at the very least, public neutrality) will be forthcoming if this is needed. The legal ramifications of present-day trucking contract negotiations, for example, have necessitated for the union the employment of its huge corps of lawyers, who have become collectively known as the "Teamsters' Bar Association." Through their high levels of remuneration former Teamster president Hoffa could claim to have "doubled the average standard of living for all lawyers in the past few years," although the personal legal problems of Hoffa (who mysteriously disappeared in mid-1975, presumably a victim of gangland action) undoubtedly accounted for some of the high statistics. For the importance of public relations to both parties in the railroad industry, one need look no farther than to the myriad of full-page newspaper advertisements placed separately throughout the 1960s and 1970s by the railroad unions and managements to state their respective labor relations cases to the general citizenry in advance of the bargaining.

For both management and union, bargaining preparation also involves more mundane matters. Meeting places must be agreed upon and the times and lengths of the meetings must be decided. Ground rules regarding transcripts of sessions, publicity releases, and even "personal demeanor" (a designation that in labor relations can deal with a spectrum extending from the use of profanity to appropriate attire for the negotiators) are sometimes drawn up. Payment of union representatives at the bargaining table who must take time off from work as paid employees of the company must also be resolved. Only on rare occasions have the parties reached a major prebargaining impasse on such issues as these, but where relations are already strained between union and management such joint decision making can be a time-consuming and even an emotion-packed process.

THE BARGAINING PROCESS: EARLY STAGES

No manager who is prone to both ulcers and accepting verbal statements at face value belongs at the labor relations bargaining table. Negotiations often begin with the union representatives presenting a long list of demands in both the economic and noneconomic (for example, administrative clause) areas. To naïve managements, many of these avowed labor goals seem at best unjustified, and at worst to show a complete union disregard for the continued solvency of the employer. Although extreme demands, such as the appointment of union officers to the company's executive board and free transportation in company cars to and from work for all employees, are rarely taken seriously, the company negotiators may be asked for economic concessions that are well beyond those granted by competitors, and noneconomic ones that exhibit a greater use of vivid imagination than that shown by Fellini or Hitchcock.

Recently, for example, the local police association in Rockville Centre, Long Island, demanded from its employer municipality eighty-five concessions, including a gymnasium and swimming pool; seventeen paid holidays, including Valentine's Day and Halloween; and free abortions. And these public servants hold no record for ambitiousness. Walter Reuther used to open automobile bargaining with so many holiday demands that on one occasion his management counterpart at General Motors is alleged to have asked, "Walter, wouldn't it be faster if you merely listed the days on which you would like to work?"

The experienced management bargainer, however, takes considerable comfort in the fact that the union is, above all, the *political* animal that the preceding chapter has depicted: There is no sense in the union leaders alienating constituents by throwing out untenable but "pet" demands of the rank and file (beyond what the various screening committees have been able to dislodge) when the company representatives stand fully ready to do this themselves and thus to accept the blame. This is particularly true when the pet union demands originate from influential constituents or key locals within the international; alienation of such sources is a job for which the employer representatives, not being subject to the election procedure, are better suited.

There are other logical explanations for the union's apparent unreasonableness. Excessive demands allow leverage for trading some of them off in return for management concessions. In addition, the union can camouflage its true objectives in the maze of requests and thereby conceal its real position until the proper time — a vital ploy for any successful bargaining.

Beyond this, labor leaders have frequently sought novel demands with the knowledge that these will be totally unacceptable to managements in a given bargaining year, but with the goal of providing an opening wedge in a long-range campaign to win management over to the union's point of view. Only in this light can, for example, Reuther's demand for supplementary unemployment benefits in the early 1950s be understood. Much more recently, "30 and out," or retirement after thirty years of service in the automotive industry regardless of age, had a similar genesis. Originally the managements in each case essentially accepted the initial union demands subject to only one condition: that implementation of what the union wanted had to be done over their dead bodies. After several years of pondering each request (and concluding that neither involved any important sacrifice of principle), however, the employers recognized both demands as desires for novel but completely acceptable kinds of employee benefits. They returned to the bargaining table fully prepared to grant them in return for union concessions in other economic areas.

Finally, since contract negotiations frequently extend over a period of weeks (on occasion, months), the union can gain a buffer against economic and other environmental changes that may occur in the interval. Technically, either party can introduce new demands at any time prior to total agreement on a contract, but the large initial demand obviates this necessity.

There is thus a method in the union's apparent madness. Demands that seem to managements to be totally unjustified and even disdainful of the company's continued existence may, on occasion, be genuinely intended as union demands; far more often, however, they are meant only as ploys in a logical bargaining strategy. They are to be listened to carefully, but not taken literally.

In fact, if imitation is the sincerest form of flattery, there is ample evidence that some managements have increasingly come to appreciate the strategic value of the large demand. Many employer bargainers have, in recent years, engaged in such "blue-skying" in their counterproposals, and for many of the same reasons as unions have (although other employers have adamantly refused to engage in this process and have even, at least partially, accepted a GE-type approach).

As a result of the premium placed on exaggerated demands and equally unrealistic counterproposals, however, the positions of the parties throughout the early negotiation sessions are likely to remain far apart.

Standing in the way of early agreement, too, is the fact that these initial meetings are often attended by a wide variety of "invited guests" from the ranks of each organization. Given a large and interested audience of rank-and-file unionists, or a union negotiating committee that is so large as to be totally unable (and unexpected) to perform the bargaining function but is nonetheless highly advisable from a political point of view, the actual union bargainers sometimes find it hard to refrain from using creative but wholly extraneous showmanship. Management representatives, too, frequently succumb to a temptation to impress their visiting colleagues as to their negotiating "toughness." And when lawyers or other consultants are engaged by either party to participate in the bargaining sessions, the amount of acting is often significantly expanded.

Even amid the theatrics and exaggerated stances of these early meetings, however, there is often a considerable amount of educational value for the bargainers. The excessive factors still do not preclude each party from evaluating at least the general position of the other side and from establishing weaknesses in the opposing position or arguments. Frequently, indeed, if negotiators are patient and observing at this point, they will be able to evaluate the other side's proposals along fairly precise qualitative lines. Thus, during the first few sessions when each side should be expected to state its position, it can often be discerned which demands or proposals are being made seriously and which, if any, are merely injected for bargaining position. Such information will be of great help later on in the negotiations.

Actually, the principle of timing in negotiations is very important. There are times for listening, speaking, standing firm, and conceding; there are times for making counterproposals, compromising, suggesting. At some points, "horse-trading" is possible; at others, taking a final position is called for. There is a time for an illustration, a point, or a funny story to break ominous tension, and there is likewise a time for being deadly serious. Through experience and through awareness of the tactics of the other side, negotiators can make use of the time principle most effectively.

THE BARGAINING PROCESS: LATER STAGES

After the initial sessions are terminated, each side should have a fairly good idea of the overall climate of the negotiations. Management should now be in a position to determine what the union is fundamentally seeking, and the union should be able to recognize some basic objectives of management. In addition, by this time, each side should have fairly well in mind how far it is prepared to go in the negotiations. Each party to the negotiations in secret internal sessions should establish with some degree of certainty the maximum concessions it will be prepared to make, and the minimum levels it will be willing to accept. Negotiators will be in a better position to bargain intelligently if certain objectives are formulated before the negotiations enter into the "give-and-take" stage. However, even at this stage it is not wise to take extreme positions and to appear inflexible in the approach to the problems under discussion. Skilled negotiators who are striving to avoid a strike—and this is the attitude of the typical management and union— will remain flexible right down to the wire. It is not a good idea to climb too far out on a limb, since at times it may be difficult, or at least embarrassing, to crawl back to avoid a work stoppage.

Indeed, after the original positions of the parties are stated and explained, skilled negotiators seldom take a rigid position. Rather than take a definite stand on a particular issue, experienced negotiators (often, where negotiation units are large, through the use of subcommittees to focus upon the major bargaining issues individually before these are dealt with at the main bargaining table) "throw something on the table for discussion and consideration." The process of attempting to create a pattern of agreement is then begun. In this process, areas of clear disagreement are narrowed whenever they can be, mutual concessions are offered, and tentative agreements are effected. Counterproposals are frequently offered as "something to think about" rather than as the final words of the negotiators. In this manner, the parties are in a better position to feel one another out as to ultimate goals. By noting the reaction to a proposal thrown on the table for discussion, by evaluating the arguments and the attitudes in connection with it, a fairly accurate assessment can be made of the maximum and minimum levels of both sides.

Actually, flexibility is a sound principle to follow in negotiations, because the ultimate settlement between managements and unions is frequently in the terms of "packages." Thus, through the process of counterproposals, compromise, and the like, the parties usually terminate the negotiations by agreeing to one package selected from a series of alternative possibilities of settlement. The package selected will represent most closely the maximum and minimum levels acceptable to each of the parties. The content of the various packages will be somewhat different, because neither side in collective bargaining gets everything it wants out of a particular negotiation. By the maintenance of flexibility throughout the negotiation, certain patterns of settlement tend to be established over which the parties can deliberate.

The package approach to bargaining is particularly important in reference to economic issues. Once the parties obtain an agreement on a total cost-per-hour figure, it becomes a relatively uncomplicated task to allocate that figure in terms of basic wage rates, supplements to wages, wage inequities, and the like. The more difficult problem, of course, is to arrive at a total cost-per-hour figure. If, for example, through the process of bargaining, the parties established $1.80 per hour as the level of agreement, they might finalize the money agreement in terms of $1.22-per-hour basic wage increase, $.20 per hour to correct any wage inequities, $.19 per hour to improve the insurance program, and $.19 per hour to increase pensions. Other subdivisions of the $1.80 would be possible depending upon the attitudes of the parties and their objectives in the negotiations.

Trading Points and Counterproposals

In establishing the content of the alternative packages, experienced negotiators employ a variety of bargaining techniques. Two of the most important are trading points and counterproposals. These procedures are best explained by illustrations.

Let us assume that management employs the *trading point* procedure. The first prerequisite in the use of this technique is to evaluate the demands of the union. Evaluation is necessary not only along quantitative lines but also along the line of the "intensity factor," which requires an assessment of the union demands to determine which of them the union is most anxious to secure. Management representatives should make mental notes of these strongly demanded issues as the negotiations proceed. For example, after a few sessions it may become apparent that the union feels very strongly about securing the union shop. At the same time, the labor organization also demands a $1.50-per-hour wage increase and nine paid holidays. Use of the trading point technique in this situation may be as follows: Management agrees to the union shop but insists that, in return for this concession, the union accept a $.70-per-hour increase and seven paid holidays.

Labor organizations also employ the trading point technique, as illustrated by the following example. Assume that, during the course of the negotiations, the union representatives sense that management will not concede to the union demand for a reduction of the basic workweek from forty hours to thirty-six. Assume further that the union feels that the issue is not worth a strike. Under these circumstances, the union may be able to employ the hours issue as a trading point. Let us say that, along with the hours demand, the union has insisted upon also securing a union shop and a $1.40-per-hour increase in pay. After the union presses the hours issue vigorously for some time (as part of the strategy, it may, of course, threaten a strike over the issue), the union negotiators agree to withdraw the hours demand in return for obtaining the union shop and the wage increase.

Counterproposals are somewhat different from trading points. They involve the compromise that takes place during the bargaining sessions. As a matter of fact, the use of counterproposals is one element the National Labor Relations Board will consider to determine whether management and labor unions bargain in good faith. However, under the established rules of the board, employers and unions do not have to make *concessions* to satisfy the legal requirement of bargaining in good faith: The implementers of public policy are more interested in whether or not there have been *compromises*. The union may request four weeks' vacation with pay for all employees. Management might counter by agreeing to two weeks' vacation with pay for employees with five years of service and one week for the remainder. A union may demand a $1.44-per-hour increase, and management may agree to a $.70-per-hour increase. At times three or four counterproposals may be made before a final agreement is reached on an issue of collective bargaining.

THE BARGAINING PROCESS: FINAL STAGES

There is almost no limit to the ingenuity that skilled negotiators use in attempting to create an agreement pattern. At more sophisticated bargaining tables, even highly subtle modes of communication may do the trick while at the same time allowing the party making a concession to suffer no prejudice for having "given in." Stevens, for example, has pointed out that

> . . . in some situations, silence may convey a concession. This may be the case, for example, if a negotiator who has frequently and firmly rejected a proposal simply maintains silence the next time the proposal is made. The degree of emphasis with which the negotiator expresses himself on various issues may be an important indication. The suggestion that the parties pass over a given item for the present, on the grounds that it probably will not be an important obstacle to eventual settlement, may be a covert way of setting up a trade on this item for some other. . . . The parties may quote statistics (fictitious if need be) as a . . . way of suggesting a position, or they may convey a position by discussing a settlement in an unrelated industry.[5]

Yet, however much the gap between the parties may be narrowed by such methods, even the most adroit bargainers frequently reach the late stages of negotiations with the complete contract far from being resolved. Given the potential thorniness of many of the individual issues involved, this should not be surprising; more than bargaining sophistication and flexibility is still generally required to bring about agreement on such delicate substantive topics as management rights, union security, the role of seniority, and economic benefits. And the fact that the bargainers seek an acceptable package that in some way deals with *all* these issues clearly makes the assignment a much more complicated one than it would otherwise be.

It is the *strike deadline* that is the great motivator of labor relations agreement. As the hands of the clock roll around, signaling the imminent termination of the old contract, each side is now forced to reexamine its "final" position and to balance its "rock-bottom" demands against the consequences of a cessation of work. And, with the time element now so important, each party can be counted upon to view its previous bargaining position in a somewhat different light.

For example, paid holiday demands, which once seemed of paramount importance to the union, may now appear less vital when pursuing them is likely to lead to the complete *loss* of paid holidays through a strike. The labor leaders may also conclude now that, although the union membership has authorized the strike should this prove necessary, a stoppage of any duration would be difficult to sustain—through either lack of membership *esprit de corps* or union resources that are insufficient to match those of management.

On its part, the management may also prove more willing to compromise as

---

[5] Carl M. Stevens, *Strategy and Collective Bargaining Negotiation* (New York: McGraw-Hill, 1963), pp. 105–6.

the strike deadline approaches. Up until now, it has sought to increase its net income by improving its labor-cost position. Now the outlook is for a *cessation* of income if operations stop.

These threats, in short, bring each party face to face with reality and can normally be expected to cause a marked reassessment of positions. The immediacy of such uncertainty generates a willingness to bridge differences that has not been in evidence at the bargaining table before.

The final hours before time runs out are, therefore, commonly marked by new developments. Frequent caucuses are held by each party, followed by the announcement from a caucus representative that his or her side is willing to offer a new and more generous "final" proposal. Leaders from each side frequently meet with their counterparts from the other side in informal sessions that are more private and have fewer participants than the official sessions themselves. These are also likely to result in new agreements. And issues that are still totally insoluble may be passed on to a newly established long-range joint study committee, with the hope that their resolution can be achieved at some later and less pressure-laden date.

Thus Stevens, in attempting to develop a systematic conceptual apparatus for the analysis of collective bargaining negotiation, has examined the implications of the deadline in the following terms:

> The approach of the deadline revises upward each party's estimate of the probability that a strike or lockout will be consequent upon adherence to his own position. . . . An approaching deadline does much more than simply squeeze elements of bluff and deception out of the negotiation process. It brings pressures to bear which actually change the least favorable terms upon which each party is willing to settle. Thus it operates as a force tending to bring about conditions necessary for agreement.[6]

Paradoxically, the imminence of the deadline can foster positive attitudes, as well as positive actions, between the parties: Its approach dramatically brings home to both groups that each will pay major costs, and thus emphasizes the existence of a common denominator. Walton and McKersie report an illustrative event occurring during the negotiations of a New Hampshire shoe company:

> The atmosphere was tense, and bargaining was definitely an adversary affair until the lights went out. Their common fate was dramatized by this incident, and the parties quickly reached settlement.[7]

Strikes do, however, occur. Sometimes the impasse leading to a work stoppage stems from a genuine inability of the parties to agree on economic or other terms; the maximum that the management feels it is able to offer in terms of dollars and

[6] *Ibid.*, p. 100.
[7] Richard E. Walton and Robert B. McKersie, *A Behavioral Theory of Labor Negotiations* (New York: McGraw-Hill, 1965), p. 232.

cents, for example, is below the minimum that the union believes it must gain in order to retain the loyalty of its members. Or, where rank-and-file ratification is required to put the contract into effect, the negotiators may misjudge membership sentiments, bargain a contract that they feel will be fully acceptable to the membership, and then see their efforts overturned by the members' refusal to approve what they have negotiated.

On other occasions, inexperienced or incompetent negotiators fail to evaluate the importance of a specific concession to the other side and refuse to grant such a concession where they would gladly have exchanged it for a strike avoidance. At times, pride or overeagerness causes bargainers to adhere to initial positions long after these become completely untenable.

And, in rare instances, one or even both of the parties may actually *desire* a strike—to work off excessive inventories, to allow pent-up emotions a chance for an outlet, or for various other reasons. The highly respected Roger Angell has not disguised his feelings that desire for a strike on the part of the owners was indeed present in the 1981 major league baseball negotiations, for example:

> . . . many of the owners privately acquiesced in the angry cries for action, for punishment, for any kind of enforced return to an older and simpler time. . . . I have heard the hard line for years now, in front offices and stadium-club bars all around both leagues. "These players are getting too much money for their own damned good," it goes. "These salaries are insane—they're ruining the game. . . . Let's stick it to them just once and see what happens. Let the season go down the tubes, if that's what it takes."[8]

The strike incidence has been almost steadily declining in the United States since the beginning of the 1960s, and strikes today, as noted earlier, idle less than 0.15 percent of total available working time. As long as workers are free to engage in work stoppages, however, it is realistic to expect that they will occasionally do so.

CRISIS SITUATIONS

It would be strange, as a matter of fact, if there were not *some* crisis items involved in *any* particular negotiation. In the typical situation, some issues will be extremely troublesome, and they will severely tax the intelligence, resourcefulness, imagination, and good faith of the negotiators. Actually, if both sides sincerely desire to settle without a strike, a peaceful solution of any problem in labor relations can usually be worked out. As previously implied, the possibility of a work stoppage is increased when both sides are not sincere in their desire to avoid industrial warfare, or when one of the parties to the negotiation is not greatly concerned about a strike. If negotiators bargain on a rational basis, keep open minds, recognize facts and sound arguments, and understand the problems of the other side, crisis

[8] Roger Angell, "Asterisks," *New Yorker*, November 30, 1981, p. 61.

situations can be avoided or overcome without any interruption to production or any impairment of good labor relations.

One way to avoid a state of affairs wherein negotiations break down because of a few difficult issues is to bypass these issues in the early stages of the bargaining sessions. It is a good idea to settle the easy problems and delay consideration of the tough ones until later in the negotiations. In this way, the negotiation keeps moving, progress is made, and the area of disagreement tends to be isolated and diminished. Thus, at the early stages, the parties might agree to disagree on some of the items. If only a few items are standing in the way of a peaceful settlement toward the close of the negotiations, there is an excellent chance for full agreement on the contract. Moreover, what might appear to be a big issue at the beginning stages of the negotiations might, of course, appear comparatively insignificant when most of the contract has been agreed upon and when time is running out. (Nonetheless, contingency plans must inevitably be made just in case. Exhibit 5-4 shows the many variables that may well have to be dealt with.)

At times, crisis situations are created not as a result of the merits of certain issues, but because some negotiators make mistakes in human relations. For example, it is good practice to personalize the things that are constructive, inherently sound, and defensible, and to depersonalize the items that are bad, destructive, or downright silly. Under the former situation, the union or the management, as the case may be, commends the other party, by saying "That is a good point," or "The committee certainly has an argument," or "Bill certainly has his facts straight." In the latter situation, it is sound policy to deal with the merits of a situation. Thus, in the face of a destructive or totally unrealistic proposal, the reaction of the other side might be something like this: "Let's see how this proposal will work out in practice if we put it into the labor agreement." It is elementary psychology that people like to be commended and dislike to be criticized. If this is recognized, rough spots and danger areas in the negotiations may be avoided.

Another way to avoid crisis situations is to be prepared in advance of negotiations to propose or accept alternative solutions to a problem. For example, suppose that the union desires to incorporate an arrangement into the labor agreement making membership in the union a condition of employment. In mapping its overall strategy for the negotiation, the union committee might decide first to propose a straight union shop but be prepared, in the face of strong management resistance, to propose a lesser form of union security. Suppose, for another illustration, that the company wants to eliminate all restrictions on the assignment of overtime. It plans first to suggest that the management should have the full authority to designate any workers for overtime without any limitation. At the same time, the company is prepared to suggest some alternative solution to the problem in the event that this proposal appears to create strong resistance. For example, it may propose that seniority be the basis for the rotation of overtime insofar as employees have the capacity to do the work in question. If both sides are prepared in advance to offer or to accept alternative solutions to particular problems, there will be less possibility for the negotiations to bog down. Instead, they will tend to

EXHIBIT 5-4
One Major Corporation's Emergency Plan Checklist for Strike Situations

```
 1. Fuel Oil
 2. Food Services
 3. Trash Removal
 4. Janitorial Supplies
 5. Mail Delivery
 6. Maintenance Supplies
 7. Security Equipment
       Cameras and Film and Tape Recorder
       Police and Guard Service
       Keys and Locks
       Passes and Parking Lots
       Portable Radios
       Flashlights/Binoculars
       Extension Cord
 8. First Aid
 9. Standby Facilities
10. Sleep-in Arrangments
11. Mechanical Maintenance
12. Electrical Maintenance
13. Emergency Transportation
14. Switchboard Operations
15. Supervisory Shift Coverage
16. Picket Line Instruction
17. Observer Teams and Forms
18. Salaried employee assignments—If/When permitted to enter facility
19. Communication Tree
20. Radio Stations to listen to
21. Vendor Notification
22. Payroll Distribution
23. Warehousing Requirements
24. Mailing Lists—labels/envelopes
25. Emergency Personnel Team
26. Hazardous Material Storage
27. Fire Brigade Team
28. Removal of necessary equipment/systems information
29. Return of all leased vehicles
30. Obtain all keys from union employees.
31. Contact local police.
32. Contact fire department.
33. Check all locks on buildings.
34. Check perimeter lighting of buildings.
35. Establish location for Company-owned vehicles.
```

keep moving to a peaceful climax. The momentum of progress is an important factor in reaching the deadline in full agreement on a new contract.

One additional procedure is available to minimize the chances of negotiation breakdowns. It has already been pointed out that many of the issues of contemporary collective bargaining are complicated and difficult. Issues such as working rules, pension plans, insurance systems, and production standards require study and sometimes are not suitable for determination in the normal collective bargaining process. As contract termination deadlines approach, a strike may result simply because not enough time has been allowed for *jointly* attacking these particularly complicated matters in a rational, sound, workable, and equitable manner. All the *unilateral* preparation in the world still does not dispose of the problem. The parties are, however, at liberty to consider such issues by the use of a joint study group, composed of management and union representatives *during the existing contractual period.* At times, management and union may see fit to invite disinterested and qualified third parties to aid them in such a project. The joint study group does not engage in collective bargaining as such; its function, rather, is to identify and consider alternative solutions. But, by definition being freed from the pressure of contractual deadlines, such a group can gain sufficient time to study these necessarily difficult issues in a rational manner.

To work effectively, the joint study group should be established soon after a contract is negotiated; it should be composed of people who have the ability to carry out appropriate research and the necessary qualities to consider objectively and dispassionately the tough issues confronting labor and management. These are no small prerequisites, but such a procedure has worked successfully in industries such as basic steel, and modified versions of it are also currently being used with beneficial results in the automobile, glass, rubber, and aluminum industries. There is no reason to believe that other collective bargaining parties, including those bargaining on an individual plant basis, could not also profit from it in avoiding crisis situations.

Some parties have found the mediation process helpful when crisis situations are reached in negotiations. The Federal Mediation and Conciliation Service of the U.S. government, and state conciliation services, make mediators available to unions and companies. The Federal Service maintains regional offices in New York, Philadelphia, Atlanta, Cleveland, Chicago, St. Louis, and San Francisco, as well as field offices and field stations in many other large industrial centers. It employs some 300 mediators, whose services are available without charge to the participants in the collective bargaining process, and it currently mediates about 20,000 labor disputes a year.

Mediation is based on the principle of voluntary acceptance. Suggestions or recommendations made by the mediator may be accepted or rejected by both or either of the parties to a dispute. Unlike an arbitrator, the mediator has no conclusive powers in a dispute. This person's chief value is a capacity to review the dispute from an objective basis, to throw fresh ideas into the negotiations, to suggest areas of settlement, and at times to serve to extricate the parties from difficult and untenable positions. The profession constitutes, as one of the nation's more active mediators once observed,

> . . . the public or private exercise of the last alternative. It is not repression. It is not dictation or decision-making for others. It is third-party participation in the bargaining process to minimize the external manifestations of conflict and to maximize the chances of agreement. It is intended to hasten agreement in the least offensive way. A mediator's lack of the customary forms of power is his greatest asset. The power of persuasion can be more potent than the powers of compulsion or suppression.[9]

[9] William E. Simkin, *Mediation and the Dynamics of Collective Bargaining* (Washington, D.C.: Bureau of National Affairs, 1971), p. 357.

This same observer also suggested, only partly in jest, that it would not hurt the mediator a bit were he to possess

1 the patience of Job
2 the sincerity and bulldog characteristics of the English
3 the wit of the Irish
4 the physical endurance of the marathon runner
5 the broken-field dodging abilities of a halfback
6 the guile of Machiavelli
7 the personality-probing skills of a good psychiatrist
8 the confidence-retaining characteristic of a mute
9 the hide of a rhinoceros
10 the wisdom of Solomon[10]

But if the successful mediator must obviously be impartial, this does not by any means demand that he always be neutral. "He is," as Walter E. Baer has written, "not merely a badminton bird to be knocked back and forth between the parties. When he thinks a proposal is completely out of line, he tells the parties so. When the situation dictates, he offers positive leadership."[11] Under any conditions, the mediator is a potentially valuable appendage to the bargaining table process when the results of that process lead to crisis situations.

TESTING AND PROOFREADING

When all issues under consideration have been resolved, the contract should then be drafted in a formal document. Many unions and managements permit lawyers to draft the formal contract. No objection is raised against this practice provided that the lawyer writes the document so that it can be understood by all concerned. A lawyer does not perform this function effectively by including in the contract a preponderance of legal phraseology. Such a contract will serve to confuse the people affected by its terms.

Regardless of who writes the final document, the author or authors should draft the agreement in the simplest possible terms. No contract is adequately written until the simplest, clearest, and most concise way is found to express the agreement reached at the bargaining table. Whoever drafts the agreement should recognize the basic fact that unfamiliar words and lengthy sentences will cause confusion once the document is put into force and may lead to unnecessary grievances and arbitration. Hence, it is sound practice to use words that have special meaning in the plant or in the industry. Some contracts wisely include illustrations to clarify a particular point in the agreement. And it is of particular value to explain in detail the various steps of the grievance procedure. The contract is designed to stabilize labor relations for a given period. It is not drawn up for the purpose of creating

[10] *Ibid.*, p. 53.
[11] Walter E. Baer, *The Labor Arbitration Guide* (Homewood, Ill.: Dow Jones–Irwin, 1974), p. 94.

confusion and uncertainty in the area of employer–employee relations.

Before signatures are affixed to the documents, the negotiators should have the contract test-read for meaning. No person who was associated with the negotiations should be used; each individual's interpretation will be colored by his or her participation in the negotiations. A better practice is to select someone who had no part in the conference. For this purpose, the union may utilize a shop steward or even a rank-and-file member. An office employee, such as a secretary, or a foreman can serve the same purpose for management. If those who are to administer the contract were not parties to the negotiation, such people should also be used for testing purposes; this is an excellent opportunity for them to determine whether they understand the provisions before they attempt to administer the document. If the testing indicates confusion as to meaning, the author must rewrite the faulty clause or clauses until the provision is drafted in a manner that eliminates vagueness.

The final step before signing is the proofreading of the document by each negotiator. Particular attention should be given to figures. Misplacing a decimal point, for example, can change a sum from 1 percent to one-tenth of 1 percent. Human errors and typographical mistakes are inevitable, and the proofreading of the contract should have as its objective the elimination of any such errors.

The signing of the contract is an important occasion. Newspapers and television stations may be notified of the event. Pictures may be taken to be inserted in union and company papers. The tensions of the negotiation terminated, the parties to the conference may well celebrate. They have concluded a job that will affect the welfare of many employees, the position of the labor union, the operation of the business, and, indeed, sometimes the functioning of the entire economy. They have discharged an important responsibility. Let us hope that they did it well!

COORDINATED BARGAINING AND MULTINATIONALS

An employer who must bargain with not just one but a number of different unions can frequently capitalize upon a built-in advantage to the situation. There often exists the possibility of dividing and conquering the various unions by initially concentrating upon the least formidable of them, gaining a favorable contract from it, and then using such a contract as a lever from which to extract similar concessions from the other unions. Recent corporate trends toward merger have increased such occurrences, not only by bringing together under one company umbrella a large number of unions but also, generally, by augmenting management bargaining strength as a consequence of the greater resources now provided the company. But even without mergers, many companies have—whether because of historical accident, union rivalry, or planned and successful management strategy—enjoyed this ability to play off one union against another, often even gaining widely divergent contract expiration dates (thus blunting the strike threat of any one union) in the process.

In recent years, many unions so affected have sought to offset their handicap by banding together for contract negotiation purposes in what has come to be known as "coordinated," or "coalition," bargaining. The concept, which is still so new as to lend itself to no rigorous definition but which universally denotes the presentation of a united union front at the bargaining table and often also involves common union demands, was first applied with any degree of formality in the 1966 General Electric and Westinghouse negotiations (and has been reapplied there in each triennial negotiation ever since). By the 1980s it had also been used by organized labor as a weapon in bargaining with Union Carbide, Campbell Soup, the major companies in the copper industry, American Home Products, Olin Mathieson, and General Telephone, among others.

Such union attempts to change the traditional bargaining structure had, understandably, been received with something less than enthusiasm by the managements involved. Why, as one scholar in the field had asked, "should a company whose employees have chosen different unions to represent them open [itself up] to more encompassing strikes by agreeing to widen the bargaining basis?"[12] Ironically, however, the management opposition *had* led to strikes, and some of these had been quite lengthy. Indeed, most of the endeavors had resulted in rather long stoppages. At Union Carbide, a dozen different plantwide strikes had occurred, with the shortest of them lasting 44 days and the longest going 246 days. The bulk of the copper industry was shut down for more than eight months. One set of General Electric negotiations was marked by a strike of more than three months' duration. Nor could it be said, at the time of this writing, that particularly impressive union victories had been recorded by the new labor strategy. Generally, unions that had not previously cooperated had found it hard to adjust to a policy requiring the sublimation of their own often intensely desired demands for the common good. In addition, the uncertain legal status of coordinated bargaining had remained a force to be reckoned with for organized labor.

At the moment, cooperation between unions is, at least in the opinion of the U.S. Circuit Court of Appeals for the Second Circuit (New York), "not improper, up to a point." In a 1969 decision resulting from General Electric's refusal to negotiate with a union's bargaining committee that included—as nonvoting members—representatives of other unions of the company's employees, the court upheld an earlier NLRB finding that such an inclusion was consistent with the employees' statutory right to select their own bargaining representatives.[13] The court did, however, caution that such a labor strategy would be sanctioned only as long as there was no "substantial evidence of ulterior bad faith" and only if the negotiations were exclusively on behalf of the workers under a specific union contract. Only a few months prior to the ruling, moreover, an NLRB trial examiner had ruled that the ten-union-member bargaining coalition in the copper industry dispute *had* run afoul of the law by insisting upon common expiration dates for the (separate) labor agreements, common terms, and simultaneous settlements. A U.S.

[12] Herbert R. Northrup, "Boulwarism v. Coalitionism—the 1966 G.E. Negotiations," *Management of Personnel Quarterly*, 5, No. 2 (Summer 1966), 8.
[13] *General Electric Co., 173* NLRB 46 (1968).

appeals court later rejected this NLRB ruling, deciding that the union's demands for similar contracts weren't "evidence of an attempt to merge the bargaining of separate units,"[14] and the U.S. Supreme Court in late 1972 refused to disturb this lower-court decision. But consequently, despite these ultimately favorable rulings from the union viewpoint, the somewhat mixed verdicts and absence of a clear-cut Supreme Court ruling to dispose of this issue once and for all has meant that the legally permissible boundaries of coordinated bargaining still remain unclear. They will doubtless stay there until, at some later date, an all-but-inevitable definitive Supreme Court decision based on another (as yet nonexistent) case disposes of the issue with more authoritativeness than was offered in 1972.

Generally speaking, spokespersons for those unions that have thus far used the coordinated bargaining approach seem to be encouraged by its results for their specific situations and optimistic about its general growth prospects, but at the same time they appear to be realistic in assessing its general applicability. The view of one union observer is reasonably typical:

> Coordinated bargaining is no panacea for the bargaining process. It is a tool which adapts itself to the facts of modern industry and one which can be used wisely or poorly. . . . Certainly, the development of the skills to use the new tool is in its infancy. With the growing complexity of corporations, the diversity of the unions that deal with them, and the multiplicity of new problems, this instrument will continue to grow and will be perfected.[15]

On the other hand, the long-lasting failure of the United Steelworkers to form a genuinely strong multiunion coalition to bargain with the major copper companies because of internal schisms cannot be overlooked as a guide to the future, either. Many copper unionists, both leaders and rank and file, have vocally preferred their bargaining here to be at the local level and have been especially fearful that the Steelworkers would force "carbon copies" of its settlements elsewhere on them.

Whatever the future may bring, coordinated bargaining has grown relatively little lately. Although trying to advance it now consumes about 25 percent of the AFL–CIO Industrial Union Department's $4 million annual budget and such bargaining does currently affect a not inconsequential 750,000 employees,[16] IUD officials freely admit that they had hoped for greater growth in the almost two decades since the concept was first applied. Company resistance and union parochialism are generally given most of the blame by the latter, who continue to view the recent corporate merger trend with much alarm.

Nor is organized labor happy about another growing phenomenon—that of the U.S.-based "multinational," or corporation operating plants in various countries. For many years, unions have watched fearfully as such firms—attracted by

---

[14] Affirmed by the full NLRB in *AFL–CIO Joint Negotiating Committee* (Phelps Dodge), 184 NLRB 106, 1970.

[15] Industrial Relations Research Association, *Proceedings of the 1968 Annual Spring Meeting,* p. 517.

[16] *Wall Street Journal,* December 14, 1982, p. 1.

a combination of tax concessions, lower-cost labor abroad, and accessibility to vital materials—have expanded their employment well beyond not only the borders of the United States but also, quite probably, the reach of U.S. labor law. By any estimate, thousands of jobs each week are being exported in this fashion by U.S.-based multinationals, and it is of no consolation at all from the viewpoint of displaced workers (or those who because of the exporting have never been employed at all) that "multinationals" often make huge sense if corporate return on investment is the criterion applied.

The UAW was the first major union to be touched by this threat, long before other labor leaders noted any grounds for alarm, indeed, but Walter Reuther's resulting advocacy of "one big global union" was all but universally believed to be unrealistic. Given the continuing absence of international collective bargaining laws, the wide disparity in union strengths and ideologies throughout the world, the millions of totally unorganized workers, and interunion rivalries, it still is. American labor's counterattack to date has essentially been confined only to loose consultation with the unions and union federations abroad. And if the rationales for worldwide bargaining expiration dates, global strikes and boycotts, and international exchanges of information have all been intensively discussed, after two decades no move toward genuine international collective bargaining at the global level can be even remotely detected.

It is not very conceivable that the American labor relations systems and its NLRB protection will prove to be of much help to unions even though their target employers are American-based themselves (in most cases). Actions taken by U.S. unions could well turn out to be illegal secondary boycotts, and most American laws could hardly be expected to bind Japanese, British, or German workers in any event. An "unbridled and immensely powerful adversary" for unionism, as Windmuller and Baderschneider have justifiably called it,[17] the "multinational" is something that to date has caused only frustration for the labor movement in the United States.

RECIPROCAL CHARACTER OF COLLECTIVE BARGAINING

The fact that collective bargaining is a two-way street is clearly evidenced in negotiation sessions. Some people hold the view that the give-and-take of the bargaining process involves only the management's giving and the union's taking. On the contrary, as earlier portions of this chapter have noted, the management will frequently resist and refuse to concede some issues. And when the employer believes that the stakes are extremely important, it will take a strike rather than concede a particular union demand. Thus, one function of management in collective bargaining is to review union demands in terms of the functions that management

---

[17] John P. Windmuller and Jean A. Baderschneider, "International Guidelines for Industrial Relations: Outlook and Impact," in *Proceedings of the Thirtieth Annual Winter Meeting, Industrial Relations Research Association*, December 28–30, 1977, p. 81.

must perform in the operation of the plant. It will presumably resist when it believes that the union demands could impair its ability to operate on a dynamic and efficient basis. In addition, most managements play a positive role in the negotiations by making demands on the union. Skilled negotiators on both sides of the table recognize that companies do and should get something out of the negotiations.

Management demands, of course, will be dictated by the character of a particular collective bargaining relationship. In some cases, for example, management will have reason to demand that the labor agreement be negotiated for a longer period than twenty-four months; that the union be more responsible for the elimination of wildcat strikes; that the employer have more freedom in the assignment of workers to jobs; that skilled employees get a larger proportionate increase in wages than unskilled and semiskilled employees; that certain provisions of the labor contract that have served to interfere unnecessarily with the efficient operation of the plant or have established "featherbedding" practices be eliminated; or that job descriptions be revised in the light of changing plant technology. Collective bargaining sessions are normally as productive in terms of protecting the basic interests of management as they are in protecting the legitimate job rights of employees. This result, however, cannot be accomplished when management remains constantly on the defensive.

Management demands need not be simulated. Over the course of a contractual period, events will arise that will provide the basis for legitimate management demands. Experienced union negotiators recognize their responsibility to agree to employer demands that are sound and fair, just as they expect such behavior on the part of the management representatives in reference to union demands. To the extent that management and unions recognize in good faith that collective bargaining is a reciprocal process, the negotiation sessions and the ensuing labor agreement will be conducive to serving the interests of all concerned. In this manner, the labor contract will be not a dictated peace treaty but a document that will establish a rational relationship between the employees, the union, and the employer.

BOULWARISM: A DIFFERENT WAY OF DOING THINGS

It can be argued with some justification that, for all its ultimate ability to effect a contract with which both parties can live for a fixed future period of time (even on the relatively infrequent occasions when a strike interrupts the negotiations), the conventional bargaining pattern is a highly inefficient one. With its exaggerated opening demands, equally inflated counterproposals, and particularly its seeming inability to motivate the parties into making satisfactory concessions until the fixed strike deadline is approached, it consumes the time and talents of many people for weeks, if not months, in a role-playing exercise that is often theatrical and almost always heavily larded with ritual. Could not the parties, it could well be asked, devise a system that comes to the point more quickly and deals with reality from the very beginning? The General Electric Company has had no doubts that such a system could be initiated. It sincerely believes, in fact, that its bargaining approach for almost three decades attempted to do exactly this.

From the 1940s until the 1970s GE religiously pursued a policy of (1) preparing for negotiations by effecting what company representatives described as "the steady accumulation of all facts available on matters likely to be discussed"; (2) modifying this information only on the basis of "any additional or different facts" it was made aware of, either by its unions or from other sources, during the negotiations (as well as before them); (3) offering at an "appropriate," but invariably a very early, point during the bargaining "what the facts from all sources seem to indicate that we should"; and (4) changing this offer only if confronted with "new facts." In short, the company attempted "to do right voluntarily," if one accepts its own description of the process. It alternatively engaged in a ruthless game of "take it or leave it" bargaining, if one prefers the union conclusion.

Aided by a highly favorable combination of circumstances—chief among them the presence of several competing unions, major internal friction within its most important single union (the International Union of Electrical Workers), a heavy dependence of many of its communities on the company as the primary employer, and an abundance of long-service (and thus less mobile) employees— GE was highly successful with this policy, known as Boulwarism after former GE Vice President of Public and Employee Relations Lemuel R. Boulware, until the late 1960s. With essentially no exceptions, the company offer in its original form was transformed into the ultimate labor contract. Constantly communicating to both its employees and the general citizenry of the various General Electric communities on the progress of the negotiations as these evolved—another major part of the Boulwaristic approach—the company could point with pride to the efficacy of its policy.

For their part, GE's unions attacked Boulwarism not only as an unethical attempt to undermine and discredit organized labor but as an illegal endeavor in refusing to bargain. Triggered by charges lodged by the IUE following the 1960 negotiations, the NLRB did in fact (in 1964) find the company guilty of bad-faith bargaining in those negotiations. And almost five years later the U.S. Court of Appeals at New York upheld this NLRB ruling, as did the U.S. Supreme Court shortly thereafter by refusing to disturb that decision. But the facts on which these judicial actions were taken were, of course, those pertaining only to 1960, and it appeared that Boulwarism itself was far from dead.

By 1969, however, other changes had started to work against Boulwarism. The long-competitive GE unions had (as mentioned earlier) been able to coordinate their efforts. The IUE itself had been rescued from its intramural warfare by a new slate of officers. The GE communities had broadened their industrial bases and hence were no longer as dependent as they had been on the company's goodwill. And the high number of long-service employees on the GE payrolls had, by the normal processes of attrition, been greatly reduced. These factors all served to lessen the company's ability to transfer its offer in pristine form into the final contract. In 1969, indeed, a long and bitter strike did motivate GE to adjust its offer somewhat, with the strike itself being the only visible "new fact" in the picture. And in the 1973 negotiations, the original company offer was also modified in the course of the negotiations. Both the 1969 and 1973 changes were relatively minor and seemed to lie far more in the packaging than in the substance, but they presaged a new approach to the bargaining.

In the late 1970s and early 1980s, this new approach came to fruition. The 1976, 1979, and 1982 bargaining sessions were all conducted without one serious accusation of Boulwaristic practice being levied at the company. And while an Armed Truce philosophy could still be said to characterize the relationship, the old "doing right voluntarily"/"take it or leave it" strategy was completely supplanted by the far more typical pattern of proposals, counterproposals, and ultimate compromises in all three of these contract negotiation years.

Yet there remained at GE many executives who believed that the old ways, having given the company so much success for so long, had been prematurely relinquished. They hoped that Boulwarism could still, in the 1980s, be drawn upon in GE labor relations. And it is of relevance, too, that more than a few other managements had at least partially utilized the Boulwaristic pattern in *their* bargaining in the more recent past. Employers at AMF, Timken, Allis-Chalmers, J. P. Stevens—and those in the worlds of both professional baseball and professional football—had acknowledged some indebtedness to the approach even in the 1980s. Many smaller and less visible organizations had also embraced Boulwarism in these years, without any fanfare at all.

Whether or not such efforts as the latter represented anachronisms or—with the tougher stance of management in general in the 1980s—the shape of things to come, Boulwarism even at the time of this writing thus could not be entirely disregarded. Whatever its deficiencies, it was at least a different concept that, certainly in the case of one major corporation, for a time operated with enormous efficiency. Such successes, however temporary, are never totally forgotten.

MUTUAL AID PACTS

"Management's strikebreaking combines in the airline and railroad industries have certainly been weakened," wrote a long-time labor editor for the AFL–CIO not long ago, "but the same tactics remain alive and dangerous in other industries." He was referring to mutual aid pacts, which he deemed with reasonable justification, "a weapon born of management determination to overpower unions through economic might."[18]

Such pacts, geared toward helping individual companies hold out against strikes through the use of industrywide strike funds—or, in some cases, by strike insurance—understandably are not widely publicized by their participants. Thus,

---

[18] Sam Marshall, "Curbing Mutual Aid Pacts," *AFL–CIO American Federationist*, February 1979, pp. 9–10.

except only for the airline plan (which required the approval of the Civil Aeronautics Board), neither the extent of their existence nor the specifics of each pact are generally widely known. It is known that both the trucking and basic steel industries have given thought to using such plans, but those industries had not by the time of this writing implemented them. It is also a matter of record that such managerial mutual aid has in fact been implemented in the rubber, newspaper, and papermill industries, as well as in the two transportation sectors cited above, and in the world of baseball, where the major league owners purchased $50 million worth of strike insurance prior to the 1981 work stoppage in that sector.

The airline Mutual Aid Pact, established in 1958, was designed to reimburse struck airlines for business lost to competitors because of the strike. Between 1968 and 1978, it paid out $500 million in benefits, over half of this amount to two frequently struck airlines, National and Northwest, and caused some unionists (and some CAB members) to question whether such income guarantees had in fact reduced the incentives of such airlines to settle strikes rapidly once they had begun, since the money flowed in anyhow. By 1978 both Pan American and Eastern Airlines (both of which had paid far more into the pact in this period than they had received from it) had resigned from the arrangement, and in the same year Congress outlawed the existing pact and placed such strict constraints on any future ones as to—at least for the time being—dampen any motivation for starting a new one.

The existence of a counterpart plan on the railroads became widely known in 1978 when it was revealed that seventy-three railroads were paying $800,000 per day into an insurance fund to support the Norfolk & Western Railway in its Brotherhood of Railway and Airline Clerks strike. The union's contention that it was legally able to strike all seventy-three carriers because of their support was subsequently upheld by the courts. Because of this, many believed that the plan would not extend to future railroad situations.

On the other hand, an ambitious mutual aid pact in the rubber industry, whereby companies that had not been struck exchanged not only cash but tire production for those struck, appeared to be very much operational at the time of this writing. Firestone's 1979 withdrawal from the pact, initially expected to kill the pact because of the influence of that company as one of the industry's two largest tiremakers, had not in any way done so.

And in printing, publishing, and among the owners of papermills, such plans (or variations thereof, involving the purchase by the industry of strike insurance from outside—often foreign—insurance companies) continued in high gear. Fully legal, at least to date, they had justified their retention in those sectors (for over four decades in the case of some newspapers) because they had demonstrably allowed their participants to hold out against strikes and to achieve more advantageous settlements in their bargaining. To the managements utilizing these mutual aid weapons, the cause of collective bargaining equality was also served in that union strike funds could otherwise place labor at a definite advantage.

Thus, although some of the vehement opposition of unions to these plans was surely based on emotion rather than economics, much also was entirely rational. And whether or not such plans would in fact spread, the labor movement even amid its airline and railroad victories viewed the whole topic with anything but equanimity.

SOME FURTHER COMPLEXITIES

Generalizations such as those offered in the bulk of this chapter cannot, of course, do justice in accounting for a *specific* contract settlement or strike. To appreciate adequately the complexities and variations involved in the negotiation process, one must turn to the interdependent variables that are apt to be influential in determining bargaining outcomes.

The *current healths of both the economy and the industry,* for example, have been of major effect in determing the relative settlements of the United Automobile Workers and major car manufacturers throughout the past three decades. In 1955, a boom year, management resistance to union demands was weak, and the UAW gains were consequently significant ones. The strike threat meant relatively little to the companies in 1958, a recession year, and the union could improve the 1955 contract only slightly and after considerable frustration. In 1961, economic conditions were somewhat better than they had been in 1958, and the union demands fared correspondingly better. And in both 1964 and 1967, when automobile-company production and profitability set new all-time records, the management quest for uninterrupted production led the companies to grant terms that dwarfed even those of 1955. In 1970, company costs were way up and sales (owing primarily to foreign car inroads) were way down at the same time that union members felt themselves badly hurt by inflation. A strike (at General Motors, the target employer of the UAW) was probably inevitable as a result, and the union, even after sixty-seven days of striking, achieved a settlement that was so relatively unexciting to its members that for a while its ratification was in definite doubt. In 1973, a rather intermediate year for both the economy and the industry, union gains were moderate. In 1976, the economy and the industry had rebounded nicely from a lean period a year earlier, and the union fared well indeed, particularly with the negotiation of an additional twelve days off with pay annually to counter any future threats of unemployment. In 1979, an average economy produced average gains. And in the 1982 bargaining round, hard times unknown to the industry since the 1930s generated mammoth economic concessions (to be described in Chapter 7) from the union in its desperate quest for maximum job retention. A Rip Van Winkle awakening after many years could without much difficulty discover how the overall economy had fared in the interval (assuming that he cared to, of course) simply by learning the extent of union successes while he was asleep.

Paradoxically, in 1983, when most unions were relatively pleased to come away with wage increases of 6 percent per year, Eastern Air Lines granted the Machinists a whopping 32 percent over three years—not because it was rolling in wealth, however, but because it was so relatively poverty-stricken that it simply could not afford a strike: By its own admission, a strike would have caused severe cash problems for it within two weeks.

On the other hand, the shoe industry has been plagued by consistently poor economic conditions for many of its specific employers for years, and, in the face of this variable and its persuasive logic, the Shoe Workers have shown considerable bargaining self-restraint for over two decades. And when the Brewery Workers struck several breweries in 1981, they undoubtedly regretted the actions (forced on the leadership by militant memberships) far more than did the employers: The industry had been hard hit by too much beer-making capacity and slumping sales—particularly, indeed, involving several of the struck facilities—and, not urgently needing the plants in operation, the managements basically felt no great pressures to settle.

Technological innovations—running a wide gamut from turbojet aircraft to computerized newspaper typesetting—have been the primary cause of many recent major bargaining stalemates and subsequent strikes, as even the cursory follower of current events is well aware. (In turn, job insecurity, resulting partly from improved technology in such competitive industries as trucking and the airlines, has made railroad workers a particularly touchy group to deal with in the past several years.) In 1980, the Screen Actors Guild and the American Federation of Television and Radio Artists struck for a share of the industry's profits on video-cassettes and videodiscs, something that they could hardly have done a few years earlier when these new forms of technology were barely visible and anything but lucrative.

The influence of other major variables, all of them noted earlier in this book, can be illustrated. The *relative strengths of the two sides* can be decisive in particular negotiations, as in those between the aforementioned over-the-road truckers and the Teamsters Union, and in almost all recent negotiations involving the International Ladies' Garment Workers Union and any of its many highly competitive and marginal employers. Some negotiations have not been easily resolved because of *political problems within the union:* The very public rancor between the State, County and Municipal Employees' national president Wurf and the powerful New York district leader of AFSCME, Victor Gotbaum, throughout the 1970s is still a major topic of conversation when AFSCME members get together: New York area public officials with whom the union bargained were frequently caught in the cross-fire between the two men. And in the 1980s, the rank and file of an increasing number of unions—the Steelworkers and Mine Workers conspicuously among them—have supported the charges of their local leaders that the bargainers were ignoring local problems, by temporarily refusing to ratify their negotiated settlements. On occasion, they have engaged in protest work stoppages as well.

Hostility between different unions may, of course, also cause problems, as in 1981 when the three biggest postal unions (the Postal Workers, the Letter Carriers, and the Mail Handlers) were for a while barely on speaking terms. This situation made the achievement of labor peace, although it was ultimately brought about, quite elusive for the U.S. Postal Service as it sought to negotiate contracts that would be fair to all parties.

Heterogeneity among managers in an industrywide bargaining situation may also play a large role in complicating negotiations. The team owners in major league baseball, for example, have widely varying degrees of financial strengths. By and large, they are strong-willed property holders and personal animosities abound. Some of this friction, indeed, cannot be divorced from the financial factors (for example, many American League owners harbor a suspicion that their National League counterparts—on the whole, a wealthier class—are selfishly resistant to needed changes in the game). Other rifts are not as clearly rooted to money: the owner of the Atlanta Braves, for example, is unpopular in the inner circles because of his "unpredictability." Either way, negotiating a contract that will be acceptable to a majority of these mutually suspicious owners has been anything but easy for the owners' chief negotiator, in enormous contrast to the union side where Players Association Executive Director Marvin J. Miller enjoyed all but total confidence from his more than six hundred constituents until his retirement in 1982.

The *personalities* of labor and management representatives often have a major bearing on the outcome. The 111-day coal mining strike in 1977–1978 (as Chapter 3 has indicated) was surely lengthened and possibly triggered in the first place by the sheer weakness of United Mine Workers leadership. Totally unprepared in any way for the union presidency when he was elected to it in 1972 at the head of a reformist ticket, Arnold Miller by all accounts trusted almost no one, delegated almost nothing, forced many able young staff assistants whom he deemed to be "insubordinate" to resign, and generally thwarted any agreement with the coal operators because nothing could be done without his approval and his near-paranoia prevented him from bestowing this. More commendably, the political and personal security of President A. F. Grospiron of the Oil, Chemical, and Atomic Workers appears to have been critical in effecting a 1979 oil industry settlement that was both peaceful and, given the government's wage guidelines at the time, responsive to the requests of the U.S. government for settlement at a "noninflationary" level.

In professional football, on the other hand, the eight-week 1982 strike clearly had many causes—not the least of them a deep desire on the players' part to move away from being the least well paid of all major league athletes—but a widespread belief by the owners that the chief negotiator for the 1,500 players was nothing if not power-hungry undoubtedly prolonged it. The owners, not exactly shrinking violets themselves as individuals, strongly resented Edward R. Garvey's aggressiveness and adamancy. They ultimately took their last offer directly to the players, undercutting Garvey's base, and were successful in this tactic.

For negotiators whose bargaining can in any way be construed to affect "an entire industry or a substantial part thereof" in such a manner as to "imperil the national health or safety," there may be at least one further possible determinant. Under the Taft–Hartley Act of 1947, as Chapter 3 has explained, the president of the United States has the authority to postpone for eighty days a strike consistent with the specifications above. It will be recalled that other forms of *government intervention* may also be present in such cases: suggestions to uncooperative bargainers that restrictive legislation might be enacted should a strike take place, statements by public officials aimed at throwing the weight of public opinion to one side or the other, mediation by high-level personnel of the Federal Mediation and Conciliation Service or respected private citizens, and a variety of other devices. The possibility that any of these forms of intervention may be used can, of course, influence the actions of the negotiators at the bargaining table. Steelworker Union settlements in the 1960s and 1970s, for example, were both peacefully arrived at and relatively mild in their economic increases (that is, "noninflationary"). Many observers have explained this situation, somewhat ironic in view of the turbulence accompanying steel negotiations as recently as 1959, by asserting that the government, which did, indeed, play a reasonably active role in all these settlements, would have it no other way.

And the railroad operating unions, as a second illustration in this area, were widely accused of being unwilling to compromise in their longstanding work-rules dispute of the past decade with the railroads. This was said to be due to their (accurate) belief that government intervenors would ultimately decide these rules anyhow—and possibly on better terms than the unions could extract from their employers. In at least one railroad situation, another motive also appears to have been present: In 1982, it is widely agreed, the president of the Brotherhood of Locomotive Engineers privately sought governmental intervention because he wanted to see the negotiations, which had dragged on for eighteen months, resolved one way or another. He achieved his goal, although he had to take the union out on strike for four days before the government actually moved in.

The preceding examples are only a few of the many that could have been chosen to illustrate each category of variable. In any given contract negotiation, one factor might be of major importance—or of no significance at all. The degree of importance of each also, of course, changes over time. And, clearly, many (or none) of these variables can be at play at one time on the bargainers. Contract negotiation is, in short, no more susceptible to sweeping statements than are the unions and managements that participate in the process.

The foregoing *has* indicated, however, that the negotiation of the labor contract in the contemporary economy is a complex and difficult job. The negotiators are required to possess a working knowledge of trade union principles, plant organization and operations, economics, psychology, statistics, and labor law. They must have the research ability to gather the data necessary for effective negotiations. Negotiators must be shrewd judges of human nature. Often, effective speaking ability is an additional prerequisite. Indeed, the position of the negotiator of the modern contract demands the best efforts of people possessing superior ability. Modern collective bargaining sessions have no place for the uninformed, the inept, or the unskilled.

Discussion Questions

1 Assume that a large, nationwide company is negotiating a contract at the present time. What economic, political, legal, and social factors might be likely to exert some influence upon these negotiations?

2 It has been argued by a union research director that "a fact is as welcome at a collective bargaining table as a skunk at a cocktail party." Do you agree?

3 Evaluate the statement that "in the absence of a strike deadline, there can be no true collective bargaining."

4 What might explain the frequently heard management observation that "highly democratic unions are extremely difficult to negotiate with"?

5 How do you account for the fact that the joint study approach still remains confined to a relative handful of industries?

6 From the viewpoint of society, is there anything to be said in favor of strikes?

7 Of all the personal attributes that this chapter has indicated are important for labor relations negotiators to have, which single one do you consider to be the most important, and why?

8 "Successful labor contract bargaining should no longer be viewed as an 'art.' It is far more appropriate today to refer to it as a 'science.' " Discuss.

Selected References

BANKS, R. F., and JACK STIEBER, *Multinationals, Unions and Labor Relations in Industrial Countries*. Ithaca, N.Y.: New York State School of Industrial and Labor Relations, 1977.

BOULWARE, LEMUEL R., *The Truth about Boulwarism*. Washington, D.C.: Bureau of National Affairs, 1969.

BRECHER, JEREMY, *Strike!* San Francisco: Straight Arrow, 1972.

CHERNISH, WILLIAM N., *Coalition Bargaining: A Study of Union Tactics and Public Policy*. Philadelphia: University of Pennsylvania Press, 1969.

DOUGLAS, ANN, *Industrial Peacemaking*. New York: Columbia University Press, 1962.

FLANAGAN, ROBERT J., and ARNOLD R. WEBER, eds., *Bargaining without Boundaries: The Multinational Corporation and International Labor Relations*. Chicago: University of Chicago Press, 1974.

GRANOF, MICHAEL H., *How to Cost Your Labor Contract*. Washington, D.C.: Bureau of National Affairs, 1973.

MILLS, DANIEL QUINN, *Industrial Relations and Manpower in Construction*. Cambridge, Mass.: MIT Press, 1972.

RUBIN, JEFFREY A., and BERT R. BROWN, *The Social Psychology of Bargaining and Negotiation*. New York: Academic Press, 1975.

SCHELLING, T. C., *The Strategy of Conflict*. Cambridge, Mass.: Harvard University Press, 1960.

SIMKIN, WILLIAM E., *Mediation and the Dynamics of Collective Bargaining*. Washington, D.C.: Bureau of National Affairs, 1971.

SLOANE, ARTHUR A., "Collective Bargaining in Major League Baseball: A New Ball Game and Its Genesis," *Labor Law Journal,* April 1977, pp. 200–10.

STAGNER, ROSS, and HJALMAR ROSEN, *Psychology of Union–Management Relations*. Belmont, Calif.: Wadsworth, 1965.

STEVENS, CARL M., *Strategy and Collective Bargaining Negotiation*. New York: McGraw-Hill, 1963.

THIEBLOT, ARMAND J., JR., and RONALD M. COWIN, *Welfare and Strikes: The Use of Public Funds to Support Strikers*. Philadelphia: University of Pennsylvania, Wharton School of Finance and Commerce, 1972.

WALTON, RICHARD E., and ROBERT B. McKERSIE, *A Behavioral Theory of Labor Negotiations*. New York: McGraw-Hill, 1965.

YOUNG, ORAN R., ed., *Bargaining Theories of Negotiations*. Urbana: University of Illinois Press, 1976.

6

Administration
of the Agreement

When agreement is finally reached in contract negotiations, the bargainers frequently call in news reporters and photographers, smilingly congratulate each other (as the cameras snap), and announce their satisfaction with the new contract. The exact performance, of course, varies from situation to situation. In general, however, such enthusiastic phrases as "great new era" and "going forward together for our mutual benefit" are often heard.

There is a minimum of sham in these actions. Public relations are, as has been stressed at several earlier stages in this book, important to both sides; and both management–stockholder and union leader–union member relationships are also not overlooked by the company and union participants, respectively, as they register their happiness with their joint handiwork. But typically the negotiators are genuinely optimistic about what they have negotiated: Compromise and statesmanship have once again triumphed.

It will be some time, however, before one can tell whether this optimism is justified. The formal signing of the collective bargaining agreement does not mean that union–management relations are terminated until the next negotiation over contract terms. After the new labor agreement goes into effect, management and union representatives have the job of making the contract work. The labor agreement establishes the general framework of labor relations in the plant; it spells out in broad language the rights and benefits of employees, the obligations and rights of management, and the protection and the responsibilities of the union. But during the course of the contractual period, many problems will arise involving the *application* and the *interpretation* of the various clauses in the labor agreement.

The application of the contract is, in fact, a daily problem. Representatives of management and the union normally devote a considerably larger share of their time to the administration of the labor agreement than to its negotiation. Moreover, the climate of labor relations in the plant will be determined to a large extent by the manner in which management and union representatives discharge their obligations in the day-to-day application of the labor contract. Whether there will be good or bad labor relations depends to a significant degree on the character of the administration of the labor agreement. For these reasons, it is vital that the parties to a collective bargaining relationship understand thoroughly the problems and the responsibilities that grow out of the application of a contract.

The source of many administrative problems is in the language of the labor agreement. Owing to the conditions under which bargaining takes place, many contractual clauses are themselves written in rather broad terms. The day-to-day job in labor relations is to apply the *principles* of the contract.

Many problems can arise under a single clause of the labor agreement. For example, a contract may limit the right of management to discharge for "just cause." An employee is discharged for talking back to a foreman in harsh terms. Is this just cause within the meaning of the agreement? In another case, a seniority arrangement may provide that the employee with the longer service in the plant will get the better job, provided that he or she has ability to perform the job equal to that of any other employee who desires the position. Whether or not the employee with longer service *is* awarded the job is an administrative problem. Or the parties may have agreed that employees will be expected to perform jobs falling within their job description. An emergency arises in the plant, and the company directs some employees to work outside their job description. Did the company violate the agreement? Or, as a final example, the labor agreement provides that wage rates of new jobs created in the plant are to be established in a manner that is equitable in terms of comparable jobs. Does a rate established for such a job in fact compare fairly with that for kindred jobs?

These illustrations suggest the multitude of problems that can arise in connection with the operation of a labor agreement on a day-by-day basis. Practically every provision in a collective bargaining contract can be the basis for problems that must be resolved.

GRIEVANCE PROCEDURE

Problems such as those posed above are handled and settled through the grievance procedure of the labor contract. The grievance procedure provides an orderly system whereby the employer and the union can determine whether or not the contract has, in effect, been violated. Only a comparatively small number of violations involve willful disregard of the terms of the collective bargaining agreement. More frequently, employers or unions pursue a course of conduct, alleged to be a violation of the collective bargaining agreement, that the party honestly believes to conform with its terms. In any event, the grievance procedure provides the mechanism whereby the truth of the matter will be revealed. Through it, the parties have an opportunity to determine whether or not the contract has actually been violated. Such a peaceful procedure, of course, is infinitely superior to a system that would permit the enforcement of the contract through the harsh vehicle of the strike or lockout. Each year, literally hundreds of thousands of grievances are filed alleging contract violations. Indeed, industry would be in a chaotic state if the strike or the lockout were utilized to effect compliance with the contract instead of resorting to the peaceful procedures of the grievance mechanism.

The best way to demonstrate the working of a grievance procedure is through an actual circumstance. For this purpose, a case that actually occurred in industry will be utilized, although fictitious names for the participants will be used.

Tom Swift, a rank-and-file member of Local 1000, had been employed by the Ecumenical Bagel Company for a period of five years. His production record was excellent; he caused management no trouble; and during his fourth year of employment he received a promotion. One day, Swift began preparations to leave the plant twenty minutes before quitting time. He put away his tools, washed up, got out of his overalls, and put on his street clothes. Jackson, an assistant foreman in his department, observed Swift's actions. He immediately informed Swift that he was going to the front office to recommend his discharge. The next morning, Swift reported for work, but Jackson handed him a pay envelope that, in addition to wages, included a discharge notice. The notice declared that the company discharged Swift because he made ready to leave the plant twenty minutes before quitting time.

Swift immediately contacted his union steward, Joe Thomas. The steward worked alongside Swift in the plant and, of course, personally knew the assistant foreman and foreman of his department. After Swift told Thomas the circumstances, the steward believed that the discharge constituted a violation of the collective bargaining contract. A clause in the agreement provided that an employee could be discharged only for "just cause." Disagreeing with the assistant foreman and the front office, Thomas felt that the discharge was not for just cause.

The collective bargaining contract covering the employees of the Ecumenical Company contained a carefully worded grievance procedure. It was through this procedure that Thomas was required to protest the discharge of Swift. The steward was aware that the requirements of the grievance procedure had to be carried out if he intended to take appropriate action to effect reinstatement of the union member. The grievance procedure provided that all charges of contract violation must be reduced to writing. Consequently, the steward and the discharged worker filled out a "grievance form," describing in detail the character of the alleged violation.

The steps in processing the complaint through the grievance procedure were clearly outlined in the collective bargaining agreement. First, it was necessary to present the grievance to the foreman of the department in which Swift worked. Both Thomas and Swift approached the foreman, and the written grievance was presented to him. The foreman was required to give his answer on the grievance within forty-eight hours after receiving it. He complied with the time requirement, but his answer did not please Swift or Thomas. The foreman supported the action of the assistant foreman and refused to recommend the reinstatement of Swift.

Not satisfied with the action of the foreman, the labor union, through Thomas, the steward, resorted to the second step of the grievance procedure. This step required the appeal of the complaint to the superintendent of the department in which Swift worked. Again the disposition of the grievance by management's representative brought no relief to the discharged employee. Despite the efforts of the steward, who vigorously argued the merits of Swift's case, the department superintendent refused to reinstate the worker. Hence the second step of the grievance procedure was exhausted, and the union and the employee were still not satisfied with the results.

Actually the vast majority of grievances are settled in the first two steps of the grievance procedure. This is a remarkable record, indicating the fairness of employers and labor unions. The employer or the union charged with a contract violation may simply admit the transgression and take remedial action. On the other hand, the party charged with violating the collective bargaining agreement may be able to persuade the other party that, in fact, no violation exists. Frequently, both parties might work out a compromise solution satisfactory to all concerned. Such a compromise may serve the interests of sound industrial relations, a state of affairs that the grievance procedure attempts to produce.

In the Swift case, however, the union refused to drop the case after the complaint was processed through the second level of the grievance procedure. Grievance personnel for the third step included, from the company, the general superintendent and his representatives; and for the labor union, the organization's plantwide grievance committee. The results of the negotiations at the third step proved satisfactory to Swift, the union, and the company. After forty-five minutes of spirited discussion, the management group agreed with the union that discharge was not warranted in this particular case. Management's committee was persuaded by the following set of circumstances: Everyone conceded that Swift had an outstanding record before the dismissal occurred. In addition, the discussion revealed that Swift had inquired of the department foreman whether there was any more work to be done before he left his bench to prepare to leave for home. The foreman had replied in the negative. Finally, it was brought out that Swift had had a pressing problem at home that he claimed was the motivating factor for his desire to leave the plant immediately after quitting time.

The grievance personnel reached a mutually satisfactory solution of the case after all the factors were carefully weighed. Management repeatedly stressed the serious consequences to production efficiency if a large number of workers prepared to leave the plant twenty minutes before quitting time. Recognizing the soundness of this observation, the union committee agreed that some sort of disciplinary action should be taken. As a result, it was concluded that Swift would be reinstated in his job but would be penalized by a three-day suspension without pay. In addition, the union committee agreed with management's representatives that better labor relations would be promoted if a notice were posted on the company bulletin boards stating that all workers would be expected to remain at their jobs until quitting time. Union and company grievance personnel were in agreement that the notice should also declare that violations would be subject to penalty. Thus the grievance procedure resulted in the amicable solution of a contract violation case.

What would have occurred, however, if the company and the labor union had not reached a satisfactory agreement at the third step of the grievance procedure? In this particular contract, the grievance procedure provided for a fourth step. Grievance procedure personnel at the fourth step included, for the company, the vice president in charge of industrial relations or a representative, and, for the union, an officer of the international union or a representative. It is noteworthy that this particular contract provided four chances to effect a mutually satisfactory disposition of a complaint alleging a contract violation.

All collective bargaining contracts do not provide for the same structural arrangements as the one described in the Swift case. Some contain only three steps while others may have as many as seven or eight; in still others, the time limits may be different; or the particular company and union personnel participating at the various steps of the grievance procedure may be somewhat different, as in Exhibit 6-1, illustrating a different but still quite common third-step situation. If their structural arrangements vary slightly from contract to contract, however, the fact remains that the essential characteristics of grievance procedures are similar. All have as their basic objective the settling of alleged contract violation cases in a friendly and orderly manner. In each there is provided a series of definite steps to follow in the processing of grievances. A certain time limit is placed on each step, and an answer to a grievance must be given within the allotted time. Failure to comply with the time limits could result in the forfeiture of the grievance by the errant party. For example, where a union fails to appeal a grievance within the stipulated time limit, the employer may deny the grievance on that basis. Where such cases go to arbitration, the arbitrator may under appropriate circumstances hold that, since the union did not comply with the time limit, the grievance is not· arbitrable. That is, the arbitrator may deny the grievance on these grounds and without inquiry into the merits of the employee's complaint. *(Case 1, found at the end of this chapter, deals with the time limit problem. It is the first of fourteen cases offered by this volume to illustrate specific problems in labor relations.)*

GRIEVANCE PROCEDURE: ITS FLEXIBILITY

Since management officials and union officers make up grievance procedure personnel, people intimately connected with the work will decide whether or not a particular pattern of conduct violates the terms of the collective bargaining agreement. Obviously, these people are in a favored position to make such a determination. Frequently, some of them helped negotiate the collective bargaining con-

EXHIBIT 6–1

LOCAL 117

RECORD OF GRIEVANCE

Date: _____August 18, 1981_____

Name _____John Williams_____ Home Phone _____

Address _____ Status: Regular _____ Seasonal _____

Date of Hire _____ Pay Rate _____ Job Class. _____

Department _____ Supervisor _____

NATURE OF COMPLAINT (Give dates) ____I was discharged for fighting on company property.____

I feel that this is unfair and unjustified because the company does not fire everyone for fighting.   I ask to be

reinstated with back pay and seniority.

Steward or Business Representative __Fred Wells__

COMPANY RESPONSE: _____Grievance denied.   Rule # 39 in the "Employee Handbook" outlines the

amount of discipline to be administered for violation of this rule.   This grievance is untimely.   Incident

occurred on 7/15/81.

Date __8/19/81__   Plant Manager __J. Wyner__ tract itself. Such participation in the contract-making negotiations should result in a clear understanding of the meaning of particular contract terms. Not only do grievance procedure personnel normally possess a thorough and firsthand knowledge of the meaning of the contract, but they are well aware of the character of the conduct alleged to be a violation. Grievance cases are at times complex in nature. The line dividing "lawful" from "unlawful" conduct under a collective bargaining contract is not always sharply drawn. Clearly, people actually associated with the situation in which the alleged violation occurred can best decide these difficult cases.

The local character of grievance procedure personnel serves to make this contract-enforcing technique highly flexible in character. These people are well aware of the environmental context in which the alleged violation occurred. Weight can be given to human or economic factors involved in alleged violations. This does not mean that an "explainable" violation will go unchallenged. However, the grievance procedure personnel might resolve an "explainable" violation in a different manner from one in which no extenuating circumstances were involved.

Since grievance procedure personnel are closely associated with the plant, they are in an excellent position to anticipate the effects of the disposition of a grievance on employers, on the union, on union leadership, and on plant operations. To promote sound industrial relations, management and union grievance procedure personnel, as noted, frequently compromise on the solution of grievance cases. It is not unknown for management to allow the union to "win" a grievance case to bolster the prestige of union leadership in the eyes of union membership; the state of industrial relations may be improved when union leaders have the confidence of the membership. On the other hand, a labor union may refuse to challenge a company violation of a contract when the employer engages in conduct absolutely essential for the operation of the plant.

Contrary to the seniority provisions of an existing collective bargaining contract, for example, a company recently laid off longer-service employees and retained shorter-service employees. Such action constituted a direct violation of the particular contract. However, the union representatives agreed with the company, when the case was resolved through the grievance procedure, that the retention of the shorter-service workers was vital to the continued operation of a crucial plant department. Union and management grievance procedure personnel concluded that had the longer-service workers been retained and the shorter-service employees been laid off, the plant, the union, and all employees of the company would have suffered irreparable damage.

It is not intended here to create a false impression of the operation of the grievance procedure. Certainly, the mechanism does not function to condone employer, employee, or union violations of collective bargaining contracts. In the overwhelming number of cases disposed of through the grievance procedure, practices inconsistent with the terms of the agreement are terminated. At times, retroactive action must be taken to implement rights and obligations provided for in the contract. Thus, the employer may be required to reinstate with back pay a worker who had previously been discharged in violation of the discharge clause of the labor agreement. Or perhaps a union caused damage to the company's property while on strike; to comply with a particular contract provision, this union might be required to pay the company a certain sum of money.

Without detracting from the fact that the primary objective of the grievance procedure is to enforce the terms of the collective bargaining contract, it remains true that this mechanism is singularly adaptable for the settlement of contract disputes to the maximum satisfaction of all concerned. Interests of all parties can be considered. Its flexible and personalized character permits compromise when this is deemed the best way to settle a particular grievance. Extenuating circumstances can be given weight. Precedent can be utilized or disregarded, depending on the particular situation. Effects of the manner of disposition of a contract violation case are clearly understood by grievance procedure personnel. In short, the flexible character of grievance procedure is its outstanding merit. Solutions to problems can be reached that will serve the basic interests of sound industrial relations. These observations lead to one conclusion: Resort to the grievance procedure provides management and unions with the most useful and efficient means of contract enforcement.

Grievance Procedure and Harmonious Labor Relations

As suggested above, the grievance procedure, by providing the parties to the labor contract with an excellent opportunity whereby complaints of workers, employers, and unions can be aired and discussed, may be regarded as supplying the "psychotherapy" of industrial relations. Small problems can be discussed and settled promptly before they become major and troublesome issues in the plant. Serious problems can be analyzed in a rational manner and resolved speedily, peacefully, and in keeping with the terms of the collective bargaining contract. The rights of employees, employers, and unions guaranteed in the labor contract can be protected and implemented in a prompt and orderly fashion. Not only does the grievance procedure serve as a means for the enforcement of the labor agreement, but it also provides the parties with the opportunity of establishing the *reasons* for complaints and problems.

Indeed, depending upon the attitudes of the management and the union, the grievance procedure can also be used for functions other than the settlement of complaints arising under the labor agreement. Many parties, for example, use the grievance machinery to prevent grievances from arising as well as to dispose of employee, union, and employer complaints. Major grievances are viewed here as symptomatic of underlying problems, and attempts are jointly made to dispose of these problems to prevent their future recurrence. In other cases, the parties may utilize the scheduled grievance meeting time, after the grievance itself has been dealt with, to explore ways of improving their general relationship and also as an avenue of bilateral communication on matters of interest to both institutions (such as new employer plans, the economic prospects for the industry, or the upcoming union election).

In the last analysis, in fact, the grievance procedure should be regarded as a device whereby managements or unions can "win" a grievance only in the most narrow of senses. It should also be viewed as a means of obtaining a better climate of labor relations, rather than as the machinery whereby either the employer or the union can exercise authority over the other. This does not mean that rights guaranteed in the labor contract should be waived or compromised, but that in discharging obligations under the grievance procedure, the parties should understand the broader implications involved. Employer and union representatives who regard the grievance procedure in this light gear their behavior, arguments, and general approach toward the objective of the improvement of labor relations.

This objective is not realized when representatives of management look upon their obligations under the grievance procedure as burdensome chores, as wastes of time, or as necessary evils. Likewise, it is not attainable to the extent that unions stuff the grievance procedure with complaints that have no merit whatsoever under the collective bargaining contract.[1] It cannot be achieved when the parties regard the grievance procedure as a method to embarrass the other side or to demonstrate authority or power. In addition, the opportunities for more harmonious labor relations through the use of the grievance procedure cannot be realized to the extent that the system is used to resolve internal political conflicts within the union or the management. If the grievance procedure does not contribute to a better labor relations climate, the fault lies not with the system, but with the representatives of unions and management who either misunderstand or distort the functions that the procedure plays in the industrial relations complex.

ARBITRATION

The vast majority of problems that arise as the result of the interpretation and application of collective bargaining contracts are resolved bilaterally by the representatives of management and the labor organization. Through the process of negotiation, the parties to a contract manage to find a solution to grievances at some step in the grievance procedure. Such a record testifies to the utility of the grievance procedure as a device for the speedy, fair, and peaceful solution of disputes growing out of the application of the collective bargaining contract. It also shows rather clearly that the great majority of management and union representatives understand fully the purpose of the grievance procedure and discharge their responsibilities on the basis of good faith.

Indeed, in healthy union–management relationships, the great bulk of grievances is disposed of at the lower levels of the procedure. This is as it should be; were most such complaints merely bucked up the union and management hierar-

---

[1] Many unions specifically instruct their stewards and grievance committee members not to process grievances that have no merit under a labor agreement. Thus, in one union manual, "After you have thoroughly investigated the case, if you decide that no grievance exists, it is your duty to the worker and the union to state this, and to take time to explain why."

chical ladders, the time and efforts of the more broadly based officials would be hopelessly drained. Lower-step settlement also helps maintain the status of lower supervision and assures that the grievance is allowed treatment by the people who are apt to be most familiar with the circumstances under which it arose.

Under even the most enviable of labor relationships, however, there will undoubtedly be some grievances that prove themselves completely incapable of being solved by *any* level within the bilateral grievance procedure. Each party genuinely believes that its interpretation of the contract is the right one, or the parties remain in disagreement as to the facts of the case.

There may also, on occasion, be less commendable reasons for a stalemate. The union leadership may feel that it cannot afford to "give in" on an untenable grievance because of the political ramifications of doing so. Management may at times prove quite unwilling to admit that the original company action giving rise to the grievance was in violation of the contract, even though in its heart it realizes that the union's allegation is right. The union may, the remarks previously offered in this connection notwithstanding, seek to "flood" the grievance procedure with a potpourri of unsettled grievances, with the hope of using the situation to gain extracontractual concessions from the company. The employer may, in turn, seek to embarrass the union leadership by making it fight to the limit for any favorable settlement. And grievances involving such thorny issues as discipline, work assignment, and management rights are sometimes accompanied by emotional undercurrents that make them all the more difficult to resolve by the joint conference method of the grievance procedure.

In short, the amount of challenge that management can expect through the grievance procedure can vary widely because of the existence of such complex variables as (1) the wisdom and extent of development of the legislated policy that is embodied in the labor agreement itself (and, no less important, the degree of operating policy development that the employer has effected to supplement the labor agreement); (2) the political environment and militancy of the local union; (3) the caliber of the management's personnel administration and supervision; (4) the nature of the existing union–management relationship; and (5) economic and related variables affecting employment and working conditions.

Given all these variables, it is, in fact, a tribute to the maturity of labor–management relations that the great majority of all grievances are in fact settled by the joint process.

Nonetheless, some contractual provision must be made by the parties to handle the relatively few issues for which the grievance procedure proves unsuccessful—those occasions upon which the parties to the labor contract are still in disagreement over a problem arising under the contractual terms after all bilateral steps in the grievance procedure have been exhausted. To break such deadlocks, the parties have the opportunity to resort to the arbitration process. An impartial outsider is selected by the parties to decide the controversy. This person's decision is invariably stipulated in the contract as being "final and binding upon both parties."

As a method of dispute settlement, arbitration is anything but new. King Solomon was an arbitrator—and, from all accounts, a first-rate one—some three thousand years ago. Arbitration (sometimes wth more than one arbitrator) was also used to settle disputes between towns in ancient Greece and was an accepted avenue for resolving controversy in ancient Babylon, the early Islamic civilization, and under Roman law. Not to be outdone, the Confucian Chinese used it, too, and so did the medieval Germans. In the United States, George Washington showed his high regard for the concept by providing for binding arbitration in his will (should any disputes arise concerning the intent of the latter).

As American unionism grew, the advantages of arbitration became visible in this sector, also. Above all, it was seen that the arbitrator could resolve the labor dispute in a peaceful manner. In the absence of arbitration, the parties might use the strike or lockout to settle such problems, a process that not only is costly to the management, the union, and the employees but would tend to foster embittered labor relations. Impressed by these arbitral facts of life, some 96 percent of all U.S. labor agreements provide for arbitration as the final step in the grievance procedure. This national percentage is significantly greater than it was in the early 1930s, when fewer than 8 to 10 percent of all agreements contained such a clause. And even by 1944, arbitration provisions had been included in only 73 percent of all contracts.[2]

Not surprisingly, the statistics involving arbitration case loads have been of no small order of magnitude. In 1981, for example, arbitrators serving under the auspices of the Federal Mediation and Conciliation Service issued 6,967 awards compared with 2,840 in 1971.[3] The American Arbitration Association also experienced a similar large increase in the number of awards.

(If it were not for the U.S. Supreme Court's decision in *Vaca* v. *Sipes*,[4] the number of cases submitted to arbitration would have been much larger. In that case, the high court held that a union is not obligated to process every grievance to arbitration. If that were required, the arbitration process would break down— it could not possibly handle such a case load, let alone the financial burden placed upon unions and employers. Fortunately, the Supreme Court held that a union is not liable for damages unless its refusal to carry a grievance to arbitration is based on bad faith. In the absence of the latter, a union may not be required to arbitrate a grievance even if it arguably has merit.)

In an era of uncertainty as to the future growth of union membership totals, moreover, there is no collective job insecurity in the profession: The case load for arbitrators keeps increasing annually. Much of the impetus for growth was provided by a major judicial decision of the late 1950s: In June 1957, the U.S. Supreme Court held that the federal courts may apply the Taft–Hartley law to enforce arbitration clauses. Under this ruling, an employer may not refuse to arbitrate

---

[2] "Arbitration Provisions in Collective Agreements, 1952," *Monthly Labor Review*, March 1953, pp. 261–66.
[3] Federal Mediation and Conciliation Service, *Thirty-fourth Annual Report*, 1981, p. 36.
[4] 386 U.S. 171 (1967).

unresolved grievance disputes when the labor agreement contains an arbitration provision.[5]

The "Trilogy" Cases

In mid-1960, the U.S. Supreme Court handed down three other decisions that provide even greater integrity for the arbitration process.[6] These decisions are commonly referred to as the "Trilogy" cases. Each of them involved the United Steelworkers of America, and each demonstrates that the system of private arbitration in the United States has now received the full support of the highest court in the land.

In the *Warrior & Gulf Navigation* case, the Court held that in the absence of an express agreement excluding arbitration, the Court would direct the parties to arbitrate a grievance. To put this in other terms, the Court would not find a case to be nonarbitrable unless the parties specifically excluded a subject from the arbitration process. The Court stated that a legal order to arbitrate would thenceforth not be denied "unless it may be said with positive assurance that the arbitration clause is not susceptible to an interpretation that covers the asserted dispute. Doubts should be resolved in favor of coverage."

More precisely, the courts will not decide that a dispute is *not* arbitrable unless the parties have taken care to *expressly remove* an area of labor relations from the arbitration process. This could be accomplished by providing, for example, that "disputes involving determination of the qualifications of employees for promotion will be determined exclusively by the company and such decision will not be subject to arbitration." But, needless to say, not many unions would agree to such a clause, since management would then have the unilateral right to make determinations on this vital phase of the promotion process.

In so ruling, the *Warrior & Gulf Navigation* decision eliminated a course of action that some companies had followed. When faced with a demand by a union for arbitration, some employers had frequently gone to court and asked the judge to decide that the issue involved in the case was not arbitrable. On many occasions, the courts had agreed with the company, with the effect of sustaining the company position in the grievance, and denying the union an opportunity to get a decision based on the merits of the case.

In the instant case, the Warrior & Gulf Navigation Company employed forty-two men at its dock terminal for maintenance and repair work. After the company had subcontracted out some of the work, the number was reduced to twenty-three. The union argued in the grievance procedure that this action of the company violated certain areas of the labor agreement—the integrity of the bargaining unit, seniority rights, and other clauses of the contract that provided benefits to workers.

[5] *Textile Workers* v. *Lincoln Mills*, 353 U.S. 488 (1957).
[6] *United Steelworkers of America* v. *Warrior & Gulf Navigation Co.*, 363 U.S. 574 (1960); *United Steelworkers of America* v. *American Manufacturing Co.*, 363 U.S. 564 (1960); *United Steelworkers of America* v. *Enterprise Wheel & Car Corp.*, 363 U.S. 593 (1960).

On its part, the company claimed that the issue of subcontracting was strictly a management function and relied on the management rights clause in the contract, which stated that "matters which are strictly a function of management should not be subject to arbitration." When the Supreme Court handled the case, it ordered arbitration because the contract did not *specifically* exclude such activity from the arbitration process. It stated:

> A specific collective bargaining agreement may exclude contracting-out from the grievance procedure. Or a written collateral agreement may make clear that contracting-out was not a matter for arbitration. In such a case a grievance based solely on contracting-out would not be arbitrable. Here, however, there is no such provision. Nor is there any showing that the parties designed the phrase "strictly as a function of management" to encompass any and all forms of contracting-out. In the absence of any express provision excluding a particular grievance from arbitration, we think only the most forceful evidence of a purpose to exclude the claim from arbitration can prevail, particularly where, as here, the exclusion clause is vague and the arbitration clause quite broad.

One additional important point must be made relative to the significance of this court decision. It does not mean that private arbitrators do not have the authority to dismiss a grievance on the basis of its nonarbitrability under a contract. Arbitrators before and after the decision have frequently held that a grievance is not arbitrable under the contract. Indeed, the authors, at times after the *Warrior & Gulf Navigation* decision, have upheld the arguments of companies that grievances were not arbitrable under the labor agreement. The major importance of the *Warrior & Gulf Navigation* doctrine is in its ruling that courts may not hold that grievances are not arbitrable *unless* specific and clear-cut language exludes the matter from the arbitration process. The private arbitrator is still fully empowered to dismiss a grievance on the basis of nonarbitrability. *(Case 2, found at the end of this chapter, deals with the problem of substantive arbitrability.)*

In the second case, *American Manufacturing*, the issue of arbitrability was also involved, but in a somewhat different way from that of *Warrior & Gulf Navigation*. The American Manufacturing Company argued before a lower federal court that an issue was not arbitrable because it did not believe that the grievance had merit. Involved was a dispute involving the reinstatement of an employee on his job after it was determined that the employee was 25 percent disabled and was drawing workmen's compensation. The lower federal court sustained the employer's position and characterized the employee's grievance as "a frivolous, patently baseless one, not subject to arbitration." When the U.S. Supreme Court reversed the lower federal court, it held that federal courts are limited in determining whether the dispute is covered by the labor agreement and that they have no power to evaluate the merits of a dispute. It stated:

> The function of the court is very limited when the parties have agreed to submit all questions of contract interpretation to the arbitrator. It is then confined to ascertaining whether the party seeking arbitration is making a claim which on

its face is governed by the contract. Whether the moving party is right or wrong is a question of contract construction for the arbitrator. In these circumstances the moving party should not be deprived of the arbitrator's judgment, when it was his judgment and all that it connotes that was bargained for.

Essentially, this means that the courts may not hold a grievance to be non-arbitrable even if a judge believes that a grievance is completely worthless. It is up to the private arbitrator to make the decision on the merits of a case. The arbitrator may dismiss the grievance as being without merit, but this duty rests exclusively with the individual arbitrator, and not with the courts.

In the third case, *Enterprise Wheel & Car Corporation*, a lower federal court reversed the decision of an arbitrator on the grounds that the judge did not believe that his decision was sound under the labor agreement. The arbitrator's award directed the employer to reinstate certain discharged workers and to pay them back wages for periods both before and after the expiration of the collective bargaining contract. The company refused to comply with the award, and the union petitioned for the enforcement of the award. The lower court held that the arbitrator's award was unenforceable because the contract had expired. The Supreme Court reversed the lower court and ordered full enforcement. In upholding the arbitrator's award, the Court stated:

> Interpretation of the collective bargaining agreement is a question for the arbitrator. It is the arbitrator's construction which was bargained for; and so far as the arbitration decision concerns construction of the contract, the courts have no business overruling him because their interpretation of the contract is different from his.

The significance of this last decision is clear. It shows that a union or a management may not use the courts to set aside an arbitrator's award. The decision, of course, cuts both ways: It applies to both employers and labor organizations. Whereas the other two decisions definitely favor labor organizations, this one merely serves to preserve the integrity of the arbitrator's award. Thus, even if a judge believes that an arbitrator's award is unfair, unwise, and not even consistent with the contract, that judge has no alternative except to enforce the award.

Thus, the Trilogy cases demonstrate that the private arbitration system has been strengthened by the judiciary. They establish the full integrity of the arbitration process. As a result of these decisions, managements and unions must be more careful in the selection of arbitrators. This is one reason why they have increasingly voiced a desire to use seasoned and experienced arbitrators.

Post-"Trilogy" Developments

In 1974, however, one cloud appeared on the horizon to cause some concern about the efficacy of the arbitration process. At that time, the U.S. Supreme Court decided *Alexander* v. *Gardner–Denver* and held that an arbitrator's decision is not final and binding when Title VII of the Civil Rights Act is involved.[7] An arbitrator

---

[7] 415 U.S. 36 (1974).

sustained the discharge of a black employee on the grounds that he was terminated for just cause. The employee claimed, however, that he was discharged for racial reasons in violation of Title VII. Lower federal courts upheld the decision of the arbitrator, in line with the Trilogy doctrine. However, the Supreme Court remanded the case to the federal district court to determine whether or not the employee's rights under Title VII were violated. What *Gardner–Denver* means, therefore, is that if an employee loses a case in arbitration, the employee may still seek relief from the courts, provided that Title VII rights are involved.

Following the *Gardner–Denver* precedent, in 1981, the U.S. Supreme Court held that an arbitrator's decision involving rights established by the Fair Labor Standards Act may be reviewed and reversed by the federal courts.[8] Given these two cases, the high court has sounded a clear signal that an arbitrator's decision is not final and binding when the issue falls within the scope of any federal law.

In 1976, the Supreme Court decided *Anchor Motor Freight*,[9] which also represents a departure from the finality of an arbitrator's award. In this case, the court held that an arbitrator's decision is subject to reversal by a federal court when a union does not provide fair representation to employees involved in the arbitration. An employer discharged eight truck drivers for allegedly submitting inflated motel receipts for reimbursement. Their union took the discharges to arbitration, but the union failed to heed the employee's request to investigate the motel employees. After the arbitration, in which the discharges were sustained, evidence turned up that a motel clerk was the guilty party. He had been making false entries in the motel register and pocketing the difference.

Thereupon, the employees sued the employer and the union. A lower federal court upheld the arbitrator's award on the basis of *Enterprise Wheel*. However, the U.S. Supreme Court ruled that when a union fails to provide fair representation to employees involved in arbitration, they are entitled to an appropriate remedy. Obviously, the truck drivers were not discharged for just cause, and elementary fairness should dictate their reinstatement to their jobs with full back pay. The arbitrator's award should not stand in the way of providing justice to the discharged employees. *Anchor Motor Freight* put the union on notice. In effect, the court has said that the courts have the authority to upset an arbitration award when a union commits a gross error in the representation of employees in arbitration or when unions are dishonest or show bad faith in the arbitration process. Such conduct could prove to be very costly to labor organizations. In 1983, the U.S. Supreme Court held in *Bowen* v. *Postal Service* that the union unfairly refused to arbitrate a grievance of a wrongfully discharged employee.[10] As a result, the union was ordered to share in the back pay due the employee. As a matter of fact, the high court directed the union to pay $30,000, and the employer only $23,000. One consequence of this policy is that unions may elect to arbitrate unmeritorious grievances rather than risk exposure to the greater liability mandated by the decision.

---

[8] *Barrentine* v. *Arkansas–Best Freight System, Inc.*, 450 U.S. 728 (1981).
[9] *Hines* v. *Anchor Motor Freight*, 424 U.S. 554 (1976).
[10] *Bowen* v. *U.S. Postal Service*, U.S. Sup. Ct. Case No. 81-525, January 11, 1983.

One should not believe, however, that the high court intends to undermine the arbitration process just because of these decisions. It would not be correct to conclude that they demonstrate the Court's intent to upset arbitration decisions on a wholesale basis. In fact, the courts have sustained an NLRB policy that makes private arbitration an even more important feature in labor relations.[11] In 1971, the NLRB held, in *Collyer Insulated Wire*,[12] that it would defer some cases to arbitration even though they contained elements of unfair labor practices. In these cases, contractual provisions were arguably involved, and the NLRB believed that private arbitrators could not only decide whether or not the contract was violated but also determine the unfair labor practice issue. Though this *Collyer* decision has been criticized on the grounds that the NLRB should not abandon its statutory duty to enforce the Taft–Hartley Act, the fact remains that the doctrine makes arbitration an even more viable instrument for the settlement of labor–management disputes.

For the arbitrator, the Trilogy and *Collyer* decisions are equally important. Private arbitrators bear an even greater degree of responsibility as they decide their cases. Not only is the post one of honor, in which the parties have confidence in the arbitrator's professional competency and integrity, but the arbitrator must recognize that for all intents and purposes his or her decision is completely "final and binding" upon the parties. Indeed, if the system of private arbitration is to remain a permanent feature of the American system of industrial relations, arbitrators must measure up to their responsibilities. Should they fail in this respect, managements and unions would simply delete the arbitration clause from the contract and resolve their disputes by strikes or by going directly to court. These are not pleasant alternatives, but the parties may choose these routes if they believe that arbitrators are not discharging their responsibilities in an honorable, judicious, and professional manner. Arbitrators should not feel so smug as to believe that their services are indispensable to labor unions and employers. They are as expendable as last year's calendar.

Limitations to Arbitration

If employers and unions support the arbitration process as an accepted method of disposing of disagreements relating to problems arising under the terms of a labor contract already in existence, there is almost no approval on the part of industry and organized labor for using arbitration as the means of breaking deadlocks in the negotiations of *new* agreements. Most employers and unions would rather have a work stoppage than refer such disputes to arbitration. Many reasons are advanced in support of this position, but the chief consideration lies in the parties' extreme aversion to having an outsider determine the conditions of employment, the rights and obligations of management, and the responsibilities and rights of the union.

[11] *Nabisco, Inc.* v. *NLRB*, 479 F (2d) 770 (CA 2, 1973).
[12] 192 NLRB 837 (1971).

Employers and unions almost invariably believe that, since the labor agreement will establish their fundamental relationship, they should have the full authority to negotiate its terms. For these reasons, the use of arbitration during the negotiation stage of a labor contract is rare. In only a very few industries, such as basic steel, have the parties ever surrendered their rights to negotiate new contracts and establish arbitration as the method to break deadlocks.

It is also important to note that in the United States the system is one of *private and voluntary arbitration*. That is, the government does not force the parties to include arbitration clauses in their labor agreements. They do so voluntarily as they negotiate the latter. Either party can refuse to incorporate any arbitration provisions at all, as has been the case in the building construction industry, where the duration of the job is deemed too brief to make use of a neutral feasible, and in much of the trucking industry, where the Teamster hierarchy has traditionally insisted that neutrals "attempt to please both sides and actually please nobody."

Equally significant is the fact that arbitrators are private rather than government officials. Most of them are lawyers and college professors. As a matter of fact, the Federal Mediation and Conciliation Service and some state agencies that provide mediation services will not permit their mediators to serve as arbitrators.

Characteristics of Arbitration Hearings

Since the decision of the arbitrator *is* final and binding, arbitration is quite different from mediation, a process wherein the parties are completely free to accept or reject the recommendations or suggestions of the mediator. Whether the arbitrator rules for or against a party to the arbitration, that decision must be accepted. This is true even when the losing side believes that the decision is not warranted by the labor agreement, by the evidence submitted in the hearing, or on the basis of fairness or justice. Frequently, an arbitrator's decision will establish an important precedent in the plant that must be followed by the company, the union, and the employees. At times the party that suffers an adverse ruling in an arbitration case will attempt to change, during the next labor contract negotiations, those sections of the labor agreement that proved to be the basis of the decision. Obviously, the side that is benefited by the decision will be reluctant to alter those features of the labor agreement that were interpreted and applied by the arbitrator.

These considerations tend to show the seriousness of arbitration as a tool of labor relations. When the decision to arbitrate is made, the employer and union representatives are undertaking a deep responsibility. To discharge this responsibility in a competent and intelligent manner, it is necessary to put the arbitrator in such a position that the arbitrator can make a decision in the light of evidence and of the relevant contractual clauses. Consequently, the parties have the obligation of preparing fully before coming to the hearing. This means the accumulation of all evidence, facts, documents, and arguments that may have a bearing on the dispute. Careful preparation also means the selection of witnesses who can give relevant testimony in the case.[13] Management and union representatives should leave no stone unturned in preparing for the arbitration.

At the arbitration hearing, each side will have full opportunity to present the fruits of its preparation. Normally, although arbitration hearings are much more formal than grievance procedure negotiations, they are considerably less formal than court proceedings. In addition, the rules of evidence that obtain in the courts of the land do not bind the conduct of the arbitration.[14] This means that the hearing can be conducted not only more informally but much faster than a case in court. However, the parties should not be deluded into believing that the arbitrator's decision will not be based on evidence and facts. Even though the arbitration proceedings might be regarded as semiformal, the fact remains that the arbitrator's decision will most likely be based *strictly* on facts, evidence, arguments, and the contractual clauses that are involved in the proceedings. Arbitration cases are not won on the basis of emotional appeals, theatrical gestures, or speechmaking. The arbitrator is interested in the facts, the evidence, and the parties' arguments as they apply to the issues of the dispute. Such material should be developed in the hearing through careful questioning of witnesses and the presentation of relevant documents.

The parties cannot, moreover, take too much care to make sure that they have presented *all* evidence that might support their case. Representatives of unions and managements who have dealt with a problem in the grievance procedure, and who therefore are fully aware of all the facets of a case, will at times not fully present their case because they believe that the arbitrator is likewise familiar with the facts and issues. Unless prehearing briefs are filed by the parties, it should be recognized that the arbitrator knows absolutely nothing about the case at the time of the hearing. It is the responsibility of the parties to educate the arbitrator about the issues, the facts, the evidence, the arguments, and the relevant contractual clauses. Clearly, if the arbitration process is to have a significant positive value in the area of labor relations, the parties to the arbitration must discharge their obligations fully and conscientiously. They must be indefatigable in their efforts to prepare for the arbitration and absolutely thorough in the presentation of their case to the arbitrator.

Responsibilities of the Arbitrator

The arbitrator, of course, is the key person in the arbitration process, possessing the cold responsibility for the decision in the case. The arbitrator decides, for example, whether a discharged employee remains discharged or returns to work, which of two workers gets the better job, whether the employer placed a correct

---

[13] A competent elaboration of this topic is contained in Frank and Edna Elkouri, *How Arbitration Works*, 3rd ed. (Washington D.C.: Bureau of National Affairs, 1973).

[14] Thus, the rules of the American Arbitration Association provide as follows: "The parties may offer such evidence as they desire and shall produce such additional evidence as the Arbitrator may deem necessary to an understanding and determination of the dispute. . . . The Arbitrator shall be the judge of the relevancy and materiality of the evidence offered and conformity to legal rules of evidence shall not be necessary." *Voluntary Labor Arbitration Rules* (New York: American Arbitration Association, 1973), p. 5.

rate on a new job, whether an employee worked outside his or her classification, whether the company rotated overtime correctly, or whether an employee forfeited seniority under the contract. Few members of the profession have ever rendered a decision that even remotely approximates a 1982 one of Sidney A. Wolff in its direct financial ramifications: In a case involving the Pabst Brewing Company and the Teamsters, he ordered Pabst to negotiate a new plant-closing settlement that cost it some $18 million in back pay. But arbitration is always of critical importance to everyone who is a party to it—or at least those who are asked to arbitrate must operate under that assumption—and it is beyond argument that one of the most important jobs that a person can receive is the assignment by an employer and a union to an arbitration case.

In discharging their responsibilities, arbitrators are expected to adhere to a strict code of ethics. The decision must be based squarely on the evidence and the facts presented. The arbitrator must give full faith and credit to the language of the labor contract at the time of the case. It should be recognized by all concerned that the language of the labor agreement binds the employer, the union, the employees, *and the arbitrator.* It is not within the scope of the arbitrator's authority to decide whether or not a particular contractual clause is wise or unwise, desirable or undesirable. The arbitrator's job is to apply the language of a labor contract as he or she finds it in a particular case. To follow any other course of action not only would be a breach of faith to the parties but would create mischief with the labor agreement. The arbitrator must regard the collective bargaining contract as a final authority and give it full respect. If a case goes against a party because of the language of the contract, the responsibility for this state of affairs lies not with the arbitrator but with the parties who negotiated the agreement.

If the language of the contract is clear-cut and unequivocal, the arbitrator's job is not too difficult. Under these circumstances, the award will favor the party whose position is sustained by the precise contractual language. Of course, there are not many cases of this type, since, if the language is clear-cut and precise, the dispute should not have gone to arbitration. It should have been resolved in the grievance procedure on the basis of the contractual language.

What complicates the arbitrator's problem is contractual langauge that is subject to different shades of meaning. That is, impartial people could find that the language involved may be reasonably interpreted in different ways. Under these circumstances, what is called "past practice"—the way in which the language has been applied in the past—serves as the guide for construction of the ambiguous contractual language. *(Case 3 deals with this topic.)*

The idea behind past practice is that both parties have knowledge of the practice and both expect that the practice will be honored as the basis of administration of the relevant contractual language. Thus, when the arbitrator is confronted with contractual language that is ambiguous, the decision will normally be based on the evidence demonstrating practice. However, if the language is unambiguous and unequivocal, and the practice conflicts with the clear-cut contractual language, the arbitrator will normally base the decision on the language rather than on the practice. That is, unequivocal contractual langauge supersedes practice when the two conflict.

Also, arbitrators generally recognize that past practice should not be used to restrict management in the changing of work methods required by changing conditions. Thus, past practice is normally not used to prevent management from changing work schedules, work assignments, workloads, job assignments, and the number of workers needed on the job. The key to such an arbitration principle is that changing conditions have made the practice obsolete. Of course, there may be written contractual language that would forbid the management's making such changes in work methods. Under these circumstances, the arbitrator's decision would be based on the written contractual langauge; but past practice would not normally be used to block management action when conditions change. Despite these limitations, past practice is frequently used as the basis for arbitrator decisions, particularly, as stated, when contractual language is subject to different shades of meaning.

Much has been said and written about the necessity of the arbitrator's being "fair" in making a decision. A decision is fair only when it is based on the evidence of a case and the accurate assessment of the relevant provisions of the labor agreement. Furthermore, fairness does not mean charity, compromise, or an attempt to please both sides. At times, a management and a union arbitrate a number of different grievances in one hearing. An arbitrator who deliberately decides to compromise or "split" the grievances is not worthy of the confidence of the parties. An arbitrator who is a "splitter" not only violates the ethics of the office but causes untold confusion and damage to the parties. What managements and unions desire in arbitration is a clear-cut decision on each grievance, based on the merits of each dispute; they do not want splitting. They are invariably unhappy with an award that appears to have been shaped from the formula $AA = (E + U)/2$, where AA = arbitrator's award, E = employer's position, and U = union's position. The parties can divide by 2 themselves and presumably have no desire to go to the trauma, expense, and uncertainty of the arbitration process for this kind of result (even while recognizing that on occasion—rare occasion—it is nonetheless inevitable).

Compromise or "horsetrading" of grievances may be accomplished in the grievance procedure. However, once grievances are referred to arbitration, every one of them must be decided on its own merits. Clearly, a "split-the-difference" approach to arbitration can do irreparable harm to the parties, the collective bargaining contract, and the arbitration process. Companies and unions would quickly lose confidence in arbitration if cases were decided not upon their merits but upon the determination of the arbitrator to "even up" his or her awards.

In fact, before hearing a case, each arbitrator normally takes a solemn oath of office to decide the dispute on the evidence, free from any bias. Any arbitrator who transgresses this oath by striving to decide a case on a split-the-difference formula has absolutely no business serving as an arbitrator. A famous and respected baseball umpire once said he called them as he saw them. Even though umpiring a baseball game is quite different from arbitrating a labor dispute, and although the qualifications for baseball umpires are quite different from those for arbitrators in labor relations, the homely statement "call them as you see them" has real significance for arbitration of any kind of dispute.

Additional responsibilities and personal qualities are required in the person serving as an arbitrator. The latter not only must be incorruptible, free from any bias, and aware of the principles of arbitration but must also have a deep and well-rounded understanding of labor relations. It takes more than honesty asnd integrity to serve effectively as an arbitrator. Arbitrators who are not trained in labor relations matters, even though they may be paragons of virtue, can cause irreparable damage to the parties by decisions that do violence to the collective bargaining contract.

At the hearing, the arbitrator should treat both sides with the dignity and the respect that is characteristic of the judicial process. The arbitrator should be patient, sympathetic, and understanding. Experienced arbitrators do not take advantage of their office by being arrogant or domineering. Arbitrators who have a tendency to exaggerate their own importance should be aware of the fact that arbitration, although important, plays a distinctly minor role in the overall union–management relationship. The arbitrator should permit each side to the dispute the fullest opportunity to present all the evidence, witnesses, documents, and arguments that it desires. While a desire for relevancy is, as Justice Oliver Wendell Holmes once wrote, a "concession to the shortness of life," experienced arbitrators frequently lean over backward to permit the introduction of evidence that may or may not be relevant to the dispute. This procedure is better than a policy that could result in the suppression of vital information.

The arbitrator also has the responsibility for keeping the hearing moving. When there is a deliberate or unconscious waste of time by either or both of the parties, the arbitrator is obligated to take remedial action. This does not mean that the arbitrator should not permit recesses, coffee breaks, or the occasional telling of a humorous story; what it means is that part of the arbitrator's fee is earned by conducting a fair, orderly, thorough, and speedy hearing. To this end, the arbitrator, while at all times demonstrating the qualities of patience and understanding, must remain in full *control* of the hearing.

Perhaps J. Paul Getty was overdoing it a bit in declaring that "the meek shall inherit the earth but not its mineral rights," yet there is at least some relevancy in that observation to arbitral obligations. Anyone who unwittingly or by design attempts to take over the hearing must be dealt with courteously but firmly. Of course, if the arbitrator is not experienced, is unsure, or for some reason cannot or will not make definite decisions, the hearing can get out of hand.

The arbitrator also has an obligation to the witnesses called upon to give testimony in the hearing. Even though they should be subject to searching examination, the arbitrator should make sure that they are treated in a courteous manner by the examining party, or by the arbitrator if it is necessary to ask questions of witnesses to clarify a point. The arbitrator should not permit witnesses to be "badgered" or insulted. Even in cross-examination, where the examining party has more leeway with witnesses than it does in direct examination, they should be treated with decorum.

Finally the arbitrator has a responsibility to the parties relative to the award. One significant advantage of arbitration is the comparatively fast disposition of disputes. Thus the arbitrator has an obligation to get the decision in the hands of the parties in a prompt manner after the end of the hearing. Unless unusual conditions are involved, the American Arbitration Association requires awards to be submitted not more than thirty days from the date of the hearing. The Federal Mediation and Conciliation Service is less demanding on arbitrators appointed under its jurisdiction. Under its rules,

> arbitrators are encouraged to render awards not later than 60 days from the date of the closing of the record as determined by the arbitrator.[15]

Of course, when the parties elect to file posthearing briefs, the arbitrator's time tolls from the receipt of such briefs. In discharge cases, the interest of the parties and the employees would be best served by decisions rendered even more promptly than in other types of cases, perhaps in about fifteen days. Arbitrators who are constantly late in their awards do a disservice to the arbitration process. As a matter of fact, under the FMCS rules, the failure of an arbitrator to render timely awards "may lead to his removal from the F.M.C.S. Roster."[16]

The award should be clear and to the point. There should be no question in the minds of the parties as to the exact character of the decision in the case. If the grievance is denied, the award should simply state that fact. Under these circumstances, some arbitrators in the decison also mention the contract provision or provisions that the company did not violate. For example, in a work-assignment case, the award might read as follows:

> The grievance of Mr. Elmer Beamish, Grievance No. 594, is denied on the basis that the company, under job description for Tool- and Die-makers, Class A, Code 286, and for Maintenance Men, Class A, Code 263, and without violating Article XVI of the Labor Agreement, may properly assign either category of employees to repair the classes of machinery in question in this case.

When a case is decided in favor of the union, the award should clearly and specifically direct the employer to take action to bring it into compliance with the contract. In addition, to avoid any misunderstanding, the decision should require the action within a certain number of working days after the receipt of the award. For example, in a "bumping" case, the award might read as follows:

[15] *FMCS Procedures for Arbitration Services,* Rule 1404.15.
[16] *Ibid.*

> Within three working days after the receipt of this award, the Company is
> directed to place the grievant, Reva Snodgrass, into the job of Spray Painter,
> Class "B," Labor Grade No. 7, and to make her whole for any financial loss
> that she suffered because of the refusal of the Company to permit her to roll
> into the aforementioned job on the grounds that the Company violated Article
> IX, Section 7, Paragraphs A and B of the Labor Agreement.

In addition to the incorporation of a clear award, arbitrators are charged with
the responsibility of writing an opinion to support their decision. Although technically opinions are not required to explain a decision, the fact is that arbitrators
almost universally write an opinion. What is more important in this connection,
the parties expect their arbitrators to write them, and so do agencies such as the
Federal Mediation and Conciliation Service and the American Arbitration Association, which submit to managements and unions the names of arbitrators.

In the opinion, the arbitrator sets forth the basic issues of the case, the facts,
the position and arguments of the parties, and the reasons for the decision. The
arbitrator deals with the evidence presented in the case as it relates to each decision.
Arbitrators are frequently extraordinarily careful to deal in an exhaustive manner
with each major argument and piece of evidence offered by the losing side. Patently,
the arbitrator has an obligation to tell the losing side just why it lost the case. Since
normally the losing side will be very disappointed with the decision, the arbitrator
should at least indicate in a careful manner the reasons for the adverse ruling. This
will probably not make the losing side feel any better, but at least an opinion that
is carefully written and covers thoroughly the major arguments and areas of evidence will demonstrate that the character of an arbitration opinion is a guide to
the amount of time, energy, and thought the arbitrator puts into the case.

Many years ago, a prominent arbitrator speculated upon his calling in the
following manner:

> Arbitration is an art rather than a body of knowledge. It cannot be learned in
> college, nor from books and speeches. It is not something that every lawyer can
> do, nor even learn. Nor is every judge a good arbitrator and, much less, every
> professor or clergyman. . . . There is much about arbitration that can be learned
> from books, from experience in industry, from personal contacts with aspects
> of the problems to be decided, and from the experiences of others. A well-
> rounded education and quite likely also special training . . . are valuable. But
> the best teacher is probably experience.[17]

It is hard to see even now how these words could be improved upon.

Selection of the Arbitrator

After the parties decide to arbitrate a dispute, the problem of the selection of the
arbitrator arises. To solve this problem, most labor agreements provide that the
parties will select the arbitrator from a panel of names submitted by the Federal
Mediation and Conciliation Service or the American Arbitration Association. When

---

[17] Edwin E. Witte, "The Future of Labor Arbitration—A Challenge," in *Selected Papers from the First Seven
Annual Meetings of the National Academy of Arbitrators* (Washington, D.C.: BNA Books, 1954), pp. 16–17.

Form Approved
OMB No. 23-R0004

FEDERAL MEDIATION AND CONCILIATION SERVICE
WASHINGTON, D.C. 20427

ARBITRATOR'S REPORT AND FEE STATEMENT

FILE NO. _____   **ARBITRATOR** _____   DATE OF AWARD _____

                                       (Name)

1. COMPANY _____

                                (Name)   *(City)*   *(State)*   *(Zip Code)*

2. UNION _____

                                (Name)   *(Local No.)*   *(Affiliation)*

3. ISSUES: *(Please check either a or b, and complete c and d)*

a. ☐ New or reopened contract terms

b. ☐ Contract interpretation or application

c. Issue or Issues *(Please check only one issue per grievance)*

1. ☐ Discharge and disciplinary actions
2. ☐ Incentive rates or standards
3. ☐ Job evaluation
4. ☐ Work assignment
5. ☐ Job classification
6. Seniority:
   a. ☐ Promotion and upgrading
   b. ☐ Layoff, bumping and recall
   c. ☐ Transfer
   d. ☐ Other
7. Overtime:
   a. ☐ Overtime pay
   b. ☐ Overtime distribution
   c. ☐ Compulsory overtime
   d. ☐ Other
8. ☐ Union officers—superseniority and union business
9. ☐ Strike or lockout issues *(excluding disciplinary actions)*

10. ☐ Vacations and vacation pay
11. ☐ Holidays and holiday pay
12. ☐ Scheduling of work
13. ☐ Reporting, call-in and call-back pay
14. ☐ Health and welfare
15. ☐ Pensions
16. ☐ Other fringe benefits
17. Scope of agreement:
   a. ☐ Subcontracting
   b. ☐ Jurisdictional disputes
   c. ☐ Foreman, supervision, etc.
   d. ☐ Mergers, consolidations, accretion, other plants
18. ☐ Working conditions, including safety
19. ☐ Severance pay
20. ☐ Rate of pay
21. ☐ Discrimination
22. ☐ Management rights
23. ☐ Job posting & bidding
24. ☐ Wage issues
25. ☐ Arbitrability of grievances
26. ☐ Miscellaneous

d. Was arbitrability of grievance involved? ☐ Yes ☐ No   If yes, check one or both ☐ Procedural ☐ Substantive

4. HEARING:

a. Were briefs filed? ☐ Yes ☐ No   If yes, give date _____

b. Was transcript taken? ☐ Yes ☐ No

c. Number of grievances _____

d. Dates of Hearing: _____

e. Date of grievance _____

f. Was there any waiver by parties on date the award was due?
☐ Yes ☐ No

5. FEES AND DAYS: For services as Arbitrator

No. of Days: _____ + _____ + _____ = _____ × $ _____ = $ _____
             Hearing   *Travel*   *Study*   *Total*   *Per Diem Rate*   *Total Fee*

Expenses: Transportation $ _____ + Other $ _____ = $ _____
                                                    Total Expense

Amount payable by Company $ _____

Amount payable by Union $ _____

TOTAL $ _____

6. PUBLICATION: If either party or arbitrator objects to publication of award, check here _____
(If not checked, please forward four copies of award)

7. PANEL: If tripartite panel or more than one arbitrator made the award, check here _____

8. Date of this report _____   Signature _____

(Please attach to this report copies of the submission agreement and the award)

Please do not write below this line

DATE CLOSED: _____   **REVIEWED BY:** _____

U.S. GOVERNMENT PRINTING OFFICE 1974—O—538-235

251

called upon by the parties to an arbitration, these agencies will supply the management and the union with a list of names, and the parties, in accordance with a mutually acceptable formula, will select the arbitrator from the list. Under some labor agreements, the Federal Mediation and Conciliation Service and the American Arbitration Association have the authority to select the arbitrator on a direct-appointment basis in the event that none of the names in the panel is acceptable.

The Federal Mediation and Conciliation Service is administered independently from the U.S. Department of Labor. It maintains a roster of arbitrators totaling about 1,200.[18] About 60 percent are lawyers or law professors. Thirty percent are college professors not in law schools. The remainder are a mixed bag, mainly clergymen and consultants. Consistent with the significant growth in arbitration volume, requests for FMCS panels have sharply increased. In 1971, the service received 12,327 requests as compared with 30,050 in 1981.[19] Upon the selection of the arbitrator, the service withdraws from active participation in the case, and the relationship thereafter is between the parties and the arbitrator, although (as Exhibit 6-2 shows) the latter must ultimately file a report with the service.

Unlike the FMCS, the American Arbitration Association is a private organization. In its formative years, it devoted itself almost exclusively to the promotion of commercial arbitration, but since 1937 its Industrial Arbitration Tribunal has become increasingly active in labor disputes. In addition to furnishing the parties with arbitrator-selection aid similar to that of the Mediation Service, it administers arbitration hearings in accordance with a number of formalized rules. The association's panel of available arbitrators currently contains about 1,500 names, although most of the work is actually done by fewer than 500 active arbitrators, and the heavy majority of these are the same people that are listed on the FMCS roster. The AAA's arbitration workload is also expanding rapidly.

Other methods are utilized to select arbitrators. Some parties directly contact one of the almost 600 arbitrators listed in the membership directory of the highly prestigious National Academy of Arbitrators, the major society of the profession and an organization to whose ranks only the most experienced of neutrals are admitted.[20] In some contracts, a person of unimpeachable integrity is designated to select an arbitrator. Under such arrangements, the parties have confidence that the person so designated will select a qualified arbitrator. Thus, under some labor agreements, a federal district judge, the president of a university, or a high-ranking public official will be called upon to appoint the neutral.

Regardless of the method, the majority of labor contracts provide some definite procedure for the appointment of the arbitrator. At times, managements and unions find that in practice they cannot agree on any arbitrator when the contract merely states that an arbitrator "mutually acceptable" to the parties will decide

---

[18] Federal Mediation and Conciliation Service, *Twenty-ninth Annual Report,* 1977, p. 47.

[19] Federal Mediation and Conciliation Service, *Thirty-fourth Annual Report,* 1981, p. 36.

[20] Most of the National Academy's members are also registered with the Mediation Service and AAA and can be engaged by the parties on this basis as well.

the dispute. It is sound procedure to incorporate some method for the selection of arbitrators by an outside agency when the parties are unable or unwilling to agree on a neutral on a mutual-acceptance basis.

Some employers and unions solve the problem of selection by appointing a permanent arbitrator under the terms of a labor agreement. Under this arrangement, one person will decide each dispute that is arbitrated. However, companies and unions are not in agreement on the use of a permanent arbitrator as against the ad hoc method of selection, in which a different arbitrator may be chosen for each case. Some employers and unions, as a matter of policy, will use a different arbitrator for each dispute; others find it a better practice to use the same arbitrator. The permanent arbitrator is used most frequently when a management has a number of different locations. Such a procedure makes for uniformity of labor policy within the different operating units of the enterprise.

Actually, there are advantages and disadvantages to each method. Perhaps the chief argument in favor of the ad hoc method is that the parties will not be "stuck" with an arbitrator whom they do not want. The parties can simply dispense with an arbitrator who proves incompetent or otherwise unqualified, even though it appears unlikely that a management and a union would have selected such a person to arbitrate on a permanent basis in the first place. Balancing the chief advantage of the ad hoc system are several disadvantages. The time and effort required to select an arbitrator for each case delays the rapid disposition of the grievance, sometimes to the detriment of employee morale. At times, out of desperation, a person who has little or no experience or real qualifications is selected to serve as an arbitrator. Such a choice may be made because he or she is the only person available who has not handed down an award somewhere at some time that the employer and the union do not like. Moreover, because each new arbitrator must be educated in the local conditions, a comparatively long period may sometimes be required to conduct the hearing.

Perhaps the chief disadvantage of ad hoc arbitration, however, is the fact that this method does not assure consistency in decisions or the application of uniform principles to contract construction. No arbitrator is bound by any other arbitrator's decisions or principles of contractual construction. Consequently, disputes involving fundamentally the same issues could be resolved in as many different ways as there are arbitrators chosen to decide cases. Thus, there is no assurance that a particular decision will bring stability to labor relations. It may have precedent value only until the next time the issues involved in the case are tested before another arbitrator.

The latter consideration indicates the greatest advantage of the selection of permanent arbitrators. The parties have the assurance of consistency and uniformity of decisions and consistent contractual interpretation. As a result, precedent will be established, the parties will know what to expect, and cases dealing with essentially the same issues as contained in a grievance previously decided in arbitration can be settled in the earlier stages of the grievance procedure. In addition, the permanent arbitrator becomes familiar with the labor agreement, the technology of the plant, and the "shop language." This means that cases can frequently be expedited much more effectively than under circumstances of ad hoc arbitration.

Perhaps the chief disadvantage of the permanent selection method is that the parties involved may tend to arbitrate more disputes than are absolutely necessary, rather than first exhausting the possibilities of settling them in the grievance procedure. This is particularly true when arbitrators are paid a set fee for a year and are obligated to arbitrate any and all cases submitted to them.

This possibility, of course, is a serious charge against the permanent selection method. As stated before, arbitration should be employed only after the parties have honestly exhausted every possibility of settling disputes in the grievance procedure. One method that might be effective in obtaining the advantages of the permanent method without incurring the possible disadvantages of excessive arbitration would be to compensate the permanent arbitrator on a per diem or a per case basis, rather than on an annual fee basis. In the last analysis, however, the amount of arbitration needed by a management and a union depends upon the attitudes of the parties rather than on the method of selection or the procedure of payment.

ARBITRATION COSTS AND TIME LAG

In recent years, arbitration has been criticized as being unduly expensive and involving too much time, but beyond these two criticisms the process has always been criticized for other reasons. Parties complain when they lose a case that they believe should have been decided in their favor. The criticism may not have much validity, but justified censure involves an arbitrator who ignores unambiguous contractual language and thereby rewrites the labor agreement. At times, opinions are confusing, leading to unnecessary discord between the parties; and, indeed, there are instances where the opinion does not even reflect the award. As one dissatisfied party has said, "We won everything except the decision." Sometimes arbitrators include so-called "dicta" (gratuitous remarks not required for a decision in a case) in their opinions, which could lead to serious problems the next time a labor agreement is negotiated. And, obviously, it is understandable why the losing side believes it has been treated unjustly when the arbitrator does not conduct a fair and impartial hearing, or fails to deal with major arguments, or ignores material evidence.

However, the most vocal criticism recently has pertained to the costs and the delays associated with arbitration. Even though alternatives to arbitration—a strike or court enforcement of a labor agreement—would be far more expensive, arbitration costs, at least on the surface, appear to be quite high.

For 1981, the Federal Mediation and Conciliation Service reported that the arbitrators who served under its jurisdiction charged an average of about $300 per day. The average cost per case for that year amounted to $1,132, normally shared equally between the parties. This figure included not only the charge for the hearing day and the arbitrator's expenses (travel, hotel, meals) but also payment for the time devoted to the analysis of the evidence and the writing of the arbitrator's opinion. Beyond the fee and expenses of the arbitrator, there are other costs. Some parties use lawyers and also may have a stenographic transcript prepared of the proceedings, and there is the payment of personnel on both sides who take part in the arbitration hearing.

There are ways to cut arbitration costs. Grievances that are of minimal importance to the parties, particularly those that go to arbitration for political and tactical purposes, should be eliminated from the process. Other suggestions include the use of local arbitrators to save on expenses, elimination of the transcript and attorneys when they are not necessary, and the consolidation of grievances of the same type to be determined in one hearing. To reduce costs, the parties may instruct their arbitrators not to write an opinion but merely to issue an award. The writing of an opinion takes considerable time, even after the arbitrator has carefully reviewed the evidence and has reached a decision. Of course, there is genuine value in a carefully written opinion, as pointed out earlier, but there are cases where the merit of cost saving outweighs the advantages of an opinion.

One delay is not attributable to arbitrators or the process but to dilatory tactics of the parties. This involves the time before arbitration is requested on a grievance. For example, recently one of the present authors handled a case in which three years had elapsed before the parties invoked the arbitration process. Such an incredible delay is not usual, but grievances commonly vegetate for many months before the parties decide to take them into arbitration. The time-lag criticism properly starts from the point at which the parties request arbitration. For 1981, the Federal Mediation and Conciliation Service reported that, on the average, 168 days elapsed from the time the parties requested a panel of arbitrators until the award was issued.[21] This is much too long, and the parties understandably wonder if the process really constitutes a viable forum for the disposition of grievances in arbitration. One consequence of the delay is the lowering of the morale in the plant, in the same way that the morale of students suffers when their teachers take much too long in returning examination papers. Employees become impatient waiting for the award; their resentment could have an adverse impact on the quantity and quality of their work, and, frequently, they badger their union representatives about the problem. Employers could also suffer a large financial loss (should they lose their case) if the arbitrator directs a monetary remedy for a contractual violation.

One way to deal with the time problem is for the parties to use comparatively new arbitrators rather than requesting the services of so-called "mainline," or veteran, arbitrators. Since the latter group receives the lion's share of the cases, its members may be unable to provide prompt hearing dates. Indeed, in fiscal 1981, the FMCS reported that 71 days elapsed between the time an arbitrator was appointed and the day of the hearing. It follows that arbitrators with small case loads might be able to offer more prompt hearing dates. The problem, of course, is to convince the parties to use new arbitrators rather than those with considerable experience. It is true that there is no substitute for experience, but it is equally true that new arbitrators could be just as qualified as those who have been in the

---

[21] FMCS, *Thirty-fourth Annual Report*, p. 39.

profession for many years and who have handled a great number of cases. Many veteran arbitrators would agree with this and would encourage employers and unions to provide opportunities for the comparatively newer arbitrators.

To avoid the delay associated with the use of arbitrators from the FMCS or the AAA, a growing number of employers and unions are making use of a *permanent panel* of arbitrators. That is, they choose a number (seven is perhaps modal) of arbitrators when they negotiate the labor agreement; when grievances are ready to be arbitrated, one of the members of the panel is selected through some agreed-upon procedure. This could save considerable time, since the use of the traditional agencies for the selection of arbitrators necessitates some delay: A letter goes from the parties to the Federal Mediation and Conciliation Service or the American Arbitration Association; the agency then sends a panel of arbitrators to the parties; additional time elapses while the parties decide which one of the arbitrators on the panel is to be used; then they write the appointing agency of the choice; the agency notifies the arbitrator; and then the arbitrator must write the parties to arrange a hearing date. For fiscal 1981, the FMCS reported that 47 days elapsed between the time a request for arbitration was made to the agency and the appointment of the arbitrator. By the use of the permanent panel, most of this delay is avoided. A telephone call or a single letter sent directly to the selected arbitrator is all that is needed.

Not only could costs be reduced by relieving the arbitrator of the responsibility of writing an opinion, but the same practice is a time saver. To reduce the time lag, stenographic transcripts of the proceedings and posthearing briefs could be eliminated. (Indeed, one of the authors is currently serving on a permanent panel of arbitrators of a major airline and a labor organization, and by contractual agreement transcripts and posthearing briefs are expressly prohibited.) Transcripts and posthearing briefs delay the process; it is not unusual to wait a month or longer for a transcript, and then another month for the briefs. In the "normal" case, these are not really needed. The arbitrator simply takes his or her own notes at the hearing and provides the opportunity to the parties to offer an oral argument at the close of the hearing. To be fair about it, however, there are some cases where a transcript is valuable, and a posthearing brief could be helpful to the arbitrator in reaching a decision.

Finally, there is the matter of the dilatory arbitrator. As stated before, it is customary, and indeed directed by the FMCS and the AAA, that an arbitrator's decision is due within a specified number of days after the close of the hearing or the filing of posthearing briefs. Unfortunately, there are arbitrators who take much longer than this allowed time—chiefly because they are handling so many cases that they cannot meet this deadline.

Mini-Arbitration

First applied in the basic steel industry in 1971, "mini-" or expedited arbitration has been adopted by other employers and unions, including the U.S. Postal Service and the postal labor organizations, the League of New York Theatres and Actors' Equity, and the UAW and the automobile manufacturers. The chief value of the mini-arbitration process is the sharp reduction of the time element and costs. Under the steel plan, the hearing must be held within ten days after the appeal to arbitration is made, and the arbitrator's decision must be made within forty-eight hours after the close of the hearing. No transcripts or briefs are permitted, and the arbitrator is expected to provide the parties with a short but precise award. Costs are also much lower than in regular arbitration. A fee is paid only for the hearing day, and this fee is only about $50 to $100 for each party per case.

To provide for such rapid service at an economical charge, the steel corporations and the United Steelworkers of America use a battery of about 200 inexperienced arbitrators, including a significant number of blacks and women. The panel includes relatively young lawyers or a local university's faculty. One advantage of the new process, therefore, is to train new arbitrators.

Indeed, this spinoff from the mini process is of significant value to arbitration. Arbitrators may not as yet, to paraphrase the UAW secretary–treasurer's previously cited remark regarding labor leaders, look like a wax museum collection when they hold a meeting, but the bulk of the profession is hardly made up of youngsters nowadays. Many still-active arbitrators entered the field on the strength of their experiences in the War Labor Board days of World War II and are now nearing the end of their careers. Unless newcomers can rather quickly be developed at this point, the field will be in some trouble.

Not all cases, however, are disposed of in the mini process—only, in general, those of the more simple and routine type—with the regular arbitration process still being used for those cases of difficult nature and representing substantial interest to the parties. In addition, either the employer or the union may demand that a case go through the regular arbitration process.

In any event, the mini procedure has generally worked successfully, not just in the steel industry but in the several other sectors where it has been tried. Undoubtedly, there is a place for it within our system of labor relations. It provides a swift and economical forum for the determination of grievances that are well within the capability of inexperienced arbitrators. It is likely that the process will spread. The most difficult problem is to determine which grievances should go the mini- and which the regular arbitration route; but this problem is not insoluble, since skilled and mature labor relations representatives on both sides can easily spot those grievances that can best be handled through the expedited procedure.

Discussion Questions

1 "The handling of workers' grievances on the job is perhaps the single most important function of modern unionism." How accurate is this statement?

2 It is generally agreed that a low grievance rate does not necessarily prove the existence of good union–management relations and that a high grievance rate does not necessarily prove the existence of poor relations between the parties. Why might the grievance statistics be misleading as a guide to the quality of the relationship?

3 From the employer's viewpoint, what advantages and disadvantages might there be in reducing a grievance to writing?

4 Harold W. Davey has argued that "a genuine grievance requires an airing, even if it is not strictly in order under the existing contract." What considerations, again from the employer's point of view, might justify this opinion?

5 Why might (a) a management or (b) a union prefer *not* to have an arbitration provision in the contract?

6 Dunlop and Healy have pointed out that although it is often said that "arbitration is an extension of collective bargaining," it is also frequently held that "arbitration is a judicial process." What are your own feelings regarding these two apparently inconsistent descriptions?

7 Given the fact that arbitrators have no compulsion to follow any other arbitrator's award or line of reasoning, how do you account for the fact that there are available at least three widely distributed publications that feature arbitration awards from all over the country? On the surface, would it not appear that such publications are a waste of time and money, since each arbitrator is in effect a law unto himself?

8 How could the present system of labor contract administration, as described in general terms in this chapter, be improved?

9 Beyond the authors' ideas to reduce arbitration delays and costs, can you offer additional suggestions to accomplish this goal?

10 Do you believe that arbitrators, like doctors and lawyers, should be certified by government before they could be permitted to arbitrate labor cases? Defend your position.

11 Indicate what standards a competent arbitrator would use in the decision-making process. What considerations would this arbitrator not use?

Selected References

BAER, WALTER E., *Practice and Precedent in Labor Relations.* Lexington, Mass.: Heath, 1972.

BUREAU OF NATIONAL AFFAIRS, INC., *Grievance Guide* (6th ed.). Washington, D.C.: Bureau of National Affairs, 1982.

ELKOURI, FRANK, and EDNA ELKOURI, *How Arbitration Works* (3rd ed.). Washington, D.C.: Bureau of National Affairs, 1973.

FAIRWEATHER, OWEN, *Practice and Procedure in Labor Arbitration* (2nd ed.). Washington, D.C.: Bureau of National Affairs, 1983.

FLEMING, R.W., *The Labor Arbitration Process.* Urbana: University of Illinois Press, 1965.

HILL, MARVIN, JR., and ANTHONY V. SINICROPI, *Remedies in Arbitration.* Washington, D.C.: Bureau of National Affairs, 1981.

————, *Evidence in Arbitration*. Washington, D.C.: Bureau of National Affairs, 1980.

POPS, GERALD M., *Emergence of the Public Sector Arbitrator*. Lexington, Mass.: Lexington Books, 1976.

PRASOW, PAUL, and EDWARD PETERS, *Arbitration and Collective Bargaining*. New York: McGraw-Hill, 1970.

SLICHTER, SUMNER H., JAMES J. HEALY, and E. ROBERT LIVERNASH, *The Impact of Collective Bargaining on Management*, pp. 692–806. Washington, D.C.: Brookings Institution, 1960.

STONE, MORRIS, *Labor Grievances and Decisions*. New York: Harper & Row, 1965.

TROTTA, MAURICE S., *Handling Grievances: A Guide for Management and Labor*. Washington, D.C.: Bureau of National Affairs, 1976.

ARBITRATION CASES

As in the eleven other cases that follow in later chapters, the three arbitration cases presented here are drawn from the authors' own experiences. They are actual cases; but since arbitration is a confidential process, the names of the employers and unions have been deleted. Also, to maintain confidentiality, fictitious names have been used for the witnesses.

In six of the fourteen cases, you will play the role of arbitrator. To reach a proper decision, be sure that you fully understand the basic facts and contractual provisions. Clearly establish the reasons for your decision in each case. In the discussion of these cases, your instructor will probably tell you the actual arbitrator's decision. These decisions can be found in the *Instructor's Manual.*

In eight cases, the complete case is presented, not only the factual background and material contractual language but also the arbitrator's entire decision. Students are urged to read the cases. A great deal can be learned about the practical day-to-day problems of labor relations by faithful study of them. They show how a professional arbitrator handles cases submitted by the parties. Whether you agree with a decision is not really important. Rather, the value is to learn how arbitrators apply and interpret contractual language, evaluate evidence, apply commonly accepted principles of contractual construction and arbitration practices, and defend their decisions with what they would like to believe is logical and unassailable reasoning.

If you desire to read additional arbitration cases, thousands have been published by the Bureau of National Affairs, *Labor Arbitration Reports,* and Commerce Clearing House, *Labor Arbitration Awards.* These services have been available for many years. (In keeping with the confidentiality of the arbitration process, the employer and the union involved must agree to publication.) However, the published cases represent only a small percentage of the cases decided by arbitrators; the vast majority are found only in the private files of the arbitrators and the parties.

Each of the fourteen cases has been placed at the end of the chapter in which the reference to the case is made. As a result of their unusual character, and the interest that they generated, two cases from the previous edition have been repeated. They are Case 8, "The Case of the Life-Support System," and Case 13, a discharge case, "The Case of the Employee Who Was Paid and Not Required to Work." Aside from these two cases, the others are new and have not appeared in previous editions.

Carefully selected questions follow the eight cases that are reproduced in their entirety. In the other six cases, the basic question is implicit: If you had been the arbitrator, what would you have decided and why?

Time Limits:
The Case of the Injured Employee

Cast of characters:*

Small	*Grievant*
Alvis and Watt	*Grievant's Physicians*
Cagle	*Personnel Superintendent*
Love	*Plant Manager*
Henry	*Union President*
Moore	*Employee Relations Manager*

Should a union fail to comply with the time limits stipulated in the grievance procedure, it could lose a grievance that might have merit. Equally, depending upon the contractual language involved, an employer who ignores time limits could be required to grant a grievance that otherwise might not have merit. Time limits are incorporated into the grievance procedure to ensure that a grievance will be processed properly. To accomplish this purpose, both sides are under a time pressure to keep the grievance moving expeditiously through the various steps of the grievance procedure.

In the following case, the employer claimed that the employee and the union did not comply with the time limits stipulated in the grievance procedure. It asserted that although the employee was discharged on December 22, 1980, his grievance was filed on November 30, 1981. Under the time limits, the employee and/or the union had five working days to file a grievance. Note that the presentation here does not deal with the merits of the grievance. We are concerned here only with the time-limit issue. If the grievance were denied on this basis, it would not be necessary to determine the merits. On the other hand, if the grievance were held as "filed timely," the arbitrator would then be required to decide whether the employee was discharged for just cause.

GRIEVANCE

In protest against his discharge, Small filed a grievance, dated November 30, 1981, which stated:

_____

* A "cast of characters" in this form is, of course, not contained in arbitration cases. It appears here to aid the student in the reading of the cases.

I feel the company is using discrimination, untimely discharge and unfair labor practices to keep me from returning to work from a job related injury.

As a settlement, he requested:

I want my job back with all seniority, back pay, holiday pay, vacation pay, health insurance, life insurance beginning Nov. 25, 1981.

When the Company denied the grievance, it stated:

The grievance filed on behalf of Small was done so on an untimely basis as outlined in the current labor agreement. Mr. Small concurred that he was talked to about his discharge due to his failure to continue rehabilitation and see his doctor for his injury in February of 1981. There has been no discrimination or unfair practices involved in his case. . . .

As a result of the failure to settle the dispute in the Grievance Procedure, the Parties convened this arbitration for its determination.

LABOR AGREEMENT

ARTICLE III. FUNCTIONS OF MANAGEMENT

The Company retains the exclusive rights to manage the business and the operation of the plant and to direct the working forces. All of the rights, powers, and authority that the Company had prior to the signing of this Agreement are retained by the Company, except those specifically abridged, delegated, granted, or modified by this Agreement or any supplementary agreements in the future.

The Company, in the exercise of such rights, shall observe the provisions of this Agreement.

ARTICLE VI. GRIEVANCE PROCEDURE

Section 2 Grievances must be presented to the first step within five working days from the date of the supervisor's answer. In the event a grievant is off due to illness or vacation or bona fide leave of absence, the five day time limit will commence with his return to work.

ISSUES

1 Was the grievance filed timely under Article VI, Section 2, of the Labor Agreement?
2 If the preceding issue is determined in the affirmative, the issue then is whether or not the Company discharged Grievant Small for just cause. If not, what should the remedy be?

BACKGROUND

The Accident

On April 14, 1977, Small, hired on February 7, 1972 and classified as a Cutter in the Cutting Department, injured his right hand while operating a die press. There was also damage to muscles in his arm, shoulder, and wrist. After the accident, he was treated by Dr. Alvis, who eventually referred him to Dr. Watt, Specialist in Hand Surgery.

In November 1978, Dr. Watt released the Grievant for light work. On February 9, 1979, the physician placed additional restrictions on him which made Small unavailable for any job. As it turned out, February 9, 1979, was the last day the Grievant worked in the plant.

Cagle, Personnel Superintendent, testified that he contacted Dr. Watt's office in April 1980 and was told that Small had not been seen in the doctor's office after September 1979. Cagle was also told that Small canceled appointments and a surgical procedure scheduled to be performed on February 29, 1980.

Letter from California

During the last week in February 1980, Small testified, he went to California where his mother had had a heart attack, returning to the local area about the end of April 1980. While in California, Small wrote the following letter to the Company:

> I'm living in Hollywood CA right now. I'm having therapy done on my right hand here. I have a real good Doctor. Why I wrote is because I need my WD-2 forms for income tax. I need the years 1978 and 1979 WD-2 forms. Please send them to my address above. I need it real soon. I appreciate it.

Dr. Watt's Letter: October 7, 1980

In a letter dated October 7, 1980, Dr. Watt supplied the following letter to the Company. It was sent after Cagle requested information about the Grievant's status. The letter stated:

> This is in response to your telephone request concerning the above named patient.
>
> Mr. Small was last examined in our office on September 20, 1979. At that time, he was scheduled for release of web space contracture and groin flap as well as second stage take-down and inset flap. This was scheduled for February 29, 1980; however, it was not performed.
>
> We have not seen Mr. Small since September 1979.
>
> If we may be of any further assistance, please do not hesitate to contact our office.

Discharge of Grievant: Company Testimony

According to Love, Plant Manager, and Cagle, on December 22, 1980, the Company by letter notified Small of his discharge. They said it was sent to the Grievant's local address. This letter, or a copy of it, however, was not submitted as evidence in this proceeding. Cagle said his secretary mailed the letter, and he did not know whether it was sent by certified mail. Henry, Union President, testified that he checked the local post office and was advised that no certified letter was sent to the Grievant during December 1980.

According to Love, when discharge letters are sent to employees, a copy normally goes to the Union. Henry testified he did not receive a copy of the December 22, 1980, letter. Small said he did not receive such letter notifying him of his discharge.

In any event, Love stated the reasons for the Grievant's discharge:

> On the basis of all the information we received from Dr. Watt, Small was not meeting his appointments with the doctor, not taking therapy, did not see his doctor for about over a year, and canceled his surgery. Also he was not keeping us informed where he was living.

According to Love and Cagle, on December 22, 1980, each of them at separate times orally notified Henry of Small's discharge at the Union President's work station. Henry denied he was informed at that time, testifying that the first time he was orally told of the Grievant's discharge was shortly before Thanksgiving 1981, when Moore, Employee Relations Manager, so advised him.

Small's Plant Visit: February 1981

In February 1981, the Grievant visited the plant and had conversations with Cagle and Love. As to this matter, Love testified:

> I verbally told him he was discharged. Small said that he had legal advice and was not worried about it, and did not ask for Union representation. He did not question the discharge.

Cagle's testimony was essentially the same as that offered by the Plant Manager.

According to the Grievant, the session went this way:

> I came to Love's office in February 1981. I told him I had an operation scheduled for May 1981. He said I was no longer on the payroll; I was taken off the payroll by Neenah.* Nothing was said about me being discharged.

Dr. Watt's Letter: November 25, 1981

On November 25, 1981, Small gave Cagle a letter written by Dr. Watt, dated November 25, 1981. It stated:

> Mr. Small was last seen in our office 10/26/81, at which time the patient was released to return to us only if a problem developed.

_____

* Neenah, Wisconsin, is the headquarters of the corporation of which the local Company is a Division.

It is our opinion that Mr. Small is able to return to work with no lifting restrictions.

If his job would cause him difficulty he should schedule an appointment for reevaluation.

Cagle acknowledged receipt of Dr. Watt's statement but testified he did not instruct the Grievant to obtain it because

he was previously discharged and there was no need for the letter. I did not tell him to bring it in.

Meeting December 4, 1981

As noted, Small filed his grievance on November 30, 1981. On December 1, 1981, Cagle sent the following letter to Henry:

This is to advise you that the Company considers the grievance filed in behalf of Mr. Small untimely on the basis that it has been filed over eleven months after Mr. Small was terminated. The Labor Agreement specifically states that grievances must be presented in a timely manner; see Article VI of the current agreement. Both you and Mr. Small were informed of his termination. Mr. Small was terminated on December 22, 1980, after being off work since April 1977. For a period of over one year Mr. Small had not seen his physician and did not notify the Company of his whereabouts when he moved out-of-state.

Although we consider the grievance untimely, we are willing to set up meetings to discuss the situation outside of the grievance procedure. I will set up the appropriate meetings in the near future.

On December 4, 1981, a meeting was held dealing with the Grievant's status. As to the events of this meeting, Love and Cagle testified that the Grievant admitted he was informed of his discharge in February 1981. In addition, Cagle testified that Small said he received the discharge letter the Company claimed it sent him on December 22, 1980; and he agreed that he had canceled the surgery scheduled in February 1980.

Henry recalled the events of the meeting this way: It lasted about one to two hours. Most of the time was devoted to discussion of doctors' statements concerning the Grievant. After he said that a different doctor should examine Small, the Company said that might help. No one from the Union agreed that the Grievant had been told that he was discharged prior to November 1981.

POSITIONS OF THE PARTIES

As for its position, the Company states:

The filing of the grievance on November 30, 1981, on behalf of Small because of his discharge on December 22, 1980 was an untimely filing and therefore it is not arbitrable; and, in addition, there is no violation of the Labor Agreement, the discharge of Small was for just cause, and if ruled as filed timely, the grievance should be denied on its merits.

In the view of the Union:

. . . the Company failed to meet the burden of proof that the grievance was untimely and Small was terminated for just cause.

ARBITRABILITY OF GRIEVANCE

Time Limits under Labor Agreement

In the final analysis, the determination of the timeliness issue depends on whether the Company discharged Small on December 22, 1980, and/or in February 1981. As the record demonstrates, and as included in the Parties' arguments, they disagree on the application of the time limits established in Article VI of the Labor Agreement. Section 1 provides that an employee may discuss any matter with his immediate supervisor. If as a result of such discussion the matter is not satisfactorily resolved, the employee and/or his Union representative may file a grievance. Section 2 requires that grievances must be submitted to the first step within five (5) working days of the supervisor's answer.

Given this language, the Union contends that the grievance was timely filed. There was no discussion between Small and his immediate supervisor, and no answer given by his immediate supervisor. Under these circumstances, the Union claims that the grievance was timely filed even though it may be assumed the Grievant was discharged in December 1980 or February 1981, and the grievance not filed until November 30, 1981.

In contrast, the Company asserts that grievances must be filed within five (5) working days from the time the incident occurs which gives rise to a dispute. Assuming the Grievant was discharged on December 22, 1980, Small had five working days from that date to file his grievance. The same observation applies if in fact he was discharged in February 1981.

For purposes of this case, there is no need to resolve this controversy. If in fact the Company discharged Small on December 22, 1980, and/or in February 1981, the grievance was filed much too late for it to be timely under the terms of Article VI. If he was discharged on December 22, 1980, his grievance was submitted about eleven (11) months later. If he was discharged in February 1981, his grievance was filed about nine (9) months later. Regardless of what interpretation of the time limits language may be correct, either that of the Company or Union, the grievance was filed far too late. When an employee sits on his rights for such a long period of time, the doctrine of *laches* applies, and he may not seek to avoid forfeiture based upon contractual language which is in dispute.

As the record shows, the Company has enforced time limits in the past. It submitted evidence to demonstrate denial of many grievances based upon time limits violation. This is not a case where time limits have not been enforced, or enforced inconsistently. Rather, here there has been uniform and consistent enforcement of the time limits governing the arbitrability of grievances.

In the light of these observations, therefore, the critical issue involves the claim that the Grievant was discharged on December 22, 1980, and/or in February 1981. If the evidence demonstrates that happened, the grievance shall be denied as not arbitrable under the Labor Agreement.

Letter of Discharge: December 22, 1980

Cagle testified he prepared a letter notifying the Grievant of his discharge effective December 22, 1980, his secretary mailed the letter, and it was sent to his local address. Cagle did not recall whether the letter went certified mail, return receipt requested. Henry testified he checked the local post office and learned that no certified mail had been sent to the Grievant in December 1980. Love said he was aware of the discharge letter sent to the Grievant by Cagle's secretary.

Small testified he did not receive the letter, and Henry said the Union did not obtain a copy of it. *The Company did not produce a copy of the letter which it claimed was sent to the Grievant.* Had the Company produced a copy of the letter, this case would be terminated at this point, the grievance denied on the basis of time limits. As incredible and strange as it may be, the Company could not produce a copy of the letter. In all candor, the Arbitrator must say that in his arbitration experience, now just short of thirty (30) years, during which time he has handled about 200 discharge cases, this is the first instance in which such a vital evidentiary paper was not produced. This, of course, complicates the determination of the time limits issue and Company proof demonstrating that it discharged the Grievant on December 22, 1980.

In a discharge case, the employer, of course, bears the burden of proof, an arbitration principle well settled. As the Elkouris state:

> Discharge is recognized to be the extreme industrial penalty since the employee's job, his seniority and other contractual benefits, and his reputation are at stake. Because of the seriousness of this penalty, the burden generally is held to be on the employer to prove guilt of wrongdoing, and probably always so where the agreement requires "just cause" for discharge.*

Applying this recognized principle to this case, the Company must demonstrate by competent evidence it discharged the Grievant on December 22, 1980. A copy of the discharge letter would have been sufficient proof. It is not an issue of questioning the integrity of Cagle or Love.

As a matter of fact, Cagle testified that it was his secretary, and not he, who mailed the letter. She did not testify in the arbitration. Love did not have direct

* Frank Elkouri and Edna Elkouri, *How Arbitration Works,* 3rd ed. (Washington, D.C.: Bureau of National Affairs, 1973), p. 621.

knowledge of the letter—only testifying he was aware that it had been sent.

Maybe the letter was sent as the Company witnesses testified, but there is no proof that either the Grievant or the Union received it. Apparently the letter was not sent certified mail, as Henry's testimony on that issue appears to show. Thus, it is possible that the letter was sent by ordinary mail, but never delivered. It would not be the first or last time the United States Postal Service lost a letter. Obviously, as Small or the Union did not receive the letter, a grievance could not be filed protesting the discharge. Even if the Company's construction of the material language—five (5) working days from the date of the occurrence—is accepted, a grievance could not be filed in the absence of knowledge of discharge.

Meeting of December 4, 1981

Absence of documentary proof that the letter was sent and/or received may not be remedied by Cagle's testimony that the Grievant acknowledged that he received the letter during the meeting of December 4, 1981. Small did not testify that way in the arbitration, stating that the first he knew about his discharge was when Henry called him around Thanksgiving 1981. Once again, the Arbitrator does not question Cagle's integrity. This is not the issue at all; what is critical is that there must be solid and hard evidence that the Company discharged the Grievant on December 22, 1980.

Obviously the stakes in this dispute are very high. It is a vital case for all concerned. In this light, to deny the grievance on the basis of time limits, the evidence must be clear to the point of certainty that the Company discharged the Grievant on December 22, 1980. Such proof may not be established by unilateral testimony of what the Grievant might have said, or not said, in the December 4, 1981, meeting.

Notification to Union

Nor does the Company meet its burden of proof by its testimony that Cagle and Love separately and on different occasions notified Henry of the Grievant's discharge on December 22, 1980. Their testimony in this respect was denied by Henry, who testified he had first heard of the Grievant's discharge when Moore told him just prior to Thanksgiving 1981. Once again the problem here is not the truthfulness of the three witnesses. Rather the issue is absence of solid and hard evidence demonstrating that the Company notified the Union of the discharge at the time claimed by its witnesses.

To be sure, the Arbitrator is fully aware of the familiar tests of credibility. However, in this dispute, all have much to gain and lose. Small has his job at stake; the Union is concerned with its legal obligation of fair representation; and the Company's problem could be costly liability resulting from the reinstatement of a disabled employee whose industrial accident may be aggravated by further work in the plant.

Conclusions: *Claimed Discharge of December 22, 1980*

In short, the Company did not meet its burden to prove it discharged the Grievant on December 22, 1980. Maybe it did discharge him on that date, but the evidence falls far short of demonstrating with certainty that that was done.

Perhaps the Company did send the discharge letter; but if it did, the proof does not establish that it was received by either the Grievant or the Union. Perhaps the Company did orally notify the Union on December 22, 1980, of the Grievant's discharge. On this issue, however, the evidence is contradictory and may not properly be used to establish with certainty that that was done.

As a result, since the evidence falls far short of proving with certainty that the discharge occurred on December 22, 1980, neither Small nor the Union was obligated to file a grievance within five (5) working days following that date to satisfy the time limits contained in the Labor Agreement.

Plant Visit: *February 1981*

As noted earlier, Cagle and Love testified they orally told the Grievant he was discharged when he showed up in the plant in February 1981. Without questioning the integrity of the Company witnesses, the fact remains that the evidence once again is contradictory. True, Small testified that Love told him that Neenah took him off the payroll. However, he also testified that the word "discharge" was not used at that time. In the Company's view, the statement that the Grievant acknowledged he made was sufficient to demonstrate that he was notified of his' discharge. It asserts:

> . . . However, Small appeared at the plant in February 1981 at which time both Love and Cagle again informed him of the discharge. Small testified at the hearing that in February 1981, he did have a meeting with Love and that he was told he was "taken off the payroll in Neenah, no longer employed."

This statement, however, does not establish that Small was put on clear and certain notice of his discharge. He certainly was not surprised to learn that he was not on the payroll. Indeed, he was off the payroll except for a short time after April 14, 1977. Likewise he was not surprised to learn that he was "no longer employed," since he was not actively employed after the time of his accident. In labor relations parlance, an employee may very well be taken off a payroll without being discharged. As a matter of fact, Henry testified that employees are taken off the payroll without being discharged for a variety of reasons, including layoffs, disability, military duty, and retirement.

As we view the evidence dealing with February 1981, there could have been a problem of communication. It is possible that Love intended to convey to the Grievant that he was discharged when he told him he was taken off the payroll. Unfortunately for the Company, however, what might have been intended by Love does not add up to clear and affirmative notice of discharge. In other words, the

Grievant might have interpreted the Plant Manager's statement in a way not intended by him.

In any event, the evidence does not show with positive assurance that Love told Small clearly and affirmatively that he was discharged. Of course, what might have resolved the issue would have been a written document given to the Grievant at that time to notify him of his discharge. Whatever the reason, the Company did not elect to do that, relying instead on oral discussion subject to contradiction and misinterpretation.

As with the case of the December 22, 1980, letter, Cagle and Love testified that the Grievant admitted that he was told of his discharge of February 1981 in the December 4, 1981, meeting. It must be stressed again that the Grievant did not testify that way in the arbitration. Indeed, given his testimony in the arbitration, what the Grievant might have said in the meeting is that Love told him that he was off the payroll. To repeat, discharge of an employee and being taken off a payroll are not necessarily the same thing for purposes of labor relations.

Based upon this careful analysis of the evidence, the conclusion must be that the Company did not offer sufficient evidence proving that it discharged the Grievant on December 22, 1980, and/or in February 1981. As a result, the grievance filed on November 30, 1981, following Small's discharge was timely filed under the material provisions of the Labor Agreement. Thus, a determination must be made concerning the merits of the discharge—that is, did the Company discharge the Grievant for just cause?

Questions

1 Do you believe that it would have made a difference to the decision if Cagle's secretary had testified in the arbitration that she had mailed the discharge letter? State your reasons.

2 What was the controversy between the parties concerning the application of Article VI, Section 2, the time limit provision of the labor agreement? Evaluate how the arbitrator dealt with this problem.

3 Do you believe that the grievant's letter sent from California deals more with the merits of the grievant's discharge than with the time-limit problem? State your reasons.

4 What evidence did the company offer to prove it discharged the grievant on December 22, 1980, and in February 1981? Why did the arbitrator rule that the company's evidence was not sufficient to prove that it had discharged the grievant at either of these two times?

The Case of Substantive Arbitrability

Cast of characters:

Donald	*Union President*
Jenkins	*Company President*
Quality, Inc.	*Company Directly Involved in Case*
A & B Printers and Fine Print	*Other Companies Involved in Case*

At times an employer requests that a grievance should be denied because it believes that the substance of the grievance is not covered by the labor agreeement, a different matter from that where an employer argues that a grievance should be denied on the basis of time limits (as illustrated in the previous case). When time limits are involved, the question deals with procedural arbitrability. When an employer claims that the issue of a grievance is not covered by a labor agreement, the question involves substantive arbitrability. Though Warrior and Gulf Navigation *sharply limited the federal courts in the matter of determining substantive arbitrability, arbitrators deny grievances when they believe that the issue raised by a grievance is not covered by a labor agreement. The Supreme Court decision was directed at the courts and not at arbitrators.*

In the following case, the employer argued that the labor agreement did not cover the grievance in question. Its position was that the National Labor Relations Board had the exclusive jurisdiction to determine the issue raised by the grievance. As a result, the employer requested that the grievance be denied on the grounds that the arbitrator lacked jurisdiction to deal with the issue. On its part, the union claimed that the substance of the grievance was covered by the labor agreement and that the arbitration process was the proper forum to seek relief from the alleged employer violation. Note that the case does not deal with the merits of the grievance. It deals exclusively with the arbitrability issue. If the employer's position were to prevail, the labor organization could seek relief only from the National Labor Relations Board. If the union's position prevailed, it could in another procedure seek relief in arbitration. As you read the case, keep in mind the fundamental issue and how and why the arbitrator reached his decision.

BACKGROUND

Demand for Arbitration

On June 28, 1979, Donald, Union President, sent the following letter to Jenkins, Company President:

> I am writing to you as President of the Union. It has been reported to the Union that your company, Quality, Inc., has a financial interest or arrangement with non-Union printing establishments in the greater Chicago metropolitan area.
>
> Be advised that it is the Union's position that our Collective Bargaining Agreement covers all composition work performed by Quality, Inc., in the Greater Chicago metropolitan area. This contract cannot be circumvented by transferring work to non-Union shops under the effective control of your Company.
>
> The non-Union shops reported to me are:
>
> A & B Printers
>
> Fine Print
>
> Therefore, it is necessary that the Union receive the following information in detail:
>
> 1 Do any of the owners of Quality have a direct or indirect financial interest or arrangement with A & B Printers or Fine Print? If so, please specify the nature of that interest or arrangement.
> 2 Has Quality performed any composition work for A & B Printers or Fine Print within the past year? If so, please specify.
> 3 Has A & B Printers or Fine Print performed any composition work for Quality within the last year? If so, please specify.

Fine Print is an Illinois corporation incorporated on June 28, 1969. Its principal office is located at 160 East Hudson Street, Chicago, Illinois, and it was organized to engage in the printing business and related fields. Annual Reports of Fine Print show that Jenkins serves as an officer of that corporation.

A & B Printers is an Illinois corporation incorporated on April 8, 1978. Its principal office is located at 2620 Circle Avenue, Chicago, Illinois. A purpose of the corporation is to engage in the typographical business. Annual Reports of A & B Printers show that Jenkins is an officer of that corporation.

Between May 1, 1977, and April 1, 1980, the number of Quality, Inc., composing room employees declined from 111 to 87.

On February 4, 1980, Donald wrote Jenkins demanding arbitration, stating:

> Quality, Inc., has violated provisions of the current contract between this Union and your Company, including but not limited to Articles III, VI, IX and the subcontracting provision of the contract now in effect.
>
> This Union hereby raises an issue with Quality, Inc., under the Grievance–Arbitration Procedure clause, Article IV, of the contract.

On August 11, 1980, Donald requested from Jenkins information for use in the arbitration scheduled for September 25, 1980. In reply, on August 25, 1980, Jenkins wrote Donald, saying:

> In response to your demand for information dated August 11, 1980, received by me on August 18, 1980, please be advised that your demand for arbitration by letter of February 4, 1980, is replete with general and vague allegations of violations of the Collective Bargaining Agreement by Quality, Inc. You do not allege any specific instances or facts to indicate in what manner Quality, Inc., has violated the agreement.
> Until we receive such written enumerations, we are unable to ascertain the validity of your demand.

Subpoenas

At the request of the Union, on August 27, 1980, the Arbitrator issued subpoenas *duces tecum* to Quality, Inc., A & B Printers, and Fine Print. In the subpoena issued to Quality, Inc., the Union requested:

1 Copies of any and all documents, drafts, vouchers, letters, and paper writings whatsoever, that can or may afford any information or evidence describing your involvement and relations with A & B Printers and Fine Print, and any other printing or typesetting operations, whether your involvement is of a financial or advisory nature, and to what extent you are involved in a financial and/or advisory capacity;
2 Copies of any and all records of work transfers for jobs which Quality, Inc., had wholly or partially performed by A & B Printers and Fine Print, or any other operation in the graphics arts field, including but not limited to paid invoices from such other operations for services rendered, with job description, and Quality, Inc.'s, correlative purchase orders.

Subpoenas issued to Fine Print and A & B Printers called for essentially the same kind of information.

On September 9 and 10, 1980, the subpoenas were served on the appropriate officials of the three corporations.

POSITIONS OF THE PARTIES

Quality, Inc., refused to comply with the subpoena on the grounds that the material requested relates to an issue that is not arbitrable under the Labor Agreement.

Unlike the Employer, the Union claimed that the Arbitrator has authority to determine the merits of all issues raised by its demand for arbitration, including the so-called "jurisdictional" matter.

At the close of the second day of hearing, January 8, 1981, the Arbitrator, over the Union's objection, granted the Company the opportunity to file a written statement relating to the jurisdictional issue. Subsequently, the Employer filed a statement, and later the Union submitted a reply statement.

The burden of the Company's argument is that the issue raised by the Union is not arbitrable under the Labor Agreement, falling within the exclusive jurisdiction of the National Labor Relations Board. On that basis, it requests that the aforesaid subpoena be quashed and the issue raised by the Union be dismissed as not arbitrable.

In contrast, the thrust of the Union's argument is that the issue it raised is a proper subject for arbitration under the Labor Agreement, falling within the legitimate scope of the Arbitrator's jurisdiction. On that basis, it requests that the Company should be required to supply the information called for in the subpoena. It further requests that the issue it raised be determined on its merits in arbitration.

BASIC QUESTION

The basic question to be determined in this arbitration is framed as follows:

> Given the circumstances of this case, did the Union raise an arbitrable issue under the Labor Agreement?

Depending upon the determination of this question, an appropriate order regarding the subpoenas shall be directed.

LABOR AGREEMENT PROVISIONS

ARTICLE III.   JURISDICTION PROVISIONS

Jurisdiction of the Union and the appropriate unit for collective bargaining is defined as including all composing room work performed for the employer covered by this agreement by employees . . .

ARTICLE IV.   GRIEVANCE–ARBITRATION PROCEDURE

Section 1   (a) . . . Both parties agree that whenever any differences of opinion as to the rights of either under the agreement shall arise, or whenever any dispute as to the construction of the agreement or any of its provisions take place, such difference or dispute shall be promptly resolved in the manner provided in this Grievance–Arbitration Procedure. . . .

ARTICLE XV.   PARTIES TO CONTRACT

Section 2   It is agreed that the only parties to this agreement are the Union and Quality, Inc.

DETERMINATION OF ARBITRABILITY ISSUE

I

If the issue raised by the Union is related solely to the scope of the bargaining unit, and not based on the Labor Agreement, the proper forum for adjudication would be the National Labor Relations Board. Rights and obligations established under the National Labor Relations Act fall within the exclusive jurisdiction of the

N.L.R.B. That agency has the exclusive authority to enforce rights and obligations which are rooted solely in the National Labor Relations Act.

As the Company asserts:

> These decisions buttress the view that resolution of issues which would require what are essentially bargaining unit determinations are for the Labor Board, not the arbitrator. Indeed, in those cases in which an arbitrator has undertaken to make bargaining unit determinations, the Board has repeatedly declined to defer to the arbitration proceedings or the arbitration award. *See, e.g., Massachusetts Electric Co.*, 248 NLRB 155, 156 (1980) ("We reject the [Union's] contention that we should defer to the pending grievance proceeding involving [the] Union and the Employer. The Board has consistently declined to leave to an arbitrator the responsibility for determining unit questions such as whether a newly acquired plant is an accretion to an existing bargaining unit covered by a collective-bargaining agreement."); *International Brotherhood of Teamsters Local 814*, 213 NLRB No. 71 (1976) (Board would not defer to decision of joint labor–management board finding that certain employees were an accretion to an existing bargaining unit). *See also Consolidation Coal Co.*, 253 NLRB No. 14 (1980) ("disputes, like the instant one, about the fundamental *existence* of an agreement between the parties, as opposed to disputes about the *interpretation* of any such agreements, are not subject to deferral by the Board."). (Emphasis in original)

In Quality, Inc.'s view, the issue raised by the Union relates strictly to bargaining unit matters, and not one that is covered by the Labor Agreement. Therefore, the Union has not raised an arbitrable issue, but instead one that falls within the exclusive jurisdiction of the N.L.R.B. The Company argues:

> It is Quality, Inc.'s position that this issue does not arise under the Contract between it and the Union and, therefore, is outside of the scope of the arbitration clause. Instead, the issue which the Union raises relates to the scope of the relevant bargaining unit, a matter within the primary and exclusive jurisdiction of the NLRB.
>
> It is plain that the issue which the Union attempts to raise here is one over which the NLRB has traditionally exercised jurisdiction in unit determination, unit clarification and unfair labor practice proceedings. . . .
>
> . . . the real issue here turns not on interpretation of the Contract, but on questions of federal law within the exclusive jurisdiction of the NLRB. . . .
>
> The Supreme Court has held that Union ploys to circumvent rights guaranteed by the National Labor Relations Act "by asserting . . . claims in a #301 suit to compel arbitration rather than in an unfair labor practice context cannot be permitted." *Howard Johnson Co.* v. *Detroit Local Joint Executive Board*, 417 U.S. 249, 262 (1974). Similarly, an attempt to "end run around . . . the Act . . . under the guise of contract interpretation" was rebuffed by the court in *Local No. 3-193, International Wood Workers of America* v. *Ketchikan Pulp Co.*, 611 F.2d 1295, 1299 (9th Cir. 1980). It is respectfully submitted that that is precisely the ploy of the Union here. . . .

Should it be held that the Union has not raised an issue covered by the Labor

Agreement, the aforesaid Company assertions would obviously control the arbitrability matter.

II

Apparently the Company believes that to find an arbitrable issue under the Labor Agreement, the contract must contain a provision that expressly covers A & B Printers and Fine Print. Thus:

> Plainly nothing in the Contract between Quality, Inc., and the Union evidences any intention on the part of the parties to extend the contract to other companies. The agreement unequivocally states that "the only parties to this agreement are the Union and Quality, Inc." In this regard, it is certainly relevant that the Union's own evidence establishes that one of the corporations which the Union now attempts to ensnare was first organized in 1969, long before the Quality Contract was signed. The jurisdictional clause which the Union claims "might relate" to the issue it attempts to arbitrate refers in the singular only to 'the employer covered by this agreement." Nothing within the four corners of the Contract or in the bargaining history leading up to it gives even colorable support to the Union's claim that the issue it attempts to raise is an arbitrable dispute arising under the Contract.

To the contrary, to find that the Union has raised an arbitrable issue, it is not necessary to establish that the Labor Agreement covers the other two corporations. It is self-evident that the Labor Agreement is exclusive between the Parties. A & B Printers and Fine Print are not signatories to the contract. However, the Union's position need not be rejected on these grounds provided it has raised an issue which is covered by the Labor Agreement.

By the same token, to find an arbitrable issue, the Arbitrator need not determine the scope of the bargaining unit. It is not necessary to establish that the Union represents the employees of A & B Printers or Fine Print. Equally, it is not necessary to establish that Quality, Inc., A & B Printers, or Fine Print constitute a single employer, or that those two corporations stand as an accretion to the bargaining unit covered by the labor Agreement.

Nor are the merits of the Union's claim to be determined here, or the character of the remedy, should it be held subsequently that the Company has violated the Labor Agreement. *The issue in this proceeding is limited exclusively to the determination of whether the Union has raised an arbitrable issue.* Other matters are not material for that determination.

III

To lend support to its position, the Company refers to the following material developed in the arbitration:

> The Arbitrator: . . . Why don't you file charges?
>   Union Attorney: There's a couple of reasons. One is that if we file charges

with the National Labor Relations Board, the burden is on the charging party to come up with the evidence. There is the subpoenas and the threshold question is the responsibility of the Employer to provide the information.

Secondly, the issue before the Board on the question of assuming there's some arbitration concept on the accretion issue, it will not be based on the Collective Bargaining Agreement and the jurisdictional language. So, ultimately it would have to be involved in the interpretation of the contract. It is our view that the best and proper form for that consideration is arbitration of the provisions of the contract.

Based upon these remarks, the Company says:

Thus, the Union virtually admits that the issue it attempts to raise does not involve interpretation of the Contract, but instead questions of the federal labor law. Those questions are not proper matters for the Arbitrator.

The cited Union remarks may not properly be viewed as a virtual admission by it that arbitration is not a proper forum to have its claim adjudicated. If it felt that way, the Union would not have resorted to arbitration. If it believed that the matter falls within the exclusive jurisdiction of the N.L.R.B., it would, of course, have filed unfair labor practice charges in the first place. Rather than conceding the jurisdictional issue, the Union merely pointed out that if it had resorted to federal law for relief, the N.L.R.B. would naturally apply federal law. To regard the aforesaid Union statement within the context in which it was made as a virtual concession of the jurisdictional issue is not warranted.

IV

With full deference to the Company, it is the Arbitrator's judgment that the Union has raised a clearly arbitral issue within the meaning of the Labor Agreement. The issue is one that is properly the subject of arbitration. It is not one that falls within the exclusive jurisdiction of the National Labor Relations Board. To say that the Union attempts a "ploy" or an "end run" around federal labor law ignores the material contractual language under the circumstances of this dispute.

Under Article III of the Labor Agreement, the jurisdiction of the Union and the unit for collective bargaining is defined as including all composing room work performed by the Company. Employees cited in the provision have the exclusive right to perform such work.

Whether meritorious or not, the Union charges that Quality, Inc., has violated Article III, undermining the integrity of the bargaining unit, by transferring work, rightfully that of its employees, to A & B Printers and Fine Print in which Jenkins has a financial interest. Thus:

. . . The Union has stated the issue to be that the Employer has violated the jurisdiction and other provisions of the contract by transferring bargaining unit work to non-union establishments with which the Employer has financial ties.

In other words, the Union charges a violation of Article III of the Labor Agreement. In Article IV, the Employer and Union agreed that should *"any dispute"* as to the construction of *"any of its provisions"* of the Labor Agreement take place, such dispute shall be resolved in the manner provided for in the Grievance–Arbitration Procedure.

A dispute has arisen concerning the application of Article III of the Labor Agreement under the circumstances of this case. The Union charges a violation of Article III because of the alleged improper conduct of the Company. Such an issue is clearly covered by the arbitration provision. *Nothing in this contractual clause, or for that matter in any other provision of the Labor Agreement, removes that issue from the scope of the arbitration provision.* As the United States Supreme Court held in the *Trilogy Cases*:

> an order to arbitrate the particular grievance should not be denied unless it may be said with positive assurance that the arbitration clause is not susceptible of an interpretation that covers that asserted dispute.*

Where in the Labor Agreement is there an express provision that removes the "asserted dispute" from the coverage of the arbitration provision? The Company stresses that

> the only parties to this agreement are the Union and Quality, Inc.

The Arbitrator fully agrees that they are the only parties to the Labor Agreement. The issue raised is whether the Employer violated the terms of the Labor Agreement. The issue is not whether A & B Printers or Fine Print violated the Labor Agreement. These two corporations are involved in this case only to the extent that the Employer may have used them to subvert the integrity of the jurisdiction of the Union as guaranteed by Article III of the Labor Agreement.

Article IV, Section (i), states that the Grievance–Arbitration Procedure is

> limited exclusively and specifically to differences in the interpretation and enforcement of the terms of this contract.

Clearly, this provision does not prevent a determination of the merits of the Union's claim. It does not because a dispute has arisen dealing with the "interpretation and enforcement" of Article III of the Labor Agreement.

V

In short, what we have here is an allegation by the Union that the Company has violated the terms of the Labor Agreement. Such a dispute is a matter of contractual interpretation and application, the natural grist of the arbitration process. What

---

* *United Steelworkers* v. *Warrior & Gulf Navigation Co.*, 363 U.S. 564 (1960).

we have here is a dispute that is rooted to the Labor Agreement, and not one that is rooted to rights and obligations established under federal law.

In the *Trilogy Cases*, the United States Supreme Court stated:

> The function of the court is very limited when the parties have agreed to submit all questions of contract interpretation to the arbitrator. It is then confined to ascertaining whether the party seeking arbitration is making a claim which on its face is governed by the contract. Whether the moving party is right or wrong is a question of contract interpretation for the arbitrator. In these circumstances the moving party should not be deprived of the arbitrator's judgment, when it was his judgment and all that it connotes that was bargained for.*

In the case at hand, the Parties have agreed to submit all questions of contractual interpretation to arbitration. The question is whether the Employer violated Article III of the Labor Agreement. The Union has raised an issue pure and simple which falls under the Labor Agreement. It is entitled to have the merits of its claim adjudicated in the arbitration process.

VI

Since the Union has raised an arbitrable issue, the Company shall be directed to comply with Paragraphs 1 and 2 of the subpoena. Moreover, since A & B Printers and Fine Print may have information necessary to establish whether the Employer violated Article III of the Labor Agreement, these two corporations shall also be directed to comply with Paragraphs 1 and 2 of their subpoenas.

Under the United States Arbitration Act and the Illinois Uniform Arbitration Act, the Union is entitled to subpoena documents and all material relevant to this dispute. The merits of the Union's claim cannot possibly be determined in the absence of such documents.

Questions

1 Assume that the company appealed to the federal courts to vacate the decision and that you were the judge. How and why would you deal with the appeal?

2 Despite the fact that the *Trilogy Cases* apply to the federal courts, how do you account for the arbitrator's use of them in his decision?

3 In the final analysis, what was the arbitrator's major reason for finding that the grievance was arbitrable under the labor agreement?

4 Establish a set of conditions in terms of contractual language or union demands in which the grievance would be held to be not arbitrable.

---

* *United Steelworkers* v. *American Manufacturing Co.,* 363 U.S. 564 (1960).

Past Practice:
The Case of the "Monthly Men"

Cast of characters:

Ohl, James, Pitts   *Grievants*
Nix   *A Union Witness*
Wills   *General Supervisor*
Rogers   *District President*

In this case, the union claimed that the grievance should be granted on the basis of past practice, stating that the practice in question had been in effect for 40 years! On its part, the employer, not challenging the union's evidence dealing with past practice, asserted that the grievance should be denied on the basis of unambiguous contractual language. As you read the case, you will see that the critical issue involved a past practice that conflicted with clear-cut contractual language. Under these circumstances, contractual language normally prevails over the practice. Underlying the arbitration principle is this: When an employer and a union adopt unambiguous contractual language, or renew such language in a labor agreement, they intend the language to prevail over custom and practice. The principle is a two-edged sword: Depending upon the circumstances of a particular dispute, it may help or hurt either the employer or the union.

You are the arbitrator in this case. Clearly establish your reasons for the granting or the denial of the grievance. In the discussion of the case, your instructor will probably tell you the decision of the actual arbitrator.

GRIEVANCE

Ohl, James, and Pitts, the Grievants in this dispute, filed a grievance which generated this arbitration. The grievance is not dated, though it shows that a Step 2 meeting was held on January 13, 1981. The grievance states:

> Management has said that they will honor the Terre Haute strip mine agreement.
> In that agreement the monthly men on shovels shall get 22 starts a month less
> Sundays and Holidays. We did not get 22 starts in the month of Nov. 1980. We
> are demanding pay for the shifts we didn't get.

The Mine Committee supported the grievance, relying on the Terre Haute Strip Mine Agreement, effective April 1, 1941, and Article XXVI, Section b, of the 1978 Labor Agreement. When it denied the grievance, the Mine Management stated:

> The above men were paid for 22 days during November. Two of these days were holidays and they were paid for these; therefore denied.

POSITIONS OF THE PARTIES

The Union contends that the Grievants are so-called "monthly men." As a result, they are guaranteed 22 starts in a month excluding holidays and Sundays. Thus, should the employees covered by the grievance not be scheduled for 22 days, say only 21 days, the Company is obligated to award them a day's pay even though they did not actually perform work on that day. In addition, the Union claims that a paid holiday does not count against the 22 days. So, within a month in which a paid holiday falls, says Veterans Day and Thanksgiving Day, the monthly men must still be scheduled for 22 starts. If in that month, should the employees only work 21 days, the Company must pay them for a day even though they received holiday pay.

Classifications covered by the grievance are Stripping Machine Operators and Oilers and Coal Loading Shovel Operators. These classifications, the Union argues, are to receive the monthly scale (22 days' pay) should they not be scheduled for 22 starts within a month.

To support its position, the Union argues:

> We have before us today a case where past practice has prevailed for 19 negotiated contracts, totaling over 40 years. We have statements where the monthly scale was paid within two months of this grievant's case; thus proving that the past practice *did* exist! (Emphasis in original)
>
> The monthly scale was a negotiated item in the 1941 Terre Haute Strip Mine Agreement between the United Mine Workers of America and the Indiana Coal Producers Association and has been carried forth ever since.

In contrast, the Company claims that the grievance does not have merit because the provision in the Terre Haute Strip Mine Agreement establishing a monthly scale conflicts with material contractual language contained in the Labor Agreement providing a daily standard rate of pay. The Company states that such a conflict started with the 1971 Labor Agreement.

Thus:

> Also appearing in the 1968 Agreement is the language relating to the Joint Commission on Wage Rates. The culmination of this Joint Commission was the language of Article IV, Section (e) of the 1971 Labor Agreement.
>
> Whereas in the rate schedules of the 1968 agreement the monthly men's

rates are shown, in the 1971 Labor Agreement, the monthly men rates are conspicuously absent. Management contends that the purpose of the 1968 Joint Commission was to eliminate inequities and discrepancies among the various districts one of which was the monthly men wage scale. Instead the negotiators intended the standard daily wage rate system to apply uniformly across the districts in the 1971 agreement and subsequent wage agreements. The standard daily wage rate continues to appear in the 1978 agreement.

Beyond its argument based upon conflict, the Company claims that the grievance has no merit for another reason: Since April 1, 1966, employees have been paid for recognized holidays. A paid holiday, the Company says, should be counted as a turn earned by the monthly men.

CONTRACT PROVISIONS

Though reference to additional contractual language shall be made later on in this Opinion, at this time the following provisions will be cited:

TERRE HAUTE STRIP MINE AGREEMENT (EFFECTIVE APRIL 1, 1941)

ARTICLE I.   SCALE OF WAGES AND CLASSIFICATIONS

Section 1   Monthly men's wages shall be based on a calendar month less Sundays and holidays. While this contract is based on a 7-hour day (See Article V, Sec. 1), monthly men working on shovels shall receive wages as stated below for 8 hours work per day, except as specified. A day's pay is 1/22 of the monthly pay (see Article I, Sec. 3).

Classification	Rate Per Day Hours	Per Day Rate	Per Mo.
Shovel Operator	$11.77	8	$258.94
Shovel Craneman	10.73	8	236.06
Shovel Fireman	9.69	8	213.18
Shovel Oiler	8.96	8	197.12
Tipple Engineer	7.79	7	171.38
Groundman about shovel	8.50	8	. . .

Section 4   The above monthly wage scale is based on a twenty-two working day month, and for the purpose of computing overtime and docking for any month, the daily rate shall be 1/22 part of the monthly rate.

LABOR AGREEMENT (EFFECTIVE MARCH 27, 1978)

ARTICLE 4

Section (e). Standard Daily Wage Rate   The standard daily wage rates paid for work performed under this Agreement and set forth in Appendix A and the job titles within the respective classifications are grouped in Appendix B, Part I, which includes the five grades for underground jobs in deep mines, Appendix

B, Part II, which includes the five grades for jobs in strip and auger mines, and Appendix B, Part III, which includes the four grades for jobs in preparation plants and other surface facilities for deep or surface mines. The standard daily wage rate for each job classification shall be the standard daily wage rate for all job titles included in such classification. The list of job titles within each classification indicates only the rates to be paid to Employees bearing such job titles. No Employer shall have authority to introduce any job title or any classification into a mine in which it does not presently exist, except when ordered to do so by an arbitrator as set out in this section.

DISTRICT AGREEMENTS

ARTICLE XXVII

Section (b). Prior Practice and Custom   This Agreement supersedes all existing and previous contracts except as incorporated and carried forward herein by reference; and all local agreements, rules, regulations and customs heretofore established in conflict with this Agreement are hereby abolished. Except where abolished by mutual agreement of the parties, all prior practice and custom not in conflict with this Agreement shall be continued. . . . Whenever a conflict arises between this Agreement and any District or local agreement, this Agreement shall prevail.

Within six (6) months following the effective date of this Agreement, the Employers and all the UMWA District presidents shall provide to the International Union and to the Bituminous Coal Operators' Association, copies of all District agreements in their possession. All District agreements which are not provided to the International Union and B.C.O.A. during the first six (6) months of this Agreement may not be relied upon by any Employer or the Union in any grievance proceeding which may occur during the balance of this Agreement.

BASIC ISSUE

The basic issue to be determined in this dispute is framed as follows:

Under the circumstances of this case, did the Company violate the provisions of the Terre Haute Strip Mine Agreement and the provisions of the 1978 Labor Agreement? If so, what should the remedy be?

BACKGROUND

Development of Material Contractual Language

As noted earlier, the 1941 Terre Haute Strip Mine Agreement established the monthly scale for the classifications involved in this dispute. Such a wage practice was continued in subsequent contracts including the one effective October 1, 1968, which stated:

> All mine workers . . . whether employed by the month or day shall receive effective October 1, 1968 . . .

In the wage schedule of the 1968 Labor Agreement, compensation was specified for the "monthly men."

The Labor Agreement, effective April 1, 1966, for the first time provided eight (8) paid holidays for employees paid by the month or the day. Before the 1968 Labor Agreement went into effect, employees were paid twice a month. With the advent of the 1968 contract, employees are paid at least every two weeks.

In the 1968 Labor Agreement, the Parties established the Joint Commission on Wage Rates. It was charged with the responsibility for investigating the wage rates and classifications in the various districts for the purpose of

> determining whether there are wage rates for all classifications of work, whether there are any existing discrepancies or inequities in rates within the districts or among the districts and other related problems.

The 1971 Labor Agreement

On November 12, 1971, the 1971 Labor Agreement became effective. With respect to wages, the contract stated:

Standard Daily Wage Rate

> The standard daily wage rates paid for work performed under this agreement was set forth in Appendix A and the job titles within the respective classifications grouped in (1) the six grades for underground at deep mines; (2) the six grades in strip and auger mines and (3) the five grades for preparation plants and other surface facilities for deep or surface mines are set forth in Appendix B. The list of job titles within the respective classifications only indicates the rates to be paid to employees bearing such job titles. This is not authority to introduce such classifications in areas where they do not presently exist.

Reference was also made to the results of the Joint Wage Commission on Wage Rates:

> The reorganization of the wage structure in the bituminous coal industry, which was the basis for the classification regrouping in Appendix A and Appendix B, was based on work of the Joint Commission on Wage Rates which was created by the Labor Agreement of 1968.

Appendix A, Part II, of the 1971 contract established the wage structure for Strip Mines. With regard to the classifications involved in this dispute, Stripping Machine Operators and Oilers and Coal Loading Shovel Operators, the Parties established a standard daily rate ranging between $39.00 and $50.00 per day for the term of the contract. Nothing in the 1971 Labor Agreement within its body or wage appendix provided for a monthly scale for any classification.

In the 1978 Labor Agreement, the classifications in question, as specified by Appendix A, Part II, were to be paid a standard daily wage rate ranging between $67.25 and $77.77 per day during the life of the contract. Nothing in the 1978 Labor Agreement within its body or wage appendix established a monthly scale for any classification.

Practice and Custom at Mine

James, Ohl, and Nix appeared as Union witnesses in the arbitration. As to service at the Mine, James had 36 years; Ohl, 18 years; and Nix, 7 years. They testified that from the start of their service until the circumstances of this dispute arose they were regarded as "monthly men," and were paid the monthly scale when they were not scheduled for 22 starts in a month. At times, the Company failed to pay them when they were short the required number of shifts, but they were paid for the missed days when the problem was called to the attention of the Company. The monthly scale was in effect when employees were paid twice a month and remained in effect after the pay period was changed to at least every two weeks. They were scheduled for 22 starts per month even in those months in which a paid holiday occurred.

In addition, the Union witnesses testified that when the circumstances of the dispute arose, the Company did not announce its intention of discontinuing payment of the monthly scale. In September 1980, James was scheduled for 21 starts. Later on, before the instant grievance was filed, the Company paid him for the missed day.

Wills, General Supervisor of the Mine, testified that he was regarded as a monthly man when he was in the bargaining unit. When the pay period was changed to at least every two weeks, the Company scheduled the classifications in question on the basis of 22 days per month rather than 11 days in a pay period, as was the case when the employees were paid twice a month. At one time, the Company had the discretion to select employees for the monthly men classifications. Since 1968 or 1971, he said, the Company lost this discretion, the job openings being posted as any other job. At one time, when a monthly man worked more than 22 shifts, say 23, the Company would not pay for the extra day. After 1974 or 1976, he said, the Company ceased not paying for the extra day worked.

Like the Union witnesses, Wills declared that at times the Company failed to pay him for 22 days. Under these circumstances, he would remind supervision and received payment for the missed days. To determine whether payment was proper to monthly men who claimed they were shorted, payroll records were checked.

As required by Article XXVI, Section (b), of the Labor Agreement, Rogers, current President of District 11, took appropriate action for the continuation of the Terre Haute Strip Mine Agreement.

chapter 7

Wage Issues under Collective Bargaining

Almost all contract negotiations pivot upon, and most grievances and arbitration procedures thus ultimately deal with, four major areas: (1) wages and issues that can be directly related to wages; (2) employee benefits or economic "fringe" supplements to the basic wage rate; (3) "institutional" issues that deal with the rights and duties of employers and unions; and (4) "administrative" clauses that treat such subjects as work rules and job tenure. In this chapter and the three that follow it, each of these areas will be discussed in turn. As in the preceding chapter, arbitration cases will also be used, where appropriate, to illustrate particular problems.

Probably no issues under collective bargaining continue to give rise to more difficult problems than do wages and wage-related subjects. When negotiations reach a stalemate, they frequently do so because management and union representatives are not able to find a formula to resolve wage disputes. And wage controversies are, for that matter, by far the leading overt cause of strikes: Over the past decade, for example, they have accounted for over 40 percent of all such work stoppages.[1]

This record highlights the vital character of wage negotiations in collective bargaining and also suggests that in the area of wages much can be done to decrease management–labor conflict substantially. In any area of human relations, ignorance breeds suspicion, distrust, and conflict; this principle of human behavior is fully applicable to wage negotiations under collective bargaining. To the extent that

[1] Data furnished by the Bureau of Labor Statistics, U.S. Department of Labor.

understanding is substituted for ignorance, there will be a greater opportunity for peaceful settlement of wage controversies, even if conflict of interest in such matters never disappears.

It is not difficult to understand why wages do play such an important and controversial role in labor relations. For workers, wages are normally the only source of income, and the standard of living of the employee and his family is determined almost exclusively by this source. For workers' families, the weekly paycheck establishes the character and quality of their dwelling, food, clothing, education, recreation, and all other items that are included in the concept of standard of living.

But if, from the point of view of the worker wages are income that establishes a standard of living, from the viewpoint of the company wages are a cost of production. And here is the heart of the wage controversy. On the one hand, employees press for higher and higher wages with the objective of raising their standard of living; on the other hand, employers are confronted with increasing pressures on the cost of production. When wages are a significant element of cost of production, when wage increases are not offset by such economic phenomena as increased efficiency, and when the union has been unable (or unwilling) to extract equal wage concessions from all competitive firms, wage increases tend to place the firm in an undesirable economic position. A company so placed might not be able to survive for long in the competitive struggle. Under such a state of affairs, union wage policy, instead of advancing the standard of living of its members, could plunge them into economic oblivion.

In fact, as is the case perhaps with no other area of collective bargaining to that extent, wage problems test the skill, understanding, and attitudes of negotiators. The latter are, as we know, now confronted with a legion of wage issues, including the establishment of the basic wage rate, wage differentials, overtime rates, and wage adjustments during contractual periods, as well as with the thorny problems involved in the negotiation of the so-called fringe, or supplemental, wage payments, which will be discussed in the next chapter. It is hoped that the following discussion of some of the principles, practices, and trends concerning these several wage and wage-related areas will contribute to a better understanding of them.

DETERMINATION OF THE BASIC WAGE RATE

If union and management representatives are exhibiting an ever-greater willingness to deal with factual information at the bargaining table, there is still no single standard for wage rate determination that has anything approaching a "scientific" base. Both the bargaining parties, indeed, commonly utilize at least *three different* such standards, each of which has definite advantages from the viewpoint of achieving an "equitable" settlement but also significant limitations: the "comparative-norm," ability-to-pay, and standard-of-living criteria.

Comparative Norm

The basic idea behind the "comparative-norm" concept is the presumption that the economics of a particular collective bargaining relationship should neither fall substantially behind nor be greatly superior to that of other employer–union relationships, that in short it is generally a good practice to keep up with the crowd, but not necessarily to lead it.

The outside observer would very probably agree with this principle, at least on the surface. When a firm is operating with a highly competitive product or in highly competitive labor markets, there is safety for employee relations in keeping labor costs and wage rates consistent with the local and industrial pattern, but not necessarily any need to exceed this pattern. Unions tend to maintain harmony and contentment among the rank and file as long as wage conditions are uniform; on the other hand, it is at times quite difficult and embarrassing for union leaders to explain to the membership why their economic terms of employment are not at least equivalent to those of other unionists (particularly where one local of an international union falls substantially behind another local of the same international). In short, the comparative-norm principle is often valid for economic, sociological, and psychological reasons.

Thus, the parties frequently make a careful and comprehensive study of the community and industry wage structure before negotiations begin and then compare these rates with the rates in existence at the location involved in the negotiations. The strategic implications of such comparisons, already cited in Chapter 5, are quite obvious. If the plant rates are below the community or industry pattern, the union can be expected to argue for a wage increase on this basis. When the plant rates are in excess of the community or industry pattern, the employer has an argument *against* a wage increase.

Notwithstanding these considerations, there are limitations to this approach to the bargaining process. Not all firms have the same capacity to meet economic demands. This is the case not only for firms in different industries but also for companies operating within the same industry. Even though economic forces are at work that tend to place firms operating within the same industrial grouping on the same economic footing, many other factors—such as imperfections in the product market, technological differences, location, stage of economic development, and financial resources—may, at any one time, place such firms on different economic levels. From this it follows that at any one time firms may be quite different in their individual capacities to meet economic demands and that the optimum wage level for one firm of a particular industry could be quite low (or quite high) in comparison with that of the industry in general.

Negotiations in the steel industry serve to illustrate this point. Most of the basic steel manufacturers, whether large or small, are organized by the United Steelworkers of America. So, too, are most steel fabrication firms, which purchase their steel from the basic steel companies, fabricate it, and then sell the resultant steel products directly to other industrial plants or to private consumers. The membership of the union is, in fact, divided about equally between employees who work in these two sectors of the steel industry.

In negotiations with the basic steel companies, the union's highest national officers deal directly with a small employer committee agreed upon by the larger of these companies (United States Steel, Bethlehem, Republic, and similar large producers). From this key negotiation, a "pattern" or comparative norm is established. The union then officially tries to gain about the same wage settlement individually from the smaller basic steel plants and the steel fabrication firms. Clearly, however, the financial and market circumstances of the large basic steel producers are quite different from those confronting the other types of managements—and the inevitable result is a wide variety of different degrees of pattern following and pattern deviation in what is nonetheless still referred to as the "steel industry."

Many other examples could be used to demonstrate the same principle. Within the rubber industry, the economic conditions, and thus the wage-paying abilities, of the large firms oriented toward the rubber tire market are quite different from those of the smaller footwear manufacturers. And highly competitive rubber heel plants, for example, normally settle with the Rubber Workers for considerably less than the rubber tire pattern established with Firestone, Goodrich, and similar rubber tire titans, even though many of the latter firms also manufacture footwear. Large meatpackers are generally in better positions to allow higher wage levels than are their smaller competitors. In the automobile industry, there are obviously significant economic differences between General Motors and American Motors. These considerations must be recognized before one accepts the proposition that the comparative-norm principle of wage determination should be used as the exclusive, or the most desirable, standard for wage settlements in collective bargaining.[2]

There are at least four other factors to be considered in regard to the comparative-norm principle. *First,* not only do firms within a given industry at any given time have unequal capabilities to meet economic demands, but frequently it is quite difficult to classify a firm in a particular industrial grouping for wage comparison purposes. Some firms may logically be classified in two or more industries, because of the products they manufacture or the services they provide. Likewise, even if a firm is classified within a particular industry, there are frequently significant subgroupings in each major industrial classification. Within the oil industry, for example, there are large, medium, and small producers of oil, and producers can be classified considerably further in terms of exact product and nature

---

[2] Recognition of the differences between firms and industries should also be taken into account when the *nonmoney* items of collective bargaining are negotiated. A seniority system, for example, that is suitable for one employer–union relationship may not fit the needs of the employer and employees of another plant. Union security formulas, checkoff arrangements, managerial prerogative systems, grievance procedures, discharge and disciplinary arrangements, and the character of union obligations should be geared fundamentally to the particular collective bargaining relationship. Company and union representatives are at times astonished to learn of the contractual arrangement of another employer–union relationship. The fact is, however, that such a formula can frequently be explained logically in terms of the environment of that firm.

of operations. Such complicating circumstances illustrate the difficulty of classifying a particular firm in a particular industry or in a segment of an industry for purposes of wage determination.

A *second* limitation involved in the use of the comparative-norm wage principle for collective bargaining is the fact that it is at times misleading to compare employees within a particular job classification, because the content of jobs may be substantially different among plants within the same labor market. The duties of an employee classified as a "subassembler, B" in one plant may be quite different from those of an employee classified identically in another plant. The fact is that job classifications within industry have not been standardized. As long as this situation exists, and there is reason to believe that it will continue to exist, the usefulness of the comparative-norm wage principle is proportionately reduced.

This wage criterion is limited in its applicability by still a *third* complication. It is difficult to use the principle when comparing workers who are within the same job classification but who are paid by different systems of wage payments. Some workers are paid on a straight hourly rate basis, others on an individual incentive system, and still others on a group incentive plan. The kind of wage system in operation can in itself have a significant impact upon wage rates.

Briefly described, incentive wages constitute a method of wage payment by which earnings are geared more or less directly to actual output instead of to time spent on the job. Employees are thus granted a relatively clear-cut financial motivation to increase their outputs, essentially by increasing the effort on which such outputs depend.

On the other hand, determination of the actual rate of pay for each "piece" or unit of output is, of course, open to union–management controversy; the management's conception of an appropriate rate is typically somewhat less liberal than is the union's. And the problem is compounded when the original job on which the rate has been set is in any way "modified" (as virtually all jobs ultimately are, because of a host of factors ranging from worker-implemented shortcuts to management job reengineering) and each party seeks a new rate that is beneficial to its own interests.

Some unions have historically opposed such plans from their inception, through fear of management rate cutting (for example, artificial reconstruction of the job in order to pay it a lower rate) and because of a deeply harbored suspicion that there is nothing "scientific" to *any* established rates. But managements that have yielded too readily to union requests for higher rates have also suffered, in inequities between earnings and effort, and in consequent problems involving not only finances but also employee morale. Increased automation of industry to the point where many workers cannot control their output rates has caused some further deemphasis of incentive plans in recent years. However, about one-quarter of all production plant workers in the United States continue to be paid under such plans, and it is obvious that the presence of such workers can make the comparative-norm principle severely misleading.

Fourth, and finally, consideration must be given to the existence of the wide variety of fringe benefits previously cited. These benefits are not distributed equally throughout industry. Thus it could be wrong to conclude that workers in different plants are not equal in terms of net economic advantage where one group earns a lower basic wage rate but surpasses another group in terms of paid holidays and vacations, retirement, social insurance, and the like.

These considerations do not mean that the comparative-norm principle is of no value in collective bargaining. Its utility is demonstrated by its widespread use. But bargainers who utilize this avenue of wage comparisons without recognition of the several problems and limitations involved in its implementation do so only at their peril.

Ability to Pay

A second leading criterion involved in wage determination under collective bargaining is the ability of the firm or industry to pay a wage increase. The outcome of wage negotiations is frequently shaped by this factor, and many strikes occur where there is disagreement between company and union negotiators relative to the wage-paying capacity of the enterprise. Careful consideration and better understanding of this factor of wage determination is no less imperative for reducing the area of disagreement between industry and organized labor than is familiarity with the comparative-norm factor.

The level of profits is one indicator of the wage-paying ability of the firm involved in the negotiations. If a firm is earning a "high" rate of profit, union representatives will frequently claim that the company can afford all or most of the union wage demand. If the firm is earning a "low" rate of profit, management negotiators will frequently argue that the firm does not have the financial capacity to meet the union's wage demands. But the heart of this controversy is, clearly, the determination of what constitutes a rate of profits sufficient to meet a given union wage demand. Unfortunately, no economic formula can answer this question with precision and exactness.

As in the case of the preceding criterion, the problem is complicated by further considerations. In the *first* place, it is not certain whether a given rate of profits earned by a company over a given time in the past will hold for the future. Future profits may fall or rise depending upon the behavior of a number of economic variables that are themselves uncertain: Changes in sales, output, productivity, price, managerial efficiency, and even the state of international relations will all bear upon the future profit experience of a particular firm or industry. Thus, a wage rate negotiated in the light of a given historical profit experience may not be appropriate in the future. Moreover, if profits are to be used as an indicator of the firm's ability to meet a given wage demand, consideration must be given to anticipated government tax structures. The wage-paying ability of the firm may be quite different before and after the payment of the federal income tax, as many business administrators can testify. There are additional elements of the never-static national and state tax programs that tend to have an impact on the wage-paying ability of industry.

Second, the use to which a company intends to put its profits also has a vital bearing upon this problem. Since profits are frequently used to promote capital growth and improvement, the future plans of the enterprise itself must receive consideration by the negotiators. The problem of whether profits should be used for growth and improvement, for lower commodity price, or for higher wages is one of the most troublesome issues in industrial relations. Concepts of "fair treatment"—always subjective—are inevitably involved. And so are a host of fundamental business decisions whose optimal resolution is vital to the very survival of the organization. Dealing with this determinant of wages alone is, in short, anything but child's play.

Third, although the level of profits is an important factor in the determination of a firm's ability to pay wages, it is not the only factor. Other considerations that have an important bearing on the problem are the ratio of labor costs to total costs, the amount of money expended for the financing of fringe benefits, the character of the product market in which the firm operates, the degree of elasticity of demand for the firm's product, and the ability of the company to increase productivity.

The ratio of labor costs to total costs particularly conditions the ability of a firm to afford increased wage rates. An employer is in a better position to grant higher wages when the firm's labor costs represent a comparatively small part of the total costs. For example, a 10 percent increase in wage rates will result in a 1 percent increase in total costs when wage costs are 10 percent of total costs (as they are, for example, in portions of the petroleum industry). Where, however, wage costs are 50 percent of total costs (as in segments of the leather industry), a 10 percent increase in wage rates will result in a 5 percent increase in total costs. This illustration, of course, is based on the assumption that there is no increase or decrease in labor productivity after the wage rates are negotiated. If output increases faster than the wage rise, labor cost per unit of production tends to decrease. The reverse is true when labor productivity does not increase with higher wages.

Moreover, the ratio of labor cost to total cost cannot by itself be taken as conclusive evidence of the wage-paying ability of a particular firm. Firms with a low labor cost do not necessarily have the capacity to pay higher wages. By the same token, it would not be accurate to conclude that firms with a high labor cost can never afford wage increases. All that can be said with some degree of accuracy is that if all economic variables were held constant, a firm with a low labor–cost ratio could afford to pay higher wages more easily than a firm with a high labor–cost ratio.

As in the case of the comparative-norm principle, it should also be reemphasized that an employer's total wage bill includes not only direct wage costs but costs incurred in providing employees with so-called "fringe" benefits. Even though basic wages constitute the major labor cost, industry each year pays a considerable amount of money in financing supplements to the basic wage bill. Into this category fall such items as sickness, accident, hospital, and dental insurance; pensions; severance pay; and paid holidays and vacations.

Employer payments for such benefits have been rising rapidly, as Chapter 8 will relate with documentation. Rising at approximately 1 percent of payroll per year ever since the late 1940s, such benefits represent a growing percentage of total payroll. As this was being written, a recent study conducted by the U.S. Chamber of Commerce and covering 983 firms had revealed that employers were spending an average of $6,627 per worker on fringe benefits, or 37.3 percent of total payroll.[3] To put it in more graphic terms, in the early 1980s fringe benefits cost employers more than $350 billion per year.

The ease with which a company can pass on the costs of a wage increase in the form of higher prices to other firms or to the consuming public is still another determinant of its wage-paying ability. Some firms (in the brewing and cigarette industries, for example) operate in a highly competitive selling market. Under these circumstances it is very difficult, if not impossible, for an employer to shift the burden of a wage increase to the consumer. Even a slight increase in price could result in a significant decrease in sales, since consumers would simply buy from other sellers. To the degree that a firm sells its products in a highly competitive market, it will find strong consumer resistance to price increases. In contrast, some companies (for example, newspaper publishers in single-newspaper cities) operate in monopolistic markets. Under these circumstances, companies have a greater degree of freedom to raise prices without experiencing a sharp decrease in sales. This would be particularly true where the product in question is sold under conditions of inelastic demand. Such a demand characteristic would apply to goods that are necessities or to those for which there are few satisfactory substitutes. Thus, if a company is operating in a monopolistic market and is selling a product for which the demand is relatively inelastic, it has an excellent opportunity to shift the costs of wage increases to other firms or to the general public in the form of higher prices.

Negotiators at times take advantage of such an economic environment. Wage increases are agreed upon and the result is higher prices. From the public's point of view, it would be much more desirable if unions and employers could work out an arrangement whereby wages could be increased without price increases. Certainly, a wage agreement that increases the prices of basic economic commodities and thereby generates a general inflation of the price level cannot be regarded as socially sound.

Wage and Price Controls

Throughout history, governments confronted with major inflationary movements have imposed some kind of limit on wage and price increases. Almost four thousand years ago, King Hammurabi of Babylonia set the annual wages of field workers at eight gur (75 bu.) of corn and those of herdsmen, whose job was presumably less valuable to society, at six gur (56.25 bu.). The Roman Emperor Diocletian in A.D. 301 established price maximums for transportation by camel and for artichokes

---

[3] *Wall Street Journal*, November 24, 1982.

and he meant business: Anyone caught charging more was put to death. In the United States, a wage and price controls program during World War II was itself a major industry: It needed 60,000 full-time officials and almost five times that many volunteer checkers for its implementation.[4]

And in more recent years, the federal government has also turned on more than one occasion to labor-related controls of one kind or another in an effort to thwart large rises in the general level of prices.

VOLUNTARY WAGE GUIDEPOSTS   In 1962,the president's Council of Economic Advisers successfully argued that labor cost increases should be limited to the nationwide annual rise in labor productivity (as measured by output per labor-hour). Over the prior few years, according to CEA statistics, this annual productivity increase for the economy had averaged 3.2 percent, and the council consequently urged that contract settlement, through "voluntary restraint" by the bargaining parties, remain below this figure, or at a level that would presumably negate the need for price increases. The council guideposts (or "guidelines," as they were also called) were viewed by government officials as a mechanism for advancing national prosperity, aiding the nation in its balance-of-payments problems, and generally protecting the broader public interest.

Neither managements nor labor organizations, generally speaking, gave much endorsement to these wage-price guideposts. Managers tended to view them as a not-very-subtle form of government intervention, even as a harbinger of ultimate price controls. Company spokespersons also argued that the CEA's recommendations would stifle business initiative and that, in addition, the current national levels of unemployment, unused plant capacity, and domestic and foreign competition were sufficient in themselves to ward off inflation.

To many unionists, the guideposts appeared to ignore "special situations," such as that existing in the automobile industry prior to the 1964 negotiations there: With auto profits at record highs in that year, the UAW leadership vociferously argued that the industry could pay considerably more than 3.2 percent to its workers and still cut prices, thereby making a settlement noninflationary. The union finally settled for about 4.8 percent. Labor spokespersons also attacked the guideposts as inequitably "freezing" worker shares in the income-distribution pie at their pre-1962 levels, in the absence of a convincing reason why such wage income shares should not be *increased*. And, as their counterparts on the management side, they also viewed with some alarm the increased government intervention implicit in the guideposts. It was said by one leading unionist that the 3.2 percent guideposts were "as welcome to organized labor as 3.2 beer."

Given this wave of opposition, it is doubtful that the guideposts ever had any significant influence on inflation. As President Nixon's Council of Economic Advisers could comment in reviewing these earlier years from the vantage point of 1970, the policy was applied during "years of considerable slack in the economy,

[4] *Time*, February 25, 1980, p. 77.

relatively high unemployment, and stable or declining farm prices"—conditions that independently tended to favor price stability. When inflationary pressures—owing particularly to the exigencies of the war in Vietnam—increased after mid-1965, the guidepost policy "clearly did not work. . . . Labor and business were being asked to act as if prices were not rising, when in fact they were. As it became evident that steps necessary to keep prices from rising were not being taken, it also became more obviously unrealistic and inequitable to make these requests in specific cases."[5] By late 1965, indeed, settlements reached in many industries had all breached the 3.2 percent in varying degrees, and a few months after this, the guidepost policy, being widely perceived as unsuccessful, was allowed to quietly fade away.

NIXON'S MANDATORY WAGE AND PRICE CONTROL PROGRAM On August 15, 1971, however, Richard Nixon ordered a ninety-day freeze on wages and prices, followed by a mandatory wage and price control program, in an effort to restrain surging prices.

To deal with a 5.9 percent unemployment problem (of some political urgency, since by August 1971, the 1972 presidential election was only fifteen months away), the Nixon administration reversed its monetary and fiscal policies of the preceding two years and sought to increase aggregate demand. So that the new Nixon policy would not aggravate the inflation problem, the mandatory wage and price control program was put into effect. Despite criticism (largely from the AFL–CIO) that the price side of the program was not enforced fairly and effectively, the rate of inflation subsided in 1971 and 1972. Prices increased by 4.3 percent in 1971 and by only 3.4 percent in 1972 after rising at a 5.9 percent rate in 1970. At the same time, unemployment was reduced to 5.6 percent in 1972.

POLICIES OF THE PAY BOARD To administer the wage control program, a Pay Board was established, composed of fifteen members, divided equally among representatives of business, labor, and the public. However, in March 1972, all labor members except Frank Fitzsimmons, president of the Teamsters, resigned, charging that the wage and price control program was not being administered fairly. George Meany, one of the four labor members who resigned, stated:

> We will not be part of the window dressing for this system of unfair and inequitable government control of wages for the benefit of business profits.[6]

The core of board regulations was a standard of 5.5 percent as the maximum allowable increase in pay. Added to this figure was a 0.7 percent allowable increase in certain fringe benefits. Thus, the basic standard was a 6.2 percent increase in direct wage and fringe increases. However, the Pay Board permitted basic wage

---

[5] *Monthly Labor Review*, 93, No. 3 (March 1970), 2.
[6] U.S. Department of Labor, Bureau of Labor Statistics, *Monthly Labor Review*, 95, No. 5 (May 1972), 63. For a detailed account of the Pay Board's policies, see Office of the Federal Register, National Archives and Records Section, General Services Administration, *Code of Federal Regulation—Economic Stabilization*, June 1, 1972.

rates to rise 7 percent as a "catch-up," to cover employees who had received less than a 7 percent increase per year over the preceding three years. In some exceptional cases, the Pay Board permitted increases beyond its maximum standards.

Of course, Pay Board allowable increases were not required; they were maximums. Where unions were involved, wage and fringe benefit increases had to be negotiated in collective bargaining within the framework of the Pay Board standards. The record shows that the Pay Board was effective in holding down wage rate increases. Whereas average negotiated wage rates increased by 11.6 percent in 1971, the increase was 7.3 percent in 1972 and 5.8 percent in 1973.

The wage control program had another definite effect upon labor relations. Whereas multiyear labor agreements are common in collective bargaining, the impact of the wage control program resulted in the negotiation of one-year labor agreements. The reason, of course, was that unions wanted to be free to negotiate higher wages once the control program ended. Within the construction industry, 81 percent of all contracts were negotiated for one year in 1972, compared with only 7 percent in 1970. In nonconstruction industries, 15 percent of the contracts were of one year duration in 1972, in contrast to 8 percent in 1970.[7]

Their capability in the wage area checked by the control program, many unions also emphasized negotiation in the allowable fringe benefit area. In addition, many unions paid particular attention to the negotiation and the enforcement of employees' job rights, such as protection against arbitrary discharge, promotion matters, and paid time while not actually working. Undoubtedly, the impact of the program resulted in fewer strikes, since the wage issue was largely removed as an item of conflict. The amount of production time lost because of all strikes dropped to 0.14 percent of estimated working time in 1972, as compared with 0.37 percent in 1970.

END OF NIXON WAGE AND PRICE CONTROL PROGRAM   In January 1973, following his record-breaking victory in the 1972 presidential election, Nixon abandoned the mandatory wage and price control program. This abrupt change in policy came as a surprise to many people, since the price level had increased by only 3.4 percent in 1972 even though price controls had not been enforced with total vigor. With the exception of the food, health-care, and construction industries, employers and unions were placed on the honor system to hold down price and wage increases so that overall price level increases would not exceed 2.5 percent for the year.

When the mandatory program terminated, however, George P. Shultz, then secretary of labor, stated that the administration retained an "ability to bring the big stick out of the closet" to enforce unacceptable wage–price behavior. He also stated that the voluntary nature of the program would be aided by "the knowledge that people who don't abide by the program may get clobbered."[8]

---

[7] Daniel Mitchell, "Phase II Wage Controls," *Industrial and Labor Relations Review*, 27, No. 3 (April 1974), 373.

[8] U.S. Department of Labor, Bureau of Labor Statistics, *Monthly Labor Review*, 96, No. 2 (February 1973), 63.

Experience proved the voluntary program to be a complete failure. The stick never came out of the closet and no one got clobbered. Indeed, by June 1973, the cost of living increased by about 9 percent. And, embarrassing as it must have been to the Nixon administration, another wage and price freeze was instituted from June 13, 1973, through August 12, 1973. Despite this freeze, prices increased by 8.8 percent for the entire year. Wage rates, however, increased at only 5.8 percent, resulting, of course, in a decline in real income for the average American employee. Inflation surged even higher during the first quarter of 1974, increasing at the rate of about 15 percent!

On April 30, 1974, the entire program terminated when Congress did not renew the authority of the president to impose mandatory wage and price controls. The legislative basis of the program was permitted to die because no pressure was put on Congress. Unions, dissatisfied with employees' experience under the program, cheered at the burial; business, enjoying once again the free market and the capability to increase profits by increasing priced, did not weep; and Nixon himself did not urge Congress to renew his authority to impose mandatory wage and price controls.

But even though these interested parties did not resist the abolishment of the program, the consuming public felt the sting of almost unprecedented inflation in 1974. In that year, the price level increased by 12.2 percent and wage rates increased by 9.8 percent, once again resulting in the decline of real income for the average worker.

Inflation cooled somewhat in 1975, rising by 9.1 percent largely as a result of the worst unemployment rate since the Great Depression. It is conceivable that had the wage and price controls been maintained, improved by eliminating the most visible inequalities on the wage side and by more effective enforcement on the price side, the nation might not have suffered simultaneous unacceptable rates of inflation and unemployment.

CARTER VOLUNTARY WAGE AND PRICE CONTROLS Inflation also seemed to be under control in 1976. For that year prices increased by 5.8 percent, a significant improvement over the previous three-year pattern. But this brief respite ended with mounting prices in 1977 and 1978: By the fall of 1978, in fact, the price level soared to almost a double-digit rate, and inflation was commonly identified as the most critical domestic economic issue.

To deal with this problem, President Carter in October 1978 launched still another voluntary program despite the failure of previous efforts to control wages and prices on a voluntary basis. Before and after the program was implemented Carter, as Nixon had, repeatedly assured the nation that he would not impose a mandatory program.

Under the Carter program, employees were limited to a 7 percent annual increase in total compensation, that is, wages and fringe benefits. In a multiyear labor agreement, wage and fringe benefit increases which averaged no more than 7 percent annually over the life of the contract complied with the pay standard.

However, no more than an 8 percent increase could be paid in the first year of a multiyear contract.

Certain exceptions to the 7 percent standard were authorized. Unions and employers could negotiate more than that amount to maintain a historical tandem relationship to another company that increased wages and fringes before October 24, 1978, the date on which the Carter program officially went into effect. Increases in compensation could exceed the standard if warranted by changes in work rules and practices resulting in improvements in productivity of equal or greater value. Workers receiving less than $4.00 per hour were not subject to the standard.

On the price side, the guidelines restricted price increases to no more than half a percent (0.5%) below the average price increase for the firm for 1976–1977. The objective of the Carter program was to limit the rate of inflation to "the range of 6 to 6-½ percent" for 1979.

THE STICK Though advertised as voluntary, the Carter program contained elements of compulsion. To be eligible to sell goods or services to the federal government, a firm had to certify that it was complying with the wage and price guidelines. Such certifications were required for firms whose business with the federal government exceeded $5 million annually. In addition, the federal government was prepared to establish a "blacklist," asking the public to boycott any business violating the compensation and price guidelines.

Contending that such enforcement tactics had no place in a voluntary program, the AFL–CIO in the spring of 1979 filed suit in federal court requesting an injunction to stop the federal government from denying contracts to firms that gave their workers a pay raise above the 7 percent guideline. It stressed that the legislation that established the Council on Wage and Price Stability, under which legislation Carter had established his voluntary guidelines, had specifically forbidden mandatory wage and price controls.

In May 1979, a federal district court agreed with the labor organization, holding that the president's authority under the Procurement Act of 1949 to promote "efficiency and economy" in government through its purchasing activities did not provide the necessary legal basis for contract debarment.

A few weeks later, however, the U.S. Circuit Court of Appeals for the District of Columbia reversed the district court and ruled that President Carter had the power to enforce his wage and price guideline program by withholding contracts to firms not in compliance.

The federal appeals court reasoned that if there were compliance with the wage and price standards, inflation would be reduced or slowed, and there would be a corresponding reduction in government expenses, the purpose of the Procurement Act.

EXPERIENCE WITH PROGRAM Even the staunchest supporters of the Carter program had little occasion to rejoice in the months following its announcement and implementation. One blow against the program was delivered by the Teamsters, who, after a twelve-day April 1979 strike and lockout, negotiated a settlement far above the pay guideline.

However, what shocked the defenders of the Carter program was the soaring price level after October 1978. In the next six months or so, prices increased to dougle-digit levels, and into the summer of 1979, they were escalating at the rate of about 13 percent—about double the figure that the administration contemplated when the program started.

Such inflationary experience prompted George Meany to call again for a mandatory price–wage program and as early as October 1978, the AFL–CIO urged

> . . . the President to draft a legislative program of full (mandatory) controls, covering every source of work—profits, dividends, rents, interest rates, executive compensation, professional fees, as well as wages and prices. It is our belief that this matter is of such urgency that the President should call a special session of the Congress for the development of a full and fair controls program. It must be a program that treats all Americans equally . . .[9]

It said also that such a program should last "only for the duration of the emergency" and that the federation would support a fair and equitable program that would impose "equal sacrifice" on all people of the nation.

In short, the AFL–CIO believed that the nation's workers would be better off under a mandatory program that would place strict limits on prices. In a mandatory program most firms, particularly the large ones, would have to receive government approval before increasing prices. Under the Carter program, the AFL–CIO complained, employers "enforced" the 7 percent guideline, often telling their workers that although they might be sympathetic to a higher settlement, the government ceiling on compensation must be observed.

Whatever success employers had with this ploy, however, did not deter the larger unions from obtaining compensation in excess of the wage standard. For the first half of 1979, the Bureau of Labor Statistics reported that unions representing bargaining units of 5,000 or more members negotiated wages and fringes averaging 9.2 percent and thus compensation was escalating at a much higher rate than the target figures. Some defenders of the program said that inflation could be worse without the standards, though they did not offer any concrete evidence to support their views.

In any event, the administration continued the program for a second year, under a Pay Board composed of an equal number of business, union, and public members. The function of the Pay Board was to recommend pay standards to the Council of Wage and Price Stability, and in early 1980 the Pay Board recommended that that allowable wage increase fall within a range of 7.5 to 9.5 percent.

Given an 11.5 percent inflation rate increase for 1979 and 13.5 percent for 1980, the pay standard could not be realistically less. Indeed, even with the more

---

[9] Statement by the AFL—CIO Executive Council on Anti-inflation Program, October 31, 1978.

generous pay standard, employees' real income decreased for those two years. In 1979, those covered by major collective bargaining contracts (1,000 or more employees) received a 7.5 percent wage increase and 9.5 percent for 1980.

These numbers demonstrate the failure of the Carter voluntary program. Even before the Council on Wage and Price Stability was abolished in January 1981, the agency conceded that its effort had been a "dismal failure." [10] Searching for some justification for its two-year operation, COWPS claimed in its final report that it had reduced pay increases for those two years by one percentage point and had reduced price increases by half a percentage point.[11] That is hardly a record calling for a celebration! As other programs before it, the Carter experience clearly shows that a voluntary price and wage control program simply does not work in this nation.

THE TRUITT DECISION   In 1956, the U.S. Supreme Court handed down an important and still applicable decision dealing with the legal obligation of employers who argue that they cannot afford wage increases.[12]

At times, a company that is confronted with a wage request by a union will claim that it lacks the financial capacity to meet such a demand. When an employer takes this position, labor organizations will ordinarily request that the company furnish them with information bearing upon the company's wage-paying ability. In *Truitt Manufacturing Company*, the Supreme Court held that when the employer argues that he lacks the economic ability to meet a particular wage demand, that employer must make financial information available to the union. In justifying this policy, the high court stated that "if such an argument is important enough to present in the give and take of bargaining, it is important enough to require some sort of proof of its accuracy."

The *Truitt* decision, of course, does not mean that the company must capitulate to union wage demands. In fact, the company can refuse to meet the union request even if the information elicited by the union shows conclusively that it *has* the ability to pay the wages demanded by the union. In addition, the Supreme Court did not specify that the employer must automatically produce proof in every instance where he pleads inability to pay. The Court held that each case must turn upon its own merits and that the judicial inquiry must always be "whether under the circumstances . . . the statutory obligation to bargain in good faith has been met."

Nor did *Truitt* establish a hard and fast rule as to the character of evidence that the employer must show when he pleads lack of ability. As is apparent from the general tone of the Court's decision, this determination would also be made on a case-by-case basis, as indeed has been the practice in the years since *Truitt* was decided. These considerations, however, do not detract from the important principle established in the *Truitt* decision. The fact is that employers who argue

---

[10] *Wall Street Journal*, January 19, 1981.
[11] *Monthly Labor Review*, 104, No. 4 (April 1981), 9.
[12] *NLRB v. Truitt Manufacturing Co.*, 351 U.S. 149 (1956).

economic inability to meet union wage demands must now generally be prepared either to produce relevant evidence to substantiate this position or to face charges of unfair labor practice.

Standard of Living

Orientation of the plant wage structure to community and industry levels and ability to pay are not only criteria utilized for wage determination in contemporary industry. Many management and, particularly, labor representatives are concerned with the problem of the adequacy of wages to guarantee workers "a decent standard of living." Disagreements arise, however, as to what constitutes such a standard.

The problem is most often resolved by personal judgment and opinions of the negotiators. More objective information is, however, at the disposal of the parties, and it has frequently been used to support demands and counterdemands at the bargaining table.

At the present time, the most widely publicized source of standard-of-living information is that published by the U.S. Department of Labor's Bureau of Labor Statistics. First developed in 1946–1947 at the request of Congress, and revised periodically since that time, the BLS's "City Worker's Family Budget" attempts to describe and measure a "modest but adequate standard of living." It is necessarily selective, restricting itself to a measurement of the income needed by a family of four (a 38-year-old employed husband, a wife not employed outside the home, and two children of school age—a 13-year-old boy and an 8-year-old girl), living in a rented dwelling in a large city or its suburbs. By studying the prices of a "representative list of goods and services" presumably purchased by such families, for about forty representative cities (weighted according to their populations), the BLS endeavors to show the cost of "a level of adequate living standards prevailing in large cities of the United States in recent years."

To make the "City Worker's Budget" more relevant, the Bureau of Labor Statistics provides levels for three standards of living—"low," "intermediate," and "high." Naturally, employees who earn sufficient wages to live at the high level enjoy more of the good things of life as compared with the workers whose wages can claim only the goods and services at the low level.

In 1982, the low budget required an annual outlay of $15,323, whereas the intermediate one demanded $25,407 and the high budget required a rather formidable $38,060. Food costs had increased about 7.5 percent in each of the budgets from the previous year, but—since they absorbed a larger percentage of total living costs at that lower budget level—they obviously had a larger effect on total costs at that level and made it all the less likely that the lower-budget families would buy any chateaubriand or even, on a frequent basis, eat meat meals at all.

As expected, the amount required varies considerably depending upon the city involved. The most expensive city to live in is Honolulu, followed by Anchorage (Alaska), New York, Boston, and Washington. Dallas is the cheapest major city in which to live; slightly more expensive are Atlanta and Houston. In all cases, however, the overall weighted averages at the time of this writing were sufficiently beyond those earned by most workers to make the budget an attractive bargaining weapon for union negotiators. Labor spokespersons had not been hesitant about arguing the "need" for substantial wage increases to reach the budgeted levels while also pointing out that the overall weighted average was required to meet the necessities of life, pay taxes, and enjoy a few amenities—but that it contained no allowance for luxuries or savings.

Employers, equally logically, had taken bitter exception to this most recent "City Worker's Budget." They had argued that the items used in computing the budget were far too generous to warrant the description "modest but adequate"; frequently cited in this regard were the budget's annual allowance for gifts and contributions, and certain of its provisions for furniture, appliances, automobiles, and recreation. In addition, they pointed out that wage earners do not have uniform responsibilities in terms of dependents (with many, of course, having no dependents), and that many families have more than one wage earner.

The arguments and counterarguments can be expected to continue indefinitely, without mutual agreement as to their validity; the line of demarcation between "luxury" and "necessity" has never been susceptible to exact location, and the concept of "decency" allows much room for emotion. Moreover, despite the increasingly frequent use of the standard-of-living criterion at the bargaining table, it does not carry as much weight as the other wage factors analyzed in the previous sections of this chapter. After all, an employer who truthfully cannot pay wages that will realize the "modest but adequate standard of living" may be entirely sympathetic to the worker's needs, but the cold realism of economic life will not persuade him to grant the additional wages. Likewise, a union will not stop at the level of wages required of the budget if it can get more from the employer because of the operation of the other wage criteria; indeed, under these circumstances, the union will probably argue that the items of the budget are too meager.

But use of such standard-of-living information as that provided by the BLS—and by such other sources as the Census Bureau, Federal Reserve Board, Department of Commerce, and independent studies of the parties themselves—is still to be preferred to total recourse to personal opinion on the subject. The data may not be accepted, but even in rejecting them the recalcitrant party is forced to deal with information that is more objective than mere individual sentiment.

COST OF LIVING: ESCALATOR AND WAGE-REOPENER ARRANGEMENTS

In addition to the comparative-norm, ability to pay, and standard-of-living principles, experienced negotiators pay close attention in wage negotiations to the status of the *cost of living*. This economic phenomenon is important because trends in the cost of living have an important bearing upon the real income of workers. Increases in the cost of living at a given level of earnings result in decreased capacity of workers to buy goods and services. By the same token, real income tends to increase with decreases in the cost of living at a given wage level. Real income for a particular group of workers also increases for a time when money wages increase faster than the cost of living.

As a matter of fact, during the soaring inflation in the 1978–1981 period, the cost of living was the major determinant for wage negotiations, as union leaders raced to keep up with higher and higher prices to protect the real income of their members. Of course, as explained above, to the extent that wage rates exceeded productivity, negotiated wages aggravated the inflation problem. If the lessons of inflation teach us anything, it is that a stable price level is the way to achieve the negotiation of noninflationary wage rates.

It is beyond the scope of this volume to analyze the multitude of factors that influence the cost of living in the American economy. This cost is affected by a variety of forces, including the general climate of business activity, productivity, the financial and monetary policies followed by financial institutions, the rate of new investment, and the propensity of consumers to spend money, as well as by the wage policies that are followed under collective bargaining itself. Government policies relating to interest rates, tariffs, the lending capacity of national banks, taxation, and agriculture also have an impact upon the cost of living. And, of course, as we have come to realize in recent years, rising energy costs constitute another important factor for higher prices. When the OPEC nations increased the cost of oil from about $5 per barrel at the beginning of the 1970s to more than six times that figure by the end of the decade, the effect was felt not only in increasing gasoline prices but in other goods manufactured by petroleum-chemical industries.

The uncertain character of the forces determining the cost of living makes it very difficult to predict with certainty its future trends. The difficulty inherent in using the cost of living as a determinant in wage negotiations is simply this: Wages are negotiated for a *future* period, whereas cost-of-living data are *historical* in character. It is a comparatively simple task to adjust wages for historical trends in the cost of living if this is the desire of the negotiators. The criterion is of limited usefulness, however, in the attempt to orient wage rates to future trends in the Consumer Price Index. The capricious character of the index makes forecasting extremely hazardous. In any event, for intelligent utilization of this wage determinant, it becomes necessary not only to have accurate information on historical trends but also to make an assessment of the future trends of the factors that determine the Consumer Price Index.[13] It cannot be emphasized too much that such predictions are fraught with difficulties and uncertainties.

Some parties in labor relations have, however, adopted one or both of two procedures—escalator clauses and wage reopeners—that take into account the capriciousness of the cost of living and likewise recognize the importance of trends

---

[13] The Consumer Price Index (CPI) is the index that is almost universally utilized in collective bargaining by employers and unions. It is prepared and published by the Bureau of Labor Statistics and appears each month in the Bureau's *Monthly Labor Review*.

in the Consumer Price Index as they relate to the real income of employees and to the financial position of companies.

Escalator Clauses

The philosophy behind the incorporation of so-called "escalator clauses," also known as cost-of-living adjustment (COLA) provisions, in labor agreements is that wages of workers should rise and fall automatically with fluctuations in the cost of living. The escalator arrangement first attained national prominence in the 1948 General Motors–United Automobile Workers collective bargaining agreement. As a result of the anticipated price inflation growing out of the Korean War, many other companies and unions soon negotiated similar arrangements, and by 1952 such arrangements covered about 3.5 million workers—concentrated mainly in the automobile, railroad, textile, aircraft, agricultural implement, and flat-glass industries. They also appeared in a wide variety of other manufacturing and non-manufacturing industries.

Since 1952, use of the wage escalator clause appears to have depended to a great extent on the upward movement of the cost-of-living index. By 1955, for example, three years of comparatively steady prices had elapsed, and the number of workers covered by such escalator clauses had dropped considerably, to about 1.7 million.[14] In 1956, on the other hand, the Consumer Price Index moved strongly forward, and a study conducted late in that year estimated that approximately 3.5 million workers were once again covered by escalator arrangements.[15] The incorporation of an escalator formula in the 1956 basic steel contract—covering 600,000 workers—alone accounted for almost one-third of this increase.

With relatively modest annual price movements from 1956 through mid-1965, interest in the escalator once more temporarily waned. By 1965, the railroads, electrical industry, and (ironically) basic steel had completely abandoned the device, and only about 2 million workers—concentrated mainly in automobiles and automobile parts, farm and construction equipment, trucking, and meatpacking—were covered by escalator clauses in the latter year.[16] On the other hand, the significant surge in the price level after mid-1965 had brought another half-million employees under coverage by 1969. And the enormous surge of prices in 1973 and 1974 again stimulated the growth of cost-of-living escalator clauses. By the end of 1974, 5.1 million workers were covered by the arrangement. At this writing, it is safe to say that approximately 9.1 million workers are covered.[17]

Perhaps the greatest single reason why the figures above are nonetheless not

---

[14] "Wage Escalation—Recent Developments," *Monthly Labor Review*, 77, No. 3 (March 1955), 315.

[15] Bureau of National Affairs, ed., "What's New in Collective Bargaining Negotiations and Contracts," No. 300 (November 30, 1956), p. 4.

[16] "Deferred Increases Due in 1965 and Wage Escalation," *Monthly Labor Review*, 87, No. 12 (December 1964), 1384. Some employees in chemicals, retail trade, and public transit also remained covered by escalator clauses.

[17] For 1979, the BLS reported that 5.6 million workers under major labor agreements were covered by COLA contracts. This number underestimated coverage because it applied only to "major contracts" or those covering 1,000 employees or more (*Monthly Labor Review*, 102, No. 1 [January 1979], 22–23). In August 1981, the BLS estimated that 9.1 million employees were covered (*Wall Street Journal*, August 5, 1981).

spectacular, even for the pronounced U.S. inflation following 1965, lies in the intense historical management opposition to the escalator concept. Employers have voiced fears that prices could not be commensurately raised without undesirable effects on profits. They have also argued what they view as the inequities of a system that allows workers to benefit without effort of any kind on their part: One mid-1960s increase in the cost-of-living index, for example, was attributed by government spokespersons primarily to increases in sugar and cigarette prices—a situation that even the most sugar-consuming and chain-smoking work force could not noticeably influence. Still other managers have stressed the potential inflationary ramifications of the escalator in opposing its use. Above all, however, employers have attacked the constant "freezing" of cost-of-living allowances into basic wage rates: Most labor contracts ultimately make such allowances a permanent part of rates when the agreements are renegotiated and to many workers the allowances are, consequently, really additional wage increases temporarily couched in other terms. Not only do cost-of-living allowances realistically become a part of basic wage rates, but frequently they are also "rolled" into pay for vacations, holidays, and other employee benefits tied to basic wage rates. Thus, not only are employers' direct wage costs increased, but also costs associated with a variety of fringe benefits.

Managements could, understandably, be expected to generate greater enthusiasm for the escalator in the event of a prolonged national period of markedly *downward* prices, but this appears an unlikely possibility for the foreseeable future. Even in the continuing absence of such a situation, however, and even if one disregards the current aggressive attempts of unions to gain the escalator device in the face of inflation, it is possible that some impetus will be provided for the escalator in the general gradual lengthening of the terms of labor contracts.

The evidence that contracts are becoming longer—such temporary regressions in the trend as in the case of the wage controls of the early 1970s notwithstanding—is persuasive. Whereas in 1948 about 75 percent of collective bargaining agreements were for one year or less, by 1963 the proportion of contracts running for longer than one year had increased sharply—to as much as 86 percent, by some estimates, and by 1983 as many as 90 percent of all contracts may have been for more than one year. Longer-term contracts lend greater stability to labor relationships, and by definition they reduce the problems of negotiation and the traumas of frequent strike threats. However, as contracts are negotiated for longer periods of time, negotiators must recognize the necessity of providing some method for the adjustment of wages during the contractual period. Some authorities believe that increasing awareness of this situation, together with the continuation of the trend to contracts of longer duration, will lend greater allure to the escalator formula, even in the face of continuing managerial opposition to the whole idea.

Although there is a wide variety of escalator arrangements, all contain a number of common principles. The most significant characteristic of the escalator formula is its automaticity. For the duration of the labor agreement, wage changes as related to cost of living are precisely determined by the behavior of a statistical index—almost always the Consumer Price Index. Wages are increased or decreased in accordance with comparatively small changes in this index. For example, the labor agreement might provide, as many recent ones have, for a $.01-per-hour adjustment of wages for every 0.26-point change in the CPI.

Each escalator arrangement specifies the time at which the CPI is reviewed. At the time of the review, a determination is made as to whether the index increased sufficiently to trigger a wage increase. Of the workers covered by escalators in 1982, quarterly reviews were by far the most common, covering about 50 percent compared with about 25 percent each for annual or semiannual reviews.[18] Though only a matter of academic interest in a period of inflation, escalator provisions normally specify the floor to which wages can fall in response to a decline in the cost-of-living index. On the other hand, the escalator formula does not normally contain a *ceiling* on wage increases occasioned by increasing prices. In 1982, only about 20 percent of the workers covered by the arrangement were subject to a ceiling, also called a "cap," on their cost-of-living wage increases.[19] When the labor agreement provides for a cap, it means that wages can only increase by a certain specified amount during the contractual period regardless of the size of the increase in the Consumer Price Index. Needless to say, when a cap appears, the employer and not the union insisted on it at the bargaining table. When an escalator arrangement contains a cap, the employer is in a better position to estimate the firm's labor costs for the contractual period. Employer resistance, of course, increases during periods of economic recession. As will be made clear later on in this chapter, this occurred during the economic recession of the early 1980s. Faced with declining sales, employers demanded caps on the operation of COLA.

Finally, the escalator method of wage adjustment is often accompanied by a definite and guaranteed increase in wages for each year of a multiyear labor agreement. Such an increase is popularly called the *annual improvement factor*. These increases are not offset by any increase generated by an escalator clause. By the same token, any increase triggered by an escalator clause is not reduced by the payment of the annual improvement factor. For example, a recent three-year contract negotiated by the Allied Industrial Workers of America states:

> Effective as of April 24, 1981 and April 23, 1982 each employee covered by this Agreement shall receive an annual improvement factor of twenty-one cents ($.21) per hour added to his hourly rate.

Those employees are guaranteed the 21-cent increase on each anniversary date of the agreement regardless of the results of the escalator provision. As expected, when a labor agreement does not contain an escalator clause, the annual improvement factor normally calls for a higher increase as compared with a contract that includes a cost-of-living adjustment provision. In the former situation, it is understandable that union leaders press for a much higher annual increase, recognizing

[18] *Monthly Labor Review*, 105, No. 1 (January 1982), 20.
[19] *Ibid.*, 102, No. 1 (January 1979) 24.

that inflation affects adversely the real income of the members. When an escalator clause is contained in the contract, the union's leaders need not be so aggressive in the matter of the annual improvement factor. *(As Case 4 demonstrates, disputes occur in the administration of a COLA program.)*

However, it should be noted that the operation of escalator arrangements *does not* provide employees with 100 percent protection against inflation. For 1968–1977, it was determined that the average escalator yield only met 57 percent of the inflation occurring during those years. In not one year did the yield match the CPI increase.[20] This will come as a genuine surprise to many who believe, in error, that escalator provisions provide the employee full protection against the ravages of inflation.

Wage Reopeners

A second method for wage adjustments during the life of a labor agreement involves a provision that permits either the company or the union to *reopen* labor agreements *for wage issues* at stated intervals. Where such a procedure is employed, labor agreements normally provide that contracts that are negotiated for one year may be reopened for wage issues after six months. Contracts that are written for two-year periods or longer are customarily open for wage negotiations once each year.

Two major characteristics of the wage-reopening clause arrangement distinguish it from the escalator principle as a method of wage adjustment. The most important involves the fact that whereas the escalator arrangement provides for an *automatic* change in wages based on a definite formula, under wage reopeners the parties must *negotiate* wage changes. This could be an advantage or a disadvantage, depending upon the particular circumstances of a given collective bargaining relationship. In addition, the wage-reopener arrangement can be utilized to take into account determinants of wages other than the cost of living. The fact that both the escalator and the reopener arrangements are frequently used in industry indicates that both procedures apparently fill the needs of employers, employees, and unions. What may be suitable for one collective bargaining relationship, however, clearly might be unsuitable for another company and union.

To invoke a wage-reopening clause, collective bargaining contracts require that the party that desires to change wages give a written notice to the other party within a specified period. Under the terms of the Taft–Hartley law, as we know, a party to a collective bargaining agreement desiring to modify or terminate the agreement must give sixty days' notice of its intention to do so. Following such notice, the law declares that there may be no lockout or strike "for a period of sixty days . . . or until the expiration date of such contract, whichever occurs later."

[20] Victor J. Sheifer, "Cost of Living Adjustment: Keeping Up with Inflation," *Monthly Labor Review*, 102, No. 6 (June 1979), 15. Reasons offered to explain this state of affairs are these: The formula of one cent increase for each 0.3- or 0.4-point CPI rise is not sufficient for total compensation; "caps" or ceilings on escalator increases; escalation adjustments lag behind price changes; escalator yields are at times diverted to finance other employee benefits; and some escalators do not operate until a significant increase in the CPI occurs, as in some clothing contracts that yield gains only when the CPI increases by 7.5 percent and 6 percent in the second and third contract years.

Employees who engage in a strike during this period lose their status as employees under Taft–Hartley and have no legal right to be reinstated.

These provisions of the Taft–Hartley law are important in connection with this discussion because wage-reopening arrangements invariably provide that a union may call a strike over wage issues if a settlement is not reached during the negotiation period. Such a strike takes place after the negotiation period as provided for in the wage-reopening clause but before the termination date of the entire contract. The question therefore arises as to whether or not a strike under these circumstances is lawful under the Taft–Hartley law. It is stressed that the law provides that no strike may take place during the sixty-day notice period or until the date the contract expires, "*whichever occurs later.*"

The National Labor Relations Board in 1954 dealt with this question of whether or not a strike called pursuant to a wage-reopening clause is consistent with Taft–Hartley, and held that such a strike is lawful even though it occurs before the terminal date of the entire labor contract, provided that the sixty-day notice requirement of the Taft–Hartley law is met.[21] In reaching this decision, the board was compelled to interpret the portion of Taft–Hartley that forbids a strike during the sixty-day notice period or until the date of expiration of a contract, whichever occurs later. It held in this connection that, for purposes of the law, the term *expiration date* refers not only to the terminal date of the entire collective bargaining contract but also to the date agreed upon in the contract when the parties can effect changes in its provisions.

Upon a review, however, a circuit court of appeals rejected the meaning attributed by the board to the term *expiration date*. In this court's view, the term must be held to mean "termination" date, and all strikes for modification before the contract's actual termination are unlawful. Concluding that the labor agreement had not been "terminated" within the meaning of the Taft–Hartley Act at the time of the strike, the court ruled that the employees in the strike lost their status as employees for purposes of the law and that they could be discharged by the company. Because of the obvious importance of the issues involved in the controversy between the National Labor Relations Board and the circuit court, the board appealed to the Supreme Court for a review of the case. In January 1957, the Supreme Court sustained the position of the board and held that the Taft–Hartley law permits a strike, after a sixty-day notice, during the life of collective bargaining contracts that contain wage-reopening clauses. To the date of this writing, labor relations continued to be governed by such a principle.

It is stressed that a wage-reopener provision is to be used only to negotiate a new wage structure. However, unfortunately some employers and unions use the opportunity to gain changes in other areas of the labor agreement, using the wage issue as the pretext. For example, a union might strike ostensibly for wages but send a message to the employer that the strike would terminate were the employer to grant certain concessions to the union, say in the matter of the application of

[21] *Lion Oil Co.*, 109 NLRB 680 (1954).

the seniority provisions. Such tactics are not necessarily very subtle. They can, however, be potent.

WAGE DIFFERENTIALS

Under certain circumstances, collective bargaining contracts provide for different rates of wages for different employees performing the same kind of work and holding down the same types of jobs. Such differentials are completely lawful except when used by the parties to discriminate on the basis of race, color, religion, sex, or national origin; as of July 2, 1965, the latter practices were forbidden under the terms of Title VII of the Civil Rights Act of 1964.[22] To many employers (as well as to unions), moreover, utilization of the "nondiscriminatory" differentials appears mandatory to ensure an adequate supply of willing employees for work under arduous or otherwise unpleasant conditions.

The most common of these differentials involves premium payment for work on relatively undesirable shifts—in the late afternoon, evening, night, and early morning hours. Practically all workers scheduled on late shifts receive extra pay.

In addition, under most contracts there is now a graduated increase in compensation for working the second and third shifts. All but a tiny fraction of workers in establishments where there is a third, or "graveyard," work schedule now receive a rate for it that is higher than that received by second-shift workers. But second-shift workers themselves have received relatively significant premiums for their acceptance of these working hours: Premium rates for second-shift work are now often as high as 10 percent above first-shift rates. Premiums often up to 10 percent of second-shift rates are the general rewards for the graveyard-shift workers.

The rationale for the shift differential is quite easy to understand. When an employee works a less common shift, there is obvious interference with family life and with full participation in the affairs of society. In Western society, the school system, recreational activities, cultural pursuits, and the like assume that employees work during the day. Since working the odd hours tends to interfere with the employee's family and societal affairs, the premium is designed to compensate the employee for this sacrifice. And although it is a fact of industrial life that some employees because of certain conditions may actually prefer to work the afternoon or midnight tour (under these circumstances, the employee reaps a net benefit for the shift differential premium), the overwhelming number of employees prefers the day shift, and thus the shift differential will undoubtedly always be a common feature in the collectively bargained wage package.

Under many collective bargaining contracts, special premiums are also provided for workers who handle certain supervisory or instructional duties, especially demanding tasks, or particularly hazardous, dirty, or undesirable work. For these jobs, extra pay is again granted as a premium to the basic wage rate of the worker

---

[22] Title VII did, however, grant exemptions to work forces of less than twenty-five persons.

concerned. For example, under one current agreement in the Midwest, a $1.50-per-hour premium is paid to employees who are engaged in "dirty work." Such work is spelled out in the labor agreement and includes, among other possibilities for premium-rate reimbursement, "work in oil tanks where not cleaned out." Another labor agreement provides for the regular overtime rate for employees engaged in hazardous work. This provision covers employees working at elevations "where there is danger of a fall of fifty feet or more."

In addition to these *premium*-rate practices, many collective bargaining contracts allow *lower* differentials for other situations. A number of agreements provide lower rates for workers who are handicapped, superannuated, temporary, or learners. Such differentials are rooted in the belief that these qualities make workers comparatively less productive, and even the federal government, recognizing the persuasive economic logic involved, has gone along with this employer argument to the extent of exempting such workers from the minimum wage laws. Abuses have occasionally been in evidence, however: Some "temporary" employees turn out, upon closer inspection, to be deserving of twenty-five-year pins; and some "handicapped" employees appear to have nothing more than color-blindness. Such situations notwithstanding, employer good faith in regard to these workers is far more the rule than the exception, and the differential can be defended on the grounds that the alternative to a lower rate of remuneration for such employees is, most often, unemployment.

Until passage and implementation of the Civil Rights Act, some contracts also contained lower wage rates for women than for men and for blacks than for white employees. For women, the practice was traditionally defended on such presumed grounds as a lesser productivity of women than men, a female inability to do all the tasks performed by men in accomplishing a job, and the argument that the employment of women at times involves extra costs not incurred when men are employed. Racial discrimination per se appears to have motivated the black differential, although some of the lower-productivity claims used to defend lower women's wages were also heard. Since mid-1965, neither type of differential is, understandably, promulgated by labor contracts governed by the act, although whether or not the practices involved will continue is subject to employer and union compliance, which goes well beyond the official wording of their agreements.

OVERTIME PROBLEMS

Collective bargaining agreements invariably establish a standard number of hours per day and per week during which employees are paid their regular rate of pay. For hours worked in excess of the standard, however, employers are required to pay employees overtime rates. By far the most common standards found in labor agreements are eight hours per day and forty hours per week, with only a fraction of labor agreements establishing standards differing from this formula. In the wearing apparel, printing, and publishing industries, a number of agreements do provide for a basic seven- to seven-and-one-half-hour day and thirty-five-hour workweek; and in the food-processing, retail, and service industries some contracts establish a standard forty-four-hour week; but these remain the exceptions.

The fact that the Fair Labor Standards Act provides a basic forty-hour week has undoubtedly caused the adoption of a forty-hour standard workweek under collective bargaining. Labor agreements that provide for a basic workweek in excess of forty hours without premium overtime pay presumably do not fall within the scope of this legislation, or within the reach of the many state wage and hour laws that regulate this activity within certain states for their intrastate commerce. On the other hand, nothing in the federal wage and hour law prohibits employers and unions from negotiating a workweek of *less* than forty hours, and (although thus far with more potential than actuality) the shorter workweek as a partial answer to the unemployment threats of automation loomed as a new labor relations issue in the 1980s, after years of relative quiescence. In addition, the Fair Labor Standards Act places no restriction on employers who desire their employees to work *more* than forty hours in a workweek, other than that the employees who work more than forty hours must be paid at least one and one-half times their regular rate of pay for all hours in excess of forty.

The vast majority of labor agreements provide overtime rates of exactly one and one-half times the regular rate of pay for employees who work in excess of forty hours per week, thus offering a not surprising conformity to the minimum provisions of the Fair Labor Standards Act, but a relatively small number of labor agreements do call for overtime rates of greater than time-and-one-half pay, most frequently double-time. With respect to hours worked in excess of the *daily* standard, most labor agreements also provide for time-and-one-half, although some labor agreements provide for double-time after a certain number of hours are worked or after a stipulated hour of the day or night. For example, some employers and unions have agreed that double-time rates should be paid if employees work more than four hours' overtime on any one workday. In this connection it should be noted that—since the Fair Labor Standards Act does not establish a basic work-day—if employees are to be paid for working hours in excess of a certain number per day, the parties to the collective bargaining contract must negotiate this objective.

In addition to establishing standard workdays and workweeks and providing the rate for hours worked in excess of these standards, collective bargaining contracts deal with other phases of the hours and overtime problem. Most labor agreements prohibit the *pyramiding* of overtime. This means that weekly overtime premiums are not required for hours for which daily overtime premiums have already been paid; moreover, many contracts provide that only one type of overtime premium can be paid for any one day. Also, in many collective bargaining relationships the employer also has the right to force employees to work overtime.

However, labor agreements and arbitration decisions establish certain standards which employers must follow before discipline can be assessed against employees who refuse to work overtime. For example, in the absence of some dire emergency—a flood in the plant, perhaps—the employer must give advance and proper notice and not grab an employee for overtime just as the person is about to clock out. Also, the employer must accept a "reasonable" excuse from an employee who refuses to work overtime. Of course, what is "reasonable" is subject to controversy, and arbitrators are called upon to apply the concept in the light of the particular facts of a case. Should an employee be excused from overtime because he was scheduled to be the best man at a wedding? This was the basic issue involved in a case handled by one of the authors. When the employee refused, he was suspended for three days. How would you decide this issue if you were the arbitrator? *(In Case 5, an employee was also disciplined because he refused to work overtime.)*

As in the case of the shorter-hour workweek, the issue of compulsory overtime invariably pops up during periods of excessive unemployment. For example, because unemployment was so high during the recession of 1975—a post-Great Depression high of 9.2 percent was reached during the summer of that year—some unions pressed for a flat prohibition against any overtime in an attempt to preserve job opportunities. Not too many unions succeeded in this goal. They were more successful in negotiating voluntary overtime provisions; that is, the employee could refuse the assignment without facing discipline. This development was dramatically highlighted in the 1973 basic automobile industry labor agreement. For the first time in that industry, production employees under certain circumstances gained the right to turn down overtime without penalty. Compulsory overtime was a major strike issue, and only by compromise on it did the automobile corporations and the UAW avoid open conflict.

It seemed a reasonable speculation that both the mounting union drive for outright overtime prohibition and sanction for the independent employee refusal to work overtime would grow—despite often fierce employer antagonism to both developments—should the numbers of unemployed not decrease to a more generally tolerable level. Nor, indeed, could one discount the possibility of new governmental action in the overtime arena—perhaps along the lines of an abortive 1964 proposal of the Johnson administration that minimum overtime pay rates in selected industries be increased to double-time (with the goal of lessening the national unemployment figures of that time by encouraging new hiring). Such proposals, however, were not made during the recession of the early 1980s.

Even without government limitations, moreover, the employer's overtime authority has rarely been an unrestricted one. In addition to the above standards, about half of all collective bargaining contracts provide that overtime work must be shared equally within given classifications of employees, or at least that overtime is to be rotated equally "as far as is practicable." Some agreements limit overtime to regular employees as against seasonal, temporary, part-time, or probationary employees.

By the same token, however, under many collective bargaining agreements, penalties may be assessed against employees who refuse to work overtime. Such

penalties range from discharge to ineligiblity to work overtime at the next opportunity. For all that has been said regarding union pressures for overtime discouragement, the premium earnings even of overtime at time-and-one-half remain
sufficiently attractive to individual employees on most occasions to make the in-
eligibility penalty a significant one.

Indeed, a prolific source of grievances and even arbitration is the employee
complaint that the employer has improperly, under the labor agreement, failed to
offer employees the opportunity to work overtime. Where the grievance is found
to have merit, the employer typically has the obligation of paying the employee
the amount of money he or she would have earned on the overtime tour of duty.

The employee, of course, has nothing to lose by filing such grievances, even
if the worker would have refused the assignment if offered the opportunity to work
overtime. If the opportunity has *not* been offered, the employee can file a grievance
and possibly get paid for work the grievant never intended to do in the first place.
For these reasons, employer representatives are very careful to assure that eligible
employees are afforded the opportunity to work the overtime. Where a foreman,
for example, makes an error in this regard, the company may be faced with the
situation of paying for the same work twice and at premium rates. To say the least,
the company controller would take a dim view of this state of affairs! (Exhibit 7-1
illustrates a reasonably typical overtime provision.)

Deviation from Standard: Four-Day Workweek and Flextime

Though not extensive, some deviations from the standard eight-hour-per-day, five-
day workweek on a fixed schedule basis have occurred. When an employer's production requirements permit, and when employees desire a three-day weekend,
some labor agreements compress a forty-hour workweek into four days. Employees
work ten hours a day and four days per week. Daily overtime beyond eight hours
is not paid. Perhaps as many as 2 million full-time employees are now on a four-
day workweek and unionized employees are as likely as nonunion employees to
work such a schedule.[23] To determine whether such a schedule is desirable, additional research is needed. Questions such as these should be explored: Does
worker fatigue after eight hours reduce productivity? What is its effect on family
life? Do employees on this schedule use the longer weekend for self-improvement,
leisure, or recreational activities, or just to get a second job ("moonlighting")?
Does the four-day workweek reduce absenteeism?

Preliminary data indicate that the avowed merits of such a schedule have not
entirely been realized in practice. Employees on a four-day workweek are roughly
twice as likely to hold a second job as compared with those who are scheduled on
a five-day basis. To the employer, the experience relating to absenteeism has not
been fully satisfactory. In theory, employees would be less likely to be absent

---

[23] Janice Neipert Hedges, "How Many Days Make a Work Week?" *Monthly Labor Review*, 98 No. 4 (April
1975), 29–35.

EXHIBIT 7–1

ARTICLE 34 OVERTIME

Section 1 Employees who are required to work overtime will be compensated in accordance with applicable laws and regulations.

Section 2 The Employer agrees to make a reasonable effort to distribute overtime equitably among qualified and available employees, consistent with the specialized skills and abilities necessary for the work to be performed. Adequate records of overtime will be maintained by the Employer and will be available to the Union upon request.

Section 3 In the assignment of overtime, the Employer agrees to provide an employee with as much advance notice as the situation permits. Consideration will be given, in light of the workload involved and the ready availability of other qualified employees willing to accept the assignment, to an employee's request to be excused from an overtime assignment.

Section 4 Callback overtime shall be a minimum of 2 hours.

Section 5 The Employer agrees to make a reasonable effort consistent with operational needs to avoid situations involving callback overtime or from requiring employees to work overtime on their regularly scheduled days off.

Section 6 An employee performing overtime work on his/her regularly scheduled day off shall be guaranteed 4 hours of work.

---

because they could tend to their personal problems during their three free days. In addition, recognizing that there would be a ten-hour loss of pay instead of eight hours, it was expected that employees would be more faithful in their attendance. Though in some instances absenteeism has declined, in other firms the rate returned to normal once the novelty of the four-day workweek has worn off.[24]

Such negative results have caused the discontinuation of some four-day schedules, a development also due to the fact that it was discovered at times that productivity dropped off due to the longer workday. Somewhat disappointing is that four-day workweek employees do not use their extra free time to engage in novel endeavors, such as self-improvement and educational programs or participating in public service and community affairs. According to one study, they merely expand the amount of time allocated to former free-time activities.[25] These considerations have restricted the spread of the four-day workweek. According to the Bureau of Labor Statistics, not many more employees are on it now than was the case in the middle 1970s.[26]

A more recent departure from industrial practice involves the opportunity of

[24] *Ibid.*, p. 33.
[25] David Mark Maklan, "How Blue-Collar Workers on 4-Day Workweeks Use Their Time," *Monthly Labor Review*, 100, No. 8 (August 1977), 18–26.
[26] *Monthly Labor Review*, 105, No. 7 (July 1982), 46.

employees to select within limits their daily work schedules. Daily shift hours are normally spelled out in labor contracts, and all employees are required to work the hours of the stipulated shift. These newer schedules are popularly called "flex-time." Under this innovation, all employees still must work eight hours per day. However, they have more flexibility in selecting their starting and quitting times. Typically, there is a daily fixed schedule during which all employees are expected to work. This period, called "core time," may range between four and six hours per day. Surrounding the core time, employees may select the starting and quitting times. For instance, core time may be established between 10 A.M. and 3 P.M. During those five hours all employees must work. Then within certain limits the employee may select starting and quitting times. For example, the schedule may require that all hours be worked between 6 A.M. and 6 P.M. An employee may elect to start at 10 A.M. and work until 6 P.M. or may elect to start at 7 A.M. and work until 3 P.M. to complete the eight-hour day. Thus, employees may adjust their starting and quitting times in accordance with their personal needs and preferences. One report says that

> several hundred thousand employees in this country already have some form of flexible hours system.[27]

Unions have not been overly enthusiastic about flextime schedules, though this attitude may change to make organization more attractive to women. Married women, particularly those with children, may find such a schedule fits their personal needs. In any event, in general, unions look at flextime as a managerial tool to reduce the need for overtime payment and to increase the intensity of the work pace. For example, unions charge that supervisors may encourage employees to 'volunteer" for a schedule to avoid the need for overtime. If flextime is to spread in the United States, objections raised by organized labor will have to be resolved. And of course, even if employees and their unions are willing, some employers may find flextime scheduling an impossibility under certain kinds of operations. To produce effectively under certain types of technology and operations, all employees must be present at the same time.

JOB EVALUATION AND JOB COMPARISON

Thus far we have been dealing with *general* changes in the level of wages under collective bargaining. The comparative-norm, ability-to-pay, standard-of-living, and cost-of-living principles—as well as the principles relating to wage differentials and overtime rates—rather than affecting any particular jobs apply either to all jobs within the plant or to all jobs that fall within certain widely delineated areas (for example, night work, "dirty work," and overtime work).

---

[27] John D. Owens, "Flextime: Some Problems and Solutions," *Industrial and Labor Relations Review*, 30, No. 2 (January 1977), 153. The report does not distinguish between organized and nonunion employees. In the light of union objections to flextime, probably the vast majority of those employees are in the nonunion sector.

Another important problem, however, involves the establishment of *relative* wage rates (or rate ranges) for each particular job, so that wage differentials are rationalized (jobs of greater "worth" to the management are rewarded by greater pay), and the overall wage structure is stabilized on a relatively permanent basis.

Essentially, employers adopt one of two methods to achieve this goal: (1) job evaluation and (2) what, for lack of a universally accepted descriptive designation, might be best described as "job comparison."

Job evaluation in its broadest sense is actually used by all employers. It occurs whenever the management decides that one job should be paid more than another, and this is *invariably* done by organizations in the sense that some jobs obviously do deserve more pay than do others.

In the more technical sense in which it is used here, however, job evaluaton requires a more systematic approach. Briefly, job evaluation—through the use of thorough job descriptions and equally detailed analyses of these descriptions— attempts to rank jobs in terms of their (1) skill, (2) effort, (3) responsibility, and (4) working requirement demands on the jobholder. Each job is awarded a certain number of points, according to the degree to which each of these four factors (or refinements of them) is present in it, and the total number of points consequently assigned to each job (usually on a weighted-average basis, depending on the importance of each factor) determines the place at which the particular job falls in the job hierarchy of the plant. Wage rates or ranges are then established for all jobs falling within a single total point spread (usually called a "labor grade") of this hierarchy. All jobs awarded between 250 and 275 points, for example, might constitute labor grade 4 and be paid whatever wages are called for by this labor grade.

Many managements have found the appeal of such a system to be irresistible. In addition to simplifying the wage structure through the substitution of a relatively few labor grades for individual job listings, it allows the company a basis for defending particular wage rates to the union and provides a rational means for determining rates for new and changed jobs (through using the same process for these jobs, and then slotting their point totals into the hierarchy of labor grades). At least three-quarters of all American managements probably make use of such a system today.

This growth of job evaluation, at least for unionized companies, has nonetheless been accomplished only in the face of rather adamant union opposition. Only a few unions—most notably the Steelworkers—have done anything but strongly attack the system. Virtually all others have voiced deep suspicion of the technique itself and have decried the reduced possibilities for union bargaining on individual wage rates allowed by job evaluation.

Why, then, has this method of evaluation spread so pervasively to industry? Livernash conveys an authoritative opinion:

> In part, unions have been bought off. Objection was not strong enough to turn down evaluation if an increase in the rate structure was also involved. . . . In

part, unions became willing to accept less bargaining over individual job rates. . . . Unions found that job evaluation did not freeze them out of a reasonable voice in influencing the wage structure and continuous wage grievances became a union problem. Particularly when accompanied by formal or informal joint participation in the evaluation process, the technique became acceptable.[28]

Unions on these grounds have been far more receptive to the concept than a mere reading of their official statements would lead one to believe.

Job comparison is, in many cases, the manager's answer to intransigent union opposition to job evaluation where this remains a force. It has also been utilized by many companies whose job structures do not appear complex enough to warrant job evaluation, or (in some cases) where the management itself is divided on the efficacy of the evaluation technique. Although it has certain refinements, it most frequently involves (1) the establishment of an appropriate number of labor grades with accompanying wage rates or ranges, and (2) the classification of each job into a particular labor grade by deciding which already classified jobs the particular job most closely resembles. The systematic approach of the evaluation method is, in short, dispensed with—and so are the many subsidiary advantages of such an approach. By the same token, however, whatever deficiencies the management or unions see in evaluation are also bypassed. The procedure, a not-too-satisfactory compromise between evaluations and individual rates for each job, is not now common in industry and, for the reasons indicated in the discussion of evaluation, can probably be expected to become increasingly less so in the years ahead.

ECONOMIC RECESSION: CONCESSIONARY BARGAINING

Organized labor officially marked its one-hundredth anniversary in 1981, but it was hardly a time for rejoicing. Starting in the summer of that year, the nation slid into the worst recession since the Great Depression. Unemployment soared from 7.2 percent in July 1981 to 10.8 percent in December 1982, the highest level since 1940. Added to the 12 million officially counted as unemployed under the government definition, about 1.6 million ceased looking for jobs because of discouragement, and 6.6 million were involuntarily working part-time. For 1982, the rate of business failures rose to the highest level since the 1930s, and factory utilization fell to the lowest level in the thirty-five-year history of that statistical series.[29] The only bright spot was the decrease of the rate of inflation to 6.0 percent in 1982,[30] a not unexpected development given the depressed state of the economy.

Never before had collective bargaining contracts been negotiated under such adverse economic conditions. In previous post–World War II recessions, the pace of wage increases and gains in other benefits slowed, but there were no wholesale

[28] Summer H. Slichter, James J. Healy, and E. Robert Livernash, *The Impact of Collective Bargaining on Management* (Washington, D.C.: Brookings Institution, 1960), pp. 563–64.
[29] *Monthly Labor Review*, 106, No. 1 (January 1983), 28.
[30] *Ibid.*, No. 3 (April 1983) 70.

concessions granted employers at the bargaining table. Now there were. In the effort to save jobs, unions made concessions on wages, fringe benefits, work rules, and other conditions of employment. Employees forfeited benefits enjoyed for as long as forty years. At times, union leaders were put in the awkward position of urging members to accept lower standards of employment. Frequently these concessions were negotiated before the expiration date of labor agreements. As a UAW spokesperson put it:

> All of the things we win at the bargaining table don't mean a thing to someone without a job.[31]

First-year wage increases under multiyear major collective bargaining contracts negotiated in 1982 averaged 3.8 percent, the lowest in the seventeen-year period during which the Bureau of Labor Statistics had been publishing such data. Over the life of these multiyear contracts, wage increases averaged 3.5 percent per year.[32] The principal reason for the low 1982 averages was that about a third of the workers covered by such contracts *did not receive any wage increase*. In contrast, for 1981, the first-year increase was 8.3 percent, and 6.4 percent over the life of the multiyear contracts.

Under the circumstances, a new vocabulary arose describing the trend. Words such as "take-aways," "give-backs," and "concessions" became commonplace in the industrial relations lexicon.

Wages Frozen and Reduced

Frequently wage rates were frozen or actually reduced. In March 1982, even the mighty Teamsters negotiated a thirty-eight-month wage freeze with several over-the-road employer associations. The then Teamster president, Roy L. Williams, hoped that the contract would

> preserve the jobs of those now employed and will help regain the thousands of jobs lost through layoffs and business failures in the trucking industry.[33]

A Louisville-based Graphic Arts union agreed to a five-year wage freeze in exchange for the employer's promise to try to remain in that city.[34] The Airline Pilots Association negotiated wage freezes and pay cuts with several major carriers.[35] For a three-year period, the United Rubber Workers agreed to a basic wage freeze with the major rubber firms, and at the Akron Goodrich plant wage cuts of up to 81 cents per hour went into effect.[36] In the meatpacking industry, the

[31] "Give Backs by Unions—How Far Will They Go," *U.S. News and World Report*, February 1, 1982, p. 65.
[32] "Collective Bargaining in 1982: Results Dictated by Economy," *Monthly Labor Review*, 106, No. 1 (January 1983), 28.
[33] *Monthly Labor Review*, 105, No. 4 (April 1982).
[34] *Ibid.*, No. 5 (May 1982), 603.
[35] *Ibid.*, 106, No. 1, (January 1983), 33.
[36] *AFL–CIO News*, May 8, 1982, p. 1.

United Food and Commercial Workers accepted a three-year wage freeze and suspension of cost-of-living adjustments for two years.[37] At several Oscar Mayer plants, not only were basic wage rates frozen until August 31, 1985, but the employees accepted a 30-cent-per-hour wage cut.[38]

Concessions in Automobile and Basic Steel Industries

The most noteworthy examples of this sort were the concessionary negotiations in the automobile and steel industries. Harassed by foreign competition and the effects of the recession, the automobile corporations pressured the United Auto Workers for major concessions. In February 1982, several months before the expiration of the prevailing contract, Ford and the UAW agreed to replace the latter with a new one.[39] For the thirty-month contractual period, basic wage rates would be frozen, cost-of-living increases deferred, and fourteen days in paid time off surrendered. Newly hired employees would be paid at lower wage rates, would have to wait longer to be eligible for certain insurance benefits, and would not be paid for certain days off. (Given the fact, however, that about 150,000 auto workers were on layoff in 1982, the latter concession did not have practical significance.) Labor cost savings resulting from the concessions amounted to an estimated $1 billion over the contractual period.

In return for these concessions, Ford employees received some job security benefits. Ford agreed to a two-year moratorium on plant closings that would have occurred as the result of so-called "outsourcing"—the purchase of parts and services from outside companies. However, closings would be permitted in the case of plant consolidations or to balance production with sales volume. A novel experiment was the selection of two plants in which 80 percent of the employees obtained lifetime job security.

Also established was a "Guaranteed Income Stream" program for employees who had at least fifteen years of service and had been laid off after the effective date of the new contract. Payments here would equal 50 percent of gross weekly pay for those with fifteen years of seniority, plus one percentage point for each additional year of service up to a maximum payment of 75 percent of gross weekly pay, or 95 percent of weekly after-tax pay, minus $12.50 whichever was less. These payments would continue until the laid-off employee retired or reached 62 years of age. During the period of coverage, the employees would be covered by health and life insurance. In addition, a profit-sharing plan was adopted starting in 1983 based on Ford's sales volume in the United States.

To provide employees with participation in management decision, "Mutual Growth Forums" were created. These forums, operating at plant and national levels, would undertake "advance discussion of certain business developments that are of mutual interest and significance to the union, the employees, and the com-

[37] *Monthly Labor Review*, 106, No. 1 (January 1983) 31.
[38] *Ibid.*, 105, No. 5 (May 1982), 61.
[39] *Ibid.*, No. 4 (April 1982), 62.

pany." At the national level, the forum would examine and discuss such items as Ford's general operation and certain business developments. Twice a year, the director of the UAW National Ford Department would have the right to address the corporation's board of directors. At the plant level, the forums would meet quarterly to discuss such things as "the plant's general operation and certain business developments."

Other provisions were intended to preserve jobs and provide benefits for laid-off employees. Substantial improvements were made in the early retirement program to encourage employees to retire before 65 years of age. To help the laid-off employees, the Supplementary Unemployment Benefit (SUB) program was made more generous. Perhaps most important of all was the establishment of a jointly managed training program to upgrade and broaden the skills of active and laid-off employees. Since a substantial number of laid-off employees would not be called back to work in the automobile and other "smokestack" industries even when the economy improved, there existed a clear imperative to train employees to take jobs in the other sectors of the economy.

One month later, General Motors signed a similar agreement with the UAW.[40] Concessions granted GM were essentially the same as those granted Ford with an estimated cost savings of $2.5 billion during the thirty-month contractual period.[41] However, GM employees fared somewhat better in job security and benefits. The corporation agreed to reopen four of the six plants it had closed when negotiations ceased in January. These four plants employed about 5,000 UAW members. Unlike the Ford contract, employees with ten years of service were eligible to participate in the Guaranteed Income Stream program. To defray the cost of the program, the parties negotiated a less liberal profit-sharing plan based on net worth and assets instead of sales volume, as was the case at Ford. General Motors employees also received a legal services plan, financed by company funding of 3 cents an hour per worker. Some of the costs of the program, however, could be reduced because of the agreement to reduce nonwage benefits for employees with excessive absentee records.

Despite gaining somewhat more job security and benefits as compared with Ford, General Motors workers approved the 1982 contract by a very slim margin. Ford workers had adopted that contract by a vote of 73 to 27 percent. The GM agreement was approved by 52 to 48 percent.[42] And with such a close vote, GM management believed it would be very difficult, if at all possible, to seek additional concessions at the plant level over such matters as work rules involving relief time, flexibility in assigning skilled workers to jobs, and production standards. It felt that the employees had given up as much as could reasonably be expected.

Different circumstances were involved in the 1982 negotiations between Chrysler and the UAW. In the three previous years, in the effort to keep the corporation in business, the UAW had agreed to massive concessions, the employees giving

[40] *Ibid.*, No. 5 (May 1982), 59.
[41] *Washington Post*, March 23, 1982, p. 1.
[42] *Wall Street Journal*, April 2, 1982, p. 1.

up $1.07 billion in wages and other benefits.[43] As a result, by 1982 there existed a $2.60-per-hour pay disparity as compared with GM and Ford.[44] To correct this situation, and to recapture some of the benefits, the UAW demanded an immediate wage increase for the Chrysler employees. A settlement was reached making a wage increase contingent upon the corporation profits. Despite the effort of UAW national officials to sell the agreement, the Chrysler workers rejected it. Negotiations resumed, and in December 1982, the parties agreed to a thirteen-month contract that provided for an immediate wage increase averaging 75 cents per hour; resumption of the cost-of-living pay adjustments; and, similar to Ford and GM, lifetime income security for employees with at least fifteen years of seniority.[45] This time the employees accepted the contract by an 80 percent majority and a strike, which would probably have been fatal to the corporation and employees, was averted.

In steel, the Steelworkers were free to strike over the 1983 contract, due to expire on August 1, 1983. And as automobile corporations did with the UAW, the basic steel companies pressured the United Steelworkers of America for major concessions. At the start of 1983, the steel industry was operating at about 52 percent of its production capability and was facing increasingly stiff competition from foreign steel producers. As a matter of fact, basic steel customers, particularly the automobile industry, made it clear that they would place orders overseas if the steel contract was not settled by March 1, 1983. Such a development would augment steel industry layoffs, which stood at about 33 percent in the early months of 1983.

In November 1982, the parties negotiated a concessionary contract, supported by the national officers but soundly rejected by local union leaders.[46] Commenting on that feature, the late Lloyd McBride, then the Steelworkers International president, said:

> I am convinced that the proposal was essential. I'm disappointed, obviously.[47]

On March 1, 1983, the target date established by the steel industry's customers, the parties negotiated another contract which was accepted overwhelmingly by the local union presidents, 169 voting for acceptance and only 63 for rejection. Steel industry analysts estimated that over the forty-one-month contract period, the concession would result in $2 billion savings in labor costs.

By far the major concession was a *wage cut* amounting to $1.25 per hour, or a 9 percent reduction of the average employee's pay. By stages, however, the reduction was scheduled to be fully restored by February 1, 1986. For 1983, the employees gave up one paid holiday and a one-week paid vacation. Cost-of-living payments were eliminated until July 31, 1984. Between August 1, 1984, and July

---

[43] *Ibid.*, August 5, 1982, p. 1.
[44] *Monthly Labor Review*, 106, No. 1 (January 1983), 29.
[45] *Ibid.*, p. 30.
[46] *Ibid.*, p. 6. Under the Steelworkers' procedure, presidents of union locals in basic steel plants have the authority to vote on proposed contracts. In this vote, the contract was rejected by a vote of 231–141.
[47] *Louisville Courier Journal*, November 21, 1982, p. 1.

31, 1985, COLA payments were to resume, but only if the Consumer Price Index increased by 4 percent over its March 1984 level. Premium pay for Sunday work was reduced from time and one-half to time and one-quarter. Extended vacations, thirteen weeks for senior workers every five years, were eliminated.

In exchange for these concessions, basic steel employees received less in job security and employee benefits as compared with employees in the automobile industry. Steel corporations pledged to apply labor-cost savings, or at least a portion of these savings, to modernize their plants. However, whether that actually occurs remains to be determined. If it does, U.S. steel companies will be in a better position to compete with foreign steel by increasing production efficiency. One factor in the decline of the U.S. steel industry has been the reluctance of its managers to invest in modern methods and plant improvement.

The 1983 contract provided a special retirement incentive designed to make early retirement more attractive to older workers so there would be more jobs available for younger employees. Also, the SUB program was improved for the benefit of laid-off employees. In contrast with the automobile industry, however, there was no guarantee against plant closings or lifetime income for senior laid-off employees. Asked why no moratorium against plant closings was contained in the contract, the vice president of the International Union, who chaired the union team in the negotiations, replied simply, "I couldn't get it."

Resistance to Concessions

Not all unions and workers, however, granted concessions, at least not before the occurrence of long and bitter strikes. In June 1982, Iowa Beef, Dakota City, Nebraska, the nation's largest beef packer, demanded that employees, represented by the United Food and Commercial Workers, agree to a four-year wage freeze, the elimination of cost-of-living increases, the right to cut wages to match any future wage reduction by competitors, and the elimination and modification of other employee benefits. The result was a sixteen-week strike marked by violence when the firm continued to operate with 1,400 replacement strike-breakers, who were being paid $2 per hour less than the starting rate provided in the expired contract. Unfair labor practices filed against the company were adopted in a complaint issued by the Kansas City regional office of the National Labor Relations Board. At that time, to avoid the delays associated with the litigation, the regular employees made an unqualified request to return to work. In the fall of 1982, Iowa Beef returned about 1,300 strikers to work and paid them the old rate.

At this writing, a strike against Brown & Sharpe, North Kingston, Rhode Island, engaged in by 1,500 members of the Machinists Union, had been in effect for almost a year. The dispute centered on the company's demand for more flexibility in the assignment of workers to jobs. Whereas the company claimed that such changes in the work rules were necessary to increase productivity, the union asserted that the management's intention in fact was to break the union by a prolonged strike. When the company hired replacements, the strike became very violent and included rock throwing and gunfire. To facilitate the use of the strike-breakers, the company employed private security officers and guard dogs, as well as off-duty local and state police.

Caterpillar Tractor Company, Peoria, Illinois, demanded a three-year wage freeze and reduction in cost-of-living payments. As a result, about 21,000 active employees (15,000 were on indefinite layoff), members of the UAW, struck in October 1982. The strike ended in April 1983, the longest UAW work stoppage in years against a multiplant corporation. The new contract froze wages for three years, and in exchange Caterpillar agreed to a profit-sharing plan and dropped its COLA demand.

In March 1982, 500 employees of Timex Clock, Ashland, Massachusetts, members of the United Electrical, Radio, and Machine Workers, struck when the company demanded to cut wages an average of 81 cents per hour. In regard to the firm's threat to move, the local union president observed:

> The company says they'll go south unless we take the cut, but we figure if they're going to move they'll go anyway, so why give them our money to travel on.[48]

Additional illustrations could be supplied to demonstrate that not all unions were prepared to grant major concessions in collective bargaining. Union officials argued that at times companies did not need such relief but were using the recession as a pretext to reduce labor standards. As one union official put it:

> I feel the company is just doing this because other companies have done it and [are] getting away with it. I believe they're just using the times, the economy, to their advantage.[49]

Only time would tell, of course, whether or not *any* of the concessions would ultimately save plants and jobs, anyhow. If they did not, employees would clearly have made unnecessary sacrifices. But what was not hypothetical in the slightest in these events of the 1980s was that, faced with economic realities, unions with the approval of a substantial number of their members had agreed to terms that would have been unthinkable not long ago.

A FINAL WORD

As this chapter has tried to show, wage rates and allied wage issues pose very difficult collective bargaining problems. But if the resultant complications do make wage controversies the leading overt cause of strikes, the fact remains that such strikes take place in only a comparatively few instances. Although the stakes can be very high and the problems formidable, employers and unions in the vast ma-

---

[48] *Wall Street Journal*, April 28, 1982, p. 1.
[49] *Ibid.*, October 13, 1982, p. 1.

jority of cases ultimately find a peaceful solution in the wage area as in other areas of bargaining.

Some of the settlements, admittedly, may not be the kind that would be advocated by economists, and some clearly fail to adjust the issues in a way that reflects equity and fairness. But the parties most often do resolve their wage disputes in a manner that proves generally satisfactory to all concerned.

It should be remembered that these wage problems are not resolved in an antiseptic economic laboratory where wage models may be constructed. If the settlements do, at times, offend the economic purist, it must be appreciated that these issues are dealt with in the practical day-to-day world, wherein pressures, motives, and attitudes cannot be isolated from the negotiations. Given such realities, it is to the credit of both parties that mutual accommodation has become increasingly visible.

Discussion Questions

1 Both industry A and industry B are extensively organized by conscientious and honestly run labor unions. Still, since 1963, the wages within industry A have risen at about three times the rate of those in industry B. How might you account for the difference in the wage situation between these two industries?

2 "Even though the actual wage rate that will be negotiated in a particular negotiation is not determinable, it is certain that the set of arguments that union and management representatives will use to support their respective positions will not change from negotiation to negotiation." To what extent, if any, do you agree with this statement?

3 Compare the methods available for the adjustment of wages during the effective period of a labor agreement, and defend what you would judge to be the most desirable arrangement.

4 "From the employer's point of view, it is inherently inequitable—the laws notwithstanding—to require the payment of equal wages to women and to men for performing the same job." Construct the strongest case that you can in support of this statement, and then balance your case with the most convincing opposing arguments that you can muster.

5 Compare and contrast the programs instituted during the early 1960s to control wages and prices with those of the Nixon and Carter administrations.

6 Recognizing the present-day circumstances in which you reply to this question, what do you believe to be the most important wage determinant in collective bargaining? Why?

7 What possible problems might confront management and unions in the negotiation and administration of contractual language dealing with overtime?

Selected References

BAUMBACK, C. M., *Structural Wage Issues in Collective Bargaining*. Lexington, Mass.: Heath, 1971.

GARBARINO, JOSEPH W., *Wage Policy and Long-Term Contracts*. Washington, D.C.: Brookings Institution, 1962.

GRAYSON, C. JACKSON, JR., *Confessions of a Price Controller*. Homewood, Ill.: Dow Jones–Irwin, 1974.

LEWIS, H. GREGG, *Unionism and Relative Wages in the United States: An Empirical Inquiry*. Chicago: University of Chicago Press, 1963.

MCKERSIE, ROBERT B., and L. C. HUNTER, eds., *Pay, Productivity, and Collective Bargaining*. New York: St. Martin's Press, 1973.

MORGAN, CHESTER A., *Labor Economics* (3rd ed.). Austin, Tex.: Business Publications, 1970.

OZANNE, ROBERT, *Wages in Practice and Theory*. Madison, Wis.: University of Wisconsin Press, 1968.

PHELPS-BROWN, E. M., *The Economics of Labor*. New Haven, Conn.: Yale University Press, 1962.

REES, ALBERT, *The Economics of Trade Unions*. Chicago: University of Chicago Press, 1962.

TOLLES, N. ARNOLD, *Origins of Modern Wage Theories*. Englewood Cliffs, N.J.: Prentice-Hall, 1964.

WEBER, ARNOLD R., and DANIEL J. B. MITCHELL, *The Pay Board's Progress*. Washington, D.C.: Brookings Institution, 1978.

Application of COLA Program:
The Case of the "Missing" Five Cents

Wylie, the union president, was the only witness called in the arbitration, and, as you will see, his testimony did not do much for the determination of the dispute. It involved the application and construction of the parties' COLA program. Indeed, during the arbitration, the parties used the time to explain their positions. Not content with that, each side filed comprehensive posthearing briefs. As you read the case, keep your eye on the particular issue presented in the dispute. Do not get tangled up in the mathematical computations. They were presented to clarify the parties' arguments dealing with the disputed five cents.

This case is unusual in one important respect. Unlike a normal escalator provision where wage adjustments are made depending upon stipulated point changes in the CPI, the parties' program, though using the course of the CPI as a factor, adopted a unique procedure to determine whether wages should be adjusted. This shows the flexibility of the collective bargaining process—objectives may be achieved in a variety of ways depending upon the creativity and innovation capability of employers and unions.

GRIEVANCE AND LABOR AGREEMENT

The dispute in this case involves the proper application of the Parties' Cost of Living Adjustment (COLA) program. In protest against the Company's application, the Union filed Grievance No. 37-80, dated December 3, 1980. It states:

> Local #802 grieves the Company's improper calculation, and application of negotiated wage and cost of living increases effective December 7, 1980 which violate the terms of Appendix 300, Article 25, Cost of Living, and others of the Agreement, and demands that all employees affected by such improper calculation be made whole for all losses and compensated at an appropriate rate of interest for all monies improperly withheld.

While denying the grievance, the Company replied:

> The Company maintains that the Wage Rates and Cost of Living Adjustment which became effective December 7, 1980 were calculated and applied in accordance with Article 25.0, Appendix 300.0 and the Cost of Living Review provision of the Labor Agreement.

LABOR AGREEMENT

ARTICLE 25.   WAGE RATES

Section 25.1   The Wage Rate Tables shown in Appendix 300.0 shall become effective as follows:

> 25.11 Appendix 300.0, April 30, 1979.
>
> 25.12 Appendix 300.0, December 9, 1979.
>
> 25.13 Appendix 300.0, December 7, 1980.

Section 25.2   A Cost of Living review will be conducted December 1, 1979 in accordance with the Letter of Understanding which appears in this Agreement.

APPENDIX 300—WAGE RATE SCHEDULE

Labor Grade	Maximum Pay Rate Effective 4/30/79	Maximum Pay Rate Effective 12/9/79	Maximum Pay Rate Effective 12/7/80
9	5.93	6.34	6.75

COST OF LIVING REVIEW

Part of the understanding reached in the Agreement effective April 30, 1979 is to review the change in the Consumer's Price Index from November 1978 to October 1979 and from November 1978 to October 1980. This is an explanation of the procedure to be followed in making such comparison.

1 Following the issuance of the Consumer's Price Index for Urban Wage Earners and Clerical Workers (Revised Series), All Cities, (1967 = 100) for October 1979 a comparison will be made as follows:

   1.1 The maximum pay rate of Labor Grade 9 as of December 1, 1979 which is $5.93 and the pay rate of Labor Grade 9 as of December 1, 1978 which was $5.32.

   1.2 The CPI for October 1979 and the CPI for October 1978 which was 200.7.

2 Comparison of the figures obtained in Item 1 will be made as follows:

   2.1 Determine the percentage increase in the pay rate of Labor Grade 9 by subtracting $5.32 from $5.93 and dividing that difference by $5.32, carrying the quotient to one decimal place. The result is 11.5%.

   2.2 Determine the percent increase in the CPI by subtracting 200.7 from the CPI for October 1979 and dividing that difference by 200.7, carrying the quotient to one decimal place.

   2.3 If the resultant percentage in 2.2 is greater than the resultant percent in 2.1, then the difference in percentage will be added to the straight time hourly rate of pay for each employee as of December 9, 1979, and will also be applied to Appendix 300 effective December 9, 1979.

   2.4 If the resultant percentage in 2.1 is greater than the percentage in 2.2, then no wage increase will be granted.

3 Similar computations made in Section 2 above will be made using the rate of pay for Labor Grade 9 as of December 9, 1979 and the CPI for November 1980. The $5.32 rate of pay and CPI 200.7 remain as the basis for computation.

4 Example in determination and application of the percentages:

   4.1 Assume the annual rate of increase for the CPI is 10% for each period. The

CPI would then be:

October 1978—200.7
October 1979—220.8
October 1980—242.8

4.2 Review at December 1, 1979

Grade 9 increased at 11.5%
CPI increased   10.0%
No wage rate adjustment

4.3 Review at December 1, 1980

Grade 9 increases 19.2%
CPI increased   21.3%
Wage adjustment of 2.1%

$$\$6.34 \times 2.1\% = \$.13 \text{ per hour}$$

Pay rates effective December 7, 1980
would be increased $.13 per hour.

BASIC QUESTION

The basic question to be determined in this dispute is framed as follows:

Did the Company violate the Cost of Living Adjustment provisions contained in the Labor Agreement? If so, what should the remedy be?

BACKGROUND

Negotiation of Cost of Living Adjustment Program

For the first time, the Parties adopted a COLA program when they negotiated the current Labor Agreement. Previous contracts did not contain such a program. On December 6, 1978, the Company proposed a COLA arrangement. With respect to calculations, including the use of base data, the proposal was the same as the one that the Parties eventually adopted. However, it called for only one review of the course of the Consumer Price Index (CPI) and wage rate progression. The review was to be made on December 1, 1980, and any adjustment was to be added to the employees' wage rates effective December 7, 1980.

It contained two examples of how the program would work. Assumptions were made as to the course of the CPI. In one example, there would be no adjustment, and in the other example, wage rates effective December 7, 1980 would be increased because the CPI was assumed to increase higher than wage rates.

With regard to the Company's original proposal, the Union said:

It was part of the Company's economic package. It was to review the CPI after the first two years of the contract to see if wage increases were adequate to keep up with the cost of living. If the wage increase was adequate, there would be no adjustment in the wage rates. If wages did not keep up with the cost of living, the difference would be granted to the employees.

In any event, the Union membership rejected that Company proposal because it provided for only one review during the life of the contract.

A strike started on December 10, 1978 and ended on April 30, 1979. During the strike, on March 1, 1979, the Company proposed another COLA program. Unlike the first proposal, this one provided for two reviews of price and wage data. The first review would take place on December 1, 1979, and the second on December 1, 1980. Calculations and base data were the same as contained in the original proposal and as appears in the current Labor Agreement. This proposal contained two examples, one which assumed an increase of the CPI not sufficient to generate a wage increase. In the second example, a wage adjustment was indicated because of an assumed increase in the CPI. Both examples provided for a review on December 1, 1979.

With regard to this proposal, Wylie, current Union President, who at that time was Recording Secretary and member of the Union Bargaining Committee, testified:

> We requested more examples, examples which would be more expressive than the previous examples.

As a result, on March 16, 1979, the Company furnished another example pertaining to the review on December 1, 1980. It assumed an increase in the CPI sufficient to yield a wage increase to be added to the wage rates effective December 7, 1980.

On the same day, March 16, 1979, the Parties agreed to the COLA program which appears in the current Labor Agreement.

Review of December 1, 1979

On this date, a cost of living review was made which generated an increase of five (.05) cents. This amount resulted from the procedures and calculations specified in the program. No dispute exists between the Parties as to the propriety of this review.

The five cents were added to the hourly rates effective December 9, 1979. As a result, the maximum rate for Labor Grade 9 was increased to $6.39. Without the cost of living additive, the rate of Labor Grade 9 would have been $6.34 per hour. Similarly, the five cents were added to the maximum rates for all labor grades and classifications as appearing in Appendix 300.

In short, starting on December 9, 1979, all employees in the bargaining unit had their wage rates increased by five cents, and the maximum rates for each labor grade and classification were increased by the same amount.

Review of December 1, 1980

Events that developed in connection with the COLA review on this date produced the dispute involved in this case. By October 1980, the CPI increased by 53.4 points from October 1978. In October 1978, the base month, the CPI was at 200.7. By October 1980, it increased to 254.1, or 26.6 percent.

Using the Labor Grade 9 rate for December 1, 1978 as the base, $5.32 per hour, it was determined that as of December 9, 1979, the hourly rate for that labor grade increased by $1.07, or 20.1 percent. To arrive at that figure, the Company used $6.39, the rate that was effective as of December 9, 1979. That amount included the five cents increase generated by the COLA review of December 1, 1979.

Based upon such price and wage data, it was determined that as of December 1, 1980 the CPI increased 6.5 percent higher than the percentage increase in wage rates (26.6 percent − 20.1 percent = 6.5 percent). This percentage difference, 6.5 percent, was used by the Company to increase wage rates effective December 7, 1980. It resulted in a 42 cent increase ($6.39 × 6.5 = 42 cents).

Effective December 7, 1980, the maximum rate of Labor Grade 9 was $6.75. Under the Company procedure, it increased this maximum by 42 cents resulting in a new maximum of $7.17. So, an employee in Labor Grade 9 at the new maximum rate would earn $7.17 per hour for the balance of this contract period. The same amount, 42 cents, was added to the maximum rates for all other labor grades and classifications as appearing in Appendix 300.

Character of Dispute

The dispute arises because the Union believes that the Company should have increased the maximum rates effective December 7, 1980, as appearing in Appendix 300, by an additional five cents. The basis for its position is that the five cent increase resulting from the review of December 1, 1979 should have been added to the maximum rates effective December 7, 1980. It was not sufficient to increase the maximum rates effective December 9, 1979. The five cent additive should also have been applied to the maximum rates effective December 7, 1980.

In accordance with the Union position, therefore, the maximum rate of Labor Grade 9 effective December 7, 1980 should have been $6.80 per hour and not $6.75. The Company should have added the 42 cents to $6.80 resulting in a new maximum of $7.22 for Labor Grade 9 effective December 7, 1980.

POSITIONS OF THE PARTIES

In essence, therefore, this dispute involves a determination of whether or not the five cent COLA additive resulting from the December 1, 1979 review should have been added to the maximum rates effective December 7, 1980. Whereas the Union claims that the five cents should have been added to those rates, the Company's position is that the five cent additive applies only to the maximum rates effective December 9, 1979 and not to those rates effective December 7, 1980.

To support their respective positions, the Parties offered their arguments at the close of the arbitration. To the extent necessary and appropriate, such arguments will be referenced in the following portion of this Opinion.

ANALYSIS OF THE EVIDENCE

Section 2.3 of COLA Program

Both Parties agree that the proper application of this provision is critical to the determination of this dispute. Section 2.3 states that an additive resulting from the December 1, 1979 review will be added to the hourly rates effective December 9, 1979 and "will also be applied to Appendix 300 effective December 9, 1979." Each side believes that this language supports its position.

> In this regard the union argues Section 2.3 does not say that the five cents should be added only to the rates effective December 9, 1979. It says that the additive should be applied to Appendix 300. There is no limit to that application to only December 9, 1979. It does not say the additive should be applied only to Appendix 300 for rates effective December 9, 1979. When the provision says the five cents should apply to Appendix 300, it means that it should be added to Appendix 300 for all purposes. Therefore, the Company should have added the five cents to the maximum rates effective December 7, 1980.

The Union argues further:

> When the Company did not add the five cents to the maximum rates effective December 7, 1980, as Section 2.3 says that it must, it means that the employees received no benefit of that increase in the third year of the contract. The five cents disappeared by the Company's failure to carry that amount to the third year of the contract as required by Section 2.3. The Company gave us the five cents and then it took it back. This is what really happened in this case. There is no basis in Section 2.3 that once the five cents was applied, it was ever to be taken back. Section 2.3 does not permit the Company to deduct and subtract the five cents after the employees received that benefit.

In the Company's view, it applied Section 2.3 in a proper manner. With regard to that provision, the Company contends:

> Section 2.3 does not say to add the five cents to rates effective December 7, 1980. It provides that the additive shall be applied to rates effective December 9, 1979 and shall be applied to Appendix 300 rates effective December 9, 1979. It directs that the five cents will be added only to Appendix 300 rates effective December 9, 1979. It does not say "and will be added to the December 7, 1980 rates."

With regard to the Union's charge that the Company took back the five cent additive, or that it deducted that amount, the Company claims that:

> We applied the COLA program in a proper manner. It calls for two independent reviews, the first on December 1, 1979 and the second on December 1, 1980. We did that and the calculations were in accordance with the provisions. We did not deduct or subtract the five cents as the Union charges. The very sug-

gestion that the Company would deprive our employees of five cents or even a penny is repugnant.

Section 2.3 Ambiguous

As we review the language contained in Section 2.3, both Parties may be correct in their interpretation of the provision. As the Union argues, the provision does not expressly state that the December 1, 1979 additive shall apply only to the rates effective December 9, 1979. In the absence of such exclusionary language, it could be, as the Union argues, that the December 1, 1979 additive should be applied to the December 7, 1980 rates. Since the language does not expressly state that the December 1, 1979 additive shall be applied strictly and only to the December 9, 1979 rates, it could be reasonable to conclude that the five cents in question should be applied to Appendix 300 so as to increase those rates effective December 7, 1980.

On the other hand, a reasonable construction of Section 2.3 could also support the Company's position. If the Parties intended that the December 1, 1979 additive should be applied not only to rates effective December 9, 1979, but also to those effective December 7, 1980, they would have adopted express language to accomplish that purpose. As the Company argues, since the language says

will be applied to Appendix 300 effective December 9, 1979,

and does not mention December 7, 1980, the additive of December 1, 1979 is limited to those rates effective on December 9, 1979.

In other words, both sides have presented reasonable constructions of the language contained in Section 2.3. Either one could be adopted as the basis of a decision. To accept one construction, and not the other, would mean the rejection of an equally reasonable construction.

What this means, of course, is that Section 2.3 is inherently ambiguous as to the issue raised in this dispute. It does not tell us expressly and specifically that the December 1, 1979 additive shall be applied only to the December 9, 1979 rate, and equally it does not tell us expressly and specifically that such additive is to be applied to the December 7, 1980 rates. If it did one way or the other, there would be no dispute and no arbitration.

At times, past practice is used to apply contractual language that is ambiguous. This is not possible in this case because the Parties for the first time adopted their COLA program. So the problem involved in this dispute obviously did not occur in the past.

In short, it would be strictly improper for the Arbitrator to decide this case based upon the language contained in Section 2.3. Though both Parties agreed that the provison is critical to the dispute, the ambiguity in it precludes a determination of the fundamental issue involved in this dispute based upon a construction of the provision. In all candor, the Arbitrator would feel uncomfortable in selecting either version as the basis of his decision.

What this means is that a legitimate basis must be established to resolve the dispute aside and separate from the language contained in Section 2.3.

Company's Original Proposal

Had the Union accepted the Company's original COLA proposal, offered on December 6, 1978, the additive would have been 47 cents per hour effective December 7, 1980. Recall that this proposal called for one review to be made on December 1, 1980. As of that time, the CPI increased by 26.6 percent over the base period. Between December 1, 1978 and December 1, 1980, the Labor Grade 9 wage rate increased by $1.02 per hour, or 19.2 percent ($6.34 $-$ $5.32 = $1.02, or 19.2 percent). The percentage difference between the CPI and the wage rate increase would have been 7.4 percent (26.6 percent $-$ 19.2 percent = 7.4 percent). Applying the percentage difference to $6.34 per hour, the result would be an increase of 47 cents ($6.34 $\times$ 7.4 percent = 47 cents). Thus, under the Company's original proposal, 47 cents would have been added to the maximum rates effective December 7, 1980.

Forty-seven (47) cents is the amount that the Union claims should have been used to increase the maximum of Labor Grade 9 and other labor grades and classifications listed in Appendix 300 effective December 7, 1980. Since the original Company proposal would have generated that amount, the Union suggests that its position in this dispute should be sustained on that basis.

Notwithstanding the ingenuity and adroitness of this argument, it is not acceptable. It is not acceptable because the Union membership rejected the Company's original proposal. It was rejected because the Union members wanted two reviews and not only one review. Given two reviews, the issue arose as to whether the five cent increase generated by the December 1, 1979 review should be added to the maximum rates effective December 7, 1980. In no way does the application of the Company's original proposal resolve the issue presented in this case. The Company's original proposal, rejected by the Union membership, simply is not relevant to the problem presented to the Arbitrator.

Though not material to the issue involved in this dispute, it may be pointed out that if the Union membership had accepted the Company's original proposal, the employees would not have received the five cent COLA additive effective December 9, 1979. They indeed would have received a 47 cent increase effective December 7, 1980. However, they would have forfeited the five cent increase they received between December 9, 1979 and December 7, 1980.

In any event, the Company's original proposal does not provide a legitimate basis to determine the issue involved in this dispute. The problem arose because the COLA program as adopted by the Parties calls for two reviews and not only one as was contained in the Company's original proposal.

Company Examples

As the Union argues, none of the examples that the Company offered on March 1 or March 16, 1979 presents the problem involved in this dispute. In this respect, it says:

> If it was the Company's intention to refuse to apply the December 1, 1979 additive effective December 9, 1979 to the rates effective December 7, 1980, this should have been explained to the Union. The Union asked for examples, more vivid examples than the Company offered. None of the examples the Company showed us deals with what actually happened in this case. It had an opportunity to do so, but it did not.

In other words, the Union's position should prevail because the Company did not present an example that reflects the circumstances of this dispute. Though there may be some merit to this argument, it does not provide a legitimate basis for a decision favorable to the Union. If the Company failed to present an example on the issue involved in this dispute, it is just as logical to say that the Union failed to raise the issue now before us. If the Company had the opportunity to make clear how an adjustment in the December 1, 1979 review would be handled for the rates effective December 7, 1980, the Union had equal opportunity to ask how the matter would be handled.

Clearly, there is no basis to find that the Company deliberately and with malice withheld from the Union information that it says the Company should have given to it. There is no reason to believe that the Company engaged in bad faith collective bargaining. Instead, what probably happened in negotiations is that neither the Company nor the Union anticipated the problem that sparked this arbitration. This is understandable because it was the first time that a COLA program was negotiated. Rather than believing that either side was negligent—the Company for not presenting the problem or the Union failing to ask about it—what appears credible is that the problem was just not anticipated. As with any new program adopted in collective bargaining, it is difficult to look to the future and anticipate every problem that might arise. Indeed, if employers and labor organizations could do that, there would be less need for arbitration!

Purpose of the COLA Program

So far, therefore, the dispute concerning the five cents in question may not be determined on the basis of the language contained in Section 2.3, the Company's original proposal, or events that happened or did not happen in the negotiation of the COLA program. Given these circumstances, it is necessary to consider the fundamental purpose of the program—to protect employees' earnings from the ravages of inflation. As noted, at the outset of the arbitration, the Union identified the objective of the program in that way:

> It was to review the CPI after the first two years of the contract to see if wage

increases were adequate to keep up with the cost of living. If the wage increase was adequate, there would be no adjustment in wage rates. If wages did not keep up with the cost of living, the difference would be granted to the employess.

Though the statement was made in reference to the Company's original proposal, it obviously applies to the program that was eventually adopted. After all, that is what the Union was seeking—a program to assure that the employees' wages would not be eroded by the inflation as measured by the Consumer Price Index.

Using its fundamental purpose as the basis, the COLA program adopted by the Parties does that *and indeed more* even though the five cents in question is not added to the wage rates effective December 7, 1980. Between October 1978 and October 1980, the CPI increased by 26.6 percent. In essentially the same period of time, December 1, 1978 through December 7, 1980, the maximum Labor Grade 9 rate went from $5.32 to $7.17 per hour, a $1.85 per hour increase, or 35 percent ($1.85 divided by $5.32 = 35 percent). In other words, during the measurement period established in the COLA program, employees' wage rates increased higher than the CPI *by more than 8 percent.*

On this basis, it follows that employees' wages more than kept up with the cost of living. Even if the five cents in question is not added to the wage rates effective December 7, 1980, employees' real income increased.

Indeed, the COLA program adopted by the Parties, even disregarding the five cents in question, proved to be much more effective than what is normally found in collective bargaining contracts. Such programs normally increase wage rates by one (.01) cent per hour for each 0.3 or 0.4 point increase in the CPI. Wage rates are adjusted either on a quarterly, semi-annual, or annual basis. A study of such programs covering the period between 1968 and 1977 demonstrated that the average COLA yield met only 57 percent of the inflation occurring during those years. In not one year did the yield match the CPI increase.*

Conclusions

The Arbitrator well understands that the Union and its members will not be assuaged by the previous observations. They feel in good faith that the five cent increase in question should have been added to the maximum rates effective December 7, 1980. Never mind that the COLA program generated a sufficient yield to more than match the increase in the CPI during the measurement period of the program. Never mind that the program did more than meet its fundamental purpose—to protect the employees against the inflation. In their view, the five cents in question disappeared and/or was subtracted away because the December 7, 1980 wage rate maximums were not increased by that amount. It is recognized that nothing that the Arbitrator has said or could say will change that attitude.

* Victor J. Sheifer, "Cost of Living Adjustment: Keeping Up with Inflation," *Monthly Labor Review*, U.S. Department of Labor, Bureau of Labor Statistics, 102, No. 6 (June 1979), 14–17.

Though the Arbitrator fully understands all of that, under the circumstances of this case, he could not in good conscience determine this dispute except on the basis of the fundamental purpose, theory, and philosophy of the Parties' COLA program. As demonstrated earlier, the language contained in Section 2.3 is so ambiguous that it could support either of the constructions asserted by the Parties. It simply did not provide a basis for a decision that the Arbitrator could support in his mind and conscience. Though under the Company's original proposal, the maximum rates effective December 7, 1980 would have increased by 47 cents, the fact remains that the Union membership turned down that proposal. A rejected proposal clearly cannot serve as a legitimate basis for a decision. Finally, the events of the COLA negotiations as to what occurred or did not occur do not provide the basis of a supportable decision one way or the other.

Given these considerations, the Arbitrator was driven to the consideration of the fundamental purpose of the COLA program as the basis for his decision. All other circumstances were not acceptable for a decision for reasons stated previously and indeed restated here. In short, when measured against the purpose of the COLA program, its fundamental objective and philosophy, the grievance has no merit and shall be denied on this basis.

Questions

1 In your own words, state the fundamental issue involved in this dispute as it pertains to the disputed five cents per hour.

2 Why did the arbitrator say that the dispute could not be determined on the basis of the language contained in Section 2.3 of the parties' COLA program?

3 How did the arbitrator reply to the union's argument that the company during contract negotiations should have presented an example demonstrating the issue involved in the arbitration? Do you believe that the arbitrator was right or wrong on this issue? Explain your answer.

4 What reasoning did the arbitrator use to support his decision? If you were an employee, would you be satisfied with his reasoning? Why or why not?

Mandatory Overtime:
The Case of the Disciplined Employee

Cast of characters:

Kemp	*Grievant*
Mills	*Foreman*
Tabor	*Foreman*
Rolf	*Director of Labor Relations*
Lee, Oliver, Rose, Hill, Diltz, Burns	*Union Witnesses*

Despite the success of unions in limiting the right of employers to force employees to work overtime, employers retain this prerogative under many collective bargaining contracts. These employers reject limitation of this right on the grounds that at times the operation of an efficient business depends in part on the requirement of overtime. It should also be recognized that in some cases employers find it cheaper in terms of labor costs to pay premium overtime rates compared with the employment of more workers.

Here is a typical mandatory overtime case. An employee was disciplined when he refused to work overtime. To defend the employee, the union argued that the company did not have the contractual right to force employees to work overtime. In this regard, it cited features of the overtime provision dealing with the selection of employees for overtime. Also, the union claimed discrimination, presenting evidence that other employees refused to work overtime and were not disciplined. As you read the dispute, you will note that the arbitrator was compelled to deal with the employees' right to privacy. In the light of Watergate, he said, "the right to privacy has become a matter of national policy." Another aspect of this case involves a labor relations principle governing employee conduct—"Work, then grieve."

GRIEVANCE AND LABOR AGREEMENT

After Kemp received a written reprimand for refusal to work overtime, he filed Grievance No. 78-11, dated June 19, 1981, which states:

> On 6-16-81 all employees in Dept. 645 was [*sic*] notified by Mills the Foreman that on 6-19-81 through 6-22-81 overtime was to be worked by everyone. On

6-19-81 I did not work the overtime because of personal reasons. Therefore I was given a written reprimand which consisted of a layoff and or discharge if I failed to work anymore overtime during this period. Also an absentee slip from 3:30 P.M. to 5:00 P.M. against me.

After receiving this warning notice I feel unjustly treated because other employees have refused overtime, and within a period of 30 days (more or less) of this occurrence. I also refer to 5.8 of the current contract which does not stipulate compulsory overtime which was stated in the warning. Past practice by the Company has been to ask an employee if they wish to work overtime without threat or harassment from supervisors.

With other employees involved in overtime, past practice plus language of the current contract—then in my opinion an act of discrimination and unfair labor practice has been used against me.

I am asking for the absentee slip, warning notice, and all statements pertaining to this incident be withdrawn from my records.

In pertinent part, the Labor Agreement provides:

ARTICLE 5.   HOURS OF WORK AND OVERTIME

Section 5.8. Overtime Assignment   In the event overtime is to be worked it will be offered in the following manner:

   A To the most senior employee in the Department who regularly performs the job within the classification. If such employee does not work the overtime, others with the classification in the department who can perform the job will be offered the overtime work according to their seniority.

   B Employees capable of performing the job within the department on the basis of seniority.

Section 5.10. Overtime Notice   Employees will be expected to work necessary overtime to provide an adequate work force at all times. The Company will give the employee at least twenty-four hours advance notice when possible.

ARTICLE 20.   MANAGEMENT

The Management and Organization of the Company, the formulation of Company policies, the determination of the number and location of its plants, the products to be manufactured, their quality, the materials to be used, the direction of the products and means of manufacture, the direction of the working forces, including the right to discipline, suspend or discharge for proper cause, to hire, promote, demote, reward for merit, layoff, determine the number, duties and work assignments of employees, formulate and enforce rules not inconsistent with the provisions of this Agreement are vested exclusively in the Company except as these rights may be limited by any of the provisions of this Agreement.

BASIC QUESTION

The basic question to be determined in this proceeding is framed as follows:

Under the circumstances of this case, was Grievant Kemp reprimanded for proper cause? If not, what should the remedy be?

BACKGROUND

When the circumstances of this case arose, Grievant Kemp, hired by the Company in 1966, was assigned to the first shift in Department 645, Final Assembly. In this Department, fabric and hardware are installed on the doors and then released to the Shipping Department. Kemp was assigned to Final Assembly in April 1978.

On Friday, June 16, 1981, Mills, Foreman of the Department, scheduled overtime for all Final Assembly employees for the following week. Normal hours for the first shift are between 7 A.M. and 3:30 P.M. Overtime was scheduled for one and one-half (1½) hours, 3:30 P.M. to 5 P.M. As originally planned, the employees were scheduled for overtime from Monday, June 19 through Thursday, June 22. As it turned out, however, overtime was worked only on Monday, June 19 and Tuesday, June 20.

Overtime was scheduled because starting on June 25 the plant was to be shut down for a two-week vacation. Customer orders were to be completed before the shutdown. The Company's busiest season is in the summer months because a large share of its sales are in the construction industry.

In mid-afternoon on June 16, Mills notified each of the 35 employees assigned to Final Assembly of the scheduled overtime. Lee told the Foreman that she could not work overtime on the following Tuesday. Mills testified that Lee told him that she could not work overtime because she had a baby-sitting problem. Lee has two children, 8 and 9 years of age. On her part, Lee testified that she told the Foreman on Friday that she could work overtime the following week with the exception of Tuesday. She said that she had "things planned" for Tuesday and could not work overtime on that day. Lee testified further that she did not tell the Foreman that she had a baby-sitting problem for the following week.

In any event, no one else told the Foreman on Friday that he or she could not work the scheduled overtime.

On Monday, June 19 at about 3:15 P.M., Kemp told Mills that he would not work the overtime scheduled for that day. According to the Foreman, the conversation between the two went this way:

> Kemp told me that he was not going to work the overtime. I asked why not. He replied that he had "personal business." I asked Kemp what was the personal business. He said it was "personal." I read Article 5, Section 5.10 of the contract to him, and explained the whole department was scheduled to work overtime. Kemp said "Well, you can't work me over 40 hours per week." I told him "of an act against you" if he did not work the overtime.

As to this conversation, Kemp testified:

> I told the foreman I had personal business to take care of and could not work the overtime. He told me that he expected me to work overtime, and said if I did not work overtime, it would go on my record.

Kemp left the plant at 3:30 P.M. and did not work the overtime on Monday, June 19.

On Tuesday, June 20, Mills gave Kemp a written reprimand. In part, the document stated:

> You are being given this written reprimand as an opportunity to correct your improper conduct in the future and I expect that hereafter you will fully perform and meet all the duties and responsibilities required of you on your job. Should you fail to do so, you will subject yourself to further disciplinary action up to and including your discharge.

Considerable testimony was offered by Union witnesses as to previous overtime assignments. This material will be dealt with later on in this Opinion.

POSITION OF THE PARTIES

Whereas the Company requests that the grievance be denied, the Union urges that it be granted. Both Attorneys offered arguments at the close of the arbitration, and to the extent necessary and appropriate, such arguments will be referred to below.

ANALYSIS OF THE EVIDENCE

Contractual Language

At the outset it is necessary to determine whether or not the Labor Agreement permits the Company to force employees to work overtime. If it does not, the inquiry shall be terminated on this basis, and the grievance granted. On the other hand, should it be held that under the Labor Agreement the Company has the right to mandate overtime, the inquiry shall proceed to other matters.

In the view of the Union, the Labor Agreement does not provide for compulsory overtime. In this regard, Union Counsel argues:

> The Company would like the Arbitrator to read something in the contract that is not there. Nothing in the Labor Agreement distinguishes between a request and an order to work overtime. It does not distinguish between the methods of overtime. All that it says is overtime. The Company should not hide behind the Management Rights' clause. It is limited by other provisions in the Labor Agreement, and nothing in the contract requires overtime. There is nothing in the contract which specifies the different types of overtime situations. If an employee refuses to work overtime, nothing in the contract requires him to work overtime.

With full deference to the Union and its Attorney, the Arbitrator disagrees with that analysis of the Labor Agreement. It is true that the right of the Company to manage the plant, including the right to direct the working forces, is limited "by any of the provisions of this Agreement." In other words, under the Management provision, the Company has the exclusive right to direct the labor forces except where a particular right is limited by some other provision of the Labor Agreement.

Included in the right to direct the labor forces is the right to require overtime. If this right is to be limited, there must be an express provision in the Labor Agreement to achieve this objective. In this regard, it is material that many labor agreements contain an express provision making overtime voluntary on the part of the employee. Those contracts make it clear that the employer's inherent right to direct overtime has been abolished. When a labor agreement expressly provides for voluntary overtime, the employer, of course, has surrendered his right to compel overtime.

Article 5, Section 5.8

In the instant Labor Agreement, no such restriction has been negotiated by the Parties. Where in the contract is there an express provision that makes overtime voluntary? Just because Section 5.8 of Article 5 establishes a system for the selection of employees for overtime does not mean that the Company surrendered its right to mandate overtime. For the purpose of contractual construction, there is a vast difference between a system for the selection of employees for overtime opportunities and the right of an employer to require overtime. In Section 5.8, the Company surrendered its right to determine unilaterally the employee selected for an overtime opportunity. However, Section 5.8 would be distorted as to its purpose and intent to find that under that provision the Company waived its right to compel overtime.

It is true that Section 5.8 contemplates employee refusal of overtime because it establishes a procedure to fill overtime opportunities when the senior man in a department does not work the overtime. In the event of senior employee refusal, the employees will be offered the overtime based upon the established criteria. This does not mean, however, that the Company may not force overtime should no employee in a department or classification accept the overtime opportunity. Undoubtedly, the overwhelming number of overtime opportunities are filled voluntarily and in accordance with the system established in the provision. However, the Company is not powerless to require overtime should all refuse because there is nothing in the Labor Agreement that expressly makes overtime voluntary. Indeed, it has been held that even when an employer has been lenient in exercising his right to require overtime, or when overtime has been voluntary in the past, absent contractual language to the contrary the employer may require overtime where the volunteer approach does not supply a sufficient number of employees for overtime work. (*Roberts Brass Manufacturing*, 53 LA 703; *Champion Bait Co.*, 51 LA 287; *American Body & Equipment Co.*, 49 LA 1172; *Michigan Seamless Tube*, 48 LA 1077.) Additional citations could be supplied to underscore this labor relations principle.

In addition, what about a situation such as the one involved in this case when there is need for an entire department to work overtime? Under these circumstances, Section 5.8 is not involved because the provision contemplates the offer of overtime to individual employees within a department.

Article 5, Section 5.10

As a matter of fact, the previous analysis is not even required to demonstrate that the Company has the contractual right to require overtime. The Union position collapses in the light of the plain language contained in Article 5, Section 5.10. Not only does the Labor Agreement fail to contain an express limitation on the Company's right to compel overtime, but also Section 5.10 expressly authorizes the Company to require overtime. *Instead of an express provision making overtime voluntary, the contract contains language that expressly makes overtime compulsory.*
Section 5.10 states that

> employees will be *expected* to work necessary overtime to provide an adequate work force at all times. (Emphasis supplied)

To accept the Union's argument would mean that the Arbitrator would ignore plain and unequivocal language making overtime compulsory. If it is argued that Section 5.10 does not provide for compulsory overtime, how do we account for the fact that under the provision the Company must provide the employee expected to work overtime at least 24 hours' advance notice, when possible, before he is compelled to work overtime? The second sentence of the provision states:

> The Company will give the employee at least twenty-four hours advance notice when possible.

If overtime is purely voluntary, as the Union argues, advance notice would not be required. Clearly, when overtime is voluntary, there would be no need for advance notice since regardless of the time at which the overtime is offered, the employee could refuse it. So that employees may make adjustments in their personal affairs, Section 5.10 provides for at least 24 hours' notice before the employee would be expected to work overtime. If the Company fails to carry out its notice obligation, the employee, of course, would not be required to work overtime.

In all candor, the Arbitrator wonders how the Union could seriously argue that overtime is purely voluntary, given the express language of Section 5.10, let alone the fact that the Labor Agreement does not contain an express limitation on the Company's right to require overtime. Though the Union may choose to ignore the language contained in Section 5.10, the Arbitrator must give the provision full faith and credit to discharge the responsibilities of his office in a proper manner.

In the case at hand, the Company gave more than 24 hours' notice to the Grievant. Like all other employees in the Department, he was notified Friday afternoon of the overtime to be worked on the following Monday.

Reasonable Excuse

It is recognized that an employer must use his right to compel overtime in a reasonable manner. Not only is advance notice normally required, a problem not involved in this dispute, but also an employer must accept a reasonable excuse when an employee refuses to work overtime. Kemp told Mills that he could not work overtime on Monday because of "personal business." When asked to explain the nature of his personal business, the Grievant refused to elaborate.

In this regard, the Arbitrator fully understands an employee's right to privacy. An employer may not arbitrarily inquire into the employee's personal affairs or business. Indeed, in the wake of Watergate, a person's or organization's right to privacy has become a matter of national policy. On the other hand, to hold the Grievant's excuse valid would make it impossible for the Company to require overtime. Any employee would be relieved of the obligation by merely saying he has "personal business."

To resolve the conflict between an employee's right to privacy and the employer's right to compel overtime, an employer may ask the *general nature* of the employee's personal business. For example, if an employee refuses overtime because of a doctor's appointment, the employer would invade the employee's privacy by demanding to know the specific reason for the doctor's appointment. If an employee refuses overtime because of a court appearance, the employer may not inquire into the specific nature of the court appearance. An employer may not inquire into the specific business of an employee when he says that he has an appointment with an attorney.

It is, of course, difficult to draw the precise line between the employee's right to privacy and the employer's allowable right to inquire into an employee's personal affairs. In this matter, common sense and good faith must be demonstrated by the employer and employee. The preceding examples are only illustrative and, of course, do not establish a formula for all situations when an employee refuses to work overtime because of personal business. In any event, it is proper to find that an employee does not offer a reasonable excuse when he merely offers "personal business or affairs" without identifying its *general character*. On this basis, Kemp did not offer a reasonable excuse for his refusal to work overtime on Monday, June 19.

The Issue of Discrimination

So far, therefore, we have determined that the Company has the right to compel overtime; it provided the advance notice required in Article 5, Section 5.10; and the Grievant did not offer a reasonable excuse for his refusal to work the overtime in question. What remains is to determine whether the penalty assessed against him should be revoked on the basis of discrimination. Recall that Kemp raised this argument in his grievance, charging that other employees have refused overtime and received no penalty. Based upon the testimony of Union witnesses, to be considered below, Union Counsel says:

It is not fair to Kemp to be penalized when in the past this was not done with other employees who refused overtime. The daily practice of the Company shows that employees were not reprimanded or disciplined when they turned down overtime. Union witnesses testified that they frequently refused overtime and were not reprimanded or disciplined.

Challenge to Company's Authority

As a threshold observation in this respect, it is material that Kemp did not use discrimination or past practice as an excuse when he was asked to work overtime on June 19. Mills testified that Kemp told him that the Company could not work him more than 40 hours per week. On the next day, June 20, Kemp testified, he told the General Foreman that the Labor Agreement does not require overtime. In this light, it appears that the Grievant was challenging the right of the Company to compel overtime under the Labor Agreement. As a result, he assumed a risk by his refusal to work overtime. At the time of his conversations with Mills and the General Foreman, what was in the Grievant's mind was not refusal based upon discrimination or past practice, but his conviction that the Company did not have the contractual right to force him to work overtime.

If Kemp believed that the Company was without such authority, he should have complied with the Company's order to work overtime on Monday and then filed his grievance challenging such Company authority. We are all aware of a fundamental principle of labor relations that when an employer gives an employee a direct order—"Work, then grieve."

Apparently Kemp's personal business was not complicated in nature, whatever it was, because he told us that he had the problem cleared up by Tuesday. He was directed to work only one and one-half hours of overtime, until 5 P.M. Could he not have resolved his problem after 5 P.M.? Why was it crucial for him to leave precisely at 3:30 P.M.? Though we do not know the general character of his personal business, from the facts in evidence it is plausible that he could have worked the 90 minutes of overtime and then filed a grievance alleging that the Company was without authority to compel overtime. If he had followed this precedent course of action, he would not have received the reprimand, and would have preserved his right to challenge the Company, and preceeded without apparent prejudice in resolving his personal business.

Analysis of Union Witnesses' Testimony

In any event, let us deal with the Grievant's charge of discrimination based upon the testimony offered by Union witnesses. In general, the latter said that they frequently turned down overtime and were not reprimanded or otherwise disciplined. On the other hand, there are some elements in their declarations which tend to distinguish past overtime experience from the circumstances of this case. Over the objection of the Company, the Arbitrator permitted Oliver, Machine

Shop employee, to testify about an overtime experience that occurred after the date of the instant grievance. He said that on Friday afternoon, December 8, 1981, his Foreman requested him to work overtime on the following Saturday. Oliver refused, and was not reprimanded. However, the Company could not compel Oliver to work overtime on that Saturday because he was not asked until Friday afternoon. Recall that the Company may not require overtime unless it gives at least 24 hours' advance notice. Oliver, unlike the Grievant, was not given the necessary advance notice. Oliver also testified that before June 19, 1981, the date upon which the Grievant refused to work the overtime in question, his Foreman, Tabor, frequently asked him to work overtime, and he refused without penalty. However, he said: "Usually the foreman would ask me on Friday for Saturday." Once again the Company did not provide him with 24 hours' advance notice, the prerequisite for compulsory overtime. Under these circumstances—when the Company fails to provide at least 24 hours' advance notice—the employee not only is not required to work overtime but also need not furnish a reason for his refusal.

Thus, to the extent that any Union witness testified that he was asked to work overtime without the required advance notice, these instances do not count in the Grievant's attempt to show discrimination.

In addition, some Union witnesses refused overtime without penalty, but they offered a reasonable excuse for the refusal. Rose, another Machine Shop employee, testified that many times, dating back to the 1960s, he refused overtime without penalty. Note, however, his testimony:

> I told my foreman in the 1960s, and told Tabor (his present Foreman) in 1974 that I never work overtime because of my farm.

Normally, work on an employee's farm constitutes a reaonable excuse when overtime is refused and particularly since Rolf, Director of Labor Relations, testified that the Company

> accepts any sort of a reasonable excuse when an employee refuses overtime.

Hill testified that he had been asked to work overtime in the past and refused without reprimand or other discipline. However, he testified:

> I have to pick up my kids at school because my wife works. One time my group worked overtime each day in a week, but I did not. I guess *my foreman knew my situation*, and did not ask me for a reason. (Emphasis supplied)

To the extent that Union witnesses testified that they had furnished reasonable excuses for their refusal, they placed themselves in a different category as compared to the Grievant because he did not offer the Company a reasonable excuse for his failure to work overtime on June 19.*

---

*There was a contradiction in the testimony of Mills and Lee concerning the baby-sitter issue. The Foreman testified that she told him that she could not work Tuesday, June 20 because of a baby-sitter problem. Lee denied that she had offered this excuse, testifying that she merely told the Foreman that she had "things planned for Tuesday." Whatever may be the truth of the matter, the Arbitrator has no basis whatsoever to resolve the contradiction one way or the other. To resolve it to support either the Company's or the Grievant's position would be improper.

Hill and Diltz testified to an overtime situation that occurred in about 1974–75. Before May 15, 1977, the Carpenters' Union represented the bargaining unit. The current Labor Agreement was the first one negotiated between the Company and the instant Union. In any event, the testimony offered by these two employees is material because the same contractual overtime language, including Article 5, Section 5.10, was in the previous contracts. In addition, practices in labor relations are not expunged absent special contractual language just because there is a change in the bargaining agent or in the management or ownership of a firm.

Hill and Diltz testified that in 1974–75 a notice was posted on the bulletin board stating that an employee would be counted as absent between 3:30 P.M. and 7 P.M. should an employee refuse to work overtime. The notice also stated that a sufficient number of absentee slips accumulated by an employee could result in discipline. Apparently, no one was disciplined on the basis of the notice. However, their testimony in this respect is not probative because there is no showing in the record how many times employees refused overtime when the Company directed it or, if they did refuse directed overtime, the evidence does not show whether the Company gave the required advance notice or whether they offered a reasonable excuse if they did refuse.

In short, at least some of the Union testimony does not reflect the circumstances of the instant case. Either employees were not given sufficient advance notice or they offered a reasonable excuse for the refusal to work overtime. As a matter of fact, given the character of the Union witnesses' testimony, it is difficult to pick out evidence that proves conclusively that past practice experience was the same as involved in this dispute. Burns, a Press Room employee, came the closest to relating an overtime experience that parallels the circumstances involved in Kemp's refusal. He said that on Friday, December 16, 1981, his Foreman scheduled his entire Department for overtime starting on the following Monday. Thus, sufficient advance notice was given. Burns told his Foreman that "I couldn't work overtime any day of the following week." He did not tell his Foreman why he could not work overtime. Thus, like Kemp, Burns did not offer a reasonable excuse. Burns did not work overtime in the following week and was not reprimanded or disciplined.

To prove that the Company surrendered its right to compel overtime, the Union was required to show frequent and regular employee refusals to work overtime under exactly the same circumstances as Kemp's refusal. A careful search of the record does not demonstrate the necessary proof to establish such a past practice. Even if we give the Union the benefit of the doubt, at best there may have been a few refusals such as testified to by Burns. However, one, two, or a few instances do not add up to a past practice as this concept is used in labor relations. To fall within the scope of past practice, an event must occur frequently and regularly. Clearly, the record does not demonstrate frequent and regular refusals such as Kemp's refusal of the overtime in question. It is true that the evidence shows that employees frequently turned down overtime, but under circumstances distinguishable from the Grievant's refusal. As stated, either sufficient advance notice was not given or the employees offered a reasonable excuse.

Since the evidence does not establish that the Company surrendered its right to compel overtime on the basis of past practice, it had the authority to compel the Grievant to work overtime. On these grounds, the Grievant's defense of his conduct based upon discrimination is not acceptable.

Conclusions

Should Kemp's grievance be granted, the Arbitrator would wipe out the Company's right to compel overtime. In the final analysis, this is what the Union really attempts to gain from these proceedings. Earlier it was abundantly demonstrated that the Company has such authority under the clear terms of the Labor Agreement. Given the terms of the material contractual language, it would be a massive and unpardonable error on the Arbitrator's part to deny to the Company a clear contractual right. If the Union believes that overtime should be voluntary, it must gain that objective at the bargaining table and not in arbitration.

Neither is the Grievant's claim that he suffered discrimination supported by the evidence. The record does not show that as a matter of past practice the Company surrendered its right to compel overtime. It does not demonstrate that employees refused overtime regularly and frequently under the same circumstances as the Grievant's refusal. Thus, when the Company ordered Kemp to work overtime, it had the contractual authority to do so.

In addition, for reasons expressed earlier, the Grievant had the obligation to accept the overtime and then file a grievance alleging that the Company did not have the right to compel overtime. Rather than following the commonly accepted labor relations principle—"Work, then grieve"—Kemp challenged the Company's authority and refused the assignment.

Finally, it is material that Kemp only received a written reprimand. He suffered no loss of pay, only receiving a warning notice that under proper circumstances the Company may require employees to work overtime. That the warning accomplished its purpose is made clear by his working overtime on the day after he refused the assignment. It should be noted that employees involved in other arbitration cases have received much stiffer penalties for refusal to work overtime, even discharge. In short, given Kemp's offense, the Company properly reprimanded him for proper cause and enforced its right to compel overtime in a reasonable manner.

Questions

1 At times arbitrators do not follow the "Work, then grieve" principle, revoking discipline when an employee does not comply with a supervisor's order. For example, an employee may properly refuse to follow an order when a job assignment could endanger the employee's physical safety. Explain why the arbitrator held that Kemp should have followed the principle in this case.

2 How did the arbitrator deal with the grievant's contention that the company discriminated against him under the circumstances of this dispute?

3 Suppose that Section 5.10 was *not* in the labor agreement. Under this condition would you, serving as the arbitrator, uphold the discipline assessed against the grievant? Explain your answer.

4 Other than the examples supplied by the arbitrator, indicate additional circumstances where an employer would improperly invade an employee's privacy by demanding a reasonable excuse for refusal to work overtime.

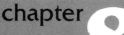

Economic Supplements under Collective Bargaining

The incorporation of employee supplementary economic benefits—from paid vacations to pension plans—in collective bargaining contracts is widespread throughout American industry. Such benefits have increased dramatically since World War II, both in their value to the employee and in their variety. And, since these supplements to the basic wage rate are now commonly equivalent to over 37 percent of payroll, it is understandable that some managers express hostility when the once accepted designation *"fringe* benefits" is used to describe this area. Nor does the adjective seem particularly applicable when it is realized that such benefits were costing employers close to $500 billion annually by the mid-1980s. Habits are not easily broken, however, and "fringe" will probably still be utilized even when the benefits approach one-half of payroll, as—since they have been steadily rising at the rate of about 1 percent of payroll per year for many years now—they most likely will do within the next decade and one-half.[1]

Many of these benefits are not new to personnel administration, and indeed, some of them were introduced by employers on a unilateral basis before the advent of unionism. However, such benefits now play a much more important part in labor relations than was ever the case in the past. By the end of World War II, many unions had succeeded in bargaining vacations and holidays for their members; the federal government's regulation of wages during 1942–1945 had proven influential in guiding the labor negotiators in this direction. And in the four decades since the war, many other benefits have found their way into labor documents with

---

[1] The percentage of payroll figures are, it is true, generally a bit less impressive for smaller firms. The figures above pertain to large- and medium-sized firms, the only ones studied intensively thus far.

increasing regularity and employer largesse: pension plans; various health insurance arrangements, including life insurance and hospital and other medical benefits; accidental death and dismemberment payments; and dismissal and reporting pay, among many others. Supplementary unemployment benefit plans, a somewhat more recent major collective bargaining issue, also may properly be regarded as a supplement to the basic wage rate.

Beyond all this, many labor agreements contain special benefits, ones that are either absolutely unique or at least not widely prevailing as guaranteed benefits in the working world. Resort hotels in Hawaii grant free use of their golf courses to their International Longshoremen's and Warehousemen's Union members. Clerks at a West Coast supermarket chain can receive almost unlimited use of free psychiatric services and so, too, under certain conditions, can every member of their families. Some employers provide workers with help in filling out their income tax returns; others emphasize tuition subsidization for college-attending children of employees. Some unionists—Steelworkers conspicuously among them—are eligible for comprehensive alcohol- and drug-addiction rehabilitation, going well beyond the token benefits offered in many other employment settings. Day care for employee children has become more common as a contractually granted benefit. And many teachers can receive additional compensation for helping out in extracurricular activities. *(Case 6, at the end of this chapter, is an unusual one in that the teacher involved was not permitted to give this benefit up!)*.

Prepaid group legal plans, too, have taken root in recent years. An estimated four thousand such arrangements now offer free routine services such as uncontested divorces, wills, title transfers, and help with landlord–tenant problems, and some even provide free counsel for (limited) criminal offenses. It is possible that such a benefit will burgeon in the years ahead: In the recent past, the UAW has implemented legal services plans with both General Motors and Chrysler, and UAW activities have, of course, often proven influential in generating trends. Many benefit trend watchers predict that such plans, which generally cost employers only several cents an hour per worker, will become as commonplace as health insurance and pensions before many more years have elapsed. On the other hand, even a free will may prove to have limited appeal as compared with, for example, more money in the pay envelope. And, in any event, this chapter focuses on the more currently widespread and thus presently costly economic supplements.

PENSION PLANS

Private pensions began to be a labor relations issue of some consequence in the late 1940s. A definite boost was given such plans by the U.S. Supreme Court's 1949 *Inland Steel* decision that employers could not refuse to bargain with their unions over this issue.[2] Managers still did not have to grant such employee benefits,

---

[2] *Inland Steel Co.* v. *United Steelworkers of America*, 336 U.S. 960 (1949).

but they could no longer legally dismiss union demands for them out of hand.

Other factors, particularly in more recent years, have also contributed to the growth of the pension plans. One of them is the modest level of benefits provided by the Social Security System. Another is the population's increased longevity and a commensurate lengthening of the number of postretirement years. Still a third, it is generally agreed, is the spread of union-spawned seniority and related provisions in labor contracts, making it all but impossible to terminate employment for older bargaining unit members *except* by pension.

Perhaps above all, there has been a growing managerial awareness—on the part of nonunion employers as well as unionized ones—of an organizational obligation to employees after their retirement. The typical present-day employer is willing to consider pensions a part of normal business costs, something to be charged against revenues in much the same way that, say, insurance of plant and machinery is so charged.

Not that there is unanimity on details. Some managers insist that employees help pay for their pensions by making regular contributions to the pension fund during their working years. There are, understandably, wide differences of opinion among executives as to appropriate payment levels for pension plans. Some employers argue that their lack of financial resources rules out the establishment of any pension plan even though they would otherwise be happy to have one. Many smaller employers (in particular) have also cited the long-term character and unknown aspects of pension costs as justification for strengthening other fringe benefits in lieu of pensions. And most, but not quite all, managements have never even remotely thought of extending pension privileges to the part-time work force.

All of these facts notwithstanding, the moral imperative of providing some kind of private pension to the retired full-time employee if at all possible is no longer seriously questioned by any responsible management at the labor relations bargaining table.

From a modest beginning in 1946, pension plans in American industry have grown phenomenally. Roughly 10 million employees were covered by the end of the 1940s, but this figure had doubled to 20 million by 1960, and the most recent Bureau of Labor Statistics information shows some 30 million wage and salary workers, about half of them in the ranks of unions, currently encompassed by private pensions.

In sheer dollar amounts, virtually all pension plan benefits have also risen dramatically in recent years. But, in contrast to the growth of the plans themselves, this latter fact can be quite misleading when one takes the considerable inflation of many recent years into account. On the average, UAW monthly pensions in the automobile industry increased 27 percent to $700 between 1973 and 1979, for example, but the cost of living rose far more than this, by 47 percent in the same period, and retirees thus suffered significantly in terms of real pension receipts. A study made by the authoritative Bureau of Labor Statistics of 131 plans found that, in response to both the inflation and the requirements of the 1974 Employee Retirement Income Security Act (to be discussed below), the average projected pension increased 20.6 percent between late 1974 and early 1978, but that, since the Consumer Price Index rose 23 percent over this period, real benefits actually dipped a bit.[3]

Even the $1,500 monthly pension negotiated a few years ago by a Teamster local in New Jersey for all members who had twenty-five years of service and chose to retire at age 65—possibly the highest industrial pension in the nation—does not seem particularly lavish in view of all this, and it is at any rate clear that the average retiree is not in an enviable situation given what inflation can do.

Major Pension Features

Until national legislation banning mandatory retirement before age 70 went into effect, on January 1, 1979, in an amendment to the Age Discrimination in Employment Act of 1967, most plans set the required age for retirement at 65. The change was not expected to make much practical difference, however, since as a general statement the heavy preponderance of employees have not chosen to work to age 70 if allowed even minimally acceptable pensions prior to that. Certainly, this is the present belief of the U.S. Department of Labor, which recently estimated that only about 200,000 more people annually would continue working as a result of the legal change.

The Labor Department was aware, in making this estimate, that of the 41,631 workers who retired from federal positions in a recent year for reasons other than disability, only 1,773 had to be terminated at the (existing) federal age limit of 70.[4] Possibly, it also knew of such other relevant situations as that at the Northrop Corporation, where each year only about one in fifty employees has chosen to stay on beyond age 65, and that at Chicago's Bankers Life and Casualty Company, which has had voluntary retirement for over three decades but where only 3.5 percent of the 3,900 home-office employees are over 65.[5]

Nor have many unions—particularly in manufacturing (where the size of recent-year unemployment figures has been of significant influence) done anything to discourage voluntary early retirement. In fact, labor organizations have increasingly sought to open up further job opportunities in the face of automation and changing market demands even before age 65, and some provision for this benefit is now made under the pension stipulation of many contracts.

The UAW, for example, has for several years now prided itself on a "30 and out" policy in the automobile industry, whereby workers can retire as early as age 47, with relatively generous monthly pensions. In a typical year, approximately 70 percent of these UAW members do choose retirement as soon as they can gain it, and the average retirement age at General Motors is a not very ancient 59.[6]

Under the steel industry arrangement, there is a variant of "30 and out," but

[3] *Monthly Labor Review*, 102, No. 4 (April 1979), 32.
[4] *Business Week*, June 19, 1978, p. 75.
[5] *Ibid.*
[6] *Ibid.*, p. 74. In recent years of rampant inflation, however, the percentage of voluntary retirements is understandably lower: Working still yields a good deal more income than any pensions for UAW members.

the Steelworker approach has been to encourage at least skilled workers in that sector (always at a premium) to stay on at a minimum until age 62, and those who choose to retire prior to that age receive reduced benefits in return for their decision. The steel industry benefit reduction system for voluntary early retirement is more common than the automobile situation of having identical benefits for all workers, regardless of age, subject to their meeting minimum service requirements. But contracts in the clothing, maritime, and mining industries—to name only three of a fast-growing number—have adopted the latter arrangement. If workers in these industries meet most often thirty years of service (and invariably at least 20), they have nothing to gain in the way of pension size by staying on (although, again, soaring prices could always be a greater dissuader to those otherwise tempted to leave the payroll).

Under plans that provide for pension benefits to workers who have been permanently disabled and who have not reached the normal retirement age, it is also usually required that such workers have a specified number of years of service with the company to be eligible for such benefits. Under many of these contracts, ten to fifteen years of service is required before an employee may expect to draw pension benefits because of permanent disability.

The question of who is to finance the pension plans—the employer alone or the employer and the employee jointly—has been an important issue ever since collectively bargained pensions attained prominence, and it continues to pose problems at the bargaining table. At the present time, in about three out of four plans, employers finance the entire cost of retirement benefits (and the plans involved are therefore called "noncontributory," in recognition of the lack of expense to the employee); the remainder are financed jointly (and thus on a "contributory" basis). Jointly financed plans remain common in some manufacturing industries (notably textiles, petroleum, and chemicals), as well as in the worlds of finance and teaching.

Arguments can be, and are, erected in favor of either position. In favor of noncontributory plans, it is frequently contended that (1) the average employee cannot afford to contribute; (2) the employee is already making a contribution to another retirement program, that of Social Security, and enough is enough; (3) the employer should exclusively bear the costs of pensions because these are no less important than depreciation expenses for machinery and plant; (4) the return to the management from the plan in terms of lower labor turnover rates (the pension acting as an inducement to stay) and increased efficiency justifies the cost; and (5) employers can charge their pension plan contributions against taxes, whereas employees cannot.

On the other, or procontributory plan, side of the ledger, proponents claim that (1) since there is a definite limit to the economic obligations that employers can assume at a given time, employee contributions ensure better pensions; (2) employees will appreciate plans to which they contribute, as they might not appreciate the noncontributory arrangement, and hence the contributory plan is psychologically better for the organization in terms of heightened morale and loyalty; and (3) when workers contribute, they have a stronger claim to their pensions as a matter of right.

Most employees and their unions, having heard both sets of arguments, have preferred the first one.

Whether the plan is contributory or noncontributory, of course, it must be financed so that the benefits that have been promised upon retirement are indeed available at that point. If the money is simply not there, or if the employer is unwilling for whatever reason to make the counted-upon disbursement, it is of small consolation to the retiree that the plan was a noncontributory one. The same statement, needless to say, applies if the employer vanishes from the scene by virtue of going out of business.

Funded pension plans—those in which pensions are paid from separated funds, isolated from the general assets of the firm and earmarked specifically for retirees—ensure that the benefits are in fact guaranteed. *Unfunded* plans depend strictly upon employer ability and willingness to comply with the pension plan provisions by making pension payments out of current funds. As such, the latter can offer no assurances at all.

Vesting refers to the right of workers to take their credited pension entitlements with them should their employment terminate before they reach the stipulated retirement age. The member of the organization's labor force who is permanently laid off or who quits without possessing a nonforfeitable vesting right is obviously no better off than the employee who has stayed all the way to stipulated retirement only to find that lack of appropriate funding has made the pension a cruel hoax.

As pensions spread in the 1950s and 1960s, improvements in both of these areas took place. Only 7 percent of all workers covered by private pension systems belonged to unfunded plans even as early as 1960,[7] and even fewer did a decade later. As for vesting, where only 25 percent of the plans studied by the Department of Labor in 1952 allowed it, 67 percent of those surveyed eleven years later did so, however much the vesting privilege remained qualified,[8] and by common estimate the figure exceeded 80 percent by the 1970s.

Yet a blatant amount of abuse with respect to private pension plans had nonetheless developed by the 1970s. Many employees who had counted on a pension simply, if tragically, did not receive the benefit. Hearings held by the Senate Labor Committee at this time disclosed that in some cases funded pension plans had been plundered or misused by their administrators. Another abuse involved the discharge or permanent layoff of employees just before they would have (having qualified under age and service requirements) been entitled to vesting. Situations such as these were unfortunately widespread.

Even more often, however, neither plunder nor specific immorality was involved, but rather the simple inability of the employer to pay. Such a case was

---

[7] *Monthly Labor Review*, 86, No. 12 (December 1963), 1414.
[8] *Ibid.*, 87, No. 9 (September 1964), 1014.

that of the Studebaker Corporation, which permanently stopped its operations in the United States in 1964 and because it had never had a funded plan was unable to offer its many terminated employees the pension benefits established in the Studebaker collective bargaining contracts. As one source could quite justifiably say about the general situation, "In all too many cases, the pension promise shrinks to this: 'If you remain in good health and stay with the same company until you are sixty-five years old, and if the company is still in business, and if your department has not been abolished, and if you haven't been laid off for too long a period, and if there is enough money in the [pension] fund, and if that money has been prudently managed, you will get a pension.' "[9]

There were too many contingencies in all of this for Congress to ignore, given the importance of the subject to so many, and in late 1974 it enacted a major piece of legislation (the Employee Retirement Income Security Act [ERISA]) that was designed to deal with the obstacles to pension payment.

To deal with the abuse involving the age and service requirements, ERISA provides that the employer must select one of three methods for vesting. Under one option, pension rights are vested in the employee starting with 25 percent after five years of service and increasing with additional years of service until the pension is fully vested after fifteen years of service. The second choice is to provide 100 percent vesting after ten years of service. The third method, called the "Rule of 45," provides that an employee with at least five years of service have a 50 percent vesting right when his or her age and service add up to 45. The percentage of vesting increases annually by 10 percentage points thereafter, until the 100 percent figure is reached after fifteen years of service.

So that funds will be available upon employees' retirement, the law requires that all newly adopted pension plans be fully funded to pay the benefits due retired employees. For those plans in existence before the law became effective, employers have the obligation to fund for past service obligations over a period of specified time. To ensure further that employees would receive the pension benefits upon retirement, the 1974 law established a Public Benefit Guaranty Corporation, a government agency that in 1983 guaranteed pensions up to a maximum of $1,517 per month should a company go out of business and/or terminate the plan. To raise the necessary funds to provide the guarantee, employers were initially required to pay annually $1 per worker for single-employer plans (the requirement is currently up to $2.60) and 50 cents for multiemployer plans. Other safeguards, involving the placing of a fiduciary responsibility on the administrators of pension plans, the reporting and disclosure annually to the Secretary of Labor of financial information showing the operation of the plan, and the right of each employee each year to receive information concerning his or her vesting and accumulated benefit status, are included in the law.

ERISA may not have deserved the description given it by one of its sponsors,

[9] James H. Schulz and Guy Carrin, *Pension Aspects of the Economics of Aging: Present and Future Roles of Private Pensions* (Washington, D.C.: United States Senate Special Committee on Aging, 1970), p. 39.

Senator Jacob K. Javits of New York, when it was enacted. He called it "the greatest development in the life of the American worker since Social Security," and other developments, including many of the ones directly involving labor–management relations and thus outlined in earlier portions of this book, might strike the student as having been even "greater." It is difficult to arbitrate in these matters of taste.

It is safe to say, however, that the law has already gone a long way toward protecting employee interests. Over 600,000 pension plans, encompassing the 30 million workers noted above and a staggering $250 billion in assets, are now covered by ERISA. The scandal-ridden $1.4 billion Central States Pension Fund of the International Brotherhood of Teamsters has essentially been cleaned up and more improvements—inspired by the Labor Department—will undoubtedly come. The federal standards have certainly given pension fund trustees a better sense of what their responsibilities are, and the vesting and guarantee features of ERISA have also worked in no small measure in favor of workers.

The impact of the law has, it is true, increased the cost of pension programs and thus in some cases led to smaller benefits. A smaller but guaranteed pension, however, is better than no pension at all for an employee who has devoted all or most of a working life to a company.

VACATIONS WITH PAY

Vacations with pay for wage earners also constitute, as was noted earlier, a comparatively new development in American history. Prior to World War II, only a fraction of workers covered by collective bargaining contracts received pay during vacation periods, and, at that time, other employees were permitted time off only if they were willing to sacrifice pay. By contrast, vacations with pay are now a standard practice in practically every collective bargaining contract, and this has been true for some time. As far back as 1957, in fact, a Department of Labor study of 1,813 agreements, each covering more than 1,000 workers, found that only 8 percent of these contracts did not provide some form of paid vacation;[10] today, the employer not furnishing this type of pay for time not worked is a true individualist.

In addition to the influence of the National War Labor Board's wage controls in spearheading the spread of paid vacations, a growing recognition by employers, employees, and unions of the benefits of such a policy (in terms of worker health, personal development, and productivity) has contributed to the growth. And as job security considerations have become more important over the past decade, employee representatives have also seen in vacations (as they have in holidays) a way to preserve existing jobs. This has been especially true in such troubled industries as automobiles, steel, and rubber, and it has in fact been in these sectors

[10] U.S. Bureau of Labor Statistics, *Paid Vacation Provisions in Major Union Contracts, 1957,* Bulletin No. 1233, June 1958.

that vacations, the most expensive of all payments for time not worked, have received particular priority in the bargaining. Once liberalized there, they have gone on to exert pressures (by their very visibility in these major industries) on other unions, and on nonunion employers who would be just as happy remaining nonunion, to expand them where *they* operate.

One eye-catching vacation experiment, however, has not spread very far. In 1962, the Steelworkers and metal can manufacturers negotiated a "sabbatical" paid vacation of thirteen weeks' duration, allowed all employees with fifteen or more years of service every five years, and the following year the basic steel industry incorporated essentially the same agreement for the senior half of its work force. After two decades, the concept had had no other takers, perhaps because its lavishness in terms of both leisure time and cost to the employer had made it too much of a good thing (and it is now no more—a victim of the bargaining concessions of the 1980s—even in steel). Its very creation, however, says something about vacation appeal.

Paid vacations have thus undergone steady liberalization as a worker benefit. In recent years, an annual five-week vacation (normally requiring twenty years of service or more) has been bargained by the parties in some situations, and while this length of paid leisure time is still enjoyed by less than one-half of all unionists, it is relevant that such a vacation was all but nonexistent until the late 1960s. Six-week vacations for employees with high seniority are, in fact, now beginning to emerge as a vacation entitlement of some visibility, and there are even seven-week vacations at American Metal Climax, Rockwell International, and Boise Cascade and in the rubber industry (among other places). Four-week vacations (usually after at least fifteen years) are today included in 90 percent of all agreements, or more than triple the 1960 frequency. Of more significance to shorter-term workers is the three-week vacation, provided for in over 95 percent of contracts (as against 78 percent in 1960) and most frequently requiring ten years of service (where fifteen years was the modal prerequisite a very few years ago). Virtually all employees, moreover, can count on a two-week vacation after building up five years of seniority, and contracts increasingly allow this length of time off after only one or two years of service. The only stagnation that has occurred is, in fact, in the one-week vacation area: One year of service has entitled most employees to a single week of vacation with pay for well over a decade now, and the next frontier relating to the one-week vacation will probably be its total abolition in favor of the two-week vacation after one year—an arrangement that is even now granted by perhaps as many as one-quarter of all agreements.[11]

In qualifying for vacations, most labor agreements require that an employee must have worked a certain number of hours, days, or months prior to the vacation period, and failure of the employee to comply with such stipulations results in the forfeiture of the vacation benefits. The rate of pay to which the employee is entitled

---

[11] All the information cited in this paragraph is based on data furnished by the Bureau of Labor Statistics, U.S. Department of Labor.

during a vacation is ordinarily computed on the basis of the regular hourly rate, although in a comparatively small number of agreements vacation benefits are calculated on the basis of average hourly earnings over a certain period of time preceding the vacation, and, in some agreements, vacation pay is calculated as a specified percentage of annual earnings; usually this latter figure amounts to between 2.0 and 2.5 percent of the annual earnings.

A problem arises involving the payment of workers who work during their vacation periods. In some contracts—as in the case of the steel and can provisions alluded to previously—the employees have the option of taking the vacation to which they are entitled or of working during this period. Other labor agreements allow the company the option of giving pay *instead of* vacations if production requirements make it necessary to schedule the worker during the vacation period. No less than in the case of the sabbaticals, when employees work during their vacation periods either upon their own or the company's option, the principles upon which paid vacations are based (health, productivity, and so on) are, of course, violated. In any event, the question arises as to how to compensate employees for their vacation time when they work during this period. In most labor agreements, employees under these circumstances are given their vacation pay plus the regular wages they earn in the plant. In a few cases, particularly when the employer schedules work during a vacation period, the wage earned by the employee working during a vacation period is calculated at either time and one-half or double the regular rate. Such earnings are in addition to the employee's vacation pay.

In a majority of contracts, management has the ultimate authority to schedule the vacation period. Under an increasingly large number of agreements, however, the company is required to take into consideration seniority and employee desires. A fairly sizable number of labor agreements permit management to schedule vacations during plant shutdowns.

An additional vacation problem involves the status of employees who are separated from a company before their vacation period. In some collective bargaining agreements, these employees are entitled to accumulated vacation benefits when they leave the employment of companies under certain specified circumstances, such as permament layoff, resignation, and military duty. In a comparatively small number of contracts, workers discharged for cause may also claim vacation benefits. (Exhibit 8-1 is drawn from one current, not atypical, contract.)

HOLIDAYS WITH PAY

Similar to paid vacations, paid holidays for production workers were not a common practice before World War II. When a plant shut down for a legal holiday, the workers simply lost a day of work and were basically no better off than Bob Cratchit, in the employ of Scrooge, on Christmas. And, also as in the case of vacations with pay, the National War Labor Board permitted employers and unions to negotiate labor agreements providing for paid holidays under its wartime wage regulations.

As a result, paid holidays became a common feature in collective bargaining contracts during World War II, and the practice continued after hostilities terminated. At present nearly 100 percent of all labor agreements incorporate some formula for paid holidays, with some construction contracts being the only conspicuous exceptions at this point.

The modal number of such holidays granted in 1983 was ten. There was almost universal agreement among the contracts on at least four of these specific holidays: More than 98 percent allowed paid time off for Independence Day, Labor Day, Thanksgiving, and Christmas. And well over 96 percent of all contracts paid for holidays on New Year's Day and Memorial Day. Wider variation takes place where more than six holidays are sanctioned, but half-days before Thanksgiving, Christmas, and New Year's Day are frequently specified, and in an increasing number of cases some holidays are oriented on an individual basis, such as the employee's birthday, the date on which the employee joined the union (in some Transport Worker contracts), and "personal" days off. Under this latter agreement, the company by definition is not penalized with whatever inefficiencies may result from a plant shutdown, and this is probably the major reason why it has become increasingly popular: Almost 50 percent of all contracts now sanction such an arrangement, up from just under 40 percent as recently as 1980. Many agreements also recognize any of a variety of state and local holidays, ranging from Patriot's Day in Massachusetts to Mardi Gras in parts of the South. Company—and even union—picnics are declared occasions for paid holidays in a somewhat smaller number of contracts.[12] (The Electrical Workers [IUE] at the Newport, Tennessee, plant of Electro-Voice, Inc., may be absolutely unique, however; a few years ago they won as a new paid holiday February 2, Groundhog Day.)

In addition to the trend toward the "personal" holiday, there has been a steady movement toward three-day weekends. The latter owes its genesis to Congress, which in 1968 enacted a Monday Holidays Law, shifting the observance of four holidays (President's Day, the third Monday in February; Memorial Day; Columbus Day; and Veterans Day) to Mondays for employees of the federal government. Not binding on any other employers, there has nonetheless been a decided tendency for the latter to follow suit, frequently in accommodation of union demands, in the years since the congressional action.

A definite shot in the arm to the spread of paid holidays was also effected in 1976, by the so-often-influential UAW. Alarmed by declining employment for automobile workers and buoyed on by its own estimate that production in 1990 would be almost 50 percent higher than in 1976 but that only 5 percent more workers would be needed to yield this higher output ("How long," asked the UAW president, "can we go on providing higher and higher benefits for fewer and fewer workers?"),[13] the union negotiated seven "personal paid holidays" in addition to thirteen existing regular holidays. By this action, which was obviously geared fully

[12] Data from the Bureau of Labor Statistics, U.S. Department of Labor.
[13] *Business Week,* October 25, 1976, p. 116.

EXHIBIT 8-1
Article 7—Vacations

Section 1. Eligibility

1 After one (1) year of continuous service, an employee shall be eligible for vacation benefits as follows:

Service	Time	Vacation Pay at Rates According to Section 2
1 year	2 weeks	80 hours
7 years	3 weeks	120 hours
15 years	4 weeks	160 hours
20 years	5 weeks	200 hours

2 The employee with the greatest seniority in the vacation scheduling group shall have first preference in selection of his vacation. Vacation quotas will be applied by classification, unit or division, and across shifts.

Section 2. Vacation Year

1 The vacation year begins on the anniversary date of employment. Each employee becomes eligible for the revised vacation schedule in his next anniversary date. Vacations must be taken during the year. They are not cumulative.
2 If an employee is ill during his scheduled vacation period and the illness extends beyond his anniversary date, the employee has the option—upon notification to his supervisor, of either being paid for unused vacation or taking this unused vacation prior to returning to work.

Section 3. Emergency Cancellations

1 In case of an emergency the Company may, at its option, require any or all employees to work in lieu of receiving a vacation from work, and in such event an employee shall receive two (2) times his normal base rate for time actually worked. Wherever possible, reasonable advance notice of an emergency will be given to the employee and a Union officer. It is clearly understood any employee who worked the emergency time shall not be required to work any other emergency work that may occur within their anniversary period and shall have the right to vacation selection by seniority preference or elect to take vacation pay in lieu of time off.
2 In the event an employee must work due to the emergency, the Company shall reimburse the employee for provable losses of deposits, license fees, and reservations.
3 In the event a cancellation exceeds the anniversary date, employee will have an additional sixty (60) days in which to take vacation. In any case an employee must take all vacations or forfeit the remainder.

Section 4. Vacations During Planned Shutdowns

1 It is the Company intent to schedule planned maintenance shutdowns during the summer months whenever feasible in order to provide employees an opportunity to schedule summer vacations. The Company shall post its intended shutdown schedule on or before March 1.

2 Employees, in affected units, who do not schedule vacations for the shutdowns shall be assigned according to the temporary transfer language.

3 These provisions shall not be construed to limit the Company's right to schedule planned maintenance shutdowns at any other time.

Section 5. Approval

1 All vacations must be scheduled in increments of one full week except that employees with at least three weeks' vacation eligibility may schedule up to one week of their vacation in one-two-or three day increments with advance approval.

2 A vacation scheduling list will be posted on or about January 15 of each year. Final vacations will be awarded according to plantwide seniority within the vacation selection group on March 31. The vacation scheduling period shall cover the full payroll weeks beginning in April through year end. The Company will schedule vacations in the first quarter on a first-come, first-served basis. The vacation quota shall not be less than 10 percent.

3 All requests for one day vacations must be made in writing to the immediate supervisor at least 48 hours in advance and not more than thirty (30) days in advance. The request will be honored providing that the operation in any work area is not seriously affected.

4 If an employee is absent due to an emergency beyond his control, he may request on his first day back, vacation time for the absence using only those single day vacation days allotted to him. All answers to emergency vacation requests will be made by the end of the Division Manager's second scheduled shift following the day the request is made. (Failure to comply on a timely basis will result in automatic approval).

Section 6. Vacation Pay upon Retirement or Termination

Upon retirement or termination, employees will be paid for vacation earned during the period worked beyond their anniversary date in accordance with the following formula—calendar days between anniversary and retirement date divided by 365 days multiplied by normal vacation benefits and defined in Article 7 of the present Agreement.

Section 7. Vacation Pay upon Death

The estate of a deceased employee will be paid for all vacation earned during the period worked beyond his anniversary date in accordance with the following formula—calendar days between anniversary and date of death divided by 365 days multiplied by normal vacation benefits as defined in Article 7 of the present Agreement.

to job security and not directed a whit toward increased leisure time per se, the UAW claimed to have created 11,000 new jobs just at General Motors alone. It expected that in future bargaining (not only its own but, by a process of coercive comparison, the bargaining of other unions) such acts of creation would be expanded.

Most labor agreements place certain obligations upon employees who desire to qualify for paid holidays, with the common objective in this respect being that of minimizing absenteeism. The most frequently mentioned such requirement is that an employee must work the last scheduled day before and the first scheduled day after a holiday. The obligation is waived when the employee does not work on the day before or after the holiday because of illness, authorized leave of absence, jury duty, death in the family, or some other justifiable reason. Under some collective bargaining relationships, illness must be proved by a doctor's certificate, by nurse visitation, or by some other device. *(Case 7 deals with an employee's eligibility for holiday pay when absent from work on his first scheduled workday after a holiday.)*

Production requirements and emergency situations at times require that employees work on holidays, and such circumstances raise the problem of rates of pay for work on these days. About three-quarters of all labor agreements provide for double-time for work on holidays, and a small number of contracts now call for triple-time. In the continuous operation industries, such as hotel, restaurant, and transportation sectors, labor agreements frequently substitute another full day off with pay for a holiday on which an employee worked.

An additional problem involves payment for holiday time when the holiday falls on a day on which the employee would not ordinarily work. For example, if a plant does not normally work on Saturdays and if in a particular year July 4 (a paid holiday under the collective bargaining agreement) falls on a Saturday, the question arises as to whether employees are entitled to holiday pay. Another aspect of the same general problem involves a paid holiday falling during an employee's vacation period. Some unions claim that pay for holidays constitutes a kind of vested benefit to employees, regardless of the calendar week on which the holiday occurs. Thus, if the holiday falls on a regular nonworkday, some unions ask that another day be designated as the holiday or that the employee be given a day's wages; or if the holiday falls during an employee's vacation period, that the employee receive another day's paid vacation or wages for the holiday. The opposing view holds that payment for holidays falling on a day on which employees do not regularly work violates the basic principle underlying paid holidays, which is protection of employees from loss of wages. Many labor agreements reflect the thinking of the labor unions on this issue and designate, for example, another day off with pay if a holiday falls on a nonworkday, but a large number of labor agreements do not treat the problem one way or the other, and frequently because of the nature of the language establishing holidays with pay, controversies in this respect are settled in arbitration.

NEGOTIATED HEALTH INSURANCE PLANS

Health insurance plans are now a common feature of collective bargaining contracts. These plans provide for one or more of the following: life insurance or death benefits; accidental death and dismemberment benefits; accident and sickness benefits; and cash or services covering hospital, surgical, maternity, and medical care. Recently the boundaries of the package have been extended to such areas as major medical insurance (often defraying all such expenses up to 80 percent of their total), dental insurance, and psychiatric treatment benefits. The vast majority of workers under collective bargaining contracts are covered, although in widely varying degrees, by some or all parts of this overall insurance mechanism.

A number of factors provide the basis for the spread of insurance plans under collective bargaining. Insurance programs were also a major fringe issue in the period of wage control during World War II, although to a far smaller extent than were vacations and holidays. Many employers and unions have, moreover, increasingly recognized that industrial workers—particularly with health costs rising rapidly in recent years—are not prepared to meet the risks covered by such plans. The Internal Revenue Service has also given incentive to the spread of such insurance, by permitting employers who contribute to these programs to deduct payments as a business expense for tax purposes, where such plans conform to the standards of law for tax relief. In addition, group insurance permits purchasing economies not available to individuals. Finally, the fact that the Social Security program has not provided protection for most risks covered by these insurance plans has made the private insurance system a widely sought one.

Today's typical bargained health and welfare package is of no small dimensions. There is a strong likelihood that it includes life insurance for an amount approximating twice the employee's annual salary; disability and sickness benefits of at least $200 weekly for six months; semiprivate hospital room and hospital board for as long as ninety days, together with such add-ons as drugs and medicines, X-ray examinations, and operating-room expenses (under either Blue Cross or a private insurance company plan); surgical expenses up to a $2,000 maximum for contingencies not covered by workmen's compensation legislation; and coverage for the employee's dependents as well as himself or herself for all or most of these benefits. And, as in the cases of pensions, vacations, and holidays, these emoluments are continuing their own process of liberalization, with discernible trends in recent years involving an increase in the amount and duration of the benefits; the extension of the benefits to retired workers, as well as to those dependents not yet covered; defrayal of the expenses of at least some medically related drugs; and the added protection for catastrophic illnesses and accidents, and addition of dental and mental health benefits cited previously. *(Case 8 involves an unusual problem relating to a group life insurance program.)*

There has been a commensurately strong trend toward exclusive employer financing of the health benefit package: 21 percent of all unionized employers paid the full cost in 1949; roughly 40 percent did so in 1956;[14] and well over two-thirds currently pay all expenses for the greatly enlarged package of today. With the continuing union emphasis on health expense defrayal, no reversal of this trend seems to lie on the horizon.

DISMISSAL PAY

Unlike all the wage supplements discussed above, dismissal, or "severance," pay is still not a common product of collective bargaining. According to Bureau of Labor Statistics information, only about 30 percent of all contracts provide such a benefit at the present time and this figure portrays a standstill in the growth of dismissal pay, since two decades ago some 30 percent of the agreements studied by the bureau also did so. And on an industrywide basis, the practice remains largely confined to contracts negotiated by the Steelworkers, Auto Workers, Communications Workers, Ladies' Garment Workers, and Electrical Workers—although many sectors of the newspaper and railroad industries also have such plans.

Dismissal pay provisions normally limit payments to workers displaced because of technological change, plant merger, permanent curtailment of the company's operations, permanent disability, or retirement before the employee is entitled to a pension. Workers discharged for cause and employees who refuse another job with the employer normally forfeit dismissal pay rights, as do workers who voluntarily quit a job.

The amount of payment provided for in dismissal pay arrangements varies directly with the length of service of the employee. The longer the service, the greater the amount of money. Ordinarily, a top limit is placed upon the amount that an employee can receive. Although labor agreements vary in respect to the payment formula, as a general rule low-service workers receive one week's wages for each year of service prior to dismissal, with higher than proportional allowances for high-service employees (up to 60 weeks' pay, for example, for fifteen or more years of service and as high as 105 weeks' pay for workers with twenty-five or more years).

A problem involving dismissal pay occurs when an employee is subsequently rehired by the company. There is little uniformity in collective bargaining contracts relative to the handling of this problem. Actually, a large number of labor agreements that provide for dismissal pay are silent on whether employees must make restitution to the company upon being rehired or whether they may keep the money paid to them when their employment was originally terminated. Some agreements, however, specifically provide that such employees must return the money; for example, one telephone industry collective bargaining contract stipulates that such employees must repay to the company any termination payment, either in a lump

[14] U.S. Department of Labor, Office of Welfare and Pension Plans, *Welfare and Pension Plan Statistics, 1960* (Washington, D.C.: Government Printing Office, 1963), pp. 3–4.

sum or through payroll deduction at a rate of not less than 10 percent each payroll period until the full amount is paid.

Since the dismissal provision is designed to cushion the effects of employment termination through technological change, merger, and cessation of business (as well as through involuntary retirement due to personal health misfortunes), it is logical to conclude that this benefit, too, will spread in the years ahead despite its plateau in recent years. The acceleration of technological business operations changes beginning in the 1950s and continuing through the 1960s was itself responsible for a considerable increase in the dismissal pay statistics in those years; only 10 percent of labor agreements had such a provision in 1949.[15] Given the continuing presence of these causative factors, there is little reason to believe that the spread of dismissal pay has run its course.

REPORTING PAY

Under the provisions of over 90 percent of the collective bargaining contracts currently in force, employees who are scheduled to work, and who do not have instructions from the employer *not* to report to their jobs, are guaranteed a certain amount of work for that day or compensation instead of work. Issues involved in the negotiation of reporting pay arrangements are the amount of the guarantee and the rate of compensation, the amount of notice required for the employer to avoid guaranteed payment, the conditions relieving the employer of the obligation to award reporting pay, and the conditions under which such pay must be forfeited by employees.

Labor agreements establish a variety of formulas for the calculation of the amount of the guarantee. Reporting pay ranges from a one-hour guarantee to a full day. About 60 percent of labor contracts dealing with this issue provide for four hours' pay; approximately 10 percent call for eight hours' pay. These rates are calculated on a straight-time basis. However, under circumstances where workers are called back to work by management outside of regularly scheduled hours, such employees are frequently compensated at premium rates, ordinarily at time-and-one-half the regular rate. Such reimbursement, popularly styled "call-in" pay, might be awarded a worker, if, for example, the worker is called back to work before having been off for sixteen hours. Thus, if the employee regularly works the first shift and is called back under some emergency condition to work the third shift, the labor agreement might require that there be payment at premium rates. In the event that the employee reports for such work only to find that the company no longer has need for his services, the employee will still be entitled to a certain number of guaranteed hours of pay calculated at premium rates.

In most agreements providing for reporting pay, an employer is relieved of the obligation to guarantee work or to make a cash payment to employees when

---

[15] "Dismissal Pay Provisions in Union Agreements, 1949," *Monthly Labor Review*, 70, No. 4 (April 1950), 384.

the employer notifies employees not to report to work. Contracts frequently provide that such notice must be given employees before the end of the workers' previous shift, although in some cases the employer may be relieved of the obligation by giving notice a certain number of hours before employees are scheduled to work. Eight hours' notice is provided in many labor contracts. In addition, employers are relieved of the obligation to award reporting pay when failure to provide work is due to causes beyond the control of the management. Thus, when work is not available because of floods, fires, strikes, power failures, or "acts of God," in most contracts either employers are fully relieved of the obligation to award reporting pay or the amount of the pay is substantially reduced. Of course, there are many questions of interpretation involved in this situation. For example, does power failure resulting from faulty maintenance relieve the employer of the obligation to award reporting pay? As in so many previous cases, such questions are resolved through the grievance procedure and at times through arbitration.

Under certain circumstances, employees forfeit reporting pay. If employees, for example, fail to keep the company notified of change of address, reporting pay is forfeited under many labor agreements. Other forfeitures might result if employees refuse to accept work other than their own jobs, leave the plant before notice is given to other employees not to report to work, or fail to report to work even though no work is available.

SUPPLEMENTARY UNEMPLOYMENT BENEFIT PLANS

One of the most interesting developments in employee benefits under collective bargaining has been the supplementary unemployment benefit (SUB) plan. This area attracted national attention in 1955 when such a plan was negotiated by the United Automobile Workers and the basic automobile manufacturers, and again in 1956 when the basic steel corporations and the United Steelworkers of America included such a plan in their new labor agreement. There is not much evidence of plans protecting workers' income during periods of unemployment prior to 1955, although a few such arrangements had been established in sectors of the consumer goods industries.

Essentially, SUB plans constitute a compromise between the "guaranteed annual wage" demanded by many unions in the late 1940s and early 1950s, and a continuing management unwillingness to grant such relatively complete job security as the "guaranteed wage" designation would indicate. The plans are geared primarily to two goals: (1) supplementing the unemployment benefits of the various state unemployment insurance systems and (2) allowing further income to still-unemployed workers after state payments have been exhausted. And they implicitly recognize at least one weakness in the state system: Since the states started paying benefits in the late 1930s, the average ratio of these benefits to average wage levels of employees when working has steadily dropped from approximately 40 percent then to somewhat less than 35 percent today.

According to the Bureau of Labor Statistics, half of all manufacturing workers in the United States now have some kind of SUB plan. Almost total coverage has been achieved in the rubber and plastics industries, where 95 percent of all workers have such a benefit. In second place are automobile and aerospace employees, some 82 percent of whom are covered. Other industries now granting significant SUB protection are "primary metals" (steel and aluminum, in particular), where the coverage statistic is 70 percent, and apparel, 61 percent of whose employees have an SUB arrangement. In all of these heavily unionized sectors—as well as in the glass, farm equipment, electrical, can, printing and publishing, petroleum, and maritime industries, where significant but lesser proportions are covered—there are some major elements of similarity.

All SUB plans, for example, require that employees have a certain amount of service with the company before they are eligible to draw benefits; the seniority period varies among the different plans—with a one-year requirement in the basic auto and can contracts contrasting with a five-year prerequisite (the most extreme) in a few contracts negotiated by the Oil, Chemical, and Atomic Workers Union. In addition to seniority stipulations, virtually all plans require that the unemployed worker will be willing and able to work. The test in this latter connection is, most often, the registration for work by the unemployed worker with a state unemployment service office; for example, under the automobile plan, workers are not qualified to obtain benefits unless they register for work with the appropriate state office and do not refuse to accept a job deemed suitable under such a state system. Beyond this, the plans invariably limit benefits to workers who are unemployed because of layoff resulting from a reduction in the work force by the company. Workers who are out of work because of discipline, strikes, or "acts of God" cannot draw benefits. Nor can workers do so whose curtailment of employment is attributable to government regulation, or to public controls over the amount or nature of materials or products that the company uses or sells.

Under the most prevalent type of SUB agreement, all employees (including those just hired) start to acquire credit units at the rate of one-half unit for each week in which they work. When they complete enough service to qualify for the benefits (the one to five years cited in the preceding paragraph), they are officially credited with these units, which they can then trade off for SUB pay when unemployed up to a maximum unemployment duration. Most plans now have set this maximum at fifty-two weeks, and consequently, an automobile or steel industry worker with two years of continuous employment has achieved the maximum amount of SUB coverage. Under about half the current plans, however, the ratio of credit units to weeks of benefit can be increased when the SUB fund falls below a certain level, thereby shortening the duration of benefits. Another common variation is to adjust the ratio in such a way that laid-off workers with long service are protected for a proportionately longer length of time than are shorter-service employees.

Almost universally, employees are entitled to draw benefits only up to the amount of credits that they have established and can receive no benefits—no matter how large the amount of their credits—during the first week of unemployment, a stipulation that is consistent with the one-week waiting period under most state unemployment insurance plans. In addition, credit units are canceled in the event of a willful misrepresentation of facts in connection with the employee's application for either state or SUB income.

Benefit formulas under most layoffs currently set a normal level of payments at 60 to 65 percent of take-home pay (gross pay minus taxes) for all eligible employees. This level comprises payments from both the negotiated benefit plan and the state system. If, for example, a worker whose normal take-home amount is $220 is laid off, a plan calling for 65 percent of his take-home pay allows him $143. And if the worker's state unemployment compensation totals $75 weekly, the SUB plan would then pay him the weekly sum of $68 to make up the difference. There is some debate even among the most rabid advocates of SUB plans as to whether the level should be pushed much beyond this 65 percent figure, for even at this percentage several plans have experienced the ironic situation of workers' preferring total layoff to work. Under UAW contracts in the automobile industry, workers with the minimal years of seniority now actually receive 95 percent of their after-tax wages while on layoff (minus $12.50 for such work-related expenses as transportation, work clothing, and lunches) for up to fifty-two weeks—and almost invariably prefer such a well-remunerated enforced leisure period to their normal work assignments! The same preference for layoff has been amply in evidence in steel, where since 1977 senior workers have been guaranteed SUB payments of up to $235 per week for two full years—and after that either a job at another plant or a pension.

To establish the fund for the payment of supplementary unemployment benefits, most plans require that the employer—who invariably exclusively finances all SUB plans—contribute a certain amount of money per work hour. Many agreements call for a cash contribution of 10 cents per hour, although several go as low as 5 cents and about the same number require 20 or more cents. The payment into this fund most often represents the *maximum* liability of the company, however. Typically, a maximum size of the fund is defined, and company contributions for any one contractual period stop completely when this limit is reached and maintained; the objectives, aside from relieving the companies of too rigorous payments, are to prevent too large an accumulation of fund money and to encourage the companies to stabilize their employment levels. On the other hand, when fund finances fall below the stipulated amount, because of SUB-financed payments the employer must resume payments at the rate required by the plan. In addition, many SUB plans—including most of those negotiated by the Steelworkers—require a further company liability: When the SUB fund reaches the "maximum" level, companies continue to make contributions—first to a Savings and Vacation Plan (to keep its benefits fully current) and then once again to the SUB fund—until approximately $250 per employee is accumulated. Only at this point do company contributions cease.

There seems to be little question that SUB plans not only warded off individual hardship but also maintained a good deal of consumer purchasing power in the United States during the several general recessions of the past quarter-century. Without them, the bleak economies of countless cities and states with a heavy dependence on automobile, steel, rubber, and other mass-production factory employment would undoubtedly have been even bleaker.

But it is also true that such plans are quite vulnerable to long-term plant closings and mass layoffs and that in several SUB industries marked by such circumstances in the 1974–1975 and 1981–1983 recessions, the nation's two worst by far since 1955, the SUB money simply ran out. Hundreds of thousands of automobile and steel workers in particular found themselves receiving only state unemployment compensation when their employers' funds were depleted amid mammoth and long-lasting unemployment. And many of these workers, ultimately exhausting their state entitlements as well, wound up on welfare rolls.

Nonetheless, this outcome should have come as no surprise. SUB was never designed to cope with anything but normal, short-term plant closings and recessions that were relatively mild in their impact. And if the monies had been a major consolation both in lesser post–1955 recessions and in the early stages of the two major ones, it was inevitable that sooner or later the horrendous layoff statistics of the latter would cause the SUB wells to run dry. Although constantly liberalized and always replenished when good times returned, there was no way that such benefits by themselves could offer sufficient protection against large-scale and enduring unemployment, even when incurred by such historically opulent organizations as General Motors and U.S. Steel (to say nothing of their less-affluent competitors). As a valuable (and expensive) segment of the overall employee benefit package, SUB would undoubtedly be of help to the *short-term unemployed* in at least the cyclical industries where it had—not by accident—been established, and perhaps in others where it might be implemented in the years ahead. To make claims that it could do anything more than this, however, would be both unfair to the parties who had negotiated it and cruelly misleading to the employees covered by it.

At any rate, outside of the manufacturing sector, the growth of SUB plans has been far from impressive. Most craft unions continue to greet such a device with total apathy, preferring to substitute other economic improvements for its introduction. And seniority protection appears to have thus far satisfied workers in many noncraft industries sufficiently so that SUB has not become a major union demand there. But the continuing hold of SUB upon the several major industries in which it was originally negotiated, and the constant improvement of SUB allowances there, remain facts that cannot be ignored, either in assessing the creativity of the collective bargaining process or in judging the potential impact of this "guaranteed annual wage" compromise should the employment instabilities that have always characterized most industries in which SUB has now been implemented spread to other parts of the economy. If SUB extensions have not been impressive in total, SUB today does exist in sectors where it is needed—namely, those where job insecurity is the greatest.

SOME FINAL THOUGHTS

If whether or not SUB will ultimately achieve the universality of pension plans, health insurance, paid vacations, and paid holidays (and such various other widespread but considerably lesser benefits as paid time off for obligations stemming from death in the family, jury duty, and voting) thus remains an open question, even in the case of SUB, a broader issue does not. It appears to be all but axiomatic to collective bargaining that *any* benefit, once implemented by the parties, becomes subject through the years to a process of continuous liberalization from the workers' viewpoint. Even supplementary unemployment benefits have undergone this process in the years since 1955, when the automobile industry's maximum of $30 weekly for no more than twenty-six weeks was considered generous.

Many of these benefits continue to allow the same cost advantages to the parties, in terms of both "group insurance" savings and tax minimization, that they did at the time of their various inceptions. Generally tight labor markets have further led employers to amass attractive benefit packages, to be placed in the front window as recruitment devices. And considerations of worker retention, productivity, and pure pride have also undoubtedly stirred both managers and union leaders in their bargaining on these economic supplements. As the new worker needs and wants in the benefit area have become active, the collective bargaining parties have clearly responded to the challenge.

However, neither for the bargaining parties nor for the nation as a whole is this situation an unmixed blessing. Increasing caution from both managements and unions will, in fact, be required as the liberalization process continues, and at least six caveats appear warranted.

In the first place, many improvements in the benefit portfolio automatically present potentially troublesome sources of union grievances that would otherwise be absent. Increasing latitude for employee choice of vacation time, by the incorporation of a "seniority shall govern, so far as possible, in the selection of the vacation period" contractual clause, for example, carries far more potential for controversy than a clear-cut statement reserving vacation scheduling strictly for company discretion. As a second example in this area, with two weeks the maximum vacation allowance, there is usually no question of carry-over credit from year to year; workers are not confronted with "too much of a good thing" and normally do not seek to bank unwanted vacation time until it may be worth more to them. Under a more liberal allowance, however, the question does arise, as many employers and unions can testify, and policies must be both established and consistently adhered to if problems on this score are to be averted.

The list of such newly created grievance possibilities could be extended considerably, to virtually all the benefit sectors. Who qualifies as a dependent under an expanded health insurance plan that now accommodates such individuals? What religious credentials must be established to authorize paid time off "as conscience may dictate" on Good Friday or Yom Kippur? Is a suddenly decreed national day of mourning an "act of God," relieving the company of an obligation to grant reporting pay, or do its circumstances compel the employer to pay such amounts? How many hours or weeks of work—and under what conditions—constitute a year, for purposes of calculating pension entitlement within a system granting a flat monthly payment "per year of service"? In a less generous age, these and obviously a myriad of similar questions were automatically excluded.

Second, even on the now rare occasions upon which the benefits are not formally liberalized, many of them automatically become more costly simply because wages have been increased. All wage-related benefits fall into this category, and a 50-cent-per-hour wage increase will thus inevitably elevate total employment costs by considerably more than this face amount because of the simultaneous rise in the worth of each holiday, vacation period, and any other allowance pegged to the basic wage rate. This industrial relations truism would hardly be worth citing were it not so often ignored in union–management bargaining rooms, in favor of accommodating only wage increases to increases in productivity (for example) rather than wage increases plus wage-related benefit increases. The degree of danger in overlooking these inflationary ramifications, moreover, obviously rises with the increasing value of the benefit itself.

In the third place, one suspects that managements have—at least at times— generated *negative* employee motivation by implementing benefits without either participation or approval of work force representatives in the process. The day of company paternalism, fortunately, now lies far in the past for the large mainstream of American industry. But the arousal of employee ego-involvement is all the more imperative in today's sophisticated industrial world. Describing a deep and enthusiastic interest in unionization on the part of employees at a large Pittsburgh plant "that was well known as having excellent wages and working conditions, and supposedly had almost perfect employee relationships," Leland Hazard has memorably quoted the following remarks of "one attractive girl" to explain the general sentiment:

> It's about time something like this happened. We have got to stand on our own feet. They do everything for you but provide a husband, and I even know girls who they got a husband for. And them what ain't got time to get pregnant, they get foster kids for.[16]

Related to this question of negative motivation, but isolable as a fourth potential problem, must stand the very real alternative possibility of *no* employee motivation whatsoever. Not being masochistic as a class, employers logically expect some benefits from their expenditures in the wage supplement area—particularly, more satisfactory worker retention figures, an improved recruitment performance, and, above all, generally increased employee productivity. Without such returns on the benefit investment, managements would be engaging in clear-cut wastage.

One can readily locate situations in which employee benefits have obviously achieved at least some of the desired results. Particularly in those areas where

[16] Leland Hazard, "Unionism: Past and Future," *Harvard Business Review,* March–April 1958.

benefit entitlement expands with increasing seniority (pensions and vacations, for example), greater worker retention has undoubtedly often been fostered. Yet there is to this moment no convincing proof that benefits have significantly affected employee motivation on any large-scale basis in American industry—and, for that matter, the few scholarly treatments of this topic that have cropped up in the literature indicate that the extent of employee knowledge as to exactly what the benefits are is something less than awesome.[17] There is a critical need for much more research into this subject by employers and other interested parties than has thus far been conducted, for the possibility that industry may be undergoing an ever-increasing expense that may be returning very little in the way of concrete worker performance cannot as yet be safely dismissed.

Fifth, it is possible that overall employment has suffered—and conceivably will continue to suffer—from the continuation of benefit expansion of the type described in this chapter. As in the preceding case, the evidence thus far is not fully conclusive. But the increasing cost pressures and personnel administration complexities involved appear to have combined with related factors to push in this direction. Certainly Garbarino, whose exploration of such a possibility for manufacturing employees is perhaps the most thorough of its kind to date, does not dispute this point. He deems it "reasonable to conclude" that the cost and administrative considerations, as well as uncertainty as to future labor requirements and other management problems, have "contributed to minimizing employment expansion without necessarily leading to a major expansion of overtime scheduling."[18] Aside from the basic issues of society's optimum utilization of manpower and the dashed aspirations of the consequently unemployed or underemployed that are always presented by such an outcome, Garbarino's conclusion—if, in fact, "reasonable"—clearly contains further pungent considerations related to urbanized ghetto America today.

Finally, unlike wage increases (which can often be at least partially negated by such mechanisms as job reevaluation and incentive rate implementation or modification), the benefit package has a strong tendency to remain a permanent part of the landscape. Except in extreme cases of corporate financial crisis, it is quite immune from disintegration. And if any significant positive effect of benefits on employee motivation thus far remains to be proven, the annals of industrial history are replete with examples of companies that have encountered surprisingly intense worker resistance in attempting to dismantle even such relatively minor portions of their benefit packages as physical fitness programs or banking facilities. Downward revisions of the leisure time, health, and pension offerings remain several miles beyond the realm of the conceivable. In short, once the parties

---

[17] See, for example, James L. Sheard, "Relationship between Attitude and Knowledge in Employee Fringe Benefit Orientation," *Personnel Journal,* November 1966; and Arthur A. Sloane and Edward W. Hodges, "What Workers Don't Know about Employee Benefits," *Personnel,* November–December 1968.

[18] Joseph W. Garbarino, "Fringe Benefits and Overtime as Barriers to Expanding Employment," *Industrial and Labor Relations Review,* 17, No. 3 (April 1964), 439.

introduce a benefit, they can expect to be wedded to it for life, with the only important questions focusing on the timing and degrees of the subsequent benefit liberalizations.

For all the reservations expressed in the paragraphs above, employee benefits hardly warrant an evaluation similar to that given by the old railroad baron James Hill to the passenger train ("like the male teat, neither useful nor ornamental"). They do provide considerable security at minimal cost to the covered employees (whether or not the latter explicitly desire such protection in lieu of other forms of compensation), at least at times abet the employer's recruitment and retention efforts in a tight labor market, and minimize the tax burdens of both company and worker. If there is room for doubt that they also allow the employer any significant return in the form of worker morale and productivity, these other reasons alone are probably sufficient to justify their dramatic spread during the past four decades.

And because the benefit package has become so relatively standardized among employers in this time interval, too, the wage supplements probably also perform a further (if less constructive) function for managers and the unions with which they deal. Their presence in anything approaching the typical dimensions prevents invidious comparisons by both current and potential employees in evaluating the desirability of the company as an employer. The extent of worker knowledge of specific benefits may fall far short of perfection, but at the present time, because corporate pattern-following has been so prevalent in this area, the absence of nine or ten paid holidays, a three-week paid vacation after no more than ten years of service, significant medical coverage for all members of the family, satisfactory pensions, and any of the various parts of the generally conspicuous benefit portfolio are often grounds for workers' dissatisfaction.

Thus it can be predicted quite fearlessly that the years ahead will see a continuation of the benefit growth. As indicated, it appears to be all but axiomatic to industrial relations that any benefit, once implemented, through the years becomes subject to a process of continuous liberalization from the worker's viewpoint. And, while variety in these economic supplements has now become increasingly difficult to achieve, there is little doubt but that new ones (perhaps more emphatically in the areas of income stabilization and employment relief) will join the already crowded ranks.

Possibly, however, increasing awareness on the part of fringe benefits implementors as to the various problem areas outlined here will result in some slowing down of the continuous liberalization process and restrain the introduction of new types of benefits until thorough investigation—tailored to the needs of individual companies and unions—has taken place. At the very least, the future demands considerably more research into these areas than has thus far been carried out. And such an omission seems particularly blatant when one realizes that there remain few other aspects of industrial relations that have not been subjected to searching scrutiny. But one must be a pessimist on these scores: Thus far, both the research and the benefit deceleration have been notably absent.

Discussion Questions

1 "If there had been no labor unions in this country in the past quarter-century or so, the growth of employee benefits would perhaps have been only a small fraction of what it has actually been." Discuss.

2 "It is not the business of the government to protect employee pension interests. ERISA is a classic example of unjustified governmental intervention in private employer–employee matters." Comment fully.

3 "Vacations and holidays are far more important for what they do in the way of job security than for what they do in the area of leisure time." Does this statement seem valid to you? Why or why not?

4 Which set of arguments as expressed in this chapter's section on pensions carries more weight with you: the case *for* contributory plans or the case *against* them?

5 "SUB plans of the type negotiated in the automobile and steel sectors are wholly undesirable. They discourage employees in the incentive to work, replace state unemployment compensation systems, discriminate against the worker not represented by a union, place an undetermined but intolerable burden on management, are financially unsound, and can actually cause permanent unemployment among some workers." In the light of your understanding of the character of these SUB plans, evaluate this statement.

6 Paul Pigors and Charles A. Myers have argued that "management should offer employee benefits and services, not because [it has] to, not only within legal limits, and not as a camouflaged form of bribery, but because such benefits and services are in line with the whole personnel program." Do you agree? Why or why not?

Selected References

ALLEN, DONNA, *Fringe Benefits: Wages or Social Obligation?* Ithaca, N.Y.: New York State School of Industrial and Labor Relations, 1964.

BABSON, STANLEY M., JR., *Fringe Benefits—The Depreciation, Obsolescence and Transcience of Man.* New York: John Wiley, 1974.

COFFIN, RICHARD M., and MICHAEL S. SHAW, *Effective Communication of Employee Benefits.* New York: American Management Association, 1971.

EHRENBERG, RONALD G., *Fringe Benefits and Overtime Behavior: Theoretical and Econometric Analysis.* Lexington, Mass.: Heath, 1971.

FREEDMAN, AUDREY, *Security Bargains Reconsidered: SUB, Severance Pay, Guaranteed Work.* New York: Conference Board, 1978.

McCAFFERY, ROBERT M., *Managing the Employee Benefits Program.* New York: American Management Association, 1972.

MEYER, MITCHELL, *Women and Employee Benefits.* New York: Conference Board, 1978.

MUNTS, RAYMOND, *Bargaining for Health.* Madison, Wis.: University of Wisconsin Press, 1967.

SRB, JOZETTA, H., *Portable Pensions: A Review of the Issues.* Ithaca, N.Y.: New York State School of Industrial and Labor Relations, 1969.

WEEKS, DAVID A., ed., *Rethinking Employee Benefits Assumptions.* New York: Conference Board, 1978.

Teacher Contracts:
The Case of the Girls' Gymnastics Coach

Cast of characters:

Dr. Baker	*Grievant*
Rose	*Assistant Girls' Gymnastics Coach*
Crews	*Athletic Director*
Small	*Director of Personnel*
Norris	*Member of Union Negotiation Committee*
Clein	*Wrestling Coach*
Gill	*Superintendent of Schools*
Gates	*Union President*
Bock	*Stage Assistant*
Cash	*Basketball Coach*
Starr	*Basketball Coach*
Clark	*Driver Education Coordinator*

Here is the first of two public-sector cases. When a controversy arises about paid extracurricular activities in a school system, the normal scenario is the termination of a teacher charged with unsatisfactory performance. Discharged basketball and football coaches would bear testimony to that! In this case, the unusual twist is that the school system would not accept the resignation of a teacher from his coaching duties. He wanted to resign as coach but retain his regular teaching job. For reasons that will become clear to you, the school system would not permit him to quit his coaching duties unless he also resigned his teaching job.

As in the private sector, arbitrators apply commonly accepted principles of contractual construction to the public sector. Both areas are subject to the same principles of the arbitration process. In the public sector, however, the decision-making process is at times complicated by state law which must command the attention of the arbitrator. This was the situation in this dispute, since the contractual provisions dealing with teacher contracts had to be viewed in the light of Iowa law. On this issue, the parties disagreed, the school system claiming that the law applied to regular teaching contracts and those covering special duties or participation in paid extra-curricular activities while the teachers' union argued that the statute applied only to regular teaching contracts. Though other issues were involved, the determination of that controversy was central to the ultimate decision.

GRIEVANCE

When the School District refused to accept Dr. Baker's resignation as the girls' gymnastic coach, he filed a grievance, dated April 23, 1981, which stated:

> I am no longer in mutual agreement with the School District regarding the assignment of high school gymnastics duties to me. I have requested release and the district has refused.

To support his complaint, Baker cited Article V, Sections B and C, and Article VI, Section A, of the Master Contract.

As relief, he requested release from his coaching duties.

MASTER CONTRACT—SCHOOL YEAR 1980–81

ARTICLE IV. EMPLOYMENT AND ASSIGNMENT

Section A. Contracts Employees are to be employed on a continuing basis in accordance with Iowa law.

ARTICLE V. EMPLOYEE WORK YEAR

Section B. Regular Contract The in-school work year for Employees on a regular contract (exclusive of counselors) shall be 189 days, except new personnel may be required to attend an additional three days of orientation. The work year for Counselors shall be ten (10) days in addition to the days worked by Employees on a regular contract and, unless otherwise mutually agreed, the additional ten (10) days of work shall occur either immediately before and/or after the regular in-school work year.

Section C. Special Contracts The Employer and an individual Employee, by mutual agreement, may enter into a Special Contract providing for additional services to be rendered by the Employee other than during the work day or to be rendered by the Employee other than during the work year. A copy of said Special Contract shall be furnished to the Union. If the additional services are described in Addendum C, the Special Contract shall be at the salary as provided in Addendum C. If the additional services are not described in Addendum C, then additional services shall be at a salary mutually agreeable.

ARTICLE VI. EMPLOYEE HOURS

Section A. Work Day The in-school work day shall consist of seven (7) hours and thirty (30) minutes, which shall include a thirty (30) minute duty-free lunch period, but does not include extra-curricular work. Any Employee may volunteer to supervise students during the lunch period and will be paid extra compensation in an amount to be agreed upon between the Employee and the Employer. Each Employee shall report for duty thirty (30) minutes before the opening of the school day and shall remain in the classroom building thirty (30) minutes after the close of the pupil's school day, except on Fridays or on days preceding holidays or vacations when the Employees may leave the building at the close of the pupil's school day.

Employees may leave the building during their lunch period without requesting permission and may leave the building at other times with the consent of the building principal.

Addendum C

Supplemental Pay Schedule   The supplemental pay for extra duties performed outside the regular school day shall be a percentage of the base pay for Step 1 of the BA column of Addendum "B." The percentages for the respective extra duties are set forth in the following schedule and are based on teachers having a full contract teaching assignment of five (5) assignments per day at the high school and six (6) assignments per day at the junior high school and a maximum of one preparation period per day in all cases.

Girls' Athletics . . .

Gymnastics

Head	15.0%
Assistant	8.0%

IOWA PUBLIC EMPLOYMENT RELATIONS ACT

Section 279.13. Contracts with Teachers—Automatic Continuation

1 Contracts with teachers, which for the purpose of this section means all certified employees of a school district and nurses employed by the board, . . . shall be in writing and shall state the number of contract days, the annual compensation to be paid, and any other matters as may be mutually agreed upon. . . .
2 The contract shall remain in force and effect for the period stated in the contract and shall be automatically continued for equivalent periods except as modified or terminated by mutual agreement of the board of directors and the teacher or as terminated in accordance with the provisions specified in this chapter. . . . A teacher who has not accepted a contract for the ensuing school year tendered by the employing board may resign effective at the end of the current school year by filing a written resignation with the secretary of the board. . . .
3 If the provisions of a contract executed or automatically renewed under this section conflict with a collective bargaining agreement negotiated under chapter 20 and effective when the contract is executed or renewed, the provisions of the collective bargaining agreement shall prevail. . . .

Section 279.15. Notice of Termination—Request for Hearing

1 The superintendent or the superintendent's designee shall notify the teacher not later than March 15 that the superintendent will recommend in writing to the board at a regular or special meeting of the board held not later than March 31 that the teacher's continuing contract be terminated effective at the end of the current school year. . . .

Thereafter, the procedure for termination is established.

ISSUE

Under the circumstances of this case, did the School District violate the material provisions of the Master Contract and/or Section 279.13 of the Iowa Public Employment Relations Act? If so, what should the remedy be?

BACKGROUND

Resignation Rejected

When the circumstances of this case arose, Baker, 42 years of age and hired by the District in 1968, was assigned to Ward Junior High School as a science instructor, also handling one section of talented and gifted students. In 1971, he originated a girls' gymnastics program at the High School, serving as Head Coach of the team for that year and in each consecutive year until he attempted unsuccessfully to resign in the spring of 1981. For each year he signed a Teachers Contract which indicated his base salary as a teacher and additional compensation for his coaching activities. For example, for the school year starting August 21, 1980, his Teachers Contract spelled out a base salary of $22,464 and $1,755 for his coaching activities.

The gymnastics activity is carried out after regular school hours, 3:30 to 5:30 P.M. Team meets are held in the evening or on weekends. In 1978, Nancy Rose was appointed Assistant Coach of the team. Before that time, Baker operated without an assistant.

In February 1981, as a result of budget considerations, the District announced that for the next school year, 1981–82, assistant coaches would be eliminated when a sport had less than twenty participants. Rose resigned as Assistant Coach in the spring of 1981. The School Board accepted her resignation. For the school year 1980–81, and apparently in previous years, the number of gymnastics team members was less than twenty. Fourteen girls were on the squad in the school year 1980–81. Had Rose not resigned, her position would have been eliminated anyway under the District's Assistant Coach policy.

On March 19, 1981, Crews, Athletic Director, by written memorandum informed Baker that he would not have an assistant coach for the 1981–82 school year. Baker returned the memorandum, stating:

> I either have a female assistant, or I will be resigning as Head Gymnastics Coach.

Small, Director of Personnel, advised Baker that his resignation would not be accepted unless a suitable replacement was found. If that occurred, the District would recommend to the School Board acceptance of his resignation. (The School Board has the final authority to accept or reject resignations.) On March 30, 1981, the District offered a Teachers Contract to Baker for the school year starting on August 27, 1981. As in previous years, it indicated his base salary, $23,616, and additional compensation, $1,845, for his coaching duties. Baker signed the contract, but attached the following addendum to it:

> Since I have already submitted my resignation from the position of high school gymnastics coach, I am signing this contract under protest. My signature should not be considered as a waiver of my rights to process a grievance on this matter under the master contract.

The School Board refused to accept the contract because of the addendum. Subsequently Baker signed another contract for the 1981–82 school year on which he did not indicate any conditions. However, the District assured Baker that his signing of the contract would not prejudice his right to file a grievance and proceed to arbitration. Small told him that if his grievance were to prevail in this arbitration, he would be released from his coaching responsibilities. So assured, Baker signed the contract on April 22, 1981, and filed the grievance generating this arbitration on the next day, April 23, 1981.

The District attempted to find a replacement for Baker, posting the job on April 23, 1981, "Head Gymnastics—High School." On June 6, 1981, it also advertised the job in the local newspaper, the *Courier*. No one bid the job or replied to the advertisement. As a result, the School Board refused to accept Baker's resignation, and he continued the coaching duties for the current school year, 1981–82. The gymnastics team season started on November 1, 1981 and ended on March 1, 1982. Baker said that if he refused to coach after his resignation was rejected, he feared disciplinary action and the loss of his teaching certificate.

Development of Special Contract Provision in Master Contract

For the school year 1976–77, Article V, Employee School Year, stated:

> **Section A. Regular Contract** The in-school year for Employees on a base contract, other than new personnel who may be required to attend an additional three (3) days of orientations, shall not exceed one-hundred eighty-nine (189) days.
>
> **Section B. Extended or Special Contract** At the request of the Employee, the Employer may enter into an Extended or Special Contract with an individual Employee providing for additional services to be rendered by the Employee other than during the in-school work year. The Special Contract shall be at a salary and for a term which is mutually agreeable. A copy of said Special Contract shall be furnished to the Union.

For the next school year, 1978–79, these provisions were written in the exact same way.

For the 1979–80 school year, however, a change in the language appeared in the Special Contracts provision. In that year, Article V, Section C, contained the same language as is found in Article V, Section C, of the Master Contract for the school year 1980–81, the collective bargaining contract which is involved in this arbitration.

Testimony was offered in the arbitration regarding the change in the language. Norris was a member of the Union's bargaining team when the 1979–80 Master Agreement was negotiated. He said that the Union was concerned that teachers were not receiving professional pay for summer school, drivers education, and extracurricular (special) activities held after the regular school day. When he served as Chairperson of the Union Grievance Committee, teachers complained that they felt coerced to participate in such programs. At times, they received extra compensation, and at other times they were not paid.

With regard to special activities, Norris said that the Union was concerned with their number and lack of sufficient teachers to cover them. In some cases, after teachers agreed to participate, it became difficult to get out of the special activities. Clein, a Junior High School Wrestling Coach, experienced difficulty in being relieved from his coaching duties, an event that occurred about three years ago.

These matters, Norris said, were discussed in the 1979 negotiations. To deal with them, the Union proposed the following contractual language:

ARTICLE V.   EMPLOYEE WORK YEAR

Section C. Special Contracts   Employees teaching summer school courses, including drivers education, performing special curriculum work, and employed in the Community School Program, shall be paid at the respective hourly rates as provided in Addendum "C" Supplemental Pay Schedule. The Employer and an individual Employee, by mutual agreement, may enter into a Special Contract providing for other additional services to be rendered by the Employer other than during the work day or other than during the in-school work year at a salary and for a term which is mutually agreeable. A copy of said Special Contract shall be furnished to the Union.

Subsequently, the District proposed language that appears in Article V, Section C, of the 1979–80 and 1980–81 Master Contracts. Eventually the Parties adopted the District's proposal that was contained in both Master Agreements. Norris also testified:

We made it known to the School District what was meant by "mutual agreement." It means that there must be mutual agreement for special contracts. A major problem was that people were being forced to continue their special duties. So we agreed that there must be mutual consent to continue. Under the language, the extension of special contracts must be by mutual agreement. That is why the new language says "mutual agreement." We made our position clear to the District. They did not say anything to lead me to believe that they did not agree with our position.

On its part, the District did not present any witnesses who participated in the negotiations that resulted in the adoption of the 1978–79 Master Contract. Gill, Superintendent of Schools, said that though not at the bargaining table, he had consulted with District representatives who had directly participated in the negotiations. In this regard, he said:

I told them that the District could not have a condition where teachers could get out of special activities at their own will. The District was in a difficult position because of the addition of extra programs without sufficient coaches. I told them further that we would not want a contract to force persons to take a coaching job. In that we agreed with the Union. But there would be mutual agreement to be relieved from coaching duties.

Release from Special Duties: Experience in the District

With regard to this issue, Small and Gill said that teachers participating in special duties, including coaches, were not permitted to resign unless a qualified replacement was secured. Gates, President of the Union, testified that it was a "common practice" for teachers to resign from such activities.

On May 11, 1981, the School Board accepted the resignation of Bock and Cash. Bock served as Stage Assistant at the High School, and Cash was the seventh grade boys' Basketball Coach at Ward Junior High School. By August 27, 1981, replacements had not been found for those two activities. These jobs were posted on that date.

With regard to Bock, Small testified that he presented a doctor's certificate indicating that he could not perform the Stage Assistant duties. In the case of Cash, Small said that he transferred from Ward Junior High to an elementary school teaching special education for retarded children. As a result, Small said that Cash was permitted to resign without a replacement because the basketball activity would interfere with his teaching duties at the elementary school. Cash also taught special education at Ward. He had time to coach basketball there, Small said, because the retarded students were in his classroom for part of the day. At the elementary school, he testified, the children were in his classroom the whole day.

In 1972, Clein resigned as the Wrestling Coach at Ward after a replacement was secured. Gill said that later on he was asked to resume coaching duties because of the condition of the wrestling program at Ward. Clein accepted the assignment. In 1978, he submitted a resignation which was accepted even though a replacement had not been found. Gill said that Clein was permitted to resign under those circumstances because when he resumed coaching, he was promised that he could resign at his discretion and without a replacement.

Starr coached basketball at Ward. When he wanted to resign in 1976, Gill testified, he told him he could not resign in the absence of a suitable replacement. Starr filed a grievance, and was permitted to resign without a replacement. Gill declared that he was permitted to resign because Starr said that when he took the coaching job "it was not forever." Gill testified that the District decided to honor the promise made to Starr that he could resign without a replacement.

POSITIONS OF THE PARTIES

Whereas the Union requests that the grievance be granted, the School District urges that it be denied. Both Parties filed post-hearing briefs to support their respective positions. To the extent necessary and appropriate, arguments contained in them will be referenced in the following portion of this Opinion.

ANALYSIS OF THE EVIDENCE

Fundamental Issue

In the final analysis, the fundamental issue is a determination of whether or not Special Contracts specified in Article V, Section C, of the Master Contract is covered by Section 279.13 of the Iowa Public Employment Relations Act. Under its pertinent provisions, teachers' contracts shall be automatically continued

> except as modified or terminated by mutual agreement of the board of directors and the teacher. . . .

As the facts show, Baker for many years, including the school year 1980–81, signed a special contract establishing his coaching duties. When he attempted to resign, the School Board rejected his resignation. Under protest he continued to coach the girls' gymnastics team for the school year 1981–82.

Should it be determined that Section 279.13 does not apply to Special Contracts, Baker's grievance would have merit. As the Union argues, the parameters of the school day are established in Article VI of the Master Contract. Special activities, including the girls' gymnastics program, are conducted after the contractually defined school day. Under these circumstances, the Union argues:

> Initially, the employer's right to assign duties and the employee's obligation to perform such assignments is limited to assignments during the workday. . . .
>
> * * *
>
> This clause [Article VI] limits the hours during which the employer, the District, has the power to assign duties to its employees. Beyond this time, the employer does not have the unilateral right to assign duties to its employees, and outside of the workday employees are not obligated to perform special assignments but may do so upon reaching agreement with the employer.

Relying upon the testimony of Norris, the Union claims that the intent of Article V, Section C, was to provide teachers with the right to resign from special duties, including coaching positions such as held by Baker. It notes that the District did not provide a witness who directly participated in the negotiations that resulted in the language currently contained in the provision. As a result, it urges that Norris's testimony should be credited. Thus:

> Mr. Norris testified that during the course of negotiations the Union had clearly stated to the District its intent to regard this "mutual consent" language as requiring the agreement of both parties before a Union member would be obligated to accept any special duty outside the regular teaching day. He further stated that this contract language was to apply to situations such as the instant case, where a coach did not wish to enter into a special contract to coach a sport during the next contract year.

And:

> . . . Because no disagreement was raised before the master contract became effective, the District may not now attempt to alter or redefine contract terms through the arbitration process. The District is now bound by the negotiated terms of the master contract and may not deprive the Union or its members of contract benefits.

In other words, given the language contained in the Special Contracts provision, and its intent as expressed by Norris, there must be "mutual agreement" between the District and a teacher for a special contract assignment to start, and "mutual agreement" must prevail for an extension of a special contract. Under these circumstances, the District and/or School Board violated Article V, Section C, when Baker's resignation was rejected, forcing him against his will to continue to coach the girls' gymnastics team.

Special Contracts under Iowa Law

In any event, it would not be proper to determine the merits of Baker's grievance in the absence of Iowa law. Beyond a shadow of a doubt, Section 279.13 covers Special Contracts specified in Article V, Section C, of the Master Contract. For the Union to prevail in this arbitration, it must demonstrate that the grievance has merit even though Iowa law applies to Special Contracts.

That Iowa law applies to Special Contracts is fully substantiated by the evidence. In the first place, Article IV, Section A, of the Master Contract states:

> **Contracts** Employees are to be employed on a continuing basis in accordance with Iowa law.

Obviously, this provision refers to Section 279.13 and particularly to its language that mandates that teacher contracts are to be automatically continued year by year unless modified or terminated by mutual agreement. Article IV, Section A, does not distinguish between a regular teacher contract or a special contract. It merely uses the word "Contracts," embracing any kind of contract agreed to by the teachers and the School Board. To exempt a special contract from its terms would be in variance with its terms.

In addition, it is manifestly clear that the Parties changed the language of the Special Contracts provision to conform with Section 279.13. Before the Master Contract for the school year 1979–80 was negotiated, the provision stated:

> The Special Contract shall be at a salary and for a *term* which is mutually agreeable. (Emphasis supplied)

That is, the School Board and the teacher have the right to agree to the length of a special contract. Unless there was mutual agreement between them as to term or length, there would be no special contract. So, why did the Parties eliminate the word "term" when they negotiated the 1979–80 Master Contract? *Obviously they did so to harmonize the language with Section 279.13.* Under this provision, contracts are to be automatically extended unless mutually modified or terminated. Under this provision, the teacher and the School Board would violate Iowa law should they agree to a term of a special contract in conflict with the statute. In other words, the Parties were well aware of the legal requirements. By eliminating the word "term," they recognized that special contracts as well as regular contracts are covered by Iowa law.

If special contracts are not covered by Iowa law, how do we account for the circumstances resulting in the termination of Clark as Driver Education Coordinator? As a result of budget considerations, the District eliminated the position. Clark refused to resign. As a result, the District and Clark invoked the termination procedures established in Section 279.15. If his special contract as Driver Education Coordinator was not covered by Iowa law, there would be no need to implement termination procedures. It is material that the Union represented Clark in that proceeding. By so doing, did not the Union beyond Clark and the District recognize that special contracts are covered by Iowa law?

If any doubt remains that Iowa law covers special contracts, it is swept away by the plain and unambiguous language contained in Section 279.13. It says: "*contracts* with teachers . . . the *contract* shall remain in force . . ." (Emphasis supplied)

No distinction is made between regular and special contracts. If the Iowa legislature intended to limit the statute to regular contracts, it would have done so by express language. Since it did not, it follows that the statute covers all contracts, regular and special, between the School Board and teachers.

Union Argument

In short, the conclusion must be that Baker's coaching contract was covered by Section 279.13 of Iowa law. Despite this, the Union argues that he may still resign from his special contract and not from his regular teaching contract. That is, he may refuse to coach and still remain a teacher in the school system. Its argument is based upon the proposition that Article V provides for two separate and distinct contracts—the regular contract established in Section B and the special contract established in Section C. Thus:

> The applicable master contract provides under Article V for two separate contracts: regular contracts and special contracts. These special contracts are to govern the provision of services rendered other than during the workday or the work year. The in-school workday, a period of seven hours and thirty minutes, is defined in Article VI. The in-school work year, those days when pupils are in attendance, orientation days and specified required attendance days, is defined in Article V. The master contract clearly distinguishes between regular contracts governing regular workday activity and special contracts governing activities such as coaching or gymnastics. . . .

Given this distinction, the Union then argues that Baker had the right to resign his special contract since mutual agreement is required to extend it:

> . . . The language in this special contracts clause specifically states that services such as the type rendered by Dr. Baker in coaching gymnastics are required to be provided by an employee only if the employer and the employee *mutually agree*. (Emphasis in original)

Not only does the Union argue that Baker had the right to resign his special contract under the terms of the Master Contract, but also that this right is protected under Section 279.13 of the Iowa statute. This right prevails even if it is true that his teaching and coaching duties are deemed to be incorporated in a single contract. To support this view, the Union points to that portion of Section 279.13 which states:

> . . . if the provisions of a contract executed or automatically renewed under this section conflict with a collective bargaining agreement negotiated under chapter 20 and effective when the contract is executed or renewed, the provisions of the collective bargaining agreement shall prevail.

In other words, since Article V, Sections B and C, provide for two separate contracts, the Master Contract prevails over the individual contract offered by the School Board to Baker. In this respect, the Union asserts:

> . . . The provisions of Section 279.13(3) recognize and enforce the distinction made in this master contract. It is clear under the terms of the master contract that the teaching duties and the coaching duties of Dr. Baker are to be defined in two separate contracts, and that the District may not treat both duties as being part of only a single teaching contract. It therefore follows that Dr. Baker may, under the terms of the master contract, refuse to agree to perform the duties of gymnastics coach and at the same time retain his teaching position.

In addition, the Union argues that Baker's right to resign his coaching duties without jeopardizing his regular contract is protected by that portion of Section 279.13 which authorizes teachers to resign a contract at the end of the school year. Thus:

> Assuming that both contracts are subject to the provisions of Chapter 279, the second flaw in the District's argument is emphasized in Section 279.13(2). Since under the terms of Section 279.13(3) and the master contract the District has issued both a regular and a special contract to Dr. Baker, each contract must be given the same treatment under Section 279.13(2) which provides that a teacher may refuse to accept, and may resign from, a contract at the end of a school year by filing a resignation with the school district. Dr. Baker did not accept his special contract for coaching gymnastics and did resign from his gymnastics coaching duties, as admitted by both Small and Gill. It therefore follows that under Section 279.13(2) Dr. Baker has taken the appropriate steps to terminate his employment as the gymnastics coach. . . .

Purpose of Automatic Renewal and Continuous Contracts under Iowa Law

The Union's arguments herein considered are inherently logical, persuasive, and well expressed. Despite this, and with full deference to the Union, the arguments are not acceptable. To grant the grievance on these grounds would *defeat the fundamental purpose* of that portion of Section 279.13 which provides for automatic renewal of contracts unless modified or terminated by mutual agreement. For the sake of argument, let us assume that the Union is correct in its argument that Article V, Sections B and C, provide for two separate contracts—a regular and special contract.

Even under this assumption, the Union's arguments do not have merit. Article V, Section C, must be applied and interpreted in the light of Section 279.13. As demonstrated earlier, Iowa law covers special contracts.

In the final analysis, the fundamental purpose of the Iowa continuous contract law protects the interests of the District, the teachers, and the students. As far as special contracts are concerned, Section 279.13 assures that the District may not arbitrarily dismiss a teacher from a special activity. By the same token, the interests of the district and the students are protected in that a teacher once initially accepting a special assignment may not be relieved of such duties without the consent of the School Board. In the instant case, for example, Baker's unilateral resignation would have resulted in the elimination of the girls' gymnastics program since no replacement was found.

If we accept the Union's argument, it would establish two standards as far as special contracts are concerned. Whereas the teacher may unilaterally resign from a special activity, the District may not unilaterally dismiss a teacher for such an activity. Recall that in the case of Clark, formal termination procedures were implemented after he refused to resign. The School Board did not have the authority to dismiss him on a unilateral and peremptory basis.

Resignation from Both Contracts Required

However, the inherent inequity of the Union's position is not the major reason why under Section 279.13 a teacher may not resign from a special contract without at the same time resigning the regular contract (assuming that Article V, Sections A and B, of the Master Contract provide for two separate kinds of contracts). It should be clear to all concerned that the Iowa continuous contract law would be meaningless as far as special contracts are concerned if a teacher may unilaterally resign such a contract and without jeopardizing the teacher's position in the school system. If a teacher may unilaterally resign a special contract with impunity, it would be as if Section 279.13 is not applicable to special contracts, a proposition that would be in variance with its terms as demonstrated earlier.

In other words, to assure that the fundamental purpose of Iowa law, continuous contracts, is effectuated as it applies to special contracts, to be relieved from a special contract, a teacher must simultaneously resign from the regular contract.

Only such a sanction maintains the integrity and purpose of Iowa law. In the absence of such a sanction, the continuous nature of special contracts as required by Iowa law would be worthless.

Value of Article V, Section C

Given this construction of Section 279.13 as applied to Article V, Section C, of the Master Contract, the Union asserts that such a decision makes superfluous the "mutual agreement" language contained in the contractual provision. It argues:

> Clearly, therefore, the language "mutual agreement" means exactly what it says—that only when both parties, the District and the employee, agree that the employee will assume duties other than regular contract teaching duties during regular contract hours will the employee be obligated to perform such duties. Any other construction of this clause would have the effect of rendering it superfluous and would give the District the power to assign special contract duties in violation not only of the master contract but of the Iowa Code.

To the contrary, the contractual "mutual agreement" language has considerable significance even though there must be mutual consent to terminate a special contract. Under the terms of Article V, Section C, the teacher must voluntarily agree before a special contract initially goes into effect. Under such language, the District may not force a teacher to start a special activity. It is only after the initial contract becomes effective, *voluntarily signed and agreed to by the teacher,* that the continuous contract feature of Section 279.13 as applied to Article V, Section C, of the Master Contract becomes applicable.

Article VI and Intent of Article V, Section C

The proper construction of Section 279.13 as it applies to Article V, Section C, makes unacceptable other arguments raised by the Union. That special activities, such as coaching a team sport, are carried out after the contractually defined regular school day results from the nature of the activities covered by the special contract. The District does not violate Article VI, the Employee Hours provision, when a special contract requires duties after the regular school day. Since the School District did not violate Article V, Section C, when it refused to accept Baker's resignation, it follows that no violation of Article VI occurred. Employer conduct proper under one provision of a labor agreement obviously does not violate another provision of the contract. How can the same employer action simultaneously be held lawful and unlawful under the same collective bargaining contract?

Even if we credit Norris's testimony as to the intent of Article V, Section C, as negotiated for the first time in the 1979–80 Master Contract—there must be mutual agreement to extend a special contract—the Union's position on this basis does not have merit. *It does not have merit because Iowa law takes precedence over the Parties' agreement.* To the extent that collective bargaining contracts conflict with applicable state or federal law, the statute and not the contract must prevail.

Under Section 279.13, as applied to Article V, Section C, a teacher may not unilaterally terminate a special contract without at the same time terminating employment in the school system. Regardless of what the intent of the Parties may have been, it may not prevail over Iowa law.

Past Practice

The Arbitrator's construction of Article V, Section C, under Section 279.13 of Iowa law is consistent with past practice. Earlier the evidence relating to experience of teachers resigning special contracts was presented. In the Union's view, however, such evidence does not add up to a practice where the School Board permitted resignations of special contracts only when replacements were secured. In this regard, it argues:

> The past course of dealing between the parties does not establish a particular practice, but rather shows that the District has handled resignations from special duty contracts in at least three ways, those being the initiation of a termination procedure, the procurement of a replacement before resignation from a special contract was accepted, and the resignation of two coaches, Starr and Clein, before a replacement was found. This indicates that there has been no binding past practice, in that there has been no "(1) unequivocal; (2) clearly enunciated and acted upon; (3) readily ascertainable over a reasonable period of time" fixed procedure.

What the Union's argument ignores, however, is evidence demonstrating that in the few instances where teachers were allowed to resign without a replacement extenuating and special circumstances existed. The Clark incident has nothing to do with practice because it was concerned with the abolishment of a special activity. Bock was permitted to resign because of medical reasons. Cash's resignation was accepted because his new teaching duties conflicted with his coaching activities. In the case of Clein and Starr, they were permitted to resign because the District had previously promised them relief from their duties at their discretion.

Beyond these four documented instances, the Union did not present any evidence whatsoever to show that teachers resigned special activities in the absence of a suitable replacement. Indeed, what comes through loudly and clearly here is a practice supporting the policy followed by the District. Except for the four instances noted, each explained by valid special circumstances, teachers holding special contracts were not permitted to resign until a suitable replacement was found. This practice is consistent with the Arbitrator's construction of Section 279.13 of Iowa law as applied to Article V, Section C.

Baker's Reasons for Resignation

Before reaching his final conclusions, the Arbitrator carefully considered the particular circumstances of this dispute. He did not deal with the issues within a vacuum or on a purely legalistic basis. Indeed, it is recognized that under compelling circumstances a teacher should be permitted to resign a special contract without forfeiting employment in the school system. Under such circumstances, the teacher should be permitted to resign even though a replacement was not available.

In this light, consideration was given to Baker's reasons for desiring to terminate his coaching duties. He said that at his age he is more subject to fatigue and a lower energy level as compared to the time he operated without an assistant. With a lower energy level, he felt that by going it alone his performance as a coach would deteriorate. Given his success as a gymnastics coach for ten years, and an excellent state wide reputation, he did not want his reputation as a coach to suffer. Baker obviously has taken great pride in his coaching accomplishments. He would rather resign as coach than turn out inferior teams.

Unlike other sports, he explained, gymnastics places an extra physical burden upon coaches. A coach must "spot" the participants as they perform their exercises. That is, a coach must be "on the spot" to prevent injury to a participant. When Baker had an assistant, she was available to perform this duty. Also, without an assistant, he has the burden to move the equipment, some of which is very heavy, from place to place. Finally, he said that he needed a female assistant to serve as chaperon during meets.

With full respect to Baker, aware of the pride that he takes in his coaching, and even if we regard his reasons sympathetically, they do not add up to a compelling situation justifying the granting of his grievance. After mentioning his age, fatigue, and lower energy level, Baker acknowledged that he is in good health. Certainly, unlike Bock, he does not present a health reason for his resignation. It is hard to believe that the passage of three years would so affect his energy level as to impair substantially his success as a coach. Between 1971 and 1978, he gained his reputation as a successful coach without an assistant. After all, Baker is not an "old man," being 42 years of age and in good health at the time of the arbitration. Naturally, he is the best judge of his physical and energy level, and certainly not the Arbitrator. Still it does not seem reasonable to believe that the passage of three years at his age would impair substantially his performance as a successful coach.

With regard to "spotting," Baker said that at times girls on his team could help to perform that duty. Also, he said that maintenance people are available to help in the movement of heavy equipment. Team members also could be called upon to the extent of their capability to move equipment.

In short, given the character of Baker's reasons, they do not add up to compelling circumstances to justify his resignation without a replacement. It is also material that the District acted reasonably when it refused his resignation. It made a good faith effort to locate a replacement for him. The job was posted and advertised in the local newspaper. Unfortunately for Baker, no one applied for the job. Also, the District indicated that it is willing to furnish a female at its expense to serve as a chaperon for team meets.

Conclusions

To say the least, this is a critical and important case. At the core of it is a person who no longer wants to coach. Even though Baker's reasons for resignation are not compelling, it is repugnant and distasteful to force a person to coach a sport against his will. On the other hand, the right of the District to provide its students with a worthwhile activity should receive consideration. Also, the interests of the students should be recognized. In a way, they are a silent party in this dispute. After all, fourteen girls currently are participating in the sport coached by Baker. With his resignation, and in the absence of a replacement, the activity would be abolished to their detriment.

In any event, these institutional and human considerations aside, the dispute must be resolved in the light of the applicable contract language and Section 279.13 of Iowa law. When they are placed in juxtaposition, the Arbitrator is fully convinced that a teacher may not unilaterally terminate a special contract. Once a teacher voluntarily and initially enters into such a contract, the automatic and continuous contract feature of Iowa law comes into play. So that the fundamental purpose of that portion of the law is realized, it follows that a teacher may not unilaterally resign a special contract without at the same time resigning employment in the school system.

Undoubtedly Baker and the Union will be very disappointed with this decision. Should it be censured, the Arbitrator would respect and understand the criticism. Be that as it may, he attempted to be faithful to the evidence, the material contractual provisions, and Iowa law. Given these considerations, the Arbitrator is fully satisfied in his conscience and mind that Baker's grievance must be denied.

Questions

1 What evidence did the arbitrator use to show that the parties recognized that special contracts are covered by Iowa law?

2 Why was the arbitrator compelled to deal with the fundamental purpose of the Iowa law?

3 Does the decision mean that under no circumstances may a teacher resign from a special contract without at the same time terminating the teacher's regular contract? Explain your answer.

4 Why did the arbitrator hold that the evidence dealing with past practice supports his interpretation of Iowa law?

case 7

Holiday Pay Eligibility:
The Case of the Arrested Employee

Cast of characters:

Dale	*Grievant*
Earl	*Court Official*
Comer	*Personnel Manager*
Smith	*Employee*

Labor agreements usually require that to be eligible for holiday pay, the employee must work the last scheduled workday before the holiday and the first scheduled workday following the holiday. Such a requirement discourages the employee from escalating a paid holiday into a sort of mini-vacation. In the absence of such an eligibility rule, it would be difficult for the employer to operate the plant should a large number of employees be absent on the workdays surrounding the holiday.

In this case, as is common in labor agreements, an employee who has a "justifiable" or "reasonable" excuse for his absence on a qualifying day will receive holiday pay. It is counted as a day worked for holiday pay purposes. As you will see, the employee offered a required court appearance as the basis of his excuse. The court appearance resulted from his arrest charged with shoplifting. The employer did not accept his excuse as justifiable and denied holiday pay.

In cases of this sort, an arbitrator has a difficult task because there are, of course, no universal or objective criteria as to what "reasonable" or "justifiable" means. As a result, the arbitrator must make a determination in the light of the facts of a case and in his best judgment. What would you have decided if you had been the arbitrator here, and why?

GRIEVANCE AND LABOR AGREEMENT

When the Company denied him holiday pay, Dale filed Grievance No. 871, dated December 10, 1980, which stated:

> On Dec. 1, 1980 the above employee had to appear in court, he called the company and told them he would be absent for a court appearance. He also

brought papers in showing he was in court. The company still denied him holiday pay.

Material to the dispute are the following provisions of the Labor Agreement:

ARTICLE 10.   HOLIDAYS AND SPECIAL DAYS

Section 10.2 It is understood that an employee who is not scheduled to work on a holiday or a paid special day shall receive eight (8) hours' pay at his straight time hourly rate of pay including shift and group leader premium, if applicable, for each of such holidays or paid special days provided that he has completed 30 days continuous employment as of the holiday, that he has worked the full day upon the work day preceding such a holiday or a paid special day and also the full day upon the work day succeeding such a holiday or paid special day. An employee will, however, receive holiday or paid special day pay if he is absent or tardy (tardiness—not greater than two (2) hours) on only one of such times preceding or succeeding, providing the absence on such day is for medical reasons, and substantiated by a doctor's certification, or providing the absence is for another justifiable reason.

STIPULATED ISSUE

The Parties stipulated the following issue to be determined in this arbitration:

Was the reason for the Grievant not being at work December 1, 1980 justifiable?

BACKGROUND

Under the terms of Article 10, November 27 (Thanksgiving) and November 28, 1980 (Friday following Thanksgiving) are designated as paid holidays. On Sunday, November 30, 1980, at approximately 1 P.M. Dale was arrested and charged with "criminal conversion" (shoplifting). At 2 P.M., Earl, a court official, released the Grievant on his own recognizance, with instructions to report to Superior Court on Monday, December 1, 1980 at 9 A.M. The document effecting his release, signed by the Grievant and Earl, stated:

I understand that failure to appear at the above stated time or times as required will result in the immediate issuance of a Warrant for my Arrest. I agree to inform the Bail Commissioner, in writing (Room B-12, City-County Building) of any change of address within 24 hours of such change.
WARNING: Failure to appear in Court as required shall subject you to prosecution and a penalty of a fixed term of imprisonment of not more than one (1) year and fine of not more than $5,000.00.

Dale was scheduled to report to work on Monday, December 1, 1980 at 7:30 A.M. He testified that he explained to the court official that if he appeared in court at the designated time he could lose his holiday pay. According to Dale, Earl told him there was nothing he could do about setting a different date. The court official also told him about the penalty for his failure to appear in court on Monday, December 1, 1980.

Before going to court on that day, Dale called Comer, Personnel Manager of the Company. At that time, the Grievant informed him of the reason for his absence from work. When he asked about his holiday pay, Comer replied that he did not know. Dale appeared in court at 9 A.M. on December 1, 1980 and entered a plea of not guilty to the charge. He did not engage the services of an attorney, testifying that he could not afford one.

After his court appearance, Dale reported to the plant at approximately 10 A.M. He told Comer he had just returned from court and was prepared to go to work. Comer did not permit him to do so because he was more than two hours late. Effective September 22, 1980, a rule was established denying employees the opportunity to work when they report more than two hours late. Since the Grievant's shift started at 7:30 A.M., and he reported at 10 A.M., Comer, on the basis of the rule, did not permit him to work. When Dale asked the Personnel Manager about his holiday pay, Comer replied that he would check on the matter later on.

On December 2, 1980, Comer told the Grievant he would not receive holiday pay. When he received his pay check for the period covering the holiday, Dale noted that he did not receive holiday day. On December 10, 1980, Dale filed the grievance subject of this arbitration.

Company Guideline

Under the terms of Article 10, Section 10.2, to be eligible for holiday pay the employee must work the full days preceding and succeeding the holiday. When, however, an employee does not comply with the contractual requirement, he is still entitled to holiday pay providing the absence or tardiness is caused by a certified medical reason or for "another justifiable reason." Since the Company did not believe his absence on Monday, December 1, 1980 was for a justifiable reason, the Company denied the Grievant holiday pay.

As the record shows, based on Comer's testimony, the Company has established a guideline for the application of justifiable reasons as contained in the Holiday Pay provisions. Its essence is whether or not an employee's absence is within his control. If an absence is beyond his control, the employee will receive holiday pay. If the employee's absence is within his control, he will not receive holiday pay. As Comer put it:

The point of demarcation is whether the employee has control of his own fate.

Using this guideline, Comer presented examples wherein the employee received and did not receive holiday pay. Holiday pay was denied when the absence was attributable to an automobile not starting, lost keys, doctors' appointment, oversleeping, being delayed by a train, and the employee's having "gone fishing."

In addition, the Company presented the circumstances of employee Smith who was denied holiday pay. This employee did not work on September 2, 1980, the day following the Labor Day holiday because he was arrested. The Union filed a grievance, but it was dropped after the time limits specified in the Grievance Procedure expired.

On the other hand, the Company paid holiday pay when the absence was caused by an employee's automobile accident on the way to work and when an employee was subpoenaed for a court appearance. Comer distinguished that situation from the Grievant's case on the grounds that

> a subpoena requires appearance in court due to action over which the employee has no control.

POSITIONS OF THE PARTIES

Whereas the Union requests that the grievance be granted, the Company asserts that it should be denied. In the Union's view, Dale's absence on Monday, December 1, 1980 constituted a justifiable reason for his absence and on that basis he should have received holiday pay. On its part, the Company argues that his excuse for his absence was not justifiable.

case 8

The Case of the Life-Support System

Cast of characters:

Dills	*Deceased Employee*
Mrs. Dills	*His Widow*
White	*Manager of Insurance Benefits*
Paul	*Director of Industrial Relations*
Johns	*Union President*
Sykes	*Union Committeeman*

Coincidentally, this case arose in the midst of the heated public debate concerning the use of a life-support system to prevent death. Although the arbitrator did not deal directly with that problem, as you will see, the use of a life-support system was a feature of the dispute. The employee, who subsequently died as a result of injuries sustained in an automobile accident, was kept alive for a time by the use of a life-support system. Under the company's insurance policy, double indemnity (twice the amount for natural death) for loss of life resulting from an accident is paid provided that the employee dies within ninety days following the accident.

In this case, the employee died after the ninety-day period, and the employer refused to award the widow of the employee the double indemnity benefit. On behalf of the widow, the union carried the case to arbitration requesting that the arbitrator direct double indemnity despite the ninety-day rule.

GRIEVANCE AND LABOR AGREEMENT

Involved in this case is the determination of when an employee's loss of life occurred resulting from an accident for purposes of insurance. On the grounds that his loss of life occurred after the allowable time limits expired for double indemnity under its insurance program, the Company refused to pay the beneficiary of Dills the sum of $9,000.00. In protest, Dills's widow and the Union filed Grievance Number 27046, dated June 27, 1975 which states:

> **Art. XIX, Par. 98**   Every employee upon acquiring seniority with the Company will receive a life insurance policy of $9,000 plus A D and D,* provided that the employee remains in active employment. The full premium will be paid by the Company.
>
> On 6/2/75 Dills died from injuries received in an accident. Company refuses to pay accidental death benefit.

As a remedy, the Union requests that the Company pay "Mrs. Dills all monies due."

Material to the case is Article XIX, Paragraph 98, which states:

> *Group Insurance*
>
> Every employee upon acquiring seniority with the Company will receive a life insurance policy of $9,000.00 plus A D and D, provided the employee remains in active employment. The full premium will be paid by the Company.

BASIC QUESTION

The basic question to be determined in this dispute is framed as follows:

> Under the circumstances of this case, did the Company violate Article XIX, Paragraph 98 of the Labor Agreement? If so, what should the remedy be?

* "A D and D" means accidental death and dismemberment.

BACKGROUND

Death of Dills

Dills was hired by the Company on December 4, 1956. He was assigned as an Inspector in Plant 2 on the second shift. He also served as a Union Steward.

On February 5, 1975, Dills was involved in an automobile accident. He was taken to a hospital, and he eventually died on June 2, 1975, or 117 days after the accident. In his death certificate, the cause of death resulted from:

> Internal injuries with fractured left ribs, left hemathorax, and ruptured spleen—
> 2-vehicle accident.

While in the hospital, Dills underwent four (4) operations, the last of which took place on April 25, 1975. After the second operation, Dills was placed in a life-support system. This system consisted of a respirator to facilitate breathing and to keep his lungs free from fluid; a heart monitor; intravenous feeding, and blood transfusions. For one (1) week, the life-support system was removed, but after this week his condition dictated the resumption of the life-support system.

On April 28, 1975, three (3) days following his last operation, Mrs. Dills testified, the attending doctor told her:

> He will die. He is a terminal case. Only the life-support system is keeping him alive.

Dills became progressively worse, and despite the life-support system, he died on June 2, 1975.

Ninety (90) Day Limit

Hoosier Life and Casualty carries the insurance for the Company. Under the accidental death and dismemberment (A D and D) feature of the insurance program, it is stated:

> If an employee suffers a non-occupational bodily injury caused by an accident and as a direct result of such injury and, to the exclusion of all other causes, *sustains within no more than ninety days* after the date of the accident which causes such injury *any of the losses listed* in the Table of Benefits in this section, then, provided:
>
> **A** the injury occurs while insurance is in force for the employee under this Title; and
> **B** the loss resulting from the injury is not excluded from coverage in accordance with Section 2 of this Title:
>
> the Insurance Company shall, subject to the terms of this policy, pay a benefit in the amount provided for such loss in said Table of Benefits but in no case

shall more than the Principal Sum be paid for all losses sustained by an employee through any one accident.

Table of Benefits	
In the Event of Loss of	*The Benefit Will Be*
Life	The Principal Sum
A Hand	One-Half the Principal Sum
A Foot	One-Half the Principal Sum
An Eye	One-Half the Principal Sum
A Hand and a Foot	The Principal Sum
A Hand and an Eye	The Principal Sum
A Foot and an Eye	The Principal Sum
Both Hands	The Principal Sum
Both Feet	The Principal Sum
Both Eyes	The Principal Sum
. . .	

Along with the entire insurance program, the A D and D feature, including the 90-day limit, was made known to the employees in a booklet distributed to them. As indicated below, the Union was also aware of the 90-day feature governing A D and D benefits.

Following Dills's death, Mrs. Dills was paid the $9,000 life insurance death benefit. Through the Union, the widow also claimed that she was entitled to an additional $9,000 because her husband's death resulted from an accident. White, Manager of Insurance Benefits, submitted the claim, but it was denied by the Insurance Carrier. Mrs. Dills testified that the carrier denied the claim because Dills's death occurred more than 90 days following the automobile accident.

This arbitration was convened because the Union contends that an additional $9,000.00 should be paid to Dills's beneficiary on the grounds that his death resulted from an accident. Its chief argument is that the 90-day limitation contained in the insurance policy has no standing under the Labor Agreement since the Labor Agreement, including Paragraph 98, was negotiated between the Union and the Company and not between the Union and the Insurance Carrier. In other words, the Union argument is that the 90-day stricture, relied upon by the Company to deny the accidental death benefit, does not control this dispute because there is no such limitation in Paragraph 98.

Negotiations of 1974 Labor Agreement

In January 1974, the Parties were in the negotiations that eventually resulted in the adoption of the current Labor Agreement. On January 9, the Union presented the following proposal to the Company:

Under AD&D it is proposed that if medical treatment begins prior to the ninety (90) day period for the injury incurred, that it would not waive the right of collection of the principal sums listed, if loss occurs after the ninety (90) day period. Also refer to proposal #29. (Anywhere 90 day appears—rewrite.)

On April 24, 1974, while discussing the 90-day limitation in question, the following exchange took place between Paul, Director of Industrial Relations, Johns, Union President, and Sykes, Union Committeeman:

PAUL: . . . All through here, Charlie, I have forgotten how many references you people made to 90 days—90 days. I would say there was something like 8 to 10 places. Just guessing off the top of my head. Talking about the 90 days on A D & D and that type of thing. I went over this in quite some detail with the guys in Insurance. This is pretty much standard language. In almost all your insurance policies.

JOHNS: It might be standard language. But it looks like if somebody was to die and they need 90 days afterward or the fact they was to have to take an arm off, or something like that. It all has to be done within 90 days or they don't get it.

PAUL: That's right—that's exactly true. If you had 120 days, it would be the same damn problem.

SYKES: No, Marv. You take now—say a man has got his arm all messed up and hell, they're operating on it and operating on it, trying to save that arm. Now you're putting a burden on that man there, saying it gets up to 89 days and say, "Hell, hack it off." If he's got any chance at all you know they're gonna keep working on that arm. It may be . . .

PAUL: I think you're going for outside choices. I can't recall, in my brief tenure here, and we've had that happen.

SYKES: We had it on a guy's eye. It came up and he thought they were going to take it out. I don't know right now how he stands. But it was going over 90 days and they were talking about taking it out after 90 days.

PAUL: But, really, this thing . . .

JOHNS: We've got two of them. Page is about to lose his eye—about 120 days after—from a nail. Then also Goodwine, he got carbide in his eye and they had several operations on it and there's a chance he might lose it.

PAUL: This is pretty much standard. This 90-day thing is all the way through your entire program.

JOHNS: Well, what we're saying here is, if treatment starts before the 90 days period . . .

PAUL: I know what you're saying. But we've talked about it quite a lot and the consensus is that you got to stay with something so you might as well stay with the standard clause, which we've got and which is preferable among everybody else.

In any event, the Company did not agree to the Union's proposal as cited above. It rejected the Union demand that the 90-day limitation would not count if the loss of life, sight, or limbs occurs after that time period provided that medical treatment started within the 90-day period. On June 19, 1974, the current Labor Agreement became effective, and contained Paragraph 98 as cited earlier. This provision appeared in the previous Labor Agreements in its current form except that the life insurance benefit was raised to $9,000 from $7,500. In addition, the Company continued to use the same Insurance Carrier, and the policy contained the 90-day limitation for loss of life, sight, or limbs resulting from an accident.

ANALYSIS OF THE EVIDENCE

Union Position: Paragraph 98 Controls Dispute

According to the Union, Paragraph 98 establishes the merits of the claim in an unambiguous manner. It urges further that the 90-day limitation contained in the insurance policy is solely between the Company and the Insurance Carrier and may not be used to apply Paragraph 98. It argues:

> We contend that the insurance contract is not incorporated into Paragraph 98. Any provision of the insurance policy is not binding upon the Union. It may not be used to undermine the unambiguous language of Paragraph 98. The Labor Agreement is determinative and not the insurance policy which is a contract between the Company and the Insurance Carrier. Paragraph 98 says the Company shall pay the benefit. There is no ambiguity in Paragraph 98. It is clear. It says the Company will pay the benefit. It does not say the Insurance Carrier will pay the benefit.

As a matter of fact, the Union, with vigor, argues that the Arbitrator should base his decision strictly on the language of Paragraph 98. It says that evidence submitted by the Company is not material and should not be given any weight. Included in this category are the 1974 negotiations that resulted in the instant Labor Agreement, previous administration of the A D and D program,* and the booklet distributed to employees explaining the insurance program. To buttress its position, the Union refers to an arbitration decision, dated December 15, 1972, involving the Parties, rendered by Arbitrator Kess. In that case, the issue involved the application of that portion of the Labor Agreement (not Paragraph 98) which deals with weekly benefits for employees who are absent from work because of accident or illness. While granting the grievance, Arbitrator Kess observed that the controlling contractual language was "clear and unambiguous." In addition, he relied on the Union argument that the insurance policy between the Company and the Insurance Carrier was not incorporated in that area of the Labor Agreement involved in his case.

Character of Paragraph 98

It is self-evident, of course, that Paragraph 98 is an agreement reached solely by the Parties. As the Union says, the Insurance Carrier and the policy under which benefits are paid are not expressly mentioned in the provision. To this extent, the Union argument has merit—the Company and Union reached the agreement contained in Paragraph 98, and this agreement is solely betwen them and not between

---

* The Company submitted two instances demonstrating that 50 percent of the principal sum was paid to two (2) employees who each lost the sight of one eye. It points out that this benefit was paid under the insurance policy, and stresses further that Paragraph 98 does not provide for a specific amount of benefit for accidental death, dismemberment, or loss of sight. Hence, the Company argues that the insurance policy is incorporated into Paragraph 98.

the Union and the Insurance Carrier. Thus, the Union is on sound ground when it argues that Paragraph 98 should govern the dispute. If there is a conflict between the language of the provision and the contract executed by the Company and the Insurance Carrier, any such conflict should be resolved in favor of the language contained in Paragraph 98.

On the other hand, the Union argument breaks down because Paragraph 98 is not written in unambiguous terms as it relates to the dispute at hand. The provision is clear to the extent that each employee acquiring seniority will be covered by a $9,000 life insurance policy. It also is clear that the Company will pay the full premium. However, what about benefits for accidental death and dismemberment? Paragraph 98 says that each employee will be covered by a life insurance policy "plus A D and D." It does not specify the amount of any such benefit, and it does not spell out the circumstances under which such a benefit will be paid. In addition, the provision is silent as to when loss of life, limbs, or sight must occur following an accident for the benefit to be paid.

Union Counsel argues that Paragraph 98 does not say that loss of life must occur within 90 days of accident for the accidental death benefit (double indemnity) to be paid. This is true. However, it is equally true that Paragraph 98 does not specify that such a benefit will be paid regardless of when loss of life occurs following an accident.

In short, for purposes of this case, Paragraph 98 is ambiguous and unclear. Indeed, for the Union position to prevail solely on the basis of contractual language, Paragraph 98 would have to say unambiguously and unequivocally that the accidental death benefit shall be paid "regardless of when death occurs following an accident." It obviously does not say this, and Paragraph 98 by reasonable inference simply cannot be held to mean what the Union would like it to mean. Thus, the position of the Union may not prevail solely on the basis of the language of Paragraph 98. As to the material issue involved in this dispute—when loss of life must occur following an accident for accidental death benefit eligibility—the provision is obviously not clear at all. For this reason, the Kess decision does not stand as a valid precedent. Not only did the dispute arbitrated by Kess arise under a different provision of the Labor Agreement, but what is equally important, Kess held that the controlling language in his case was clear and unambiguous. In this case, it is incontrovertible that Paragraph 98 is not written in unambiguous terms as it relates to the instant dispute. To hold that the language is clear beyond reasonable doubt as to the material issue would be a masterpiece of error.

Union Recognition of 90–Day Limit

It would likewise be a most grievous error for the Arbitrator to find that the Union and the employees are not bound by the 90-day limit contained in the policy in effect between the Company and the Insurance Carrier. True, the Insurance Carrier is not a party to Paragraph 98. As mentioned earlier, Paragraph 98 is a contractual provision negotiated by the Parties. It was not negotiated between the Union and the Insurance Carrier.

Despite these considerations, *the evidence is incontrovertible that the Union recognized that the 90-day limit contained in the insurance policy is incorporated into Paragraph 98.* The best evidence for this conclusion is the fact that the Union attempted unsuccessfully to broaden the 90-day limit. In his argument, Union Counsel says that the negotiations do not count and should not be given any weight. He argues that under the *parol* evidence rule what was proposed, discussed, and rejected in negotiations should not prejudice the Union's position. Such an argument would have merit if Paragraph 98 were written in clearcut and unambiguous terms as it relates to the material issue in this case. Under these circumstances, the events of the 1974 negotiations would not count and would not prejudice the Union's case. Under the *parol* evidence rule, what was proposed, discussed, and rejected may not properly be held to vary *unambiguous* contractual language. As abundantly demonstrated, however, Paragraph 98 is ambiguous as it related to the circumstances of this dispute.

Since it is ambiguous and uncertain, the events of the 1974 negotiations are squarely material to the application of Paragraph 98. In those negotiations the Union endeavored to change the 90-day limit. It demanded that the 90-day limit not apply if medical treatment were obtained within the 90-day period. That is, if medical treatment were administered to an employee within the 90-day period, the employee would be eligible for A D and D benefits regardless of when loss of life, limbs, or sight would occur. Indeed, if the Union really believed that the 90-day limit did not apply to Paragraph 98, why in the world did it make such a proposal? Common sense alone tells us that the Union made this proposal because it recognized that A D and D benefits are not paid when loss of life, limbs, or sight occurs after 90 days following an accident. In short, the Union was fully aware of the 90-day limit under Paragraph 98, and it unsuccessfully attempted to broaden the limit. The Company rejected the Union's demand, and Paragraph 98 remains in the current Labor Agreement as it appeared in previous contracts except for the increase of the principal benefit.

That the Union knew what the 90-day limit was all about is made crystal-clear in the exchange between the Company and Union representatives in the 1974 negotiations. This entire exchange was cited earlier in this Opinion. In any event recall the following:

JOHNS: (Union President): But it looks like if somebody was to die and they need 90 days afterward or the fact that if they was to have to take an arm off, or something like that. It all has to be done within 90 days or they don't get it.

PAUL: (Manager of Labor Relations): *That's right—that's exactly true.*

In other words, the 90-day limit is a part of Paragraph 98. The Union knew it and tried without success to change it. Union Counsel cautions the Arbitrator that he would commit the cardinal sin of arbitrators if he were to read the 90-day limit into the provision. To the contrary, the conduct of the Union in the 1974 negotiations proves conclusively that it recognized the 90-day limit. *That is why it tried to remove the stricture in the 1974 negotiations.* The Arbitrator does not inject into Paragraph 98 the 90-day limit. It was there before the Arbitrator was called upon to decide this dispute. He does not read into the provision a restriction that was not previously recognized by the Union.

In the light of these observations, the Arbitrator finds that Paragraph 98 contains the 90-day limit which is in the insurance policy. Though not expressly mentioned in the provision, one would have to shut one's eyes to the most clear and incontrovertible evidence that the Union was fully aware that the 90-day limit is incorporated into the provision.

In short, the Arbitrator regards Paragraph 98 as if it expressly contained the stricture found in the insurance policy. The limitation on the payment of accidental death benefits is this: *Loss of life caused by accident must occur within 90 days after the date of accident.*

Meaning of "Loss of Life" under Paragraph 98

It should logically follow, therefore, that the grievance should be denied. Dills's accident occurred on February 5, 1975, and he did not die until 117 days later. His death certificate was executed on June 2, 1975. Though his loss of life was caused by an accident, he died beyond the 90-day limit. Understandably, the Company argues:

> The Union has failed to prove that the Company violated the contract by not paying an additional $9,000 to the widow of employee Dills.
> The Union acknowledged, by virtue of their proposal submitted to the Company during the negotiations that they recognized the 90-day limitation in A D & D and wished to broaden this limitation . . .
> It is very evident and clear that the Union is attempting to obtain in this arbitration proceeding what it could not obtain at the bargaining table of negotiations in the formulation of this labor agreement.

In other words, since the Union failed to broaden the 90-day limit, and since Dills died after the 90-day limit, the Company requests that the grievance should be denied.

Without question, Dills died on June 2, 1975. The death certificate was executed on this date. It was not, of course, executed within the 90-day limit. On these grounds, the grievance should have no standing under Paragraph 98. The fact that the Insurance Carrier denied the claim is additional proof that for purposes of Paragraph 98 Dills died after the 90-day limit.

What is involved here, however, is the construction of the term "loss of life" as contained in the A D and D feature of the insurance program. It says that in the "event of loss of life" the benefit will be the principal sum of the life insurance policy. At the risk of inviting understandable censure by the Company, the Arbitrator construes Dills's "loss of life" for purposes of Paragraph 98 as of April

28, 1975, which was within the 90-day period. On this date, the uncontested evidence demonstrates that the medical authorities said that Dills had no chance to live. Uncontested evidence demonstrates that his "life" was prolonged beyond that date by a life-support system. For all practical purposes, Dills's life expired as a human being on April 28. If the life-support system of Dills had been taken away, he would have officially died before the 90-day period expired. Only by the use of the life-support system did he linger until June 2, 1975.

For purposes of Paragraph 98, "life" means more than being maintained as a vegetable by a life-support system. "Life" means that the person can function as a human being and has a reasonable chance for recovery. We should not believe in miracles, and no miracle occurred in this case. Medical authority said that Dills had absolutely no chance to recover, and he did die as predicted. Only by the use of a life-support system did he technically "live" until after the 90 days had expired. In other words, the Company places an unrealistic construction on the term "life" under the circumstances of this case. For all realistic purposes, Dills for purposes of Paragraph 98 lost his life as of April 28, 1975. For these reasons, the Arbitrator shall grant the grievance.

Conclusions

Having reached this conclusion under the circumstances of this case, the Arbitrator cautions all concerned not to read too much into his decision. He does not write into Paragraph 98 the proposal that the Union unsuccessfully attempted to advance in the 1974 contract negotiations. The 90-day limit still applies for purposes of Paragraph 98. That is, loss of life, sight, or limbs must occur within 90 days following an accident. Nothing in this decision is intended to undermine the integrity of the 90-day limit.

Put succinctly, the Arbitrator grants this grievance solely and exclusively because of the particular circumstances of this case: Dills effectively and realistically lost his life within the 90-day period. He was maintained beyond this time by a life-support system. Beyond this, the Arbitrator establishes no precedent and makes no exception to the 90-day limit. As a result of the narrow set of facts under which the Arbitrator has applied Paragraph 98 in this particular case, the Union, of course, does not gain in arbitration what it failed to achieve in contract negotiations. What is at stake in this case is exclusively the Arbitrator's construction of "loss of life" under its particular facts and circumstances. This is the full and only extent of the Arbitrator's decision to grant the grievance.

If the Union believes that the 90-day limit is unfair and unrealistic, it must change it in collective bargaining and not in arbitration. Nothing the Arbitrator has said in this case, or intended to say, removes the 90-day limit for the purpose of the application of Paragraph 98. All that the Arbitrator has said in this case, or intended to say, is that for purposes of Paragraph 98 Dills lost his life effective on April 28, 1975. On that date, the 90-day limit had not expired.

Questions

1 Why did the arbitrator find that the ninety-day rule is incorporated into Paragraph 98 though it does not appear in the express language of the provision?

2 Was the arbitrator's decision to award the widow double indemnity consistent with his finding that the ninety-day rule was incorporated into Paragraph 98? Defend your position with cogent arguments.

3 Assume that an employee injures his hand and after ninety days the hand is amputated. To what extent would the arbitrator's decision in this case stand as a valid precedent for the employee's claim that he should be indemnified for the loss of the hand?

4 Why did the arbitrator hold that the employee lost his life within 90 days for insurance purposes following the accident even though he died on the 117th day?

chapter 9

Institutional Issues under Collective Bargaining

The modern collective bargaining contract encompasses many issues that do not fall into the general category of wages or fringe supplements. Such subjects, rather, deal with the rights and duties of the employer, the union, and the employees themselves. Some of them—such as seniority and discharge—most directly serve to protect the job rights of workers and might be most appropriately thought of as "administrative" concerns. They will be treated in such a manner in Chapter 10.

Other subjects, however, tend to supply the institutional needs of either the labor organization or the particular management—through "compulsory union membership" clauses, for example, or by provisions explicitly allowing the management the right to make decisions for the direction of the labor force and the operation of the plant. These matters will be dealt with in the paragraphs that follow in this chapter.

In considering this institutional dimension of collective bargaining, it must be recognized that the topics it encompasses can on occasion give the negotiators considerably more trouble than do the wage or fringe issues. There can, indeed, be deeply rooted conflict over basic philosophies of labor relations, the rights of management, and the rights and obligations of unions. And it is, for example, at times infinitely easier to compromise and settle a wage controversy than to resolve a heated difference of opinion as to whether or not a worker should be compelled to join a union as a condition of employment. For all the thorniness of many wage and wage-related issues, some of the longest and most bitter individual strikes have had as their source conflicts dealing with the institutional issues of collective bargaining.

This chapter will inspect, in turn, union membership as a condition of em-

ployment, the so-called "checkoff" mechanism, union obligations, managerial prerogatives, "codetermination" and the question of unions in the board of directors'
room, and so-called "Quality of Work Life" programs.

UNION MEMBERSHIP AS A CONDITION OF EMPLOYMENT

Prior to the passage of the Wagner Act in 1935, there was essentially only one way
in which a union could get itself recognized by an unsympathetic management:
through the use of raw economic strength. If the labor organization succeeded in
pulling all or a significant part of the company's employees out on strike, or in
having its membership boycott the production or services of the company in the
marketplace, it stood a good chance of forcing the employer to come to terms.
Lacking such economic strength, however, the union had no recourse—even if all
the company's workers wanted to join it—in the face of management opposition
to its presence.

The 1935 legislation, as we know, greatly improved the lot of the union in
this regard. It provided for a secret-ballot election by the employees, should the
employer express doubt as to the union's majority status. It also gave the union
the exclusive right to bargain for all workers in the designated bargaining unit,
should the election prove that it did indeed have majority support. As Chapter 3
has indicated, these new ground rules for union recognition continue to this day.

Legally fostered recognition has not been synonymous with any assured status
for the union as a institution, however. Indeed, in the many years since the Wagner
Act, unions have still been able to find three grounds for insecurity. For one, the
law has given the recognized labor organization no guarantee that it could not be
dislodged by a rival union at some later date. For a second, there have still been
many communication avenues open to antagonistic employers who choose to make
known to their employees their antiunion feelings in an attempt to rid themselves
of certified unions after a designated interval following the signing of the initial
contract. And for a third, the government has not granted recognized unions
protection against "free riders"—employees who choose to remain outside the
union and thus gain the benefits of unionism without in any way helping to pay
for those benefits. Under the law, the union clearly has not only the right but also
the obligation to represent all employees in the bargaining unit, regardless of their
membership or nonmembership in the union. Unions have particularly feared that
the "free-rider" attitude could become contagious, resulting in the loss through a
subsequent election (in which nonmembers as well as members can vote) of their
majority status and thus of their representation rights.

Consequently, organized labor has turned to its own bargaining table efforts
in an attempt to gain a further measure of institutional security. By and large, such
attempts have been successful. Today, possibly as many as 83 percent of all contracts
contain some kind of "union security" provision.[1]

---

[1] Based on unofficial information furnished by the Bureau of Labor Statistics, U.S. Department of Labor.

Such provisions, which are frequently also referred to as "compulsory union membership" devices, essentially are three in number: the closed shop, the union shop, and the maintenance-of-membership agreement. Brief reference has already been made to each of these mechanisms. A common denominator to all is that in one way or another membership in the union is made a condition of employment for at least some workers. They differ, however, in the timing for the requirement of union membership and in the degree of freedom of choice allowed the worker in the decision about joining the labor organization.

The closed shop and union shop are dissimilar in that under the former the worker must belong to the union *before* obtaining a job, whereas the latter requires union membership within a certain time period *after* the worker is hired. Under a maintenance-of-membership arrangement, the worker is free to elect whether or not to join the union. The worker who does join, however, must maintain membership in the union for the duration of the contract period or else forfeit the job.

These forms of compulsory union membership can also be viewed as differing with respect to the freedom of the employer to hire workers. Under the closed shop, the employer must hire only union members. This allows the union in effect to serve as the employment agency in most situations and to refer workers to the employer upon request. Under union shop and maintenance-of-membership arrangements, the employer has free access to the labor market. The employer may hire whomever he wants, and the union security provision becomes operative only after the worker is employed.

A final significant feature of union security is, of course, that it has received considerable attention from both Congress and the state legislatures. The laws these bodies have enacted must be taken into account at the bargaining table, and union security provisions that disregard these relevant public fiats do so only at a definite risk.

As in many other areas of collective bargaining, there are several different approaches to the union security problem. The elasticity of the process is clearly demonstrated in the varied methods that employers and unions have adopted to deal with the issue.

The *closed shop,* obviously the most advantageous arrangement from labor's point of view, appeared in 33 percent of the nation's agreements in 1946.[2] Prohibited for interstate commerce by the Taft–Hartley Act of 1947, it visibly decreased in its frequency in the years thereafter, and less than 5 percent of all contracts today contain such a provision. Many of these are in intrastate commerce, of course, but some are in the construction industry on an interstate basis. Much of the latter sector refused, rather bluntly, to abide by the Taft–Hartley stricture and in fact openly flaunted it until 1959, when the Landrum–Griffin Act recognized the special characteristics of that sector and officially allowed it a stronger form of union security that approximates the closed shop.

---

[2] Theodore Rose, "Union Security Provisions in Agreements, 1954," *Monthly Labor Review,* 78, No. 6 (June 1955), 646.

With the decrease in usage of the closed shop, the *union shop* became the most widespread form of union membership employment condition. After being part of only 17 percent of all contracts in 1946,[3] it appeared in about 64 percent of all labor agreements in 1959, and the figure is at about the 71 percent level today.

The *maintenance-of-membership* arrangement, originating in the abnormal labor market days of World War II, is still fully legal but is utilized relatively infrequently. After appearing in about one-quarter of all contracts in 1946, it steadily lost ground thereafter, and only about 3 percent of all contracts now make provision for it. Much of the loss has undoubtedly been absorbed by the gains of the union shop, which maintenance-of-membership employers, having already taken this step toward accommodating the union, have rarely resisted very adamantly. (But some of *this* loss, in turn, is not entirely real: Some arrangements have adopted the name of "union shop" but been modified in practice to equate or nearly equate to maintenance-of-membership. There is sometimes a danger in taking things at face value.)

Two other brands of union security, neither at all common, constitute compromises between the union's goal of greatest possible security and the management's reluctance to grant such institutional status. Under the *agency shop,* nonunion members of the bargaining unit must make a regular financial contribution—usually the equivalent of the union dues—to the labor organization, but no one is compelled to join the union. The money is, in fact, at times donated to recognized charitable organizations. Nonetheless, the incentive for a worker to remain in the "free-rider" class is clearly reduced in this situation, and the union thus gains some measure of protection. The *preferential shop* gives union members preference in hiring but allows the employment of nonunionists, and its efficacy seems to depend on how the parties construe the word *preference.*

Although the straight union shop thus appears to be the most popular form of union security, some employers and unions have negotiated variations of this species of compulsory union membership. Under some contracts, employees who are not union members when the union shop agreement becomes effective are not required to join the union. Some agreements exempt employees with comparatively long service with the company. Under other contracts, old employees (only) are permitted to withdraw from the union at the expiration of the agreement without forfeiting their jobs. Under this arrangement, a so-called "escape period" of about fifteen days is included in the labor contract. If an employee does not terminate union membership within the escape period, he or she must maintain membership under the new arrangement. Newly hired workers, however, are required to join the union.

Whether the straight union shop or modifications of it are negotiated, the Taft–Hartley law forbids an arrangement that compels a worker to join a union as a condition of employment unless thirty days have elapsed from the effective

---

[3] *Ibid.*

date of the contract or the beginning of employment, whichever is later. In administering this section of the law, the National Labor Relations Board has held that the thirty-day grace period does not apply to employees who are already members of the union. However, it interprets the provision literally for workers who are not union members on the effective date of the contract or who are subsequently employed. Thus, in one case, a union shop arrangement was declared unlawful because it required workers to join the union twenty-nine days following the beginning of employment. Another union security arrangement was held to be illegal because it compelled employees to join the union if they had been on the company's payroll thirty or more days; in invalidating this agreement, the board ruled that it violated the law because it did not accord employees subject to its coverage the legal thirty-day grace period for becoming union members *after the effective date* of the contract.

Whereas some negotiators have adopted variations of the straight union shop, others have devised a number of alternatives to the maintenance-of-membership arrangement. Only at the termination of the agreement are employees under most maintenance-of-membership arrangements permitted to withdraw from the union without forfeiting their jobs, and usually only a fifteen-day period is provided at the end of the contract period during which time the employee may terminate union membership. But many agreements have a considerably less liberal period of withdrawal, from the worker's viewpoint, and some contracts allow more than the modal fifteen days. If an employee fails to withdraw during this "escape" time, the employee must almost invariably remain in the union for the duration of the new collective bargaining agreement.

Under some labor agreements, maintenance-of-membership arrangements also provide for an escape period after the *signing* of the agreement, to permit withdrawals of existing members from the union. Other agreements do not afford this opportunity to current members of the union but restrict the principle of voluntary withdrawal to newly hired workers.

These modifications are fully consistent with the law in all but the twenty "right-to-work" states, which ban any form of compulsory union membership, but certain other arrangements are not. Reference has already been made to the terms of Taft–Hartley under which an employee cannot lawfully be discharged from a job because of loss of union membership unless the employee loses the membership because of nonpayment of dues or initiation fees. In spite of the existence of an arrangement requiring union membership as a condition of employment, expulsion from a union for any reason other than nonpayment of dues or initiation fees *cannot* result in loss of employment. The National Labor Relations Board will order the reinstatement of an employee to his former job with back pay where this feature of the law is violated. Depending upon the circumstances of a particular case, the board will require the employer or the union, or both, to pay back wages to such an employee.

The board has, in fact, applied a literal interpretation to this feature of Taft–Hartley. In one case the board has held that a worker actually does not have to join a union even though a union shop arrangement may be in existence.[4] The employee's only obligation under the law is the willingness to tender the dues and initiation fees required by the union. In this case, three workers were willing to pay their union dues and initiation fees but they refused to assume any other union-related obligations, or even to attend the union meeting at which they would be voted upon and accepted. As a result, the union had secured the discharge of these workers under the terms of the union security arrangement included in the labor agreement. The board held that the discharge of workers under such circumstances violated the Taft–Hartley law, ruled that both the union and the company engaged in unfair labor practices, and ordered the workers reinstated in their jobs with full back pay.

The "right-to-work" laws themselves, of course, serve as formidable obstacles to union security arrangements in the primarily southern and southwestern states in which they remain on the books. On the other hand, not only has their effect on labor relations in these states been highly debatable, but in its 1965–1966 session Congress came close to repealing the relevant Taft–Hartley Act passage permitting the enactment of such state laws (Section 14b),[5] and while there was at the time of this writing little likelihood that the repeal efforts would soon be resumed on Capitol Hill, it was a safe bet that ultimately they would be.

Were Congress to remove Section 14b, this action would nullify all right-to-work laws as far as these laws apply to interstate commerce, because of the *federal preemption* doctrine, which forbids states to pass laws in conflict with a federal statute. And in that event the right-to-work laws existing in Alabama, Arizona, Arkansas, Florida, Georgia, Iowa, Kansas, Louisiana, Mississippi, Nebraska, Nevada, North Carolina, North Dakota, South Carolina, South Dakota, Tennessee, Texas, Utah, Virginia, and Wyoming would have application only in the area of intrastate commerce. They would cease to have any effect upon firms engaged in interstate dealings.

In the other direction, there was also a strong chance as this edition approached publication that several states would be battlegrounds for new right-to-work laws. No state has passed such a law since 1976, when Louisiana did so (and the voters in Arkansas overwhelmingly voted to *keep* their longstanding right-to-work laws). But many right-to-work advocates were optimistic about near-term prospects for antiunion shop legislation in New Mexico, Colorado, Idaho, Maine, New Hampshire, and Vermont. Missouri, where in 1978 the voters had defeated a right-to-work proposal by a margin of 60–40, also could not be counted out: A bitter feud there between the national and local right-to-work forces had probably caused the 1978 result and thus may not have reflected the true popular feeling.

---

[4] *Union Starch & Refining Co.,* 87 NLRB 779 (1949).

[5] The repeal measure passed the House by a 20-vote margin, but a filibuster led by the late Sen. Everett M. Dirksen of Illinois prevented the bill from being formally considered by the Senate. AFL–CIO officials, nonetheless, claimed that as many as 56 Senate votes, or more than the majority needed, would have been forthcoming in favor of repeal had the measure been brought to a vote. In 1977, too, the AFL–CIO was optimistic (in the face of a newly-elected liberal Democratic Congress) that it could get repeal enacted; this time labor's efforts were tabled by both Houses.

And there was even an outside chance as this was being written that Pennsylvania, Illinois, and Delaware—states whose unionized percentages of the work force were greater than the national average—would have right-to-work laws on *their* books within a matter of an election year or so. If any of them in fact did, new ground would be broken in the sense of a northern industrial state joining the right-to-work states' roster: Indiana, which can fairly also be called a "northern, industrial state," did have such legislation until 1965 but repealed it in the latter year, the only state ever to throw out a right-to-work law after installing it.

Nor were the forces seeking these new right-to-work laws exactly poverty-stricken. The National Right to Work Committee, based in Fairfax, Virginia, by some estimates now receives $10 million in annual contributions (and sends out approximately 25 million letters to and on behalf of its 600,000 individual and company members). Some of the money goes to such relatively broader projects as attacks on public-sector unionism and investigations into what the organization sees as the spread of prounion materials into public schools, and the committee recently pushed hard if unsuccessfully for a congressional bill that would make the committing of violence on picket lines punishable by up to twenty years in prison and a $10,000 fine. But most of the group's money is directed to the key item on the committee's agenda, the advance of the right-to-work movement itself.

Regardless of the fate of right-to-work legislation, however, it seems very likely that the question of whether union security provisions should be negotiated in labor agreements will remain a controversial one for some time to come—among the general public and some direct parties to collective bargaining if not among the large segment of unionized industry that has already granted such union security.

This controversy actually contains three major elements: morality, labor relations stability, and power.

Whether or not it is *morally* right to force an employee to join a union in order to be able to work is not an easy issue to resolve. Unions and supporters of unionism often argue that it is not "fair" to permit an employee to benefit from collective bargaining without paying dues, given the fact that the union must under the new law represent all workers in the bargaining unit. And the argument is not without logic. Improvements obtained in collective bargaining *do* benefit nonunion members as well as union-member employees, and the union *is* compelled by law to represent nonunion bargaining unit employees, even in the grievance procedure, in the same fashion that it represents union members. Against this argument stands the equally plausible one that employees should not be forced to join a union in order to work. Such compulsion seems to many people to be undemocratic, immoral, and unjust. Almost everyone, however, has different ideas on what is "morally" correct in this controversy. Indeed, even the clergy has been drawn into the fight, and its members have exhibited the same lack of unanimity in their opinions as have other people. And if these stewards of God are not certain what is morally correct, how can two college professors make a judgment that will once and for all resolve the moral issue?

Congress itself, however, has now made a judgment as to what employees should appropriately do when they have bona fide religious beliefs against joining labor organizations or financially supporting them. In a 1980 amendment to Taft–Hartley, it decreed that such workers need not violate these beliefs.[6] Instead, in something of a variation of the agency shop, they must make a contribution equal to the amount of the dues to a nonlabor, nonreligious charity. The amendment also provides that if the religious objector requests a labor organization to handle a grievance on his or her behalf, the union may charge the employee a "reasonable" amount for such servicing.

Some observers claim that union security is the key to *stability in labor relations*. They argue that a union that operates under a union-shop arrangement will be more responsible and judicious in the handling of grievances and in other day-to-day relations with its employers because of its guaranteed status. And, again, there is some strength to this argument. At times, conflict between union members and nonunion employees does hamper the effective organizational operation, and on this basis, some employers may welcome an arrangement that forces all employees to join the union, as a way of precluding such conflicts. Moreover, unions can also claim that in the absence of a union security provision, the union officers must spend considerable time in organizing the unorganized and keeping the organized content so that they will not drop out of the union. Proponents of this position justifiably declare that if union officers are relieved from this organizational chore, they can spend their time in more constructive ways, which will be beneficial not only to the employees but also to the employer.

On the other hand, other debaters point out with equal justification that unions that do enjoy a union security arrangement sometimes use this extra time to find new ways to harass the company. The solution to this particular controversy appears to an outsider to depend upon the character of the union involved and upon its relationship with the employer. Clearly, no one would blame an employer who resisted granting the union shop to a union that had traditionally engaged in frequent wildcat strikes, continually pressed grievances that had no merit, and, in short, sought to harass management at every turn.

At times, finally, employers and unions themselves argue along morality and labor relations lines to conceal a different purpose—their respective desires for *power* in the bargaining relationship. It is self-evident that the union does have more comparative influence in the negotiation of labor agreements and in its day-to-day relationship with the employer when it operates under a union shop. And, by the same token, the employer has more comparative influence when employees need not join the union to work and may terminate their membership at any time. Or, in short, the parties may speak in terms of morality merely as a smoke screen to conceal an equally logical but less euphemistic power issue.

But "power" still remains a rather nebulous term. The old saying that in poker a Smith and Wesson beats four aces is certainly true and lucidly pinpoints exactly where the power lies, and why. However, as a general statement, depending

---

[6] Public Law 96-593, 96th Congress, effective December 24, 1980.

upon the assumptions one makes, a union could have infinitely more power than a management, and the reverse would be true under a different set of assumptions and circumstances. Given this elusiveness, as well as the unhappy connotations often placed on the word, it is perhaps not surprising that the verbal controversy over union security continues to be waged along the other lines described as well as those of power.

THE CHECKOFF

Checkoff arrangements are included in the large majority of collective bargaining contracts. This dues-collection method, whereby the employer agrees to deduct from the employee's pay monthly union dues (and in some cases also initiation fees, fines, and special assessments) for transmittal to the union, has obvious advantages for labor organizations, not only in terms of time and money savings but also because it further strengthens the union's institutional status. For the same reasons, many managers are not enthusiastic about the checkoff, although some have preferred it to the constant visits of union dues-collectors to the workplace. Once willing to grant the union shop, however, employers have rarely made a major bargaining issue of the checkoff per se. And the growth of this mechanism has been remarkably consistent with that of the union security measure: Where in 1946 about 40 percent of all labor agreements provided for the checkoff system of dues collection, this figure is, as we know, somewhat over 80 percent today.

Taft–Hartley, as was also pointed out earlier, regulates the checkoff as well as union security; under the law, the checkoff is lawful only on written authorization of the individual employee. It is further provided that an employee's written authorization may be irrevocable for only one year or for the duration of the contract, whichever is shorter.

Checkoff provisions frequently deal with matters other than the specification of items that the management agrees to deduct. Some arrangements specify a maximum deduction that the company will check off in any one month, require each employee to sign a new authorization card in the event that dues are increased, indemnify the company against any liability for action taken in reliance upon authorization cards submitted by the union, require the union to reimburse the company for any illegal deductions, and provide that the union share in the expense of collecting dues through the checkoff method. Not all these items, of course, appear in each and every checkoff arrangement; many labor agreements, however, contain one or more of them.

From the foregoing, it appears rather clear that although the checkoff is an important issue of collective bargaining, it does not normally constitute a crucial point of controversy between employers and unions. It does not contain the features of conflicting philosophy that are involved in the union security problem, falls far short of other problems of collective bargaining as a vexatious issue between the parties, and has rarely by itself become a major strike issue, since the stakes are not that high. As a matter of fact, even though the checkoff serves the institutional needs of the union, employers often find some gain from the incorporation of the device in the collective bargaining agreement. This would be particularly true where the labor contract contains a union security arrangement. Not only does the checkoff obviate the previously noted need of dues collection on company premises, with the attendant impact upon the orderly operation of the plant, but it avoids the need of starting the discharge process for employees who are negligent in the payment of dues. Frequently, without a checkoff, an employee who must belong to a union as a condition of employment will delay paying dues, and the employer and union are both faced with the task of instituting the discharge process, which is most commonly suspended when the employee, faced with loss of employment, pays the owed dues at the last possible minute. The checkoff eliminates the need for this wasted and time-consuming effort on the part of busy employer and union representatives.

Even when the union shop is not in effect, moreover, the checkoff need not necessarily be given permanent status. The employee is obligated to pay dues for one year only, and if he or she desires to stop the checkoff it is possible to do so during the "escape period." But under any circumstances, if the management believes that the union with which it deals is so irresponsible as not to deserve the checkoff, it need not agree to it as part of the renegotiated contract, and the mechanism is consequently also revocable from the company's point of view.

UNION OBLIGATIONS

The typical collective bargaining contract contains one or more provisions such as those listed in Exhibit 9-1 (drawn from a current contract between the Oil, Chemical and Atomic Workers and a medium-sized chemical company) that establish certain obligations on the part of the labor organization. By far the most important of these obligations involves the pledge of a union that it will not strike during the life of the labor agreement. Most employers will, in fact, refuse to sign a collective bargaining contract unless the union agrees that it will not interrupt production during the effective contractual period.

The incorporation of a no-strike clause in a labor agreement means that all disputes relating to the interpretation and the application of a labor agreement are to be resolved through the grievance and arbitration procedure in an orderly and peaceful manner, and not through the harsh arbiter of industrial warfare. The pledge of the union not to strike during the contract period stabilizes industrial relations and thereby protects the interests of the employer, the union, and the employees. Indeed, a chief advantage that employers obtain from the collective bargaining process is the assurance that the organization will operate free from strikes or other forms of interruption to production (slowdowns, for example) during the period of the agreement.

Managements and unions have negotiated two major forms of no-strike pro-

---

EXHIBIT 9-1
Article 2

Section 3. No Strike—No Lockout

1 During the life of this Agreement there shall be no strike, work stoppage, slow down, nor any other interruption of work by the Union of its members, and there shall be no lockout by the Company. In the event of a violation of this provision, either party to the Agreement may seek relief under the Grievance and Arbitration provisions of the Agreement or may pursue his remedy before the court or the Labor Board, as the case may be.

2 As an alternative, either party, in the event of an alleged or asserted breach of the no strike–no lockout clause, may institute expedited arbitration by telegram to the Federal Mediation and Conciliation Service and request that the FMCS designate an Arbitrator as quickly as possible. The Arbitrator shall hold the hearing as promptly as possible, notice to be served on any officer of the Company and on the President, Vice President or Secretary-Treasurer of the Union (any one of the three officers of the Union). The Arbitrator shall set the date, time and place of hearing and shall issue his award orally as soon after the completion of the hearing as possible.

3 Individual employees or groups of employees who adopt methods other than those provided in the grievance procedure for the settlement of their grievances shall be subject to disciplinary action, including discharge. Any disciplinary action taken by the Company under this clause shall be subject to review under the grievance procedure.

4 Should any dispute arise between the Company and the Union, or between the Company and any employee or employees, the Union will cooperate to prevent and/or terminate a work stoppage or suspension of work or a slow down on the part of the employees on account of such dispute. A violation of this paragraph by any employee or group of employees will give the Company the right to administer discipline, including discharge. In administering discipline, including discharge, the Company shall have the right to distinguish between those instigating or leading the work stoppage or suspension of work or slow-down and those who simply participate therein. Any disciplinary action taken by the Company under this clause shall be subject to review under the grievance procedure.

Section 4. Successors and Assigns

This Agreement, any supplements or amendments thereto, hereinafter referred to collectively as "Agreement" shall be binding upon the parties hereto, their successors and assigns.

---

visions. Under one category, there is an *absolute and unconditional* surrender on the part of the union of its right to strike or otherwise to interfere with production during the life of the labor agreement. The union agrees that it will not strike for any purpose or under any circumstances for the duration of the contract period. Employers, of course, obtain maximum security against strikes by this approach to the problem.

Under the second major form, the union can use the strike only under certain *limited* circumstances. For example, in the automobile industry the union may strike against company-imposed production standards. Such strikes may not take place, however, before all attempts are made in the grievance procedure to negotiate production standard complaints. Other collective bargaining contracts provide that unions can strike for any purpose during the contract period but only after the entire grievance procedure has been exhausted, when the employer refuses to abide by an arbitrator's decision, or when a deadlock occurs during a wage-reopening negotiation. The union cannot strike under any other conditions for the length of the contract.

In the vast majority of cases, labor organizations fulfill their no-strike obligations just as most unionized companies fulfill all their contractually delineated responsibilities. However, in the event that violations do take place, employers have available to them a series of remedies. In the first place, under the terms of the Taft–Hartley law, employers can sue unions for violations of collective bargaining contracts in the U.S. district courts. And, although judgments obtained in such court proceedings may be assessed only against the labor organization and not against individual union members, additional remedies are provided for in many collective bargaining contracts. Under some of them, strikes called by a labor union in violation of a no-strike pledge terminate the entire collective bargaining contract. In others, the checkoff and any agreement requiring membership as a condition of employment are suspended.

In addition, the employer may elect to seek penalties against the instigators and the active participants, or either group, in such a strike. Many contracts clearly provide that employees actively participating in a strike during the life of a collective bargaining contract are subject to discharge, suspension, loss of seniority rights, or termination of other benefits under the contract, including vacation and holiday pay. The right of an employer to discharge workers participating in such strikes has been upheld by the Supreme Court.

Finally, arbitrators will usually sustain the right of employers to discharge or otherwise discipline workers who instigate or actively participate in an unlawful strike or slowdown. Such decisions are based on the principle that the inclusion of a no-strike clause in a labor agreement serves as the device to stabilize labor relations during the contract period and as a pledge to resolve all disputes arising under the collective bargaining contract through the orderly and peaceful channels of the grievance procedure.

In June 1970, the Supreme Court provided employers with a powerful legal weapon to deal with strikes that violate a no-strike clause contained in a collective bargaining contract. At that time, the high court by a 5–2 vote in *Boys Markets* v. *Retail Clerks* (398 U.S. 235) held that when a contract incorporates a no-strike agreement and an arbitration procedure, a federal court may issue an injunction to terminate the strike. This decision permits employers to go into court to force employees back to work when a labor agreement contains these features. The idea behind the decision is that the grievance procedure and arbitration should be used to settle disputes that arise during the course of a collective bargaining contract.

Even though the decision of the Supreme Court could be defended on the grounds that employees should not strike to settle their grievances when arbitration is available, the 1970 decision astonished many observers of the labor relations scene, because in 1962 the Court had ruled that federal courts could not issue an injunction to stop a strike called in violation of a no-strike clause (*Sinclair Refining v. Atkinson,* 370 U.S. 195). In the 1962 decision, the high court held that injunctions could not be issued because the Taft–Hartley law did not make such strikes illegal. Since they were not made illegal, the Court reasoned, such strikes, although in violation of the labor agreement, constitute a labor dispute within the meaning of the Norris–La Guardia Act. We have learned from the study of this law that federal courts are forbidden to issue injunctions when a labor dispute exists within the meaning of the statute.

Thus, after an eight-year period, the Court reversed its position. Some people believe that the Court was wrong in this switch of policy, because Congress did not seek to change the 1962 decision through legislation. As the *Wall Street Journal* observed when the Court rendered its 1970 decision:

> As a matter of fact such legislation was introduced, but Congress so far has not seen fit to act. Congressional action, of course, would have been much the better way. However desirable the result, the Supreme Court still should restrain itself from assuming the tasks that properly belong to the legislators.

Such criticism of the *Boys Markets* decision does not, of course, mean approval of strikes in violation of no-strike agreements. As a matter of labor relations stability, and to preserve the integrity of agreements made at the bargaining table, employees and unions should resort to arbitration, not to the street, to settle disputes with their employers. Rather, the source of the criticism is the change in Supreme Court policy after an eight-year period during which Congress did not see fit to reverse the 1962 *Sinclair* decision. As the minority opinion stated:

> Nothing at all has changed except the membership of the court and the personal views of one justice.

Regardless of one's judgment of the Supreme Court's change in policy, the fact remains that it has provided employers with a potent weapon to stamp out strikes that violate no-strike agreements.

At times, strikes and other interruptions to production that are not authorized by the labor organization occur. These work stoppages, commonly known as "wild-cat strikes," are instigated by a group of workers, sometimes including union officers, without the sanction of the labor union. Under many labor agreements, the employer has the right to discharge such employees or to penalize them otherwise for such activities. At times employers impose a stiffer penalty on local union officers, including stewards and grievance committee persons, compared with rank-and-file employees who commit the same offense. Disparate discipline is justified because union officials have a greater obligation to comply and enforce the no-strike clause. In a 1983 case, however, the U.S. Supreme Court held that employers may not impose more severe discipline on union officials who commit the same offense as rank-and-file employees.[7] If both, for example, instigate a wildcat strike, engage in picketing, or encourage other employees to join the strike, an employer may not discharge the union officials while only suspending the rank-and-file employees. Should a management desire to penalize union officials more severely, it must negotiate a contract provision that specifically authorizes disparate treatment by placing special obligations on the officials. It is not likely, however, that many unions would agree to such a contractual provision.

A special problem has been created by the Taft–Hartley law in reference to wildcat strikes. Under this law, a labor union is responsible for the action of agents even though the union does not authorize or ratify such conduct.[8] Thus, an employer may sue a union because of a wildcat strike even though the union does not in any way condone the stoppage. As a result of this state of affairs, unions and employers have negotiated the so-called "nonsuability clauses" that were mentioned in Chapter 3. Under these arrangements, the company agrees that it will not sue a labor union because of wildcat strikes, provided that the union fulfills its obligation to terminate the work stoppage. Frequently, the labor contract specifies exactly what the union must do in order to free itself from the possibility of damage suits. Thus, in some contracts containing nonsuability clauses, the union agrees to announce orally and in writing that it disavows the strike, to order the workers back to their jobs, and to refuse any form of strike relief to the participants in such work stoppages.

Other features of some collective bargaining contracts also deal with strike situations. Under many labor agreements, the union agrees that it will protect the employer's property during strikes. To accomplish this objective, the union typically pledges itself to cooperate with the management in the orderly cessation of production and the shutting down of machinery. In addition, some unions agree to facilitate the proper maintenance of machinery during strikes even if achieving this objective requires the employment of certain bargaining unit maintenance personnel during the strike. Finally, it is not uncommon for unions to agree in the labor contract that management and supervisory peronnel entering and leaving the plant in a strike situation will not be interfered with by the labor organization.

Many collective bargaining contracts place other obligations upon unions, extending well beyond the area of strikes and slowdowns. Under many agreements, for example, the union obligates itself not to conduct on company time or on company property any union activities that will interfere with the efficient operation of the plant. The outstanding exception to this rule, however, involves the handling of grievances: Meetings of union and company representatives that deal directly with grievance administration are usually conducted on company time. Some agree-

[7] *Metropolitan Edison Co.* v. *NLRB,* Case No. 81-1664, April 4, 1983.
[8] Section 301(e) states: ". . . For purposes of this section, in determining whether any person is acting as an 'agent' of another person as to make such other person responsible for his acts, the question of whether the specific acts performed were actually authorized or subsequently ratified shall not be controlling."

ments also permit union officials to collect dues on company property where the checkoff is not in existence. And another exception found in many contracts involves the permission given to employees and union officers to discuss union business or to solicit union membership during lunch and rest periods.

Another frequently encountered limitation of union activity on plant property involves restrictions of visits to the company by representatives of the international union with which the local is affiliated. Still another denies unions permission to post notices in the plant or to use company bulletin boards without the permission of the employer. Where the union is allowed to use bulletin boards, many labor contracts specify the character of notices that the union may post; notices are permitted, for example, only when they pertain to union meetings and social affairs, union appointments and elections, reports of union committees, and rulings of the international union. Specifically prohibited on many occasions are notices that are controversial, propagandist, or political in nature.

MANAGERIAL PREROGATIVES

Once upon a time, a vice president for industrial relations of a large corporation was bargaining against a strike deadline with only hours to spare and making no progress whatsoever. The parties remained poles apart and the executive—not an especially calm person to start with—was approaching the condition of a nervous wreck.

Suddenly, a messenger informed him that his wife, nine months pregnant, had been taken to the hospital and the union (which had not to that point shown itself to be particularly accommodating) in no way argued with his suggestion that he make a quick trip to see her. At his wife's bedside, however, a strange contrast could be seen: The baby had not yet arrived, and she, though in considerable pain, was nonetheless amazingly calm and composed; he, without child at all, was more of a nervous wreck than ever.

The industrial relations man asked the nurse to explain his wife's commendable placidity and was told, "It must be that wonderful new tranquilizer that she's been given: Twilight Zone." The executive said, "Great! Great! Give me some, too! Give me some, too!" The nurse responded, "I'm sorry, sir, but that's only for labor." And the executive replied, "My God! Is there nothing left for management?"

That collective bargaining is in many ways synonymous with limitations on managerial authority is an observation that was offered on the earliest pages of this book. A fundamental characteristic of the process is restriction on the power of the management to make decisions in the area of employer–employee relations, and much of the controversy about collective bargaining grows out of this factor. On the one hand, the labor union seeks to limit the authority of management to make decisions when it believes that such restrictions will serve the interests of its members or will tend to satisfy the institutional needs of the union itself. On the other hand, the responsibility for efficiency in operation of the enterprise rests with management. The reason for the existence of management, in fact, is the overall management of the business, and executives attempt to retain free from limitations those functions that they believe are indispensable to this end.

The problem is, moreover, hardly disposed of simply because most union leaders assert—and normally, in good faith—that they have no intention of interfering with the "proper functions of management." Years of witnessing official union interest expand from the historical wages and hours context into such newer areas as those outlined in this portion of the book have understandably led managers to conclude that what is "proper" for the union depends on the situation and the values of the union membership.

Nor do employers find much consolation in the fact that the managerial decision-making process is already limited and modified by such economic forces as labor market conditions, by such laws as those pertaining to minimum wages and discrimination, and by the employee-oriented spirit of our society. If unionism is not by any means the only restriction on company freedom of action in the personnel sphere, it is nonetheless a highly important one for companies whose employees live under a union contract.

Beyond this, finally, the controversy is hardly confined to the personnel area, for managers can point to numerous (although proportionately infrequent) instances of strong union interest in such relatively removed fields as finance, plant location, pricing, and other "proper" management functions. In recent years, for example, some railroad unions have constantly blamed their employers' high degree of bonded indebtedness for depriving railroad workers of "adequate" wage increases; legal representatives of the Ladies' Garment Workers as well as those of several other unions have become familiar faces in courtrooms, to protest plant relocations of their union's employers; and the United Automobile Workers' interest in the pricing of cars is now all but taken for granted in automobile industry bargaining rooms (although the UAW's freely offered advice on this subject has yet to be accepted by the automobile manufacturers). Given the present state of the government's "legal duty to bargain" provisions, as Chapter 3 has indicated, no one can assert with complete confidence that such examples will not multiply in the years ahead.

In many ways, in fact, ramifications of the subject extend far beyond the two parties to collective bargaining. There is justification, indeed, for arguing that the "managerial rights" issue really pivots upon the broader question of what the appropriate function of labor unions in the life of our nation should be.

Managements have frequently translated their own thoughts on the subject into concrete action. Approximately 60 percent of all labor agreements today contain clauses that explicitly recognize certain stipulated types of decisions as being "vested exclusively in the Company." Such clauses are commonly called "management prerogative," "management rights," or (more appropriately, to many managers) "management security" clauses.

Fairly typical of management prerogative provisions is the following, culled from the 1982–1985 agreement of a large midwestern durable goods manufacturer:

> Subject to the provisions of this agreement, the management of the business and of the plants and the direction of the working forces, including but not limited to the right to direct, plan, and control plant operations and to establish and to change work schedules, to hire, promote, demote, transfer, suspend, discipline, or discharge employees for cause or to relieve from duty employees because of lack of work or for other legitimate reasons, to introduce new and improved methods or facilities, to determine the products to be handled, produced, or manufactured, to determine the schedules of production and the methods, processes, and the means of production, to make shop rules and regulations not inconsistent with this agreement and to manage the plants in the traditional manner, is vested exclusively in the Company. Nothing in this agreement shall be deemed to limit the Company in any way in the exercise of the regular and customary functions of management.

Some rights clauses, by way of contrast, limit themselves to short, general statements. These are much more readable than the one above, but considerably less specific—for example, "the right to manage the plant and to direct the work forces and operations of the plant, subject to the limitations of this Agreement, is exclusively vested in, and retained by, the Company." On the other hand, the management rights clause cited is itself a model of brevity when compared with that of at least one of its counterparts: The current agreement between the Kuhlman Electric Company of Detroit and the UAW contains one that consumes over a dozen pages; it is, as one observer commented when it was originally inserted in a prior contract, a "likely candidate for the *Guinness Book of Records.*"[9]

No matter which way management injects such clauses into the contract, however, two industrial relations truisms must also be appreciated: (1) The power of the rights clause is always subject to qualification by the wording of every other clause in the labor agreement; and (2) consistent administrative practices on the part of the company must implement the rights clause if it is to stand up before an arbitrator.

According to one point of view, moreover, the inclusion of such a clause in a labor agreement is unnecessary, and, of course, many agreements do not make any reference to managerial rights. This practice of omission is often based on the belief that the employer retains all rights of management that are not relinquished, modified, or eliminated by the collective bargaining contract. Thus, in the absence of collective bargaining, according to this view, the employer has the power to make any decision in the area of labor relations that he desires (subject to considerations of law, the marketplace, and so on). This right is based on the simple fact that the employer is the owner of the business. For example, the emloyer's right to promote, demote, lay off, make overtime assignments, and rehire may be limited by the seniority provisions of the collective bargaining contract. And the contract

[9] *New York Times,* December 12, 1976, p. F-13.

may stipulate that layoffs be based on a certain formula. However, to the extent that such a formula does not limit the right of the employer to lay off, it follows that management may exercise this function on a unilateral basis. *(Cases 9 and 10 deal with the management rights problem.)*

This concept of management prerogatives is sometimes called the "residual theory" of management rights. That is, all rights reside in management except those that are limited by the labor agreement or conditioned by a past practice. Where a management embraces the residual theory, it most commonly takes a stiff attitude at the bargaining table relative to union demands that would tend to further limit rights of management. With more elements of an "Armed Truce" than an "Accommodation" philosophy, it views the collective bargaining process as a tug of war between the management and the union—management resisting further invasions by the union into the citadel of management rights, which are to be protected at all costs as a matter of principle.

Such employers are not particularly concerned with the merits of a union demand; *any* demand that would impose additional limitations on management must be resisted. For example, such a management, regardless of the merits of a particular claim, would typically resist the incorporation of working rules into the labor agreement—rules dealing with such topics as payment to employees for work not actually performed, limitations on technological change or other innovations in the operation of the business, the amount of production an employee must turn out to hold a job, and how many workers are required to perform a job. One can also safely predict that a residualist management would strongly resist any demand that would limit its right to move an operation from one plant to another, shut down one plant of a multiple-plant operation, subcontract work, or compel employees to work overtime. In addition, such a management would quite probably try aggressively, when the occasion seemed appropriate, to regain "rights" that it had previously relinquished.

Indeed, today many employers are striving to reclaim the right to make unilateral determinations of working rules. Many recent strikes in a host of industries as diverse as the airlines, petroleum, and printing and publishing have been waged because managements desired to erase from the bargaining relationship working rules to which they had agreed in previous years. It is understandable why labor organizations resist these attempts of management: With the elimination of working rules, employees could more easily be laid off, for example. Since automation and changing market demands constitute in many relationships constant threats to job security, it is no mystery why some unions would rather strike than concede on this point.

The opposing view of the theory of residual rights is based on the idea that management has responsibilities other than to the maximization of managerial authority. It proceeds from the proposition that management is the "trustee" of the interest of employees, the union, and the society, as well as of the interests of the business, the stockholders, and the management hierarchy. Under the "trusteeship theory," a management would invariably be willing to discuss and negotiate a union demand on the merits of the case rather than reject it out of hand because it would impose additional limitations on organizational operations. Such an employer would not necessarily agree to additional limitations but would be completely amenable to discussing, consulting, and ultimately negotiating with the union on any demand that the latter might bring up at a collective bargaining session. Exhibiting an attitude of "Cooperation," the trusteeship management does not take the position that the line separating management rights from that of negotiable issues is fixed and not subject to change. Rather, it attempts to balance the rights of all concerned with the goal of arriving at a solution that would be most mutually satisfactory. As such, the "trusteeship" and "residual" theories are poles apart in terms of management's attitude at the bargaining table and even in the day-to-day relationship between the company and the union.

There is no "divine right" concept of management in the trusteeship theory, a statement that cannot be made for the residualist camp. No better summary of the differences between the two theories on this score has ever been made than that offered many years ago by the eminent Arthur J. Goldberg, then general counsel of the United Steelworkers of America:

> Too many spokesmen for management assume that labor's rights are not steeped in past practice or tradition but are limited strictly to those specified in a contract; while management's rights are all-inclusive except as specifically taken away by a specific clause in a labor agreement. Labor always had many inherent rights, such as the right to strike; the right to organize despite interference from management, police powers, and even courts; the right to a fair share of the company's income even though this right was often denied; the right to safe, healthful working conditions with adequate opportunity for rest. Collective bargaining does not establish some hitherto nonexisting rights; it provides the power to enforce rights of labor which the labor movement was dedicated to long before the institution of arbitration had become so widely practiced in labor relations.[10]

It is impossible to determine how many employers follow the residual theory of management rights and how many follow the trusteeship theory. Cross-currents are clearly at work: the previously mentioned management attempt to regain work-rule flexibility, and the equally visible trend to more employee-centered management that was described in Chapter 1. The relative infrequency of "Cooperation" philosophies would, however, indicate that trusteeship managements remain in the distinct minority. Moreover, there is no universal truth as to which would be a better policy for management to follow, or whether some compromise between the two might form the optimum arrangement. The answer to this problem must be determined by each employer in the light of the particular labor relations environment.

---

[10] Management's Reserved Rights under Collective Bargaining," *Monthly Labor Review*, 79, No. 10 (October 1956), 1172.

"CODETERMINATION" AND UNIONS IN THE BOARD ROOM

The concept of workers *directly* playing a major role in corporate decision making by means of board of director membership, or "codetermination" as it is generally called, has never taken root in the United States. At least to date, American labor leadership has preferred to oppose rather than to join in any kind of partnership with management, and the official AFL–CIO position has been one of not desiring "to blur in any way the distinctions between the respective roles of management and labor in the plant."[11] Managers act; unions react.

Yet in other countries "codetermination" has become a reality, most notably in West Germany where in 1946 the occupying British administrators in the Ruhr Valley introduced the idea to the German steel industry as something of a compromise between nationalization and free enterprise. It was extended to the coal industry in that country in 1951 and—in the face of concerted union pressure magnified by the threat of a general strike—to larger companies in all German industries one year later.

Even in Germany employees have not received literal "codetermination" powers in the typical situation. Only in steel and coal, the original frontiers, have stockholders and workers controlled an identical number of directors; in all other sectors workers were legally allowed only a one-third representation on corporate boards until 1976, and they still, under a complicated formula, lack fully equal representation in practice. But after four decades even executives in Germany seem to be wholly adjusted to the concept (particularly, of course, the heavy majority of executives who have never known anything else). They are even cooperating— as are their unions—in helping other European countries (Sweden and Denmark most notably) experiment with it, being in the main convinced that Germany's economic prosperity and generally peaceful labor relations owe something to the idea.

Why "codetermination" has nonetheless been as welcome to United States business managers as a drunkard at an Alcoholics Anonymous meeting, and not of much interest to American unionists either, can undoubtedly be explained along several lines. As Koch and Fox have written, "In Western Europe . . ., community attachments have traditionally been much stronger, and upward mobility has been more constrained than in the U.S. Together, these forces have increased the impetus for workers to pursue more actively (as compared to the U.S. situation) a better lot in their present workplace."[12] As earlier chapters in this book have outlined, the values of private enterprise, property rights, and individualism have been developed here to a degree absolutely unknown in other lands: Against this backdrop,

[11] Thomas R. Donahue, "Collective Bargaining, Codetermination, and the Quality of Work," *World of Work Report,* 1 (August 1976), 1–7.
[12] James L. Koch and Colin L. Fox, Jr., "A Proposed Model of Factors Influencing Worker Participation," in *Proceedings of the Thirtieth Annual Winter Meeting, Industrial Relations Research Association,* December 28–30, 1977, p. 389.

"codetermination" seems dangerously socialistic. Nor can the aforementioned general resistance of U.S. employers throughout labor history to unionizing efforts be completely overlooked as an explanation, either: "In a real sense," Kassalow has declared, "a conflict situation is the midwife of almost all new American unions."[13] On such adversary initial relationships are adversary later relationships often built.

Yet even in the United States the situation may finally be changing. In May 1980, the Chrysler Corporation gave the then-UAW president Douglas A. Fraser one of the eighteen seats on its board of directors. And the impressive performance that he registered in the several years following this milestone, the first instance of a major American corporation electing a union leader to such a position, had led at least some observers to predict that the future would see more such union directors.

Chrysler had not offered Fraser, despite his universal reputation as a man of considerable intellect and unimpeachable character, this seat with any notable enthusiasm. It had done so quite reluctantly, in fact, as part of the price that it had to pay to win economic concessions vital to its survival from the UAW. And even within Chrysler's managerial hierarchy itself, many people had undoubtedly shared the sentiments of General Motors Chairman Thomas A. Murphy that the move would make "as much sense as having a member of GM's management sitting on the board of an international union."[14] Nor did Fraser's acceptance of the directorship, his considerable popularity within the union notwithstanding, occur without a good deal of negative comment from his own constituents: The word "sellout" received particularly frequent mention from the UAW rank and file. Some other critics—among them, law professors—feared that a conflict of interest on Fraser's part was unavoidable, since the interests of the shareholders and those of the union would inevitably operate, at times, in opposing directions.

Within months of the UAW leader's advent to the board, however, all of these sentiments appeared to have been groundless. Chrysler itself could muster nothing but praise for Fraser's contributions, especially his ability to ask pointed, well-informed questions: "He has," corporation Chairman Lee Iacocca could assert, "stimulated our board to think."[15] Another company insider declared that "Doug [can] speak with credibility to the workers because, as a director, he [has] seen the detailed financial data."[16] And there was general agreement among all who saw Fraser in action that the UAW leader, who temporarily suspended his participation in the board meetings when UAW members in Canada struck Chrysler in late 1982, had been flawless in avoiding not only any conflict of interest but even the appearance of such conflict.

By his own admission, Fraser's chief objective in accepting the board seat had been to interpret worker thinking into managerial decision making. ("I can't

[13] Everett M. Kassalow, "Industrial Conflict and Consensus in the United States and Western Europe: A Comparative Analysis," *Proceedings of the Thirtieth Annual Winter Meeting*, p. 120.
[14] *Time*, May 19, 1980, p. 78.
[15] *Wall Street Journal*, March 12, 1981, p. 33.
[16] *Ibid.*

represent my members if I'm always reacting to management decisions," he had said, ". . . we can bring an important resource to the board. People in the plants will tell me things they won't tell management").[17] More than three years later his tenure on the board as judged by this standard had clearly been a successful one.

And, to some extent, it had spawned interest in duplicating such union participation elsewhere. At the time of this writing, only Pan American World Airways among major corporations had followed Chrysler's lead in electing a union-proposed director. But union representatives had been placed on the boards of several smaller employers, such as Connecticut's Waterbury Rolling Mills, Inc., and many more such companies were opening their books to the unions with which they dealt, in some cases as a first step toward union leader board membership. The Rubber Workers, whose president had also advocated a board seat for labor, achieved not only the right to audit Uniroyal's books but, in a move that also appeared to presage full board membership, the right to have their president appear before the Uniroyal board at least once a year. The Communications Workers, among others, were also seriously studying the union board membership idea.

Most American companies, it is true, remain adamantly opposed to such union activities. "The pure and simple notion of opening the books and being a member of the board is a cure for which there is no known illness," one not atypical company negotiator has said.[18] And many managers also continue to advance the argument, presumably in all sincerity, that having a unionist on the board would expose the corporation to lawsuits for conflict of interest, Fraser's performance notwithstanding. Moreover, it is not irrelevant that virtually every employer that has granted unions the greater privileges has been, as Chrysler, confronted with significant financial problems at the time of the offering and has sought some kind of union pay concession in return. Nor does any reputable authority in the field see anything that remotely resembles full West German style "codetermination" in the United States as being closer than several million light-years away.

But for the first time some thoughtful students of the subject are starting to believe that the Chrysler innovation will spread. Past Industrial Relations Research Association president Douglas A. Soutar, a managerial industrial relations careerist, has declared that

> it is likely to be the "in" thing for the future. Under union pressure, some companies might think it is a forward-looking thing to do in terms of broadening corporate accountability and responsibility in the same way they did when they put women and blacks on boards. I myself can see some situations where it could be a good thing, particularly for corporations that are in trouble. I do not have a knee-jerk reaction against it, though if I advocated it now in my own company I'd get thrown out the 37th floor window.[19]

And former Federal Reserve Board chairman Arthur F. Burns, a conservative economist and a man never accused of harboring prounion sentiments, has gone

17 *Business Week*, November 22, 1982, p. 30.
18 *Ibid.*, February 1, 1982, p. 17.
19 *New York Times*, April 27, 1980, Sec. 3, p. 14.

even further. He applauds Fraser's entry onto Chrysler's board and both feels and hopes that the concept will spread elsewhere. "We want to educate some of these labor leaders," he said. "I work on the theory that, by sitting in on board meetings and studying the company's affairs, they will learn something about the company's needs and problems and especially its need for profits."[20]

It seems safe to say, under any conditions, that whether or not the Fraser precedent ever becomes a normal part of American corporate governance, the topic can never again really be ignored.

QUALITY OF WORK LIFE PROGRAMS

Something else that may be changing in labor–management relationships is the historic unwillingness of both parties to allow joint worker and management problem solving of workplace problems. An increasing number of unions, either on their own initiative or on the employer's, have become involved in so-called "Quality of Work Life" activities, denoting a movement whose title has no fully acceptable simple definition but basically connotes direct participation by workers in day-to-day decision making on the job.[21] Most often, employees get a voice in work scheduling, quality control, compensation, a determination of the job environment itself and/or other significant working factors, and the goal is a twofold one: increased productivity and improved union–management relations.

It is impossible to know how many organizations currently have such programs, since not only is there no formalized record keeping but many "QWL" programs go by some other name. The list of unionized users even now, a mere decade after the first major implementation, is nonetheless impressive. All of the nation's automobile manufacturers have a QWL program, most notably General Motors, which has one in each of sixty-six plants; Westinghouse has worker–management "quality circles," small groups that meet regularly to discuss product quality improvement, in fifty facilities (sixty-three such groups are in its Baltimore defense complex alone); the major steelmakers have a variety of "labor–management participation committees"; and the entire Bell System is experimenting with QWL principles. Programs have also been installed in coal mining, retail food, and the government (federal, state, and local), among others; and it is generally agreed that a 1983 Department of Labor listing of QWL programs in about 700 plants owned by some 180 organizations covered at best no more than half the actual total.

Many nonunion organizations have had such worker involvement efforts in place for years, often with the thought that such projects might help preserve nonunion status by improving employee morale. But unions have almost unanimously opposed the idea, partly because of fear that membership loyalty to the

---

[20] *Ibid.*

[21] Glenn Watts, president of the Communications Workers of America, is one of many involved leaders who uses exactly this definition. See his thoughtful article, "QWL: CWA's Position," in *QWL Review*, March 1983, pp. 12–14.

labor organization might be weakened by closer exposure to management and partly because of a suspicion (often fully justified) that the concept constituted a direct effort on the employer's part to pave the way for ultimate nonunion status. ("You've got to put up or shut up," one union chief executive told a group of major industrial leaders not long ago on this subject. "You can't ask unions to walk hand in hand into the unknown land of worker participation while going full speed ahead with union-bashing antilabor programs. There has to be a greater acceptance of unions in this country. I want very much to cooperate in consensus-building and problem-solving, but management can't expect cooperation when the hand it puts around my shoulder has a knife in it.")[22]

Why, then, the new collaboration? One reason has certainly been the same factor that has generated offers of board membership to unionists: economic adversity. Most, if not all, of the unionized organizations have suffered financial hardship and jobs have definitely been at stake. According to one scholar in the field, Jerome M. Rosow, employees recognize that if they can improve quality and productivity; "they'll be more competitive, they'll increase their company's share of the market, and, in the final analysis, they'll keep their jobs."[23] Another reason for the collaboration seems to be an increasing awareness on the part of unions (and managements) of a trend toward a dehumanization of work in many situations: Kahil Gibran may have called work "love made visible" and the Benedictines may say that "to work is to pray," but most people have always been less than enthusiastic about their own jobs and in recent years the level of discontent amid new technology and an ever-lessened worker control over the working environment appear to have grown appreciably. Many unions have been willing to explore new solutions in the face of this development.

The possibility that the growth of QWL may also reflect—even primarily—nothing more than a fad cannot be dismissed, however. As the respected president of the Communications Workers has pointed out, "packaged, narrowed participation programs [have been] the hottest selling item in the management consulting field"[24] over the past few years, and it is reasonable to expect that if no satisfactory rewards for both managements and unions can be attributed to QWL, the latter's tenure on the collective bargaining landscape may be short-lived. To date, even amid econmic hard times that cannot be expected to continue indefinitely, the returns have not been particularly impressive, indeed, in terms of documented major improvements in either morale or productivity. And it must be recognized again (as it was in Chapter 1) that the United States has never been a particualrly fruitful territory for the genuine union–management cooperation that QWL obviously requires if it hopes to survive.

John F. Kennedy frequently declared to proud parents who presented him with their new baby for what was at least for them a memorable moment, "It looks

---

[22] A. H. Raskin, "Frustrated and Wary, Labor Marks Its Day," *New York Times*, September 5, 1982, p. F-6.

[23] *Business Week*, June 30, 1980, p. 101.

[24] Watts, "QWL: CWA's Position," p. 12.

like a nice baby. We'll know more later." The same statement can perhaps be made on behalf of Quality of Work Life programs.

CONCLUSIONS

If unions and management are viewed as institutions, as distinct from the individuals they represent, the issues considered in this chapter take on special meaning. Institutions can survive long after individuals have perished, and in a real sense the problems of union security, union obligations, and management rights are related to the *survival* of the bargaining institutions. Union security measures preserve the union per se (although in so doing they may also allow it to do a better job for the members of the organization). Similarly, to survive and function as an effective institution, management must be concerned with its prerogatives to operate the business efficiently. It must also be concerned with union obligations as these might affect its continued effectiveness.

In principle, therefore, the devices of collective bargaining that feed the institutional needs of the union and the firm are cut from the same cloth. They are designed to assure the long-run interests of the two organizations. The objectives of labor unions and companies are quite different, but to carry out their respective functions both need security of operation. Business operates to make a profit and thus must be defended against encroachments of organized labor that might unreasonably interfere with its efficiency as a dynamic organization in the society. And although firms clearly differ in their philosophical approach to this problem, as witness the sharp differences between the residual and trusteeship concepts of management rights, the typical management position is the fundamental one that the business unit must be permitted to operate as efficiently as possible within the collective bargaining relationship. Its insistence upon management prerogatives stands as a bulwark of defense in this objective.

But unions also justify themselves as institutions on the American scene in their attempting to protect and advance the welfare of their members, and union security arrangements are an important avenue toward the realization of this objective. Although there may be philosophical objections to compulsory union membership, there cannot be any question that union security arrangements serve the long-run survival needs of organized labor.

If we view in retrospect the labor relations environment over the years, the conclusion appears irrefutable that business and unions have been relatively successful in reconciling these fundamental objectives, however much the verbal controversies continue to rage (and however foreign to both of their philosophies the idea of full "codetermination" may be). Businesses that have engaged in collective bargaining relationships have by and large not only been able to survive but have often flourished. Many of the most influential and prosperous firms in this country (the automobile companies, at least in normal years, and the airlines come immediately to mind) have, as we know, been highly unionized for years. Likewise, organized labor not only has survived but has grown appreciably in strength over the years, the contemporary unexciting performance of union membership totals being accountable chiefly by causes other than management destruction. Moreover, if institutional survival and growth of unions is measured by the quality of employee benefits, one would have to conclude that in most relationships, unions have succeeded in defending and promoting the welfare of their members. Although the objectives of the two institutions are quite different, and although occasional major impasses are reached by unions and managements in their bargaining on these issues, sufficient protection for both organizations has been provided in the vast majority of unionized industry.

Discussion Questions

1 Arguing in favor of "right-to-work" laws, a publication of the National Association of Manufacturers has expressed the view that "no argument for compulsory unionism—however persuasive—can possibly justify invasion of the right of individual choice." Do you agree or disagree? Why?

2 "From the viewpoint of providing maximum justice to all concerned, the agency shop constitutes the optimum union security arrangement." To what extent, if any, do you agree with this statement?

3 "Good unions don't need compulsory unionism: bad unions don't deserve compulsory unionism." Comment.

4 Evaluate the opinion of a former Steelworker Union president that "nothing could be worse than to have . . . management appease the union, and nothing could be worse than to have the union appease management," relating these remarks to the areas of management rights and union security.

Selected References

AFL–CIO, *Union Security: The Case against Right-to-Work Laws*. Washington, D.C.: AFL–CIO, 1958.

CHAMBERLAIN, NEIL W., *The Union Challenge to Management Control*. New York: Harper & Row, 1948.

CHANDLER, MARGARET K., *Management Rights and Union Interests*. New York: McGraw-Hill, 1964.

DEMPSEY, JOSEPH R., *The Operation of Right-to-Work Laws*. Milwaukee: Marquette University Press, 1961.

HAGGARD, THOMAS R., *Compulsory Unionism, the NLRB, and the Courts*. Philadelphia: University of Pennsylvania Press, 1977.

MCDERMOTT, THOMAS J., "Union Security and Right-to-Work Laws," *Labor Law Journal*, November 1965, pp. 667–78.

MEYERS, FREDERIC, *Right to Work in Practice*. New York: Fund for the Republic, 1959.

MEYERS, SCOTT, *Managing without Unions*. Reading, Mass.: Addison-Wesley, 1976.

STONE, MORRIS, *Managerial Freedom and Job Security*. New York: Harper & Row, 1963.

SWIFT, ROBERT A., *NLRB and Management Decision Making*. Philadelphia: University of Pennsylvania Press, 1974.

Management Rights:
The Case of the Part-Time Employees

Cast of characters:

Dana, Sanders, Shinn, Yost	*Grievants*
Case	*Foreman*
Solt	*Company Vice President*
Spicer	*Union Steward*
Roll	*Union President*
Strong	*Union International Representative*
Smith	*Company Attorney*

Nothing is more critical in arbitration than cases in which a union challenges the right of an employer to manage the plant. To promote efficiency, employers constantly introduce new methods, adopt technological improvements, and make more effective use of the labor force. In the typical labor agreement, a management prerogative clause guarantees the employer the sole right to adopt measures calculated to ensure the efficient operation of the plant. Disputes arise, however, when a union claims that the exercise of such a management right violates terms and conditions of employment specified in the labor agreement. In general, the rule is that an employer may make any decision in the operation of the plant or in the direction of the labor force unless such decision violates provisions of the collective bargaining contract. In such cases, the arbitrator's responsibility is to determine whether or not a violation has occurred. The arbitrator reviews the material provisions of the labor agreement and the relevant evidence in the light of the employer's action. In the event that a violation is found, the arbitrator will restore the status quo and award back pay if that issue is involved in the dispute. On the other hand, a grievance protesting the right of the employer to manage the plant and direct the labor force will be denied when it is determined that no violation has occurred.

This case and the next illustrate the management prerogative problem. In Case 9, the employer used part-time employees to perform certain work on the second shift instead of assigning the work to regular first-shift employees on an overtime basis. Such as assignment resulted in lower labor costs—it would have been more expensive to pay overtime rates to the regular employees. In protest, the regular employees filed a grievance, claiming that the company violated the labor agreement. The union's problem was that no contract provision expressly prohibited the employer's action. Not content to drop the grievance on that basis, the union claimed that the employer violated the overtime provision. Among other problems, the arbitrator's task was to determine whether the overtime provision and experience under it prevented the use of part-time employees on the second shift instead of regular employees.

In Case 10, after making certain improvements in the operation in question, the employer abolished a job classification. Because of the improvements, the employees in the classification performed only about two or three hours per day on the job. For efficiency purposes, the employer assigned the remaining work of the abolished classification to another classification of employees. As a result, the union claimed that the employer violated the labor agreement. You are the arbitrator in each of these cases.

GRIEVANCE AND LABOR AGREEMENT

On August 3, 1982, Dana, Sanders, Shinn, and Yost filed the grievance that generated this dispute. It states:

> Part time employees were called in to work on Company products in the Paint Dept. The full time employees were denied the overtime. When the other departments have extra hours to be worked the day people work the overtime. They don't hire outside help.

As a remedy, the Grievants request that the employees of the Paint Department be

> paid for all lost time. Also Company follow contract on overtime and posting it.

Material to the dispute are the following provisions of the Labor Agreement:

ARTICLE III. MANAGEMENT

The Union recognizes the Company's right to control and manage the plant in the traditional manner, which rights and responsibilities belong solely to the Company. Without limiting the generality of the foregoing, the Company retains the right to hire, direct, and control schedules, operations, and facilities; to determine the amount and quality of work necessary; to determine and designate the products to be manufactured, the schedule of production, the methods, processes and means of manufacturing, the control and selection of raw materials, semi-manufactured and finished parts, which may be incorporated into the products manufactured; to lay off employees because of lack of work or for other legitimate reasons; and to manage the properties in the traditional manner; provided, however, that in the exercise of such functions, the Company shall comply with the terms of this Agreement where applicable.

ARTICLE IX.   HOURS OF WORK AND OVERTIME

Section 1. Regular Work Day and Work Week   Eight (8) hours shall constitute a regular day's work and five (5) days (Monday through Friday) shall constitute a regular week's work. Hours of work shall be consecutive except when an unpaid lunch period is provided in accordance with prevailing practices. A work day shall be defined as a consecutive twenty-four (24) hour period, beginning with the time the employee starts work or is scheduled to work, whichever is earlier. The provisions of this paragraph are not intended and are not to be construed as a guarantee of a full work day or a full work week.

ARTICLE XIV.   SENIORITY

Section 12. Assignment of Overtime   In the event the Company determines that overtime work is required, such overtime shall be assigned to the employees having the longest period of seniority in the department involved. In the event no employee within the department desires to work overtime, the overtime shall be offered to employees based upon plant-wide seniority, subject to the fitness and ability to perform the work to be done. As to work which by its nature involves the entire operation of the plant, and if such work is to be done on overtime, the Company will assign such work to employees on the basis of plant-wide seniority.

Section 13. Posting of Overtime   When overtime work is required, the Company shall post by job classification and by noon of the day on which the overtime is to be performed, and employees desiring to work such overtime shall sign such overtime posting by no later than 3:30 P.M. and overtime shall be assigned in accordance with the provisions of Section 12.

BASIC QUESTION

The basic question to be determined in this arbitration is framed as follows:

Under the circumstances of this case, did the Company violate the material provisions of the Labor Agreement? If so, what should the remedy be?

BACKGROUND

Basis of Grievance

Involved in this dispute are regular and part-time employees assigned to the Paint Department. Regular or full-time employees work a normal eight (8) hour day on the day shift. When the Company establishes a second shift in the Paint Department, it is manned by part-time employees who work four (4) hours after the day shift ends. Part-time employees are included in the bargaining unit, represented by the Union, and receive the same wage rate paid to regular employees. No regular employee is assigned to the second shift, and no part-time employee is assigned to the day shift. Of the Company's four (4) departments, a second shift is established only in the Paint Department. A separate seniority list is maintained for regular and part-time employees.

On August 1, 1982, the Company established a second shift in the Paint Department. It remained in effect until January 1, 1983, the period covered by the grievance. During this period, six (6) part-time employees were assigned to the shift, working 5:30 to 9:30 P.M. five (5) days per week.

On the second shift, the part-time employees painted Company products and also castings sent to the Plant for painting by the N. A. Foundry. During the period of the grievance, the part-time employees devoted 90 percent of their work to the painting of Company products and 10 percent to the painting of the outside firm's castings.

Since part-time employees were used to paint Company products on the second shift, the opportunity for overtime by the regular day shift employees was reduced. The Union and the Grievants contend that part-time employees should not have been assigned to the painting of Company products, and, instead, the regular employees should have been given the opportunity to paint such products on an overtime basis. No objection is made to the painting of the castings by the part-time employees. Castings are painted exclusively on the second shift. Since the regular employees paint Company products on the day shift, they charge that they have the right to that job when they are painted on the second shift. Regular employees worked overtime during the period of the grievance only when the part-time employees did not report to work.

Grievant Dana testified:

> When the grievance was filed, I wanted to work the overtime. After I worked my 8 hours, I was sent home. Then the night crew (part-time employees) took over my job. I desired the overtime, but was denied the right to paint Company products on the second shift.

History of Second Shift

Starting in 1960, the Company from time to time has used a second shift in the Paint Department. Case, Foreman of the Paint Department since 1962, testified that he began his employment with the Company in 1960 and worked on the second shift between 5:30 and 9:30 P.M. for two years. Until 1970, the second-shift part-time employees exclusively painted Company products. In 1970, the Company started to paint castings for the N.A. Foundry on the second shift. Since that year, the part-time employees painted Company products and the N. A. Foundry castings, devoting 80 percent of their time to Company products and 20 percent to the castings.

Solt, Company Vice President, testified that a second part-time shift has been used over the years when the regular day shift employees could not handle the workload. He said:

> If there was a lot of work to do, we used a second shift with part-time employees.

He said further that part-time employees are normally used on the second shift each year of the peak season, between the summer and fall of the year. When castings come in for painting in the off-season, Solt said that part-time employees are called in on the second shift to accomplish that work.

Spicer, Union Steward, has worked for the Company for ten (10) years. She said that a second part-time shift has been used during her tenure of employment. With respect to the work performed on the second shift, she testified:

> The part-time employees painted castings and Company products. When the part-time employees did not report for their 5:30–9:30 P.M. shift, the regular day shift employees were offered overtime.

Negotiations of 1980 Labor Agreement

This grievance arose under the current Labor Agreement. Roll, Union President, participated in the negotiations that produced that contract. She testified that Strong, Union International Representative, raised the issue of part-time employees and said further that the "Union wants to get rid of them altogether."

Attorney Smith represented the Company in the 1980 negotiations. Roll testified that when the Union raised the issue of part-time employees, Smith said he

> did not want to discuss anything about the part-time people.

In any event, in the 1980 negotiations, Roll declared, no agreement was reached to eliminate the part-time employees.

case 10

Management Rights:
The Case of the Abolished Job Classification

Cast of characters:

Gill	*Manufacturing Superintendent*
Gaber	*Grievant*

GRIEVANCE AND LABOR AGREEMENT

When the Company abolished the Refire Unloader classification and assigned its duties to the Kiln Drawer classification, Grievance Number 33-74, dated November 12, 1982, was filed. It states:

The Union asks that the original employee be replaced back on his job: Unloading Refire Line, Operation 5941.

Material to the dispute are the following provisions of the Labor Agreement:

ARTICLE II.   PURPOSE AND SCOPE OF AGREEMENT

It is the intent and purpose of the parties hereto that this Agreement will promote and improve industrial and economic relations between the Employer and its Employees and to set forth herein the basic agreement covering rates of pay, hours of work, and conditions of employment.

ARTICLE VII.   ADJUSTMENT OF GRIEVANCES

Section 7(e) The jurisdiction of the Arbitrator shall be strictly limited to deciding grievances which conform to the definition set forth in Section 4 of this Article. The Arbitrator shall have no authority to add to, subtract from, or in any way alter or amend the provisions of this Agreement.

ARTICLE XII.   WAGES

Section 1 Hourly incentive and piecework wage rates as well as all job classifications in effect as of the effective date of this Agreement shall remain in effect for the duration of the Agreement.

Section 2 Management shall retain the right and responsibility of deciding the basis on which wages shall be paid, such as piecework, daywork, hourly rates or rates on an incentive basis. Insofar as practicable, jobs that are not now on piecework shall be put on piecework.

Section 3 When new processes, new job duties or new fixtures are to be established which would result in a substantial change in job duties or requirements, piecework prices or hourly rates will be established by the Employer based on prices of comparable fixtures of like size, weight, design or other factors affecting the work required to produce and process such fixtures.

Section 5 In the event Management makes an installation of equipment or changes an operation or establishes a new job which is impracticable to continue on piecework, the Union may, if it disagrees, process this issue through Article VII of the Basic Agreement in conformance with the ten (10) day time requirement of Section 5. If the issue is processed through arbitration, the Arbitrator's decision will be limited as to the practicability of establishing the operation(s) in question on an incentive and/or piecework basis. The Arbitrator will not have jurisdiction to determine the rate to be paid for the work.

ARTICLE XV.   MANAGEMENT

Section 1 The Management of the Plant, including but not limited to the establishment of factory rules and vacation rules not to conflict with this Agreement, the direction of the working forces, the right to hire, promote, transfer, suspend or discharge for cause, the right to relieve employees from duty because of lack of work, or for other legitimate reasons, and the right to determine the extent to which the Plant shall operate or be shut down, the products to be manufactured, the schedule of production, and the methods, processes and means of manufacturing, are solely and exclusively the responsibility of the employer, except as defined and modified in the Agreement.

Section 2   The Employer reserves the right to introduce new or improved facilities or methods of production.

BASIC QUESTION

The basic question to be determined in this arbitration is framed as follows:

Under the circumstances of this case, did the Company violate material provisions of the Labor Agreement? If so, what should the remedy be?

BACKGROUND

Under the Labor Agreement, the Union represents employees of the Company in plants located in Kokomo, Torrance, San Pablo, Tiffin, Trenton, New Orleans, and Plainfield. This dispute involves the Kokomo plant. Within the Kokomo plant, about 160 employees are in the bargaining unit, and they manufacture a variety of products, including toilet tanks, bowls, urinals, and lavatories. After the products are molded, they are dried and sprayed. Thereupon, they are fired in a kiln, inspected, assembled, packed, and shipped.

Two classifications are involved in this dispute. They are Kiln Drawer and Refire Unloader. The latter classification is paid at a day rate and the former classification is paid on a piece rate basis. Before the circumstances of this case arose, the Kiln Drawer unloaded rail cars after they came from the kiln. He placed the parts on a truck, and moved the vehicle adjacent to the work station of the Inspectors. After he unloaded his truck, the Kiln Drawer returned to the kiln area and repeated the cycle.

When the Inspector deemed a product to be salable, he placed it on the proper conveyor belt. Should the product be deemed defective, it was carried along a different conveyor belt to be "refired." It is at this point in the process that the Refire Unloader performed his duties. He removed the defective product from the conveyor belt, and placed it on another conveyor belt. To perform this task, he walked about 12 feet to the Refire conveyor belt. In short, the Refire Unloader unloaded defective products from one conveyor belt and placed them on another conveyor belt which eventually carried the off-quality products to a repair process. Gill, Manufacturing Superintendent, testified that originally the Refire Unloader was occupied with the duties of his job for 5–6 hours per day. He said this was determined on the basis of a time study. For the remaining hours, the Refire Unloader performed odd jobs, such as clean-up work. Gaber, the Grievant in this dispute, held the Refire Unloader classification until it was abolished.

In 1980, the Refire Unloader per week handled about 5,000 pieces of product.

As a result of a change in product mix, and quality improvement, the volume of pieces handled by the Refire Unloader decreased. Gill testified that in the week of July 8, 1981, Gaber handled 2,539 pieces; 2,723 in the week of November 10, 1981; and 2,694 pieces in the week of November 6, 1982. In other words, when the classification was abolished, Gaber was handling about 50 percent fewer pieces as compared to the time before the change of product mix and quality improvement in the plant. As a result, whereas he originally spent about 5–6 hours per day performing the duties in his classification, by November 1982 this time was reduced to about 2–3 hours per day.

In the week of November 10, 1982, the Company abolished the Refire Unloader job. Gaber was assigned to another job classification, but did not suffer any reduction in pay. With the elimination of the Refire Unloader classification, the Company assigned the duties of that classification to the Kiln Drawer. That is, the Kiln Drawer would not only perform the duties of his regular classification, but would assume the duties of the Refire Unloader classification.

POSITION OF THE PARTIES

The position of the Union is that the grievance should be granted. As a remedy, it requests:

> The award must be for the Union. The Company must eliminate the Unloading work from the present job classification of Kiln Drawer and must restore the Unloader's job as it existed when this contract began.

In contrast, the Company requests that the grievance be denied.

10

Administrative Issues under Collective Bargaining

Provisions relating to seniority, discipline, employee safety, and the various other "administrative" areas of the labor relationship have, as in the case of institutional provisions, the common characteristic of falling into the noneconomic classification of collective bargaining. They nonetheless have a profound influence upon the economic welfare of the employer and the economic status of the employees.

The character of a seniority clause, for example, can have a vital impact upon the efficient operation of the productive process. And the protection afforded an employee as a result of a discharge clause can be of much greater importance than any of the rights enjoyed as a result of the negotiation of wage rates or fringe benefits. It matters little to the worker who has been discharged for an obviously unfair reason that the wages called for by the labor contract are very generous.

Moreover, in the 1980s, technological change is of overriding importance in many labor relationships, dwarfing even the subject of wage issues in such instances. Literally thousands of jobs are being eliminated by such change each week in the economy, and it is a rare union that does not see the development, now an accelerating one indeed, as a formidable one from the viewpoint of job security. This volume has already dealt with union economic demands that are rooted at least partially in this problem: early retirement, severance pay, and SUB plans, among others. As we shall see, many administrative issues also flow from workers' fears that amid rampant technological innovation their jobs are very vulnerable.

In short, as important as the negotiation of economic issues may be, one cannot ignore these nonwage administrative issues of collective bargaining. Both are interwoven in the contemporary labor relations environment, and to ignore or slight either—or, clearly, the institutional area of the contract as well—would represent a distortion and an incomplete picture of present-day labor relations in the United States.

The following discussion indicates the nature of these problems, the manner in which employees and unions handle them in collective bargaining, and recent trends in administrative clause negotiations.

SENIORITY

The principle of seniority, under which the employee with the greater length of organizational or organizational subunit services receives increased job security and improved working conditions (and, commonly, greater entitlement to employee benefits), is not new either to the world of work in general or to American industry. As Gersuny has pointed out, over a thousand years ago promotion in the Chinese civil service was governed by time in grade, and two centuries ago it was rigorously applied in the Prussian bureaucracy to determine personnel advancement as the only alternative to the corruption that was almost a national pastime of the period. And while in the British civil service in the mid-nineteenth century promotion was theoretically to be based on "merit," in practice seniority was the dominant factor— again, as an antidote to favoritism by decision makers.[1]

In the United States, the armed forces have emphasized it from the days of Andrew Jackson, and the railroads and printing trades have stressed it for almost a century.

For at least three reasons, however, seniority has received increasing stress in labor contracts over the past few decades. In the first place, both management and employee representatives have become convinced that there is a certain amount of justice to the arrangement, especially in terms of work contraction or recall opportunities after layoffs. Second, the application of seniority is an objective one, calculated to avoid arbitrariness in the selection of personnel for particular jobs and consequently less irksome for the labor negotiators to deal with than alternative devices. Third, the employee benefit programs that have mushroomed in these years have been geared almost exclusively to seniority—often, to make them more acceptable to the companies by restricting the number of employees entitled to the benefits.

Almost every labor agreement now includes some seniority formula, and this practice has become a deeply imbedded feature of the collective bargaining process. It is a chief method whereby employees obtain a measure of security in their jobs. It also limits the freedom of management to direct the labor force and influences considerations of plant efficiency. A seniority structure that approaches the ideal would be one that affords protection to employees in their job rights and at the same time does not place unreasonable restrictions on the right of management to make job assignments without sacrificing productivity and efficiency in the plant. This objective can best be realized to the extent that a seniority system is constructed

[1] Carl Gersuny, "Origins of Seniority Provisions in Collective Bargaining," in *Proceedings of the 1982 Spring Meeting, Industrial Relations Research Association*, April 28–30, 1982, p. 520.

to fit a particular plant environment. It must be tailored to fill the requirements of the technology, the kinds of jobs, the skills and occupations of the employees, and the character of labor relations of a specific company. A seniority formula that might be desirable in one industrial situation might not be suitable to another plant environment. In addition, perhaps no other phase of the collective bargaining relationship demands so much of company officials and union leaders in terms of common sense, good faith, and reciprocal recognition of the problems of management, the labor organization, and the employees.

As a result of the nature of the seniority principle, many problems are inherent in the formulation and application of a seniority structure. Among the major problems, beyond the crucial determination of the phases of the employment relationship that are to be affected by the length-of-service principle, are: establishment of the unit in which employees acquire and apply seniority credits; identification of circumstances under which employees may lose seniority; determination of the seniority status of employees who transfer from one part of the bargaining unit to another, or who leave the bargaining unit altogether; and the fixing of certain exceptions to the seniority system. As can be expected, these problems are handled in a multitude of fashions in collective bargaining relationships. Some labor agreements, moreover, attempt to cover all these issues, and some deal with only certain ones of them.

The heavy majority of all labor agreements, for example, provide that seniority play a part in the determination of layoffs, in rehiring, and in promotions. But, as discussed below, the same labor agreement might use one seniority system to govern layoffs and rehiring and a different one in connection with promotions (where considerations of ability and physical fitness are often as important as, and in many cases more important than, length of service). Where a fixed-shift system exists in a plant, labor agreements may permit workers their choice of shifts on the basis of seniority, and factors such as personal convenience, wage or hour differentials, and the kind of job itself may dictate the senior worker's choice in this respect. Under other contracts, however, seniority plays no role in shift assignments.

Units for Seniority

There are three major systems relating to the unit in which an employee acquires and applies seniority credits: company- or plantwide, departmental or occupational, and a combined plant and departmental seniority system.

Under a *company- or plantwide seniority system,* the seniority status of each employee equals that person's total service with the firm. Thus, transfers from job to job within the establishment or transfers from one department to another have no effect on an employee's seniority standing. Subject to other features of the seniority structure, an employee under the company- or plantwide system will apply his or her seniority for purposes covered by the seniority system on a strictly company- or plantwide basis. In actual practice, this system is not used in companies in which it would be necessary for an employee to undergo a considerable training period when the employee takes a new job to replace a worker with less seniority. It is practicable only for companies in which the jobs are more or less interchangeable. A companywide system obviously gives the greatest protection to employees with the longest length of service. On the other hand, depending upon the other features of the seniority structure, it could serve as a deterrent to the efficiency and productivity of the plant.

Under *departmental* or *occupational seniority systems,* separate seniority lists are established for each department or occupational grouping in the plant. If such a system does not have any qualifications or limitations, employees can apply seniority credits only within their own department or occupation. Such a system facilitates administration in large companies employing a considerable number of workers. It minimizes the opportunity for large-scale displacement of workers from their jobs in the event of layoffs or discontinuation of particular jobs because of technological innovations, or because of permanent changes in the market for the products of the company. On the other hand, additional problems arise as the result of the use of this kind of seniority system. If layoffs in one department become necessary, or if certain jobs in such a department are permanently discontinued while other departments are not affected, a state of affairs could develop wherein employees with long service in a company would find themselves out of a job while employees with less seniority were working full time. In addition, under a strict departmental seniority structure, transfers between departments tend to be discouraged because a transfer could result in complete loss of accumulated seniority.

As a result of the problems arising from a strict company or departmental seniority system, many managements and unions have negotiated a number of plans combining these two types of seniority structures. Under a combination system, seniority may be applied in one unit for certain purposes and in another unit for other purposes. Thus, seniority may be applied on a plantwide basis for purposes of layoffs, whereas departmentwide seniority is used as the basis of promotion. A variation of this system is to permit employees to *apply* their seniority only within the department in which they are working but to *compute* such seniority on the basis of total service with the company. In addition, although the general application of seniority is limited to a departmental basis, employees laid off in a particular department may claim work in a general labor pool in which the jobs are relatively unskilled and in which newly hired employees start out before being promoted to other departments. At times, a distinction is drawn between temporary layoffs resulting from lack of business or material shortages, and permanent layoffs resulting from changes in technology or permanent changes in the products manufactured by the company. Under the former situation, seniority may be applied only on a departmental basis, or seniority might not govern at all (as in the automobile industry), whereas under the latter circumstances, employees have the opportunity to apply their seniority on a plantwide basis. Other variations of the combination system are utilized within industry as determined by the circumstances of a particular plant.

Limitations upon Seniority

Regardless of the type of system under which seniority credits are accumulated and applied, many collective bargaining agreements—possibly as many as one-third of them—place certain limitations and qualifications upon length of service as a factor in connection with layoffs. In some cases, seniority systems provide for the retention of more senior employees only when they are qualified to perform the jobs that are available. In considerably fewer labor agreements, a senior employee will be retained in the event of layoffs in the plant only when the employee is able to perform an available job "as well as" other employees eligible for layoff.

Although a large number of labor agreements permit employees scheduled for layoff to displace less-senior employees, limitations on the chain displacement or "bumping" process are also included in many labor agreements. Employers, unions, employees, and students of labor relations recognize the inherent disadvantages of seniority structures that permit unlimited bumping. Such disadvantages are manifested in many ways. Bumping could result in serious obstacles to plant efficiency and productivity to the detriment of all concerned, could cause extreme uncertainty and confusion to workers who might be required to take a number of different jobs as a result of a single layoff, and could result in serious internal political problems for the labor organization.

For these reasons, careful limitations are usually placed on the bumping process. Many labor agreements allow an employee to displace a less-senior worker in the event of a layoff only when the former employee has a minimum amount of service with the company. Other contracts circumscribe the bumping process by limiting the opportunity of a senior employee to displacement of a junior worker from a job that the employee with longer service has already held. Under this system, the worker comes down in the same fashion that he went up the job ladder. Under other seniority systems, the area into which the employee may bump is itself limited: It may be stipulated that employees can bump only on a departmental or divisional basis, or can displace workers only with equal or lower labor grades. In addition, the objective of limiting the displacement process is achieved by permitting the displacement of only the *least*-senior employee in the bumping area and not of any other less-senior employees.

Most labor agreements provide for rehiring in reverse order of layoffs—the last employee laid off is the first rehired. In addition, laid-off employees are given preference over new workers for vacancies that arise anywhere in the plant. However, such preferences given employees with longer service are frequently limited to the extent that the employee in question is competent to perform the available work. In this connection, the problem of the reemployment of laid-off workers becomes somewhat complicated when a straight departmental seniority system is used. In such a case, although a labor agreement might provide for the rehiring of workers in the reverse order of layoffs, production might not be revived in reverse order to the slack in production, and thus employees with shorter service might be recalled to work before employees with greater seniority. To avoid such a state of affairs, some labor contracts provide the older employee in terms of service with the opportunity of returning to work first, provided that the person has the ability to carry out the duties of the available job.

Length of service as a factor in promotion is of less importance than it is in layoffs and rehiring, and in only a relative handful of contemporary labor agreements is length of service the sole factor in making promotions. The incidence is low because all parties to collective bargaining realize that a janitor, for example, in spite of many years of service in this position, is not qualified to be promoted to, say, a tool-and-die-maker's job. But if such a criterion is rarely the sole factor in the assignment of workers to higher-rated jobs, the vast majority of labor agreements now require that seniority along with other factors be given *consideration*. In many contracts, seniority governs promotions when the senior employee is "qualified" to fill the position in question. Under others, seniority becomes the determining criterion in promotions when the senior employee has the ability and physical fitness for the job in question "equal to that" of all other employees who may desire the better job. Under the latter seniority structure, length of service is of secondary importance to the ability and physical fitness factors, however. (*Case 11 deals with the application of seniority for promotions.*)

In practice, management makes the decision about which worker among those bidding for the job gets the promotion; and in the heavy majority of cases, this decision of the company is satisfactory to all concerned, usually because the senior employer *is* best qualified for the job in question or because the employer is completely willing to give preference to the senior employee when ability differences among employees are not readily discernible. At times, however, when the management passes over a senior employee in favor of an employee with shorter service in making a promotion, the union may protest the action through the grievance procedure. For example, the union may argue that the senior employee bidding for the better job has equal ability to that of the worker whom the management tapped for the promotion. The problem in such cases is to evaluate the comparative abilities of the two workers. Such a determination involves the study and appraisal of the entire work record of both workers. Consideration here is usually given to such items as the previous experience of the workers on the actual job in question or on closely related jobs; the education and training qualifications of the workers for performing the job in question; production records of the employees; and absenteeism, tardiness, and accident records, when relevant. Ordinarily, such disputes are resolved on the basis of these considerations. At times, however, the parties are still in disagreement, and the matter is then most often referred to an impartial arbitrator, who will make the decision in the case.

Seniority in Transfers

Another seniority problem involves the seniority status of employees who transfer from one department to another. As stated above, interdepartmental transfers do not create a seniority issue under a straight plantwide seniority system. To the extent that seniority is acquired or applied on a departmentwide basis, however, the problem of transfers becomes important to employers, unions, and employees;

reference has been made to the fact that interdepartmental transfers are discouraged when employees lose all accumulated seniority upon entering a new department. Some contracts deal with this problem by allowing a transferred employee to retain seniority in the old department while starting at the bottom of the seniority scale in the new department; under these circumstances, such an employee would exercise seniority rights in the old department in the event that the employee were laid off from the new department. Some contracts even permit such an employee to further accumulate seniority for application in the old department in the event that he or she is laid off from the new department. Another approach to the problem permits the transferred employee to carry seniority acquired in the old department to the new department. This is a common practice where the job itself is transferred to a new department, where the job or the department itself is permanently abolished, or when two or more departments are merged.

Still another seniority problem arises under the circumstances of an employee's transferring entirely out of the bargaining unit. This issue is particularly related to the seniority status of workers who are selected by management to fill the foremen's jobs. There are three major approaches to this problem. Under some contracts, a rank-and-file employee who takes a supervisory job simply loses accumulated seniority. If for some reason the supervisory job is terminated and the employee desires to return to a job covered by the collective bargaining contract, he or she is treated as a new employee for purposes of seniority. Another method is to permit such an employee, when serving as a foreman, to retain all seniority credits earned earlier. Under this approach, if the employee transfers back to the bargaining unit, the employee returns with the same number of seniority credits as before the transfer. Finally, under some contracts, an employee taking a supervisor's job accumulates seniority in the bargaining unit while serving as a foreman. If the employee returns to the bargaining unit, that worker comes back not only with the seniority credits acquired before taking the supervisory job but with seniority credits accumulated while serving as a foreman. Rank, at times, does have its privileges.

Obviously, the seniority status of foremen is not a problem when management fills its supervisory posts by hiring outside the plant. On the other hand, the problem is a real one when the company elects to fill such jobs from the rank and file. It is apparent that a worker with long seniority in the bargaining unit would hesitate to take a foreman's job if doing so would forfeit accumulated seniority. In recognition of this situation, many employers and unions have agreed that workers promoted from the bargaining unit to supervisors' jobs may at least retain the seniority they accumulated while covered by the labor agreement. Whatever approach unions and managements take to this problem, it would generally be desirable to spell out the method in the labor agreement. Confusion, uncertainty, and controversy could arise when the contract is silent on this issue.

At times seniority may be used as the basis of a transfer to a job within the same wage classification. Such an opportunity may be used by an employee who desires to move to a different shift, for instance from the night to the day shift. Or if the employee and the foreman cannot get along, the employee may exercise transfer rights to a job in another area of the plant or to a different shift. Under these circumstances, the transfer would be beneficial to the management and the employee. Normally, however, there are restrictions on employee transfer rights. When the transfer is within the same wage classification but to another job, the employee must have qualifications to perform the work. It is common for different jobs to be grouped within the same wage classifications. Transfer provisions also do not ordinarily permit bumping. Before a transfer may occur, there must be a job vacancy. Recognizing that promiscuous transfers could be harmful to plant efficiency, employers insist that the employees' right to transfer be limited. For example, some contracts require that an employee be within a job classification, often for six months or a year, before the employee may exercise transfer rights. In addition, when two or more employees desire to transfer to the same job, normally labor agreements will give preference to the senior employee provided that the senior bidder has qualifications relatively equal to those of a junior service employee.

Exceptions to the Seniority System

Under many collective bargaining contracts there is provision for some exemptions from the normal operation of the seniority structure. One of these involves the issue of "superseniority" for union officers. Some managements and unions have agreed that designated union officers may have a preferred status in the event of layoffs. Such employees are protected in employment regardless of their length of service. They are entitled to such consideration strictly by virtue of the union office they hold, however, and lose their superseniority status when their term of office is terminated.

One obvious problem involved in the negotiation of a superseniority clause is the designation of the employees who are to have this status. Frequently, labor agreements limit this protection to the comparatively major local union officers. If too many employees are covered by a superseniority status, the effective and fair operation of the seniority structure might be prevented. In any event, it is common practice to specify exactly which officers of the union are to be included under the superseniority clause.

Another problem concerns the bumping rights of employees protected under such an arrangement. Contracts are usually clear as to just what job or jobs such employees are entitled to when they are scheduled for layoff. In addition, it is common practice to make clear the rate of pay that the employee will earn in the new job. Thus, if a worker protected by superseniority takes another job that pays a lower rate than his or her regular job to avoid layoff, the contract specifies whether or not that employee will get the rate of the job filled or the rate of the regular job. Obviously, when these problems are resolved in the labor agreement, there is less chance for controversy during the hectic atmosphere of a layoff itself.

Some labor agreements also permit management to retain in employment during periods of layoff a certain number of nonunion-officer employees regardless of their seniority status. Such employees are designated as "exceptional," "specially skilled," "indispensable," or "meritorious" in collective bargaining contracts. As in the case of superseniority, problems growing out of this exception to the seniority rule are normally resolved in the collective bargaining contract. Problems in this connection involve the number of employees falling into this category, the kind of jobs they must be holding to receive such preferential status, their bumping rights (if any), and the rate of pay they shall earn in the event that they are retained in employment in jobs other than their regular ones.

Another general exception to the normal operation of a seniority system involves newly hired workers. Under most labor agreements, such workers must first serve a probationary period before they are protected by the labor agreement. Such probationary periods are frequently specified as being from about thirty to ninety days, and during this period of time the new worker can be laid off, demoted, transferred, or otherwise assigned work without reference to the seniority structure at all. However, once such an employee serves out this probationary period, seniority under most labor agreements is calculated from the first day of hire by the employer.

Under the terms of many collective bargaining contracts, employers may lay off workers on a *temporary* basis without reference to the seniority structure. Such layoffs are for short periods of time and result from purely temporary factors, such as shortages of material and power failures. It is, of course, vital in this connection that the labor agreement define the temporary layoff. At times, contracts incorporate the principle that employers may lay off without reference to seniority on a temporary basis but fail to specify what is meant by the term *temporary layoff*. Some agreements define the term as any layoff for less than five or even ten working days. Other contracts, however, specify that the seniority structure must be followed for any layoff in excess of twenty-four hours. Whatever time limit is placed on the term, the labor agreement should specify the duration of a temporary layoff. By this means, a considerable amount of future argument will be avoided.

Finally, virtually all seniority structures specify circumstances under which an employee loses seniority credits. All employees should fully understand the exact nature of these circumstances and the significance of losing seniority credits. Under the terms of most collective bargaining contracts, employees lose seniority if they are discharged, voluntarily quit, fail to notify the management within a certain time period (usually five working days) of an intention to return to work after the employer recalls employees following a layoff, fail to return to work after an authorized leave of absence, neglect to report to work within a certain period of time (usually ninety working days) after discharge from military service, or are laid off continuously for a long period of time, usually from about twenty-four to forty-eight months.

An Overall Evaluation

However qualified it may be in particular situations, there can be no denying the current acceptability of the seniority criterion in regulating potential competition among employees for jobs and job status. The traditional arguments that seniority fosters laziness, rewards mediocrity, and crimps individual initiative are no longer automatically brought into play by managers to oppose this length-of-service criterion. And the on-balance benefits of seniority, both in improving employee morale and in minimizing administrative problems, are no longer seriously questioned by progressive companies, *if* length of service is limited by such other factors as ability when these are relevant. Although it is probably true that in general a seniority system tends to reduce the efficiency of operations to some extent, if care is taken to design a system to the needs of the particular organization, and if length of service is appropriately limited in its application, the net loss to efficiency is normally not very noticeable.

Beyond this, many would argue that efficiency, despite its obvious importance, should not be the only goal of American industry. The advantages of providing a measure of job security to employees, and thereby relieving them of the frustrations of discrimination and unfair treatment, cannot be easily quantified. But human values have become the increasing concern of modern management, and the judicious use of seniority clearly serves the human equation.

Seniority Versus Affirmative Action

Because seniority is such a major factor in layoffs—almost 50 percent of all contracts now use it as the exclusive criterion in such circumstances, indeed, with another 30 percent commanding that it be a determining layoff factor—it has generated considerable tension between white male workers and minority and female ones. Generally having been more recently hired, both of the latter kinds of employees have also been, in accordance with seniority, the first to go when work forces are pared to accommodate hard times. Thus, amid declining economic conditions of both the mid-1970s and the early 1980s, many workplaces within months became once again as white and as male as they had been years earlier.

Equal opportunity had, of course, finally come to minorities and females in the 1960s and 1970s. It had had many causes—among them, certainly, more progressive mores of society and more enlightened attitudes on the part of the new breed of industrial leader. But, patently, one factor had been paramount: Title VII of the Civil Rights Act of 1964, with its ban on job discrimination by race, sex, color, religion, or national origin and its application to all corporations, state and local governments, labor organizations, and employment agencies having more than fifteen employees. Following this landmark legislation, blacks and other minority group members, as well as women, had been hired and promoted, often in some abundance, into jobs for which even in an expanding economy they had generally been treated like wallflowers at an orgy.

To the Equal Employment Opportunity Commission, charged (together with the Justice Department) with enforcing Title VII and empowered to sue the title's violators, what employers should do in the face of the need for layoffs was clear: give special protection to the newly recruited groups to compensate them for past discrimination. At least as clear, however, was the fact that union contracts commanded respect for the seniority principle and its "last in, first out" principle. And, all but universally, the second of these Hobson's choices was embraced by the management community as the economy sank to its lowest levels since the Great Depression of the 1930s in a 1975 tailspin that would be exceeded in its enormity only by the impact of the 1981–1983 recession.

As court dockets became clogged with consequent affirmative action vs. seniority suits (with the EEOC lending its full weight to minorities and women, and the U.S. Department of Labor generally supporting seniority), most experts felt that seniority would ultimately triumph—at the U.S. Supreme Court level, where the issue would inevitably wind up. For one thing, the 1964 Civil Rights Act itself specifically approved "bona fide" seniority systems in layoffs (although it omitted any helpful interpretations as to what was "bona fide"). For another, with only one exception the lower courts had already consistently upheld the seniority system, most notably in the case of *Jersey Central Power and Light Co.*, where a U.S. appeals court judge ruled that Congress had not mandated such a sweeping remedy as that proposed by the EEOC and that only Congress could do so. And for a third, layoff by seniority was specifically sanctioned even on the occasion of the EEOC's most conspicuous victory: in 1973, when, by a consent decree, the American Telephone and Telegraph Company agreed to pay $51 million in back wages and raises.

On the other hand, predictions as to the ultimate judicial fate of this critical issue would also have to take into consideration the 1976 Supreme Court decision (in *Franks* v. *Bowman Transportation Company*) that if victims of hiring prejudice later were hired by the offending employer and could prove the original discrimination, they must be granted seniority retroactive to the date of their original rejection for the job. This decision, relating as it did only to victims of bias who were (1) later hired and (2) could prove this original action, was clearly limited in its application, however. And some observers thought that a harbinger of future Supreme Court action was contained in the dissenting opinion (in this 5–3 ruling) of Chief Justice Warren E. Burger. He was not exactly enthusiastic about granting seniority to some workers at the expense of others and wrote "I cannot join in judicial approval of 'robbing Peter to pay Paul.' "

For a time, the harbinger proved to have been accurate. In two complex 1977 decisions involving United Air Lines stewardesses and truck drivers employed by T.I.M.E.–D.C. Inc., the court ruled by 7-to-2 margins that although it might perpetuate the effects of past discrimination against women and minorities, an otherwise "neutral" seniority system did not violate the Civil Rights Act. Specifically, the Court drew upon the act's own approval of "bona fide" seniority systems to assert that Congress had allowed no recourse for those who claimed that the discrimination occurred before the law took effect on July 2, 1965. And it added that even charges of discrimination since 1965 might themselves be moot unless they were made in a "timely" way.

But this was not to be the last judicial word on the subject. In mid-1979 the Supreme Court ruled on a major new "reverse discrimination" suit, brought by a white worker at a Kaiser Aluminum plant in Louisiana on the grounds that he had been discriminated against by being turned down for a company training program designed to increase the number of blacks in skilled craft jobs. The worker, Brian F. Weber, pointed out that he had been rejected even though two black workers who were accepted had less seniority. The case stemmed from a 1974 company–union agreement to establish a new skilled job program, open to blacks and whites on a 50–50 basis until blacks had achieved a 39 percent representation in such skilled jobs (39 percent because this equaled their current representation in the area work force).

The Court decided against Weber. By a 5-to-2 majority, it declared that an employer could give preference to minorities (and women) in hiring and promoting for "traditionally segregated job categories" and that it didn't matter that the employer had never practiced discrimination. In so doing it greatly relieved Kaiser Aluminum (and, obviously, many other employers) of an understandable worry: Up until this decision the Civil Rights Act had appeared to allow remedial discrimination only where past discrimination had been proven, and if Kaiser, amid this circumstance, had admitted any such past discrimination it would have opened itself to all sorts of lawsuits from injured employees.

Yet the decision was decided on rather narrow grounds. As Justice William Brennan pointed out in writing the majority opinion, the only key was whether the Civil Rights Act forbade *voluntary* endeavors of the Kaiser variety. The decision that it did not was hardly tantamount to *requiring* employers to establish affirmative action programs.

The true impact of *Weber* was not clear a half-decade later. Some employers *had* been encouraged to set up affirmative action programs with the fear of reverse discrimination suits by white males such as *Weber* now considerably lessened. Others, having had affirmative action almost as a way of life for years, did not seem to be much affected. Most managements, in no way having been required to engage in affirmative action by the Supreme Court decision, also went on as usual and did nothing in the way of affirmative action. And, essentially because of the numerical domination of the latter, women and minorities did not fare appreciably better when the widespread need for layoffs arose in the 1981–1983 period than they had in 1975. Nor were they encouraged by a 1984 Supreme Court decision involving the city of Memphis and its firefighters: When layoffs are involved, said the judges there, the terms of a bona fide seniority system take precedence over an affirmative action plan.

Yet whatever the ultimate inroads of affirmative action into the arena controlled by seniority for so long might be, it was hard to disagree with the opinion of UAW general counsel Stephen I. Schlossberg as registered during the first economic downturn. He asserted that "remedying past discrimination is hard enough without pitting worker against worker during a recession. That is not the way you make progress. You have to do it when the economy is expanding."[2]

The expanding economy in the decade following 1964 had certainly made the

---

[2] *Business Week,* May 5, 1975, p. 67.

employment progress of both minorities and women easier. And the post-1975 economic boom had allowed their reabsorption into the labor force to be no trouble at all as long as *it* had lasted. It was equally to be hoped by all of goodwill that new economic recovery in the middle 1980s would do even more. Ideally, it would be so long lasting and deeply rooted that women and minorities would be firmly established on future seniority ladders and the major issue of the late 1970s and early 1980s—seniority vs. affirmative action—would be of interest only to historians.

DISCHARGE AND DISCIPLINE

To the naked eye, in the absence of a collective bargaining agreement, the employer is relatively unfettered in applying discipline. Actions cannot be taken, to be sure, that conflict with federal, state, or local labor laws. The government has also, as we know, been anything but bashful in dealing with the subject of discrimination against individuals on a variety of grounds, and clearly the disciplinary efforts cannot run afoul of these constraints either. Except only for such considerations, however, the management is as free to deal disciplinarily with its payroll members as it chooses—even if it chooses to act quite arbitrarily, inconsistently, autocratically, and harshly. The employer can discipline for any reason or, indeed, for no reason at all.

The advent of the union changes all of this, in the sense that *specific standards* are now established for the discipline. Generally, labor–management contracts state that employers may discipline only for "just cause" (or "just and proper cause" or "proper cause"); and even where they do not, such a stricture is assumed to be implied if there is no concrete language to the contrary. And the critical interpretation of just cause is accomplished through industrial practice and common sense, as well as (if need be) the grievance procedure and the arbitration process.

A large percentage of arbitration cases involve discipline, most frequently discharge situations, and this is entirely understandable. The right of the employer to discipline is essential to operating a successful enterprise, but—as one arbitrator phrased it in ruling against a company in a discharge case:

> If the Company can discharge without cause, it can lay off without cause. It can recall, transfer or promote in violation of the seniority provisions simply by invoking its claimed right to discharge. Thus, to interpret the Agreement in accord with the claim of the Company would reduce to a nullity the fundamental provision of a labor–management agreement—the security of a worker in his job.[3]

In addition, the stigma of discharge would hardly make it easier for the former

---

[3] *Atwater Mfg. Co.,* 13 LA 747.749., as quoted in Frank Elkouri and Edna A. Elkouri, *How Arbitration Works,* 3rd ed. (Washington, D.C.: Bureau of National Affairs, 1973), p. 611.

employee to find another job. Thus, discharges have even more serious consequences for workers than do permanent layoffs.

Although the majority of contracts contain only the previously noted general and simple statement that discharge can be made only for just cause, many labor agreements list one or more specific grounds for discharge: violation of company rules, failure to meet work standards, incompetence, violation of the collective bargaining contract (including in this category the instigation of or participation in a strike or a slowdown in violation of the agreement), excessive absenteeism or tardiness, intoxication, dishonesty, insubordination, and fighting on company property. Labor agreements that list specific causes for discharge normally also include a general statement that discharge may be made for "any other just or proper reason."

In addition, many contracts distinguish between causes for immediate discharge and offenses that require one or more warnings. For example, sabotage or willful destruction of property may result in immediate discharge, whereas a discharge for absenteeism may occur only after a certain number of warnings. In recognition of the fact that not all employee infractions are grave enough to warrant discharge, lesser forms of discipline are imposed at times under collective bargaining relationships. Into this category fall oral and written reprimand, suspension without pay for varying lengths of time, demotion, and denial of vacation pay. Frequently, union and management representatives in the grievance procedure will agree upon a lesser measure of discipline even though the employer presumably has the grounds to discharge an employee for a particular offense. At times, the union and the employee in question will be willing to settle a case on these terms rather than risk taking the case to arbitration.

A very large number of collective bargaining contracts specify a distinct procedure for discharge cases. Many of them require notice to the employee and the union before the discharge takes place. Such notification is generally required to contain the specific reasons for the discharge. A hearing on the case is also provided for in many labor agreements, typically requiring the presence of not only the worker in question and an appropriate official of the company but also a representative of the labor organization. Frequently, collective bargaining agreements provide for a suspension period before the discharge becomes effective. The alleged advantage of this procedure is that it provides for an opportunity to cool tempers and offers a period of time for all parties to make a careful investigation and evaluation of the facts of the case.

In 1975, the U.S. Supreme Court decided a case that has an important bearing on the right of employees to union representation when discipline is an issue.[4] In *Weingarten,* the Court held that an employee has a right to the presence of a union representative at employer-conducted investigatory interviews that the employee may reasonably believe could lead to disciplinary action. At times, employers conduct a "fact-finding" interview with an employee to determine whether or not

---

[4] *NLRB* v. *J. Weingarten,* 416 U.S. 969 (1975).

such action should be imposed. In such a session, the employer does not impose a penalty but obtains information to decide whether the employee should be disciplined. Since it is an investigation session, some employers have refused requests by employees for union representation. However, under the Court's rule, the employer must grant an employee's request for union representation in such a session. Failure of an employer to obey this doctrine violates the rights of employees protected by Taft–Hartley, and the National Labor Relations Board may direct the reinstatement of the employee to the job with back pay despite the offense. In a 1982 decision that must have astonished employers, the NLRB applied the *Weingarten* doctrine to *nonunion* firms. When the employer discharged an employee for refusal to participate in an interview after the employee had requested the presence of a co-worker and had been denied, the NLRB held that the employer had violated the law and reinstated the employee.[5]

Part of the procedure for discharge cases is provided for in the general grievance procedure of the collective bargaining contract. As suggested, almost every labor agreement provides for appeal of discharge cases, and this appeal is taken through the regular grievance procedure, since the appeal is looked upon as a grievance. If, for example, the labor agreement provides that the employee or the union must appeal a discharge within a certain number of days, such appeal must be made during this period or the discharge may become permanent regardless of the merits of the case. Likewise, a management that neglects its obligation to give an answer to the appeal within the stipulated number of days may find that it has lost its right to discharge the worker regardless of the justice of the situation.

Frequently, labor agreements also provide that a discharge case has a priority over all other cases in the grievance procedure. Some of them even waive the first few steps of the grievance procedure and start a discharge case at the top levels of the procedure. In these arrangements, employers and unions recognize the fact that it is to the mutual advantage of all concerned to expedite discharge cases. Workers want to know as quickly as possible whether or not they still have a job. The management also has an interest in the prompt settlement of a discharge case, because of the disciplinary implications involved and because labor agreements normally require that the employer award the employee loss of earnings where a discharge is withdrawn.

From the foregoing, it should be clear that under a collective bargaining relationship, the employer does not lose the right to discipline or discharge; it is, however, more difficult for management to exercise this function. There must be just cause, a specific procedure must be followed, and, of course, management must have the proof that an employee committed the offensive act.

If a case does go to arbitration, in fact, the arbitrator will be particularly concerned with the quality of *proof* that management offers in the hearing. On many occasions, employers have lost discharge cases in arbitration because the evidence they have presented is not sufficient to prove the case for discharge. At

---

[5] *Materials Research Corp.*, 262 NLRB No. 122 (1982); *Interstate Security Service*, 263 NLRB No. 2 (1982).

times, the management's case against the employee has simply been poorly prepared; at other times, the management has not been able to assemble the proof despite the most conscientious of company efforts. (One difficulty in this latter regard, as all arbitrators are well aware, is that employees dislike testifying against other employees who are charged with some offense.)

If the arbitrator did not demand convincing proof before sustaining discipline, however, the protection afforded employees by the labor agreement would be worthless. The same situation prevails in our civil life, wherein juries have freed criminals because the state has not proved its case. Such courses of action reflect one of the most cardinal features of our system of justice, the presumption that people are innocent until proven guilty, and this hallmark of our civil life plays no less a role in the American system of industrial relations. This situation has undoubtedly resulted in the reinstatement to their jobs with full back pay for employees who are in fact "guilty," but it is beyond argument that an employer bears the obligation to prove charges against employees it has displaced. In the absence of such an obligation, this most important benefit allowed employees under a collective bargaining contract, protection against arbitrary management treatment, is obviously negated. *(Cases 12 and 13 involve the discharge of employees. Case 13 is particularly called to your attention because of its strange circumstances.)*

And, fully as important, the rules must be *clear* and *specifically communicated* or employees simply cannot be held responsible for violating them. It is generally agreed that this stricture need not apply where the conduct involved is so obviously wrong on both moral and legal grounds that a specific rule is not needed: There is certainly no need, for example, to have an explicit rule banning employees from threatening supervision with a knife, and falsification of one's work records is—again—so clearly reprehensible that workers need not be given advance notice that this constitutes unacceptable behavior. On the other hand, it cannot be taken for granted by the employer that employees will always know what is expected of them and most often specific communication is essential to sound discipline. It is better to saturate the landscape with such information than not to give enough.

Machinery for conveying behavioral expectations abounds in organizations. Employee handbooks, bulletin board postings, company house organs, special memorandums from the management, and incorporation of the rules into the union contract are common avenues of communication. So, too, is oral publicity, by the personnel office (during orientation, for example) and also by supervision (perhaps simply as reinforcement of the original exposition). Consistent enforcement of the rules, let it not be forgotten, lends another kind of visibility to them.

What is important, however, is obviously not the exact methodology by which the rules are made known, but rather the fact that they *are* made known. No employee, when confronted with discipline, should be able to argue credibly that he or she did not realize that the conduct involved was forbidden, or—for that matter—that *changes* in the rules or a managerial intention to apply an existing rule more strictly had not been brought to the attention of the work force.

Finally, in assessing penalties, the arbitrator will fully weigh *extenuating* or *mitigating circumstances*. Is it appropriate, for example, to discipline an employee, who, at the company Christmas party, gets drunk, throws the contents of a can of beer in the face of the industrial relations manager, and makes the air purple with obscene remarks in the process? One would certainly think so, but a case involving exactly this set of circumstances reached the arbitration stage a while ago, and the arbitrator overturned the thirty-day suspension that the employee had been given for his behavior by the company and ordered that he be given full back pay as well. The decision was based primarily on the following considerations: (1) the man had worked for the company thirty-three years without a prior incident of insubordination; (2) the offense had been committed neither during working hours nor under plant disciplinary conditions, and the employee's conduct appeared to stem from his consuming too much alcohol rather than being connected with the employment relationship; and (3) although there had been prior incidents of drunken fights at the Christmas party, the company had continued to give out free and unlimited liquor and it consequently ran the risk of "predictable consequences."[6]

Mitigating circumstances—here, of course, three of them—completely changed the outcome from what might have been expected. Whether or not there is a labor arbitrator in the picture, a sound disciplinary policy commands nothing less than that these circumstances be carefully scrutinized where they exist.

Particularly when it is notably superior or glaringly inferior, a *past record,* for example, can make a large difference in evaluating the severity of a given offense. Even incidents that by themselves may hardly warrant much of a penalty at all, much less discharge, may generate a termination of employment under the most enlightened of disciplinary policies if they form a "last straw" in a long history of similar incidents. The alcoholic employee who has been warned on many occasions about his bad attendance record (as well as counseled about his underlying problem) and then is suspended for five days with the understanding that one more similar absence will cause his discharge and who then absents himself for the same drink-related reason may be said to illustrate this category. On the other side of the scales, a worker who might otherwise be terminated for a very serious offense—using abusive language in talking to a supervisor, let us say—could conceivably be given a lesser penalty in view of the worker's eleven years of superior performance (and absence of disciplinary infractions within it) in the service of the company.

In fact, *length of service,* in its own right, irrespective of its quality, can serve as a mitigating circumstance. Arbitrators have regularly accepted long service as something working in the disciplined employee's favor and so, too, in general have nonunion employers. Longevity itself presumably deserves some reward, but there are other considerations as well: As Elkouri and Elkouri assert, "[it is] recognized that the loss of seniority may work great hardship on the employee, and that it is not conducive to the improvement of relations between other workers and management."[7]

---

[6] *Grievance Guide,* 4th ed. (Washington, D.C.: Bureau of National Affairs, 1972), p. 30.
[7] Elkouri and Elkouri, *How Arbitration Works,* p. 641.

Still another kind of extenuating circumstance at times lies in the *behavior of management personnel* themselves. The employer is on very thin ice in attempting to enforce a rule against solicitation by employees on company premises if it is known that supervisors regularly peddle merchandise within the building, and the employer deserves no better fate in administering an antiobesity rule if members of management tip the scales at significantly more than their allotted poundage. Employees can hardly be expected to observe rules that are so obviously ignored by their superiors.

SAFETY AND HEALTH OF EMPLOYEES

Few people would argue that employees do not have a real interest in the area of industrial safety and health. After all, it is the worker and the worker's family who suffer the most devastating consequences of neglect in this area, in terms of accidents, sickness, and even death. And although most employers can sincerely claim that they, too, are deeply interested in safe and healthy working environments, such concern cannot restore to life a person killed on the job, or restore an employee's limbs, or succor an employee's family when an employment-caused accident or illness leads to a long-term disability. Indeed, this consideration is at the root of a longstanding policy of the National Labor Relations Board that safety and health demands of unions are mandatory subjects of collective bargaining. Employers must bargain on these issues even though working conditions are also subject to the many safety regulations imposed by federal and state statutes.

Not surprisingly, then, most collective bargaining contracts contain explicit provisions relating to the safety and health area, although such provisions take one of two routes, depending upon the particular contract.

On the one hand, many contracts merely state in general terms that the management is required to take measures to protect the safety and health of employees. At times, the term *measures* is qualified by the word *reasonable*. When a contract contains such a broad and general statement, the problem of application and interpretation is obviously involved, and disagreements between the management and union in this regard are commonly resolved through the regular grievance procedure, or by the operation of a special safety committee.

The second category of contracts provides a detailed and specific listing of safety and health measures that obligate the employer. Thus, many agreements stipulate that the latter must provide adequate heat, light, and ventilation; control drafts, noise, toxic fumes, dust, dirt, and grease; provide certain safety equipment, such as hoods, goggles, special shoes and boots, and other items of special clothing; and place guards and other safety devices on machines. In addition, under many contracts, the management must provide first-aid stations and keep a nurse on duty. Of course, whether or not a collective bargaining contract contains safety rules, an employer must comply with the federal and state safety and health laws applicable to its operations.

Many labor agreements impose obligations on employees and unions as well as on employers in the matter of safety. Such provisions recognize the fact that safety, despite the individual employee's crucial stake in it, is a joint problem requiring the cooperation of the management, employees, and union. Under many labor agreements, employees must obey safety rules and wear appropriate safety equipment, and employees who violate such rules are subject to discipline. In some labor agreements, the union assumes the obligation of educating its members in complying with safety rules and procedures of the plant. And some agreements, in the interest of safety, also establish a joint union—management safety committee. Many of these committees serve as advisory bodies on the general problem of safety and health; others, however, have the authority to establish and enforce safety and health rules, allowing the union a considerably more active role.

The Occupational Safety and Health Act and Its Consequences to Date

A high point in the area of employment safety and health was reached in the last days of 1970 with the enactment of the Occupational Safety and Health Act, generally referred to (as is the federal agency primarily charged with administering it) as OSHA. Under it, the federal government assumed a significant role in this area for the first time in history, and individual states were allowed to share jurisdiction if their plans for doing so could meet with the approval of Washington. OSHA inspectors were granted authority to inspect for violations (without prior notice to the employer) at the nation's 5 million workplaces and to issue citations leading to possibly heavy fines and even, as a last resort, jail sentences.

AFL–CIO president Meany applauded OSHA's enactment as "a long step down the road toward a safe and healthy workplace"; Richard M. Nixon, in signing it as president, referred to the act as "a landmark piece of legislation"; and the normally unemotional *Monthly Labor Review* passionately proclaimed it a "revolutionary program."[8] Great expectations, in short, accompanied passage.

Yet disillusionment was quick to set in and, within a very few years, OSHA appeared to be all but friendless, its critics coming in almost equal numbers from the ranks of labor and management. By the end of the 1970s, the administrator of OSHA could sadly point out that the legislation had succeeded in alienating both sides. "Business and labor," she declared, "have criticized OSHA for nit-picking and the stringent enforcement of so-called nuisance standards. . . . Organized labor has complained that OSHA has been excruciatingly slow in adopting major health standards to protect large numbers of workers from widespread threats to their health."[9]

The complaints were justified. With fewer than 3,000 inspectors available to visit the 5 million places of work, the average employer could expect to see an

---

[8] George Perkel, "A Labor View of the Occupational Safety and Health Act," *Labor Law Journal*, August 1972, p. 511.

[9] Eula Bingham, "The New Look at OSHA: Vital Changes," in *Proceedings of the 1978 Annual Spring Meeting, Industrial Relations Research Association*, May 11–13, 1978, p. 488.

OSHA agent roughly every seventy-five years. Yet when they did show up, these civil servants, as the administrator also pointed out, "were citing violations of regulations on everything from coat hooks to split toilet seats."[10] Moreover, OSHA's 325 pages of safety and health standards were so technical as to be unintelligible to the vast majority of employers without professional (and thus costly) help: In its first months alone, the agency had adopted almost 5,000 "consensus" safety standards. And the standards themselves were under any conditions expensive to satisfy, OSHA's noise-control demands alone potentially costing management anywhere from $13 billion to $31 billion (depending upon the final severity of these rules). OSHA, as one by no means atypical employer said of it at the end of its first decade, "is to a management what a knife is to a throat."

On the other hand, the agency's penalties for violations had averaged a not very punitive $25 each, with companies convicted of criminal violations being so rare as to be essentially invisible. And for all the "safety" standards, only three major "health" standards and a fourth one covering fourteen carcinogenic substances had been promulgated by the 1980s.

And it was the latter trend—only—that continued after the inauguration of Ronald Reagan as the nation's chief executive in 1981. Budgetary cuts reduced the meager inspection staff by more than half, to a far more meager 1,100 within a year. Under a presidential executive order, health and safety standards and regulations were weakened by a requirement that benefits be weighed against costs (although a subsequent Supreme Court ruling, in a dispute involving worker exposure to cotton dust, commanded that worker health must remain the overriding consideration even in such circumstances). Three of every four manufacturing firms were exempted from routine safety inspections (in the interests of more governmental concentration on high-hazard manufacturing industries). And much emphasis was generally placed on voluntary employer compliance.

"You want to know about whither OSHA?" asked the head of the AFL–CIO's Occupational Safety and Health Department in assessing these actions, "Just take out the first 'h' in whither,"[11] With no more restraint, the federation's magazine commented, "Students of public administration may well rate the Reagan Administration's emasculation of the Occupational Safety and Health Administration as its greatest bureaucratic coup."[12] And even the editors of *Business Week* could remark that "by all accounts, the Reagan Administration's [OSHA] is the acknowledged front-runner in Washington's current 'regulatory relief' sweepstakes."[13]

Yet for all of this, OSHA continued to have an impact, and in fact a very significant one, on employee health and safety. Despite the cutbacks, most of OSHA's formidable standards still governed, and their very presence had—and has—generated enormous expenditures on capital investments linked to this area.

[10] *Ibid.*
[11] *Business Week*, April 6, 1981, p. 33.
[12] AFL–CIO, *American Federationist*, April–June 1982, p. 16.
[13] *Business Week,* April 27, 1981, p. 48.

By some estimates, as much as $6 billion annually is being spent by managements for health and safety, representing a doubling of the annual rate of a decade ago, and there is no question that the employer community's willingness to correct hazards and improve such vital environmental ingredients as ventilation, noise levels, and machine safety is much greater now than it was before OSHA's passage.

Essentially all experts also agree that because of OSHA employers know far more about such dangerous substances as asbestos, vinyl chloride, cotton dust, and many other actual or probable carcinogens than they formerly did and that appropriate actions to protect workers from these have been taken. It is also a widely held belief among OSHA watchers that simply by pressing the issue of employee safety and health, OSHA has made employers much more aware of workplace dangers than they would otherwise have been.

From organized labor, the activity has been even more pronounced. Ironically, the growing dissatisfaction with OSHA's enforcement has added impetus to labor's efforts, and literally hundreds of recent major contract innovations can be traced to this impetus. Such innovations include the establishment of Oil, Chemical, and Atomic Worker–oil company agreements of local joint health and safety committees with not only access to company data but the right to arbitrate unresolved safety controversies. They encompass also the training of local UAW officials as full-time paid health and safety monitors in the automobile industry and a requirement won by the Steelworkers that when steel and aluminum industry workers are transferred out of dangerous jobs to lower-paying ones because of the hazards of continued exposure to toxic substances they must be paid at the higher rate. And the Rubber Workers have now won access to the lists of chemicals used by most rubber companies; the union also now has a program whereby rubber companies are required to contribute 1 cent-per-hour worked for research (conducted by both Harvard and North Carolina) into potential health hazards.

Many unions, possibly most, are still not much more active than they have historically been in the area of safety and health. Others do no more than the minimum required to prevent membership outbursts. But the momentum set in motion, first by the high hopes for OSHA and then by the fears of the act's inadequacies, shows no sign of abating. Most probably then, the years ahead should see even more activity and expenditure both at the bargaining table and (from all concerned groups) in lobbying efforts toward a goal that all but the most selfish segments of society can applaud: the minimization of occupational hazards in the American workplace.

PRODUCTION STANDARDS AND MANNING

Certainly one of the most important functions of management is that of determining the amount of output that an employee must turn out in a given period. So important is this area to management's objective of operating an efficient plant that employers at times suffer long strikes to maintain this right as a unilateral one.

It is easy to understand why employers have such a vital interest in production standards. To the degree that employees increase output, unit labor costs decline. With declining labor costs, employers make a larger profit, or else they can translate lower labor costs into lower prices for their products or services with the expectation of thereby increasing the total volume of sales and strengthening the financial position of the company.

There is still another way to look at production standards in the operation of the firm. If employees produce more, the employer will have to hire commensurately fewer additional employees, or may even be in a position to lay off present employees on a temporary or permanent basis. Indeed, with a smaller labor force, the management could also save on the number of foremen needed to supervise the work of its employees.

Production standards are thus directly related to the manning of jobs or to the question of how many employees are needed to carry out a specific plant assignment. But even when contractual commitments or past practices obligate the company to assign a certain minimum number of workers to a given operation at all times, significant economies can be realized by management if it is able to impose higher production standards upon this inflexible crew.

If the interest of management in production standards is understandable, however, it is no less understandable that employees and their union representatives have an equal interest in ensuring "reasonableness" and "fairness" in this phase of the firm's operation. Before the advent of unions, employers could require employees to produce as much as management directed. Failure to meet these production standards could result in the summary dismissal of the employee. At times, employees suffered accidents, psychological problems, and a generally shortened work life in meeting the standards of the employer. And although modern and enlightened management does not normally impose production standards that employees cannot reasonably attain, unions and employees are nonetheless still vitally concerned with the amount of production that an employee must turn out in a given length of time because of the patent ramifications of job opportunities and union membership.

There is no simple solution to the problem of how much an employee must produce to hold a job or to earn a given amount of pay. At times, the determination of a solution is purely subjective in character; a supervisor's individual judgment is the criterion adopted to resolve the problem. To this, unions argue that the judgment of employees or labor union officers is as good as that of the management representatives.

More sophisticated methods of determination are available, but these techniques, too, are hardly so perfect or "scientific" as to end the controversy. Such techniques fall under the general title of time and motion studies. That is, having been shown the most efficient method of performing a job, so-called "average" employees, who are presumably thus working at average rates of speed, are timed. From such a study, management claims that the typical employee in the plant should at least produce the average amount in a given period. Where incentive wage systems are in effect, as we know, the employee receives premium pay for output above the average. However, production standards are important even when employees are paid by the hour, since failure to produce the average amount could result in employee discipline of some sort—ranging from a reprimand to discharge, with intervening levels such as a suspension or a demotion to a lower-paying job. Unions are far from convinced that time and motion studies constitute the millennium in the resolution of the production standards problem. They claim that the studies are far from scientific, since they still involve human judgment, and that employees who are timed are often far better than average, so that their rate of speed is consequently unrealistically fast.

With few exceptions (most notably in the garment industries), unions have pressed for an effective means of review of employer establishment of production standards, rather than toward seeking the right to establish such standards initially. Organized labor has generally believed that employee and union institutional interests are served as effectively, and without the administrative and political complexities of initial standard establishment, if there is a union opportunity for challenge of the management action, either through arbitration or by the exercise of the right to strike during the contractual period in the event of unresolved production standards disputes.

Some unions have historically preferred the right to strike to arbitration in this area. The United Automobile Workers has, for example, steadfastly refused to relinquish its right to strike over production standards disputes, and although the UAW now agrees to arbitration on virtually all other phases of the labor agreement, it is adamant in its opposition to the arbitration of standards. The international neither distrusts arbitrators nor challenges their professional competency. Rather, it believes that a union cannot properly prepare and present a case in arbitration that can successfully challenge production standards. It contends that the problems are so complicated, the proofs so difficult to assemble, and the data so hard to present in satisfactory form that arbitration is not the proper forum for resolving production standards disputes. In essence, it claims that employers have an advantage in any arbitration dealing with production standards, and the union does not intend to turn to this process because it would jeopardize the interests of its members.

On the other hand, most unions have now agreed to the arbitration of production standards. Beyond reflecting the general contemporary acceptance of the arbitration process itself, this course of action has behind it a highly practical reason: Frequently, production standards are protested by only a small group of employees in the plant. For example, the employer may have changed the standards in one department (because of improved technology, equipment, or methods) but left unaltered at least temporarily the standards in all other departments. Without arbitration, the only way in which the affected employees could seek relief would be for the entire labor force to strike—at times, a politically inopportune weapon for the union to use, because the employees in the other departments are satisfied and do not care to sacrifice earnings just to help out employees in a single department. Arbitration avoids this situation, while still allowing a final and binding decision on the grievance of the protesting employees.

There is, however, probably no area of labor relations in which management and organized labor still stand any further apart than in production standards. There is no magical solution to such controversies when they arise. Standards lie at the heart of the operation of the plant and are vital to the basic interest of the employees and unions. To say that they should be established "fairly" and "reasonably" is to recognize only an unrealizable ideal, since in the give and take of day-to-day operations deep and bitter conflicts are still bound to arise. The stakes are very high, and as long as management seeks efficiency and the union seeks to protect the welfare of its members, there exists no easy way out of the problem. Certainly nothing approaching a panacea for it has yet been discovered by the parties to collective bargaining.

TECHNOLOGICAL CHANGE

"I essentially hoped to shuffle off to a quiet demise," declared AFL–CIO president Lane Kirkland a while ago, "without ever having learned what a computer is all about or the intricacies of microwave transmission or low-frequency transmission or cable TV and satellite TV and all of those things. But I am aware that a revolution is going on."[14]

An unparalleled revolution, he could have added. In both the factory and the office technological change is affecting employment needs so greatly that it is now estimated that some 45 million existing jobs in the United States (45 percent of all jobs, indeed) will be directly touched by the year 2000.

The industrial robot, characterized by mechanical arms connected to reprogrammable computers, is probably the most dramatic symbol of this revolution. The silicon chip, itself an obvious part of the new era, too, has "thrust robots from fantasy to reality"—as two observers of this "robot revolution" have phrased it[15]—and graphic statistics concerning the new phenomenon abound even now in the earliest years of the robot age. The General Electric Company recently launched an ambitious program that is ultimately expected to lead to the replacement of half of its 37,000 assembly-line workers with robots and almost immediately to the elimination of 2,000 blue collar positions. A study conducted at Carnegie–Mellon University has found that today's robots have the technical ability to perform millions of existing factory jobs and that sometime after 1990 it will be technically possible to replace *all* manufacturing operatives in the automotive, electrical equipment, machinery, and fabricated metals industries—some 7.9 million of them—with robots. The study also declares that some 3 million of these jobs may actually

---

[14] *New York Times,* November 15, 1981, p. E3.
[15] Sar A. Levitan and Clifford M. Johnson, "The Future of Work: Does It Belong to Us or to the Robot?" *Monthly Labor Review,* September 1982, p. 11.

be lost.[16] And while only about 5,000 robots are currently in use in this country, the figure represents approximately a tripling in a two-year period, with the robot sales curve only now, with the new capabilities of its product, starting to take off. It is not hard to find industrial analysts who expect as many as 100,000 robots to be in use by 1990, and it is obvious that the robot can no longer be shrugged off as something reserved to science fiction.

Least of all can the advent of the robotic age be taken lightly by organized labor. The threats to job security are nothing if not awesome, and most scholars in the field generally share the views of MIT's labor expert Harley Shaiken that "new technology based on computers, as symbolized by robots, will be one of the—if not *the*—collective bargaining issues of the coming decade."[17]

This opposition on labor's part will nonetheless be something new in the case of robotics. Up until now, with only modest numbers of robots in operation, many of them quite restrained (in the pre-silicon-chip age) as to what they could do and economic growth in all but the most recent years preventing significant job losses in any event, unions were quite lackadaisical on the subject. "When you take into account the need robots have to be maintained and fed parts [to work on]," as a UAW official could say as recently as 1980, "I don't consider this a great threat to working people."[18] And it did not go unnoticed by unions, either, as one journalist could observe, that robot applications had "relieved people of work that is hazardous, dirty, or monotonous: loading stamping presses, spraying paint in confined areas, and making the same spot welds day in and day out."[19] With the advent of the robot revolution, such favorable evaluations for the robot from union quarters were becoming increasingly less evident.

The robot hardly stands alone, moreover, as a form of changing technology significantly affecting the work force. Examples abound to show the impact of other forms of automation—broadly defined as a system of automatic devices that integrate the entire productive process—as well. At the Port of New York Authority waterfront, for example, where over 85 percent of all general cargo now moves in containers, fewer than 10,000 workers now handle the same volume of freight that 30,000 did two decades ago. In its last years, before being broken up into smaller independent companies in 1984, the American Telephone & Telegraph Company cut some 120,000 jobs from its payrolls, at least primarily because of automation. In railroading, the automatic dispatching of freight cars has made the human dispatcher about as visible as the steam locomotive. And job obsolescence has already been the fate, too, of thousands of workers even in retail trade, as symbolized by one mail-order house in which a computer now handles over 100,000 tallies each day, keeping an automatic record of the 12,000 items sold by the employer in the process. Nor has governmental employment been immune from automation's in-

---

[16] *Wall Street Journal,* October 26, 1981, p. 1. If anything, this may be a conservative estimate. The consulting firm of Arthur D. Little, Inc., has placed the loss figure at 4 million factory jobs.
[17] *Business Week,* June 9, 1980, p. 63.
[18] *Ibid.*
[19] *Ibid.*

roads: The 450 U.S. Treasury Department clerical employees who were not long ago replaced by a single computer that can accommodate the half a billion checks issued by the federal government every year are far from unique among the casualties of technological change in that sector.

Not all of the jobs involved are, of course, unionized ones. Retail trade is, as we know, hardly a hotbed of organized labor, and (although the Treasury clerks in the above example happen to have been union members) clerical work, too, is clearly far more nonunionized than it is unionized. But the fact remains that the blue collar worker in mass-production industry—automobiles, steel, electrical, and other bastions of collective bargaining—has been the most visible victim to date of the new era of rampant technological change. The robot and other computer-based automation have a natural affinity for these sectors and, whatever the future brings, job totals here have already suffered most notably.

In the typical automated radio manufacturing establishment, for example, only two employees produce 1,000 radios per day, where standard hand assembly called for a labor force of 200. Fewer than twenty glass-blowing machines have for some time produced almost all the glass light bulbs used in the United States and, still having time on their hands, all the glass tubes used in radio and television sets (except for the picture tubes). New technology has already eliminated thousands of automobile industry jobs, with robots—costing a mere $6 hourly to operate and able to do the work of two $20-an-hour human workers—ever more tempting given the financial problems of that sector. And in steel the inroads of technology have combined with foreign competition to cut the 500,000 production workers of two decades ago approximately in half.

For all of these labor-displacement and related skill-rating effects, there are clearly some offsetting advantages. The employer implementing the changes presumably benefits, either by gaining a competitive edge or by closing a competitive gap. The increased productivity that is created raises national living standards immensely: The average family income in the United States, at constant dollars, is now expected—for example—to reach an impressive $30,000 annually by the year 2000, up from only half that figure today. Jobs are invariably made safer, with materials handling and other relatively dangerous occupational aspects either considerably minimized or eliminated altogether. Product quality is frequently improved, since the automatic machine has little room for human error. And even an improved national defense can be said to have been generated, with modern warfare now so dependent upon the most advanced technology.

Most importantly, it can be argued with considerable justification that everyone, in the long run, benefits from scientific progress. There are infinitely more people working in the automobile production and servicing industries (even now) than there ever were blacksmiths, for example. And the number of employees associated with the telephone industry vastly exceeds the highest labor force totals ever achieved by the town-crier profession.

All these arguments, however, are of small consolation to the employee actually being displaced or threatened by technology. Just as logically, the employee can echo the irrefutable statement of Lord Keynes that "in the long run, we are all dead." And one can often balance the fact that technology has generally improved working conditions by pointing to undesirable features of the problem that have an impact upon the workers: greater isolation of employees on the job, with less chance to talk face to face with other workers and supervisors; a greater mental strain, particularly since mistakes can now be much more costly; the deterioration of social groups, since it requires considerably less teamwork to run the modern operation; and the fact that jobs in the automated plant (or office) are fast becoming much more alike, with less on-the-job variety also often the case, and attendant psychological and social implications stemming from this situation.

But most worrisome of all to the industrial worker is the threat of displacement, or at least of severe skill requirement downgrading, through *future* technological change. The results of one employee survey with which the authors are personally familiar showed that almost three-quarters of all respondents, asked whether they believed that "automation is a good thing for workers," replied in the negative (and many of them added that the new methods constituted a "real job threat"). Such findings have been echoed in countless other studies.

The fears appear to be well grounded. If technological change undeniably creates new jobs and even industries, the possibility remains that at the present time, it is destroying more jobs than it creates. Even placing all government and private estimates at their rock-bottom minimums, it is likely that 20,000 jobs are eliminated *each week* in this manner. And however many of the displaced are ultimately reabsorbed into the employed labor force, the increasing skill requirements of an automated world leave little room for at least the unskilled worker to join their ranks; at the time of this writing, with a national rate of unemployment seemingly inflexibly fixed above 8 percent, the rate for unskilled workers has steadily exceeded 20 percent in recent years.

Thus, while by far the greatest organizational problem of unions involves the organization of the white collar sector in the face of the automation-caused changing complexion of the work force, within the current arena of collective bargaining, organized labor—both as the blue collar worker's representative and for its own institutional preservation—has inevitably been forced toward the promotion of *measures minimizing job hardship for blue collar workers.*

Accordingly, unions have in recent years pushed hard, and with much success, for several devices geared explicitly to cushioning the employment impact of technological change. Some of these—SUB, pension vesting, severance pay, extended vacation periods, extra holidays, and early retirement provisions—have already been discussed as "economic supplements" (see Chapter 8). They have frequently been negotiated to satisfy goals other than adjustment to automated change: A desire for greater leisure purely and simply sometimes motivates vacation and holiday demands, for example, and severance pay implementation or liberalization may be triggered by, say, a union wish to protect workers unable to work because of permanent disability. In addition to these devices, several that tend to be more directly related to technological change deserve attention:

1 *Advance Notice of Layoff or Shutdown.* Such advance notice, impracticable for management in the case of sudden cancellation of orders and various other contingencies, is far more feasible where technological change is involved, since many months may be required to prepare for the new equipment and processes. An increasing number of agreements now call for notice considerably in excess of the few days traditionally provided for in many contracts, with most of the liberalizations now providing for six to twelve months.

Managements independently have often agreed with the advisability of such liberalization—to maintain or improve community images, to dispel potentially damaging employee rumors, and, frequently, because of a desire to develop placement and training plans for displaced workers. Very often, in fact, the actual notice given by management exceeds that stipulated in the contract. There seems to be little doubt, however, that unions have been instrumental in inserting longer advance-notice provisions in some contracts—as in portions of the meatpacking, electrical, and electronics industries—that might otherwise not have modified traditional practices. Such certainly appears to have been the case in the 1982 General Electric and Westinghouse negotiations, where the companies agreed to give six months' notice before shutting down product lines (and sixty days' notice before installing robots). Recent bargaining in the telephone industry has resulted in comparable contractual obligations for the employer, and for the same reason.

2 *Adoption of the "Attrition Principle."* An agreement to reduce jobs solely by attrition—through, in other words, deaths, voluntary resignations, retirements, and similar events—by definition gives maximum job security to the present jobholder, although it does nothing to secure the union's long-run institutional interests. As a compromise, it has appealed to many employers as an equitable and not unduly rigorous measure. Managements have proven particularly amenable to this arrangement when the voluntary resignation rate is expected to be high, when a high percentage of workers is nearing retirement age, or when no major reduction of the labor force is anticipated in the first place (and the number of jobs made obsolete by automation is consequently small to begin with). In other cases, unions have been the major force behind introduction of the principle—usually, however, with some modifications more favorable to the union as an institution placed upon it. Thus, the current agreement between the Order of Railroad Telegraphers and the Southern Pacific Railroad places an upper limit of 2 percent upon the jobs that can be abolished for any reason in a given year. Good faith is obviously required in such cases, however: If employers later feel that the upper limit is too severe for them to live with, given a bleak economic climate or other adverse conditions, they could understandably be tempted to encourage additional workers to leave by implementing unreasonable working conditions or otherwise lowering the employee happiness level in violation of the spirit of the agreement.

In recent years, many railroad workers have received the protection of the "Attrition Principle," as have both newspaper printers and printing-pressworkers throughout the country (but most conspicuously in New York) and postal service employees, among others.

3 *Retraining.* An expanding but unknown number of bargaining relationships now provides opportunities for displaced employees to retrain for another job in the same plant or another plant of the same company. The same protection is also increasingly being extended to employees for whom changes in equipment or operating methods make it mandatory to retrain in order to hold their current jobs. Often, such retraining opportunity, which is most commonly offered at company expense, is limited to workers who meet certain seniority specifications. General Electric workers, for example, must have at least three years of continuous service in order to qualify. At other times, preference but not a promise for retraining is granted senior workers, as in one Machinist union contract that provides that such employees "shall be given preference for training on new equipment, provided they have the capabilities required."

Where such provisions have significantly mitigated displacement, not unexpectedly, they have been implemented by companies whose operations have been expanding in areas other than those causing the initial displacement. "Retraining for *what?*" is a pertinent question when such expansion is not in evidence or at least is not highly likely. Lack of employee self-confidence or lack of worker interest sufficient to meeting the new skill requirements have also been known to make the retraining opportunity an essentially valueless one for employees permitted to utilize it. The 52-year-old with a quarter-century's experience as a blast furnace operative and the grizzled veteran of two decades on the automobile assembly line often have little optimism that they can successfully be retrained for jobs in the sales, health, clerical, and other fields where positions *are* being created. And they frequently have no greater amount of interest in finding out in any event. Thus, for example, when General Motors and the UAW cooperated in a 1982–1983 venture to train laid-off employees at two California automobile facilities for jobs in data processing (as well as aerospace), there were few takers: Only 1,522 of the 5,400 eligible workers signed up; many of the others thought that they might be rehired when GM and Toyota jointly began building new cars in the area and preferred to take their chances in this direction.

Nor can the United States government, it would seem, realistically be expected to do much to help the retraining efforts. Even the $3.5 billion Job Training Partnership Act, which took effect in late 1983 and was expected to train some 100,000 displaced workers (in addition to 1 million disadvantaged teen-agers and adults), was widely perceived as a very modest effort in view of the numbers of people covered, the fact that only 70 percent of the monies would actually go for training, and—again—the immobility, real or imagined, of those displaced.

It appeared that retraining for positions outside the employer's operations, however appealing its theory, would remain in practice anything but a powerful answer to the job losses caused by technological change.

4 *Restrictions on Subcontracting. Subcontracting,* the term that stands for arrangements made by a company (for reasons such as cost, quality, or speed of delivery) to have some portion of its work performed by employees of another company, can obviously have major work-opportunity ramifications for the first company's employees. There is probably no completely integrated company in the nation, and some measure of subcontracting has always been accepted by all unions as an economic necessity. But when the union can argue that union member employees could have performed the subcontracted work, or that such work was previously done by bargaining unit employees, it can be counted upon to do so. And when disputes do arise over this issue, they are, as Chapter 4 has pointed out, often of major dimensions. In the face of automation-caused job insecurity, there has been an observable recent trend toward union control over many types of subcontracting; the battle has tended to move from open interunion competition to the union–management bargaining table.

So thorny is the subcontracting problem that more than 75 percent of all major contracts still make no direct reference to it in a special contractual section, and thus situations such as those depicted in Exhibit 10–1 constitute minority ones. But an increasing number of contracts are incorporating into various of their other sections (ranging from union recognition clauses to seniority articles) or in separate "memoranda of understanding" certain limitations on the procedure.

The limitations are of several kinds: (1) agreements that subcontractors will be used only on special occasions (for example, "where specialized equipment not available on company premises is required" or "where peculiar skills are needed"); (2) no-layoff guarantees to current employees (as in "no Employee of any craft, which craft is being utilized by an Outside Contractor, shall be laid off as long as the Outside Contractor is in the plant doing work that Employees in such craft are able to do"); (3) provisions giving the union veto power over any or all subcontracting; and (4) requirements that the company prove to the union that time, expense, or facility considerations prevent it from allowing current employees to perform the work.

Subcontracting remains an area of large controversy in collective bargaining, and in a time of widespread worries over jobs it can realistically be expected to spread. If more attention is being paid to it at the present time, this is not because there is more agreement on its appropriate use. It seems a safe prediction, indeed, that management will fight even more vigorously to preserve its work assignment ability as foreign competition and cost pressures become more intense, and that organized labor will continue to push for limitations on the employer's subcontracting flexibility. Only when more adequate solutions to the problems of technological change are formulated can one expect the conflict in this area to abate. *(Case 14, the final case in this volume, involves the subcontracting issue.)*

5   *Other Measures.* Unions have also unilaterally attempted to minimize the administrative, institutional, and other problems of technological change through increasingly successful, if still limited, bargaining table campaigns for (1) shorter workweeks, often with a prohibition against overtime work when qualified workers are on layoff or where the overtime would result in layoffs; (2) the requirement of joint labor–management consultation prior to the introduction of any automated change; (3) the overhauling of wage structures with job upgrading to reflect the "increased responsibility" of automated factory jobs; and (4) special job and wage

---

EXHIBIT 10–1
ARTICLE 19—SUBCONTRACTING

Section 1. General

1 Whenever a contractor or subcontractor performs work on Company premises which would ordinarily be performed by employees covered by this Agreement, the Company will include a provision in the applicable contract requiring the contractor to pay (1) not less than the rates of pay provided for in this Agreement for the same character of work, and (2) one and one-half (1½) times the employees regular rate of pay for hours worked in excess of forty (40) hours per week.

Section 2. Maintenance Subcontracting

1 Whenever the Company contemplates contracting out any type of work normally performed by maintenance employees it shall inform the President, Chairman of the Grievance Committee and the affected Shop Steward of its intentions prior to making a decision to award the contract.

2 It is further agreed that the Union retains the right to examine any existing or new subcontracting agreement for the purposes of checking wage scales and the specific work contracted.

3 The Company shall not subcontract the work of any maintenance employee when the total number of maintenance employees falls below:

    a 22 percent of the total active permanent workforce (excluding short-term disability, LTD, laid-off employees, and summer employees). For example, if the total hourly active workforce is 160, then the Company may not subcontract if the maintenance force falls below 35 (22 percent of 160). The maintenance force shall be counted in the same manner as the permanent workforce.

    b For the purposes of this paragraph Maintenance employees shall exclude Storehouse Clerks and Salvage Section.

4 The Company will provide the Union quarterly reports summarizing subcontracting performed in the prior three (3) months plus a three month projection of anticipated major subcontracting projects, including a review of total workload.

5 The Company further agrees:

    a The purchase requisition will require designation of whether outside repairs or construction services will be required.

    b Contractors will not perform a significant amount of work outside the original scope of a job unless an additional subcontract notification is submitted.

    c The Company will submit a list of service contracts to the Union by January 31 of each year.

    d The Company will notify the Union as soon as practicable of any outside vendors called in for trouble-shooting that are not on service contracts.

provisons for downgraded workers, to minimize income losses suffered by such workers, or to offset them entirely. In addition, unions have in some cases sought to facilitate new employment through the development of their own training, place-ment, and referral services. And, perhaps more visibly, they have often waged highly ambitious political lobbying campaigns (both on the international and AFL–CIO levels) for: a vast array of employment-generating public works programs; far-reaching tax programs and expanded Social Security benefits (to increase con-sumer purchasing power and lessen the burden on those most likely to be displaced); and innovative federal and state training programs.

As judged by short-run goals—the insertion of the various contract provisions within labor agreements and, in the latter case, the enactment of the lobbied-for legislation—unions have achieved a considerable measure of triumph (if less in the relatively penny-pinching governmental years of the 1980s than earlier). And the fact that they have frequently been aided in such campaigns by increasingly social-minded employers in no way detracts from this success. Although union aggressiveness and creativity have varied widely, there can be no denying that many unions have considerably alleviated the burdens of technological change for many workers.

Yet neither singly nor in combination have these measures, or the host of other automation-adjustment methods cited earlier, provided anything approaching a full solution for the basic problems with which they deal. The displacement and displacement threats continue, now actually in accelerated form, as the march of technology continues to prove that it is both a blessing and a curse for society. Indeed, a case can be made that a vicious circle is involved: Virtually all these measures increase labor costs for the companies concerned, giving the employer even further motivation for automating, and often thus causing the represented employees to lose jobs all the more rapidly.[20]

There appears to be rather general agreement among all segments of our society on at least three relevant points, however. First, most of us concede that technological change is a product of society. It is not caused only by individuals, single firms, or groups of firms, but rather it is an expression of our cultural heritage, of our educational system, and of our group dynamics. As such, unlike other problems affecting collective bargaining, it requires not only a private (labor–management) solution but a supplementary public (government) one. Second, we are essentially in agreement that no single group should bear the entire burden but that we should all bear it by making sure that the benefits of the increased productivity allowed by technology are shared by all. Without such a philosophical basis, automation and other such changes would mean that some would make spectacular gains, and others would shoulder the full burden. We do not want automation to divide the nation into "haves" and "have nots." Third, we share general unanimity that this is a time for daring innovation in social dynamics and

[20] This is, of course, true only if the costs are incurred in any event. If they occur *only* if one automates, they reduce the saving and in some cases could make automation unprofitable.

social engineering and that, although the problem is great, we fortunately have within our capacity the power to deal with the issues within a system of free enterprise. Since old methods will not work, we must innovate and pioneer.

The increasing attention being given to the consequences of technology at the bargaining table (and by the bargaining parties in the public arena) can thus be viewed as recognition of a great but not necessarily insurmountable challenge.

PLANT CLOSINGS

If, as noted above, there has been something of a trend to liberal advance notice on the part of the employer in the case of both layoffs and the closing of some product lines stemming from technological change, much advance notice when entire plants are to be permanently closed (whether because of outmoded technology, foreign competition, or any other reason) is still a relative rarity. According to the Bureau of Labor Statistics, only about 10 percent of all contracts contain such a provision, and even these frequently call for little more than a month or so in the way of notification.

Managements have some very rational reasons for keeping their shutdown intentions confidential. Employees who realize that even with the best performance on their part they are destined to lose their jobs have been known to engage in excess absenteeism and tardiness, and even vandalism by some such workers has sometimes occurred (presumably in an effort to get even). Moreover, as McKersie has pointed out, "If they know a firm or plant is about to close down, bankers may refuse to extend credit, while customers, worried about the flow of spare parts, will stop making new orders."[21] Stock market considerations, too, may dictate playing it close to the vest when a shutdown is contemplated. Generally, organized labor has not only understood all of this but been relatively sympathetic to it through the years.

Yet as plant closings have accelerated in the past few years—especially in such hard-pressed older industries as automobiles, rubber, steel, and meatpacking—unions have become much more active in attempting to block them, particularly when they view the closings as mere vehicles for switching jobs to plants with lower wages in the middle of union contracts, as has often in fact been the case.

To date, labor has been unable to win any kind of federal or state legislation barring such closings. But it has already achieved some success by drawing on existing legislation. Under Section 8(d) of Taft–Hartley, neither party can force the other to modify an existing contract before it expires, and unions have now won two victories by relying on this stricture. In 1979, a federal appeals court enforced a National Labor Relations Board decision against the Los Angeles Marine Hardware Company which had transferred a unionized sales division to a

[21] Robert B. McKersie, "Advance Notice," *Wall Street Journal*, February 25, 1980, p. 20.

nonunion shell company in another location by agreeing that the employer had acted illegally. The latter, said the court, could not "tear up the agreement simply because the bargain . . . it struck turned out to be disadvantageous."[22] And in late 1982 another federal court enjoined the Bohn Aluminum Corporation, a Gulf & Western subsidiary, from moving to a plant with lower labor costs after agreeing that Bohn had "no real intention" of negotiating concessions to the UAW to preserve the jobs at the original location.[23]

Companies, contending that they should be absolutely free to close down operations in the absence of an express contractual ban on their doing so, had reacted vigorously by pushing for more favorable treatment through the courts. And until a definitive Supreme Court ruling dealt with the matter, it could not be said with any assurance that they could not move operations in midterm, or—for that matter—that they could. Obviously, waiting until the contract expired would prevent them from running afoul of the existing law. And so, too, presumably, would moving for a reason other than labor costs—assuming, needless to say, that the management could prove this. Until the courts had had their full say on the matter, however, only sleepless nights would seem to await employers who intended to pursue what many managers had long believed to be an unequivocal managerial right: the freedom to phase out work as they and they alone saw fit.

A CONCLUDING WORD

Despite the preceding section, it can fairly be said that the mutual accommodations to the hard issues of collective bargaining that the parties have displayed in regard to wages, employee benefits, and institutional issues are no less in evidence when one inspects the current status of the administrative issues in our labor relations system. Management has increasingly recognized the job-protection and working-condition problems of the industrial employee and has made important concessions in these areas. At the same time, however, there has been reciprocal recognition on the part of unions that the protection of the employee cannot be at the expense of the destruction of the business firm. The axiom that employees cannot receive any protection from a business that has ceased to exist appears to have been fully appreciated by all but the extreme recalcitrants of the labor movement, and workable compromises have usually been possible with respect to the areas of seniority, discipline, and most of the various other dimensions discussed in this chapter no less than in the case of previous topics.

Clearly, there is considerable room for future progress, and, on occasion, the conflicts between the parties on the administrative issues can be very serious. Production standards, subcontracting, and—increasingly—plant shutdowns remain highly visible sticking points. And strikes do, of course, at times result. There should be no illusion that the sensitive matters of collective bargaining are adjusted

---

[22] *Business Week,* January 24, 1983, p. 25.
[23] *Ibid.*

without painful struggle. Even standing alone, however, this chapter demonstrates rather irrefutably that managers and unionized employee representatives have increasingly recognized each other's positions. It offers additional evidence of the growing maturity of the American labor relations system, a theme that in one way or another has marked so much of this book.

Discussion Questions

1 It has generally been agreed that the increased use of the seniority concept in industrial relations has lessened the degree of mobility among workers. What can be said (a) for and (b) against such a consequence?

2 "The typical labor agreement's disciplinary procedures contain as many potential advantages for management as they do for unions and workers." Comment.

3 Jack Barbash has commented that "management's perception of technological change is producing an offensive strategy; the union's perception is in general producing a defensive strategy." Confining your opinion to automated changes, do you agree?

4 The several devices noted in the "Technological Change" section of this chapter constitute the major existing avenues for minimizing employee resistance to such change. Can you suggest other measures that might be utilized in an attempt to realize this goal?

Selected References

BACOW, LAWRENCE S., *Bargaining for Job Safety and Health*. Cambridge, Mass.: MIT Press, 1980.

BAER, WALTER E., *Discipline and Discharge under the Labor Agreement*. New York: American Management Association, 1972.

BLACK, JAMES MENZIES, *Positive Discipline*. New York: American Management Association, 1970.

BRODEUR, PAUL, *Expendable Americans*. New York: Viking, 1974.

DONOVAN, RONALD, and MARSHA J. ORR, *Subcontracting in the Public Sector: The New York State Experience*. Ithaca, N.Y.: New York State School of Industrial and Labor Relations, 1982.

GERSUNY, CARL, *Punishment and Redress in a Modern Factory*. Lexington, Mass.: Heath, 1973.

KENNEDY, THOMAS, *Automation Funds and Displaced Workers*. Boston: Harvard University, Graduate School of Business Administration, 1962.

NORTHRUP, HERBERT R., et al., *The Impact of OSHA*. Philadelphia: University of Pennsylvania Press, 1978.

REDEKER, JAMES R., *Discipline: Policies and Procedures*. Washington, D.C.: Bureau of National Affairs, 1983.

SHILS, EDWARD B., *Automation and Industrial Relations*. New York: Holt, Rinehart and Winston, 1963.

SHULTZ, GEORGE P., and ARNOLD R. WEBER, *Strategies for the Displaced Worker*. New York: Harper & Row, 1966.

SIEGEL, ABRAHAM J., ed., *The Impact of Computers on Collective Bargaining*. Cambridge, Mass.: MIT Press, 1969.

SLOANE, ARTHUR A., *Personnel: Managing Human Resources,* pp. 396–418. Englewood Cliffs, N.J.: Prentice-Hall, 1983.

SOMERS, GERALD G., EDWARD L. CUSHMAN, and NAT WEINBERG, eds., *Adjusting to Technological Change*. New York: Harper & Row, 1963.

THOMIS, MALCOLM I., *The Luddites: Machine-Breaking in Regency England*. New York: Schocken Books, 1972.

TOBIN, JOHN A., *A Positive Approach to Employee Discipline*. Wheaton, Ill.: Hitchcock, 1976.

WEINSTEIN, PAUL A., ed., *Featherbedding and Technological Change*. Boston: Heath, 1965.

Relatively Equal Ability:
The Case of the Illinois Prison

Cast of characters:

Falk	*Grievant*
Bair	*Assistant Warden*
Hill	*Warden*
Moore	*Chief Engineer*
Bolt	*Junior Service Employee*
Ohl	*Another Employee*
Scott	*Hearing Officer*
Curtis Falk	*Grievant's Father and Union Vice President*

This is the second public-sector case. Unlike Case 6, "Teacher Contracts: The Case of the Girls' Gymnastics Coach," it was not complicated by state law. As a result, the arbitrator applied the same contractual principles developed in the private sector. The dispute centered on the application of the seniority provision to the facts of the case. The prison management selected the junior service employee for the job in question, asserting that the selection was proper under the terms of the provision and the circumstances of the dispute. In contrast, the senior employee and the union claimed a violation of the provision. The evidence clearly demonstrated that the junior employee had greater experience in carpentry work. Once again, you are the arbitrator.

GRIEVANCE

When Falk was not selected to fill a vacancy in the Corrections Maintenance Craftsman classification, he filed Grievance No. 6-196-81, dated March 4, 1981, which stated:

> Management is in violation of the RC-6 contract agreement filling the vacancy of Corrections Maintenance Craftsman. Failure to comply with Article XVIII, Section 2A is a direct violation of this contract agreement. Therefore, I ask to be placed in the position of Corrections Maintenance Craftsman with all monies due to me as of March 1, 1981.

His grievance was denied in the Grievance Procedure, and this arbitration was convened to decide the dispute.

LABOR AGREEMENT

ARTICLE XVIII.   SENIORITY

Section 1. Definition   Seniority for RC-6, for the purposes stated in this Agreement, shall consist of the length of service of an employee within a department.

Section 2. Application   (a) For employees in the RC-6 bargaining unit, in all applications for seniority under this Agreement the ability of the employee shall mean the qualifications and ability (including physical fitness) of an employee to perform the required work. Where ability and qualifications to perform the required work are, among the employees concerned, relatively equal, seniority as defined in Section 1 above shall govern.

ISSUE

Under the circumstances of this case, did the Employer violate Article XVIII, Section 2(a), of the Labor Agreement? If so, what should the remedy be?

BACKGROUND

Recommendation of Panel

When the circumstances of this dispute arose, Falk, hired on February 2, 1978, was classified as Corrections Officer assigned to the Correctional Center. Bair served as Assistant Warden, Operations, and Hill was the Warden. The resident population was about 900 prisoners and 275 employees were assigned to the institution.

On January 20, 1981, a vacancy was posted for Corrections Maintenance Craftsman, day shift, with a salary range between $1,255 and $1,600 per month. The posting said:

DESIRABLE REQUIREMENTS: Requires knowledge, skill and mental development equivalent to completion of four years of high school. Requires experience necessary to qualify as a journeyman in one of the maintenance or automotive repair trades.

Its assignment was to the Carpenter Shop of the Maintenance Department. Two carpenters are assigned to the Carpenter Shop. Moore, Chief Engineer, supervisor of the Carpenter Shop, and other maintenance operations, described the job as "general carpentry work" involving general repair, construction of portable buildings, typing tables, and hanging of door frames and facings. Beyond performing carpenter work, the employee also instructs and supervises prisoners in the trade. Between four and twelve residents are assigned to the Carpenter Shop.

Seven employees applied for the job, including Bolt, hired on October 19, 1978, also classified as a Corrections Officer. Moore and two Assistant Engineers constituted the panel that interviewed the applicants. As it turned out, only the interviews of the Grievant and Bolt are material to the dispute. Moore's notes of the interview state:

Bolt
Mr. Bolt states that he has 6 yrs. experience in carpenter and construction business. At one period of time, he was self-employed, operating his own construction and remodeling business. He also worked for Cumberland Const. Co. and for Beckman Const. Co. He states he was never a union member of the carpenter trade.
When questioned about tools and materials used in the carpenter trade, he answered in a satisfactory manner. He was somewhat vague on some terminology.
He appears to be well qualified and should be able to handle the position without difficulty.

Falk
It is difficult to determine the exact amount of experience that Mr. Falk has had, as he worked with his grandfather (Heath Construction Company, Raber, Illinois) for 5½ yrs., this being part time and summers, etc.
He has one (1) year of woodworking in grade school and one (1) year in high school. He has 4 credit hours of college in real estate and possesses a real estate salesman's license. He states he is able to read blueprints. When questioned about tools and materials of the carpenter trade, he answered satisfactorily, but was somewhat vague on terminology.
In our opinion, Mr. Falk would qualify for the Carpenter Shop position.

On February 18, 1981, in a memorandum addressed to Bair, Moore on behalf of the panel recommended that Falk be awarded the vacancy, stating:

We also feel that Mr. Falk and Mr. Bolt are equally qualified for the carpenter shop position, and therefore we must abide by the RC-6 contract and recommend Mr. Falk for the Corr. Maintenance Craftsman (Carpenter Shop) position because of seniority.

With regard to the interviews of the Grievant and Bolt, Moore testified:

Bolt did not sell himself. He was quiet and humble. We felt that Bolt had more experience than he was telling us. We could not draw him out. Falk was a good talker. He sold himself to us.

Bolt Selected for Job

Bair did not accept the panel's recommendation. He testified that he interviewed Bolt when he was hired as a Corrections Officer, and knew that he had been a carpenter in the building trades. As a result, on February 19, 1981, the Assistant Warden sent a memorandum to the applicants requesting them to provide him with

a detailed list and verification of experience which qualifies you for the Corrections Maintenance Craftsman position that you have applied for. I will need the list and verification of experience by Monday, February 23, 1981.

In compliance with Bair's instructions, Falk and Bolt supplied the required information, accepted in the record as Joint Exhibits 7 and 8 respectively. (The experience of the two employees in carpenter work will appear later on in this Opinion.)

On February 27, 1981, in a memorandum addressed to Warden Hill, Bair recommended Bolt for the job, stating:

> However, in reviewing the recommendations for promotions, it is my opinion that the two candidates that Mr. Moore has rated as equal for the Carpenter's position were, in fact, not equal in their experience. Therefore, I notified each and every applicant who applied for the Carpenter's position to further document their experiences to me and have the documentation to me no later than Monday, February 23, 1981. These notifications were sent out to all applicants on Friday, February 20, 1981. On February 23, 1981 I reviewed the documentation of experiences which I had received, of which there were only three. Correctional Officer Falk documented his experiences as well as Correctional Officer Bolt and Correctional Officer Ohl. In reviewing the documentation, it is my opinion that Correctional Officer Bolt has more experience working in the building trades and as a carpenter than the other two individuals. Correctional Officer Falk's experiences were a composite of part-time experiences over several years. However, Correctional Officer Bolt's experiences were as a full-time employee.

Hill accepted Bair's recommendation and Bolt was assigned to the Carpenter Shop as Corrections Maintenance Craftsman. Bolt said that he started in the Carpenter Shop on a temporary basis on March 1, 1981. Effective April 1, 1981, he was assigned to the classification on a regular basis.

Subsequent Events

On March 4, 1981, Falk filed the grievance that generated this arbitration. According to Curtis Falk, the Grievant's father and Vice President of the Union, he had a conversation with Hill on or about March 6, 1981 in the Yard Office. At that time, Curtis Falk testified, Hill told him that

> he would admit that the Grievant and Bolt were equal in experience, but it is Management's choice to make the promotion.

Curtis Falk testified that no one else was present when the conversation took place. Hill did not appear in the arbitration.

A Third Level Grievance Procedure meeting was held on April 21, 1981, conducted by Scott, Labor Relations Administrator, Department of Corrections. Several Union officers were present, including Curtis Falk. Only Bair appeared on behalf of the Employer. According to the Union Vice President, Bair said in the session:

These two people were exactly equal in qualifications, but it is Management's choice.

Bair denied that he made that statement, testifying that in the Second Level Grievance Procedure meeting, held on March 13, 1981, he stated: "In my opinion, their experience is not equal."

In any event, Scott recommended that the grievance be denied, stating:

> Recommendation: Management closely evaluated the qualifications of both candidates, giving particular emphasis to the previous experiential qualifications due to the importance of full knowledge of the carpentry skills to fill this position. Based on this important criteria, Management determined Mr. Falk was not relatively equal to Mr. Bolt due to Mr. Bolt's having had considerable more varied, as well as quantity of, experience. Management, therefore, using contractual provisions of "relatively equal," chose Mr. Bolt. I believe Management has substantiated that. Bolt and Falk are not relatively equal, and, therefore, recommend the grievance be denied.

Previous Experience in Carpentry Work

In compliance with the Assistant Warden's instructions, Falk and Bolt supplied statements about their previous experience. Since the vacancy called for carpentry work, some of the experience listed by both employees was not relevant. Bolt had a job in the flying service business and Falk was a laborer, welder, and real estate salesman. Those jobs have nothing to do with the requirements of the job in question and will be disregarded.

With respect to carpentry work, Bolt said he

> worked full-time from 1971 to late 1977 and earned living as a carpenter and other Building Trades

And:

> My experience as a carpenter consists of about 6 years of experience. During this time, I have laid out homes from the ground up and performed about every carpenter job there is in building a home.

As to his experience, Falk stated that

> in high school, I took two courses in carpentry. In April 1974, I started to work for Heath Construction Company, Raber, Illinois, which was owned by my grandfather. While in high school, I averaged 20–25 hours per week, and averaged 50–60 hours per week during the summer vacations.

Falk graduated from high school in May 1977. Between April 1977 and February 1978, he was employed by Tri-Star, and worked for Heath Construction in the evenings, averaging 20–25 hours per week. Falk started at the Correctional

Center on February 2, 1978. Since that time, and to the present, he works for Heath Construction in the evenings and his day(s) off, averaging between 20 and 25 hours per week.

While employed at Heath Construction, Falk performed carpenter work, including building and hanging cabinets; roofing homes; hanging drywall and paneling; installing windows and doors; building garages, attached and unattached; and hanging interior doors and trim.

This work was performed on the fourteen homes built by Heath Construction between 1974 and 1981. Falk said he performed "all aspects of carpentry work on these homes."

While employed by Heath Construction, the Grievant also built grain bins, hog houses, pole barns, and machine sheds, and installed roofs on sheds and barns. Heath Construction owns a thirteen-apartment complex, the Grievant performing some aspects of carpenter work connected with them, including panel and window installation.

Between May and August 1980, when not on his job at the Correctional Center, Falk was employed by Thull Construction Company, Raber, Illinois. In his document, he stated:

> I assisted the company in the building of houses from start to finish. For example, some of the work was hanging drywall, paneling and remodeling of older homes, siding homes and residing of older homes, roofing homes and barns, and cabinet building.

Additional Material

Additional material developed in the record indicates that Bair and Bolt apparently are personal friends. Curtis Falk, the Grievant's father, testified:

> It is common knowledge in the Corrections Center that Bair and Bolt are friends.

About a year ago, Bolt helped Bair in the building of the Assistant Warden's home. After Bair issued the memorandum dated February 19, 1981, requesting documentation of the employees' experience, Bair advised Bolt how to make out the form after Bolt asked him. Bair did not converse with Falk prior to the time the selection was made.

For the three months Bolt served in the carpenter job prior to the arbitration, the Employer rated his work as superior and awarded him a wage increase.

Bair verified the carpentry experience of Bolt, but did not check out the experience offered by the Grievant. With regard to this feature of the case, Bair said Bolt at his request furnished W-2 federal income tax forms to prove he worked for the employers that he listed in his statement. The Assistant Warden also found such employers' telephone numbers listed in the "yellow pages" of the Raber, Illinois, phone directory.

With regard to the Grievant, Bair testified:

Falk listed about 7 years of experience in his document. When he started here, he was only about 20 years of age. Yet he said he had experience covering the whole gamut of construction work. I could not see how he could have had that amount of experience at his age. So age was a factor when I made my selection.

I did not verify the Grievant's experience because he listed Heath Construction which is owned by his grandfather. I figured that his grandfather would not dispute the experience which he listed.

Finally, during the arbitration, both employees testified to carpentry work that was not listed in the written documents supplied by the Assistant Warden. For example, Falk said that he built his own home, and Bolt declared he had carpentry experience not listed on the document.

---

cases *12* & *13*

The following two cases deal with the discharge of employees. In Case 12, an employee was discharged because he carried a gun into the plant. It was not loaded and the employee brought the weapon into the plant for an innocent purpose. Certainly he did not intend to shoot someone. In his decision, the arbitrator said that "the Grievant is a good person, surely not dangerous, and he certainly meant no harm when he brought the gun into the plant." However, a plant rule called for discharge of employees bringing a firearm into the plant. Though there are other aspects of the dispute, the fundamental problem of the arbitrator was to determine whether the employee, despite his qualities and innocent intent, should be discharged under the plant rule.

Case 13 is surely one of the strangest cases in the annals of arbitration. A comparatively small telephone company was owned privately by its president. For about one year, the employer paid an employee full wages and fringe benefits though he did not require the employee to work! Then the employee was discharged, the company alleging that his productivity was deficient and that he was psychologically unfit to work. Despite the odd character of the dispute, the arbitrator attempted to apply sound arbitration principles as the basis of his decision. As you read the case, try to determine the real reason for the employer's paying the employee though the employee was not required to work.

Discharge of Employee:
The Case of the Prohibited Gun

Cast of characters:

Dash	*Grievant*
Batz, Sitz, Neely	*Employees*
Spear	*Plant Superintendent*
Mills	*General Foreman*
Kone	*Chief, Plant Security*
Yost	*Labor Relations Manager*
Murphy	*Division Employee Relations Manager*
York	*Employment Manager*

GRIEVANCE AND LABOR AGREEMENT

On July 14, 1980, Dash was discharged because he brought a gun to the plant. In protest, he filed Grievance No. 858, dated July 14, 1980. It states:

> I have been unjustly discharged. And as settlement for this grievance ask that I be made whole for all moneys lost. And be reinstated with full seniority and benefits.

Material to the dispute are the following provisions of the Labor Agreement:

ARTICLE II. MANAGEMENT

Section 1 In pertinent part, under this provision the Company has the right to discharge for "proper cause" and "establish and enforce Company rules."

Section 6 The Company agrees to maintain safe, clean and healthful conditions in the plants and on Company premises.

Section 7 The Company shall institute and maintain reasonable and necessary precautions for safeguarding the health and safety of its employees in accordance with the Federal Law and Federally approved State Law. Both the Company and the Union recognize their mutual objective to assist in the prevention and elimination of reasonably avoidable hazards and unhealthy working conditions.

COMPANY RULES

Also material are the Company Rules contained in a booklet given to all employees entitled "Welcome to the Industrial Machinery Division." The Rules are divided into two categories: "No. 1 General Rules of Conduct" and "No. 2 General Rules of Conduct." As a preface to the No. 1 Rules, the following appears:

> *No. 1 General Rules of Conduct*
>
> The following rules are designed to promote the welfare of both the Company and the employees. These rules are to be followed by all employees:

Thereafter are listed thirteen (13) Rules to guide employee conduct. Before the No. 2 Rules, the following appears:

> There are certain activities that affect the welfare of all and are, therefore, *subject to immediate disciplinary action or dismissal.* They are: (Emphasis in original)

Then are listed ten (10) Rules governing employee conduct. Of material importance to this case is Rule No. 5 which states:

> Carrying firearms or other dangerous weapons on Company premises.

BASIC QUESTION

The basic question to be determined in this arbitration is framed as follows:

> Under the circumstances of this case, was Grievant Dash discharged for proper cause? If not, what should the remedy be?

BACKGROUND

Gun Brought into Plant

When the circumstances of this case arose, Dash, hired on March 12, 1979, was classified as Helper on the 606 Milling Machine. On Wednesday, June 25, 1980, he brought a gun onto Company premises. It was a 38-caliber two-barrel derringer pistol concealed in his lunch box. Dash said that the weapon was not loaded and that he did not bring shells for it.

According to the Grievant, he brought the gun to the plant intending to sell it to Batz, another employee. After Batz looked at the gun, he refused to buy it, and Dash returned it to his lunch box. Dash also said that about a month prior to June 25, he purchased the gun from another employee, Sitz, testifying that the transaction occurred in the plant.

Conversation with Spear

On the day in question, Spear, Plant Superintendent, was informed that Dash had the gun. Spear, Mills, General Foreman, and Kone, Chief of Plant Security, approached the Grievant at his machine. When Spear asked him, the Grievant denied the gun was at his machine. Dash replied: "I am not that stupid" when Spear asked him if he had brought a gun onto Company premises. Then Dash told Spear the weapon was in his car.

Later on the same day, Dash was summoned into Spear's office. Kone was in the office when the Grievant arrived. At first, Dash again denied that he had brought the gun into the plant. Spear told the Grievant that it would be best to be honest. He also told Dash that he was going to order him to leave the plant. Then Dash told the Superintendent that he had a family and had to work. At that point Dash acknowledged that he had the gun at his machine. Spear instructed the Grievant to get the weapon, telling him he would escort him out of the plant. Spear also told him that after the gun was off plant premises he could return to work, and further that Personnel need not have to be involved in the matter once the gun was out of the plant.

Grievant Returns to Work

Thereupon, Dash walked to his machine, got the gun from his lunch box, and placed it in one of a pair of gym shoes which he had. Spear and Kone escorted the Grievant to the gate. While still on Company premises, Dash handed the gun to Spear who placed it into an envelope.

As it turned out, Dash did not have his car at the plant. That morning he rode to work with another employee. Apparently while in the Superintendent's office he asked another person for transportation. When the car arrived, Spear returned the weapon to Dash, and Dash was driven to his home.

The person who transported Dash to his home did not return Dash to the plant because his car broke down. The Grievant called the plant and spoke to Mills. Informed of the situation, the General Foreman drove to the Grievant's home and returned him to the plant. Dash completed his shift on June 25.

Grievant Discharged

Dash worked the next day, Thursday, June 26. Starting on Friday, June 27, the plant shut down for its annual vacation period, operations resuming on Monday, July 14. However, Dash was permitted to work during the first week of the shutdown.

Yost, Labor Relations Manager, was not in the plant on June 25. On Thursday, June 26, he returned to work and Spear and Kone informed him about the gun incident. Yost did not take any action against the Grievant on June 26, testifying that he wanted time to investigate the matter and he was too busy to do so on that day, being concerned with the problems of the shutdown scheduled for the next day. However, Spear, Murphy, Division Employee Relations Manager, and York, Employment Manager, were in the plant on June 26.

On Monday, July 14, when the plant resumed operations, Yost discharged the Grievant after he consulted with Murphy. On the same day, Dash filed his grievance, claiming that he was not discharged for just cause and requested reinstatement with back pay and full contractual rights.

Other matters involved in this case will be explored later on in this Opinion.

POSITIONS OF THE PARTIES

The position of the Company is that the grievance should be denied, and the Union requests that it be granted. Both Parties filed post-hearing briefs. Arguments contained in them will be cited later on in this Opinion to the extent necessary and appropriate.

ANALYSIS OF THE EVIDENCE

Application of Rule 5

At the outset it is required that a determination be made as to whether or not the Grievant violated Rule No. 5. If he did not, the grievance shall be granted, making unnecessary further analysis of the dispute. On the other hand, should it be held that he did violate the Rule, consideration must be given to other features involved in the dispute.

Not even the Union contends that Rule No. 5 does not represent a reasonable exercise of the Company's authority to establish plant rules under Article II, Section 1, the Management provision. As is well-known, such a rule is common in industry and sanctioned by collective bargaining contracts. Indeed, the reasonableness of the Rule is also supported by the Company's obligation under Article II, Sections 6 and 7, to provide a safe workplace and maintain reasonable and necessary precautions for safeguarding the health and safety of its employees. This fact need not be labored because all concerned recognize the obvious purpose of a rule forbidding firearms in the plant.

Though recognizing the need for Rule No. 5, the Union believes that the Grievant did not violate it under the circumstances of this case. It argues:

> At no time did Dash come under the terms of "carrying firearms" (to carry arms). There was no question on this matter. It was undisputed that the empty weapon that Dash had, remained in his dinner bucket the complete time except for those moments that Batz looked at it. It was undisputed that employee Dash had brought the weapon inside the plant for another employee.

Holding in abeyance the significance of the Grievant's testimony that he purchased the weapon in the plant, and with full deference to the Union, the argument that it presents is not acceptable. As a threshold observation in this respect, the Grievant said that he was aware of the Rule, but felt that he did no wrong when he brought the gun into the plant. He testified:

> I knew of the Rule, but I thought it was O.K. to bring it into the plant because I did not have it loaded and I previously bought it in the plant from another employee.

Contrary to the Union's position, the Rule does not distinguish between a gun that is loaded or not loaded. It flatly forbids firearms in the plant. Whether the weapon was loaded or not loaded does not make any difference for the proper application of the Rule. Moreover, the Union is in error when it claims that the Grievant did

> at no time . . . come under the terms of "carrying firearms" (to carry arms).

The pistol was obviously a "firearm" under the meaning of the Rule. If it was not a "firearm" what should we call it? He carried it into the plant within the meaning of the Rule because he brought the gun into the plant. Does the Union suggest here that to "carry arms" for purposes of the Rule an employee must carry it like a shotgun over his shoulder? Clearly, the Arbitrator does not believe that the Union could mean that though he puzzled at length about its assertion that the Rule did not apply to the Grievant. The fact that the gun was concealed in the Grievant's lunch box except when shown to Batz does not exculpate him from the coverage of the Rule. The bottom line is that Dash brought the gun into the plant. Where he kept it does not relieve him from the application of the Rule.

Still another argument of the Union is not acceptable. It says:

> The grievant made a bad error in judgement, but should the grievant be disciplined with discharge for his error in judgement? The Union says "No." The Union has to agree that employees have responsibility to abide by reasonable rules and regulations. Discharge as being the discipline administered in this case is too extreme. A lesser penalty should have been administered.

Whether or not discharge was the proper penalty shall await determination. At this point it is sufficient to say that Dash does not escape from the Rule on the grounds that he used "poor judgment." Rather than passing off what he did as merely "poor judgment," the conclusion is inescapable that he knowingly violated the Rule. He was fully aware of the Rule, but still brought the weapon into the plant. Indeed, the very fact that he carried the gun into the plant concealed in his lunch bucket demonstrates that he knew that he was committing a violation. If he did not, why did he not carry it in a more exposed position, say in his pocket or even in his hand? He did not do that because he wanted to conceal the weapon from observation by other persons. The lunch bucket served his purpose.

Grievant's Intent

Full recognition is given to the Grievant's testimony that he brought the gun to the plant with the intention of selling it to another employee. Apparently the Union believes that the Rule does not apply to such a situation, arguing:

> The instant grievance concerns an employee who brought an unloaded weapon into the plant with the intention of selling said weapon to another employee.

Clearly, if the Grievant is to be excused from the Rule because of his intent, there would be no way in the world whereby the Company could enforce the Rule. The word would get out that it is permitted to bring firearms into the plant as long as you intend to sell them! Under these circumstances, the plant could become a veritable gun swap shop. More seriously, an accident could conceivably happen. An employee brings his gun into the plant, but forgets to unload it. In his enthusiasm to sell the weapon, showing the potential buyer its merits, the employee accidentally presses the trigger and a tragedy results. This consideration is not as far fetched as it would seem at its first reading. Barely a day passes when we do not read or hear about a person injured or killed by a gun going off by accident.

Beyond these observations, Rule No. 5 does not make any exception for intent. It forbids firearms in the plant regardless of intent. Of course, only a lunatic would bring a gun into the plant to shoot someone. So, are we to limit coverage of the Rule by holding that guns are forbidden only if you intend to kill someone? That would be the logical end of applying the Rule in terms of intent. The fundamental purpose of the Rule is to keep firearms out of the plant. Once we draw a distinction between innocent and evil intent, the enforcement of the Rule and its purpose would be seriously, if not completely, undermined. Such a distinction would indeed open a Pandora's box.

Unless one shuts his eyes to the incontrovertible evidence, or a desire to interpret the Rule literally out of existence, the conclusion is inescapable that the Grievant violated the Rule when he brought the gun into the plant. To find that he did not on the basis of his intent would constitute a masterpiece of error.

What remains, therefore, is to determine whether or not there exists a valid mitigating circumstance, or a compelling reason to set aside the discharge despite the Grievant's violation of the Rule.

Conversation Between Grievant and Plant Superintendent

Of significance here is the statement by Spear to the Grievant to the effect that if Dash removed the gun from the plant the Personnel Department would not become involved in the matter. In its defense of the Grievant, the Union stresses this point, arguing:

> Dash stated that Mr. Spear, the Plant Superintendent, told him that he didn't see any reason for Personnel to get involved if he got the weapon out of the plant.

In other words, the suggestion here is that the Plant Superintendent promised the Grievant that he would not be disciplined if he removed the gun from the plant premises. The Arbitrator was concerned about this matter because an employer should not make a promise to an employee and later violate that promise.

After due reflection on this feature of the case, the Arbitrator does not believe that the discharge should be set aside on the basis of what the Superintendent told the Grievant. In the first place, the Superintendent's statement did not add up to an ironclad promise. He said that Personnel "need not" become involved. That may not be regarded as positive assurance that Personnel would not become involved.

More important than that, the Superintendent's major objective was to get the gun out of the plant as fast as possible, with minimum disturbance, and without undue embarrassment to the Grievant. The Company, of course, had other ways to remove the gun if the Grievant did not voluntarily agree to do so. It could have searched the Greivant and his possessions. It could have called the police to make a search and possibly have the Grievant arrested for carrying a concealed weapon. Obviously these are ugly methods causing delay, disturbance, and embarrassment to the Grievant.

Given these considerations, it is understandable why the Superintendent made the statement in question. It was an expedient way to get the gun off the premises as fast as possible and without resorting to ugly alternative options.

Delay of Discharge

As the facts show, the incident occurred on June 25 and Dash was not discharged until July 14. He was permitted to complete his shift on June 25, having been picked up at his home by the General Foreman and driven to the plant; he worked the next day; and he then was permitted to work the first week of the shutdown.

In regard to these events, the Union argues:

> Witness Yost stated he was not at the plant the day of the incident but he was working the day after. He stated he was informed of the incident, but Personnel was too busy to get involved in it at that time because of the plant shutdown starting and they didn't want to make a snap decision. However, on cross he exposed the fact that Superintendent Spear was in contact with the Chief of Personnel who had 32 years of experience. York, another Personnel Manager, was also there and available. It would appear that a decision cannot be given without the presence of this witness.
>
> If this was such a serious and major crime, why did the Plant Superintendent, Chief of Personnel Murphy, and Personnel Manager York permit this employee to return to work the day in question—the following day—and the following week?
>
> Dash called a friend because he had no car. His friend drove him and the gun home. He was to drive Dash back to work but his car broke down. Dash calls the Company and tells them he will be late because of this. The call is transferred to General Foreman Mills who in turn drives to the grievant's house and brings him back to work. Does that incident alone indicate the character

of the grievant; does that incident indicate that this employee has complied with Article II, Management, Section 2? There can be only one answer, that being positive.

Though the Company permitted the Grievant to work after the incident, it does not mean that it condoned his offense. He was permitted to work because the Company did not regard him as a dangerous person unfit to associate with his fellow workers and supervision. Indeed, Yost testified that Dash is not a dangerous person; he did not appear that way to the Arbitrator who had an opportunity to observe him under trying circumstances. For sure, the Grievant was not discharged because he is a dangerous person. Rather, he was discharged because he violated Rule No. 5. In any event, just because the Company permitted him to work after the incident does not amount to condonation of his offense.

In addition, it is not unusual in industry, and particularly under a collective bargaining relationship, that the Director of Industrial Relations must approve a discharge before it takes place. Though other Company officials were in the plant on June 26, and apparently not preoccupied with the matter of the plant shutdown as was Yost, they apparently did not have the authority to discharge. In addition, it is understandable why Yost waited until the first day of operation after the plant shutdown to approve the Grievant's discharge.

Of greater importance, the delay in the discharge did not harm the Grievant or prejudice his rights. He and the Union had the same opportunity to defend against the discharge. Clearly, his defense would not have been any stronger had the discharge occurred on the same day of the incident or the next day. In short, to reinstate the Grievant just because he was not discharged until July 14 would not be proper.

Knives and Guns in the Plant

In its continuous search for a valid basis for the Grievant's reinstatement, the Union also produced evidence that employees have brought knives in the plant. Yost testified:

> I saw knives in the plant. Some employees make knives in the plant and take them home.

There is no showing in the record that any employee has been disciplined for having a knife on plant premises.

Rule No. 5 not only forbids firearms but also forbids "other dangerous weapons." So, the Union says that since a knife can be regarded to be a dangerous weapon, and since no one has been disciplined for having a knife in the plant, it follows that the Grievant's discharge should be set aside on that basis.

Though there is some inherent logic to this Union argument, it may not be successfully used to set the discharge aside. In this dispute, we are concerned with guns and not knives. Though a knife may be regarded as a dangerous weapon, there are differences between a knife and a gun. A knife can be used for legitimate purposes and not as a weapon to do harm to another person. A gun, particularly the kind that the Grievant brought into the plant, has only one purpose—to injure or kill a person. Most of all, *a knife unlike a gun does not go off by accident.*

With respect to guns, when the Company had knowledge of their presence on plant premises, it discharged the employee. As a matter of fact, other than the instant case the Company had knowledge of only one other instance when an employee carried a gun into the plant in an unauthorized manner. That occurred in 1969, and the employee, Neely, was discharged. The Union claims that this should not count as precedent because Neely was a probationary employee and the gun was loaded.

As noted earlier, Rule No. 5 forbids guns in the plant whether loaded or unloaded. Obviously, though a probationary employee, Neely was discharged because he brought a gun into the plant. There is no showing in the record of any other reason for his discharge. In short, there is no evidence that when the Company had knowledge that an employee carried a gun onto its premises that it did not discharge the employee. Therefore, the Greivant may not properly claim that he was singled out for discharge in a discriminatory manner.

In two instances there is evidence that employees brought guns into the plant, but were not discharged. However, the *Company did not have knowledge of the incidents.* How could the Company act when it had no knowledge of the offense? One instance involves the testimony of the Grievant that he purchased the gun in question from Sitz. In error, the Grievant used that transaction as part of his belief that he did not violate the Rule. Clearly, that is not a valid precedent because the Company did not have knowledge that Sitz had brought the gun into the plant. The second instance occurred many years ago when Yost was in the bargaining unit. He testified that an employee brought a shotgun into the plant and showed it to other employees. However, here again, there is no evidence that the Company was aware of the incident. It is possible that other employees have brought guns into the plant. However, for discharge to occur, the Company must have knowledge of the offense.

Violations of Other No. 2 Category Rules

We now turn to what is perhaps the major Union argument calculated to save the Grievant's job. It presented evidence that employees committed violations of other category No. 2 Rules and were not discharged. In some cases, the employees received only a warning and in other cases a short suspension.

With regard to this matter, the Union points out:

> The Union does not believe the infraction of the rule committed by employee Dash of bringing an unloaded weapon to sell is any worse of an offense than when:
>   . . . employee . . . was given a written warning for two different occasions for coming to work under the influence. How many machine operator's lives and health were in jeopardy; or when

... employee ... was given a written warning for outright refusing to do a job on the order from the foreman and was later caught on the same day in question in an area without permission; or when

... employee ... was given a 2 day suspension for purposely destroying company property with the intent to steal; or when

... employees ... were all involved with fighting in one manner or another and were disciplined with warning letters or a 5 day suspension; or when

... employee ... threatens his foreman twice in a four (4) month period and received only a written warning; or when employee ... threatened his foreman on the job and followed him to his house and again threatened him there and received only a two (2) day suspension; or when

... those employees who stole time and money or falsified the records and received at most the discipline of a two day suspension.

After detailing these incidents, the Union argues:

All of these are industrial crimes on Page 22 of General Rules of Conduct. Were there arbitrations and grievance cases over the aforementioned infractions? Of course the answer is "No." Just discipline was administered. Was "just" discipline administered in the instant case? We say it wasn't. Employee Dash should have received no less or no more than the other employees as demonstrated in the Union's Exhibits.

Though the Arbitrator recognizes the vigor and sincerity of the Union's argument, it cannot be used as a basis to reinstate the Grievant. With the possible exception of the employee who reported to work under the influence of alcohol,* the offenses committed by the employees covered by the Union's exhibits *did not present the potential danger to the plant community as compared to a gun.* In its indefatigable search for a valid basis for the Grievant's reinstatement, the Union loses sight of the purpose of Rule No. 5. It is designed not only to protect the Company interests, but also serves to protect all persons in the plant from being injured or killed by a gun. As such, Rule No. 5 is distinguishable from all other Rules in the No. 2 category. Given its fundamental purpose, the Company may reasonably distinguish between penalties for offenses of Rule No. 5 as compared to penalties for the other category No. 2 offenses. In short, Rule No. 5 is in a class by itself and is distinguishable from the other No. 2 Rules.

Conclusions

To put it up front, and in all candor, the Arbitrator refuses to dilute the enforcement of the Rule in question. He refuses to take the first step by establishing a precedent that could conceivably result in the injury or death of a person by gunfire. Such would be the potential consequences of the reinstatement of the Grievant. With his reinstatement, other employees would be encouraged to bring guns into the

---

* Note, however, that he was sent home and did not drive his truck. He was removed as a potential danger to himself and all employees.

plant. In no way does the Arbitrator desire to be a party to such a state of affairs which could result in tragedy to a person and the family involved.

Be assured that the Arbitrator does not take any personal joy in this decision. He fully understands the importance of the Grievant's job to himself and his family. This is particularly true in these days of serious unemployment. What makes this case so sad is that the Arbitrator believes that the Grievant is a good person, surely not dangerous, and he certainly meant no harm when he brought the gun into the plant. In any event, the bottom line is that he violated the Rule, and knew that he was doing so when he concealed the weapon. Though this decision is painful, the Arbitrator must support the full integrity of a Rule designed to protect the plant community from injury or death by gunfire.

Questions

1 How did the arbitrator handle the union's argument concerning the discipline of employees who committed other offenses calling for discharge under Rule 2?

2 What was the fear expressed by the arbitrator if he applied Rule 5 in terms of the intent of the employee?

3 In a letter sent to the arbitrator by the union, it was said that the arbitrator overreacted and was too dramatic in his decision and reasoning. Do you believe that the union's censure was justified? If you were the arbitrator, how would you answer the union's letter?

4 Suppose the union appealed to the federal courts to set aside the decision? What arguments would the union use? If you were the federal judge, how would you rule on the union's petition? State your reasons.

The Case of the Employee Who Was Paid and Not Required to Work

Cast of characters:

Hall	*Discharged Employee*
Jones	*A Union Witness*
Thomas	*President of Company*
Fells	*Superintendent*

GRIEVANCE AND LABOR AGREEMENT

In protest against his discharge, effective October 1, 1975, Hall filed a grievance dated October 2, 1975. It states:

> In reference to letter received by aggrieved employee Sept. 30, 1975 from employer stating that his job would be terminated Oct. 1, 1975 for violation of Paragraph 2, Page 1, of Contract. Aggrieved employee has not violated Paragraph 2, Page 1, of Contract and has no knowledge of why he is accused of doing so or for what reasons the Company has for stating that his job would be terminated Oct. 1, 1975.
>
> He requests that he be reinstated to his regular and/or normal job with full seniority and made whole for any and all monies and benefits due him in accordance with terms and conditions of contract.
>
> The employer has not found proper cause to discharge aggrieved employee.

Having failed to settle the dispute in the Grievance Procedure, the Parties convened this arbitration for its final and binding determination.

Material to the dispute are the following provisions of the Labor Agreement:

PURPOSE

> **Paragraph 2** The Union agrees that its said members will individually and collectively, at all times perform loyal and efficient service, comply with the terms and working conditions of this Agreement, use their influence and best efforts to protect the property of the Company and all its employees to such ends.

Paragraph 3(b)   Subject to the provisions of this Agreement, the Company shall have the right to schedule and assign work, to hire, promote, recall, demote, suspend, transfer, lay off and for proper cause to discharge employees.

GRIEVANCE PROCEDURE AND ARBITRATION

Paragraph 16   The arbitrator or arbitrators shall have no authority to add to, subtract from, or modify any provision of this Agreement, or to rule on any questions except the ones submitted for arbitration.

BASIC QUESTION

The basic question to be determined in this arbitration is framed as follows:

Under the circumstances of this case, was Grievant Hall discharged for proper cause? If not, what should the remedy be?

BACKGROUND

Grievant Hall was hired by the Company on June 6, 1966. On August 4, 1974, he broke a leg while riding a horse. Though the Labor Agreement does not contain a sickness–accident program, paying employees for nonwork-related accidents or sickness, employee Jones said that it was the policy of the Company to pay employees about six or seven weeks' pay when they were disabled as a result of such circumstances.

Some time in September 1974, Hall called Thomas, President of the Company. The Grievant testified that two weeks prior to the call he had received four days' pay, and a week before the call, he did not receive any pay. He testified that the purpose of the call was to discuss the problem with Thomas.

According to the testimony of Thomas, at one point in this phone conversation Hall said to him:

The only reason I work for a S.O.B. like you, is because I have a wife and children to support.

As to this event, the Grievant denied that he made the aforecited statement attributed to him by the Company President. Hall testified that he said to Thomas:

I have a wife and two children who depend on me and that is why I work.

Hall declared that Thomas replied:

If you don't like to work for me, why don't you work for a good guy?

On or about October 14, 1974, Hall reported to work though he still had a cast on his leg. Fells, Superintendent, assigned him to driving a truck. However, at times, Fells said, the Grievant buried cables, using a vibrator and a back-hoe. On November 18, 1974, Hall buried cables for nine hours.

The next day, November 19, 1974, Fells called the Grievant and told him to bring his truck in for repairs. He did so and had a conversation with the Superintendent. Hall testified that he told Fells that work was falling behind, and asked for another truck. Fells refused. Instead, Fells told the Grievant to go home and wait until he was called back to work. In this regard, Hall testified:

> Fells told me that my truck needed repairs. He told me to go home and wait until I was called.

Also, Fells told the Grievant that he would get full pay for all the time he did not work. As events turned out, the Company paid the Grievant his full pay and fringe benefits from November 19, 1974 until October 1, 1975 on which date he was discharged. In other words, for about one year, the Company paid the Grievant although he did not work. During this period of time, Hall periodically executed a Daily Time Report. On this report, he would write: "Waiting on truck." These reports were sent to Fells, who approved them, and the Company paid the Grievant although he did not actually perform work for his employer.

Thomas explained the reason for such a state of affairs. He testified:

> I heard for a long period of time many complaints from my customers. This indicated to me that Hall was not working. Also, after he called me in September, 1974 and said "the only reason I would work for a S.O.B. like you is because I have a wife and children to support," I assumed that he did not want to work for me. I decided that we would be better off to leave him on the payroll and not have him work. I did not want any more customer complaints. He was impeding the progress of other employees. But the precipitating cause for this action (pay and no work) is that he simply did not want to work for me. It was in the best interest of the Company for us to take a $20,000 loss by paying him for not working than to assume the risk of having him work.

In addition, Thomas said the reason why the Grievant was not discharged on November 19, 1974 was that "I was not certain about the problems of terminating an employee."

Superintendent Fells also explained why the Company paid the Grievant though he did not perform any work. He said:

> We were unhappy with him because of his work performance. We did not think we were getting the job done. It was our judgment that he was not producing enough. He took too much time on a job.

During the period of time in which the Grievant was paid though he did not perform any work, there was no contact between the Grievant and the Company except the sending of his paychecks by the Company, the acceptance of them by the Grievant, and the filing of periodic Daily Time Reports. The Company did not call or write him, nor did Hall come to the Company, or write or phone.

In any event, effective October 20, 1975, the Grievant was discharged. Thomas wrote him:

> Mr. Hall:
> Paragraph 2 in the contracts (*sic*) reads:
> The Union agrees that its said members will individually and collectively, at all times perform loyal and efficient service, comply with the terms and working conditions of this Agreement, use their influence and best efforts to protect the property of the Company and all its employees to such ends.
> It is because you have violated these terms of this contractual agreement, you are hereby terminated effective October 1, 1975.

Thomas disclosed the circumstances which prompted him to discharge the Grievant. It so happened that an employee of the Company had a son with some degree of mental deficiency. The employee asked Thomas to hire his son. Thomas did not hire the young son because he feared that he might have an accident. In the light of this event, Thomas said:

> I had a man [Grievant] who was not working and drawing full pay. The boy could probably have performed more work than Hall. After serious thought, I wrote the termination letter.

During the processing of the grievance, Thomas made two offers to settle the dispute. On October 15, 1975, he offered to pay the Grievant his full wages until July 1976, at which time Hall would qualify for early retirement. Under the applicable early retirement provisions of the Labor Agreement, the Grievant would then receive $210.00 per month for life. The offer was refused by the Grievant.

A second offer was made in the middle of December 1975. Thomas proposed that he would return the Grievant to his job provided that Hall visit a psychological social worker weekly. Such treatment, Thomas explained, would be at the Company expense. Hall refused this offer. In the Company brief, Thomas stated:

> If I could have come up with any other new and better ideas to help this man, I would have done so. As I explained at the hearing, we are operating with a Humanitarian philosophy of business management, and we care for the people who work for us.

ANALYSIS OF THE EVIDENCE

Strange Character of Case

To say the least, this is a very strange case. In the quarter of a century of the Arbitrator's experience, he knows of no situation in which a company paid an employee, and did not require that person to perform any work. The fact that this was done for about one year underscores its extraordinary nature. It was not a situation where the Grievant was physically disabled and received accident benefits. For about five weeks before his discharge, Hall was working, though he had a cast on his leg. Also, in February 1975, Hall was released by his doctor demonstrating that his leg was fully healed. Thus, during the year or so in question, Hall was physically qualified to work, and received full pay and fringe benefits, but the Company did not require him to work.

In any event, the uniqueness of the dispute should not serve to mask its substantive issues. As the Company's termination letter demonstrates, Hall was discharged on the grounds that he violated Paragraph 2 of the Labor Agreement. Under this provision, the Union agreed that its members will perform loyal and efficient service for the Company. Should the evidence demonstrate that Hall violated his obligations under this provision, it would follow that his discharge was for "proper cause" under the terms of Paragraph 3. Of course, if Hall engaged in conduct that offended his obligations as an employee, he could be discharged for "proper cause" without reference to Paragraph 2.

Grievant's Work Performance

As Company testimony demonstrates, one charge against the Grievant was that he did not satisfactorily perform his job. Fells testified that Hall "was not producing enough," and that he "took too much time on a job." Thomas said that he received customer complaints about the Grievant. In other words, when the Grievant was actively working for the Company, he failed to produce satisfactorily. His productivity did not measure up to acceptable standards.

As a threshold observation, it may be stated that an employer may properly discharge an employee under such circumstances. An employer must produce satisfactorily, or face the consequences. Indeed, the Arbitrator has sustained the discharges of employees who failed to meet reasonable production standards. Professional arbitrators have recognized that to keep a job, an employee must satisfactorily meet reasonable standards of productivity.

Thus, the first question to be determined is whether or not the evidence demonstrates that the Grievant produced satisfactorily. In this respect, the Company has the obligation to provide competent and convincing evidence to prove that Hall did not measure up to reasonable production standards. As countless arbitration decisions demonstrate, in a disciplinary case the employer bears the burden of proof. In short, the employer must supply convincing evidence that the employee committed the offense for which he was discharged. It is up to the employer to prove the employee "guilty," and not the employee who must prove himself "not guilty." This is a rock-bottom principle of arbitration, and so familiar that no citation of arbitral precedent is necessary.

Quality of Company Evidence

Applying this principle to the circumstances of this case, the conclusion is inescapable that the Company failed to prove that the Grievant did not produce satisfactorily. All that the Company supplies in this respect is the judgment of its two officials that the Grievant failed to produce adequately. With respect to the customer complaints against Hall, Thomas testified that he received two phone calls from the Company's customers complaining about the Grievant. He said:

> These two complaints were from women who complained that the Grievant was in the coffee shop. I probably got these calls in 1974.

Note that the Grievant was employed by the Company for about nine years. Even if the complaints were fully justified, the occurrence of two complaints of this nature in a nine-year period does not demonstrate that the Grievant was not a satisfactory employee. Beyond this, the Company apparently did not regard these two complaints to be of much consequence because it did not call them to the attention of the Grievant.

In addition, the judgment of the Company officials that the Grievant was taking too much time on his jobs and/or did not produce enough is not backed up by objective evidence. Note the testimony of Fells:

> It is our *judgment* that he was not producing enough. He was taking too much time on his jobs.

Though the judgment or opinions of supervision deserve consideration, they are not of much evidentiary value unless supported by objective evidence. Any supervisor can testify that in his opinion or judgment an employee is not doing his job. In this respect, the Company has not provided any evidence whatsoever to support the judgment or opinions of its officials. Daily time sheets are filled out by the employees, and these documents are inspected by the Superintendent. Such time sheets show the kinds of jobs performed by the Company's employees and disclose the time spent on such jobs. In other words, there exists objective evidence to demonstate the productivity of the employees. However, before the Company discharged the Grievant, no reference was made to such documents. Fells testified: "I did not examine his time sheets before we discharged him."

Progressive Discipline

Added to these considerations, the record shows that at no time did the Company ever warn the Grievant that his production was not satisfactory. During his nine years of service, Hall did not receive any warnings, reprimands, or suspensions. In fact, Fells testified that his work was "average,"* and that "I never told him that his work was taking too long."

It is a matter of common sense that when an employee falls below par, the worker should be counseled, warned, reprimanded, and even suspended before discharge takes place. This is what is meant by progressive discipline, a system used by employers to rehabilitate an employee. In cases of this sort, where the

---

* In all fairness, in the light of the general testimony of Fells, when he described the work of the Greivant as "average," he was apparently making the assessment in reference to the quality of the Grievant's work rather than about its quantity.

allegation is made that an employee fails to meet reasonable standards of production, the employer first counsels the employee in the effort to improve his or her performance. If such counseling, fairly given, fails to correct the employee's deficiencies, the next step is to implement discipline. Normally, the employee is first warned orally and/or in writing. If this does not induce the employee to improve production, the next step is a suspension. When all this fails, the employer then discharges the employee on the grounds that all efforts to rehabilitate the employee have failed.

In this case, even if we assume that the Grievant did not meet production standards, the Company made no effort to rehabilitate him. As a matter of fact, at no time did the Company even tell the employee that he was not producing satisfactorily. Clearly, it is a matter of common sense that when an employee does not turn out a "fair day's work" the employer calls this to his attention. If the employer does not do this, how does the employee know that his work is not satisfactory? In the absence of counseling and/or warnings, the employee has reason to believe that his or her work meets production standards.

In any event, in this case, the evidence simply does not support the charge that the Grievant was not doing his job. All that we have in the way of evidence is the unsupported opinion of the two Company officials. Beyond this, the Company did not offer a scintilla of evidence to prove the charge. Indeed, the very fact that the Company never counseled or warned the Grievant discloses that his work was satisfactory. In short, in the light of the available evidence, it would be absolutely improper to sustain the discharge of the Grievant. Such a decision would be totally unwarranted given the state of the evidence and would fly in the face of settled and recognized principles of the arbitration process.

Psychological Fitness of Grievant

In addition, the Company argues that Hall is psychologically unfit to return to work. With respect to this feature of the case, Thomas says:

> Offered early retirement of $210.00 per month, he refused. Offered his regular job provided he would see a psychological social worker on company time and at company expense, he refused this also.
> Still he persists he wants to come back to work for a man he intensely dislikes. This is not the behavior of a rational man; rather, it is the behavior of a very neurotic man. In the interest of the company and its customers, I can and will not gainfully employ anyone too sick to do an adequate job, whether it be physical or psychological.
> Hall has not always been willing to follow instructions from the company in the past. The only possible explanation for the fact that he could take full pay for doing absolutely no work for almost a year, and rather dutifully stay around Dover, because he was "waiting on truck" as ordered, and never in the entire time communicate with me is an indication of the seriousness of his neurosis.
>
> * * *
>
> What alternatives do I have where an employee is physically healthy, but

is not at all well psychologically? We accept the responsibility of taking care of our employees from their time of employment to their death. However, when one is sick, should that man get full pay? I think not, in fairness to our other employees, the company owners, and the telephone customers.

Termination was my last alternative, only because I could not think of any other options to offer Hall.

Under proper circumstances, an employer may properly terminate an employee for reasons of psychological or mental unfitness to hold a job or under proper circumstances, an employer may require an employee to be treated for mental or psychological disorders as the prerequisite for holding a job. In this case, the Company relies upon these propositions to justify the discharge of the Grievant.

To support its position, the Company says that Hall demonstrated irrational and psychologically unsound behavior because he accepted pay for about one year without performing work. It argues that this state of affairs "is an indication of the seriousness of his neurosis."

Certainly, this feature of the case demonstrates its rare and unusual character. Here we had an employee receiving full pay and fringe benefits, and the Company did not require him to work. As noted earlier, the Arbitrator has never been confronted with such a situation, and it is probably unique in labor relations. To conclude on this basis, however, that the Grievant is psychologically unsound to work is unwarranted. The bottom line is that the Grievant did exactly what the Company told him to do. On November 19, 1974, the Company told the Grievant to "go home and wait until he was called back to work." He was told that while he waited for the call he would receive full pay and fringe benefits. If it is held that it was strange behavior on the part of the Grievant to accept such payments, it was just as strange for the Company to have permitted this state of affairs to occur.

At any time, the Company had the power to stop this unusual condition. At any time, it could have directed the Grievant to return to work or discharged him as it eventually did on October 1, 1975. True, the Grievant testified that he felt "uncomfortable" when he received pay without working. But what was Hall supposed to do? He did not have the authority to work without receiving such permission to work. It was the responsibility of the Company to direct him to work. In the absence of a call to work, should he have refused payment and thereby lose the source of income to support his family? Should he have quit his job, and thereby forfeit his contractual rights gained over nine years of service? Should he have quit his job and taken his chances on getting another job given the fact that jobs are scarce because of the current national problem of unemployment? Clearly, if the Company was willing to tolerate this strange state of affairs, it was to be expected that Hall would accept payment. Indeed, it would be an irrational act on his part to refuse payment or to quit his job. In short, the Arbitrator finds that the Grievant's acceptance of payment does not demonstrate irrational behavior or show that he was psychologically unfit to hold his job, or that he required psychological or psychiatric treatment.

In support of the Company's argument herein considered, the Company also argues that Hall

> still insists he wants to come back to work for a man he intensely dislikes. This
> is not the behavior of a rational man, it is behavior of a very neurotic man.

Even if for the sake of argument we may assume that the Grievant does not like Thomas,* this does not make Hall a psychological cripple unable to hold his job. Many employees do not necessarily like their employers, but they still work for them given the realities of life. We do not have a society or an economy where employees are free to quit their jobs just because they do not necessarily like their employers. A man has to work, and he subordinates his resentment of his employer to the necessity of earning a living.

Apparently the Company regards the workplace as some sort of idyllic society wherein each member plays his or her role with contentment and where peace and harmony prevail. To the contrary, in the real world, frictions develop in the employer–employee relationship, and there does not exist a condition of love and contentment between employees and employers. Conditions develop in which employers resent employees, and employees resent employers, but still they tolerate each other. No one has as yet devised a system wherein the workplace would be converted into some sort of idealistic community in which love characterizes the employer–employee relationship. In any event, it would be a masterpiece of error to hold that the Grievant is psychologically unfit to hold his job even if it is true that he may not like Thomas.

Beyond these observations, the Arbitrator finds nothing in the record to demonstrate that the Grievant is psychologically unfit to hold his job. He testified in the arbitration in a rational manner; spoke clearly; and was in full control of his behavior. He was tuned into reality and did not demonstrate the behavior of a psychological cripple. He worked for the Company for nine years, and nothing in the record demonstrates irrational behavior while he was on the job. If it is true that the Grievant was psychologically unsound, there would have been evidence of irrational behavior while he was on the job. No such evidence was supplied by the Company.

For nine years, he had a spotless disciplinary record. At no time was he warned, reprimanded, or suspended for any employee offense. Indeed, the charge that he did not produce enough and/or took too much time to do his work was not proved by the evidence.

---

* Apparently the Company concludes that the Grievant "intensely dislikes" Thomas because of the nature of the phone conversation of September 1974. Without exploring in depth the character of this Company argument, the fact that the Grievant vented his anger about being denied sick pay (with or without justification) does not necessarily show that he "intensely dislikes" Thomas. It is not uncommon for employees to say things in anger about their supervisors. This does not necessarily prove that the employees harbor a deep-seated and irreversible hatred of their employers. Indeed, in the course of human events, we all say things in anger (even between husband and wife) that do not reflect a permanent dislike for one another. In fact, the venting of anger, some say, is a healthy psychological therapeutic device.

Conclusions

In arbitration, we base decisions on facts and evidence. We do not make decisions based upon suppositions or unsupported allegations. Indeed, the published and unpublished decisions of this Arbitrator demonstrate that he has frequently sustained discharges of employees. In those cases, he found on the evidence that employees engaged in offensive conduct of a serious nature and that the employers proved that the employees had committed the offenses for which they were discharged.

In the case at hand, the Company did not prove that the Grievant was deficient in his obligations as an employee. The evidence does not support the charge that he did not perform his work satisfactorily. The evidence does not support the charge that he was psychologically unsound in the sense that he cannot hold his job. For these reasons, the Arbitrator shall grant the grievance. In the final analysis, the Company has failed to prove that it discharged the Grievant for proper cause within the meaning of the Labor Agreement.

Questions

1 Now that you have read the case, what do you believe to be the real reason why the employee was paid for not working?

2 What evidence did the arbitrator use to show that the employee was not a psychological cripple?

3 How did the arbitrator deal with the charge that the employee's productivity was not sufficient?

4 Why do you believe that the employee refused the two offers made by the company to settle the grievance?

5 Would you have done the same thing as the arbitrator?

Subcontracting: The Case
of the Declining Number of Millwrights

Cast of characters:

Paul, Hoff	*Millwrights*
Getz	*Union President*
Hope	*Industrial Relations Manager*
Miller	*General Superintendent*

By this time you should have recognized that job security is a fundamental union objective in collective bargaining. Protection from layoff, whether temporary or permanent, is a major union goal. You should also have recognized that this union goal conflicts at times with the employer's objective—to operate an efficient business. This conflict frequently surfaces in cases involving the subcontracting of work.

In this case, where you are once again asked to serve as the arbitrator, the employer used an outside firm to perform some work on a machine. There was no question about the qualifications and ability of the regular employees to perform the work in question. On this basis, the union asserted that the employer had violated the provision of the labor agreement covering the subcontracting of work. As you read the case, try to determine the union's objective in submitting the case to arbitration.

GRIEVANCE AND LABOR AGREEMENT PROVISIONS

In protest against the Company's decision to subcontract certain work, the Union filed Grievance No. 13-M-738, dated April 18, 1981. It states:

> On Apr. 16, no. 2 paper machine was shut down for extensive maintenance work. Part of this work is being subcontracted to an outside maintenance firm. We feel that our Millwrights are qualified to do this work and should be permitted to do so.
>
> *Settlement Desired:* Payment for all man-hours worked by the outside maintenance firm personnel at one and one-half times our Millwright's job rate, divided equally among all eligible Millwrights.

Having failed to settle the dispute in the Grievance Procedure, it was submitted to arbitration for its determination.

ARTICLE 2. MANAGEMENT RIGHTS

Paragraph (a)   In pertinent part, this paragraph says that the Company has the right to "sub-contract work at the discretion of the Company (subject to Paragraph "c", Article 2)."

Paragraph (c)   Maintenance work will not be sub-contracted if the Company has sufficient qualified manpower and facilities available to perform such work.

ARTICLE 3. RECOGNITION

The Company hereby recognizes the [Union] as the exclusive representative of all the employees, as herein defined included in the bargaining unit of production and maintenance workers for the purpose of collective bargaining with respect to rates of pay, wages, hours of employment, and working conditions.

BASIC QUESTION

The basic question to be determined in this case is framed as follows:

Under the circumstances of this case, did the Company violate Article 2, Paragraph (c)? If so, what should the remedy be?

BACKGROUND

Backett Paper Company, located in Midland, Ohio, a division of Consolidated Paper Company, produces a variety of paper products. In April 1981, about 260 employees were in the bargaining unit, including 20 Millwrights, the classification involved in this case. About 26 Millwrights were in the classification in 1971.

In November 1980, the Company started to make plans, including the ordering of material, to renovate the No. 2 paper machine. As it turned out, the project involved the expenditure of $300,000. In addition to No. 2, there are two other paper machines in the Mill, No. 1 and No. 3. Machine No. 1 has not been used for approximately five years.

This dispute arose when the Company subcontracted a portion of the renovation job on the No. 2 paper machine. Specifically, the subcontractor installed nine cone pulleys, the cost of which was about $30,000. Paul, a Millwright, testified that the pulleys were in the Company's warehouse for several months before they were installed by the subcontractor. He also said that it was general knowledge in the Mill and in the Maintenance Department that "sooner or later" the pulleys would be installed on No. 2.

On April 13, No. 2 was shut down for the repair job. The subcontractor started to install the pulleys on April 16. While the subcontractor was performing that work, some Company Millwrights installed a head box and showers on the unit. Other Millwrights performed their regular duties in the Mill. On April 22, the work on the machine was completed. At that time, the subcontractor completed his job, and the machine went back into production on the next day. Thus, between April 16 and April 22, a period of seven days, No. 2 was not in production.

During the period in question, April 16 through April 22, the Millwrights were scheduled 12 hours per day. Additional overtime during the week was available for any Millwright willing to take the assignment. The Parties stipulated:

> during the days in question, that is the days when the outside contractor was in the plant, all employees of the maintenance department received overtime, in fact as much overtime as they wished to work.

One Millwright earned $750.00 in the week and another earned $806.00.

No employee in the Mill was laid off during the time when No. 2 was shut down. Production employees assigned to Machine No. 2 helped the Millwrights with the repair work. No employee in the Finishing Department was laid off though the Department is staffed with a sufficient number to handle the output of two paper machines. With No. 1 idle, and No. 2 shut down for repairs, only No. 3 was in operation during the time period in question. The Company furnished jobs for the Finishing Department employees who were not performing their regular work.

Getz, Union President, became aware of the subcontract in question in the early part of April. He was told about it by Paul and Hoff, another Millwright. On or about April 9, Getz asked Hope, Industrial Relations Manager, whether the Company intended to subcontract. After Hope told Getz that was the intention of the Company, Getz warned him that the Union would file a grievance. During that conversation, Getz testified, Hope told him that he (Hope) would set up a meeting in the following week to be attended by Hope, Miller, General Superintendent, Getz, and two Millwrights. The meeting was not held. On April 18, 1981, two days after the subcontract was started, the Union filed the grievance that resulted in this arbitration.

The Parties stipulated the following four items:

1 The bargaining unit Millwrights had full capability and qualifications to perform the work carried out by the subcontractor.
2 While the No. 2 paper machine was shut down the Company was losing 50 tons of paper per day. The Company's goal was to restore the machine to production as soon as possible.
3 Had the bargaining unit employees been assigned to the work, the No. 2 paper machine would have been out of production for an additional five days.
4 Finishing Department employees would have been laid off if the repair job would have taken longer than seven days.

During the negotiation of the grievance, Hoff told the Company that if there were now as many Millwrights as there were in 1971, they could have completed the job as fast as the subcontractor. In the arbitration, the Union argued that the

Company should hire a sufficient number of new Millwrights to restore the size of the classification to what it was in 1971.

The Union takes the position that the grievance should be granted and the Company asks that it be denied.

Concluding Statement

Will Rogers once said, in presenting his suggestion for terminating the German submarine menace to Allied shipping during World War I, that "all we need to do is heat the Atlantic Ocean up to 212 degrees Fahrenheit, then the subs will have to come to the surface and we can pick them off one by one. I know," he added, "that somebody is going to want to know how to warm up that much water. But I can't worry about that. It's a matter of detail and I am a policymaker."[1]

He may have been going too far in his scoffing at detail, but the authors can sympathize with his desire to do a bit of broad concluding, in our case particularly in view of the myriad of specifics offered on previous pages.

The following, then, expresses our more general thoughts.

The productive potential of the United States depends upon many factors, including the status of employer–employee relations. Our nation has been extremely fortunate in being endowed with a highly favorable natural environment for the encouragement of the productive process. Its virtually inexhaustible stores of natural resources, advantageous geographic location, and population growth constitute a sound basis for an expanding and dynamic economy. Despite these considerations, the fact remains that the fruitfulness of the productive process of our nation depends fundamentally upon the creativeness of the managerial function, the economic and political systems in which business and labor operate, and the industry and the spirit of the labor force. Other nations that have not attained the level of industrial development of the United States can match to some extent our

[1] As quoted in W. Willand Wirtz, *Labor and the Public Interest* (New York: Harper & Row, 1964), p. 160.

natural resources. Few people, however, equal the vigor and the creativeness of Americans in implementing the productive process. In the last analysis, the level of the standard of living of a nation depends not so much upon its stores of iron ore, coal, oil, and the like, as upon the motivation and the energy of its people, and the system of government and economics within which the productive process is accomplished.

A fundamental if implicit thesis of this volume has been that an important prerequisite for the increasing productivity of the American nation is the status of its employer–employee relations. Since we are a nation practicing free enterprise, what has thus far remained (despite a highly visible trend to increasing government interest in labor relations) the essential privacy of our employer–employee relationship is to a great degree the dominant characteristic of the industrial relations environment. A wholesome labor relations environment that encourages maximum efforts of labor and management will do much toward improving our standard of living. In contrast, the productive process will be obstructed to the extent that the employer–employee relationship is implemented in a hostile framework. From this it follows not only that the best interests of employers and employees are dependent upon the establishment of a harmonious industrial relations climate, but that the entire nation likewise has a stake in the accomplishment of this objective.

In retrospect, the evidence is clear that collective bargaining relations in the United States have improved remarkably over the years. It is well to recall in this connection that widespread collective bargaining is a comparatively recent development in this country. The earliest unions date from 1800, and unionism can hardly be viewed as a new phenomenon, but not much more than fifty years ago only a relatively few employers and employees were involved in the process, virtually none of the vital industries of the nation were characterized by collective bargaining, and unionism had not yet penetrated the major mass-production sectors. During the period of growth of collective bargaining, union–employer relations in these industries were far from satisfactory and not conducive to high levels of industrial productivity. Since the process was new and virtually untried, there was much distrust and suspicion on both sides of the bargaining table. Many employers questioned the methods and the ultimate objectives of labor unions and, in general, aggressively resisted the development of unions. In some cases, unions moved too fast in their development and failed to take into consideration the legion of problems involved in establishing collective bargaining within new industries. On a number of occasions, labor–management relations deteriorated into prolonged and violent strikes resulting in loss of life, in physical injury, and in destruction of company property. It may be argued with some validity that these events were probably unavoidable because of the newness of the collective bargaining process. Such happenings might be regarded as the "growing pains" of a new and potentially important area. Notwithstanding these considerations, the fact remains that some of the history of the development of industrial relations— particularly prior to the 1930s, but even as late as World War II—is not pleasant to recall.

With the passage of time, labor relations handled under the collective bargaining process have improved enormously. As noted earlier, social upheaval and violence in union–management relations have virtually disappeared from the American industrial scene. To appreciate this, one has only to compare the bloody Memorial Day 1937 Little Steel incident with the Ford Motor Company strike a mere three decades later. In the steel industry strike, ten lives were lost, scores of people suffered serious physical injury, and there was severe damage to property. In the automobile strike, only token picket lines were manned by the union, and there was no violence and no damage to property. The latter strike was so "civilized," indeed, that some of the plants involved in it supplied power for the TV sets viewed by employees serving on picket-line duty.

It has been said that a conservative is just a liberal with some money. And it may well be that violence (on both sides) has dwindled almost to nonexistence because the newer unionist has shunned radical activities as too risky to affluence, thus generating the tame responses from management (at least in those cases where the initial actions came from labor). More than a decade ago, George Meany said about as much: "While you have no property, you don't have anything, you have nothing to lose by these radical actions. But when you become a person who has a home and has property, to some extent, you become conservative."[2] In 1981, the long-time head of the International Longshoremen's Association predicted in much the same vein that relatively few of his members would march in that year's New York City Labor Day parade because "they will all be off in the country closing down their summer bungalows. I mean our members are not poor; they make darn good wages."[3]

And Lane Kirkland, who says that he shares with the late Sam Goldwyn the conviction that "one should never prophesy, especially about the future,"[4] has nonetheless offered a similar explanation for the relative absence of agitation on the modern labor relations front: "An institution that fights for job security and for the economic means by which its members can participate fully in community life is not likely to advocate social upheaval and confrontation for its own sake as the appropriate response to social changes."[5]

But the virtual demise of the role of extreme actions is, by the same token, only *one* of many developments attesting to the greatly improved state of labor relations in recent years. The earliest pages of this volume indicated that there has been similar progress along almost *every* basic labor–management dimension, and it is hoped that, by this point in the book, the reader stands in fundamental agreement. The facts show not only that in an overwhelming number of instances the parties have been able to negotiate under a strike deadline without reaching a stalemate, but that with respect to unauthorized, or "wildcat," strikes, the record

[2] Melvyn Dubofsky, *American Labor Since the New Deal* (Chicago: Quadrangle Books, 1971), p. 294.
[3] *Time,* September 14, 1981, p. 15.
[4] Lane Kirkland, "Labor's Challenge in the 1980s," in *Proceedings of the Thirty-fourth Annual Meeting, Industrial Relations Research Association,* December 28–30, 1981, p. 9.
[5] *Ibid.,* p. 12.

is similarly impressive. Instead of resorting to industrial warfare as the means of adjusting and settling disputes arising over the interpretation and application of an existing contract, employers and unions settle these problems through the grievance and arbitration procedure, thereby lending considerable further stability to their relationships.

Running through the preceding pages are testimonials to other types of success—from a stress on considerably more informed bargaining sessions to the attainment of a far larger measure of contracts that constitute "good compromises," and from the almost complete disappearance of Conflict philosophies to the great growth of Accommodation (if not Cooperation) ones.

Indeed, under some management–union relationships, there is now a genuine feeling of mutual trust and respect between the parties. Although contract negotiations, grievances, and arbitration cases are treated with vigor by both the management and the union, the problems are handled within a general framework of friendliness and of bilateral trust and confidence. It is obvious that such a state of development of industrial relations fosters high levels of productivity, profits, wages, and quality of product. It means that all parties to the collective bargaining process, including the public, derive benefit.

Such progress in labor relations did not develop by accident. There are cogent reasons for the great strides that have been made in the union–management relationship. Developments in management and union attitudes, in philosophy, and in procedures have been responsible.

On the part of employers, there is general acceptance, even if this is in many cases given begrudgingly, and even if at times it might appear not to be given at all in some public-sector relationships, of the process of collective bargaining. In contrast to the state of affairs four decades ago, the typical management today has no open quarrel with the existence of collective bargaining. However much it might prefer a nonunionized work force (and however greatly it might continue to oppose the union in theory), it is now preoccupied with the practical problem of getting along with its labor organization on a day-by-day basis while preserving at the same time those managerial prerogatives needed to operate an efficient and productive enterprise. Many employers operating under collective bargaining contracts sincerely believe that the protection of job rights of their employees by a labor agreement is desirable. Even though at times protection of job rights obtained through collective bargaining might diminish plant productivity, most managements and unions have found the collective bargaining contract sufficiently elastic to accommodate the objectives of both efficiency of production and the protection of job rights. The pliability of the collective bargaining process has thus far provided chances for the reconciliation of both objectives, and it is to be suspected that even the thorny problems of technological change will ultimately be resolved in the same way (although, here, most likely in conjunction with government actions). So, too, if history is any guide at all, will the still-primitive relationships that are perhaps the inevitable birth and growth pains in some (but far from all) of the public sector.

In addition, many managements have taken a realistic approach to the institutional character of unionism. They are aware that, to an extent, the collective bargaining process tends to supply the needs of the union as an institution, as well as to provide the mechanism whereby the terms of employment of workers are established. Many contractual provisions are agreed to by management on the theory that a union secure in its status may be more judicious in its behavior at the bargaining table and in grievance negotiations.

Management's recognition of the problems and needs of employees is likewise an important element in the establishment of sound relations under collective bargaining. Relations between employers and unions are bound to be more harmonious as management exhibits a genuine understanding of the problems confronted by the individual employee. A union will tend to be more aggressive and attempt to impose more limitations on the managerial function to the extent that a management, through its general behavior and personnel policies, demonstrates an unsympathetic attitude toward employees' problems and objectives. Indeed, one major reason for the establishment and the expansion of unions is that in the past, some companies did not give sufficient attention to the needs of employees. At present, the evidence is quite clear that the business community in general is vitally concerned with the welfare of its workers. One of the primary bases of the science of personnel management is the development of techniques and procedures that have at their core the sympathetic consideration of employee problems. In most organizations, the needs of employees are now given equal weight and attention with the problems of finance, production, sales, and quality control. And executives are, in fact, assigned to personnel departments to no small extent because of their ability to understand employees' problems sympathetically and to deal with employees on the basis of sound human relations. This development means that a solid foundation exists for more harmonious relations between managements, unions, and employees.

There is also a growing tendency on the part of industry to place the operation of labor relations in the hands of qualified and professional managers. Increasingly, the industrial relations department has equal prestige and status with any other division or department within the enterprise. Such a development likewise fosters better relations at the bargaining table. But because collective bargaining negotiations and the administration of labor agreements constitute a most difficult and highly responsible job, it is necessary that employers entrust such a function to executives who are qualified in terms of training, motivation, skill, and personality. Organizations that delegate these duties to unqualified personnel, or impose the duties as additional responsibilities on already busy executives, cannot expect to acquire a labor relations climate conducive to high levels of productivity.

It is also noteworthy that employers are increasingly conducting classes and other training programs involving the problems of contract administration for first-line supervisors. This appears to be an indispensable part of a sound company industrial relations program. Frequently, grievances arise because first-line supervision has not been adequately trained in the principles of labor relations and in the meaning and application of the collective bargaining contract. With the growth of the science of industrial relations, and particularly as this is cast within the framework of collective bargaining, it is imperative that the labor relations program be executed and administered correctly by all levels of supervision. To the extent that this has been recognized by the business community, the cause of harmonious and sound labor relations has been proportionately advanced.

Not only does the evidence, finally, reveal that managements in increasing numbers are giving sympathetic understanding to the problems of employees and unions, but there is also a growing awareness by union members and their leaders of the problems of management. At present, many union leaders, although they are representatives of organizations that are, above all, political, are fully conscious of the fact that in the last analysis the welfare of employees depends upon the economic prosperity of the firm. The leaders understand further that the collective bargaining process is conditioned by the economic framework surrounding the particular negotiations, and that the overall economic character of a firm or an industry relative to its competitive position, sales, profits, capital equipment, expansion requirements, and quality of production necessarily determines the economic benefits that can be provided to employees. There is increasing awareness that a company has obligations not only to its employees but also to its investors, management, and customers. These considerations do not mean that unions are less militant in collective bargaining. Negotiations are not conducted in a tea-party atmosphere. What these observations do mean is that labor relations generally improve to the degree that collective bargaining negotiations are based on factual information and rationality and are carried on in a general atmosphere of reciprocal recognition of problems and in a spirit of genuine good faith and mutual respect. Clearly, guesswork, emotionalism, preconceived notions of equity, and intransigence, whether displayed by a management or by a union in collective bargaining negotiations, are not conducive to good labor relations.

Some color has been drained away from the labor relations scene in the process of this metamorphosis to greater mutual responsibility and accommodation. Nothing, as labor scholar Robert Schrank has remarked, compares to the euphoria of a crusade and nothing motivates more powerfully than crusades do.[6] The martial refrain of labor's once-ubiquitous hymn "Solidarity Forever" ("When the union inspiration / Through the workers' / Blood shall run / There will be no power / Any greater / Anywhere beneath the sun . . .") is sung so rarely today that its chanting is almost noteworthy when it does occur. It has been a long time since workers en masse have drawn from Joe Hill's *Labor Songbook*, too, and Labor Day in the 1980s is, as the ILA leader noted earlier indicated, merely an end-of-the-summer extra day off to most unionists (as to nonunionists). Management also conducts *its* dealings with unions with infinitely less passion than it once did. The computer has no room for militancy, and five-year master plans do not normally

---

[6] See his thoughtful article "Are Unions an Anachronism?" in the *Harvard Business Review,* September–October 1979.

generate intense emotions. Excitement still abounds in union–management relations, but to a lesser extent than formerly.

Yet the new maturity in bargaining can only be deemed beneficial to all of our society, and the loss of some amount of fervor is a small price to pay.

Collective bargaining literally means the joint determination of the terms of employment. The process does not *create* the problems of the employment relationship; issues such as wages, hours and overtime, vacations, holidays, discipline, job classification, promotions, and employee safety and health exist with or without collective bargaining. Problems growing out of the employment relationship must be solved, in one way or another. In the absence of collective bargaining, they are handled and determined by the employer on a unilateral basis. The decisions that the employer makes in this respect are final; they have as their frame of reference the employer's own standards of fairness and are limited only by the marketplace and the law.

But if collective bargaining does not create the problems of the employment relationship, it does establish a definite procedure wherein they are handled and resolved. Employers and employees, through their respective representatives, negotiate the terms of employment and provide the mechanisms by which these terms can be administered throughout the contractual duration.

The growth of unions is not, as Roomkin and Juris have well put it, "a right chiseled in stone. The union as an institution evolved because individual workers needed a counterbalance to real and perceived mistreatment at the hands of management in the employment relationship."[7] From all the available evidence, millions of individual workers—whether in significantly increasing numbers or not—still feel that they do. And whatever deficiencies remain in the present system, the considerable progress that has been made in the past few decades augurs well for the future productive potential of the nation, assuming only that we can exercise sufficient patience in having our expectations for collective bargaining translated into action.

[7] Myron Roomkin and Hervey A. Juris, "Unions in the Traditional Sectors: The Mid-Life Passage of the Labor Movement," in *Proceedings of the Thirty-first Annual Meeting, Industrial Relations Research Association,* August 29–31, 1978, p. 221.

Mock Negotiation Problem

The purpose of this problem is to familiarize students with the negotiations of a labor contract. The problem is strictly a hypothetical one and does not pertain to any actual company or union. It is designed to test in a practical way the student's understanding of the issues of collective bargaining studied during the semester and the strategy of the bargaining process. The strategy and techniques of negotiations are treated in Chapter 5, and the issues of collective bargaining are dealt with primarily in Chapters 7 through 10. Before the actual mock negotiation, the student should carefully reread these chapters.

PROCEDURE AND GROUND RULES

1 Class will be divided into labor and management negotiation teams. Each team will elect a chairperson at the first meeting of the team.
2 Teams will meet in a sufficient number of planning sessions to be ready for the negotiations. Each participant will be required to engage in necessary research for the negotiation.
3 In the light of the following problem, each team will establish *not more* than eight items *nor less* than six that it will demand. *All demands must be based on the problem. No team will be permitted to make a demand that is not so based.* For purposes of this problem, a union wage demand and all fringe issues, if demanded, will be considered as only *one* demand.
4 Each team should strive to negotiate demands that it believes to be most im-

portant. This requires the weighing of the alternatives in the light of respective needs of the group the team is representing.

5 Compromises, counterproposals, trading, and the dropping of demands to secure a contract will be permitted in the light of the give and take of the actual negotiations.

6 Each team should strive sincerely and honestly in the role playing to do the best job possible for the group it represents. This is a *learning situation* and to learn there must be sincere dedication to the job ahead.

7 *Absolutely no consultation with any of the other teams, regardless of whether company or union, will be permitted. Each team must depend entirely upon its own resources.*

8 Chairpersons should coordinate the planning of each team, decide on the time and place for planning sessions, and assign work to be done to members of the team. Chairpersons, however, are not to do all the talking in the actual negotiations. To maximize the learning situation, each member of the team should positively participate in the negotiations.

9 There must either be a settlement of all issues in the negotiation or a work stoppage. *No extension of the existing contract will be permitted.* It is a question of either settlement or work stoppage.

10 Someone on each team should keep track of the settlements. Do not write out the actual contractual clauses agreed to. It will suffice only to jot down the substance of agreements.

11 There will be a general discussion of the problem after the negotiation. Each team chairperson will make a brief statement to the entire class as to the final outcome of the problem.

Herein follows the problem on which the demands will be based and which provides the framework for the negotiations. *Read the problem very carefully to size up the situation. Base your demands only on this problem.*

Representatives of the Auto Products Corporation of Indianapolis, Indiana, and Local 5000, United Metal Workers of America, are in the process of negotiating their collective bargaining contract. The current contract expires at the close of today's negotiations. (*Instructor should set the date of the mock negotiation, and the exact clock time that the contract expires.*) The negotiations cover the Indianapolis plant.[1] Auto Products also owns a plant in Little Rock, Arkansas, but the southern plant is not organized and is not a part of the current negotiations. The current contract, which covers only the Indianapolis plant, was negotiated for a three-year period. *The time of the negotiation is the present, and, accordingly, the parties are conditioned by current elements of economic trends, patterns of collective bargaining, and labor relations law.*

The Indianapolis plant has been in business for sixty-one years and has steadily expanded. At present, 3,800 production and maintenance employees are in the bargaining unit of the plant.

Except for the years of the Great Depression, the financial structure of the firm has been relatively good. Here are some financial data from the Indianapolis plant for the fiscal year preceding these negotiations:

[1] The location of the plant may be shifted to your own area to provide more local relevance.

Net sales	$200,825,900
Material costs	79,250,000
Direct labor costs (includes fringe benefits and reflects layoffs in previous fiscal year)	72,635,000
Other variable costs	13,265,000
Fixed costs	5,500,000
Total expenses	170,650,000
Income before taxes	30,175,000
Net income after taxes (federal, state, county, municipal)	9,400,000

In the past, the experience has been to distribute about 65 percent of net profits in dividends and 35 percent has been held as retained earnings. Last year the company borrowed $6.3 million from the Hoosier National Bank. The rate of interest on the loan was 11.6 percent. The proceeds of the loan were used to expand the Little Rock plant. The loan is scheduled for liquidation in ten years.

The company manufactures a variety of auto accessories. These include auto heaters, oil pumps, fan belts, rear-view mirrors, and piston rings, and in the last year the company has also started production of auto air conditioners. About 65 percent of its sales are to the basic auto companies (General Motors, Ford, Chrysler, and American Motors); 25 percent to auto-repair facilities; and the rest to government agencies. The plant operates on a two-shift basis. A 25-cent-per-hour premium is paid to employees who work the second shift.

The employees of the company were unionized in 1937, as a result of the CIO campaign to organize the mass-production industries. In August of that year, the union was victorious in an NLRB election. As a result of the election, certification was awarded, on August 17, 1937, to Local 5000, since which time Local 5000 has represented the production and maintenance workers of the company. The first collective bargaining agreement between the company and Local 5000 was signed on November 14, 1937.

Only one contract strike has taken place since the union came into the picture. It occurred in 1940; the issues were the union's demands for a union shop, increased wages, and six paid holidays. The strike lasted six weeks. When it terminated, the union had obtained for its members a 4-cent hourly wage increase, retroactive to the day of the strike (the union had demanded 7 cents), and four paid holidays. The union failed in its attempt to obtain any arrangement requiring membership in the union as a condition of employment. Also, the current contract does not include a "checkoff." At the time of these negotiations, all except 400 workers in the bargaining unit are in the union.

The average wage for the production workers in the Indianapolis plant is $8.50 per hour. Of the 3,800 employees, there are 175 skilled maintenance employees (electricians, plumbers, carpenters, mechanics, and tool and die makers), and their average rate is $11.20 per hour. The existing contract contains an escalator (COLA) clause providing for the adjustment of wages in accordance with changes in the Consumer Price Index. There is no "cap" on the amount of the increase. It provides for a 1-cent change in wages for each 0.4-point change in the CPI. The escalator arrangement is reviewed on a semiannual basis. The current wage rates include the increases generated from the escalator clause and the annual improvement factor. During the term of the three-year contract, workers received a 50-cent increase in wages: 20 cents from the operation of the escalator clause and 30 cents from the operation of the annual improvement factor (a 15-cent increase on the anniversary date of the contract in each of the past two years).

The Little Rock plant was built five years ago. It started with a modest-size labor force, but during the past three years the southern plant expanded sharply, and it now employs about 1,500 production and maintenance workers. Efforts to organize the southern plant have so far been unsuccessful. The union lost an NLRB election last year by 300 votes. Of the 1,500 employees, 1,300 cast ballots, with 800 voting against the union and 500 voting for it. The average wage in the Little Rock plant is $6.40 per hour. Currently, 450 employees in the Indianapolis plant are on layoff. It is no secret that one reason for this has been the increase of output in the Little Rock plant. Another reason was the decrease in sales at the Indianapolis plant. In Little Rock, essentially the same products are made as in Indianapolis. Of the 450 on layoff, reduction in sales caused by the state of the automobile industry accounts for 300, and the remainder is attributable to the southern situation. There is talk in the plant that some laid-off employees will never be recalled to work. Of the 450 laid-off employees, 75 have exhausted their benefits under the Indiana Unemployment Compensation Act. The present contract does not provide for a supplementary unemployment benefit program.

In general, the relations between the management and the union have been satisfactory. There have, of course, been the usual disagreements, but all in all, relations have been quite harmonious. However, last month there was a wildcat strike, the first one since the union came into the picture. It occurred in the Oil Pump Department, and the alleged cause was the discharge of the steward of the department on the grounds that he shoved a foreman while he was discussing a grievance with him. The union disclaimed all responsibility for the strike, and its officers stated that they did all they could to get the men back to work. However, the employees in the Oil Pump Department picketed the plant, and the incident, which lasted two days, shut down all production in the plant for these two days. There is a no-strike clause in the contract that states:

> There will be no strikes, slowdowns, or other interruptions of production because of labor disputes during the contract period. Employees who engage in such prohibited activity are subject to discharge.

The company threatened to sue the union for damages under the Taft–Hartley law, but management finally decided not to go to court after the employees returned to work. No employee was disciplined because of the strike; however, at present, the steward remains discharged, and the union has demanded that he be returned to his job. Under the contract, the company has the right to discharge for "just cause." The steward is 64 years old and was one of the leading figures in the earlier years of the union. He is known affectionately by his fellow workers as "Old Joe."

The existing contract contains a standard grievance procedure and provides for arbitration for all disputes arising under the contract, except production standards, which management has the unilateral right to establish. During the last contractual period (three years), 275 written grievances were filed by employees protesting "unreasonably" high production standards. As required by the contract, the company negotiated the production standard grievances, but the union did not have the right to appeal to arbitration or to strike over them. In three cases sparked by the production standard grievances, the company reduced the standards. In all other cases, the company denied the grievances. The management rights clause states in effect that the company retains all rights except as limited by express provisions of the labor agreement.

Provided in the contract are a series of fringe benefits: eight paid holidays; a pension plan similar to the one negotiated in the basic automobile industry; a paid vacation program wherein employees receive one week's vacation for one year of service, two weeks for five years, and three weeks for twenty or more years of service; an excellent medical insurance program including physician and hospital services (except that it does not cover employees laid off for more than thirty consecutive days—of the 450 on layoff, 80 percent have been laid off for more than thirty consecutive days.) The total costs of the fringe benefit program amount to $2.20 per hour. Under the current pension program, employees may retire at age 65 and receive full benefits, though retirement is not required at any age. The average age of the employees in the plant is 39. About 8 percent are over 65 years of age.

The current seniority clause provides for promotions based on length of service and ability. That is, seniority governs when the senior employee has qualifications reasonably equal to those of junior employees who bid on the job. During the contract period, twenty-one grievances were filed by employees who protested against the company's filling jobs with junior service employees. The company's position in these grievances was that the junior employees had far more ability than the senior employees. Five of these grievances went to arbitration, the company winning four and the union winning only one. Promotions are bid for on a departmental basis.

The seniority area of the existing contract provides for plantwide application of seniority credits for layoffs and recalls, provided that the senior employee has the necessary qualifications to perform the available work. During the recent period in which layoffs occurred, the company, as required by the contract, laid off many junior employees rather than senior employees because of the plantwide system. Foremen have complained to management that, in many cases, the junior employees who had been laid off were more efficient than the senior employees who had to be retained because of the plantwide system.

Also, the current contract provides that an employee whose job goes down, or whose job is preempted by a more senior employee, may bump any junior employee in the plant, provided that the preempting employee has the qualifications to fill the job. During layoff periods, the company became aware that this situation caused a great deal of expense because of an unreasonable amount of job displacement. Also, the current contract does not contain a temporary layoff clause. This means that displaced employees may exercise their bumping rights based on their plantwide seniority regardless of the length of the layoff. Foremen have complained to the management that employees should be laid off without regard to seniority when the layoff is for a short period of time.

The existing contract provides for "superseniority" for stewards and other union officials. This provision protects the stewards and union officials only from layoffs. There are sixty stewards in the plant. Last year, stewards spent, on the average, about ten hours each per week on grievance work, for which they were paid by the company. There are no limitations on stewards for grievance work. Foremen have complained that some stewards are "goofing off," using "union business" as a pretext not to work. All the stewards deny this. In fact, the stewards claim that it is the unreasonable attitude of foremen that provokes grievances and complaints. Also, the stewards claim that there cannot be a true measure of their time on the basis of the number of written grievances (a total of 450 grievances, including the production standard complaints, were filed during the last three years), since a good share of their time is spent discussing grievances on an oral basis with employees and supervisors before a written grievance is filed. There is no record to show how many of these oral discussions ended problems without written grievances being filed.

Last year, because of an unexpected order from the government, the plant worked Saturday and Sunday overtime for a period of two weekends. Under the existing contract, the company has the right to require overtime. About 200 employees refused to work overtime and did so only because the company threatened to fire them if they refused. These 200 employees have been raising a lot of trouble in the union about this overtime affair. Also, the company has the right to select the employees to work overtime. Some employees have claimed that foremen are not fair, giving their personal friends the opportunity to earn the extra money and discriminating against the other employees.

For many years, by custom, each skilled tradesperson has worked only within his or her trade. Five months ago, the company required a mechanic to do a job normally performed by a plumber. The employee and union filed a grievance, and the case went all the way to arbitration. The arbitrator sustained the position of the union on the basis of the "past practice" principle.

Some maintenance people have been affected by the current layoff, with 25 laid off. They charge that the company has been subcontracting out skilled work that could be done by them. Last year, for example, the company subcontracted out electrical work while three electricians were on layoff. The subcontract job lasted six days. Under the current contract, there is no restriction on the company's right to subcontract.

The present contract, as stated, was negotiated for a three-year period. Both sides have indicated that in the future they may want to move away from this long-term arrangement for a variety of reasons. However, there is no assurance of whether this attitude indicates the parties' sincere position or is merely an expression of a possible bargaining position.

Automation has been a problem in the company for several years. About 250 workers have been permanently separated because of automation. Union and management meetings to deal with the problem during the past several years have proved fruitless. Previous discussions have centered on the rate of automation, the problem of income for the displaced employees, and the training of employees for the jobs created by automation. All indications are that the next wave of automation will cost about 390 bargaining unit jobs. The 250 employees who have been permanently separated are in addition to the 450 employees who are currently on layoff because of the southern situation and the drop in sales.

There has been considerable controversy over the problem of temporary transfers. Under the existing contract, the company may not transfer an employee to a job not in his or her job classification.

There are also problems regarding other working rules. These now include a fifteen-minute rest period every four hours; a stipulation that no supervisor may perform bargaining unit work regardless of circumstances; paid lunch periods of twenty-minute duration; and paid "wash-up" time for ten minutes prior to quitting time. The company contends that these "working rules" are costing it a lot of money. Whenever this issue has been brought up in the past, the union has refused any change.

Company records show that 60 percent of the workers have seniority up to ten years; 30 percent, between ten and twenty years; and 10 percent, more than twenty years. About 20 percent of the bargaining unit are women, and 15 percent are blacks. Some black employees have complained that they have not been given equal opportunity to get better jobs. Of the 175 in the skilled trades, only 8 are black. They have threatened to file complaints against both the company and the union under Title VII of the Civil Rights Act and Taft–Hartley. They have retained an attorney for this purpose.

FOR THE INSTRUCTOR: HOW TO USE THE MOCK NEGOTIATION PROBLEM

We have used the preceding mock negotiation problem with great success for several years. Students are uniformly enthusiastic about the problem, and there exists a friendly rivalry among the students during the weeks before the negotiation. Here are some suggestions on how to use the problem most effectively:

1 The class should be divided into union and management negotiation teams about the middle of the semester. Each management and union team should include from three to five students. The teams could be selected in random fashion, but a better method is to distribute the better students among the different teams; by the middle of the semester, the instructor should have a good idea of the

capability and the potential of the students. Each student should be assigned to a specific team, and each team should elect a chairperson as rapidly as possible.

2   The teams should be instructed to conduct the research necessary to collect the data and formulate the arguments to be used in the negotiation. The chairperson of each team should be encouraged to divide the research among the members of each team. For example, one member may be responsible for the problem of wages; another for answering the other team's demands for changes in the seniority structure; and so on. Depending upon the number of students on each team and the number of issues that are likely to be negotiated, one student may be required to research more than one issue. The idea here is that each member of each team should be involved in the research, and the task of research should be divided as equally as possible among all members of the team. The instructor should advise students where the information can be found. The more helpful sources include the *Monthly Labor Review* of the U.S. Department of Labor; the Bureau of National Affairs' *Collective Bargaining Negotiations and Contracts;* special reports of the U.S. Department of Labor; existing collective bargaining contracts; the AFL–CIO's *Federationist;* the AFL–CIO *News;* publications of the American Management Associations and other management sources; *Labor Law Journal; Industrial and Labor Relations Review; Business Week;* and the *New York Times* and the *Wall Street Journal.*

3   Experience has shown that each team should meet in its private planning sessions about five times, for about two to three hours for each session, before the negotiation. This is in addition to research conducted on an individual basis. Because of the time involved, the negotiation could be used instead of the traditional term paper.

4   The instructor may, if he or she desires, attend some of the planning sessions, although in recent years we have not been doing this on the grounds that the full responsibility for planning should be assumed by the students. If visits are made, the instructor should not shape the overall strategy of the team but merely consult with the team on particular problems.

5   We have found that the negotiation session should last about four hours. It could be held on an evening or a Saturday morning. Announce the date well in advance of the actual negotiation—at least six weeks.

6   The negotiation should be held toward the end of the semester so that the students can use the knowledge gained during the semester. We have usually scheduled the exercise during the second-to-last week of the semester.

7   The number of negotiations depends upon the number of students in the class. In one semester, the class included sixty-six students, and, hence, there were six negotiations going on simultaneously. Be sure to arrange well in advance of the exercise for the rooms in which the negotiations are to be held. If possible, the room should be of the conference type, although any room will do, provided that chairs can be arranged around a table so that the teams face each other.

8   The instructor should visit each negotiation, and the total visiting time should be divided equally among the groups. If some technical problem arises

during the negotiation, the instructor should deal with the issue. Other than this, the instructor should remain silent when observing the negotiation. *Do not give any help to any team while the negotiation is under way.* At times, we have had management and organized labor representatives visit the negotiations. Uniformly, they have been impressed with the success of the students and their competence at the bargaining table.

    9 *The teams should be instructed that the sessions must end promptly at the specified time. If the negotiations are to end at 10 P.M., they should end at 10 P.M. Do not extend the time, since to do so would result in lack of uniformity for the different teams.*

    10 When the negotiations are over, all students should meet in one room for a wrap-up session. Each chairperson should report on whether there was a strike or a settlement, the major difficulties and problems of the negotiation, and other highlights. The chief purpose of this session, however, is for the instructor to make observations based on the visits to the negotiations. This session should not exceed forty-five minutes. This meeting is usually charged with emotion, some horseplay, and friendly criticism of each other by the students. If there is not a definite time limit, it could go on indefinitely. In the instructor's analysis, the students should be treated kindly. They have worked hard and deserve congratulations and a pat on the back. Remember that this is their first experience and mistakes will be made. These should be pointed out, but in a strictly impersonal manner.

    11 Other suggestions are that (1) some arrangements should be made for the students to have coffee during the negotiations; (2) if possible, smoking should be permitted; (3) to pacify the janitorial staff, the rooms should be cleared of debris, and chairs and tables rearranged, when the negotiations are ended; (4) the instructor should permit some poetic license during the actual negotiation, but cut off a student or a team that invents too much; and (5) the instructor should not discourage some of the fun the students develop during the negotiations.

Author Index

Subject Index